Auditing the Performance of Management

LEO HERBERT, Ph.D., C.P.A.

LIFETIME LEARNING PUBLICATIONS • Belmont, California

A division of Wadsworth, Inc.

Editing, design, production supervision: Brian K. Williams
Editing: Sylvia Williams
Design: Albert Burkhardt
Illustrations: Winn Kalmon
Composition: Graphic Typesetting Service

© 1979 by Wadsworth, Inc. All rights reserved. No part of this book may be reproduced, stored in a retrieval system, or transcribed, in any form or by any means, electronic, mechanical, photocopying, recording, or otherwise, without the prior written permission of the publisher, Lifetime Learning Publications, Belmont, California 94002, a division of Wadsworth, Inc.

Printed in the United States of America

1 2 3 4 5 6 7 8 9 10—83 82 81 80 79

Library of Congress Cataloging in Publication Data

Herbert, Leo, 1912–
   Auditing the performance of management.

    Bibliography: p.
    Includes index.
    1. Management audit. I. Title.
HF5667.H397   657'.45   79-4551
ISBN 0-534-97998-X

A word about gender: Auditors, state officials, company officers, and so on, may, of course, be men or women. However, so as to avoid burdening the reader with such cumbersome devices as "he/she" or the constant use of the word "person," the author has found it necessary to use the singular pronoun "he." Most of the actions described can be attributed just as easily to women.

TO MY WIFE, RUTH

the chief motivator in my writing this
book and without whose support
it could never have been accomplished

CONTENTS

Preface   vii
Detailed Table of Contents   ix
How to Use This Book   xv

Part One. Auditing the Performance of Management

1. On Auditing the Performance of Management   3
2. Understanding the Phases of the Audit Function   19
3. Determining Efficient, Economical, and Effective Operations   33

Part Two. Getting Started

4. Planning and Programming the Audit   63
5. Reviewing Management Audit Principles Using Real-Life Situations   73
6. Applying the Principles, Policies, and Practices of Program Auditing   97
7. Understanding Management Control   121

Part Three. Making the Detailed Examination

8. Obtaining Evidence in Performance Auditing   141
9. Understanding Working Papers   161
10. Illustrative Working Papers: The Detailed Examination for a Management Audit   171
11. Illustrative Working Papers: The Detailed Examination for a Program Audit   221

Part Four. Using Specialized Techniques in Auditing the Performance of Management

12. Obtaining Audit Evidence Through Statistical Sampling   263
13. Obtaining Evidence Through Interviews and Questionnaires   281
14. Using the Computer as an Audit Tool, and Auditing the Tool Itself   307
15. Using Specialized Analytical Techniques—Using Experts and Consultants   329

Part Five. Reporting the Results of the Audit

16. Understanding the Principles of Reporting   349
17. Writing a Clear, Concise, and Objective Report   361

Appendixes   373
Notes   455
Glossary   459
Bibliography   463
AGA Bibliography on Operational Auditing   469
Index   474

PREFACE

To the best of my knowledge, this is the first book that brings together the principles and practices of performance auditing—the auditing of subjects other than financial statements.

Its purpose is to provide an introduction to—and reference for—those involved in performance auditing and anyone affected by it. That includes:

- Public accountants who have been doing financial statement examinations and who would like to become involved in performance auditing;
- Government auditors required to follow the Comptroller General's standards;
- Internal auditors who find performance auditing pertains to their work;
- Managers in business, public administrators, and other planners interested in program evaluation who want to improve the performance of their organizations;
- Accounting and public administration professors, graduate students, and advanced undergraduates (those with at least one course in auditing) who are interested in the theory and practice of auditing the performance of management.

Because the book is intended for these several different audiences, it offers the following unique features:

1. It is written in such a way that both those with accounting backgrounds and those with financial statement examination backgrounds can learn performance auditing.
2. It presents 42 actual cases, taken from both the public and private sectors, to show how the principles of performance auditing have been applied in practice.
3. It shows step by step how performance auditing is done, from start to final report.
4. It offers a common terminology useful in both the private sector concerned with efficiency and profits and the public sector concerned with the effectiveness of programs.
5. It has a self-instructional kind of organization, with learning objectives, summaries, and review questions, so that the book can be used as a self-teaching tool.
6. It offers detailed information on interviewing, writing a proposal and engagement letter, writing a report, using consultants and experts, using the computer, auditing the computer, and using quantitative techniques.
7. It provides numerous illustrative working papers, checklists, letters, and forms. In addition, there are extensive appendixes, bibliography, and glossary, conveying information on the very latest of the state of the art.

This book represents many years of experience and the contributions of many individuals. The concepts used as a foundation for writing the book grew out of a conceptual structure developed in the 1960s by three persons in the Office of Staff Management in the U.S. General Accounting Office for training GAO auditors to make performance audits—Ernest C. Anderson, Roger Kirvan, and the late Edward Breen—and I wish to acknowledge their strong contribution. Others in the GAO who played major roles in accepting the concepts and applying them to the policies and actual work of making audits of management performance are Allan Voss, William Conrardy, Hyman Krieger, Donald Scantlebury, Irwin d'Addario, and the late Ellsworth H. Morse, Jr., and Robert Rasor.

The material quoted directly from or adapted from the policies of the U.S. General Accounting Office has been used with the permission of the GAO. I especially thank Henry Eschwege and Fred J. Shafer for providing me with the working papers for the illustrative cases. I am particularly grateful to Mr. Morse, former Assistant Comptroller General, for his review of the book and for his approval of the material.

I began writing the book while with the Accounting Department at Brigham Young University, and I wish to thank members of that department for allowing me to experiment with some of the book's ideas while teaching a graduate course. Most of the book was written while I was with the Accounting Department at Virginia Polytechnic Institute and State University, and Dean H. H. Mitchell and Dr. Larry Killough were especially helpful. I am also very grateful to Ms. Karen Hrhea, who taught the book in its early stages to an advanced auditing class, and to the students in that class for their suggestions for improving the text. Finally, Ms. Lynn Sheldon and the secretaries in the Accounting Department who typed much of the manuscript have my warmest appreciation.

Leo Herbert

DETAILED TABLE OF CONTENTS

Part One. Auditing the Performance of Management: The Fundamentals

Chapter 1. On Auditing the Performance of Management   3

    Terminology   4
    Attest, Accountability, and Audit Relationships   4
    Performance Auditing   5
    Management Auditing (M-auditing)   6
    Program Auditing (P-auditing)   7
    Standards for Management and Program Audits   8
    Reporting   9
    Knowledge the Performance Auditor Needs   9
    Review Questions   11

    Case 1: Performance Audit Conclusions from an Industrial Corporation, a State Agency, and a Federal Agency   12
        Audit Scenario 1: **The Travel Advances that Advanced**   12
        Audit Scenario 2: **The Case of the Federal Grant Funds**   12
        Audit Scenario 3: **High Costs for Low Rents: The Public Housing Case**   13

    Case 2: Performance Audit Conclusions from a Federal Agency, a Corporation, and a Municipality   14
        Audit Scenario 1: **Controlling Expenditures: A Federal Case**   14
        Audit Scenario 2: **The Case of the Company Cars**   15
        Audit Scenario 3: **The Case of the Careless Cost Charges**   15

    Case 3: Performance Audit Conclusions from a City, a State Agency, and a Federal Agency   16
        Audit Scenario 1: **The Big Costs that Came in Little Packages**   16
        Audit Scenario 2: **Snow Removal Snowed Under**   16
        Audit Scenario 3: **The Employment Program that Did Not Employ**   17

Chapter 2. Understanding the Phases of the Audit Function   19

    Evidence and Audit Objectives   20
    Elements of the Audit Objective   21
    Subobjectives   22
    Summary of Discussion on Audit Objectives   23
    Phases of the Audit Function   24
    Review Questions   27

    Case 1: The Case of Too Many Workers in the Production Department at Torex   29

    Case 2: A Case of Probation in the State of Sylvania   30

    Case 3: Auditing the Uses of Equipment: A University, a Corporation   31
        Audit Scenario 1: **How They Made Copies at Sohi—and Copies and Copies**   32
        Audit Scenario 2: **Who Used the Research Equipment at Texon—and When?**   32

Chapter 3. Determining Efficient, Economical, and Effective Operations   33

    M-audits   33
    P-audits   37
    Review Questions   43

  Case 1: What Went on in the City Garage? Phases of an M-audit   46

    Audit Scenario 1: **The Preliminary Survey**   46
    Audit Scenario 2: **The Review and Testing of Management Control**   47
    Audit Scenario 3: **The Detailed Examinations**   47
    Audit Scenario 4: **The Report**   48

  Case 2: What Made the Nursing Homes Unsafe: Phases of a P-audit   49

    Audit Scenario 1: **Preliminary Survey and Review and Testing of Management Control**   51
    Audit Scenario 2: **The Detailed Examination**   55
    Audit Scenario 3: **The Report on the P-audit for Nursing Homes**   59

Part Two. Getting Started

Chapter 4. Planning and Programming the Audit   63

    Audit Planning   63
    Audit Programming   65
    Review Questions   69

  Case 1: The City Garage: Planning an M-audit   71

  Case 2: The Nursing Homes: Planning a P-audit   71

  Case 3: Planning the Audit Program: A Case in Point   72

Chapter 5. Reviewing Management Audit Principles Using Real-Life Situations   73

    Basic Principles of Management Auditing   74
    Application of Principles for an M-audit: "The Spark Plug Case"   78
    Application of Principles for the Preliminary Phases: "The Case of the Overseas Flights"   81
    Review Questions   85

  Case 1: Self-assessment Taxes in the State of Piedmont: The Case of the Lost Revenues   87

    Audit Scenario 1: **The Preliminary Survey**   87
    Audit Scenario 2: **The Review and Testing of Management Control**   91

  Case 2: Welfare in the City: The AFDC Case in Yorktown   93

    Audit Scenario: **Preliminary Survey and Review and Testing of Management Control**   93

Chapter 6. Applying the Principles, Policies, and Practices of Program Auditing   97

    Basic Principles of P-auditing   99
    Principles of P-auditing Applied: "The Indian Education Case"   105
    Review Questions   109

  Case 1: The Valley City Jails   111

    Audit Scenario 1: **The Preliminary Survey**   111
    Audit Scenario 2: **The Review and Testing of Management Control**   114

Detailed Table of Contents / **xi**

    Case 2: The Mass-transit Grant 117

      Audit Scenario 1: **The Preliminary Survey** 117
      Audit Scenario 2: **Additional Data on Management Control** 118

Chapter 7. Understanding Management Control   121

      Introduction to Management Control 121
      Meanings of Internal Control and of Management Control 121
      Distinctions and Similarities Between Internal Control and Management Control 124
      Objectives of the Entity 124
      Plan of Organization 125
      Appropriate Policies and Practices 131
      A System of Review 131
      Review Questions 133

    Case 1: The City Garage: Management Control in an M-audit 135

      Audit Scenario 1: **Plan of Organization of a Large City Garage** 135
      Audit Scenario 2: **Flow Chart of Transactions Concerning Usage of Spark Plugs** 135
      Audit Scenario 3: **Acceptable Standards of Management Control** 135
      Audit Scenario 4: **Starting an Audit** 135

    Case 2: The Nursing Homes: Management Control in a P-audit 136

      Audit Scenario 1: **Plan of Organization for Nursing Homes** 136
      Audit Scenario 2: **Flow Chart of Fire-Prevention Program at Alpha Nursing Home** 136
      Audit Scenario 3: **Standards for Fire Prevention** 136
      Audit Scenario 4: **Testing Transactions** 136

    Case 3: Nonresident Tuition in the Fernwood Schools 136

    Case 4: Collections at the Local Church 137

Part Three. Making the Detailed Examination

Chapter 8. Obtaining Evidence in Performance Auditing   141

      Facts and Information as Evidence 141
      Quality and Reliability of Evidence 143
      Sources of Audit Evidence 146
      Further Considerations on Evidence 149
      Review Questions 149

    Case 1: The School Voucher Project at Alum Rock 151

    Case 2: The Workplace Inspection Program 155

Chapter 9. Understanding Working Papers   161

      What Working Papers Are 161
      The Purpose of Working Papers 162
      Working Papers as a Record of Evidence on the Objective 163
      Recording Evidence in Working Papers 165
      Working Papers as a Record of Competency of Evidence 165
      Working Papers as the Basis for the Report 167
      Other Uses of Working Papers 168
      Review Questions 169

Case 1: The City Garage: Audit Working Papers for an M-audit   170

Case 2: The Nursing Homes: Audit Working Papers for a P-audit   170

Chapter 10. Illustrative Working Papers: The Detailed Examination for a Management Audit   171

GAO Standards for Work-paper Preparation   171
The Importance of Summaries   173
Illustrative Working Papers: The Case of the Overseas Flights—The Detailed Examination   177
Example: Level II Summary   178
Analysis of the Work Papers   180
Peer and Supervisory Review   209
Review Questions   209

Case 1: State Self-assessment Taxes: The Detailed Examination for an M-Audit   210

Case 2: City Welfare: The Detailed Examination for an M-audit   214

Chapter 11. Illustrative Working Papers: The Detailed Examination for a Program Audit   221

Illustrative Working Papers: The Indian Education Case—The Detailed Examination   221
The Summary Schedule of Responses by School Officials to Key Questions   226

Case 1: The Valley City Jails: The Detailed Examination   249

Case 2: The Mass-transit Grants: The Detailed Examination   253

Part Four. Using Specialized Techniques in Auditing the Performance of Management

Chapter 12. Obtaining Audit Evidence Through Statistical Sampling   263

Little Need for Auditor to Review Every Item   264
Sampling Principles Related to Principles of Auditing and Evidence   265
Sample Objectives   266
Precision   266
Confidence and Risk   267
The Size of the Sample from a Formula   270
The Size of a Sample from a Table   271
Attribute Sampling   273
Homogeneous Universe   275
Random Selection   275
Review Questions   277

Case 1: Estimating the Assets of Mammoth City   279

Audit Scenario 1: **Estimating Asset Values in Mammoth City**   279
Audit Scenario 2: **Determining Adequacy of Procurement Internal Control**   279

Case 2: Classifying Civil Servants in the State of Landia   279

Chapter 13. Obtaining Evidence Through Interviews and Questionnaires   281

Interviews: Use of Oral Information   281
Sources of Interview Information   282
Planning and Preparing for Important Interviews   283
Beginning an Interview   283
Written Record of Interview   285

Confirmation by Interviewee   285
Illustrative Working Papers for Interviews   286
Questionnaires: Advantages and Disadvantages   295
Planning for Use of Questionnaires   296
Design   296
Selection of Responders and Distribution of Questionnaires   297
Tabulating Answers   297
Review Questions   298

Case 1: Indian Education: Analyzing Information from Interviews   299

Case 2: Computer Security: Can a Questionnaire Help?   299

Chapter 14. Using the Computer as an Audit Tool, and Auditing the Tool Itself   307

Computers, Computer Usage, and Computer Auditing   307
Using the Computer as a Specialized Audit Tool   309
Auditing Computer Operations   310
Relying on Information from the Computer   314
Extending Audit Procedures to Assure Competency of Evidence   316
More Advanced Computer Auditing   317
Review Questions   319

Case 1: Analysis of a Complete Audit: Improvements Needed in Managing Automated Decision Making by Computer   320

Audit Scenario 1: **The Preliminary Phases**   320
Audit Scenario 2: **The Detailed Examination and the Report**   322

Case 2: The Computers that Were Converted in the State of New Kent   327

Chapter 15. Using Specialized Analytical Techniques—Using Experts and Consultants   329

Specialized Analytical Techniques: Several Models   330
Probability Models   330
Experimental Models   332
Balancing Models   333
Optimizing Models   335
Other Mathematical Models   340
Using Experts and Consultants   340
Use of Experts and Consultants in the Normal Audit Organization   341
Use of Experts and Consultants as Members of a Task Force   341
Review Questions   342

Case 1: Ranges for Measuring Risk and Uncertainty in Cost Estimates   344

Case 2: Procuring M.D.s for the Service: A Cost-effectiveness Analysis   345

Part Five. Reporting the Results of the Audit

Chapter 16. Understanding the Principles of Reporting   349

Standards of Reporting   349
Logical Organization of the Report: Two Patterns   351
Background Information   352
Reporting the Results of the Audit   354
Recommendations   356
Scope of the Audit   356

Peer Reviewing and Referencing 356
Relationship Between Work Done and the Report 357
The Report Summary or Digest 357
Chapters 357
Review Questions 357

Case 1: Organizing Two Audit Reports 359
Audit Scenario 1: **The City Garage** 359
Audit Scenario 2: **The Nursing Homes** 359

Case 2: State Self-assessment Taxes: The Report 359

Case 3: City Welfare: The Report 360

Chapter 17. Writing a Clear, Concise, and Objective Report 361

Readers of Audit Reports 361
Style of Writing 362
Level of Importance of Each Item in the Section 362
The Right Word 362
Sentences and Paragraphs 363
Edit the Report 364
Review Questions 365

Case 1: The Valley City Jails: The Report 367

Case 2: The Mass-transit Grant: The Report 367

Case 3: Indian Education: A Reaudit 368

Appendixes

I. GAO Standards for Audit of Governmental Organizations: Programs, Activities, and Functions 373
II. Checklist Prepared by the American Institute of Certified Public Accountants 375
III. The Proposal and Engagement Letter 377
IV. Illustration of Assignment Approval, with Tentative Report Digest 383
V. Illustration of Analysis Needed for Continuing Assignment Authorization: Review of Food Stamp Program Service and Administration 391
VI. Selected Policies for a GAO Program Audit 399
VII. Developing the Report: Selected Policies from the U.S. GAO Report Manual 403
VIII. Illustrative Report with Appendixes: Fuel Savings and Other Benefits Achieved by Diverting Department of Defense Passengers from Chartered to Scheduled Overseas Flights 405
IX. Writing the Report: Selected Policies from U.S. GAO Report Manual 433
X. Illustrative Audit Report: Indian Education Program 437

Notes 455

Glossary of Selected Terms 459

Selected Bibliography 463

AGA Bibliography on Operational Auditing 469

Index 474

HOW TO USE THIS BOOK

This book is really three books in one:

1. It is an *introduction* to the whole subject of auditing the performance of management. The flow chart (*next page*) gives an overview of how a performance auditor proceeds. Because it is an introduction, the book is therefore organized as a *self-teaching tool*. Each chapter opens with an overview—a *list of objectives*—that tells you what tools and concepts you will understand after you have finished reading the chapter. Many chapters end with a *summary* of what you have just read. Each chapter is followed by a list of *review questions*, each carefully cross-referenced back to the discussion within the chapter so that you can quickly refresh your memory.
2. It is a series of *cases*. At the end of each chapter are several cases, and many of the cases include different "audit scenarios." Some of the cases are carried throughout the book, to illustrate how concepts are developed and applied. Accounting professors in particular will find these case studies invaluable instructional aids.
3. It is a *resource* or *reference* book. Experienced performance auditors will find the 10 appendixes and the extensive bibliography on this emerging subject extremely useful.

OVERVIEW OF PERFORMANCE AUDITING

Start: Auditor has no idea where to go or what to do. Determines total areas (universe).	Auditor finds he has many areas to choose from. Selects area.	Auditor selects area from universe of areas. Does preliminary survey.	Determines objective of specific activity —very tentative. Also determines tentative alternatives. Reviews and tests management control.
Obtains general knowledge of total responsibilities. Leads to total areas that can be audited.	Background and general information on areas (such as dollars spent, executive interest, legislative interest, public interest) leads auditor to select a specific area to be audited.	Background and general information from area leads auditor to tentative audit objective by some evidence and assertions. Possible alternative tentative objectives considered.	Tests of management control give auditor evidence to support firm objective.
			Possible tentative report could be prepared at this time. Also program for the detailed examination is prepared, if audit is to continue.

Selects firm audit objective

Gathers sufficient relevant material, and competent evidence on audit objective to come to a conclusion on that objective. Does detailed examination.

Summarizes evidence in working papers, sufficient to support conclusion on objective.

From summarized evidence, prepares report, including conclusion and recommendation. Report is the final product of the audit.

Obtains sufficient, relevant, material, and competent evidence to support the conclusion on the audit objective, including any evidence obtained in prior phases.

Summarizes all evidence in working papers on the objective in order to have a workable amount for the report and to support the auditor's conclusion.

Uses summarized evidence to support conclusion and recommendations.

PART One

Auditing the Performance of Management: The Fundamentals

In Part 1, chapters 1 through 3, you will be introduced to the basic information needed for your study of auditing the performance of management. You will learn the terminology used in the field, definitions used in this book, and the areas of management that can be audited for better performance. You will learn how to start an audit, including how to develop audit objectives. You will see how the audit continues from phase to phase until it results in the final report. Then you will learn how to apply each of these phases of an audit to the various types of performance audits.

CHAPTER 1

On Auditing the Performance of Management

After you have read this chapter, studied the review questions, and worked through the cases, you will understand:

- The terms used in performance auditing.
- The attest, accountability, and audit relationships inherent in any auditing situation.
- The definitions of performance auditing, management auditing, and program auditing.
- How to classify the results of any audit into whether it is for efficiency and economy (a *management audit*) or effectiveness (a *program audit*).
- The audit standards that apply to government organizations, activities, programs, and functions.
- The three elements found in the conclusion to any audit aimed at improving management performance.
- The need to know certain types of knowledge for performing audits of management performance.

No one knows when the first audit was made, but there is evidence that even early civilizations provided some form of reviewing and reporting on the accountability of one person or group of persons to others. But auditing today is considerably different from what it was during early Chinese, Hebrew, and Roman times or, for that matter, from that practiced during the early twentieth century. Whereas the purpose of accounts examination used to be to detect fraud and certify the accuracy of records, the primary purpose now is to express opinions on the *fairness* of presentation of the financial statements. And whereas the purpose of auditing the performance of management used to be to ensure compliance with laws, policies, and regulations, the primary purpose today is to improve managerial performance, to determine whether an organization, activity, or program has been managed economically, efficiently, or effectively.

Performance auditing can be used to cover all types of management activities—planning, marketing, production, selling, research, warehousing, personnel, and accounting. It can also cover all types of programs, both commercial and noncommercial—the services of health, welfare, medical, education, and environment, for instance, or products such as highways and missiles. Being involved with so many different organizations, activities, and programs often leads auditors into a dilemma of terminology. Let us consider, therefore, the terms we will use in this book.

Terminology

Internal auditing was probably the first term to be used that indicated auditing that went beyond the field of financial-statement examinations. This kind of auditing, which was concerned with whether managers or employees adhered to prescribed policies, today generally implies that the auditors are employed by an organization rather than are independent of it. Internal auditors perform financial-statement examinations; audit for efficiency, effectiveness, and economy; and ascertain whether employees are complying with the organization's policies and regulations.

Compliance auditing has been a term used in government since 1776. The early purpose of government auditors was to determine whether government employees complied with prescribed laws and regulations. While some governmental units still require such detailed compliance audits, most, when they are significant, are absorbed into efficiency, economy, and effectiveness audits.

In recent years, *operational auditing* has become the buzz word for the audits of activities other than those pertaining to financial statement examinations. Operational auditing has been more concerned with the economy and efficiency of management's operations than with the effectiveness of the programs management has been carrying out.

Management auditing is the term now used for evaluating the efficiency and economy of a given operation. Since the term is both descriptive and suitable, we will use it to describe such an audit. We will further simplify the term by calling management auditing **M-auditing.**

The auditing of effectiveness, on the other hand, has had many terms applied to it since it became one of the requirements for full-scope auditing of governmental programs, functions, activities, or organizations. The Comptroller General often uses the term *program results audits*. Other common terms used are *program audits* and *program evaluations*, as well as *mission-oriented results audits* or *mission-oriented audits*. Recently, however, literature in both the private and government sectors has been using the terms *programs* and *programming*. The one term we consider most appropriate is **program auditing**, and we will use it to describe effectiveness-type audits. We will further simplify the term by calling program auditing **P-auditing.**

The one obvious term that should be used for the whole field of auditing to improve the performance of management is **performance auditing**, and it will be used throughout this book.

Since we have been using various terms to define and describe the audit function, let us now place these in proper focus.

Attest, Accountability, and Audit Relationships

The words *accountability* and *attest* are often found in auditing literature and sometimes are used to mean the same thing. While related, the three functions of auditing, accountability, and attesting are not the same.

Persons or groups of persons in all organizations are accountable and report to some outside or higher level of authority. If reliability and acceptability are needed in the information given by the accountable party to the outside or higher-level party, then some independent person attests to that information and does so through an audit.

The auditor is often called the first party. Management or employees of an organization who are accountable to a third party are often called the second party. The third party, the one who receives the report, can be any one of several groups: higher levels within the same organization, the board of directors, the stockholders, the Congress, the public, the press, investors—any individual or group, in fact, to whom the second part is accountable.

This relationship is represented graphically in Figure 1.1.

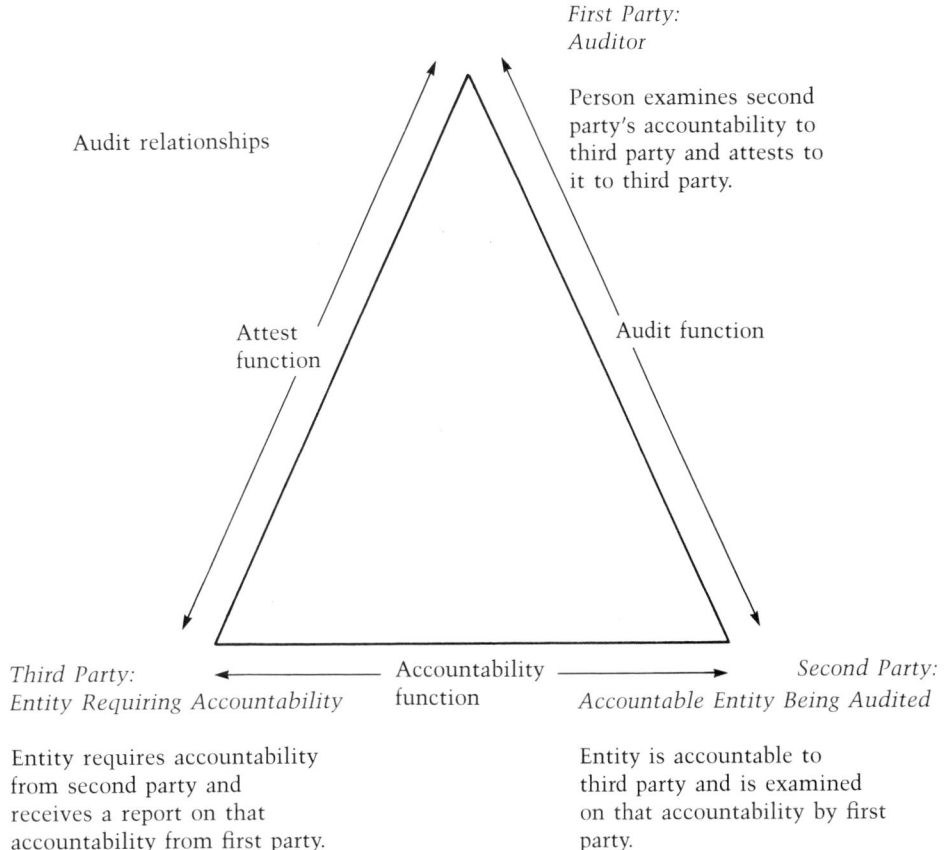

Figure 1.1 Audit relationships

Performance Auditing

A recent book on auditing has said:

> ... for an activity to be properly called an audit there must be:
>
> 1. An auditor, auditee, and audit recipient;
> 2. An accountability relationship between the auditee (subordinate) and the audit recipient (higher authority);
> 3. Independence between the auditor and auditee; and
> 4. An examination and evaluation of certain of the auditee's accountable activities by the auditor for the audit recipient.[1]

This is an excellent description of an audit. For our purposes, however, a conceptual definition of auditing is needed so that all types of performance auditing can be related, whether they be of auditing management activities or of auditing program activities. This conceptual definition is as follows:

6 / Auditing the Performance of Management: The Fundamentals

> **Performance auditing is:**
> 1. Planning for, obtaining, and evaluating sufficient relevant, material, and competent evidence,
> 2. By an independent auditor,
> 3. On the audit objective of
>   a) whether an entity's management or employees have or have not accepted and carried out;
>   b) appropriate accounting, management, or operational principles, policies, or standards;
>   c) for effectively, efficiently, or economically using its resources;
> 4. From this evidence on the audit objective, the auditor comes to an opinion or conclusion and reports to a third party.

Using this definition, we can further define and describe the two basic types of performance audits: (1) management auditing and (2) program auditing.

Management Auditing (M-auditing)

Management within the context of management auditing includes all internal operations of an organization accountable to some higher level. It includes, but is not limited to, operations for accounting, purchasing, producing, personnel, research, or any other activity conducted by the organization. M-auditing attempts to determine for the accountable entity the best use of the second party's manpower, material, machinery, and information.

The best use of resources can be determined by holding the revenue or benefits constant and reducing the costs or expenditures, by holding the costs or expenditures constant and increasing the revenue or benefits, or by increasing the revenue or benefits at a faster rate than increasing the costs or expenditures.

In the examination of financial statements by an independent auditor, the profession has clearly established the responsiblities of both the auditor and management. Within its responsibility for *all* actions, including those of financial statements, management must determine and apply generally acceptable standards of operation for the best use of its resources. In the audit function, however, it is often the auditor who must determine the appropriate standards so that he may gather evidence on the audit objective.

The auditor has the responsibility to inform third parties whether or not the management and operations being evaluated have been accomplished efficiently and economically. In a management audit, *findings* is the term generally used to define both the conclusion and the evidence that supports it.

Our primary conceptual definition of performance auditing (given above) can now be used as a basis for defining management auditing:

> **Management auditing (M-auditing) is:**
> 1. Planning for, obtaining, and evaluating sufficient relevant, material, and competent evidence,
> 2. By an independent auditor,

> 3. On the audit objective of
>   a) whether an entity's management or employees have or have not accepted and carried out;
>   b) appropriate laws, regulations, policies, procedures, or other management standards for properly using its resources;
>   c) in an efficient and economical manner;
> 4. From this evidence on the audit objective, the auditor comes to an opinion or conclusion and reports to a third party,
>   a) with sufficient evidence in the report to convince the third party that the conclusion is accurate; and
>   b) with a recommendation for the possible correction of any deficiencies.

Program Auditing (P-auditing)

In a business or industrial enterprise, a program is concerned with the *end results* of the enterprise. The end results, often called *objectives* or *expected results*, should form the basis for determining the direction an organization takes to develop the means for producing a product or rendering a service, rather than allowing the means to determine the end results. Usually, the end results are directly related to a particular product or service when there are many products or services provided by a particular organization. Thus, if the enterprise is to accomplish the objective of the program effectively, the expected results need to be known before starting to develop a process for producing the product or rendering the service.

Let us illustrate programs in this context, using an organization with only one product and hence only one program. Suppose the owner of the Buggy Whip Manufacturing Company had as his objective making a profit for the year of $50,000 manufacturing buggy whips. But there is no demand for his particular type of buggy whip, even though he may be the most efficient producer of buggy whips in the world. He could not, then, effectively accomplish his profit objective by producing buggy whips. A program is thus concerned with the end results from producing a product or rendering a service; these end results are the reason for the existence of the enterprise.

In government also, programs are concerned with accomplishing desired results, as the Urban Institute definition makes clear:

> ... a federal *program* is defined as the provision of federal funds and administrative direction to accomplish a prescribed set of objectives through the conduct of specified activities. Typically the federal money goes to intermediaries rather than to final recipients of services.[2]

As distinguished from M-auditing, then, P-auditing evaluates and reports on an entity's effective use of its resources in accomplishing intended results. The program entity, in contrast to the well-defined hierarchical structures of most organizations, may be unduly scattered and not at all well defined. It may even be difficult to determine who has the responsibility for managing the program. For example, most universities have a program in accounting, which might encompass accounting given by engineering schools, medical schools, and public administration schools. The head of the accounting department should certainly guide the total accounting program, but often he is not even called in when the engineering school decides to give a course in cost accounting.

The program, however, must be defined even though it is not well structured, as is the case with many educational and health programs. Much of the financial support, for example, given to state education departments for their educational programs comes from the federal government, and both state and local levels must carry out the intended educational results.

Many corporate entities, too, are becoming program oriented, thus losing hierarchical structures. For example, the payroll function at one time was carried out entirely by the payroll department; a timekeeper from the payroll department kept time even in the plant. Now, this operating department becomes a part of the payroll program. Likewise, equal employment opportunity programs, social programs, and environmental programs are scattered throughout the organization, even though one individual or organization may have overall responsibility.

Sometimes the results intended are given by the highest level of authority. The Congress, for instance, may give the results intended for certain federal programs; the chief executive officer, for a corporation; the legislature, for a state program; and the city council, for a municipality.

At other times, however, the results intended may not be given or even known. What, for example, is the expected outcome of certain educational programs? Although a program manager should know and communicate the results intended before starting operations, many program entities actually begin before determining what they specifically intend to accomplish. Before starting a P-audit, then, the auditor must insist upon determining the results intended, with the concurrence of the program manager, of course.

Using again our primary conceptual definition of performance auditing, we can now define program auditing as follows:

Program auditing (P-auditing) is:

1. Planning for, obtaining, and evaluating sufficient relevant, material, and competent evidence,
2. By an independent auditor,
3. On the audit objective of
   a) whether an entity's management, employees, or delegated agents have or have not accepted and carried out;
   b) appropriate standards for achieving the results desired by a higher level authority;
   c) in an effective manner;
4. From this evidence on the audit objective, the auditor comes to an opinion or conclusion and reports to a third party,
   a) with sufficient evidence in the report to convince the higher level authority that the conclusion is correct; and
   b) with a recommendation for possible improvements in the effectiveness of the program.

Standards for Management and Program Audits

Like auditors of financial statements, those who audit management activities and programs in government must follow some generally accepted standards that have been developed for all governmental organizations, activities, programs, and functions by the Comptroller General of the United States in cooperation with other federal, state, and local auditing organizations, as well as such organizations as the American Institute of Certified Public Accountants. (See Appendix I.) While not compulsory, these standards are excellent. Anyone engaged in performance auditing should consider carefully those that apply to the audits of management and program activities.

Reporting

Auditing standards stress the attest or reporting function, and our primary definition of performance auditing states that from the evidence on the audit objective auditors come to an opinion or a conclusion on that objective, which they then report to a third party.

In reporting conclusions for performance audits, the GAO standards state that auditors should provide sufficient evidence so that the reader will come to the same conclusion as the auditor: "Detailed supporting information should be included in the report to the extent necessary to make a convincing presentation."

Although conclusions depend upon the evidence obtained on the audit objective, both management and program audit conclusions are based on three common elements: (1) an *appropriate standard*, (2) the *actions of individuals or organizations* that did or did not follow the standard, and (3) the *results* brought about by the actions of organizations or individuals following or not following the standard. These three elements can be illustrated by showing a conclusion from a fictional M-audit:

> We estimated that $50,000 could be saved annually (results) if the agency that provides the policy, and the organizations that use the vehicles (actions of organizations), were to use state gasoline outlets instead of private gasoline stations to the maximum extent practicable (appropriate standard).

The same three elements can be illustrated in a conclusion from a GAO P-audit, this one pertaining to the improvement of Indian education in schools:

> Little progress has been made (results) by the agency in the accomplishment of its stated goal of closing the education gap between Indians and other Americans (actions of organizations) by raising the academic achievement level of Indian students up to the national average within 5 years (appropriate standard).

Not only the conclusion in the audit report but the objective on which the evidence is gathered contains the same three elements. The auditor who can recognize these in any given report conclusion is on his way to learning and understanding what must be done to make a good performance audit.

Knowledge the Performance Auditor Needs

Auditors who examine financial statements leave their formal educational process with a basic knowledge of accounting and auditing, and upon graduation from college seldom have specific knowledge of any particular company's accounting system. Nevertheless, before starting an examination, they must learn that particular system.

Similarly, auditors who examine management performance have a general knowledge of management, production, personnel, information systems, computers, quantitative methods, and other related subjects upon graduation from college; yet they too seldom know just how any one particular activity or

10 / *Auditing the Performance of Management: The Fundamentals*

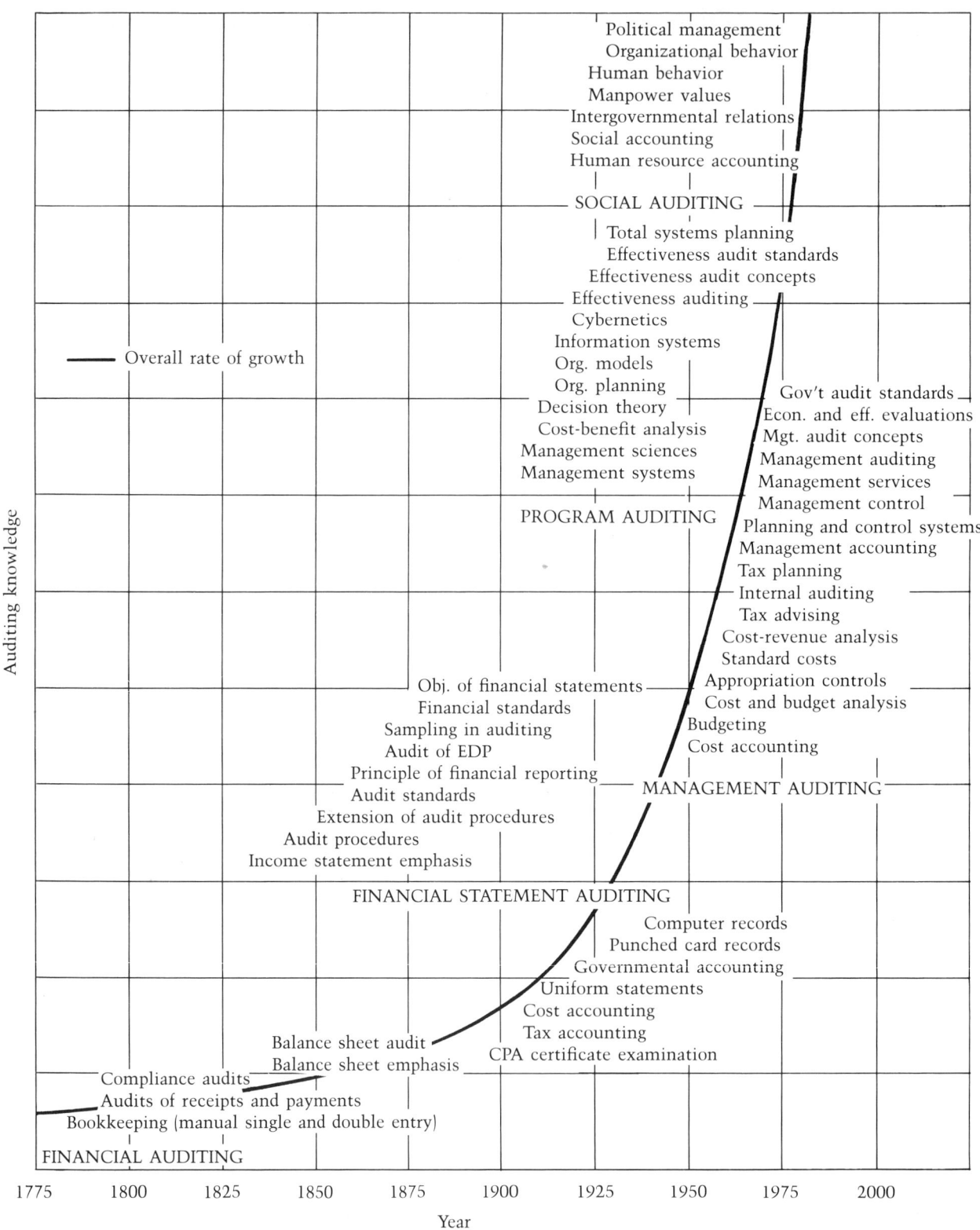

Figure 1.2 Growth of knowledge needed for the auditing function, 1775–1979.

program is carried out. They learn this information on the job just as financial statement auditors do.

All auditors need to continue their professional development. Figure 1.2 illustrates particular subjects that auditors may encounter today; and with the rapid expansion of knowledge in the auditing field, new ones will constantly be added to such a chart.

This wider knowledge can be gained in several ways:

- By additional study of the subject during formal education,
- By additional study through courses taken after formal education,
- By reading and studying journals and articles in the particular field of interest,
- By study of the program and organization being audited, and
- By using experts on the audit who bring special knowledge to bear on the job and also train auditors.

REVIEW QUESTIONS

1. Describe the general trend that the purposes of auditing have taken since the start of this century to today. (See p. 3.)

2. Describe some of the terms used in auditing the performance of management. (See p. 4.)

3. What terms will be used in this book for: Economy and efficiency type audits? Effectiveness type audits? For the whole field of auditing management's performance? (See p. 4.)

4. Auditing is concerned with three parties. Identify and explain their relationships in terms of auditing, accountability, and attesting. (See pp. 4–5.)

5. Performance auditing encompasses all types of managerial activities. Define performance auditing and within this framework discuss the distinguishing features of an M-audit and a P-audit. (See p. 4.)

6. Management within the context of M-auditing includes all internal operations of an organization. Define M-auditing and explain its purpose. (See pp. 6–7.)

7. The program entity, as contrasted to an organization's well-defined structure, may be unduly scattered and not well defined. Define P-auditing. What does a P-audit attempt to accomplish? (See pp. 7–8.)

8. Does the person who audits programs have any responsibility for determining the objectives of a program? (See p. 8.)

9. From evidence on the audit objective, the person who audits comes to a conclusion on a performance audit. That conclusion is reported to a third party. What three elements are present in all conclusions? (See p. 9.)

10. Looking at Figure 1.2, are there any subjects that you may need to review for your study of performance auditing? (See p. 10.)

CASE 1

Performance Audit Conclusions from an Industrial Corporation, a State Agency, and a Federal Agency

Required
1. Classify the following performance audit scenarios into (a) an M-audit or (b) a P-audit.
2. Explain the reasons for your classifications.
3. For each of the audit scenarios state (a) the appropriate standard used as a basis for the audit, (b) the actions of individuals or organizations that did or did not follow the standards, and (c) the results brought about by the actions of individuals or organizations that did or did not follow the standards.

AUDIT SCENARIO 1
The Travel Advances that Advanced

Funds for authorized travel were advanced to employees of the Romad Company in amounts greater than necessary or reasonable to meet travelers' requirements pending periodic reimbursements. Certain of these advances were allowed to remain outstanding for extended periods during which no travel occurred.

Our review of travel advances showed that a total of $10,000 had been made to 40 sales department employees by June 30, 1978, and we found that advances issued to 20 of the employees were in excess of their needs. These advances ranged from $120 to $500 and totaled $6,600, of which $4,400 was in excess of the travelers' needs. During the fiscal year ending on June 30, 1978, some of these 20 employees did not travel. Other employees' travel ranged from 1¾ days to 61¼ days, and their travel vouchers averaged from $42 to $147. Our review also showed that 2 employees were holding travel advances at June 30, 1978, although they had not traveled for 13 and 24 months, respectively.

AUDIT SCENARIO 2[3]
The Case of the Federal Grant Funds

A state auditor, Alan Good, reported that a state education agency was not complying with the provisions of its federal grant.

Title I of the Elementary and Secondary Education Act states that grants obtained as a result of this act should not result in a decrease of state or local funds that would otherwise be available to a project area in the absence of Title I funds. The U.S. Office of Education guidelines state that Title I funds

> ... are not to be used to supplant State and local funds which are already being expended in the project areas or which would be expended in those areas if the services in those areas were comparable to those for non-project areas....

Our audit of the state agency for Mr. Good found a decrease in state and local fiscal effort. Title I funds, estimated at $520,750, were used to supplant state and local funds that were already being spent for services in project areas. We question whether this amount is allowable under the grant, and the agency may be required to refund this amount or provide additional services.

The agency officials advised us that, with the exception of administrative reviews performed by program monitoring officials, no effective means existed to evaluate the comparability of services.

We recommend that this agency review other grant programs to determine whether similar deficiencies exist. On the basis of this review, if similar deficiencies exist, the agency should develop policies and procedures and issue them to all local education agencies in order to insure that similar deficiencies do not recur.

AUDIT SCENARIO 3

High Costs for Low Rents: The Public Housing Case

The low-rent housing program is designed to make decent, safe, and sanitary dwellings available to low-income families at rents within their financial means. HUD provides financial and technical assistance to Local Housing Authorities (LHAs), which develop and/or acquire, own, and operate low-rent public housing projects to accomplish this aim.

To provide low-rent public housing, LHAs use several methods—conventional construction, turnkey, direct acquisition of existing privately owned dwelling, and leasing.

Use of Direct Acquisition Method Does Not Increase Housing Supply

We reviewed HUD's and LHAs' practices and procedures relating to the direct-acquisition method of obtaining existing, occupied standard structures and found that, although the method was expedient, it has certain disadvantages that tended to make it less desirable than other methods.

By using the direct-acquisition method, the LHAs increased the supply of low-rent public housing but did not directly help to achieve the national housing goal of increasing the housing supply.

Our review of 15 projects in 8 selected cities or metropolitan areas showed that LHAs had expended about $80 million to acquire the projects without increasing the supply of standard housing by a single unit. HUD's analyses of housing-market conditions showed that, in 7 of the 8 cities, a need for both subsidized and nonsubsidized standard housing existed when these projects were acquired. The LHAs' action, therefore, did not improve the overall condition of the housing market. It appears that, in such cases, the construction of new housing and the rehabilitation of substandard housing would be the preferred method and would use federal funds more effectively by adding to the supply of standard housing.

We proposed that HUD limit its financial assistance to LHAs to the acquisition of privately owned standard housing where the supply of such housing exceeds the demand, terminate the acquisition of existing, occupied, privately owned standard housing in the planning or early development stages, and use the funds instead to finance the construction of new low-rent public housing projects or to purchase and rehabilitate existing substandard housing.

HUD did not agree because it felt that such a practice would be too restrictive. HUD commented that, despite an overall demand for unsubsidized housing in a community, some structures would not meet the demand for various reasons.

We agreed that, if certain standard housing had a high vacancy rate and could be purchased at an acceptable price, acquisition of such housing by an LHA would be beneficial. Of the 15 projects reviewed by GAO, however, all had low vacancy rates.

Acquired Units Are Not Being Used to House Those Most in Need

Our review showed that the acquisition of privately owned standard housing generally had not substantially reduced the number of families or persons living in substandard housing, because many of the occupants of the acquired housing units had previously lived in standard housing. Some of the families occupying the acquired units had incomes exceeding the established limits entitling them to public housing. Also, some persons were occupying units larger than those suggested in HUD's guidelines.

Because only a relatively small number of the occupants of the acquired housing projects included in review had previously occupied substandard housing, there appeared to be a need for specific standard admission policies to insure that those families or persons most in need are given preference.

We suggested that the Congress might wish to require that LHAs give preference for admission to public housing to occupants of private substandard housing over those who are occupying private standard housing.

Hardships to Former Occupants of Acquired Properties

The acquisition of privately owned standard housing has provided standard housing to certain low-income families sooner than it could have been provided under the other methods, but it has resulted in (1) hardships to former occupants of acquired projects who were forced to move, and (2) loss of tax revenues to local governments. In some cases, the people forced to move were not

14 / *Auditing the Performance of Management: The Fundamentals*

assisted in relocating, although HUD regulations so provided. Other displaced occupants were subjected to various physical and financial hardships.

We recommended that HUD, prior to approving LHAs' acquisition of occupied, privately owned standard housing, require LHAs to demonstrate adequately that housing of comparable quality and rent existed in the area and that adequate relocation assistance would be available for tenants to be displaced.

Because it is awaiting the results of its housing studies, HUD took no action on our recommendation.

Need to Insure that Prices of Acquired Properties Are Reasonable

Our review indicated that HUD needed to improve its procedures to provide adequate assurance that the prices of acquired properties are reasonable. We recommended that HUD establish appraisal requirements for the direct acquisition method similar to those established for the turnkey method, which requires that two independent cost estimates be obtained; and further that the total price be no greater than the average of the cost estimates. Although HUD agreed with this recommendation, it took no action pending the results of the housing studies.

CASE **2**

Performance Audit Conclusions from a Federal Agency, a Corporation, and a Municipality

Required
1. Classify the following performance audit scenarios into (a) an M-audit or (b) a P-audit.
2. Explain the reason for your classifications.
3. For each of the audit scenarios state (a) the appropriate standard used as a basis for the evaluations, (b) the actions of individuals or organizations that did or did not follow the standards, and (c) the results brought about by the actions of individuals or organizations that did or did not follow the standards.

AUDIT SCENARIO 1
Controlling Expenditures: A Federal Case

We found that the Pacific Region of the agency has expended approximately $267,000 for goods and services that either were unnecessary or were unjustifiable in part, considering conditions existing at the time and the very negligible benefits that accrued to the government.

1. A sound/alarm system for the region headquarters building in Honolulu was leased for 10 years at an annual rental of about $10,600 or $106,000 for the 10-year period. According to the agency, this procurement was justified by the need for sounding the alarm signal for possible fire, tidal wave, or enemy attack, and for transmitting official messages and background music throughout the building. Inasmuch as (a) the lessor of the sound/alarm system has also installed a fire alarm system in the building and (b) the State of Hawaii had installed a civil defense warning system near the building, we questioned the need for the lease of the sound/alarm system.

2. The region purchased 148 clothes dryers at a cost of about $12,500 for use by employees housed on Wake Island. Because of inadequate planning, the dryers remained in storage for about a year. An additional $25,000 had to be spent to modify and properly equip the housing in order to use the dryers.
3. On June 29 and 30, 1978, the region placed orders totaling about $15,600 for library books under conditions indicating that the principal objective was to obligate available funds prior to the end of the fiscal year rather than to order books for which there was real or urgent need.
4. Numerous other purchases—totaling about $46,000—were made at the end of fiscal years 1977 and 1978, the necessity of which appeared questionable.
5. Various items of equipment and supplies for major repairs were purchased for Canton Island at a cost of about $27,000, even though complete phaseout of the installation had been under consideration for some time.
6. The region incurred costs of over $30,000 directly related to ceremonies dedicating new facilities at 3 locations. We questioned whether the dedication ceremonies provided benefits to the government commensurate with their costs.

AUDIT SCENARIO 2
The Case of the Company Cars

Our review of travel procedures at three divisions of the corporation showed that the divisions had not been furnished information on the cost of operating motor pool cars at various mileage levels. They therefore were not in a position to consider adequately the alternative of providing motor pool cars to high-mileage drivers who drove their own cars on official business.

Our more detailed reviews at the offices of the Production Division, the Planning Division, and the Internal Auditor's Office showed that the annual cost of reimbursing high-mileage drivers for official travel exceeded the cost of operating motor pool cars by about $20,000. If the mileage patterns observed were typical, the annual costs for the entire corporation of reimbursing high-mileage drivers for official travel would exceed the cost of operating motor pool cars by about $100,000.

As a result of our proposals, the comptroller revised the corporation's travel regulations to provide policy guidelines for division management to determine (a) when it is beneficial to the organization for employees to use their own cars for official business, and (b) what reimbursement employees are entitled to if they are authorized to use their own cars on official business when such use is for their own personal convenience.

AUDIT SCENARIO 3[*]
The Case of the Careless Cost Charges

The city auditor found that a federal agency was not making office space payments in accordance with an adopted cost-allocation plan. The agency occupies a city-owned building consisting of 4,180 square feet of space.

The city developed a cost-allocation plan and implemented this plan for charges to all governmental agencies that occupied space in the city's buildings, effective September 1, 1977. The plan provides for the space costs (buildings and capital improvements) allocated to the various city departments and other agencies on a straight-line depreciation basis at an annual rate of 2.5 percent (40-year life). This charge amounted to 30 cents per square foot.

Before adopting the cost-allocation plan, the city's policy was to establish rental rates comparable to local space rates. The cost criteria requires consistent application of the city's accounting policies and procedures for costs to be applicable for all agencies occupying city space.

Prior to the adoption of the cost-allocation plan, the city charged the agency 20 cents per square foot. The agency made the proper payments of $836 per month (4,180 square feet at 20 cents per square foot) through August 31, 1977, and continued to make the same payments through August 31, 1978.

We estimate that the agency is underpaying the city $418 per month, or $5,016 per year. This underpayment will continue until the federal agency begins to pay its proper share of rent for the space it occupies.

16 / Auditing the Performance of Management: The Fundamentals

CASE 3

Performance Audit Conclusions from a City, a State Agency, and a Federal Agency

Required
1. Classify the following performance audit scenarios into (a) an M-audit, or (b) a P-audit.
2. Explain the reason for your classifications.
3. For each of the audit scenarios state (a) the appropriate standard used as a basis for the audit, (b) the actions of individuals or organizations that did or did not follow the standards, and (c) the results brought about by the actions of individuals or organizations that did or did not follow the standards.

AUDIT SCENARIO 1[5]
The Big Costs that Came in Little Packages

In our audit of the city's program for purchases by schools and other institutions, we found that considerable savings could be realized if larger sizes of packaged commodities were used when possible.

The city's purchasing department has instructed the city schools and other institutions to purchase commodites in the most economical size packages. When commodities are available in packages of more than one size, the instructions require that the agencies and institutions requisition the commodities to the maximum extent practicable in large-sized packages—such as 50-pound containers.

In seven institutions covered by our review, the agencies were purchasing foodstuffs in small-sized packages instead of large-sized packages.

A substantial part of the costs of providing flour, shortening, and nonfat dry milk could be saved if the schools and institutions purchased the commodities in larger containers. We estimated that in the 1979 calendar year, $50,000 could have been saved if the various institutions had purchased various types of foodstuffs in larger containers than the ones they did buy.

In view of the possible savings that could be made by buying commodities in large-sized packages, we recommend that the purchasing department review purchasing actions of the various institutions and vigorously enforce their requirement for purchases to be made in the most economical size packages.

AUDIT SCENARIO 2[6]
Snow Removal Snowed Under

A state auditor, Mary Forbes, found that the state's snow and ice removal program was not accomplishing its objectives because legislation made the state department of transportation's operations difficult.

Goal of the Program

The commissioner of the state department of transportation is responsible for removing ice and snow from state roads.

Condition Found by the Auditor

Ms. Forbes found that Article 12 of the State Highway Law authorizes the commissioner of the department of transportation to contract with counties for removing snow and ice on state roads. The statute also permits counties to select sections of state roads to plow or sand or to apply other abrasives or chemicals. The department of transportation is obligated to service the remaining road mileage. This feature of the legislation is referred to as the first-preference clause.

Effect of Not Meeting the Goals

Under the first-preference clause, counties have elected to service one section of state highways but not an adjoining section, and then resume service at another point on the road. This skip patchwork operational pattern often results in state roads that have not been properly cleared of ice and snow. A county crew may spread salt on one portion of the state's highway only to have it removed later by the state's plow crews. Also, the state's work crews may not be able to plow or sand sections of highways until the county has serviced its portions.

Cause that Contributed to Failure to Meet the Goal

The first-preference clause is permitting counties too much flexibility in location, amount of mileage selected, and in type of service performed. As a result, the department of transportation is unable to do adequate long-range planning for equipment purchases and staffing work forces.

This report contained no recommendations. However, the state's first-preference clause should obviously be amended.

AUDIT SCENARIO 3[7]

The Employment Program that Did Not Employ

Federal auditors reported the following situation where the objectives of a state employment program were not realized:

The Department of Labor's Concentrated Employment Program (CEP) was designed to combine, under one sponsor and in a single contract with one funding source, all manpower training and other services necessary to help persons move from unemployability and dependency to self-sufficiency. CEP seeks to accomplish this objective among persons in a designated target area by (1) making intensive outreach efforts to bring persons into work-training programs; (2) presenting a variety of job-training opportunities to applicants; (3) providing such supporting services as day care for children, transportation, and health care; and (4) placing applicants in jobs.

From December 1968 through February 1970, of the 6,732 persons enrolled in the program, 3,333 received some training or work experience and 2,586 were placed in jobs. About one-half of those placed in jobs, however, did not receive any orientation, training, or work experience. Often they were limited to the same types of low-skill jobs they held before joining the program.

Many placements were only temporary. Only 56 percent of the persons placed were employed six months later. Many had changed jobs during the six-month period.

Many enrollees were placed in jobs requiring similar or lower-level skills than those required in previous occupations. Only about one-half of the jobs increased the wages employees were receiving before entering the program.

Job placement was not always related to the type of training an enrollee received. For example, a person trained as a welder was placed as a janitor, an offset printer as a mail clerk, and an automobile mechanic as a maintenance man.

About $14 million was spent on CEP in the Mississippi Delta from June 1967 through December 1971.

CEP's effectiveness was hindered by:

- economic slowdown that closed or cut back operations of some companies in the area,
- the special nature of the disadvantaged residents of the area—minority-group farm workers accustomed to seasonal employment,
- a stagnant economy,
- an insufficient labor demand,
- a labor force consisting largely of black farm workers without necessary educational and vocational skills, and
- the large area and widely dispersed population that the program was trying to reach.

Increased mechanization has displaced many farm workers in the traditionally agricultural delta area. New job opportunities have been scarce because industries have been slow to come into the delta, and available jobs have required skills that enrollees do not have and cannot obtain reasonably.

The Congress is currently considering measures that will seek to revitalize the economy and increase job opportunities in such rural areas as the Mississippi Delta. The Secretary of Labor should try to improve the effectiveness of CEP by ensuring that skill training and other manpower services are provided with due regard to the capabilities and needs of program participants and available job opportunities and by making all possible use of work-experience programs and other subsidized employment, such as public service jobs funded under the Emergency Employment Act of 1971, for those participants who cannot be placed readily in jobs.

CHAPTER 2

Understanding the Phases of the Audit Function

After you have read this chapter, studied the review questions, and worked through the cases, you will understand:

- How to define evidence.
- How to define audit objectives.
- How to define the conclusion to an audit objective.
- How to define the three elements—*criteria, causes,* and *effects*—found in the conclusion to an audit objective or in the audit objective itself.
- How to state an audit objective for either an M-audit or a P-audit, including identifying the three essential elements of the objective above.
- That audit objectives have subobjectives and be able to state a subobjective for an M-audit or a P-audit.
- There is a reason for starting any audit.
- The four phases of any audit.
- What is included in and how to obtain background information on any organization, program, activity, or function.
- The steps needed to perform a preliminary survey.
- The purposes for reviewing and testing management control.
- That the detailed examination is the phase of an audit normally called the audit, but the preliminary survey and review and testing of management control phases are just as important as the detailed examination phase.
- That the work of an audit leads to the report to a third party—and this phase is so important that extensive work must be done to understand the process for reporting.

According to the definition of performance auditing given in Chapter 1, auditors make performance audits to come to a conclusion on a management's activities or programs. To reach a conclusion, auditors must thoroughly understand, in theory and in practice, how to plan for, obtain, and evaluate audit evidence as it relates to the performance audit objective, as well as how to present the evidence convincingly.

Auditing, including even the examination of financial statements, has never had a complete body of theory developed on audit evidence. However, the American Institute of Certified Public Accountant's "Statements on Auditing Standards" for financial-statement examinations has some valuable information on the subject, and the Comptroller General's standards for auditing governmental organizations, activities, programs, and functions set forth a good rationale for evidence:

Sufficient, competent, and relevant evidence is to be obtained to afford a reasonable basis for the auditor's opinions, judgments, conclusions, and recommendations.[1]

In spite of lacking a complete theory on audit evidence as it applies to performance auditing, we will develop one for our use in this chapter and in Chapter 8, which treats the subject of evidence in depth. The basic ideas relating to evidence in such fields as law, logic, history, and journalism will prove useful here even as we keep in mind that our chief concern is audit evidence.

Evidence and Audit Objectives

Any definition of evidence, whether it comes from financial-statement examinations, law, logic, or elsewhere, states something comparable to the following:

1. Evidence is the
2. facts or information used
3. to prove or disprove
4. a proposition.

Before an auditor can gather facts or information, he must have a proposition. All planning for, gathering of, and evaluating of evidence begins with the proposition, a term auditors seldom use, preferring the word *objective*. Since, in fact, the audit function is concerned with the relationship between the auditor and the entity being audited, *audit objective* or simply *objective* will be our term to mean the point of issue, the proposition to be proved, the question to be answered, the hypothesis to be proved, the allegation to be proved—all terms used by other disciplines.

When the auditors plan for, gather, and evaluate evidence on the audit objective, the result is the proof or answer. Auditors seem to dislike the words prove, disprove, or answer as much as they do proposition. Perhaps proof gives too much assurance or certainty, while answer implies absolute correctness. Similarly, the word inference seems to imply too much uncertainty, while judgment seems too Godlike. Findings is used, but the words most often found in audit literature are *opinion* for the results of examining financial statements, and *conclusions* for the results of auditing management performance. These are the words we have used in our definition of auditing and will be used to mean the proof, answer, judgment, findings, or any other such term.

As related to performance audits and to auditors' terminology, audit evidence is:

1. The facts or information used
    a) To come to a conclusion
    b) On the *audit objective* of
        (1) whether an entity's management, employees, or designated agents have or have not accepted and carried out
        (2) appropriate accounting, management, or operational principles, policies, or standards
        (3) for effectively, efficiently, or economically using its resources, and
2. The facts or information used to demonstrate to a third party that the conclusion the auditor came to is the correct conclusion.

Elements of the Audit Objective

You remember we learned in the preceding chapter that all conclusions to performance audits always have three elements: an appropriate standard, employees actions based on whether the appropriate standards were or were not carried out, and the results of either carrying out or not carrying out the appropriate standards. The audit objective likewise contains these same three elements. Thus, the objective on which evidence is gathered and on which the conclusion is determined must be related to certain appropriate standards, management and employee actions, and results.

For clarity, let us use a particular word for each as follows: *Criteria* will represent any appropriate standard, standards, or group of standards—for either a management or a program audit, and it will be used both as a singular and a plural word. *Causes* will represent management or employee action or actions that took place, as well as actions that should have taken place to carry out or not to carry out the appropriate standards. In most cases, causes will represent actions that carried out some standard other than the appropriate standard. *Effects* will represent the results obtained through the measurement of the causes against the criteria. Effects will be the results obtained when management or employees carry out actions based on improper standards and those actions are measured against the appropriate standards.

To illustrate these terms from an M-audit, suppose the policy of a company was to recap tires, at an average cost of $10 per tire, for its fleet of 400 automobiles and trucks rather than to buy new tires (criteria). During the year the employees of the company, assuming that the policy was always to buy new tires, purchased 40 new tires at an average cost of $60 per tire. Obviously, there was a lack of proper supervision of these purchases (causes). The action of the employees, based on an assumed policy measured against the appropriate policy, would thus be a bad or deficient action, resulting in a loss to the company of $2,000 (effects).

The significance of the effects is an important element in determining the audit objective and the audit conclusion. Two thousand dollars may or may not have been a significant amount to the company. Yet it often makes the difference as to whether or not a report is issued; or more importantly, whether an audit is even started unless the significance can be determined. Furthermore, unless the criteria are acceptable both to the auditor and to the person being measured, and the causes can be measured against the criteria, then the effects cannot be determined with any degree of certainty.

Thus, each audit objective will have these three essential elements: criteria, causes, and effects. The objective can be stated either in the form of a question or in the form of a simple declaration. Let us illustrate an audit objective from the audit information given above in the form of a question:

> Have the employees in the National Company in charge of procurement of tires purchased new tires (causes) instead of recapping tires (criteria) at a cost to the company of approximately $2,000 (effects)?

You can see that facts and information can be planned for, gathered, and evaluated on this audit objective in order to conclude whether the company spent more money than necessary for buying new tires instead of recapping the old tires. Here is another example taken from Case 3, Audit Scenario 1 of Chapter 1, about uneconomical package sizes:

> The city's purchasing department has instructed the city schools and other institutions to purchase commodities in the most economical size

packages. When commodities are available in packages of more than one size, the instructions require that the agencies and institutions requisition the commodities to the maximum extent practicable in large-sized packages, such as 50-pound containers (criteria).

The agencies were purchasing foodstuffs in small-sized packages instead of large size packages (causes).

A substantial part of the costs of providing flour, shortening, and nonfat dry milk could be saved if the schools and institutions purchased the commodities in larger containers. We estimated that in the calendar year 1979, $50,000 could have been saved if the various institutions had purchased various types of foodstuffs in larger containers than the ones they did buy (effects).

In the form of a question, the audit objective on which evidence was gathered and analyzed in order to come up with the conclusion to the above report would have been stated somewhat as follows:

> Have the purchasing agents in the various schools and institutions in the city purchased foodstuffs in small containers (causes), thereby not following the city's purchasing department instructions to buy foodstuffs in large-sized packages to the maximum extent practicable (criteria), and resulting in overexpenditures of $25,000 or more (effects)?

Notice that the effects stated in the audit objective are those that the auditor would consider significant. Thus, the audit function would be for the purpose of obtaining evidence on all three elements of the audit objective in order to come to a conclusion. The conclusion would show that there were more dollar effects than was stated in the audit objective. Also, the conclusion based on evidence gathered on the audit objective would always show that some individual or organization has or has not followed particular standards that brought about significant efficient or deficient results.

For our next illustration, let's state an objective for a P-audit. Remember that in a P-audit, the effects pertain to the effectiveness of the program; that is, whether the results intended are, or are not, being accomplished. This example is taken from Audit Scenario 2, Case 3 in Chapter 1, and is also posed as a question:

> Have the Commissioner of the State Department of Transportation, those county agents with whom he has contracted, and the legislature that provided the laws (causes) made the roads safely passable (effects) by adequately and properly removing snow and ice from the state roads (criteria)?

By gathering sufficient relevant, material, and competent facts and information on all three elements of the above audit objective, the auditor would have a conclusion that could be reported to a third party. When you read over this scenario on snow removal (p. 16 ff.), notice that quite a bit of the evidence is stated in the auditor's report.

Subobjectives

Very few audits have only one level of audit objectives. In an audit, each subobjective must be directly related to the primary objective and the conclusion on that subobjective must always be evidence on one of the causes for the primary objective either being properly or not properly carried out. For example, in the illustration on uneconomical package sizes, several agencies were purchasing foodstuffs in small-sized packages. The conclusion on the actions regarding each of the various agencies purchasing small-sized packages of commodities could be evidence on causes of the primary audit objective concerning all of the agencies that purchased the commodities.

Moreover, the question or statement that proposes the audit subobjective should always contain the same three elements—criteria, causes, and effects—as are found in the primary audit objective, and still directly relate these to the criteria of the primary audit objective. As an illustration, the auditor's subobjective for the audit on a city's purchase of small-sized packages could be stated in the form of the following question:

> Has the purchasing agent for City Hospital purchased foodstuffs in small containers (causes) thereby not following the city's purchasing department instructions to buy foodstuffs in large-sized packages to the maximum extent practicable (criteria) and resulting in overexpenditures of approximately $5,000 (effects)?

We can also illustrate the use of subobjectives in a P-audit with the case on snow removal. If the auditor was interested in the results in one county, which eventually would be consolidated into the total audit, the audit objective for that county would be somewhat as follows:

> Has the county agent in Madison County, with whom the Commissioner of the State Department of Transportation contracted (causes) made the state roads in the county safely passable (effects) by adequately and properly removing snow and ice from the state roads (criteria)?

The conclusion on this subobjective would be additional evidence on causes of the primary audit objective, a type of evidence often called *analytical evidence*.

Summary of Discussion on Audit Objectives

Every audit objective—the question to be answered, the proof to be developed, the issue to be judged, the results to be expected—always has three elements: criteria, causes, and effects. Each element should always be stated in the audit objective. The criteria are appropriate standards that individuals in an organization should have followed in carrying out their responsibilities. The auditor uses them to measure the actions of those persons as they actually do carry out their responsibilities. The criteria of the audit objective should be stated in such a way that they can be used to measure the actual actions of management and employees, which they either properly chose and carried out or improperly chose and did not carry out when compared to the appropriate standards. Causes are the actual actions. Effects are the results of measuring the actual actions against the appropriate standards; that is, measuring the causes (the actual actions) against the criteria (the standards for appropriate actions).

Most performance audits have subobjectives as well as primary objectives. A subobjective is a breakdown of the primary objective into individual audit parts, each one of which has the same three elements as does the primary objective. Since the subobjective is a breakdown of the primary objective, the criteria of the subobjective should be based on and should be an expansion of the primary audit objective. The conclusion the auditor derives by obtaining evidence on the subobjective is always evidence on the causes of the primary objective. This type of evidence is often called analytical evidence.

Now we are ready for a discussion on how we use audit objectives in the various phases of the audit function.

Phases of the Audit Function

In Chapter 1 we defined the three separate and distinct functions of performance auditing: the audit function, the attest and communication function, and the accountability function. In this chapter so far we have defined evidence and objectives, and identified the three essential elements of an audit objective: criteria, causes, and effects.

You can easily see, then, that the auditor making a performance audit always goes through at least two phases: making the audit, and preparing the report. During the audit phase, the auditor gathers evidence on an objective and comes to a conclusion on that objective. During the report phase, the auditor develops the conclusion into a report. Sufficient evidence should be presented in the report to convince the reader that the conclusion is correct. The report is then transmitted to a third party to accomplish the communication and attest function.

Are these two phases the only ones auditors go through in making a performance audit? How, for instance, and when do they learn what activity or organization to audit? Where, when, and how do they arrive at an audit objective? For auditors to develop an assertion into a firm audit objective, they must do more than simply state that they have an audit objective, just as in financial-statement examinations CPAs must know what is wanted by the agency or activity. Governmental auditors or internal auditors may have a law, regulation, or policy that tells the audit group what type of work they will do, but it does not tell them which activity or organization to examine.

Thus, whether governmental, internal, or private, the auditor must determine the specific activity or organization to examine; and to make this determination, certain factors should be considered. They include:

1. Specific statutory or policy requirements for audits;
2. Legislative, audit committee, or executive department requests;
3. Importance of the program, activity, or organization judged by such measures as size of expenditures, investments in assets, and amounts of revenue;
4. Knowledge by the auditor of the agency and its system of internal and management control;
5. New programs or activities that need careful watching; and
6. A request for a proposal to audit a specific activity or function.

You can see now that to reach the audit objective, the auditor must include two additional steps, which we will call a preliminary survey and a review and testing of management control. There are thus four phases in any audit function, each of which we will discuss in detail. They are:

1. The preliminary survey,
2. The review and testing of management control,
3. The detailed examination, and
4. The report development.

Note that these four phases are comparable to the five steps given by the American Institute of Certified Public Accountants for conducting performance evaluations:

1. Ascertaining the pertinent facts and circumstances,
2. Seeking and identifying objectives,
3. Defining problem areas or opportunities for improvement,
4. Evaluating and determining possible improvements,
5. Presenting findings and recommendations.[2]

The Preliminary Survey

The purpose of the preliminary survey phase of the performance audit function is for the auditor to obtain background and general information in a relatively short period of time on all aspects of the organization, activity, program, or system being considered for examination in order to have a working knowledge of that entity. At this point in time, such knowledge is not evidence, but simply descriptive information. It includes historical and operating information for the activities of private and governmental organizations as well as legislative information on the activities of governmental organizations. To illustrate, let us consider appropriate background and general information for three different entities, as follows:

1. For an organization
    a) its location,
    b) its management,
    c) its history,
    d) the number of its employees,
    e) the type of examination to be made,
    f) the organization's policies,
    g) its legal requirements,
    h) its charter or changes in charter, and
    i) its obligations.
2. For an activity
    a) the type of activity,
    b) its location,
    c) persons responsible for the activity,
    d) policies pertaining to the activity, and
    e) specific procedures for accomplishing the activity.
3. For a program
    a) purposes and objectives of the program,
    b) interrelationships among the organizations used for accomplishing the objectives,
    c) policies and procedures for accomplishing the program, and
    d) administrative regulations related to the program.

CPAs, or other management consultants engaged in performance auditing, especially for governmental organizations, approach the preliminary survey a little differently from governmental auditors. They must often plan for a request for proposal for the contract for the engagement, as well as prepare for gathering background and general information. The American Institute of Certified Public Accountants has prepared for CPAs who may go into this type of work a checklist that sets forth important points concerning the proposed contract and the CPA's ability to perform the contract in addition to points pertaining specifically to the audit. This checklist is reproduced as Appendix II.

From the background and general information obtained, the auditor should now have a good working knowledge of the organization, activity, program, or system being considered for examination, and should thus be able to make a preliminary determination as to the audit objective, even though that objective is still tentative. If there are possible areas of weakness, then the auditor is identifying only *relevant* evidence on a tentative objective, not necessarily evidence that is sufficient, material, or competent. And often only one element of the audit objective has been identified with evidence, not all three. The auditor would have to assert the other two elements even to have a tentative objective. Before continuing, then, the auditor will need to be certain of obtaining sufficient evidence, which is also material, competent, and relevant, on all three elements of the audit objective, in order to complete the examination and arrive at a reportable conclusion.

At this point, however, the auditor would not move toward obtaining more evidence unless fairly certain the audit should be continued. In fact, withdrawing from the examination is one of the possible conclusions the auditor can reach in this phase. For example, the client may want the auditor to express a favorable conclusion on the effectiveness of a program with only a limited examination. The auditor would have no recourse but to withdraw from the examination.

We can see, thus, that the auditor will not move directly toward obtaining sufficient evidence to arrive at a reportable conclusion until sure, first, that there was enough evidence on all three elements to have a specific and workable objective; and second, that the evidence to be obtained from the entity will be competent.

When the conclusion on the preliminary survey phase is converted to a question or statement, it then becomes the objective for the review phase. It also becomes the basis for determining how to obtain the evidence and how much evidence is needed for the phase that reviews and tests management control.

The Review and Testing of Management Control

Having arrived at only a tentative objective in the preliminary survey phase, the auditor must make it into a firm objective in order to continue the examination of the particular activity or program. This is the purpose of the second phase, which we term the review and testing of management control. It's function is twofold: (1) to obtain evidence on all three elements of the tentative audit objective by actual testing of management control transactions of the entity, and (2) to determine that the evidence obtained from within the entity would be competent if the audit were extended into a more detailed examination. If not competent evidence, the evidence the auditor would need would have to be obtained from alternative sources. The auditor should identify those best possible alternative sources.

The term *management control* as used here embraces the entire system of organization, including the planning, policy, and procedures determination, as well as the actual practices carried out in managing an entity's affairs. It promotes the effective carrying out of assigned responsibility in the manner and with the results intended.

Management control often goes beyond the internal management of a company. For example, when an independent CPA audits the financial statements of an organization, that CPA reviews the internal control of the company. Internal control usually includes only the accounting control, but can also include administrative actions related to accounting control. Management control includes *all* activities of management, whether related to accounting or not, and thus includes external activities of management as well as internal activities. An independent CPA who is reviewing financial statements becomes a part of the external management control system but should not be a part of the entity's internal management control. In the area of accounting alone, internal management control and internal control mean the same thing, whereas performance auditing relates as well to many other matters.

By obtaining evidence on each element of the tentative audit objective, the auditor can determine whether there will be a firm audit objective that can be used as a basis for the detailed examination. By determining the competency of the evidence during the review and testing of management control, the auditor also will be able to determine the reliability of the information to be obtained from the management systems.

The Detailed Examination

The detailed examination phase of the audit function is the phase normally thought of as the audit. The prior two phases, however, are just as important as the detailed examination because those two phases determine what is to be done in the detailed examination and how it is to be done.

The evidence in this phase will have to be sufficient as well as competent, material, and relevant in order for the auditor to arrive at an acceptable conclusion on the audit objective and then report that conclusion to a third party.

Report Development

All work done in the audit function leads to this phase. Its purpose is to take the conclusion to the audit objective, which has been developed in the detailed examination phase from evidence gathered in that phase, and convert it into a form that an interested third party can accept and understand.

Over the years, various means have been developed for presenting the results of an audit to a third party. For example, the short-form audit report has been developed for expressing an opinion on financial statements. No such standard way exists for presenting the results of a performance audit—either an M-audit or a P-audit. There are some basic ideas, however, on ways to present the results of performance audits; and since this subject is of such importance to the auditor, these ideas, along with illustrations for accomplishing them, will be given in Chapter 16.

REVIEW QUESTIONS

1. One of the most fundamental subjects in the education and training of a performance auditor is that of planning for, obtaining, evaluating, and reporting auditing evidence. What other fields can be used as a basis for understanding audit evidence? (See p. 20.)

2. Define evidence as used in the general definition of performance auditing. (See p. 20.)

3. Evidence is the facts or information used to come to a conclusion on an audit objective. Define audit objective. (See p. 20.)

4. The audit objective on which evidence is gathered and a conclusion expressed must be related to certain standards, actions, and results. Within this context define criteria, causes, and effects for M-auditing and P-auditing. (See pp. 21–23.)

5. Consider the following illustration of an M-audit: The policy of the store is to remove all fruit from the shelves that has been standing for over four days. The employees, however, have been allowing the fruit to remain on the shelves for almost a week. Identify the criteria and causes in this case and discuss the effects. (See pp. 21–23.)

6. Very few audits have only one level of objectives. A subobjective is also an audit objective. Discuss the relationship of each subobjective to the primary objective, and identify the three basic elements of a subobjective. (See pp. 21–23.)

7. In order to develop a firm audit objective, the auditor must determine which activity or organization to examine and the type of work to be

performed. Discuss the responsibility of the auditor in these two decisions. (See pp. 25–26.)

8. In governmental or internal auditing, certain factors should be considered before determining the audit objective. List some of the factors that help the auditor determine what agency or activity to examine. (See p. 24.)

9. What is generally considered background information for a performance audit? (See p. 25.)

10. The auditor should not move toward obtaining more evidence unless fairly certain the audit should be continued. What evidence must the auditor first obtain before gathering sufficient evidence to form a conclusion? (See p. 26.)

11. The auditor must take the tentative objective obtained during the preliminary survey phase and make it into a firm objective. What is the purpose of the phase for the review and testing of management control? (See p. 26.)

12. The detailed examination phase is normally considered to be the audit. Discuss the importance of the prior two phases in a performance audit relative to the detailed examination phase. (See p. 27.)

13. All work done in the audit function leads to the report development phase. Discuss the purpose of this phase. (See p. 27.)

CASE 1

The Case of Too Many Workers in the Production Department at Torex

Required
1. Determine whether the following audit is an M-audit or P-audit. Explain your reason for your determination.
2. State the audit objective for the audit. Label the criteria, the causes, and the effects as illustrated in the chapter.
3. How was this audit started? Discuss how the information from the preliminary phases was used to develop the audit objective.

The president of Torex, Joan Bond, requested us to review the personnel needs of the production department for the month of January 1979.

Personnel records showed that 250 employees worked in the department during the month of January 1979. The budget request for the fiscal year beginning April 1, 1979, showed the department needed an additional 25 persons, with a budgeted total of 275.

According to the department foreman, the department was often behind in its production schedule during the production crisis of the late 1970s. This information was confirmed by reference to the production records for the months of July to December 1978.

The foreman also stated that in order to assure that the department was never behind in production, he figured that they should always stay ahead about 25 employees. He also said that when employment conditions eased in 1978, he hired and trained sufficient personnel to take care of emergency conditions. He said that he thought that conditions would continue to improve so he would need the additional people asked for in the budget.

From reviewing production records and discussing the situation with knowledgeable people in the department, we believe sufficient personnel are trained to take care of any emergency that may arise in the near future. We observed many of the present employees standing around with no work to do. Several of the workers complained to us that they were not being used at all. Others said that they were only being used part time.

It is our conclusion, and the production foreman agrees with us, that the department could operate more efficiently with 25 fewer workers than they presently have. Reducing the number of employees would reduce costs of the department by approximately $250,000 each year. Thus, both total costs and unit costs in the department could be reduced.

Our recommendation to president Bond is that the department reduce the numbers of employees to its present need, 225, and hire no new employees until the total number in the department is below 225. We also recommend that the reduction in employees be accomplished through attrition rather than through layoffs. At the present turnover rate of an average of 3 a month, this could be accomplished in about 8 months.

CASE 2

A Case of Probation in the State of Sylvania

Required

1. Determine whether the following audit is an M-audit or a P-audit. Explain your reason for your determination.
2. State the audit objective for the audit. Label the criteria, the causes, and the effects as illustrated in the chapter.
3. How was this audit started? Discuss how the information from the preliminary phases was used to develop the audit objective.

Sentencing is one of the most important functions of the criminal justice system and requires accurate, complete information on offenders. Probation is the most frequent sentence in the state of Sylvania. The objectives of probation are:

1. To rehabilitate the offender,
2. To protect the community, and
3. To save incarceration costs to the state.

The state agencies involved in probation in Sylvania have not:

1. Developed acceptable minimum probation standards, goals, and guidelines or otherwise assured adequate planning to correct probation problems,
2. Insured that information systems were adequate to identify problems and assess the effectiveness of the probation,
3. Provided sufficient technical assistance to probation departments in developing and implementing programs, or
4. Established funding priorities to assure that resources were allocated to meet the needs of criminal justice systems.

In their process of sentencing, judges often lack information needed to adequately answer such questions as:

1. Who should be sent to prison and for how long?
2. Who should be granted probation?
3. Will available services benefit the probationer?
4. Will the risk to society be minimal?

The primary source of such information should be presentence investigative reports—often prepared by probation departments.

In 46 percent of the cases we reviewed, presentence investigations were not made. When they were made, 64 percent contained sentence recommendations. But few contained recommendations relating to the offender's threat to the community, the type of probation supervision needed, or the probationer's chances of being rehabilitated. In only 15 percent of the cases were professional diagnoses of the probationers' problems and needs made before sentencing.

A probationer receiving needed services will more likely complete probation successfully. If probation departments would allocate their scarce resources more effectively, they would begin more adequately to rehabilitate more offenders.

During our review, we found in only 38 percent of the cases were rehabilitation plans prepared. We also found that only 41 percent of the time were court-ordered conditions of probation and rehabilitation enforced. Allowing probationers to continue or complete probation after violating the basic conditions set at the time of sentencing seriously interferes with rehabilitation. Under these conditions, repeat offenders do not take conditions of probation seriously. And, overall, only about 23 percent of the probationers completed a treatment program.

We found that probation officers have too many cases. The individual caseload averaged 85. On the basis of a standard of 35 cases per officer (recommended by the President's Commission on Law Enforcement and Administration of Justice) the state would require 711 probation officers instead of the 292 they had.

Large caseloads force probation systems to focus services and attention on the probationers who need the most help and supervision. In this state, neither the courts nor probation departments had adequate techniques to determine how much supervision or what types of services probationers needed.

The behavior of the offenders in the community is the most critical test of achieving the objectives of a probation program.

About 26 percent of the former probationers we reviewed either had their probations revoked or were convicted of crimes involving a sentence of more than 60 days. This happened while they were on probation or during a follow-up period—which averaged 22 months—once they were off probation.

An additional 19 percent were convicted of less serious crimes while on probation. Thus, overall, 45 percent of the former probationers were convicted of new crimes during or not long after their probation period.

About half of the former probationers convicted of additional crimes while on probation remained on probation. The other half were imprisoned. Additionally, about 37 percent of the individuals who were still on probation remained on probation after being convicted of additional crimes.

Overall, the state failed successfully to deal with an estimated 55 percent of the former probationers: they fled, had their probation revoked, or were convicted of new crimes.

Our conclusion is that the state is not effectively accomplishing the objectives of the state probation system. New ideas and more positive leadership are needed to improve probation at the state level. If no action is taken, the probation system will continue to be overburdened and will deteriorate further, increasing the costs to the state and the dangers to society.

Our recommendation is:

1. The state should develop minimum standards governing such areas as workload and need for presentence reports.
2. The state should develop improved communication systems concerning probation.
3. Probationers should receive needed services.
4. Since most offenders are placed on probation, the priority given to probation in the criminal justice system must be reevaluated.
5. Allocation of competing resources in the criminal justice system should be looked at more closely.

CASE 3

Auditing the Uses of Equipment: A University, a Corporation

Required
1. In each of the following audit scenarios determine whether the audit is an M-audit or a P-audit. Explain the reason for your determination.
2. State the audit objective for each of the audit scenarios. Label the criteria, the causes, and the effects for each scenario as is illustrated in the chapter.
3. How were these audits started? Discuss how the information from the preliminary phases was used to develop the audit objective.

AUDIT SCENARIO 1
How They Made Copies at Sohi—and Copies and Copies

Our review at Sohi University showed that no standards for maximum and minimum office-copier usage had been set by the comptroller's office. The comptroller's office standards allow each academic department and each administrative division to acquire and use its own office copying machine for any activity it so desires.

Costs in the printing department show that they can reproduce copies above 25 at a cost of 1 cent per copy. Lease costs on copiers run about 3 cents per copy. Almost all of the copiers are at present leased.

We observed each department's usage of its office copier. In almost 50 percent of the cases, the department ran more than 25 copies.

We determined that if the comptroller's office standards required that individual departments and divisions send to the printing department all requests for duplication of more than 25 copies, at least $25,000 could be saved by the university each year.

AUDIT SCENARIO 2
Who Used the Research Equipment at Texon—and When?

In our review of the Research Division of the Texon Corporation, we found technical equipment that cost about $250,000, with a present market value of approximately $100,000, was either excess to needs or had not been used for an extended period. We also found that there was no pooling of infrequently used equipment, and therefore every researcher was ordering and had on hand equipment that was available but not being used by another researcher. We estimate that the corporation spent $75,000 for this excess equipment during the current year.

CHAPTER 3

Determining Efficient, Economical, and Effective Operations

After you have read this chapter, studied the review questions, and worked through the cases, you will understand:

- The various considerations the auditor will make in determining the directions he will take in his examination.
- That most management audits point to deficiencies in managerial operations.
- How to state a tentative objective for an M-audit.
- How to state alternative tentative audit objectives for an M-audit.
- How management control transactions are tested in order to firm up the tentative audit objective.
- How to state a firm audit objective that will be used in the detailed examination for an M-audit.
- That the auditor must gather sufficient relevant, material, and competent evidence on the audit objective in order to come to a conclusion on that objective so that he can report his conclusion to a third party.
- What a *program* is.
- What a P-audit is.
- That the same four phases apply to a P-audit as to an M-audit. Yet the auditor must identify the goals of the program and the interorganizational structures for accomplishing the goals in the preliminary phases of a P-audit.
- How to state a tentative objective for a P-audit.
- How to follow the flow of the management control in a P-audit in order to test it and state a firm audit objective for the audit.
- How to state a firm audit objective for the detailed examination of a P-audit.
- The flow of information and evidence concerning the audit objective for both an M-audit and a P-audit.

M-audits

The Preliminary Survey

Since an M-audit is the examination of a particular activity or organization to determine the efficiency or economy of operations, repetitive audits seldom occur. In this respect, an M-audit is quite different from a financial-statement examination, which may take place over and over, from year to year. Each phase of a management audit, therefore, is much more distinct and necessary than that of a financial-statement examination. The need is especially distinct for auditors to identify from the background and general working information, evidence that will show the direction they will take in the examination.

Some considerations an auditor will make in determining the directions to take in an examination are:

1. The amount of money received and spent: the larger the amount the better the chance that there is need for improvement in the way the money is spent.
2. Executive interest: the executive, in an overall position, often has a better view of the operations than the auditor.
3. Legislative interest: the legislature or audit committee might be considering an area for review that has a direct bearing on the area being considered for examination by the auditor.
4. Legal requirements: the law ordinarily is specific in the requirements to make an examination.
5. Auditor's personal knowledge: working around an agency or activity for a sufficient time, the auditor may have acquired a great deal of knowledge concerning an area needing examination, and this knowledge often leads to areas of known deficiencies.
6. Other considerations: public concern, current interest by the board of directors.
7. Request for proposals: often CPAs and management consultants get into an area because of a request for a proposal to make an examination. The auditor, undoubtedly, should have some reason for entering an area before starting to make a preliminary survey of that area.

Once the broad area has been determined, the auditor can obtain the information for the entity, as discussed in the last chapter. The auditor will interview responsible officials and employees at all levels of the activity or organization. The auditor will obtain all types of records, such as budget and operating information submitted to the legislature, boards of directors, or executive officials; reports prepared on the agency by outside groups; policy manuals, procedure manuals, internal audit or inspection reports, and internal management reports. Finally, the auditor will observe activities of all types, such as inspecting the physical property, seeing how an activity is actually carried on, and making a walk-through of the organization, often a revealing way to spot deficiencies in operations.

Most M-audits are those that point to a deficiency in operations. Suppose the area in a state being considered for examination was the State Administrative Agency and the auditor, Lynn Price. This agency would have responsibility for all administrative activities in the state. These would include budgeting, accounting, automobile control, purchasing, warehousing, and other activities normally considered administrative.

Quite often the evidence spotted from the background and general information points to deficient effects. Once the auditor learned from the background and general information that the State Administrative Agency had responsibility for all state automobiles and that the state had government gasoline outlets, all she would have to do in order to assert a tentative audit objective would be to see the driver of a state vehicle buying gasoline from a nongovernment outlet. Ms. Price might not know exactly how much could be saved, but she could assert that if government car operators used (causes) government gasoline outlets whenever feasible instead of private outlets (criteria), the state could save quite a bit of money (effects).

Once a particular tentative audit objective has been defined, it is easy to consider alternative objectives. For example, if the survey is concerned with automobiles, should the auditor not consider what is happening to tires, batteries, and repairs, as well as to gasoline? But she would not have a tentative audit objective unless she could obtain some evidence on whether tires were bought from retail outlets, batteries were bought from retail outlets, or repairs made in-house or by retail outlets.

At this time, the auditor would have only a tentative objective. The State Administrative Agency might in fact already have a requirement that drivers of state vehicles buy gasoline from government outlets; nevertheless, as the auditor, Ms. Price asserts that they should have that requirement.

We can easily see now that in further planning for this case, the auditor can determine what types of evidence she would need if she expected to continue the examination. She would have to have information on whether the agency had the authority to require agencies and drivers to buy gasoline from government outlets, whether the agency had any regulation or requirement presently on the books, and whether the amount of savings would be worth the time of the auditor and the agency to continue the examination. If Ms. Price decided to go on, she would have a tentative plan for testing management control.

The auditor might also find, however, that the activity is doing everything so well that there is no reason to believe that she could find enough evidence to support a significant deficiency. In that case she should stop before wasting any more time.

As has been pointed out in the above illustration, the agency might already have a regulation concerning the use of government gasoline outlets. Audits concerned with compliance with laws, regulations, or other requirements are often called *compliance audits.* As long as compliance with the law, regulation, or other requirement results in more efficient or economical operations, noncompliance with the requirement would result in a management audit report. The law, regulation, or other requirement would automatically be the criteria for the audit. Noncompliance with this appropriate standard would result in a deficiency, which, if significant, should be developed and reported.

Sometimes, in the course of a P-audit, the auditor may determine that the program is operating effectively but that certain activities of the program apparently are not being carried out efficiently or economically. These apparent or tentative audit objectives coming from a P-audit can be used as the basis for starting an M-audit.

The Review and Testing of Management Control for an M-audit

The primary purpose of the review and testing of management controls is to firm up the audit objective. To do this, the auditor obtains relevant, material, and competent evidence—not necessarily sufficient—by testing transactions in the management control system. He can thus determine whether the weaknesses identified as the tentative objective might be significant (effects), whether some particular individual or groups of individuals might cause the weakness (causes), and whether the standard used might be reasonable and firm (criteria). A secondary reason would be to evaluate the effectiveness of the management control system in order to determine the competency of any evidence that came from the overall system.

Any good management control system follows these steps: setting standards, objectives, goals, or procedures; determining whether the standards, objectives, goals, or procedures have been appropriately carried out; appraising the results of such carrying out; and then, when necessary, taking corrective action. The principle underlying these steps is that no one person should be in complete control of any important part of the operations of the system.

The basic approach to the review of management control for an M-audit is to review the specific flow of procedures and practices applied to a specific transaction or item. As an example, let us continue with the illustration concerning the buying of gasoline for state cars. In testing a transaction concerning the buying of gasoline from a government outlet, Ms. Price, the auditor, would first start that testing by determining whether the State Administrative Agency had the authority to require operators to buy gasoline from government outlets. This authority would be in the form of a law, regulation, or operating practice. By obtaining the law, regulation, or operating practice, Ms. Price would have some evidence on the criteria. If there were none, she would have evidence on the lack of a standard and would have to develop one.

She would then have to follow the transaction back to the leasing of the vehicle to the agency and ask questions. Are there instructions to the driver in the vehicles concerning the buying of gasoline? Can the operator buy wherever he wants or is he required to buy from government outlets? Then the auditor would have to trace a particular driver's actual purchases of gasoline by analyzing the credit car purchases on travel vouchers. Has the driver bought gasoline from government outlets or from retail outlets? What has the agency done to assure the purchase from a proper outlet? Who has the responsibility for this particular activity? Do purchases from retail outlets happen often? With answers to such questions, Ms. Price would have some evidence on causes.

Then, if she analyzed the transaction in terms of the amount purchased from nongovernment sources compared to that purchased from government sources, and took the difference in cost from private sources to government sources, the auditor would have some analytical evidence of the effects—not enough evidence to warrant reporting on this audit, but enough to determine the possible significance of the effects.

Thus, by tracing one particular transaction from beginning to end as described, an auditor would have evidence on all three elements of the tentative objective and would be able to determine whether the finding would be significant enough to warrant continuation of the audit to the detailed examination.

In this way, too, she would be able to determine the competency of evidence from the management control system. Does one person have overall control? Are the duties properly segregated? Are the operations actually being carried out? Are there duplicate steps? Does the system provide adequate control on costs, expenditures, receipts, or other revenue?

The Detailed Examination for an M-audit

Much of the balance of the book will be concerned with the concepts, standards, and procedures for making a detailed examination, and a great deal of this concern will be for M-audits. To further illustrate here, let us continue with the illustration pertaining to government gasoline purchases for state-owned cars.

The audit objective Ms. Price developed for this case might read somewhat as follows:

> Have drivers who use state-owned cars bought (causes) gasoline from state-owned outlets when feasible instead of private outlets (criteria) thus saving the state approximately $25,000 per year (effects)?

If the State Administrative Agency does not have a good standard for requiring the usage of government gasoline outlets, the auditor may want to go to other states or the federal government in order to have an excellent standard for measuring the present actions of buyers of gasoline for state cars; that is, she would gather additional evidence on her criteria in order to have the best standard possible. Thus, she would be able to assure that the criteria was acceptable and that it could not be rebutted.

The actions involved in this case might include the failure of the state agency to prepare an acceptable standard. Also, the agency might not have done anything to control the actions of the drivers of state cars. Ms. Price would have to gather evidence on these causes in order to present a recommendation that would correct the situation.

In addition, she would either have to gather evidence on all the transactions concerning gasoline purchases for the year, or at least make a sample that would enable her to estimate the total cost of buying nongovernment gasoline compared with buying gasoline from government outlets. This evidence would also be evidence on the causes of the loss during the year.

Once the auditor had all the information on gasoline purchasing from the many state agencies using state cars, she could make an analysis of the total savings that could be made by using government outlets rather than private ones.

The auditor would then be ready to report her findings to the appropriate state officials, such a report representing the end result of the audit of management's performance concerning efficiency and economy. Because this subject is of such importance, it will be treated at length in chapters 16 and 17, but a useful example of the graphic flow of an M-audit is shown in Table 3.1.

P-audits

The Preliminary Survey

In an industrial concern, programs are related to products produced and sold. Programs are the activities of (1) internally producing the product, and (2) externally selling the product. Industrial and commercial organizations may also have socially oriented programs, such as equal employment opportunity programs, environmental programs, public identity programs, and power usage programs.

In governmental organizations or industrial and commercial organizations with socially oriented activities, programs are related to the services in which the organization is engaged. As identified in (1) and (2) above, such programs are the activities of internally producing a service and externally providing the benefits of the service to others. For example, General Motors produces and sells Chevrolets, Oldsmobiles, Pontiacs, Buicks, and Cadillacs. Each of these could be considered a program. Likewise, the U.S. Department of Health, Education, and Welfare (HEW) produces and renders the services of health, welfare, and education. Each of these could be considered a program.

Not only are there programs at the highest level of activity, but there can also be programs much further down the line. A division of General Motors, for instance, might produce only engines, and that could be a program. Similarly, HEW might have a special program for mental health, and a city might have a program under police protection called prevention of child molestation.

Each of the programs has something in common: It is producing a product or service and selling the product or rendering that service to an outside group. You can see that from a financial standpoint, the costs of the program can be related to revenues or benefits, and there is a similar relationship of the revenues to the objectives.

In a P-audit, the auditor determines whether the organizations responsible for the program are accomplishing the intended objectives. Therefore, in most P-audits, if the costs are related to revenue or benefits and they in turn

Table 3.1 Phases of the Audit Function for an M-audit, Described by Process

A. The Preliminary Survey	B. The Review and Testing of Management Control

1. Obtain in a relatively short period of time background and general information on organization and management activity being considered for examination.
 	
2. Analyze background and general information to obtain relevant evidence—not necessarily sufficient, material or competent—on one or more elements—criteria, causes, or effects—of a possible M-audit objective.
 	
3. Assert the other element or elements in order to have a tentative M-audit objective.
 	
4. Assert alternative criteria and other elements on related management activities to establish possible alternative M-audit objective.
 	
5. If possible alternative objective is to be considered, obtain relevant evidence, if no evidence has previously been obtained, on one or more elements of the possible audit objective in order to have alternative tentative M-audit objective.
 	
6. Summarize evidence and assertions on tentative M-audit objectives.
 	
7. Conclude from relevant evidence and assertions:
  a) *that original or alternative tentative M-audit objective can be used as the objective for the review phase,* if relevant, material, and competent evidence can be obtained on all three elements of the tentative objective, and (1) what types of relevant material and competent evidence will be needed to determine the audit objective, and (2) what types and how much evidence will be needed to determine competency of evidence. Proceed to review, or
  b) *that tentative objective cannot be used* because evidence would not be available or that conditions do not warrant continuation. Withdraw from engagement.
	1. Obtain any needed additional background information.
	
	2. Obtain relevant, material, and competent evidence—not necessarily sufficient—on tentative M-audit objective by testing management control to determine:
	  a) *that there could be a reasonable criteria,*
	  b) *that some particular person or group of persons at one or more levels of responsibility could cause an inefficient operation, and*
	  c) *that the effects of the inefficient operation are significant.*
	
	3. Obtain evidence from management control system on the competency of evidence that must come from system if additional work is to be done.
	
	4. Determine that evidence could not be obtained on all three elements of the tentative M-audit objective.
	
	5. Summarize evidence and conclude:
	  a) *whether the developed tentative M-audit objective can be a firm objective to be used in the detailed examination phase,*
	  b) *whether evidence that must be obtained would be competent, and*
	  c) *what additional evidence must be obtained and from what source to have sufficient competent, material, and relevant evidence to come to a conclusion on the audit objective.* Proceed to detailed examination, or
	  d) *that auditor should withdraw from examination.*

C. The Detailed Examinations	D. The Report Development

1. Obtain any additional background data needed.
 	
2. Obtain sufficient competent, material, and relevant evidence to determine:
   a) *the acceptability of the criteria of the M-audit objective and that any argument against the criteria can be rebutted,*
   b) *the specific action or lack of action at levels involved in the management activity that caused the effects, and*
   c) *the significance of the effects.*
 	
3. Summarize evidence in terms of criteria, causes, and effects.
 	
4. Conclude from the summarized evidence that the effects in the management activity were significantly inefficient when the actions of employees and management are evaluated against the criteria. Proceed to report development.
 	
5. Conclude that sufficient evidence could not be obtained to determine an appropriate criteria on the management activity, determinable causes, or significant effects, or that other conditions warrant that the auditor should withdraw from engagement.
	1. Set the scene through background or general information or through scope of audit.
	
	2. Communicate conclusion, stating the significance of the effects caused by not following a proper standard. Sufficient evidence on criteria, causes, and effects should be given with the audit objective for the reader to come to same conclusion as the auditor.
	
	3. State recommendation, usually that the criteria should be followed in the future to obtain best results.

are related to the objective, the auditor can then determine whether the costs are reasonably commensurate with revenue or benefits. The benefits, of course, would have to be converted to a dollar value.

Some P-audits, however, are concerned with how effective the organization is in carrying out its objective in terms other than dollar values. In such cases, effectiveness must be measured from some other agreed-upon standard, based upon the objective.

The approach to a P-audit follows the same four phases identified for M-audits. The program, however, may be carried out by organizations not directly related to the one responsible for the objective. Because of these interorganizational relationships, the auditor must often go outside of the primary organization in order to determine the benefits or other measures of effectiveness in relation to the costs.

Often, too, the organization being audited and the one responsible for the program have been so involved in budgeted line-item costs such as salaries, travel, and printing expenses, that they have not considered how these costs relate to specific programs. Or even more important, they have never considered what the objectives of the program are. Therefore, if any studies concerning the development of the objective for the program have ever been made, either internally or externally, the auditor should obtain that information.

Furthermore, since the entity often has not developed specific objectives for the program, or even given the matter much thought, the auditor must use reports of consultants, as well as analytical techniques more sophisticated than those he would employ for financial-statement audits or management audits. In addition, since a program may be carried out by many organizations, gathering information and evidence from these interrelated organizations may demand the use of such techniques as questionnaires and pilot programs, which are seldom used in other types of audits.

Evaluating the building of Chevrolets, for example, may take the auditor to many organizations—for tires, engines, fenders, batteries, and so on. Selling Chevrolets, likewise, would take the auditor into many dealer organizations. If an auditor is trying to find out whether the Chevrolet program is effective, he will need criteria, based on a stated objective and usually a profit objective; causes, based on all levels of production and selling activities; and effects, based on whether the costs do or do not exceed the revenues, stated as profits in the objective.

We must remember, of course, that profits are not the only objective of an organization; there could be social objectives, for instance, not directly related to profit. Is the program polluting the atmosphere or the streams? Is the program providing jobs to the economically or socially depressed? When these activities are related to the objectives of the program, they can turn out to be important considerations, themselves often related to cost benefits. It is clear, then, that costs, as related to cost benefits, are much broader than accounting costs. For example, in a situation where the atmosphere is being polluted, the possibility of an organization going out of existence would be a cost in terms of cost-benefit considerations. For this organization, the discounted costs of long-term interest would be a cost in terms of continuing operations or buying a new building elsewhere.

These same principles apply to governmental programs. For example, the objective of a federal program might be the improvement of water quality in the rivers through grants to cities for sewage-treatment plants. But consider this: if industrial and agricultural pollution of the streams is so great that sewage treatment may have no effect on the streams, then the grants will have no effect on the improvement of water quality.

Thus, in evaluating background and general information on a program in order to come up with a tentative audit objective, the auditor has a much broader field of information than he does for an M-audit. The principle, however, is the same: obtain evidence from background and general information on one or more elements of the tentative audit objective and assert the other element(s). Let us turn to the specific case, identified above, in the area of grants to improve the quality of the environment: the auditor, Howard Green, may observe pollution of streams by industry and assert that the program for improving water quality of the streams is ineffective (effects) because those who grant money to cities for constructing sewage plants and those in the cities who build the sewage plants (causes) have not considered that grants should not be given to cities where agricultural pollution and industrial pollution is so great that sewage-treatment plants would have no effect on the improvement of water quality (criteria).

At this point, Mr. Green would have only a tentative audit objective, and he would need to do much more work before he could consider reporting on the effectiveness of the program.

The Review and Testing of Management Control for a P-audit

The accomplishment of the purposes of reviewing and testing management control for a P-audit becomes much more complex than it is for an M-audit. For example, since one purpose is to firm up the tentative audit objective, the auditor must determine the objective of the program in order to firm up a measurable criteria. Also, since the program is usually not carried out by any one organizational unit, the auditor must consider causes from multiple units. And, unless the multiple causes can be evaluated against a firm criteria, it would be impossible to determine whether the program was or was not effective.

Furthermore, since the program's system is usually composed of many units, the determination of the quality of the management control system and the information from any one of those units may cause the auditor some problems in determining the competency of the evidence from the system. Because of good management control in one unit, the evidence may be reliable; because of poor management control in another unit, the evidence may not be reliable.

Let us continue with Mr. Green, our auditor on the case concerning grants for improvement of water quality. He already has a tentative objective and wants to firm up that objective by following one transaction completely through the management control cycle.

By selecting one grant and following the transactions concerning that grant, the auditor would have a basis for determining whether he could firm up his audit objective. Is the objective of the program well stated? Does it provide for improving the water quality of the streams? Does it have a system for measuring the water quality? Are grants given on the basis of each grant improving the water quality of the stream on which the sewage-treatment plant dumps its waste? Does the grantor agency have some method for determining whether other wastes would counteract the treatment provided by the sewage-treatment plant? If all the answers to these questions are yes, the auditor would have a basis for measuring the actual operations of the sewage-treatment plant along the river.

However, let's be realistic. Seldom does a program have a well-stated objective with specific standards for measuring that objective. The auditor would then have to develop the objective and the standards for measuring the activities of the program. And since this standard will project into the future,

Mr. Green will have to determine what techniques of analysis, such as mathematical models, will have to be used, rather than limiting himself to mere gathering of evidence. To do this, an auditor usually obtains help from experts or consultants, and these advanced methods are discussed in Chapter 15.

In our case, Mr. Green might have to have a mathematical model of the river basin made in order to have a standard by which to evaluate the results of the various types of pollution on a given stream. Without this model as a standard, the auditor would have no way of measuring the results of the program; with it, or with evidence from the granting agency, he would have some evidence on the criteria.

The auditor's next step would be to follow the grant to the city. Mr. Green would observe the sewage-treatment plant and its operation. The plant may be operating in an excellent manner; but, by testing the quality of the water in the stream, he may find nevertheless that the stream is just as polluted as ever because of agricultural and industrial wastes. He would have some evidence on causes. And through analytical reasoning, he could determine that the effectiveness of the program was not being accomplished, at least for this one grant.

From this illustration you can see that the meaning of management control has been extended beyond the confines of just one organization; within the context of P-audits, it encompasses *all* activities of the program, whether within or without the responsible organization.

The Detailed Examination for a P-audit

Let us continue with our example in order to illustrate the next step in a P-audit. The preliminary survey and the review and testing of management control will have resulted in a firm audit objective, which our auditor, Mr. Green, might state somewhat as follows:

> Have the federal agency providing the grants and the various cities receiving the grants by building sewage-treatment plants (causes) been effective in the grant program (effects) by improving the water quality of the river to acceptable Environmental Protection Agency standards (criteria)?

The evidence in this program would have to come from many sources. If the auditor tested the water in the stream below each treatment plant that received grants, he might find that the water quality was far below federal or even many state standards. He would have to determine what caused this, discovering in most instances that industrial and agricultural wastes were the culprits.

At this point, Mr. Green might turn to his mathematical model of the entire river basin showing what needs to be done to control all wastes—agricultural, industrial, and human—in order to bring up the quality of the river to national standards. Having learned that treatment of one of the wastes alone was not accomplishing the purpose of improving water quality in the river, the auditor might want to consider also how the grants would have to be divided among the three different types of wastes in order to achieve the objective. He might have to recommend that additional funds would be necessary to achieve the purpose designated.

The final step, reporting the results of a P-audit, is of such importance that it will be treated at length in chapters 16 and 18; but a useful example of the graphic flow of a P-audit follows as Table 3.2.

REVIEW QUESTIONS

1. The objective of a preliminary survey for any type of audit is to obtain a working knowledge of the organization, activity, system, or program being considered for examination. Discuss how the objective of a preliminary survey for an M-audit is more distinct than that for a financial-statement examination. (See pp. 33–34.)

2. Once the audit area has been determined for an M-audit, what types of information should the auditor obtain in the preliminary survey phase? (See p. 34.)

3. An M-audit is the examination of a particular activity or organization to determine the efficiency or economy of operations. How does the auditor often determine a tentative audit objective in the preliminary survey phase? (See p. 34.)

4. What is the purpose of the phase for the review and testing of management control in a management audit? (See pp. 34–35.)

5. Explain how the auditor reviews the specific flow of procedures for management control for an M-audit. (See p. 36.)

6. Explain how the auditor determines his objective for the detailed examination for an M-audit. (See pp. 36–37.)

7. Review the audit objective for the detailed examination stated on p. 36. Can you state an objective similar to this for any of the cases given in chapters 1 or 2?

8. If during the course of a P-audit, the auditor finds that the program has no stated goal, what must the auditor do before making the audit? (See p. 40.)

9. See if you can state an audit objective for the P-audits in chapters 1 and 2.

10. Review tables 3.1 and 3.2 in this chapter. Can you follow the information on each phase as given in the chapter? These two tables can become a handy reference guide.

Table 3.2 Phases of the Audit Function for a P-audit, Described by Process

A. The Preliminary Survey	B. The Review and Testing of Management Control
1. Obtain in a relatively short period of time background and general information on program and management system being considered for examination, including purpose of program. 2. Analyze background and general information on program and management system to obtain relevant evidence—not necessarily sufficient, material, or competent—on one or more elements—criteria, causes, or effects—of a possible P-audit objective. 3. Assert the other element or elements in order to have a tentative P-audit objective on effectiveness of program. 4. Summarize evidence and assertions. 5. Conclude from relevant evidence and assertions: a) that tentative P-audit objective on effectiveness of program can be used as the objective of the review phase if relevant material and competent evidence can be obtained on all three elements of the tentative objective and (1) what types of relevant, material, and competent evidence will be needed to determine the audit objectives, and (2) what types and how much evidence will be needed to determine competency of evidence. Proceed to review, or b) that relevant evidence and assertions would lead to a more significant objective on an M-audit. Proceed to the review and testing of management control phase for an M-audit (column B, Table 3.1, p. 38, or c) that tentative objective cannot be used because evidence would not be available or that the conditions do not warrant continuation. Withdraw from engagement.	1. Obtain any needed additional background information. 2. Obtain relevant, material, and competent evidence on tentative objective (evidence may have to be obtained from auditor's use of advanced analytical techniques or from experts) to determine: a) that there could be a reasonable and firm criteria based on entity's objective, b) that action or lack of action, within or out of the organization responsible for accomplishing the objective could cause c) a significantly good or bad effect. 3. Obtain evidence on the competency of the evidence that must be obtained if additional work is contemplated. 4. Determine that evidence could not be obtained on the three elements of the tentative objective. 5. Summarize evidence and conclude: a) whether the tentative P-audit objective can be firm enough to be the detailed examination audit objective. Proceed to detailed examination, or b) whether the evidence shows that deficiencies in the management of the program could be a firm audit objective for an M-audit. Proceed to the detailed examination phase for an M-audit (column C, Table 3.1, p. 38), and/or c) whether evidence for either the P-audit or M-audit would be competent, d) what additional evidence must be obtained to have sufficient material, relevant, and competent evidence to come to a conclusion for either the P-audit or the M-audit, and e) whether to withdraw from the examination.

C. The Detailed Examination	D. The Report Development

1. Obtain any additional background data needed.
 	
2. Obtain *sufficient* competent, relevant, and material evidence on the audit objective to determine:
   a) the acceptability of the criteria and that any argument against it can be rebutted,
   b) the specific action or lack of action within or outside of the responsible organization which caused it, and
   c) the significance of the effect.
 	
3. Determine that sufficient evidence could not be obtained on criteria but evidence could be obtained on causes and effects. Consider the detailed examination phase of M-audit.
 	
4. Summarize P-audit evidence in terms of criteria, causes, and effects.
 	
5. Conclude that effects are significant when the actions are evaluated against the P-audit criteria. Proceed to report development, or
 	
6. Withdraw from engagement.
	1. Set the scene through background data or scope of examination.
	
	2. Communicate the conclusion developed during the detailed examination phase. Include sufficient relevant, material, and competent evidence on criteria, causes, and effects to convince reader.
	
	3. Provide recommendation for future appropriate action by one or more levels of the management system.

CASE 1

What Went on in the City Garage? Phases of an M-audit [1]

The chapter states that in governmental or internal auditing the auditor must determine what agency or activity he wants to examine before he can determine the specific audit objective. The following information is the reason for making a performance audit of a large city garage.

The mayor and city council of a large city were disturbed over the high costs of service at the city garage. Managers of departments using the garage complained that costs for routine servicing of vehicles were much higher than those at commercial garages. They were not dissatisfied with the service, only the cost. The mayor talked to the head of the city audit department, James O'Brien, suggesting that he look into the garage operations, especially the routine servicing performance, and report back any indications of what might be causing the high costs.

AUDIT SCENARIO 1
The Preliminary Survey

Required

Several possible audit objectives can be determined from the following background and general information. List as many possible audit objectives as you can. Be sure to include all three elements in your tentative objective. You may have to assert various elements at this time in order to come up with a possible audit objective since evidence has not been obtained on each of the elements.

Also, since the mayor was more concerned with routine servicing than other activities, keep your tentative objectives directly related to the servicing costs.

Background Data

This garage was the only one the city had for servicing all city automobiles and trucks. It had the responsibility for keeping in service approximately 5,000 trucks, automobiles, and other internal combustion equipment, such as tractors and mowers. It provided services to all departments, including police, fire, and the highway and streets department.

This prime responsibility for servicing city automotive equipment included determining requirements; buying, storing, and requisitioning parts and supplies; establishing maintenance and service standards; repairing the equipment; and disposing of unneeded new and used parts. It had the full responsibility for keeping up the equipment from purchase to final disposal.

The garage operated on a revolving fund basis and charged only the costs it incurred; it did not attempt to make a profit. Costs included overhead as well as direct costs.

The garage management prided itself on trying to discover the best parts for the least cost when repairing equipment and had experimented with several types of parts to determine which ones would give maximum service life for the cost. For example, they had determined that spark plugs with platinum tips lasted five times as long as the conventional spark plug, but cost three times as much. On the other hand, the platinum-tipped spark plugs had a reclamation and disposal value, while the conventional spark plugs cost the garage the time and effort to dispose of them. The conventional spark plugs cost $0.75 while the platinum-tipped plugs cost $2.50; the salvage value of the platinum-tipped plugs was $0.25. In order to make the determination to buy the platinum-tipped spark plugs, the management had also set a standard for usage for both the platinum-tipped plugs and the conventional ones. The conventional type was to last 10,000 miles and the platinum-tipped type,

50,000 miles, before being changed at routine servicing time.

The garage serviced the equipment at regular service periods, both by mileage and time, in addition to servicing the equipment at any failure. For example, automobiles were brought in for routine servicing, including tuning the motor, every 6,000 miles or 6 months, whichever came first. Since many of the automobiles, such as police cars, were used 24 hours a day, the average service time on automobiles was once a month. Spark plugs were one of the large items of parts cost for this routine servicing.

Mr. O'Brien and his audit team obtained all of this information by looking at cost records, by reviewing the charter of the garage, and by discussing operations of the garage with those having that responsibility. While they were making a "walk through" of the garage, they observed quite a few spark plugs in the disposal bins that appeared to be in their original containers. They also noticed that most of the plugs in the disposal bin appeared to show little wear, as if almost new. A final point of information furnished by the requirements group was that most of the plugs used were of the platinum-tipped variety.

AUDIT SCENARIO 2
The Review and Testing of Management Control

Required

An auditor at this time must make a decision whether to use any of the possible audit objectives or to start all over. Most such decisions are based on the possible significance of the effects. In this example, one objective from which Mr. O'Brien could develop a possible significant effect would read as follows:

> Have the mechanics replaced platinum-tipped plugs (causes) before obtaining maximum service life from them (criteria) at a loss to the city of $2.50 for each plug replaced too soon plus all of the costs of buying and storing the additional plugs (effects)?

Using this possible audit objective and the following evidence, determine whether the auditor would have a firm audit objective and if so state it. Refer to each of the elements in your objective by placing each in brackets, as shown above.

Evidence Obtained by Reviewing and Testing Management Control

No additional background data need be obtained at this time; but in order to continue the examination, the auditor must obtain evidence on the possible audit objective. He will only need enough evidence on each element to convince him that it is worthwhile to continue the examination. The process of reviewing management control, as we have learned, means following a transaction through the management control system. In this case, Mr. O'Brien and his team started with the determination of requirements; then looked at the purchasing, storing, and issuing of spark plugs; checked the servicing records as well as observed the actual servicing conditions; and finally observed the disposal process. They discovered that some of these transactions, such as the disposal process, had already been accomplished during the preliminary review phase.

The auditors now reviewed the records that the requirements group used in determining how many spark plugs needed to be ordered. These showed that the average service life of the platinum-tipped plugs ranged from 6,000 to 10,000 miles. They also reviewed the purchase orders of the purchasing groups, based on the requirements. These showed that orders were outstanding based on the 6,000 to 10,000 miles of usage.

The auditors reviewed the appropriate technical manual on spark-plug usage, which showed that 30,000 miles of usage was the minimum desired service life from the platinum-tipped plugs.

The records further showed that of the 5,000 automobiles and trucks given routine service maintenance several times during the year, most were 6 or 8 cylinders.

From watching the mechanics service an automobile, the auditors observed that the mechanics routinely changed the plugs every time they serviced an automobile.

AUDIT SCENARIO 3
The Detailed Examination

Required

From the following evidence, respond to these two questions:

1. What conclusion would you come to on the audit objective?
2. State your conclusion in a summary report form along with sufficient evidence to support your conclusion.

There was enough evidence to convince Mr. O'Brien and his team to continue, but it was not sufficient to report to the mayor and city council. There were still too many missing links. The auditors had to gather sufficient relevant, material, and competent evidence on the objective to convince the third party that the criteria were reasonable, acceptable, and appropriate; that they could identify the specific action or lack of action that caused the result; and that the effects were significant. Mr. O'Brien would state his audit objective somewhat as follows:

> Has the city garage, because the mechanics changed the platinum-tipped spark plugs every 6,000 miles, the requirements group determined the requirements based on the actual usage of 6,000 miles, and the purchasing group ordered the spark plugs based on the requirements group's determination (causes), lost over $1,000,000 each year (effects) because the mechanics did not use 30,000 miles as the basis for changing spark plugs, the requirements group did not determine requirements based on 30,000 plus miles of usage, and the purchasing group did not order the spark plugs based on the requirements group's determination of 30,000 plus miles of usage (criteria)?

Sufficient Relevant, Material, and Competent Evidence on the Objective

The auditors obtained reports of the tests made by technical personnel that originally convinced the garage personnel that they should use the platinum-tipped plugs. This report showed that the plugs would give a minimum of 50,000 miles of wear. The auditors also contacted other garages using these plugs and found that, once placed in the car, they would last the life of the car—up to 200,000 miles. The plugs had not been used in any vehicles over 200,000 miles; and to obtain over 100,000 miles of wear, an inexpensive cleaning and gapping machine had been used to clean, test, and regap the plugs.

The auditors also discussed with the city garage mechanics the reason for discarding the plugs and replacing them with new plugs whenever the cars were brought in for servicing. The mechanics said they had always done this for any car they serviced and saw no reason not to continue. When asked whether they knew the spark plugs they were using were special plugs that would last for at least 30,000 miles, they said that they knew something was different about them but to them they were "just spark plugs."

When the auditors discussed the reason for not obtaining more mileage from the plugs with the supervisor of the mechanics, he said that his mechanics were well-trained and he accepted their opinion as to whether or not the spark plugs needed replacing.

According to the requirements group, the spark plugs were a special order and therefore a year's supply had to be kept on hand at all times. Every 6 months the purchasing group would order a sufficient amount to keep the minimum of a year's supply by replacing the amount used the previous 6 months. In interviews with the purchasing group, they said that they were just getting ready to place an order for another 6 month's supply based on the requirement group's determination that the spark plugs had been used for 6,000 miles. The order, according to the purchasing agent, amounted to about 200,000 platinum-tipped spark plugs at a cost of about $500,000.

After seeing the computations of the auditors, the purchasing group said they would defer placing the order until further notice from the requirements group.

AUDIT SCENARIO 4
The Report

Required

Analyze your summary audit report as to whether you have stated your conclusion in a manner that would be acceptable to the third party—in this case, the mayor and city council. Have you provided sufficient evidence on each of the elements to convince the mayor and city council that your conclusion is the right one? Is it necessary to provide additional background data concerning the audit activity in order for them to understand your conclusion? If you send a draft report to the garage, would they agree with your conclusions? Have your provided a recommendation that would improve the operations?

After you have answered the above questions, draft a *revised* report to the mayor and city council—one that you believe would surely include all the elements of a good M-audit report.

CASE 2

What Made the Nursing Homes Unsafe: Phases of a P-audit[2]

The state auditor for the State of Sylvania, John Ortega, received the following letter from the governor:

Dear Mr. Ortega:

I have been concerned over the recent tragic nursing home fires in our state, which have killed approximately 30 persons.

I would greatly appreciate your assistance in investigating the reasons for the severity of the fires and your suggestions as to possible curative actions to avoid future similar situations. In addition, please investigate:

- whether a sprinkler system throughout the facilities might have put out the fires or lessened the severity;
- whether the facilities in Junction City meet the life safety code requirements for participation in our grant program;
- the State Department of Welfare's enforcement of fire safety standards in Junction City and elsewhere;
- the accuracy of state fire inspections of the Junction City facilities in question and of the Department of Welfare's validation;
- the state inspection procedure, including the qualifications of the inspectors;
- the quality of trained personnel assisting patients during the fires;
- and finally, any additional matters that in your judgment would assist with an assessment of the fires and possible action.

I am a little worried about whether we are meeting the federal government's requirements for fire safety in our nursing homes and whether they can continue to participate in Medicare-Medicaid funding if we are deficient.

Sincerely yours,

/s/ Able Baker

Governor

In January 1976, a nursing home fire in Junction City killed 23 people. Within a week, another nursing home fire just outside the city claimed the lives of 8 people.

There are about 500 nursing homes, referred to as skilled nursing facilities (SNFs) or intermediate care facilities (ICFs), depending on the level of care provided, participating in the program for nursing homes in the state.

Medicaid—authorized by Title XIX of the Social Security Act as amended—is a grant-in-aid program in which the federal government pays part of the costs (50 to 78 percent) incurred by states in providing medical services to persons unable to pay. At the federal level, the Medicaid program is administered by the Social and Rehabilitation Service (SRS) within HEW.

States have the primary responsibility for initiating and administering their Medicaid program under the Social Security Act. The act requires that state Medicaid programs provide SNF services. However, services in ICFs, which provide care to patients that do not require skilled nursing services, are optional.

Medicare, authorized by Title XVIII of the Social Security Act, is the federal health insurance program for the aged and disabled. Part A of Medicare provides hospital insurance and also pays for all covered services in a SNF for the first 20 days after a hospital stay and all but a certain amount a day, up to 80 additional days, during a benefit period. ICFs do not participate in Medicare.

About 200 of the state's SNFs participate in Medicaid, and about 100 also participate in Medicare; in addition, about 200 ICFs participate in Medicaid. During fiscal year 1975, federal and state Medicaid payments for SNF and ICF services were $100 million, and Medicare payments for SNF services were $5 million.

Standards have been established by law and regulation that must be met by all nursing facilities participating in Medicare or Medicaid. The federal requirements on fire safety, which have been incorporated in state requirements, adhere to the Life Safety Code established by the National Fire Protection Association and revised as late as 1973.

HEW regulations require that each nursing facility certified for Medicare or Medicaid be inspected at least annually by state inspectors (employed by state agencies having contracts with the federal government) to determine whether the facility is in compliance with federal requirements, including the Life Safety Code. Facilities not in full compliance with the fire safety standards may be certified for limited periods under both programs while corrections are being made, but certification may be cancelled if deficiencies have not been corrected within the specified time.

The code requires automatic sprinkler protection throughout all nursing facilities, except those of 2-hour fire-resistive construction or one-story, 1-hour protected noncombustible construction.* The fire-resistance rating of building construction varies with the susceptibility of fire damage of the building materials used and the degree of fire protection provided for the structural members.

A building classified as 2-hour fire-resistive construction is one in which the structural members, including walls, partitions, columns, floors, and roofs, are of materials having a fire-resistance rating ranging from 1½ to 4 hours. As required by the National Fire Protection Association standards, a building may be classified as 1-hour protected noncombustible if it is constructed of materials having a minimum fire-resistance rating ranging from 1 to 2 hours. The requirements for these two classifications are directed toward limiting the spread of fire and maintaining the building structure to permit adequate time to evacuate nursing home patients safely.

The Social Security Amendments of 1967 permit a waiver, in accordance with HEW regulations, of specific Life Safety Code provisions, including the automatic sprinkler requirement. Such a waiver may be issued if its rigid application might result in unreasonable hardship on a nursing home; it should be granted, however, only if it will not adversely affect the health and safety of the patients.

SNF waivers under Medicare have always been issued by HEW; and since 1972, waivers for Medicaid facilities are also issued by HEW. Under current procedures, states make recommendations for both Medicare and Medicaid SNF waivers relating to fire safety standards, but HEW regional directors make the final decisions. Waivers of code standards for ICFs, on the other hand, are issued by state agencies.

---

*The National Fire Protection Association defines the rating of building materials in terms of hours. The ratings are the result of standard fire tests in which the materials are subjected to controlled fire conditions. The performance is based on the length of time the materials maintain their structural integrity and are expressed as 2-hour, 6-hour, ½-hour, and so on.

On December 28, 1973, Congress enacted Public Law 93–204, which authorized HUD to insure loans made to nursing facilities for purchasing and installing fire safety equipment, including automatic sprinkler systems.

AUDIT SCENARIO 1

Preliminary Survey and Review and Testing of Management Control

Often in an audit, especially a P-audit, the two preliminary phases of the audit—the preliminary survey, and the review and testing of management control—are conducted at the same time. Since the criteria of the audit objective is based upon the program's goals, much of the preliminary information is designed to determine just what the goal of the program is, and what standards are used to meet that goal.

Required

From the general information previously given and the following background information

1. Determine the goal of the nursing home program. Be sure the goal you determine is for a program directly related to the questions asked by the governor.
2. State an audit objective for the audit of the nursing home program. Include in your objective each of the elements and label them. Also, be sure that your objective for your detailed examination is related to the questions asked by the governor.

The following information was obtained from a report of the House Committee on Government Operations, 1972:

> House Report 92-1321, "Saving Lives in Nursing Home Fires," published August 9, 1972, by the House Committee on Government Operations, was a part of the study on the problems of the aging begun in the latter part of 1971 by the Special Studies Subcommittee. The findings reported by the Committee included:
>
> - In the 20 years from 1951 to 1970 a total of 496 deaths in nursing home fires were reported where multiple deaths occurred, for an annual average of 25 deaths. In 1971 there were 38 such deaths and for the first half of 1972, 30 deaths occurred.
> - The combination of sparse night staff and aged residents, of whom 50 percent are disoriented and 40 percent are partially or totally nonambulatory, renders infeasible the successful evacuation of residents in case of a fire at night.
> - The use of a fire detection alarm system connected to the nearest fire department may serve to avoid a total loss of life, but it still does not prevent, as recent fires had shown, a large number of deaths occurring, notwithstanding an extremely prompt response by the alerted fire department.
> - Even fire-resistive or protected noncombustible construction does not prevent contents fires in such structures. In fact, if such construction is not carefully executed, or if at the time of a fire, doors are not closed, then such construction will not stop a fire from spreading, as demonstrated by the nursing home fires in Marietta, Ohio, in 1970 and in Buechel, Kentucky, in 1971.
> - Since most fire deaths in homes for the aged are caused by asphyxiation resulting from toxic gases rather than being caused by actual burns, the increased use of fire retardant materials and substances, which basically result in incomplete combustion to produce toxic gases, may in the opinion of one expert, increase the hazard of deaths in fire rather than reducing it.
> - According to the National Safety Council and the American Nursing Home Association, automatic sprinkler systems installed throughout a facility, not only in hazardous areas, provide the greatest "safety to life" factor available in the fire protection field, because they can automatically sound an alarm and immediately start fighting the fire when activated. When activated, they are the most reliable and effective means of fire extinguishment. Other forms of protection equipment, including automatic alarms, are not effective substitutes for automatic sprinkler systems.
> - This is basically the position of the National Fire Protection Association, which has voted to require early warning detection and automatic sprinklers in all new and existing nursing homes, regardless of the type of construction.
> - The Fire Marshals Association of North America, which has within its membership all of the State Fire Marshals as well as those serving local government, adopted a resolution in its 1965 convention endorsing the principle of complete automatic sprinkler systems for all institutions and homes caring for the aged, regardless of construction type, detection systems, or other protection.
> - The Joint Commission of Accreditation of Hospitals, in its standards of accreditation for nursing care and resident care facilities, agrees with this view and recommends that every facility be provided with a complete automatic sprinkler system.
> - The best means of avoiding multiple death fires is

- the construction of complete automatic sprinkler systems that will also transmit an alarm to the nearest fire service.
- The cost of installing an automatic sprinkler system in an existing structure will necessarily be more than the cost of including it in new construction. The Committee has, from figures received by it, concluded that the average installation cost will be about $800 a bed for existing construction. Amortization of such installation costs on a 20-year basis, at 8 percent, comes to an annual charge of approximately $80.

The following is information directly related to the fires mentioned by the governor:

On January 30, 1976, and February 4, 1976, fire occurred at the Alpha and Beta nursing facilities, respectively, which resulted in the deaths of 31 patients. Both institutions were ICFs participating in Medicaid. According to reports of investigations, these deaths occurred even though

- the nursing facilities substantially met federal fire safety requirements,
- the fire departments responded promptly to the alarms, and
- the construction of the buildings adequately confined the flames to the rooms of origin.

The deaths were reported to be caused by smoke and toxic gases rather than by flames; no fatalities occurred in the rooms of fire origin. Investigators of these fires stated that sprinkler systems would have prevented deaths in these nursing facilities; however, both facilities were classified as fire resistive and, under the Life Safety Code, were exempt from the automatic sprinkler requirement.

Alpha Nursing Home Fire

The Alpha Nursing Home fire occurred on the third floor of the facility during the morning of January 30, 1976. Alpha, an ICF in Junction City, has 28 sleeping rooms, which can accommodate 88 permanent residents. The residents included Medicaid patients.

At the time of the fire, Alpha had the following fire safety devices:

- Three alarm systems: (1) pull-box, (2) heat detectors (both of which activate alarms to the city fire department and to the nursing home staff), and (3) smoke detectors that activate an alarm only to the nursing home staff. The three alarm systems were activated at approximately the same time.
- Three portable fire extinguishers.
- A public-address system.
- A battery-operated emergency lighting system—not a significant factor because the fire occurred during daylight hours. The system reportedly would not have functioned properly because smoke residue covered, and the heat had melted, the plastic hoods on the lights.
- Solid-core doors to resident rooms that authorities considered adequate to stop the fire, heat, and smoke if the doors were closed.
- Fire-resistive floors, walls, and ceilings. These were not penetrated by the fire, although the wall coverings did burn.

At the time of the fire, 83 aged residents (many confined to wheelchairs) occupied the home. When the fire occurred, 5 nursing home attendants, a priest, and 40 residents were on the third floor of the home. Approximately 28 of the 40 residents were attending a religious service in the third-floor lounge-chapel, which does not have a door and is thus open to the corridor.

A nurse's aid discovered the fire in room 306, at the approximate center of the single corridor that serves the third floor, at about 11:40 A.M., summoned the priest, and activated a pull-box fire alarm. Initially, the priest—and later, two maintenance men and an administrator—attempted to put out the fire with extinguishers but could not contain it. Intense smoke and heat forced them to abandon the room after attempting to close the door to the corridor. The attendants and others began concentrating on evacuating residents from the lounge-chapel and the third floor.

The Junction City Fire Department arrived at about 11:46 A.M., approximately 3 minutes and 40 seconds after it received the alarm. In response to the first alarm, the fire department dispatched 39 firemen with 7 trucks (4 pumpers, 2 hook and ladders, and 1 snorkel). When the fire department arrived, intense smoke on the third floor was already affecting elderly residents; some were gasping or unconscious. In response to a special call, 18 more firemen arrived at 12:01 P.M. with special equipment, including another snorkel truck. In response to a second alarm, 44 firemen arrived at 12:04 P.M. with 1 helicopter, 1 communication van, and 8 trucks (4 pumpers, 2 hook and ladders, and 2 water-cannon turrets).

In response to special calls, both the fire and police departments and private organizations dispatched 10 ambulances to the home. The ambulances and four fire-department automobiles transported the injured to hospitals.

As of February 20, 1976, 23 nursing home residents had died from smoke inhalation, the majority of whom were in the lounge-chapel area at the time of the fire.

The fire destroyed room 306 and caused significant damage in the corridor. Moderate fire, along with intense smoke and heat, damaged the corridor, the lounge-chapel (which did not have doors), and sleeping rooms where the doors were open. Sleeping rooms with closed doors did not incur smoke or heat damage.

Beta Nursing Home Fire

The Beta Nursing Home fire occurred in room 421 on the fourth floor early in the morning of February 4, 1976. Beta is an ICF in the town Goshen, adjacent to Junction City, and can accommodate 618 residents. The residents included Medicaid patients.

At the time of the fire, Beta Nursing Home had the following fire safety devices:

- Two alarm systems: (1) pull-box and (2) smoke detectors (both of which were wired to activate alarms to the city fire department). The smoke detectors automatically closed hall smoke doors.
- Fire extinguishers and fire hoses on each floor. Because of operator error, the fire hose on the fourth floor did not operate.
- A public-address system, which was used to notify nursing home staff of the fire and its location.
- Solid-core doors to resident rooms. Authorities considered these adequate to stop the fire, heat, and smoke if the doors were closed.
- A sprinkler system on the first floor, with vertical pipes to the other eight floors. According to a nursing home official, horizontal pipes and sprinkler heads on the upper floors had not been installed because of financial considerations.

According to a patient census the previous night, 460 persons occupied the nursing facility; 24 persons could have been accommodated in the fourth floor west wing where room 421 was located.

At about 6:30 A.M., a nurse and a nurse's aide heard screams and discovered the fire in room 421. While the aid activated the pull-box alarm, the nurse evacuated two of the residents from the room. The third occupant was not in the room at the time of the fire. A security guard who responded to the alarm attempted to extinguish the fire—first with a fire extinguisher and then with a hose, which he did not operate properly—but abandoned the attempt when he was overcome by smoke. Two maintenance employees directed water on the fire from a hose operated through a fifth floor window, but they could not extinguish the blaze.

The city fire department arrived promptly at 6:44 A.M., responding to the alarm activated by smoke detectors on the fourth floor.

The smoke detectors automatically closed smoke doors at the entrance to the corridor and contained the heat and smoke in the west wing of the nursing home. Although room 421 was adjacent to the smoke doors, residents did not sustain injuries, nor did damage occur outside the smoke barrier on the west wing. Eight residents died from smoke inhalation in west-wing sleeping rooms where doors to the room were open at the time of the fire. Smoke and heat damage also occurred in these rooms and in the corridor. In another west-wing sleeping room, where the door was closed during the fire, residents did not sustain injuries and little property was damaged.

Officials of the state fire marshal's office initially attributed the fire to a faulty electric cord on a nightstand lamp.

Severity of the Fires

An official of the fire marshal's office attributed the severity of the two fires to (1) steadily burning fires, (2) combustion gases trapped by the upper walls and ceilings in the fire rooms (flashovers), and (3) ejection of flames and lethal smoke from burning plastic and vinyl in the rooms where the fires originated.

At both nursing homes, steadily burning fires in freestanding wood wardrobes generated intense heat, resulting in considerable fire damage to the rooms in which the fires originated. Heavy smoke damaged the corridors, resident rooms with open doors, and the lounge-chapel at Alpha Nursing Home.

At Alpha Nursing Home, most of the fatalities occurred in the lounge-chapel area, which did not have a door so that lethal smoke entered. The lounge-chapel was not damaged by flames; however, the plastic covers on the ceiling light fixtures were melted by heat. At Beta

Nursing Home, the fatalities and damage occurred in resident rooms with doors open to the corridor.

The fires at both facilities burned material that generated toxic smoke. At Alpha, the fire burned vinyl-chloride wall and mattress covers. Combustion of vinyl covers generates hydrogen chloride gas, which sears lung tissue. At Beta, the fire burned polyurethane foam (foam rubber) mattresses. Combustion of foam rubber generates hydrogen cyanide gas. According to experts of the National Fire Prevention and Control Administration of the Department of Commerce, all common combustible materials can generate lethal quantities of carbon monoxide when subjected to fire. Medical evidence was not available to the auditors that would identify the specific products of combustion primarily responsible for the deaths.

According to a study made by a nursing home association and an engineering firm under contract to HEW, wood wardrobe fires in simulated nursing-facility rooms can cause flashovers within 5 minutes after ignition. This conclusion is based on an experiment conducted for HEW to test the 1967 Life Safety Code.

Compliance with Fire Safety Standards

The state fire marshal's office surveys SNFs and the public health department surveys ICFs for fire safety.

To survey SNFs, the fire marshal's office has a staff of 44 inspectors, who have fire-related backgrounds, such as work experience as firemen or a degree in fire technology. New inspectors receive classroom and on-the-job training, including training in the Life Safety Code, before making inspections. All inspectors receive fire safety training each month. Inspectors normally spend 1 to 1½ days annually inspecting SNFs for compliance with the Life Safety Code and state laws; they follow up on deficiencies at 30-day intervals until each has been corrected.

Inspectors from the public health department make annual health and safety surveys of ICFs. The department's architectural section has 14 registered architects and two engineers who make fire safety surveys. The department trains its inspectors, using the Life Safety Code, and gives them on-the-job training before placing them in charge of inspections. Inspectors usually inspect a facility in 1 day and revisit facilities within a specified period to verify correction of serious deficiencies. Inspectors also follow up on minor deficiencies either by correspondence or during the next annual inspection.

The HEW regional office conducts validation reviews, which are surveys of facilities to insure the adequacy of the state inspections. These reviews are made in facilities selected at random. The office has one team to survey selected facilities from the 3,600 SNFs and ICFs in the region.

In addition, Junction City makes fire safety inspections of SNFs and ICFs. The fire department's Bureau of Fire Prevention is responsible for inspecting the approximately 100 SNFs, ICFs (including Alpha Nursing Home), and other types of nursing homes in the city. The department uses the city municipal code for fire prevention rather than the Life Safety Code. Within the bureau, a specially trained department captain and 11 lieutenants are responsible for inspecting institutional facilities such as hospitals and nursing homes. Lieutenants who are assigned to the bureau are required to attend a fire safety course at the city fire academy.

The results of recent state inspections at the two nursing homes indicated that both facilities were in substantial compliance with existing fire safety standards. The state public health department had noted two deficiencies at the Alpha ICF in its December 1974 fire safety survey. According to department documents, the home corrected both deficiencies in April 1975, and at the time of the fire had substantially complied with the Life Safety Code.

The city fire department's Bureau of Fire Prevention had inspected Alpha Nursing Home six times in 1975, noted two deficiencies that were corrected in October 1975, and did not note any further fire safety violations in the October, November, and December inspections. According to bureau officials, the nursing home employees responded properly to a simulated fire emergency situation during the December 1975 inspection.

The state public health department had noted 10 deficiencies at Beta Nursing Home in its December 1975 fire safety survey. On February 7, 1976, 3 days after the fire, the state fire marshal officials, in a special investigation of the home, noted 5 deficiencies under the Life Safety Code, and 27 conditions that needed to be corrected under state rules and regulations.

According to the department and to fire marshal officials, however, none of the deficiencies noted in either inspection contributed to the ignition or the severity of the fire.

A nurse and nurse's aide, two maintenance men, and others assisted residents during the fire.

According to officials, Beta Nursing Home holds a minimum of 12 fire drills annually, including simulations of emergency fire conditions and transmission of fire alarms.

Investigation Findings on Sprinkler Systems and Other Fire Safety Measures

Sprinkler Systems. According to officials of the state fire marshal's office, sprinkler systems prevent flashovers because they prevent the accumulation of excessive heat on the upper walls and ceiling. In the opinion of Junction City fire department officials, sprinkler systems provide the best fire protection because they signal the fire location and immediately spray 22 gallons of water a minute on fires, which activate the system. Fire department officials believe sprinkler systems would have extinguished the fires at both nursing homes and prevented deaths.

After its investigation of the Alpha Nursing Home fire, a special panel appointed by the mayor of Junction City recommended that new requirements immediately be made part of the Building and Fire Ordinance Code of the city. One requirement was that sprinkler systems be installed in all new and existing nursing homes and electrically interconnected with the fire-alarm system.

On February 4, 1976, the mayor asked the city council to require all nursing homes to have automatic sprinkler systems. The ordinance was introduced only a few hours after the nearby Beta Nursing Home fire and was approved by the council on April 7, 1976. It required all city nursing homes to install sprinkler systems by February 1977.

According to an HEW engineer's report on the Alpha Nursing Home fire, "The only alternative to a well-trained staff is a complete sprinkler system, smoke compartments, and smoke detectors." Of the area fires, another HEW report stated:

> The facilities in each case were of fire-resistive construction, but failed to provide reasonable protection. There is a need for several fire safety measures that exceed current regulations.

Furnishings. According to a report by a state fire marshal official, presented at state hearings, "The Alpha and Beta Nursing Home fires demonstrate that ignition of coverings and furnishings can turn nursing facilities into gas chambers." Other state officials indicated that federal standards were needed to regulate furnishings used in nursing facilities.

Fire Emergency Training. State and local officials emphasized the importance of fire-emergency training of nursing-facility employees. The committee, appointed by the mayor, recommended that nursing-facility employees, in addition to existing training programs, be required to participate in formal fire department emergency training every 6 months.

AUDIT SCENARIO 2
The Detailed Examination

Required

From the following evidence, respond to these two questions:

1. What conclusion would you come to on the audit objective?
2. State your conclusion in a summary report form along with sufficient evidence to support your conclusion.

It can be presumed that the goal of nursing homes is to provide safe, dependable residential care at a reasonable price to elderly patients. For this audit, the governor is not necessarily interested in all elements of the goals of the program; his special interest is a program for providing safety from fires for the patients in the nursing homes.

Originally, Mr. Ortega, the auditor, might have come up with an objective such as the following:

> Have the nursing home administrators; the fire departments in the cities affected; the Congress, the state legislature, the county commissioners, and the city council; and the executives in the agencies concerned in their carrying out of (causes) the requirements of federal, state, and local laws and regulations concerning nursing home protection from fires (criteria) effectively provided safety from fires to residents of the nursing homes (effects)?

However, the information gathered in the preliminary survey phase and the review and testing of management control phase of the audit would allow the auditor to come to the conclusion that the laws and regulations as stated were not providing safety in an effective manner. Thus, instead of using the above as his objective, Mr. Ortega would probably state his objective somewhat as follows:

> Could the actions of nursing home administrators; the fire departments in the cities affected; the Congress, the state legislature, the county commissioners, and the city council; and the executives in the agencies concerned provide (causes) effective safety from fires (effects) by providing additional safeguards from fires, such as sprinkler systems, as a part of the fire safety precautions in the nursing homes (criteria)?

Sufficient Relevant, Material, and Competent Evidence on the Objective

Many studies and reports have concluded that automatic sprinkler systems are effective in putting out fires and saving lives. About one half of the nursing homes participating in Medicare and Medicaid are not required, because of construction classification, to be protected with automatic sprinkler systems. Historically, nursing-home fires resulting in multiple deaths have had two conditions similar to the examples described: the primary causes of death were smoke and other gaseous products of combustion, and the facilities did not have complete automatic sprinkler systems. Since 1972, several congressional committee reports have recommended that all nursing facilities be fully protected with automatic sprinkler systems. Mr. Ortega and his audit team for this P-audit believe that a strong case can be made for adopting such a proposal.

The cost of installing automatic sprinkler systems will vary with factors such as building size, type of construction, method of installation, and whether installation is in existing buildings or those under construction. In several installations during 1975, the cost ranged from $393 to $625 a bed. The monthly cost of amortizing $625 a bed over a 20-year period at a 9¼ percent interest rate is $5.57 a bed each month, or about 19 cents a bed each day.

By installing an automatic sprinkler system, some savings are possible on fire insurance for both the building and its contents. In the Washington, D.C., area, for instance, estimates on these savings are up to 30 percent on building coverage and 50 percent on contents insurance, depending on type of construction. In addition, Medicare and Medicaid will bear a share of the cost of sprinkler systems through payments on behalf of program beneficiaries.

Current Federal Standards and Automatic Sprinklers. The Life Safety Code exempts, as previously noted, nursing facilities classified as 2-hour fire-resistive construction or as one-story, 1-hour protected noncombustible construction, from sprinkler requirements. As a result, about half of the nursing facilities are exempt, and these included both the nursing homes where the fires occurred.

In addition to the exemptions, HEW also has the authority under the Social Security Act to waive the automatic sprinkler requirement in any nursing facility regardless of construction type. The HEW Office of Nursing Home Affairs could not tell the auditors how many facilities were waived from the automatic sprinkler requirement as of April 1976 because information on such waivers is maintained at the regional offices.

A GAO report entitled "Many Medicare and Medicaid Nursing Homes Do Not Meet Federal Fire Safety Requirements" (MWD-75-46) dated March 18, 1975, pointed out many problems associated with the waiver procedures: Of a sample of nursing homes inspected, over 79 percent granted waivers from the automatic sprinkler requirement did not meet the HEW standards for such a waiver.

The report further stated that the HEW waiver standards, designed to insure a level of safety equivalent to that provided by automatic sprinklers, have not been established for any type of nursing home, except those of one-story protected wood frame construction. It was recommended that HEW establish waiver standards for all types of nursing homes to insure, as required by the Social Security Act, that waivers from the automatic sprinkler requirement would not adversely affect patient safety. HEW did not accept this recommendation on the basis that the propriety of a waiver should be left to the discretion of the state, with the approval of the HEW regional office.

Further Studies and Comments on the Value of Sprinklers. The National Safety Council and American Nursing Home Association's "Safety Manual for Nursing Homes and Homes for the Aged" state that:

Automatic sprinkler systems provide the greatest "safety to life" feature available in the fire protection field. Not only can they automatically sound an alarm, but they will immediately start fighting the fire when activated. Automatic sprinklers are by far the most reliable and effective means of fire extinguishment. Other forms of protective equipment, as well as automatic alarms, have their special place, but none can ever be an effective substitute for automatic sprinkler systems.

According to the National Fire Protection Association, there is no record of a multiple-death fire in any nursing home fully protected with an automatic sprinkler system.

During the summer of 1974, the American Health Care Association (formerly the American Nursing Home Association), under contract to HEW, made a series of monitored fire tests, some of which were carried out in an abandoned nursing home near Gary, Indiana. The tests were conducted by a fire safety engineering firm; and the purpose of the contract, according to an HEW official, was to validate specific fire-protection requirements contained in the 1967 edition of the Life Safety Code applicable to nursing homes. The tests were also intended to provide the basis for policy modifications regarding fire safety standards, for making recommendations for action by HEW, and for suggesting legislative amendments.

During one of the fire tests, with fire department personnel stationed throughout the building, a fire started in a wooden wardrobe burned out of control and destroyed the building. According to the project engineer for the fire safety engineering firm, as the fire developed it traveled into the concealed spaces near the roof so that the fire department could not contain it. It gradually spread through the spaces down to the second floor, and eventually worked its way throughout the building. The engineer pointed out that because fire in concealed spaces can be very difficult to reach, buildings have been lost this way many times throughout the country.

The HEW officials noted that automatic fire sprinklers were not in use for the specific test that resulted in destroying the building. The project engineer pointed out a number of conclusions from the various tests, including:

- Smoke barrier doors were effective.
- Many of the ordinary doors, such as might be found in the typical nursing homes, do a good job of containing fires for a short time.
- Automatic sprinklers generally did a good job of controlling and containing the fires. Even where it was arranged so that the water from sprinklers could not hit the fires directly, the sprinklers still contained them.
- When automatic sprinklers were used, the fires did not last long enough to be affected, even by combustible wall paneling and ceiling tiles.

Fire in Another State Nursing Home with Sprinklers Did Not Result in Deaths. The Delta Nursing Home fire occurred on February 18, 1976. This nursing home, an SNF in a southern state, can accommodate 300 residents. At the time of the fire, 224 residents, including both Medicare and Medicaid patients, occupied the home.

A nurse's aide noted smoke and a burning mattress in room 421 (no one was in the bed) and, with a nurse's assistance, evacuated the three occupants of the room. The nurse activated a pull-box alarm and closed the room door. The fire activated one of two sprinklers in the room, which sprayed water on the fire and extinguished it before the firemen arrived shortly after the alarm.

The fire did not cause any deaths or injuries to the home residents. Fire damage was confined to the mattress; little, if any, heat or smoke damage occurred.

The fire chief attributed the absence of injuries and the prompt control of the fire to the sprinkler system and the quick employee response. Because the fire was promptly controlled, it did not generate sufficient heat (160° F) to activate the second sprinkler in the room.

An official of the state fire marshal's office attributed the cause of the fire to the careless use of smoking materials by a resident.

Causes of Deaths in Nursing Home Fires. The causes of death in the Alpha and Beta Nursing Home fires were the same as those in other fires involving multiple deaths—smoke and toxic gases. There were similarities between these two fires and four other nursing facility fires in Marietta, Ohio; Buechel, Kentucky; Madison, Wisconsin; and Wayne, Pennsylvania—all studied by the Senate Subcommittee on Long-term Care. All of these facilities were classified as fire resistive; and smoke and other products of combustion, rather than flames, caused multiple deaths.

In 1972, after its investigation of multiple-death nursing-facility fires, the House Committee on Government Operations reported in House Report 92-1321 that most fire deaths in nursing homes were caused by asphyxiation resulting from toxic gases, rather than actual burns. In 1975, the Senate Special Committee on Aging reported in Senate Report 94-00 that nursing home patients present a particular problem because of their reduced tolerance to heat, smoke, and gases and that many patients are under sedation or bound with restraints. The Senate committee reported that despite the importance of smoke as the major cause of fire death in the United States, there are no national standards governing the smoke-generation properties of furnishings, including carpets and floor coverings.

Following the January 1970 Ohio fire, the *Fire Journal* commented, "Had the building been equipped with an automatic sprinkler system, all the victims could have been saved." After the Kentucky fire, the publication stated, "If the entire building (not just the rubbish and laundry chutes) had been protected with an automatic sprinkler system, the fire could have been confined to the room of origin, with very little smoke or fire damage."

The Cost of Automatic Sprinkler Systems. The cost of installing an automatic sprinkler system will vary with the size and type of facility and depend on whether it is of new or existing construction. However, to examine the impact of requiring all nursing homes to install sprinkler systems, Mr. Ortega and his team for this P-audit presented general data obtained regarding the cost of sprinklers. In February 1976, they discussed costs with a representative of the National Automatic Sprinkler and Fire Control Association, who gave a figure, including pumps, valves, piping, and alarms, of from $0.75 to $1.25 a square foot for installation of a complete sprinkler system during construction of a new building. Installation in an existing building would cost from $1.00 to $1.50 a square foot. Variables would include whether the sprinkler heads were to be concealed or exposed, whether the sprinkler heads were to be recessed, and the availability of a water supply (that is, is a reservoir necessary?). In April 1976, seven sprinkler-installation companies in the Washington-Baltimore area provided further data. According to their estimates, a sprinkler system might cost between $0.50 and $1.75 a square foot in an existing facility. Actual installations during 1975 in four existing facilities, three in Ohio, and one in Minnesota, showed costs ranging from $393 to $625 a bed, as follows:

Facility	Number of beds	Square feet	Total HEW approved cost of sprinkler system	Cost per bed	Cost per square foot
1	30	12,100	$18,744	$625	$1.55
2	34	16,481	20,072	590	1.22
3	100	35,484	42,850	429	1.21
4	150	48,040	58,917	393	1.23

Using the highest actual cost per bed, the monthly cost of amortizing $625 a bed over a 20-year period with a 9¼ percent interest rate is $5.57 a bed each month.

According to the National Fire Protection Association, automatic sprinkler heads need replacement at the end of 50 years. However, financing a sprinkler-system installation over a period of more than 20 years does not seem likely. Consequently, the P-audit computation shows the monthly payment expected over the term of a 20-year loan.

Savings for Nursing Facilities with Sprinkler Systems. Although fire insurance rates vary among states, savings are possible on both building coverage and contents insurance when nursing facilities are protected by automatic sprinkler systems. The auditors obtained information on the general rates in two states and found that savings of about 30 percent are possible in building coverage and 50 percent on contents insurance.

According to a representative of the insurance services office of one state, fire insurance premiums would be less because of the installation of automatic sprinklers in nursing facilities. With regard to fire insurance on the building, he said the rate per $100 of insurance is about 8 cents without sprinklers in ordinary construction and about 6 cents with sprinklers, for a savings of about 25 percent. In protected wood-frame construction, he said the fire insurance rate per $100 of insurance is about 16 cents without sprinklers and about 11 cents with sprinklers, for a savings of about 30 percent.

According to a representative of the insurance rating bureau in the other state, building-contents insurance premiums could be reduced by as much as 50 percent by installing automatic sprinkler systems. He quoted rates for nursing facilities of frame, ordinary, and fire-resistive construction. He stated that in buildings of frame construction, the building-contents insurance rate per $100 of insurance is about 71 cents without sprinklers and 45 cents with sprinklers, for a reduction of about 37 percent. In ordinary construction, he said the building contents rate per $100 of insurance is about 50 cents without sprinklers in contrast to about 30 cents with sprinklers, for a savings of about 40 percent. For fire-resistive construction, he quoted a building-contents insurance rate per $100 of insurance of about 20 cents without sprinklers and 10 cents with sprinklers, for a savings of about 50 percent.

To illustrate the annual savings on fire insurance premiums due to the installation of an automatic sprinkler system, consider a hypothetical example of a protected wood-frame facility insured for $500,000 on the building and $100,000 on the contents. Without a sprinkler system the facility would pay about $800 for building insurance at 16 cents for $100 of coverage and about $710 for contents insurance at 71 cents per $100 of coverage, for a total annual cost of about $1,510. With a sprinkler system the facility would pay about $550 for building insurance at 11 cents per $100 of coverage and about $450 for contents insurance at 45 cents per $100 of coverage, for a total annual cost of about $1,000. The installation of an automatic sprinkler system would thus result in annual savings for fire insurance in excess of $500.

Medicare and Medicaid Will Help Pay for Automatic Sprinklers. Nursing facilities participating in either Medicare or Medicaid will be reimbursed for part of the cost of automatic sprinkler systems through interest and depreciation.

Medicare facilities receive reimbursement of all allowance costs associated with the use of the facilities by Medicare patients. Medicare regulations (20 CFR 405.415) provide that an appropriate allowance for depreciation on building and equipment is an allowable cost. Consequently, Medicare will reimburse facilities for the cost of automatic sprinkler systems over a period of time, suggested as 25 years, based on the number of Medicare patients. In addition, Medicare regulations (20 CFR 405.419) provide that interest on both current and capital indebtedness is an allowable cost. As a result, part of the interest paid each year on sprinkler system loans can be reimbursed under Medicare.

Medicaid is required to reimburse facilities on a cost-related basis as of July 1, 1976. Under HEW-proposed regulations to implement this requirement, depreciation and interest may be included in the determination of cost, based on Medicaid patient utilization of the facility.

It is clear, thus, that over the long run, since depreciation and interest are allowable costs under both Medicare and Medicaid, part of the costs of installing automatic sprinkler systems in nursing facilities will be paid by Medicare and Medicaid. The actual amounts will vary among facilities depending on the number of residents covered by the programs.

AUDIT SCENARIO 3

The Report on the P-audit for Nursing Homes

Required

Analyze your summary audit report as to whether you have stated your conclusion in a manner that would be acceptable to the third party—in this case, the governor and the public. Have you provided sufficient evidence in the report on each of the elements of the objective to convince them that your conclusion is the right one? Is it necessary to provide additional background data concerning the audit program in order for them to understand your conclusion? Have you provided a recommendation to the agencies that would improve the operations of the program?

In answering the above questions, draft a revised report to the governor that you believe would meet the answers to the above questions.

PART TWO

Getting Started

Part 2, chapters 4 through 7, shows the auditor how to get the right start in making a performance audit.

In this part, you will learn how to plan for and prepare audit programs for each of the phases of a performance audit. You then will apply what you have learned to planning for a specific M-audit and a specific P-audit. Since you will find yourself concerned with management control in all of your performance audit endeavors, you will learn what management control is as well as how to review management control.

After reading and studying each chapter, answering the review questions, and working the cases, you should be able to accomplish the specific objectives listed at the beginning of each chapter.

CHAPTER 4

Planning and Programming the Audit

After you have read this chapter, studied the review questions, and worked through the cases, you will understand:

- How to plan for staff and time estimates for any audit.
- How to prepare an audit program for a preliminary survey, a preliminary review and testing of management control, a combined survey and review, and a detailed expamination in general form.
- How to plan for report preparation.

In any audit, but especially in performance audits, the auditor should organize his work so that he can carry it out in an efficient, economical, and effective manner; he should be as concerned with how to organize his own work as any other manager. In auditing, this "how" is often described as:

> Audit planning and programming: adequate planning for information and evidence to be gathered on the audit objective during each phase of the audit function with the proposed procedures to accomplish the plan.

The auditor, then, should appropriately determine in advance such items as:

1. The types and quantity of personnel he needs to do the work,
2. What information he should gather, how to gather it, and how to evaluate it in order to know his audit objective,
3. What evidence and how much of it he must gather, along with the means to obtain it, in order to come to the proper conclusion on the objective, and
4. What results he expects in the way of a report from the work he will do.

From his audit planning and his audit program, the auditor will then use various procedures and techniques (1) to obtain and use personnel properly, and (2) to gather information and evidence, record it in proper form, summarize it so that it can be evaluated, and then come to an opinion or conclusion on the audit objective. From this evidence on the objective and the conclusion, he develops a report, which he then presents to a third party.

Audit Planning

Any kind of audit planning involves three chief concerns that pertain to the overall audit work:

64 / *Getting Started*

      1. Staff and time estimates,
      2. Other audit planning considerations, and
      3. Report planning.

Staff and Time Estimates

The auditor is concerned with staff and time estimates for two separate and distinct periods of time: (1) staff and time for the preliminary work, and (2) staff and time for the detailed examination.

Preliminary work. Examples of work that is definitely preliminary would be the public accountant, when he is planning to bid on an audit for a governmental unit; the internal auditor, when he is determining the activity he intends to examine; and the governmental auditor, when he is determining the area, the program, or the activity he plans to audit. All these must have some time to do the necessary planning for this preliminary activity.

The management of the audit organization must plan for this preliminary activity by alloting a certain amount of time for it, and this type of time estimate becomes an overhead charge until the audit becomes a certainty.

Detailed Examination. For the detailed examination, the auditor should include in his audit program estimates of the time required to do the work. These should include both the types of personnel needed as well as the man-days estimated to do the audit. While staff and time estimates will undoubtedly need to be revised as the work goes on, an original estimate can still be useful to the audit supervisor in planning.

Other Planning Considerations

Planning for a performance audit is comparable to planning for a first-time financial-statement examination of a previously unaudited organization. The auditor needs to plan for a lot of information on the organization, its staff, and its operations before he begins to make the examination; planning for all types of audits is an important standard consideration. Concerning planning for financial-statement examination, the American Institute of Certified Public Accountants gives as its first standard of field work, "The work is to be adequately planned and assistants, if any, are to be properly supervised."[1] Planning for governmental audits also occupies an important part of the work for that type of auditor. The first standard for the examination and evaluation for governmental auditing issued by the Comptroller General is "Work is to be adequately planned."[2]

Planning for the preliminary phases of the audit is just as important as audit programming for the detailed examination. For example, the results of the preliminary survey are the basis for the audit program for the review and testing of management control; and the results of the review and testing of management control are in turn the basis for the audit program for the detailed examination.

Thus, the determination of what is wanted in a prior audit phase is most important, as the results of that determination become the basis for the program of the next phase.

In public accounting or management services, the auditor often must start his engagement with a proposal. Planning and preparing the proposal letter, which then becomes the engagement letter when signed, is discussed and illustrated in Appendix III. This discussion and illustration, from the *AICPA's Journal of Accountancy* for June 1975, pertains to management services but will apply equally to proposals and engagement letters for performance audits.

Report Planning

The auditor should be considering what he is to report on as soon as he determines that he has a firm audit objective, but the detailed evidence and the opinion or conclusion for the report will be developed during the detailed examination phase. Sufficient competent, relevant, and material evidence will be obtained on the audit objective, and each subobjective, so that the auditor should be convinced as to the appropriateness of the opinion or conclusion. He should also have obtained sufficient evidence on each element of the objective—criteria, causes, and effects—so that he can convince any ordinary reader that his conclusion is the proper one.

In preparing the report, the auditor often outlines, in advance, the final report in sufficient detail to know precisely what he is to say and the manner in which he will say it before he starts to write. If the auditor has the objective firmly stated, sufficient evidence on the criteria to show that it is the proper one and not easily rebutted, sufficient evidence on causes at the various levels involved to show that someone did or did not carry out the criteria, and sufficient evidence on the effects to show that they are significant, then his writing of the report becomes more a matter of organization than anything else.

Audit Programming

The phases of the audit function, discussed in Chapter 3, show generally what work is to be done in each phase and how it is to be done. The audit program for each phase, however, should spell out specifically, not generally, what the objective is of that phase, what must be done to accomplish the objective, as well as what will be done with the results. The auditor, moreover, should recognize that any planning documents, especially those in the early phase, should be dynamic and not static. When the auditor finds there is a reason for change, he should, with approval of his audit supervisor, make that change. He should not carry out audit steps merely for the sake of carrying them out. While this is true of every phase, it is more true of the early phases because the results of the work become the basis for the work in the next phase.

The Audit Program for the Preliminary Survey

Almost always, the auditor should have a written program for the preliminary survey phase for a performance audit. One exception is when the supervisor in charge of the audit is making the preliminary survey. Then, his notes are used as the program; but when the work is to be done by an assistant, it is essential that he have a written guideline as his audit program.

As we have said, the main purpose of a preliminary survey is to obtain background and general working information on the audit area in order to plan for succeeding phases. The auditor also makes preliminary tests of management control to identify activities warranting further attention, and we have called this identification *possible audit objectives.*

In order to obtain proper background and working information and identify a possible audit objective, it is best for the auditor to avoid future complications by writing out, in detail, during the preliminary survey phase, what background data he must obtain, where to obtain them, and what he is to do with them after he has them.

As an example, let us consider a preliminary survey for an M-audit in the area of housing provided for persons who are required to live on the premises. The auditor is Margaret Lee. She may gather information on housing provided for doctors and management personnel who are required to live at a hospital where they provide the services. When governmental activities provide housing for specific persons, there is usually a regulation that such persons must pay certain fees for that housing. Unless Ms. Lee knows that there is a regulation requiring residents to pay rental rates comparable to those charged private citizens in the area, she may not pick up that background information.

This type of background data can easily be turned into evidence on the criteria for the particular audit activity. This would be especially true in this case if the rental rates charged were either very low or exorbitant. We see, thus, that the auditor could have an important tentative audit objective—one which she might have completely overlooked if she had not been guided into the proper information.

From the evidence and the tentative audit objective obtained in the preliminary survey, the auditor can determine the specific steps she will need in the next phase. For example, if Ms. Lee obtains information on all three elements of the tentative audit objective during one visit, she may already have evidence on a firm objective and thus would plan differently; that is, she would not have to plan for gathering evidence on each element of the tentative objective in order to have a firm objective because she would already have that evidence.

Often the question is raised, "Why isn't there a uniform audit program?" We must understand that since each audit is separate and distinct from every other audit, the audit program must be prepared specifically for each audit and for each phase of that audit. Seldom should the auditor consider using a uniform audit program for any type of examination.

The Program for the Review and Testing of Management and Internal Control

The Comptroller General states:

> An evaluation is to be made of the system of internal control to assess the extent it can be relied upon to ensure accurate information, to ensure compliance with laws and regulations, and to provide for efficient and effective operations.[3]

Assessing the extent evidence can be relied upon to insure accurate information is often called determining the competency of evidence, but the auditor must go beyond this: He must also consider what evidence he still needs to assure himself that his audit objective concerning efficient, economical, or effective operations is the one that should be used. For example, in the illustration just given about government housing, the auditor may have determined that the criteria—the personnel should pay rents comparable to rents paid by residents in the neighborhood—is a good one and she has evidence on it. But, until she tests some transactions, she will not know whether rental rates paid by the medical and administrative personnel living on the hospital grounds are comparable, nonexistent, or completely out of line. In other words she has only a tentative audit objective and not a firm one.

Furthermore, it is only from the review and testing of management control that an auditor is able to determine the detailed steps he will need in his audit program to accomplish the detailed examination. Usually, the program for the testing of internal and management control includes steps for reviewing particular transactions from beginning to end.

By following a single transaction for an activity all the way through the organization, an auditor can easily determine the reliability of the information from people within the organization and from the organization's records. He can also spot any weaknesses in the particular activity that he may want to examine in greater detail himself or may wish to report to management.

In an audit program for a performance audit, the steps in the program guide the auditor not only in determining the competency of the information from the system, but also in obtaining evidence to firm up his tentative objective. By following a single transaction in the activity pertaining to the tentative objective all the way through the organization or system, he can easily ascertain whether or not the tentative weakness, previously identified, is a significant weakness that needs reporting on.

Combined Program for the Preliminary Survey and the Review and Testing of Management Control

Since each M-audit is distinct from every other one, it becomes quite important for the auditor to know exactly which activity he is to audit before placing too many resources into the audit. Therefore, most performance-audit programs include both phases—one on the preliminary survey and the other on the review and testing of management control. In other words, the auditor must have a firm objective before he seeks to obtain approval for continuing the examination. As the GAO says in its audit manual:

> Separate work programs should be prepared for the survey and review phases of an assignment.
>
> - The survey phase encompasses the work described [in the chapters] on the preliminary survey, review of legislation and preliminary review.
> - The review phase covers the work described [in the chapter] on the detailed examination.
>
> Survey programs will ordinarily be less detailed than review programs and will contain broad objectives and guidelines for attaining those objectives. Review programs should be more precise since areas warranting detailed examination will have been identified, generally, on the basis of survey work.[4]

However, whether individual audit programs are prepared for the preliminary survey and for the review and testing of management controls or one program is prepared for both phases, the program must identify a specific audit objective for the detailed examination and specific steps for accomplishing that objective.

In M-audits identified by public accountants making financial-statement examinations, the only objective identified is a tentative objective, which requires an engagement letter for approval in order to continue the examination. In most government audit agencies, since the law requires that examinations be made, the approval that must be obtained for continuing the audit is from a higher-level authority in the audit agency. Appendix IV illustrates the forms used by the GAO to approve the continuation of a proposed performance audit.

You will see that the materials in Appendix IV show that a tentative report based on the objective can be written at this stage to indicate what will be accomplished in the final report. It should be emphasized that this report is only tentative, much as an objective is tentative, and is made to illustrate to the higher-level authorities just what will result from the audit if the evidence gathered agrees with the assertions made or questions raised in the objective at this point in the examination.

You should note also that the objective may be stated differently from the illustrations given but that all elements of the objective must be presented before attempting to gather detailed evidence on it.

The Audit Program for the Detailed Examination

Once the auditor has gone through the phases for the preliminary survey and the review and testing of management controls, he should be able to spell out specifically what evidence is needed during the detailed examination. And since each account, each transaction, and each internal control activity is different from any other, you can easily see why a specific detailed program should be prepared for each examination. This detail can go as far as to spell out the specific subobjectives, and then the specific individuals to interview, the specific records to examine, and the specific actions to observe. In both an M-audit and a P-audit, it is most important that sufficient evidence be obtained on the criteria, as well as causes and effects, to assure that those criteria are acceptable and that they are not easily rebutted. Thus, evidence must be obtained on the criteria of the subobjectives as well as on the criteria of the primary objectives.

You can see, then, that each audit program for a performance audit is usually tailor-made, insofar as possible, for each specific assignment. Sometimes the same program can be used for different locations. Even then, however, conditions may differ at these locations and the program should be altered accordingly. Similarly, the program should provide for specific consideration of the development of each individual audit finding within the same assignment.

Under each audit program, the auditor should be able to apply initiative and sound judgment. The procedures prescribed in the audit program should not be so strict that the auditor cannot deviate from them, even making a decision to extend the work if he feels it necessary, and if he requests permission.

All detailed examination programs generally contain four parts:

1. Background information concerning audit,
2. Results expected from the audit work,
3. The audit procedures needed to accomplish the results, and
4. Special instructions, if necessary.

Background Information on the Audit

Whenever an auditor approaches a detailed examination, he should have sufficient information concerning the organization and the audit to understand and carry out the program. This background information is usually a brief description of the organization, its programs, its activities, and the way it carries out its procedures concerning the activity under examination. The person preparing the program seldom includes detailed narratives about the programs and activities unless some special purpose is served from this information.

The Results Expected from the Audit Work

In Chapter 2, we thoroughly discussed audit objectives. These are the end results or specific goals on which the auditor gathers and evaluates evidence from which he comes to a conclusion.

The specific results expected on each assignment should be stated as clearly as possible within the framework of the elements of the audit objective. These elements—criteria, causes, and effects—should be specifically stated and the results should be achievable from the procedures provided in the audit program.

When he has a statement of the results expected, the auditor can also use it to summarize briefly the means for accomplishing the results, the planned reporting pattern, and any other points concerning the way the audit will be managed to accomplish the results.

A tentative report digest, such as the one illustrated in Appendix IV, can also be appended to this statement to make the results clearer to those who will work on the audit.

Audit Procedures

This part of the program consists of the specific directions for carrying out the detailed examination phase of the audit. It should be subdivided into sections comparable to the sections found in a financial-statement examination for assets, liabilities, capital, income, and expenses. It should be further subdivided into subobjectives concerned with the causes of the deficiency in the operations of the activity, such as found in cash-in-bank, petty cash, and cash-on-hand as a subdivision for cash in a financial-statement examination.

Considering the primary objective, the main subdivision should be based on criteria, causes, and effects. These primary divisions should then be broken down into each further line of inquiry, and the specific objective should be stated for that subobjective along with its relationship to the primary audit objective. Pertinent information about the criteria of the objective—such as applicable laws, requirements to be met, or suggested policy—should be given if available. In addition, information on the causes and effects—such as special problems or weaknesses, prior findings, persons involved, or recommendations made—should be provided.

Each step in the program should be stated in terms of positive instructions, clearly setting forth the work to be done and the reason for doing it. In contrast to questions found in a questionnaire form of a standardized audit program for a financial-statement examination, instructions on procedures for a performance audit should be statements that require analysis and evaluation rather than superficial answers to questions. (There are times, of course, when a questionnaire-type program is appropriate.)

Along with instructions for each step, the reason for doing the work should always be given so that staff members will know why, as well as what, they are to do. This knowledge will often minimize the inclusion of unnecessary work steps.

Furthermore, the program should provide only necessary information. Often, for instance, the auditor finds that information is available at his location that he needs only as a reference but does not need to include in his audit.

In providing the suggested procedures for an audit program, the person preparing the program should consider having the organization ready documents, reports, or special analyses. Such forethought should reduce the auditor's work, although he should still test the information provided by internal auditors, or other analysts, to make sure it is reliable.

Finally, if the program for the detailed examination is prepared properly, the auditor should be able to use it as a basis for gathering appropriate evidence on the audit objective to support or deny the objective. If it supports the objective, then the auditor would be ready to report the conclusion.

Special Instructions

The fourth part of a detailed examination program should contain any necessary special instructions as to

- the procedures to be followed in handling significant or unusual developments that may arise during the audit,
- the method to be followed in indexing and filing working papers,
- the use of internal audit work and external studies by consultants, and
- other important matters not covered elsewhere in the work program.

REVIEW QUESTIONS

1. The auditor should perform the work of an audit as efficiently, economically, and effectively as possible. Describe the planning the auditor should follow in doing so. (See pp. 63–64.)

2. What two periods of time is the auditor concerned with in planning for staff and time estimates for the audit? (See p. 64.)

3. Explain how the results from one phase of the examination can be used as the basis for developing the program for the next phase. (See pp. 64, 66–67.)

4. For what purposes does the auditor develop an audit program to test management control? (See pp. 66–67.)

5. Is it possible to combine the programs for the preliminary survey and the review and testing of management control? (See p. 67.)

6. Discuss the reasons why an auditor should not use a uniform audit program for all performance audits. (See pp. 67–68.)

7. List and describe briefly the four parts that the detailed examination program should include. (See pp. 68–69.)

8. Discuss the validity of the following statement: "The audit program should generally spell out the results expected from the audit work." (See p. 68.)

9. Why is it important for the auditor to state procedures in an audit program to obtain evidence on the criteria of the subobjectives as well as the primary objective in making a performance audit? (See pp. 68–69.)

10. Discuss the reasons why there should be a special instruction section of an audit program. (See p. 69.)

CASE 1

The City Garage: Planning an M-audit

Required
 Reread Case 1 in Chapter 3 (pp. 46–48) and then complete the following exercises on the audit program:

1. Outline the steps you would take to obtain the preliminary information section of the case.
2. Outline the steps you would take to obtain the information given on the background data section of the case.
3. Outline the steps you would take to obtain the information and evidence in the section on "Evidence Obtained by Reviewing and Testing Management Control," Audit Scenario 2.
4. Outline the steps you would take to obtain the evidence on the objective given in the section on "Sufficient Relevant, Material, and Competent Evidence on the Objective," Audit Scenario 3.

CASE 2

The Nursing Homes: Planning a P-audit

Required
 Reread Case 2 in Chapter 3 (pp. 49–59) and then complete the following exercises on the audit program:

1. Outline the steps you would take to obtain the information for the section on preliminary information in the case.
2. Outline the steps you would take to obtain the information for the section on "Preliminary Survey and Review and Testing of Management Control," Audit Scenario 1.
3. Outline the steps you would take to obtain the evidence on the audit objective for "The Detailed Examination," Audit Scenario 2.

CASE 3

Planning the Audit Program: A Case in Point

Required

Since planning is such an important part of every audit, complete the following pertinent exercises:

1. Discuss the relationship of audit programs to the AICPA and GAO auditing standards.
2. You are instructing an inexperienced member of the staff on a first assignment in auditing the performance of management. This young auditor is to interview an agency official concerning appropriate usage of rental cars. How would you help this person plan for the interview? State the interview objective. State the particular approach and the steps the new staff member would take in making the interview.

CHAPTER 5

Reviewing Management Audit Principles Using Real-Life Situations

After you have read this chapter, studied the review questions, and worked through the cases, you will understand:

- The basic principles of M-auditing as first set forth in Chapter 1.
- Selected standards management may use to accomplish its work more efficiently and economically.
- How to follow any M-audit through its respective phases, including the development of tentative, alternative, and firm audit objectives.
- How to prepare an audit program for a detailed examination of an M-audit.

The person who reads new material on a technical subject needs to be provided not only with a discussion of the subject but also with examples of real-life situations that pertain. For the new subject of performance auditing, this has proved difficult to do—and understandably so. Because auditors work under many pressures and often feel they have not done a perfect job, they are wary of criticism in showing their work to outsiders. The author, in fact, found it difficult to obtain real-life cases to use in his own training programs for the GAO. Nor were mock situations the solution, for they do not really provide learning auditors with practical answers.

Since the author believes that for real-life situations there is always an answer, he is grateful to staff members and officials of the GAO who have provided him with sufficient authentic cases so that the reader of this book can see what actually happens during an audit. The author recognizes that the subject matter of the audits in the GAO may not be the same as those found in audits made by other federal audit agencies, state or local audit agencies, public accountants, or internal audit groups. The basic approach, however, is the same.

We found, for instance, that in our training programs in the GAO we could train staff members who dealt with military subjects by using situations found in civil agencies and vice versa. Also, the approach to programs concerning Indian education could be applied to programs concerning energy or health. Clearly, understanding can be transferred between types of audits when the basic principles of performance auditing are understood.

By reviewing the basic principles of performance auditing in this chapter and applying them to real-life situations, you will be able to transfer this knowledge to your own actual audit situations. Let us start first with situations concerning M-auditing.

Basic Principles of Management Auditing

In reviewing the basic principles of M-auditing, we will start by listing them, and then enlarging upon them with a discussion of practical applications. We will use a rather simple situation, the illustration from which Case 1, Chapter 3 was developed, take it from start to finish, and then move to the preliminary phases of a more complex case, which will be thoroughly developed in later chapters.

A Listing of the Four Basic Principles of Auditing Related to an M-audit

1. An M-audit is the planning for, the obtaining of, and the evaluating of sufficient relevant material, and competent evidence on the audit objective of whether an organization's management or employees have or have not accepted and carried out efficiently and economically laws, regulations, policies, and acceptable practices, or other management standards for properly using its resources. From this evidence, the auditor comes to a conclusion on the audit objective. He then reports his conclusion to a third party, along with sufficient evidence to convince the third party that his conclusion is correct.

The auditor in making an M-audit usually places most emphasis on those activities that appear to show the greatest opportunities for improvement; in other words, he is usually looking for deficiencies in management.

2. In an M-audit, audit evidence is the facts and information used by the auditor to come to a conclusion on the audit objective. The audit objective is a statement or question proposing the answer to an audit inquiry as to the economical or efficient use of an organization's resources in providing a product or rendering a service. The audit objective is always composed of three essential elements:

   a) *The criteria.* The standards, which if carried out, would result in efficient or economical use of the organization's resources in providing a product or rendering a service. In an M-audit, these standards are acceptable and appropriate standards for carrying out the activities under audit.

   No generally accepted criteria are found for all activities covered in M-auditing as is true for financial-statement examinations. Thus, for the audit of each activity of management, the appropriate standards must be determined each time an examination is made.

   b) *The causes.* The actions of management, employees, or their delegated agents being audited, who either did or did not accept or carry out the proper standards for efficiently and economically managing the activity or organization.

   c) *The effects.* The amount, measurement, or results of the actual actions of management, employees, or their delegated agents when compared with the acceptable and appropriate standards for carrying out the activity. Since the measurement is in terms of efficiency or economy, most results of the measurement can be stated as a dollar value.

The deficiencies, as revealed in the effects, are only one aspect of an M-audit. Possibly of even greater importance to the overall audit is the identification and correction of the underlying causes of any deficiencies found to exist. Thus, the auditor's purpose would be to improve the management system so as to save money, avoid improper payments, prevent other losses, and promote operational efficiency. The auditor must therefore identify, to the extent practicable, the specific individual or organizational unit responsible for the deficient result. Furthermore, the indication of a deficiency is based on some acceptable standard of performance by which to measure that weakness.

We should remember that although the general approach to an M-audit is the identification and development of deficiencies, the auditor should give recognition to work resulting in favorable effects wherever possible. This will often require the auditor to obtain additional evidence to support the favorable finding, but certainly should place the reporting in a more objective stance.

3. All evidence the auditor uses to come to a conclusion on the audit objective must be relevant, material, and competent. It also must be sufficient to convince not only the auditor but any other person who has occasion to accept the conclusion.
    a) Relevance of evidence means that the information relates to the criteria of the audit objective. Materiality means that the information is significant enough to be considered.
    b) Competency of evidence pertains to the source of the information. Therefore, evidence must be obtained on an objective as to whether the source is competent. Since much of the information in an M-audit comes from various sources—records, testimony of others, and observations—each piece of evidence must indicate that the source is competent. But, like accounting records, information from the overall records of a company can be examined for competency at one time rather than by examining each individual record. This can be done by examining the internal management control system of the organization as it pertains to those records.
    c) Sufficiency of evidence in an M-audit pertains to the amount of evidence needed by the auditor to suggest clearly and convincingly that the conclusion concerning the objective of whether there is a deficiency in operations is the proper one. In legal terminology, evidence on the criteria and the effects can be little more than a preponderance of the total. But, evidence on causes, when causes pertain to particular individuals, must be convincing enough to be beyond a reasonable doubt.
    d) Evidence in an M-audit may be obtained by sampling as well as by making detailed tests. (See Chapter 12.)
    e) The competency of the evidence that comes from computers must be determined by reviewing the internal and management control of the computers. (See Chapter 14.)

Since the auditor is an expert in the gathering and evaluation of evidence, he should be able to perform this function in technical areas just as easily as in administrative areas. Thus, his audit activities in gathering evidence can be extended to include activities throughout the entire organization, not only activities in the financial areas.

4. Each management audit has four phases as follows:
    a) *The preliminary survey.* The auditor gathers background and general information on the organization and its activities. He identifies one particular activity that has an apparent weakness, as well as possible alternative activities, and states a tentative audit objective. He then prepares a program for the review and testing of management control within the area of the activity he selects.
    b) *The review and testing of management control.* The auditor gathers relevant and material evidence on all three elements of the audit objective by reviewing the management control of the or-

ganization to determine whether the criteria are acceptable, someone caused the effects, and the effects are significant enough to have a firm audit objective. During this review of management control, the auditor can also gather evidence on the objective of whether the information from the management controls is competent and can be relied upon. He then prepares a program for the detailed examination.

c) *The detailed examination.* The auditor gathers sufficient relevant, material, and competent evidence on the audit objective of whether some individual or group of individuals carried out an acceptable standard of operation in an economical and efficient manner within the framework of a specific management activity. He summarizes and analyzes the evidence in order to come to a conclusion on that objective.

d) *Report development.* The auditor, based upon his detailed examination and the conclusion from the detailed examination, prepares a report and communicates the conclusion to a third party along with sufficient evidence to support the conclusion.

In Chapter 3, we thoroughly discussed the preliminary survey phase for an M-audit and learned that this phase is much more distinctive for an M-audit than for a financial-statement examination. Since M-audits are seldom repeated, each audit is distinctive and the determination of what activity to examine becomes extremely important.

Before determining which specific activity to examine, the auditor must first determine which area he will look into. Will he look into the administrative area, the production area, the financial area, the marketing area, the transportation area, or some other area within an organization? The choice will depend upon several factors: the amount of money received or spent, the auditor's personal knowledge of the management controls in the area, executive or legislative interest, legal or policy requirements, public concern, or other similar interests.

An auditor who understands the three elements of an audit objective can isolate some particular activity that appears to warrant further examination in several ways: by walking through the organizational area, by looking at historical records of the area, by examining statistics concerning the area, or by discussing with the employees some of the activities concerning the area.

The box below presents selected standards for managing an organization—ones that an auditor can easily see should be followed by the management of any entity.

Selected Standards by Which Management May Provide for More Efficient and Economical Operations, by Area and Activity

I. *Planning*
   A. Plan for complete purchase transaction for major transactions to avoid change orders.
   B. Make studies for make-or-buy decisions.
   C. Plan only for needed copies from computer.
   D. Plan for proper use of inventory and warehousing space.
   E. Plan for proper arrangement of machinery and equipment.
   F. Standardize buying sizes.
   G. Plan maintenance cycle for longer operation of plant and equipment.

        H. Establish economic reorder points for ordering.
- II. *Operations*
    - A. Purchasing operations
        1. Seek purchases through competitive bids.
        2. Provide time to shop market.
        3. Order from approved vendors.
    - B. Inventory operations
        1. Control slow moving inventories.
        2. Shift the carrying of inventories to supplier.
        3. Take inventory count at low level of stocks.
    - C. Travel
        1. Obtain negotiated prices for hotels.
        2. Act as self-insurer on rental cars.
        3. Determine whether owned cars are less expensive than rental cars.
        4. Use compacts rather than full-sized cars.
        5. Use coach-class rather than first-class air fare.
    - D. Personnel
        1. Do not use high-priced labor for low-priced jobs.
        2. Stabilize labor force to avoid overtime—for example, second shift.
        3. Provide sufficient and trained employees to do the job.
    - E. Production
        1. Watch for excessive machine speed and too-slow machine speeds.
        2. Watch for excessive scrap and waste of materials.
        3. Reduce insurance premiums on plant and equipment by proper compliance with insurance company inspection reports.
    - F. Financial
        1. Invest short term cash.
        2. Eliminate duplicate accounting and operating records.
        3. Check customer credit before shipment of goods.
- III. *Control*
    - A. Control travel through travel requisitions.
    - B. Control purchases through periodic review of major purchase transactions.
    - C. Use purchase orders as receiving reports.
    - D. Control discounts through timely processing of invoices.
    - E. Use self-checking capabilities of the computer as a control device.
    - F. Consider state of current facilities and equipment before investing in new facilities or equipment.
    - G. Control power costs through negotiated interruptible rates.
    - H. Control plant shutdowns from power interruption through alternate sources of supply.

Finally, in this review of M-audit principles, let us recall that each phase in a performance audit leads to the next phase but that the first two are often combined into one. Thus, the auditor can combine the preliminary survey and the review and testing of management control into one phase, which would lead to the development of the audit objective. Then the detailed examination phase would allow the auditor to gather sufficient relevant, material, and competent evidence to come to a conclusion on an objective, which would be reported to a third party.

Moreover, by providing good recommendations in the report, the auditor can help the level of management with the primary responsibility for the operations and activities of that organization. The auditor can point out means for management to achieve greater economy and improve efficiency, as well as ways for simplifying procedures, developing more effective procedures, and eliminating those procedures that involve duplication or do not achieve a result commensurate with the costs. Obviously, the auditor does not have the responsibility for managing the organization and thus the recommendations made should always be suggestions for improvements, not commandments to follow.

Now, let us see how these principles can be applied to an M-audit in a real-life situation.

Application of Principles for an M-audit: "The Spark Plug Case"[1]

This real-life example, which we will call "The Spark Plug Case," illustrates the principles of M-auditing as applied to the flow of work for an M-audit—from beginning to end. Also, this case describes what was done rather than illustrating with a display of the working papers and the report.

Introduction

A large military installation has the worldwide prime responsibility for managing spark plugs used in aircraft reciprocating engines. This responsibility includes computing requirements; buying; establishing maintenance and service standards; and disposing of used, and surplus new, spark plugs. Aircraft spark plugs may be classified broadly as massive or fine-wire electrode-type plugs. Fine-wire spark plugs generally contain platinum-tipped center and ground electrodes. Millions of both types have been bought at prices for each ranging from about $1.25 for the massive electrode to about $4.00 for the fine-wire electrode.

Spark plugs are supposed to be serviced by the using units at regular service periods or at the time of engine failure, and by the engine overhaul facility during the periodic overhaul of engines. An aircraft spark plug is considered worn out when the electrodes have worn to such a degree that the plug cannot be economically serviced and used. Using units return the worn out fine-wire plugs to the overhaul facility for disposal so that the platinum can be reclaimed or the plugs sold for salvage value. Using units that require large quantities of fine-wire plugs may requisition a relatively inexpensive spark-plug servicing kit for use in cleaning, testing, and reconditioning this type of plug.

The Preliminary Survey

Much background data for the preliminary survey has just been given in the introduction. In addition, the auditors observed during the survey an inventory of about 800,000 fine-wire plugs being processed for disposal. They also noted that a large number of the fine-wire plugs appeared to show little wear and some were new and in factory-sealed containers.

By seeing the new fine-wire plugs in disposal bins, the auditors obtained evidence on one element (effects) of the following possible audit objective, providing they asserted the other two elements (criteria and causes).

Asserted criteria: New fine-wire plugs that have been requisitioned by using units and are over their needs should be returned to stock instead of being processed for disposal.

Asserted causes: Using units sent unneeded new fine-wire plugs to overhaul facility for disposal instead of returning them to stock.

Evidence on effects: The auditors saw the new fine-wire plugs in disposal bins. If each new fine-wire plug sent by the using unit to scrap disposal would instead be returned to stock, a saving of $4.00, less salvage value, for each plug, would result. Any quantity sent to scrap disposal would soon result in a significant effect.

The auditors, observing this limited amount of evidence, would have only a possible objective on a management deficiency. Much more evidence on criteria, causes, and effects would have to be gathered before any definite conclusion could be reached on the apparent management weakness. Before continuing to gather evidence on this objective, however, they should consider alternative objectives.

By asserting, when no evidence has previously been obtained, different criteria and related causes and effects, the auditors could state three other possible audit objectives as follows:

Audit Objective 1

Asserted criteria: Additional usage should be obtained from each fine-wire plug.

Asserted causes: Using units were not obtaining sufficient life from fine-wire plugs. Purchasing unit therefore was ordering too many fine-wire plugs.

Evidence on effects: The auditors observed that many of the 800,000 fine-wire plugs were relatively unused. If using units obtained an equivalent period of service for each spark plug now being used, $4.00 would be saved, and no new plugs would have to be ordered until current stock is depleted.

Audit Objective 2

Asserted criteria: The platinum in the electrodes of the fine-wire plugs should be reclaimed and sold separately instead of disposing of fine-wire plugs as scrap.

Asserted causes: Disposal unit was selling used fine-wire plugs for scrap instead of first reclaiming platinum and selling precious metal.

Asserted effects: Savings could be made of the difference between scrap sales value and the amount received for reclaimed precious metal, plus scrap value of remaining parts of plugs less costs of reclamation.

Audit Objective 3

Asserted criteria: Massive electrode plugs should be used in place of fine-wire plugs whenever possible.

Asserted causes: Using units were employing fine-wire plugs in all equipment, such as testing engines. Requirements unit was determining, and procuring unit was ordering, too many fine-wire and not enough massive electrode plugs.

Asserted effects: Savings could be made of the difference between the cost of fine-wire plugs, $4.00; and massive electrode plugs, $1.25.

Still further possible objectives could be established by asserting criteria from other levels of responsibility: (1) proper inspection should determine that all new plugs are serviceable so that no disposal would be made of these new plugs, or (2) the complete engine should not be overhauled except at appropriate service time to save any expenses of premature repairs, or (3) carburetors should be repaired instead of replaced. In each instance, if a possible audit objective is considered, evidence must be obtained on at least one element of the objective.

After considering the appropriate alternative audit objectives, the auditors must then summarize the evidence and assertions in order to consider which, if any, of the audit objectives they will choose to gather evidence on.

Review and Testing of Management Control

From the four possible audit objectives, it would appear that if the first one on spark-plug usage were considered, there would be a greater possibility of significant effects than from the other three. In the actual audit, evidence was gathered on several of the possible objectives at the same time. Our illustration will consider only the objective on spark-plug usage.

Limited evidence has already been obtained on one element of the process, effects. The auditors observed relatively little use of the 800,000 fine-wire plugs. Now they need evidence on a firm criteria, actual causes, and the significance of the effects. The auditors reviewed the appropriate technical manual on spark plug usage, which showed that 400 hours was the minimum desired service life for the fine-wire plugs. This evidence showed that there could be a reasonable and firm criteria of 400 hours.

The auditors reviewed the records the requirements group used in determining requirements. These showed that the average service life of the plugs ranged from 188 to 241 hours. They also reviewed the procuring unit's purchase orders. These showed that orders outstanding were based on the 188 to 241 hours of usage. The evidence indicated that actions of the using units (causes) were contrary to the standards of the technical manual and that actions of the procuring unit (causes) were based on the 188 to 241 hours standards of the using units.

From the summarized evidence above, the auditors would prepare an audit program for the detailed examination in which they would list the specific audit objective and the specific steps needed to gather evidence on the objective in order to come to a conclusion.

The Detailed Examination

With this audit program as a guide, the auditors must gather sufficient competent, relevant, and material evidence on the criteria, causes, and effects of the audit objective. They obtained additional evidence on each of the following:

Additional Evidence on Criteria. The auditors obtained reports of evaluation tests made by technical personnel that demonstrated that the fine-wire plugs could be used for 300 hours and that a large percentage could then be reconditioned and used for at least an additional 300 hours. Technical personnel at one using unit told the auditors that the unit was obtaining over 600 hours from the fine-wire plugs by cleaning, testing, and regapping the plugs through the use of relatively inexpensive equipment.

Additional Evidence on Causes. The auditors found that the requirements group used records of many using units in determining requirements. These records showed that average service life ranged from 188 to 241 hours per plug. By interviewing technical personnel, the auditors determined that most using units obtained about 100 to 300 hours of service life from the plugs. After that limited usage, the plugs were returned to scrap because the using unit did not have a relatively inexpensive cleaning and testing machine. Purchase orders in the procurement department showed that orders had been placed and were to be placed to replenish spark plugs based on the service life of 100 to 300 hours.

Additional Evidence on Effects. The auditors obtained a requirements group report showing purchase computations based on an operating life of 600 hours per plug. The report showed dollar value of needed plugs for the year was overstated by $4.6 million when purchase computations were compared to the original service life of 100 to 300 hours. Of this amount, procurement records showed that $3.6 million worth were presently on order and $1 million worth were scheduled to be ordered. Procuring officials stated that on seeing the current computations, they were postponing indefinitely the scheduled orders of $1 million worth of spark plugs.

Conclusion on Objective

The auditors—or anyone else for that matter—would surely conclude from the summarized evidence the following:

The overstated purchase requirements for fine-wire spark plugs occurred because procuring officials used the 100 to 300 hours of service life obtained by most using units as the basis for determining requirements, instead of the 400 to 600 hours (or more) of service life required by technical manuals and obtained by selected using units. Relatively unused spark plugs were therefore being sent to scrap disposal.

Reporting

The auditors must now communicate their conclusion to the proper authorities. They must set the scene by giving background information on the process before a reader can readily understand the conclusion. This information usually describes the organization and its operations.

The conclusion the auditors state in the report and that in the audit are the same, although the report conclusion may follow a different rhetorical style from that in the audit. The following is an example:

> Our review disclosed a widespread practice by using activities of returning relatively unused platinum electrode spark plugs to the disposal unit for reclamation or scrap disposal. Failure of these using activities to obtain the minimum desired service life from the spark plugs resulted in an overstatement of requirements amounting to $4.6 million. Procurement officials have already ordered $3.6 million worth of spark plugs against this requirement, and following a recent recomputation, have deferred procurement of the $1 million balance of this requirement.

The evidence in the report ordinarily would be a summarized version of that shown in the audit. Depending upon the circumstances and the reader, it is possible that less evidence is needed in the report than in the audit.

A recommendation the auditors can make is to have the purchasing unit order spark plugs based on the assumption that using units will obtain from 400 to 600 hours of service life from them. A recommendation also can be made that using units procure and utilize a relatively inexpensive cleaning and testing machine to obtain longer life. The same recommendations may be suggested for other units at other locations, or other organizations.

Application of Principles for the Preliminary Phases: "The Case of the Overseas Flights"[2]

"The Spark Plug Case" showed the application of the principles of performance auditing to all phases of a rather simple type of M-audit. "The Case of the Overseas Flights" will show in more detail a much more complex situation, one which has been taken from a GAO audit and reproduced here with GAO permission.* This section illustrates the application of the principles of per-

---
*Special thanks are due to Mr. Fred Shafer, the Director of the Logistics and Communications Division of the GAO.

formance auditing to the preliminary phases of the audit. Chapter 10 will illustrate the principles applied to the detailed examination phases.

In this example, the reader should note at the outset that the majority of evidence needed in the detailed examination will be on effects, while the needed evidence on criteria and causes will be obtained during the preliminary survey and the review and testing of management control. As is true for many audits, the two preliminary phases were combined and considered as one.

Background Data and Additional Evidence

The following information, summarized from the working papers, was obtained by the auditors during the preliminary survey and the review and testing of management controls.

The Military Airlift Command (MAC), a major command of the U.S. Air Force, is the single operating agency for airlift services within the Department of Defense (DOD). MAC is responsible for providing overseas air transportation for military personnel and their dependents.

MAC headquarters at Scott Air Force Base (AFB), Illinois, directs the activities of this airlift force. Operational control is vested in the 21st and 22nd Air Forces at McGuire AFB, New Jersey, and Travis AFB, California, respectively. Components of these Air Forces in the United States and overseas carry out the day-to-day functions necessary to operate a global airlift service.

MAC, in addition to operating its own aircraft, contracts with commercial airlines for additional airlift. MAC procured about $170 million worth of airlift services in fiscal year 1975; about $140 million worth of this was for transportation of passengers.

Airlift procurement is divided among air carriers in proportion to their participation in the Civil Reserve Air Fleet program, which obligates carriers to provide specific aircraft to MAC in emergencies.

During fiscal year 1974, MAC moved over 1.1 million passengers between the United States and overseas locations. About 78 percent of these passengers traveled on chartered commercial aircraft under contract to MAC. The charter rate per passenger, established and approved by the Civil Aeronautics Board (CAB), is much less than the standard commercial fare. Under the charter arrangement, however, MAC must pay for all available seats on the aircraft, whether used or not.

Charter flights are procured both from supplemental airlines (carriers that normally do not offer regularly scheduled passenger service) and from certificated carriers (carriers that also provide regularly scheduled flights on CAB-approved routes). The charter flights usually depart from and arrive at military air bases rather than commercial facilities.

Procurement of commercial airlift is subject to CAB regulation. CAB is an independent regulatory agency with broad authority to regulate and promote civil aeronautics within the United States and between the United States and foreign countries. In carrying out these responsibilities, CAB issues regulations that have the force of law and that set forth its policies, requirements, and procedures.

In 1973, because of the fuel crisis, CAB approved applications from several certified air carriers for authority to divert military passengers from charter flights to their regularly scheduled flights at the charter flight rates and on a temporary basis. This action was to move the passengers into otherwise unoccupied space on scheduled flights, thereby eliminating the need to operate certain charter flights. Under this procedure, substitute service was scheduled several weeks in advance and DOD passengers went directly to a commercial airport.

From this background data and the additional evidence obtained during the review and testing of management control, the auditors would come up with an audit objective somewhat as follows:

> Would the Department of Defense by diverting passengers (causes) from charter flights operated by U.S. international air carriers to regularly scheduled flights of the same carriers and at the charter flight rate (criteria) (1) reduce annual operating costs by several millions of dollars, (2) save a great many millions of gallons of jet fuel, (3) reduce annual balance of payments by as much as the fuel would cost if it had to be procured overseas, and (4) improve the financially ailing condition of the U.S. international airlines by many millions of dollars (effects)?

If the audit group making the audit had to sell the audit to a higher-level authority within the organization, they might do so by stating:

> The Department of Defense could save as much as 40 million gallons of jet fuel annually, improve the balance of payments to the extent that the jet fuel saved would have been purchased from foreign sources, reduce annual costs to the DOD by as much as $3 million through better use of seats, and allow the financially ailing U.S. international air carriers to reduce annual operating costs by as much as $30 million.

The Audit Program

Upon completion of the preliminary phases of the audit, the auditors should have sufficient information and evidence to determine what additional evidence they would need to come to a conclusion on the audit objective.

The auditors would have a fairly strong basis for the criteria of the audit. Since the CAB had already given the DOD authority, on a temporary basis, to divert military passengers from charter flights to regularly scheduled flights at the charter flight rates, it is obvious that this authority would be an appropriate standard.

Likewise, in the preliminary phases, the particular operating organizations that had the responsibility for contracting for airlifts had been identified. Thus, the causes as well had been fairly well determined. Since the CAB might not be willing to grant an extension of the temporary authority to a permanent status, the auditors should consider what effect the CAB might have on the carrying out of the proposed standard.

To be assured that the CAB would approve an extension of the temporary authority, the auditors would have to discuss this matter with a CAB authority. In addition, the auditors would need assurance from the air carriers, as well as from the DOD, that they are in agreement with the suggestion and capable of carrying out the standard.

The major part of the audit program, however, would be concerned with obtaining evidence on the effects. Since the audit objective has four different effects based on the same criteria and causes, then the audit program would have to identify specifically the means of gathering evidence on those particular effects. The effects as stated in this audit objective, which we will now consider in detail, are:

1. Gallons of fuel saved,
2. Cost reductions through better use of aircraft,
3. Improved balance of payments, and
4. Reduction of costs to carriers.

84 / *Getting Started*

Gallons of Fuel Saved. In order to determine the gallons of fuel that could be saved if the DOD converted charter flights to regularly scheduled flights, the auditor would have to go through the following audit steps:

1. Determine the number of flights for base period of October 1973 to September 1974.
   a) For all flights originating and returing to McGuire AFB. (This will include all flights to and from Europe where there are regularly scheduled flights.)
   b) For all flights originating and returning to Travis AFB. (This will include all flights to and from the Far East and Honolulu where there are regularly scheduled flights.)
      Note: Instead of calculating all flights for the year, four representative months, October 1973, November 1973, August 1974, and September 1974 can be used, and this one third of a year multiplied by three to convert to a full year.
2. Convert flights to average time. This information can be obtained from the flight logs.
3. Obtain average fuel consumption for a 707 from Boeing Corporation. Average consumption from Boeing can be confirmed by PAA, TWA, and NWA.
4. Obtain average passenger load for each channel to determine if all charter flights can be converted to regularly scheduled flights.
5. If seats are available so that all passengers can be converted from charter flights to commercial flights, then the total for all fuel used for all charter flights would need to be obtained. This would be the savings for each flight converted.
6. Add together all flights:
   a) Multiply average flight time by fuel-consumed-per-hour to determine total consumption for the Pacific Region.
   b) Multiply average flight time by fuel-consumed-per-hour to determine total consumption for the Atlantic region.
   c) Combine total fuel consumption for the Pacific region with total fuel consumption for the Atlantic region to obtain total gallons of fuel that could be saved.
7. Summarize total savings in fuel consumption for the year.

Cost Reductions Through Better Use of Aircraft. Cost reductions to the DOD would be obtained when the agency utilizes an aircraft to the fullest extent. Charter aircraft are seldom fully used. If the payment-per-passenger-mile is the same on the commercial aircraft as on the charter aircraft, then any underutilization of the charter aircraft would be an additional cost to the government.

The following steps would have to be taken by the auditors to obtain evidence on this objective:

1. Determine the number of flights for the base period of October 1973 to September 1974.
   a) For all flights originating and returning to McGuire AFB. (This will include all flights to and from Europe where there are both regularly scheduled commercial flights and flights flown by charter aircraft.)
   b) For all flights originating and returning to Travis AFB. (This will include all flights to and from the Far East and Honolulu where there are both regularly scheduled commercial flights and flights flown by charter aircraft.)

Note: Again, four representative months can be used.
    c) This audit step would be the same as that for determining the amount of fuel saved. The auditors would need to cross-reference to that work paper for this information.
 2. Determine the number of miles for each flight.
 3. Determine available seating capacity for each flight.
 4. Determine passenger-mile seating capacity.
 5. Obtain the number of seats occupied on each flight.
 6. Calculate rate of occupancy for each flight.
 7. Determine unused occupancy for each flight.
 8. Calculate unused-occupancy passenger miles.
 9. Multiply unused-occupancy passenger miles by charter rate per-passenger-mile to obtain total cost of unused seats.
 10. Combine total for Atlantic region flights with total for Pacific region flights to obtain total costs of unused passenger seats.
 11. Summarize information.

Improved Balance of Payments and Reduction of Costs to Carriers. These two additional audit objectives would also need programmed steps for the auditors to derive the amount of the effects. Although these two programs are not shown, readers might find it challenging to come up with the steps they believe would help the auditors obtain the evidence necessary to come to a conclusion on each.

REVIEW QUESTIONS

1. The author states that apparently there is quite a bit of transferability of understanding between different types of audits. Discuss. (See p. 73.)

2. When an auditor locates a deficiency in the manner that management carries out its activities, he should fully consider the effects and consequences of the deficiency. Discuss the scope of this consideration, and the requirements of the auditor in discharging his responsibility in relation to these matters. (See pp. 74–75.)

3. An auditor is an expert in the gathering and evaluation of evidence. In what areas, other than financial and administrative, should an auditor be able to gather and evaluate evidence? Discuss. (See p. 75.)

4. Before determining which specific activity to examine, the auditor must first determine which areas he will look into. Give examples of factors that might influence his choice of areas, and explain how the auditor might isolate a particular activity for further examination. (See p. 76.)

5. If properly carried out, what should be the results of the preliminary phases of an M-audit? (See pp. 75, 77–78.)

6. Most M-audit programs include both the preliminary survey phase and the review and testing of management control phase in one audit program. Why? (See pp. 77–78.)

7. Explain how alternative audit objectives may be developed after the original tentative objective has been determined. (See pp. 79–80.)

8. In the detailed examination, the auditor gathers sufficient evidence on all three elements of the audit objective to prove the conclusion. Explain how the auditors gathered evidence to come to the conclusion in "The Spark Plug Case." (See pp. 80–81.)

9. Explain how the auditors would come up with the audit objective they did in "The Case of the Overseas Flights." (See p. 80.)

10. Explain how the audit steps given for the gallons of fuel saved would be developed. (See p. 84.)

CASE 1

Self-assessment Taxes in the State of Piedmont: The Case of the Lost Revenues[3]

Commenting on audits of efficiency and economy (M-audits), Chapter 1 states:

> The best use of resources can be determined by holding the revenues or benefits constant and reducing the costs or expenditures, by holding the costs or expenditures constant and increasing the revenue or benefits, or by increasing the revenue or benefits at a faster rate than increasing the costs or expenditures.

The case that follows pertains to increasing efficiency and economy by improving the revenue picture of a state agency that has the responsibility for collecting self-assessment taxes. If the costs or expenditures could be held fairly constant and the revenues improved substantially, the state could operate more efficiently and economically.

News releases and official position papers released by the governor's office and the two houses of the legislature in the state of Piedmont indicated that both the governor and the legislature were interested in improving the revenue position of the state. Indications were also given that heads of state agencies were complaining that they had too much to do without the necessary resources and thus needed increased appropriations.

Comments made by both political parties, as well as the governor, indicated that even though they understood the need for additional revenue, they considered it politically inexpedient to raise taxes at the present time. Many taxpayers were complaining that taxes were too high, and some taxpayer groups were talking about pushing for reduced taxes.

Members of state auditor George Bennett's staff, learning of these comments, decided that they should obtain information on the subject in case either the governor or the legislature should request it. The staff, which had the responsibility for auditing the organizations concerned with revenue and taxation, met with Mr. Bennett and decided that they would, with his approval, look into the matter immediately.

AUDIT SCENARIO 1
The Preliminary Survey

Required

1. Develop a preliminary survey audit program for the audit of the organization(s) that have the responsibility for self-assessment taxes in the state of Piedmont.
2. From the preliminary information and background data that follows and from your own knowledge of state income and sales taxes, identify as many possible audit objectives as you can for increasing revenues from self-assessment taxes in the state of Piedmont.

Background Information.

By reviewing the laws, legislative history, and regulations of the Department of Revenue of the state of Piedmont, the auditors found that the responsibility for collecting all self-assessment taxes for the state had been given to that department. The laws also mandated that all tax returns must be kept confidential; in gathering background information, therefore, the auditors decided not to look at any tax returns.

At one time, the state had collected real property taxes; but when the state began to collect income, sales, and personal property taxes, they relinquished this source of revenue to the cities and the counties. Almost all revenue sources from which the department collected revenues were thus currently under a self-assessment system—a system under which the taxpayers themselves originally determined whether they must file a return and then established the tax due. The state, in other words, did not do this for them as under an *ad valorem* tax system.

The Department of Revenue had collected the revenue shown below from the indicated sources during the preceding fiscal year.

Sources and Amounts of Revenue Fiscal Year 1978 (amounts to nearest millions of dollars)

Sources	Revenue
1. Sales taxes	$450,000,000

2. Individual income taxes
   a) Resident, $350,000,000
   b) Nonresident, $50,000,000
	400,000,000

3. Corporate income taxes	150,000,000
4. All other revenue sources—including unincorporated business, personal property, gift, estate, inheritance, liquor, and tobacco taxes, and grants	100,000,000
	$1,100,000,000

The organization chart of the Department of Revenue is shown in the figure on p. 89; it includes a statement of the duties of the various offices and divisions. The authorized positions and fund allotments for the various offices and divisions for fiscal year 1979 are shown in the following table.

Authorized Positions and Fund Allotments

Office or division	Authorized positions	Amount allotted for fiscal 1979 (nearest $10,000)
Office of the Commissioner of Revenue	8	$ 160,000
Office of General Counsel	25	440,000
Office of Administration	50	900,000
Data Systems Division	97	2,000,000
Tax Administration Division	350	5,900,000
Office of Treasurer	100	1,600,000
Total	630	$11,000,000

Organization chart, Department of Revenue, State of Piedmont

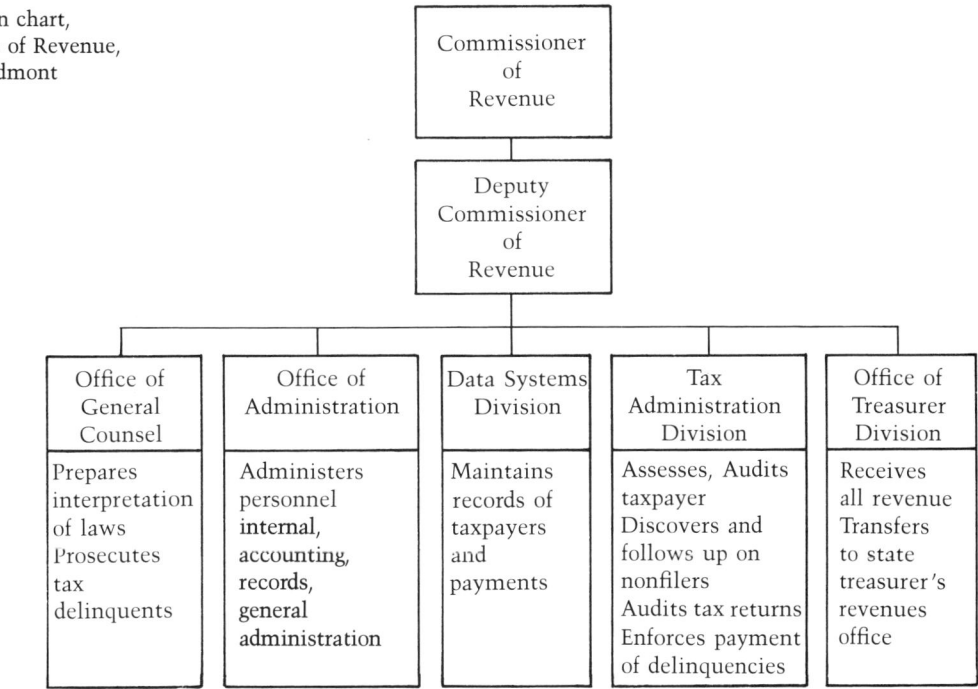

The Tax Administration Division is the organization principally responsible for assuring compliance with the tax law. It informs taxpayers of the laws and regulations, and assists taxpayers in the preparation of their returns. It also follows up on nonfilers and audits tax returns. It is organized as shown in the figure below.

Organization chart, Tax Administration Division, Department of Revenue

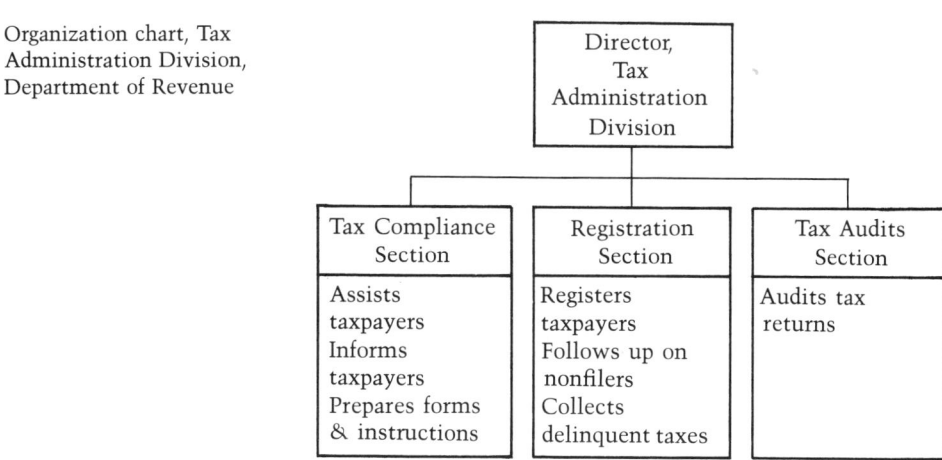

Ann Rassi, the auditor from Mr. Bennett's staff assigned to this task, obtained articles and books on self-assessment taxes and found that the assumption behind self-assessment taxes is that individuals will (1) voluntarily follow the laws, regulations, and related assessment instructions, (2) file proper tax returns, and (3) pay taxes due. Further information showed that voluntary compliance with self-assessed taxes requires adequate information concerning laws, regulations, and preparation of tax returns. Without such information, taxpayers often neglect to file returns, or file incomplete returns. Also, unless the taxpayers understand the information and forms, they are likely to become frustrated and again, fail to file a return. Although withholding may help to collect some of these taxes, it does not help when the taxpayer works in other jurisdictions or is not an employee.

During the auditor's walk through of the Department of Revenue activities, she observed several people talking on the telephone. When asked, these employees said that they were answering questions concerning preparation of individual income and business sales tax returns. Often the callers had the same problems: state income tax forms, for instance, did not agree with federal ones so that conversion was difficult. Many said also that the instructions for filling out both income and sales tax returns were difficult to understand; and the comment most frequently made was that even though they filled out the form in the best manner they knew, they were not sure that their tax was properly computed.

In the department's data systems division, a copy of the most recent list of individual and corporate income and sales-tax taxpayers was shown to Ms. Rossi and her audit team. The director of the division said that he was a long way from being sure that the list of taxpayers for any of the categories was complete. The computer, for instance, was not programmed to relate sales taxes to business income taxes or franchise taxes. Nor was he able to compare federal tax returns on the computer with state tax returns or relate withholding taxes with returns. He said that it would take only a little more time and effort to program the computer to accomplish these tasks, but at the present moment he was not sure that all taxpayers had filed—or even who should have filed.

As Ms. Rossi and her audit team passed through the Tax Administration Division, some of the tax auditors commented that they thought they had done an outstanding job auditing tax returns. The external auditors were given a statement of collections during the past two years of sales taxes and income taxes collected as a result of the audit program (see the table below).

Tax Administration Division Audited Returns, Additional Revenue, and Hours, for Years 1977 and 1978

Type of return	1977	1978
Individual		
Audited returns	25,000	23,000
Audit revenue	$2,400,000	$2,200,000
Audit hours	65,000	62,000
Withholding		
Audited returns	800	900
Audit revenue	$40,000	$60,000
Audit hours	1,700	2,000
Corporation		
Audited returns	2,100	1,700
Audit revenue	$1,300,000	$1,400,000
Audit hours	8,000	7,000
Unincorporated business		
Audited returns	800	700
Audit revenue	$165,000	$75,000
Audit hours	2,600	2,200
Sales and use tax		
Audited returns	700	800
Audit revenue	$1,900,000	$1,700,000
Audit hours	30,000	40,000

AUDIT SCENARIO 2

The Review and Testing of Management Control

Required

1. Prepare an audit program for the review and testing of management control based on the tentative audit objectives you develop.
2. Develop a firm audit objective, insofar as possible, evaluating the Department of Revenue for the possibility of increasing revenues from the self-assessing tax system of the State of Piedmont. Consider the possible steps that will be needed to gather the evidence to come to a conclusion on the objective.
3. You might want to consider yourself the supervisor on this assignment. Develop a classification and indexing system that will be needed for the working papers used to file the information gathered as evidence on the audit objective.

Background Information

In Audit Scenario 1, the preliminary survey phase, you should have come up with at least one tentative audit objective and possibly several more. You might also have made individual objectives or have made one combined objective, in a very tentative form, such as the following:

> Can the Department of Revenue through improving the state's self-assessment taxing system (causes) increase state revenue by as much as .2 percent or $2,200,000 (effects) by: (1) identifying and following up on nonfilers, (2) improving the ease with which taxpayers fill out the forms and prepare the return, (3) relating federal forms to state forms, (4) relating federal taxes with state taxes, (5) providing adequate assistance to taxpayers in the preparation of their returns, and (6) increasing the number of returns audited (criteria)?*

Each of the above six criteria could have been used as a basis for a separate objective; but causes and effects, in this situation, relate directly to each of the criteria and therefore only one audit objective need be stated. If causes or effects were related to more specific individuals or groups, or to specific amounts, then separate objectives should have been stated.

As we have emphasized in this book, when a stated objective is only a possible or tentative one, it must become firm before the auditor puts forth

---
* To keep this case within workable limits, all criteria have been related only to sales and income taxes.

---

much effort to obtain detailed evidence. To firm up the objective, the auditor will have to have some evidence on each of its elements. He might then want to revise the objectives based on his additional evidence.

To obtain the evidence on the elements of the tentative objective in this case, Ms. Rossi and her team will review and test the actual operations of the tax-assessing and collecting system—the process termed the review and testing of management control.

Additional Background Information

When the auditors started to review the management control system by testing a few transactions from beginning to end in order to collect evidence with which they could come up with a firm objective, they were interested in looking at a few tax returns. What they wanted to do was follow the process of the return, from (1) the development of the tax form and instructions, to (2) the original preparation of the return—with assistance when given—to (3) the return coming in, to (4) the tax-collecting system, to (5) the relating of taxes assessed to withholding, to (6) the relating of taxes assessed and collected to other related systems, to (7) the computer processing of returns, to (8) the auditing of returns, to (9) the determination that taxes were collected from all taxpayers required to file, and finally to (10) the collection of delinquent taxes.

They were immediately told that the law setting up the Department of Revenue specifically stated that only certain persons were allowed to look at individual tax returns. According to the department's general counsel, external auditors were not included in the category of those allowed to examine returns.

The auditing team, then, had to adopt new techniques to gather the needed evidence. Since the purpose of the review and testing of management control is to firm up the audit objective, and not to go into a full-scale examination, they only needed sufficient evidence from the management control system to determine whether to proceed with the audit or whether to stop, and they were able to obtain the following additional evidence:

Tax Forms and Instructions. The auditors reviewed the forms and instructions and found they had difficulty relating one to the other. They also determined that no relationship existed between the federal forms and the state forms.

Original Preparation of Return. Since the auditors were unable to look at the tax returns and relate them to the assistance given, they decided to talk to several individuals and business managers to obtain their views as to the problems involved in the assessment of their taxes and the preparation of their returns. Here is a sample of their responses:

> "I do not reside in this state. Since my employer withholds for both states, I have asked him to withhold for the state in which I reside. My state makes it easy to file a return. All I do is to take my federal return's adjusted gross income and start from there."

> "I can't quite tell exactly how much sales taxes I should collect. For example, do I collect sales taxes on patent medicines, since medicines are exempt. The instructions are vague. I haven't been questioned on my views, so I guess I have been doing what is right."

> "I have a small business and don't make much money. I'm sure the state would not want me to pay a small business tax or even income taxes."

> "I have not had much trouble paying my taxes. I go down to the Office of the Department of Revenue and they help me file my return. But, it does seem to me that they are more interested in collecting the maximum tax than in helping me file an honest tax return."

> "Every time I turn around, the auditors are examining my sales tax return. They haven't collected any additional taxes in five years. Why do they keep examining the same individual?"

> "It seems to me that the instructions should have some tables to help me know if I have computed and paid the right tax."

Returns Coming into the System. The auditors observed the returns coming into the system in total, but they were unable to follow individual returns in the system. They did observe that the procedures appeared satisfactory and were in accordance with good internal control procedures.

Computer-related Efforts. The auditors had been told during the preliminary survey that the manager of the division felt there were many problems in the computer-related efforts. It was not possible to relate withholding taxes to the tax form, the federal return with the state return, business taxes to sales taxes.

Auditing of the Returns. One of the tax auditors showed Ms. Rossi that the number of tax audits he made had been going up steadily, but he had no increase in collections as a result of the audits. Although he was allowed to choose any taxpayer's return he wished, he felt that if he were judged on the amount of taxes collected instead of the number of returns he audited, he might be in trouble. He suggested that the department obtain information on which types of returns needed to be audited in order to produce the greatest improvement in taxes collected. He also said that he had a backlog of audits he wanted to do; he was certain they would increase revenue but had no time to do them if he wanted to keep his production quota up to the standards that he thought he should. As far as he knew, desk audits were not considered in the number of audits made and he knew of no one making desk audits.

Finding Nonfilers. The tax auditor in charge of the section pertaining to finding taxpayers not filing returns said that her section made a determined effort to locate every such taxpayer by developing internally related information on nonfilers, although they were not allowed to go outside the department to gather this information. She also said that as far as she knew, the department had never made an attempt to determine whether nonprofit organizations should pay income or sales taxes.

Collection of Delinquent Taxes. According to the section dealing with delinquent taxes, these arise when a person files a return but does not pay the taxes; when additional assessments of taxes are made upon audit; when error in the return causes an additional assessment; when businesses collect sales and withholding taxes and then do not pay, or go out of business; and when estimated taxes are never paid.

The section chief gave the auditors a copy of the information concerning the delinquent taxes collected during the previous past two years (see the table above right).

Delinquent Collections

		1977		1978	
Action	Number	Amount	Number	Amount	
Collected	22,000	$7,000,000	18,000	$6,000,000	
Collected from prosecution	90	800,000	200	1,000,000	
Written off	8,500	800,000	8,000	800,000	

CASE 2

Welfare in the City: The AFDC Case in Yorktown[4]

One of the major costs of operation in highly populated cities and states is the cost of welfare, and a major welfare cost is aid to families with dependent children (AFDC). This case attempts to bring into focus the procedures necessary to audit for efficiency and economy (M-audit) the activity of providing AFDC.

AUDIT SCENARIO 1
Preliminary Survey and Review and Testing of Management Control

Required

1. Develop an audit program combining the preliminary survey and the review and testing of management control for the audit of the organizations that have the responsibility for AFDC in the welfare department of Yorktown.
2. Carrying out the procedures of your audit program should have provided you, as a minimum, with the information that follows. From this information, state an audit objective for the audit of the activities of the Department of Human Resources, city of Yorktown, as they relate to AFDC.

Background Information

The organization chart shown below was obtained from the Department of Human Resources (DHR), the agency that has charge of welfare in the city. (Only organizations having direct relationships with the AFDC activity are shown.)

AFDC is the major public assistance program in Yorktown. For fiscal year 1978, AFDC payments represented about 90 percent of the total welfare payments. Under the AFDC program, HEW shares in furnishing financial assistance—50 percent.

Since fiscal year 1974, the city's AFDC case load has almost doubled and total payments—federal and city—have more than doubled: in fiscal year 1974, the average monthly case load was about 16,800 and payments totaled about $40.8 million; in fiscal year 1978, the average monthly case load increased to about 30,200 and payments increased to about $86 million.

Quality Control

As a means of monitoring the AFDC program and maintaining continuous and systematic control over the incidence of ineligible

Organization chart, City of Yorktown, Department of Human Resources (DHR)

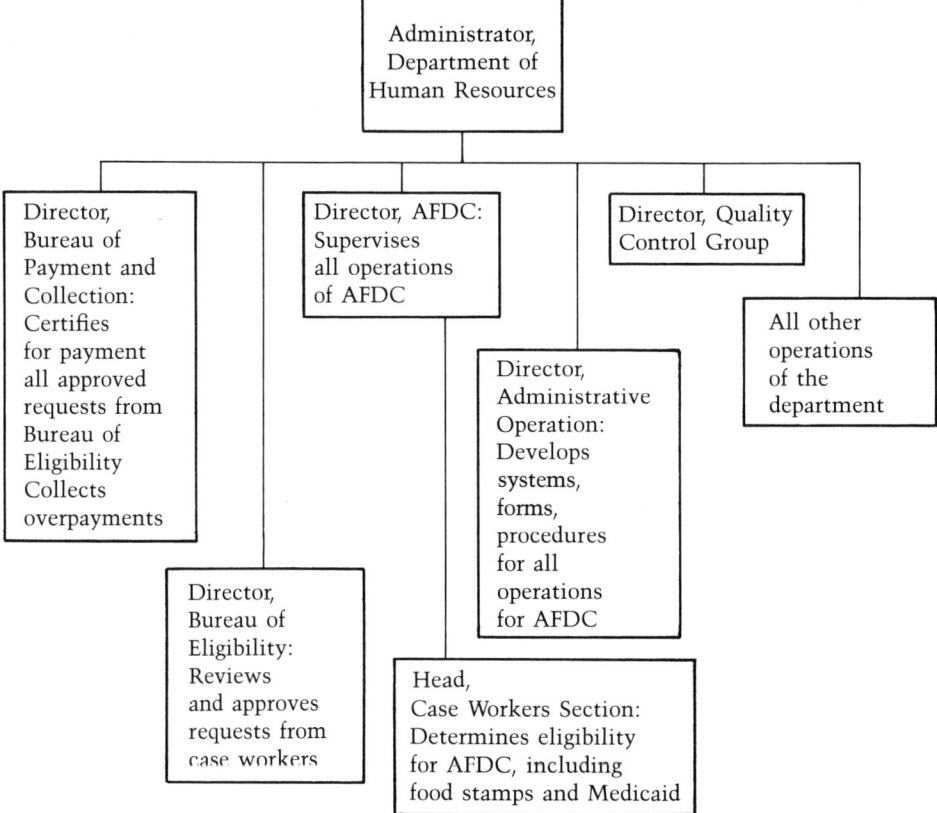

recipients and incorrect payments in the public assistance case load, HEW requires the city to have a quality control program, with the primary purpose of holding the incidence of errors in AFDC to HEW's preestablished tolerance levels. It accomplishes this purpose by:

- Reviewing a statistically reliable sample of welfare cases,
- Collecting and analyzing case findings periodically to determine the incidence of errors, and
- Using corrective action to bring the level of erroneous cases—ineligible or incorrect payments—within established levels, when tolerance levels are exceeded.

HEW's maximum acceptable error level for ineligible cases is 3 percent of the case load; for either overpayments or underpayments, it is 5 percent. HEW requires the city to sample randomly and review, every six months, a minimum number of cases based on its AFDC average case load, and to determine which number is statistically representative of all its cases. The current quality control program has been in effect for five years.

The quality control review consists of an analysis of the case records and a field investigation that independently verifies and documents factors affecting eligibility and payment by interviewing applicants and other sources, making home visits, and examining pertinent documents.

The quality control group periodically prepared a summary report on the results of its reviews showing the number of cases reviewed and the number of cases found to be in error, each classified by whether the recipient is ineligible for welfare or whether the recipient was overpaid or underpaid.

For each case in error, the group prepares a report detailing (1) whether the case is underpaid, overpaid, or ineligible, (2) the cause of the error, (3) the support to substantiate the error, and (4) whether the error was caused by the recipient or DHR.

These reports are sent to DHR's Bureau of Eligibility Determination (BED) for action. For those cases in error, BED must review the data furnished; and, if affirmed, must take action to stop or to adjust the welfare payment.

DHR procedures require that, if there are

indications of widespread errors, action must be taken to identify and correct the problem. For example, if high error rates were attributable to incomplete or inaccurate information on the amount of income reported by the welfare recipient, DHR could institute new procedures for verifying this data. Similarly, if high error rates were attributable to agency staff misapplying agency policy, DHR could require more employee training or supervisory review. DHR took no effective action on the reports by the quality control group.

Results of Quality Control Reviews

From October 1973 through December 1978, the quality control group made 11 reports on its reviews of the AFDC program. Of the 7,484 welfare cases reviewed, the group found that 2,872 cases, or 38 percent, were in error. They found that:

- 782 were ineligible for welfare
- 1,599 were overpaid, and
- 491 were underpaid.

Cases Indicating Willful Misrepresentation: A Continuing Problem

The following table shows, by calendar year, the number of cases that indicate recipients willfully misrepresenting the facts concerning their eligibility as found by the quality control group. (The results of two or more review periods have been combined.)

willful misrepresentation; in calendar year 1978, the percentage of such cases almost doubled to 13.5 percent. The principal reasons accounting for the 226 cases in 1978, as reported by the quality control group, were:

- Inaccurate reporting of earned income (62 cases),
- Children not living with specified relative (47 cases),
- Female recipient living with husband or paramour (47 cases),
- Recipients no longer living in the city (23 cases), and
- Other (47 cases).

The auditors estimate also that, on the basis of the quality control group's review results, DHR made welfare overpayments of about $10 million on willful misrepresentation cases from October 1973 to December 1978.

Potential Food Stamp and Medicaid Overpayments

People who are eligible to receive AFDC welfare payments may also receive Medicaid and food stamp benefits. If AFDC recipients are found to be ineligible for welfare and their welfare payments are terminated, their Medicaid and food stamp benefits can also be terminated. However, recipients who are terminated are advised that they may be eligible for, and can apply for, Medicaid and food stamps as nonpublic assistance

Number of Cases of Recipients Willfully Misrepresenting Eligibility

Calendar year	Cases reviewed	Cases indicating willful misrepresentation			Percent of cases indicating willful misrepresentation
		Ineligible	Overpaid	Total	
1973–74*	1,952	73	72	145	7.4
1975	1,426	90	53	143	10.0
1976	800	45	40	85	10.0
1977	1,634	113	79	192	11.8
1978	1,672	124	102	226	13.5
Total	7,484	445	346	791	

*Includes only last 3 months of 1973.

As the table shows, the problem of willful misrepresentation cases has persisted for years and has become progressively worse. For the period from October 1973 through December 1974, 7.4 percent of the cases reviewed indicated cases. In calendar year 1978, the value of Medicaid and food stamp benefits to recipients possibly ineligible because of potential willful misrepresentation could turn out to be as much as $2.5 million.

CHAPTER 6

Applying the Principles, Policies, and Practices of Program Auditing

After you have read this chapter, studied the review questions, and worked through the cases, you will understand:

- The basic principles of P-auditing, including the need for independence by the auditor.
- How the standards for evaluating program effectiveness are related to the objectives of the program.
- How to follow any P-audit through its respective phases, including the development of a tentative audit objective and a firm audit objective.
- How to develop an audit program for the detailed examination for a P-audit.

In accounting and auditing literature, such terms as program auditing, program budgeting, program evaluation, PPBS, and program analysis are all rather new. The term *program analysis* will be used in this chapter to encompass all of the above terms. We will, however, focus on P-auditing, using the other terms to define this field more clearly.

Only within the last two decades have the terms within the field of program analysis become common enough for many auditors to become familiar with them. Some auditors and accountants seldom hear the terms; others seldom have occasion to use them in their day-to-day practice, but many have begun to use them regularly even though each person may have a particular meaning for each term.

Accountants and auditors in educational, managerial, and public accounting organizations have applied many of the principles involved in program analysis without realizing that the terms they use often have the same meaning as those applied in the field of accounting commonly called *management control*. Accountants involved with management control often do not see that objectives they deal with are comparable to the objectives that program analysts deal with. The objectives of accountants and auditors are related to profits, standard costs, or a return on investment. Program analysts, on the other hand, deal with social objectives, personnel objectives, or other management objectives. Both, however, are related to what the organization or program would like as an end result.

Outside of the field of management control for profit activities in large commercial and industrial organizations, these new terms in the field of program analysis have arisen in large part in government. Because the trend of major expenditures in government within the last two decades has been towards social programs as distinguished from those in the past, which have been predominantly military and administrative programs, the need has arisen for a means to evaluate such social programs.

Since the various government entities provide about 40 percent of the gross national product, there appears little question that all types of auditors will eventually become involved in program analysis of one kind or another. Either it will be the measurement of profit or return-on-investment objectives in business; or, in government, it will be the measurement of social or other management objectives. One of the standards for governmental auditing is that P-audits be a part of the audit of any governmental organization.

Sufficient literature is available on accounting for program analysis for profit-objective entities. This chapter, therefore, will deal principally with P-audits for entities whose objectives are other than for profit.

In government, P-auditing has a counterpart in the field of military procurement. The design and procurement of military weaponry in early United States history was handled through the military bureaucracy by the use of arsenals. The expansion of military procurement came about because of various U.S. military engagements. The military began to use industrial facilities, which followed arsenal specifications, to obtain much of its basic hardware. Military procurement, therefore, became a process of obtaining the specifically designed goods through a system of military-industrial complexes.

When the military went to industry to obtain their requirements, they could measure the value of the items obtained through a normal accounting practice—through revenue-cost-profit relationships. Assuming the goods met the specifications, any audit analysis would then measure whether the goods were produced efficiently and economically, or whether the profit on the goods was too high.

As time went on, industry, instead of producing only, began to take over more and more of the entire weapons-systems program, from design to the completed product. At this point, industry had to be measured on the effectiveness of the product, as well as how efficiently or economically the goods were produced. To a certain extent, then, this process was the forerunner of effectiveness analysis—or what we have termed in this book P-auditing.

Social programs, likewise, had their start in government within the bureaucracy. In the past, the old folks' home was usually run by the county; now, with help from federal, state, and local governments, privately owned nursing homes have taken the place of these county institutions. Welfare programs, poverty programs, educational programs, and health programs are all administered by both private and governmental organizations, often using federal or state funds.

P-auditing is concerned with the evaluation of, and the reporting on, an entity's effective use of its resources in accomplishing its intended results. These intended results are usually called objectives, or goals. In accomplishing its objectives or goals, a program entity—in contrast to the bureaucracy's well-defined organizational structure—may be unduly scattered and not well defined, often carried out, in fact, by various other types of organizations.

As distinguished from program evaluation, P-auditing must be carried out by an independent auditor; furthermore, the auditor will report the results of the audit to a third party. Program evaluators may be a part of the management of the program; this responsibility could not be accepted by a program auditor. The distinction between the responsibilities of management and the responsibilities of the auditor have been made clear in the work of the financial-statement auditor, but it has not been as well stated in the field of program analysis.

In contrast to program budgeting, P-auditing must focus on the independence of the auditor. The person involved in program budgeting, while also determining the goals of the program, is a part of the management of the program, and thus focuses on only one element of an audit objective—the criteria. The program auditor, however, must focus on all three elements of the objective—criteria, causes, and effects—in order to determine whether the results intended have been effectively accomplished. The results being accomplished or not accomplished could not have been caused without appropriate resources being applied. Nor could recommendations for improvements be made without considering the causes of the program's effectiveness or ineffectiveness.

Many managers of programs do not have a stated goal with appropriate standards that can be used as criteria for measuring the results intended. Thus, the auditor must often go through the process, as he often must in M-auditing, of determining the most appropriate goal or objective for the entity in order to have measurable audit criteria.

The criteria he develops, however, must be one that is acceptable to management, since he is not a part of management. As was stated earlier, the auditor must have a criteria that cannot be rebutted before he can report on the conclusion.

The illustrative audit in this chapter serves to bring out the ideas suggested above; and again, the reader should be able to transfer much of the information to audits of a similar type he may encounter in other organizations.

Let us approach the practical applications of the principles of P-auditing to a real-life audit situation somewhat as we did in the chapters on M-auditing. We will start first with the principles and a discussion of those principles, and then go to the actual audit situation—"The Indian Education Case."

Basic Principles of P-auditing

In a P-audit, the auditor places primary emphasis on programs where opportunities for improvement exist. While the auditor may analyze a program to show that it is effectively carrying out the objectives of the program, he most often will analyze it to show that it is ineffective in carrying out the objectives. Thus, he will place most of his emphasis on ineffective programs rather than effective programs in order to provide recommendations for improvement in operations.

The indication of significant ineffectiveness in the operation of a program is only one aspect of that program. In order to provide recommendations for improvement, the auditor must identify the causes of the ineffectiveness; and since the program may be carried out by diversely scattered organizations, the causes may be much more difficult to find than those in a deficiency finding. For example, in our illustrative audit, Indian education may be scattered from Alaska to Florida. Education could be carried out by public schools, contract schools, private schools, or schools developed by the Bureau of Indian Affairs (BIA). As a reminder and review, let us list and describe some of the basic principles found in a P-audit.

The principles of P-auditing have been condensed into three:

1. The definition of auditing,
2. Evidence and audit objectives, and
3. The phases of a program audit.

Definition of P-auditing

The basic principle of P-auditing is that of the definition:

A P-audit is the planning for, the obtaining of, and the evaluating of sufficient relevant, material, and competent evidence by an independent auditor on the objective of whether an entity's management, employees, or delegated agents have or have not accepted and carried out appropriate standards for effectively achieving the results desired by the program's higher level authority. From this evidence, the auditor comes to a conclusion on the audit objective. He then reports his conclusion to a third party along with sufficient evidence to convince the third party that his conclusion is correct.

This definition brings out three general attributes of a P-audit that do not necessarily apply to other types of program analysis:

1. The auditor must be independent,
2. The auditor must have standards to measure from, based on a statement of the end results or objectives of the program, and
3. The auditor must report to a third party.

Independence of the Auditor. As we discussed in Chapter 1, each auditor must be independent of the entity he audits. This problem has been fairly well resolved in the financial-statement and management-auditing areas. In the P-auditing area, however, it is in a rather delicate state. Many program evaluators are a part of the management of the entity being evaluated. Until the clear indication of independence has been resolved in the program analysis field so that the third party can rely on the results of the audit, these results will not be accepted as thoroughly reliable.

Management needs program evaluators to help them determine the goals of the organization and the best standards for accomplishing these goals, yet they also need to be audited by auditors who are independent of the management standards and goals. This does not mean that the auditor cannot develop and use criteria for measuring the effectiveness of the program; it does mean that the criteria he uses should be those of management and acceptable to management, and not acceptable only to the auditor.

Standards for Achieving a Valid Program Objective. Before an auditor can measure the effectiveness of the program, he must first determine a valid objective. The following GAO report offers excellent guidelines:

> The objectives of the policy or program—the benefits desired to be achieved—frequently are not stated clearly and precisely. The original sponsors of the policy or program may not have had a precise idea of the end results desired. Formal statements of objectives may be intentionally ambiguous if it is easier to obtain a consensus on action. Value judgments underlying the objectives may not be shared by important groups. Consequently, the end results intended may be perceived by some as implying ill effects for them. Furthermore, explicit statements of objectives tend to imply a specific assignment of priorities and commitment of resources.
>
> To the extent feasible, statements of objectives should:
>
> 1. Capture a complete understanding of the intended benefits, including the expected level of attainment.
> 2. Identify recipients of unavoidable adverse consequences or unintended benefits.
> 3. Include important qualitative aspects, even though measuring degrees of attainment may be exceedingly difficult.
> 4. Take account of multiple objectives that may be complementary or conflicting.

The importance of taking such a comprehensive view of objectives cannot be overstated. Oversimplified statements (1) will not capture all essential aspects of the effects intended and (2) may contain implied conflicting consequences for groups other than the intended beneficiaries ... Implied objectives may represent desirable end results. For example, a summer employment program aimed primarily at increasing earnings of young people may be viewed as reducing civil disorders. Moreover, even desired end results may not all be achievable simultaneously and may be interdependent.

Oversimplified statements may result if activity milestones are contained in them ... An objective stated in this way may overly constrain an assessment of alternatives, the purpose of which is to determine efficient levels of attainment of an ultimate benefit. On the other hand, it is important that the statement be specific with respect to the nature and direction of change so that progress can be measured. A statement such as "to reduce deaths, additional complications, disability, and suffering of persons with acute injuries by improving emergency care" would satisfy these criteria. Quantitative goals or targets are also needed, but these must reflect priorities among programs. Accordingly, they can best be set as part of the budget and long-range financial planning process and should be reexamined regularly as budget priorities shift.

In appraising results of ongoing programs, if targets or activity milestones have been furnished to managers, the targets or milestones should not be accepted uncritically ... An attempt should be made to find whether deficiencies in attaining the milestones are caused by unrealistic expectations or by the way the program was implemented or operated.

A shift in objectives can occur over time and care must be taken to assure that statements of objectives currently in use are still valid. For example, the objective associated with the national 55 miles per hour speed limit now includes safety, as well as energy conservation.

Determining valid objectives is a complex and frustrating task. A study may have to proceed without fully satisfying these requirements. If this is the case, objectives should be reexamined and clarified as the study progresses.[1]

Third Party Reporting. Figure 1.1 in Chapter 1, showing the three related functions pertaining to auditing—the audit function, the accountability function, and the reporting function—illustrates graphically the auditor's responsibility for attesting to a third party the results of the audit of the second party. The third party is usually most interested in the accountability relations of the second party to the third party, and the audit function can provide an independent review of those relationships.

This third-party reporting, attesting to the accountability of the second party to the first party, emphasizes the importance of the independence of the auditor. Without it, the reliability of the attest function would often be questioned.

Evidence and Audit Objectives

The second basic principle pertains to evidence and the audit objective, which we have defined as follows:

Audit evidence is the facts and information used to come to a conclusion on the audit objective. The audit objective for a P-audit is a statement or question proposing the answer to an audit inquiry as to the effectiveness of the outputs of the program fulfilling the program's desired results. The audit objective is always composed of three essential elements. A discussion of each follows.

1. *The criteria.* The standards, which if carried out, would result in the effective accomplishment of the results desired by the higher level authority that authorized the program. The results desired of the program are often called the objectives of the program. The criteria used for measuring whether the objective has been effectively accomplished are those standards which should have been used for originally carrying out the activities of the program. For example, the end results desired of the Animal and Plant Health Inspection Service of the Department of Agriculture are the protection of consumers from foodborne illnesses caused by harmful bacteria, such as illnesses caused by salmonella-contaminated meat and poultry products. The criteria for measuring the effectiveness of the program would be whether the salmonella-contaminated meat and poultry products reached the market. If they did, whether consumers had been adequately alerted to the problem and the safeguards they must take to minimize the spread of the bacteria during food handling.[2]

It is obvious that there are no generally accepted standards for all program audits. Seldom is an audit repeated. Thus, the criteria must be determined for each particular audit. Developing standards that can be used as criteria is often difficult. The following is an excellent statement by the GAO concerning the development of standards that can be used as the criteria for measuring the effectiveness of a program:

> Valid measures of policy and program consequences are required for both appraising results and assessing alternatives. Objectives and measures of consequences are interdependent. The quality of each depends on the other. Measures should be used which cover all aspects of a given objective. Ideally, measures should
>
> - quantify the extent to which the objective(s) are or would be met—"effectiveness" measures;
> - capture qualitative aspects of the consequences—"intangible" measures;
> - quantify, to the extent possible, unintended consequences—"side-effect" measures;
> - quantify, to the extent possible, the differences of impact on the beneficiaries and the cost bearers—"distribution" measures.
>
> When appraising results, it may be decided for practical reasons to exclude side-effect and distribution measures. However, they should not be excluded if reasonable effort would produce useful data or if the decisionmaker is especially interested in these measures. For intangible measures, some qualitative indication of relative magnitude should be used (e.g., ratings by clients reflecting their satisfaction with the quality of a service).
>
> Data may not be available on the desired measures or, if available, may be obtainable only at high cost. In these cases, surrogates will have to be used. For example, the scholastic aptitude test is used to measure likely achievement in college. When surrogates are used, their validity should be established.
>
> There is a temptation to define quantifiable measures, especially of effectiveness, too rigidly or narrowly. For example, in evaluating a

public employment program, a successful participant might be specified as a person who is employed 1 year after completion of training. If the participant worked 1 day less than a year, would that person be viewed unsuccessful? Suppose the participant only occasionally held a job, but happened to be working a year after the program. Should this be counted as a success? The range and distribution of outcomes should be considered in this case. For example, data on the percentage of persons holding jobs for various lengths of time after training would provide a more meaningful picture of real outcomes. This sort of distribution is needed to judge levels of attainment or degrees of success or failure.

These four fundamental concepts are closely interrelated. A clear understanding of what is needed for the decisionmaking process, of the nature of the problem, and statements of objectives is necessary in order to assure that a meaningful and feasible set of measures has been specified.[3]

2. *The causes.* The actions of management, employees, or their delegated agents who are being audited who either did or did not accept or carry out the proper standards for effectively accomplishing the desired results. Using the criteria shown above from the GAO case on salmonella contamination, actions of the management, employees, and their delegated agents of the Food and Drug Administration and the Animal and Plant Health Inspection Service of the Department of Agriculture, who had the responsibility for protecting the consumers, would be the primary causes. Additional causes would arise from actions of packing plant management and employees, shippers, and processors of the contaminated meat and poultry products.

The element, causes, of the P-audit objective often has many levels of actions. For a P-audit, these often do not fall within the normal bureaucratic organization. For example, states and cities often carry out federal programs. Students or patients are often the recipients of money from federal programs.

3. *The effects.* The amount measurement, or results of the actual actions of management, its employees, or their delegated agents when compared with the criteria for measuring the effectiveness of the program. In many cases, the effects can be stated in dollar values. For example, in the above contaminated meat illustration, the effects were 2 million cases of salmonellosis at an estimated cost of $300 million in medical expenses and lost working days. However, in many other cases, the effects may be such as the lack of parental involvement, loss of lives of patients, lack of information, inadequate snow removal, or other similar effects when related to the desired results, many of which cannot be measured from a dollar and cents standpoint.

Sufficient relevant, material, and competent evidence must be gathered and analyzed on the audit objective in order to come to a conclusion on that objective.

Because many governmental programs are rather new, acceptable objectives and standards for accomplishing them often have not been well thought out, or tested in practice sufficiently long enough to determine whether they are appropriate and acceptable as criteria for measurements. Therefore, to obtain evidence on the criteria for a P-audit demands newer approaches than found in either financial-statement examinations or M-audits. The auditor, or

104 / *Getting Started*

consultants who are specialists in the fields of mathematical modeling, experimental designs, statistical inference, time series, or verbal scenarios, can often provide evidence on the criteria for many program audits.

Yet, in the older programs, such as suggested in the illustrations of Indian education or the contaminated meat and poultry products, sufficient experience has been obtained on these standards for accomplishment to be used as the criteria for the examination.

In addition, since the program may be carried out in many locations, rather than only one, more sophisticated techniques for gathering evidence on causes and effects may be necessary. Techniques of sampling, questionnaire design, correlation, and interviewing are usually employed in these types of audits. The computer is often used for canned programs for linear programming and computer-based models. The accountant is an expert in cost analysis. Yet, often he must relate costs to benefits or to effectiveness. Converting such items as lives, environmental improvement, or educational improvement to dollar values may be a new area of knowledge he needs to grasp.

The Phases of a P-audit

Each P-audit has four identifiable phases. The first two phases, however, are often combined into one, as we have learned.

1. *The preliminary survey.* The auditor gathers background and general information on the program, its organizations, its activities, and its objectives. He identifies one particular program objective, or appropriate level of the objective, on which there may be problems of effectively accomplishing the objective and states a tentative objective. He also identifies possible alternatives for accomplishing the objective. He then prepares a program for the review and testing of management control within the area of the program or level of program he selects.
2. *The review and testing of management control.* The auditor gathers relevant and material evidence on all three elements of the audit objective by reviewing the management control of the program to determine whether the criteria are acceptable, whether someone caused the effects, and whether the effects are significant in order to have a firm audit objective. During this review and testing of management control, the auditor can also gather evidence on the objective of whether the information from internal management controls is competent and reliable. He then prepares a program for the detailed examination.
3. *The detailed examination.* The auditor gathers sufficient relevant, material, and competent evidence on the audit objective of whether the program participants, including the entity responsible for the program, have carried out the program in such a manner that the results expected to be achieved by the program are achieved; or if not, why not. He then summarizes and analyzes the evidence and comes to a conclusion on the objective.
4. *Report development.* The auditor, based upon his detailed examination, prepares a report and communicates his conclusion to a third party along with sufficient evidence to support the conclusion.

Because of the dimensions of many P-audits, some organizations require the auditors to prepare an analysis of what they expect to find upon the conclusion of the review and testing of management control phases. This analysis helps the organization to determine whether the additional costs of making the audit will result in comparable benefits. An illustration of this type of analysis is shown as Appendix V.

Upon completing all of the field work for the P-audit, the conclusion of whether the program's objectives have been effectively accomplished must be communicated to a third party. There is no standard report for this type of audit as the conclusion must be directly related to the particular program. As a general rule, after an introduction to the background of the program, the auditor will state the conclusion first. He will then follow with the condition that caused the ineffectiveness, and then state the effects and the criteria. The pattern will be the same as that discussed in Chapter 16; and similarly, evidence must be shown in the report in order to convince the reader that the criteria the auditor used are acceptable, the causes and the condition of the causes are as stated, and the effects are significant.

Principles of P-auditing Applied: "The Indian Education Case"

The P-audit we have selected for an illustration—"The Indian Education Case"—is a GAO audit. Much of the preliminary phases work has been summarized and presented in order to lay the background for the actual working papers, which will be presented for the detailed examination. As is often true, the two preliminary phases—the preliminary survey and the review and testing of management control—have been combined into one.

Background Information

In November 1969, a Senate subcommittee concluded a two-year investigation and issued a report called *Indian Education: A National Tragedy—A National Challenge*.[4] The subcommittee outlined a number of serious inadequacies in the education programs of the Bureau of Indian Affairs (BIA). They concluded that "The present organization and administration of the BIA school system could hardly be worse."

The subcommittee recommended that the federal government commit itself to providing Indians with an excellent education, including maximum Indian participation in, and control of, Indian education programs. The subcommittee also recommended that the federal government set specific goals for rapid attainment of equal educational opportunity for Indian children, which included the goal of an achievement level for Indian high school students equal to that of the national norms.

The BIA, however, had already established certain educational goals. In 1963 their goal was to close the educational gap between Indians and non-Indians by 1970. Except for the target date, these goals, outlined in the Program Memorandums for fiscal years 1971 and 1972, have continued into the 1970s as follows: (1) 90% of all Indian youth graduate from high school, (2) by 1976 the achievement level of Indian students at least equal that for non-Indian youth, (3) 50 percent of the graduates enter college, and (4) the remaining 50 percent be either employed or enrolled in technical training.

These BIA goals appear to be consistent with the educational goals of the Indians themselves as a report of a private firm in 1969 showed. An Indian school board member, during an April education conference in 1969 at the Fort Apache Reservation in Arizona, said:

> Our ultimate goal should be to educate our children so that their qualifications for any open position will be on an equal par with, if not better than, the non-Indians. This is the goal we should strive for.

The executive branch of the government had also recommended to the Congress that they improve the fate of the Indians by passing legislation to improve their education.

During the course of the review of management controls, the auditors found that the BIA had done very little in letting the Indian schools know about their stated goals. A school in Arizona, for instance, said it had never heard of the goals and thus had not set any plans for accomplishing them.

Indian school administrators stated that they had set some goals, but these were essentially aimed to make sure Indian students were capable of holding jobs when they got out of high school. They also stated that they had no means for measuring whether they accomplished their goals, for they kept no records of students after graduation.

They further stated that their budget was so limited that they had very little chance of doing much more than they presently were doing. They could not afford to add such "frills" as counselors or tutors in subjects such as mathematics and English, which seemed to be major weaknesses of their students. Counseling was usually handled by teachers who accepted this assignment as one of their regular assigments.

As for testing, they had only limited means for academic achievement testing, or for other types of testing such as IQ and scholastic aptitude. They seldom used such tests for placement, guidance, curriculum development, or comparison with other schools.

When auditors discussed with school officials their problems about teachers who missed classes because of illnesses or other causes, officials said they had substitute teachers but not enough on call to take care of all their emergencies.

Program for the Detailed Examination

From the background information and the review and testing of management controls, the auditor should have been able to come up with an audit objective somewhat as follows:

> Are the Bureau of Indian Affairs and the schools that come under its jurisdiction in the process (causes) of accomplishing (effects) their objective of having the achievement level of Indian students at least equal to that for non-Indian youth by 1976 (criteria)?

As we know, there are many levels of causes in a P-audit. In this audit, these can be broken down into the audit areas of (1) officials in the BIA having a good management system for accomplishing the objectives, (2) officials testing for achievement or IQ, (3) officials providing remedial subjects, such as reading, (4) officials providing for special education, (5) officials providing adequate substitute teaching, and (6) officials providing for and properly using the results of counseling.

Since the criteria of the objective is acceptable, appropriate, and measurable, the above causes will be the basis for most of the detailed examination work. Approaching the audit this way will enable the auditor to see whether (1) the officials responsible have properly communicated the objective; and when they have, have the lower levels of management within the BIA accepted the objective, (2) have all levels of officials the capability to measure the results of whether the objectives have been accomplished, and (3) have all levels of officials provided the means for accomplishing the objective.

An audit program, asking questions pertaining to the above causes, would be somewhat as follows:

    A. *Management System*
        1. Are school administrators aware of BIA central office goals as set forth in 1971–72 Program Memorandums?

2. Is the school's education program designed to accomplish these goals by 1976, including the establishment of objectives, identifying all restraints, periodic milestones, and periodic evaluations?
3. Do school officials agree that if the BIA goals are to be accomplished there should be a well-organized and well-managed program specifically designed to meet them?
4. If school officials were not aware of BIA goals, to what do they attribute their lack of information?
5. Have the BIA goals been disseminated to the schools in the form of an objective or policy statement?
6. Has the school received any guidelines or instructions concerning the implementation of procedures directed toward the accomplishment of BIA goals?
7. Do school officials consider the BIA goals realistic?
8. If the answer to previous question is "no," explain why.
9. What are the educational objectives of the school as indicated by school administrators? Are they in writing?
10. What criteria have been established for measuring progress relative to accomplishment of
    a) central office objectives?
    b) school objectives?
11. Is the BIA central office aware of the school's objectives?
12. Who formulates the school's budget request?
    a) Are the teaching or counseling staffs consulted?
    b) Do the teaching or counseling staffs believe they could contribute anything worthwhile if consulted?
13. Is the school's budget based on
    a) Needs in terms of central office objectives per 1971–72 Program Memorandums?
    b) Basically prior or present programs?
    c) Other (describe)?
14. Is the school's budget request for the following items based on the needs of the total student population?
    a) Mathematics?
    b) Counselors?
    c) Substitute teachers?
15. Is the school's budget request for compensating communications program and special-education programs based on the need of the total student population?

B. *Testing*
1. What instructions have Indian schools received that set forth the program of academic achievement testing and IQ testing?
2. Do school officials believe that a testing program can provide useful information?
3. Does the school use academic achievement and IQ test results for placement, identification of student needs, curriculum development, evaluating program results, and identification of weakness in the quality of education being provided?
4. Are the following tests administered?
    a) Academic achievement tests to all new entering students.
    b) Academic achievement tests to all students annually, at about the same time each year.

c) IQ tests (organized programs, not isolated tests here and there).
d) The same or comparable academic achievement tests given from year to year.
5. Describe the school's present testing program and the programs conducted during the recent years, if any.
   a) IQ test.
   b) Academic achievement tests (all grades similar, unless otherwise indicated)
      (1) CAT—California Achievement Test.
      (2) MAT—Metropolitan Achievement Test.
      (3) SAT—Standard Achievement Test.
      (4) CRT—California Reading Test subpart of CAT.
C. *Remedial Reading, and Other Compensating Communications Programs*
   1. Do school officials believe that one of the students' primary restraints to academic achievement at national norms is their inability to communicate (read, write, speak) effectively in the English language?
   2. Does the school provide compensatory programs to overcome these restraints? Regular BIA educational program funding, or other?
   3. If the school does not provide for such programs currently, are there plans for such in the future? When? Regular BIA education program funding, or other?
   4. Are the current and planned compensatory communication programs adequate in terms of meeting the total population needs?
D. *Special Education*
   1. Do school officials believe there is a need for special education for students at their schools (students with physical, sensory, mental, or emotional problems)?
   2. Does the school provide, or plan to provide, a special education program? How funded (regular budget, Title I, or other)?
   3. Do school officials believe the programs are or will be adequate to meet the total student population needs?
E. *Substitute Teaching Services*
   1. Do school officials believe substitute teaching services should be provided (to take over classes when regular teachers are not available)?
   2. Are such services provided?
      a) If so how?
      b) Is the number on call sufficient?
   3. If the substitute teacher services are not adequate or provided, what provisions are made in the event a teacher is absent?
F. *Counseling*
   1. Are school officials in agreement with American Personnel Guidance Association (APGA)—that is, counselors should generally be involved in test administration, compilation, and interpretation of results; careers and post-high-school education guidance; identification of students' needs; curriculum development; placement of students in classes; and so on?
   2. Is counseling provided?
   3. Is organized developmental guidance provided to all students on a periodic basis?

Applying Principles and Practices of Program Auditing / **109**

4. Are counselors involved in student placement or curriculum development?
5. Do counselors give standardized IQ and academic achievement tests and use the data to identify students and curriculum needs?
6. Do counselors maintain records that adequately reflect results of counseling sessions and information concerning students' needs and progress?

REVIEW QUESTIONS

1. Many accountants have applied the principles of program auditing and program budgeting to the field of management control without being aware of it. In your own mind, distinguish between P-auditing in general, and the field of management control in terms of the nature of their respective audit objectives. (See p. 97.)

2. New terms in the field of program analysis have arisen largely in government. To get a feel for the general concept of a program, review the definition of a program. (See pp. 7–8.)

3. P-auditing is concerned with evaluating and reporting on an entity's effective use of its resources in accomplishing the intended results of the entity. Contrast effectiveness evaluation as applied to program budgeting with effectiveness evaluation as applied to program auditing in terms of focus on the elements of an audit objective. (See pp. 98–99.)

4. The audit objective for a P-audit contains the same three basic elements as do the objectives for other types of audits. See if you can define the criteria of a P-audit objective and explain why it must be determined for each audit. (See pp. 102–3.)

5. The element, causes, of the program audit objective often has many levels of actions, some of which do not fall within the normal bureaucratic organization. See if you can explain what is meant by this statement, and explain what the auditor must do to evaluate the different levels of action. (See p. 103.)

6. Once the audit objective has been determined, criteria for measuring the effectiveness of management's efforts in carrying out the program objective should be established. What characteristics do you believe an ideal measure possesses? (See p. 102.)

7. It is necessary for the auditor to have a working knowledge of the program under audit, its objectives, and its organization before too many resources are applied to the audit. One method of doing this and being sure that a meaningful result will come from the audit is to prepare a proposed report after the preliminary survey and the reviewing and testing of management control have been accomplished. Can you explain and illustrate how this can be done? (See p. 104 and Appendix V.)

8. All evidence used to reach a conclusion on an audit objective must be relevant, material, and competent. What do you think are some of the

problems, peculiar to P-auditing that the auditor has in assessing the competency of evidence. (See pp. 103–4.)

9. Identify some of the weaknesses found in the review of management control in the illustrative case on Indian Education. (See p. 106.)

10. A P-audit usually has many levels of causes. Can you identify some of the possible causes in this case? (See p. 106.)

11. Review the suggested program steps related to the element causes in the audit objective of the illustrative case, shown on pp. 106–9. Does the information and evidence obtained in the preliminary phases indicate that there is a need for these steps to obtain evidence on these particular causes? Would you add additional steps to obtain other evidence or take away some of the steps?

12. Has sufficient evidence been obtained on the criteria of the audit objective in the illustrative case to be able to use it as a basis for measuring the action of management against it in order to determine whether the program is effective? (See pp. 106, 108.)

CASE 1

The Valley City Jails[5]

AUDIT SCENARIO 1
The Preliminary Survey

Required

1. Assume you are the auditor in charge of the audit of the local jails program. Develop an audit program for the preliminary survey for that audit.
2. From the information developed in your preliminary survey, determine whether you have a possible audit objective. If so, state it.
3. If you state a possible audit objective, develop an audit program for the review and testing of management control for the local jails program.

Preliminary Information

Valley City was a fairly large city in the state. Its form of government was that of a mayor and city council, with each council member overseeing a particular functional area of city operations. The council member who had the responsibility for public safety decided that she should discuss with the mayor the anxiety she had found among several citizens concerning the local jails. Citizens believed that all of the inmates were going to be released from the jails and turned loose on society. The city had five local jails tied in to the five precincts of the police department.

The mayor suggested to the member that if the problem seemed serious enough, it should be discussed at the next council meeting; he arranged for the topic to be placed on the agenda. At the meeting, other council members stated that they also had discussed the topic with their constituency, who seemed to have the same concern. At the meeting, it came out that some localities were being required to turn the inmates loose because of the conditions of the local jails. Further discussion brought out that all members of the council, including the mayor, were in favor of having an audit made to determine whether the local jails were effectively accomplishing the purpose for which they were established.

The council authorized the mayor to contract with a local firm of certified public accountants for this audit. The local firm was familiar with the operations of Valley City because they made the financial statement examinations each year, and as well had made several special studies for the city. They were asked to come up with their results as soon as possible.

The auditors, under the leadership of firm member Robert Davis, decided to find out about the conditions of local jails nationwide before they started to gather information on the specific conditions of the local jails in Valley City. The following is a summary of the information they found:

> The need for jails will not be completely eliminated even if all communities avail themselves of such alternatives as pretrial release, halfway houses, probation, and parole, since there will always be some individuals who either are not willing to accept the constraints in community-based programs or would present too great a risk to public safety if placed in such a program.
>
> The "1970 National Jail Census"[*] stated that, of the 3,319 local jails which served counties or were located in municipalities of 25,000 or more, 86 percent provided no exercise or recreation facilities and almost 90 percent had no educational facilities. A followup survey[†] to the "National Jail Census" indicated that rehabilitative programs were very limited. For example, about 80 percent of the jails provided no inmate counseling, remedial education, vocational training, or job placement. A report by the National Advisory Commission on Criminal Justice Standards and Goals[‡] also commented on the poor physical conditions of jails and their lack of adequate services to those incarcerated.
>
> Many jails need replacing as illustrated in the following comments from selected recently issued comprehensive State plans:

[*] "1970 National Jail Census," Law Enforcement Assistance Administration, Department of Justice, February 1971, p. 1.

[†] "Survey of Inmates of Local Jails 1972: Advance Report," Law Enforcement Assistance Administration.

[‡] "Corrections," National Advisory Commission on Criminal Justice Standards and Goals, 1973, Law Enforcement Assistance Administration, pp. b41-b59.

- Many local jails are old, deteriorating, and unsafe and are located in areas too small in population and too short in resources to provide adequate correctional services.
- Inspection of facilities indicated a state of general deterioration compounded by other shortcomings, such as lack of fire extinguishers, lack of fire exits, and lack of operative fixtures—toilets, lavatories, lighting, beds, mattresses, heating, windows, painted walls, and showers. A survey of basic services provided to the offender—meals, exercise, and special custody—revealed an alarming absence of these services as well as a lack of ability to segregate offenders by age, sex, type of offense, or other special custody needs.
- For the most part, the local facilities are generally dirty, in need of paint and repair, poorly heated and ventilated, and sometimes fail to provide adequate security. As a whole, the county jails can best be described as "warehouses of human flesh" in which little or no rehabilitation efforts are made except for maintenance work.
- Many county jails and lockups are substandard. These facilities present health and safety hazards for both prisoners and staff, and many do not provide secure custody due to structural or equipment problems. In most county jails, work release is the only treatment program available.
- The majority of [the state's] jails are in such an advanced state of disrepair that the introduction of effective rehabilitation programs is impossible.

The money needed to provide adequate facilities and services to the jail population is probably much greater than local and State governments are willing to provide, especially when the taxpayers must authorize such expenditures. LEAA [Law Enforcement Assistance Administration] funding represents a limited source for the amount needed for the entire criminal justice system. In addition, for a grantee to be eligible for LEAA block grant funds, the federal grant must be matched by state and/or local funds. Therefore, the use of LEAA funds for any particular aspect of criminal justice is affected by the extent to which the state and local governments desire to or are capable of addressing the problem.

Criminal justice authorities, including the 1967 President's Commission on Law Enforcement and Administration of Justice, the National Advisory Commission on Criminal Justice Standards and Goals, and the National Clearinghouse on Criminal Justice Planning and Architecture, believe that many persons incarcerated in local jails are not a danger to society and should not be in jail. According to the National Advisory Commission, offenders are perceived as stereotyped prisoners regardless of the seriousness of the offense. Authorities stress the need to develop a broad range of alternatives to incarceration of the nonviolent offender.

Along these lines, LEAA and States are directing their effort to community-based corrections—alternative measures emphasizing community participation to reduce involvement of offenders with the institutional aspect of corrections. Although this solution may reduce the jail's population, it does not solve the problem of how to provide an adequate facility to those considered ineligible for release.

State-operated local jails

In 1973 the National Advisory Commission on Criminal Justice Standards and Goals reported that the most striking inadequacy of jails is their "abominable" physical condition. Recognizing that few local communities can be expected to have sufficient resources to resolve the problem and provide appropriate services, the Commission recommended that states take over the operation and control of local institutions by 1982.

As of late 1972, only five States operated and controlled all of their correctional facilities: Alaska, Connecticut, Delaware, Rhode Island, and Vermont. Each has only a few facilities. For example, Rhode Island has one location where it incarcerates all offenders, from pretrial to those with life sentences. Delaware has jails in three different communities, and Connecticut has 11 correctional facilities.

Regional-operated jails

The regional jail concept has been suggested as a solution to the local jail problem for some time. The 1967 President's Commission on Law Enforcement and Administration of Justice and the 1973 National Advisory Commission of Criminal Justices Standards and Goals referred to this concept under which one jail would serve multicounty or city-county needs. With the consolidation of the jail population from several counties, the size of the operation could justify a better physical plant and some rehabilitation services.

Barriers that are difficult to overcome confront efforts to regionalize jails. With emphasis on community-based corrections, criminal justice authorities believe the offender should be kept in the community into which he will be reintegrated. With a centralized facility serving multiple communities, keeping the individuals involved in their home communities would be difficult.

A second barrier acknowledged by criminal justice experts and referred to continually by law enforcement personnel contacted is a transportation problem. Under a regional system, the offenders would be subject to constant movement, particularly in the pretrial stage. The transporting of inmates would require security guards. Some of the local sheriffs indicated that they were operating with an inadequate staff; thus, because of the security required to transport offenders, a regional jail would further stretch their limited resources and would reduce the time available for actual enforcement activities.

One variation of the regional jail concept that appears to have more promise is the combination city-county jail. If a city and contiguous county determine that the offender population is large enough to justify combining the correctional facilities of only the two jurisdictions, the above-mentioned barriers do not appear to be major problems. LEAA might study the feasibility of encouraging appropriate cities and counties to consolidate their operations.

Mr. Davis requested the city attorney to prepare an analysis for him of the legal standards for maintenance and services required to be provided prisoners in local jails; Mr. Davis and his audit team received the following:

Among basic requirements, courts have included: (a) the essential elements of personal hygiene (e.g., soap, towel, toothpaste, toothbrush, and toilet paper); (b) clothing and blankets; (c) access to sinks (including hot water) and showers; (d) clean laundry (or use of laundry facilities) provided on a reasonable basis; (e) essential furnishing (elevated bed, mattress, a place to sit, and sanitary toilet facilities); (f) adequate drinking water and diet, prepared by persons screened for communicable disease in kitchens meeting reasonable health standards; (g) shelter; (h) adequate (but not excessive) heat; (i) exposure only to reasonable noise levels; and (j) light and ventilation. To the extent isolation or segregation cells may still be used at all, for punitive or administrative reasons (including a prisoner's own protection), such detention facilities should be so designed as to allow custodial (preferably, medical or psychiatric) supervision. Prisoners may not be housed in unsanitary or permanently overcrowded cells, or under conditions which may be reasonably anticipated will endanger personal safety or sanity. See, e.g., these Arkansas cases: *Finney* v. *Ark. Bd. of Corr.*, 505 F.2d 194 (8th Cir. 1974) (*Finney*), aff'g in part, rev'g in part *Holt* v. *Hutto*, 363 F. Supp. 194 (E.D. Ark. 1973) (*Holt III*), modifying *Holt* v. *Sarver*, 422 F.2d 304 (8th Cir. 1971) (*Holt II*), aff'g 309 F. Supp. 363 (E.D. Ark. 1970), (*Holt II*), 300 F. Supp. 825 (E.D. Ark. 1969), (*Holt I*).

While local jails may be exempt from compliance with local health and housing codes, prison conditions are unlikely to meet minimum community standards of decency if they totally fail to comply with essential health, safety, and housing (particularly space, ventilation, plumbing, heating, electricity, or sanitation) regulations. *Cf., Gates* v. *Collier*, 501 F.2d 1291 (5th Cir. 1974), adopting and aff'g 349 F. Supp. 881 (N.D. Miss. 1972). Similarly, courts have ordered that prison kitchen standards be made to conform with state board of public health restaurant standards. *Little* v. *Cherry*, 3 Pris. L. Rep. 70 (E.D. Ark. Jan. 31, 1974).

While the nature of appropriate medical treatment falls within the sound discretion of medical personnel, prisoners may not be deprived of competent medical and dental care. *Gates* v. *Collier*, supra; *Nerman* v. *Alabama*, 349 F. Supp. 278 (M.D. Ala. 1972). Adequate supportive facilities should be available—not necessarily within the prison—to meet reasonably foreseeable medical and dental needs, including pharmaceutical and medically prescribed dietary requirements. *Finney*, supra, 202–204; *Steward* v. *Henderson*, 364 F. Supp. 283 (N.D. Ga. 1973).

Medical care must include treatment of drug-dependent prisoners, or medically supervised drug detoxification. *Wayne County Inmates* v. *Wayne Co. Bd. of Commr.*, 1 Pris. L. Rep. 5, 51, 186 (Mich. Cir. Ct. 1971, 1972), substantive issue not disputed on appeal, sub nom., *Wayne County Jail Inmates* v. *Lucas*, 216 N.W. 2d 910 (Mich. 1974). Differences in services afforded, based on anticipated length of imprisonment, have been permitted, provided at least that classification of services afforded prisoners is rational, is based on differences in sources of available funding, and does not deny basic medical needs. *Kersh* v. *Bounds*, 501 F.2d 585 (4th Cir. 1974), cert. denied, _____ U.S. _____, 43 U.S.L.W. 3452 (U.S. Feb. 14, 1975).

Reasonable access to the courts may not be denied or obstructed. *Johnson* v. *Avery*, 393 U.S. 483 (1969). Facilities must be adequate to permit confidential attorney-client visits. A basic collection of representative legal materials (including case law and search materials) should be available, at least on a loan basis. *Gilmore* v. *Lynch*, 319 F. Supp. 105 (N.D. Calif. 1970), aff'd under the name of *Younger* v. *Gilmore*, 404 U.S. 15 (1971). Library size and number of required copies of basic materials necessarily depend on the size and character of the institution. If materials may not be removed to the cells, size and furnishings should be adequate to afford prisoners a reasonable opportunity for research and study. *Cf. White* v. *Sullivan*, 368 F. Supp. 292 (S.D. Ala. 1973); *Stone* v. *Boone*, 3 Pris. L. Rep. 285 (D. Mass., Oct. 10, 1974) (consent degree).

Prisoners must be permitted to follow the tenets of their religion, including the right to conform to dress and dietary requirements, insofar as their religious beliefs can be reasonably accommodated. *Ross* v. *Blackledge*, 477 F. 2d 616 (4th Cir. 1973). Chapel or similar facilities and religious materials must be adequate to accommodate the needs of minority faiths, if available to others. *Pitts* v. *Knowles*, 339 F. Suppl. 1183 (W.D. Wis. 1972), aff'd 478 F.2d 1405. Religious privacy must be protected with services being held in places where prisoners not choosing to attend are not made unwilling participants. *Cf. Edwards* v. *Davis*, 3 Pris. L. Rep. 54 (D.N.C. Dec. 11, 1973) (consent degree).

Prisoners are not entitled to benefits not generally recognized as rights enjoyed by the community at large. *James* v. *Wallace*, 382 F. Supp. 1177 (M.D. Ala. 1974). Adult education is not provided as a matter of right, and except as otherwise required by local law, rehabilitative services including educational or job training programs need not be provided for adult prisoners. But cf. *Holt III*, supra, 378–379; *Finney*, supra, 209.

Moreover, where local jails are used to house persons detained under civil commitment or pretrial detainees unable to raise bail, facilities must be designed and equipped to meet additional requirements. The detainee is presumed not guilty of criminal misconduct; he may not be punished without or before trial. He may be held only under conditions comprising *the least restrictive means* of achieving the purpose requiring and justifying his detention. *Hamilton* vs. *Love*, 328 F. Supp. 1182, 1192 (E.D. Ark. 1971). Note, "Constitutional Limitations on Pretrial Detention," 79 Yale L. J. 941, 949–950 (1970). Detention may not be more punitive than incarceration within the state's penal system; it should not be substantially more burdensome than detention in other State or Federal institutions used for the same purpose, in the same area. *Rhem* v. *Malcom*, 507 F.2d 333, 336–337 (2d Cir. 1974) (*Rhem III*), aff'g in part, rev'g in part 337 F. Supp. 995 (*Rhem II*), 371 F. Supp. 594 (*Rhem I*) (S.D.N.Y. 1974); *Inmates of Suffolk County Jail* v. *Eisenstadt*, 360 F. Supp. 676 (D. Mass. 1973), aff'd 494 F. 2d 1196 (1st Cir. 1974), cert. denied 419 U.S. 977 (*Eisenstadt*).

Detainees committed under civil commitment for psychiatric evaluation or treatment should be committed to facilities designed to provide suitable professional treatment and evaluation. Cf. *O'Connor* v. *Donaldson*, _____ U.S. _____ 43 U.S.L.W. 4929 (U.S. June 26, 1975) vacating *Donaldson* v. *O'Connor*, 493 F.2d 507 (5th Cir., 1974); see the latter, and cases cited therein, 518–527.

Whether or not the courts will eventually require classification of detainees, they have recognized that maximum security conditions cannot be justified as "the least restrictive means" of assuring that the great majority of pretrial detainees will appear at trial. In individual cases, courts have held that detainees were entitled: (1) to have privacy (including, in one case, the right to be locked in, as well as out of, the cell), *Rhem I, supra*, 628; in others, to single-cell occupancy, *Eisenstadt*, 360 F. Supp. 676; (2) to associate with other detainees (to assemble, *e.g.* for religious services, *United States ex rel. Jones* v. *Rundle*, 453 F.2d 147 (1971)); (3) to enjoy access to a broad range of reading and writing materials, (*Inmates* v. *Peterson*, 353 F. Supp. 1157, 1168–1169 (E. D. Wisc. 1973) (*Peterson*)); (4) to engage in recreational activities and to use recreational facilities, (*Rhem I, supra*, 594,); and (5) to have outside communication by telephone (*Brenneman* v. *Madigan*, 343 F. Supp. 128, 141), letter (*Peterson, supra*, 1167–1168), and personal contact, including visits by children (*Brenneman, supra*) and, in one case, conjugal rights arranged in a discreet and circumspect manner (*Government* v. *Gereau*, 3 Pris. L. Rep. 20, D.V.I. May 30, 1973).

Courts have ordered the reduction of jail population, the closing of nonconforming jails, or substantial alteration of existing facilities, including: (1) removal of cells to provide recreational areas, (2) dismantling of prisoner-visitor telephone systems and walls separating prisoners from their visitors, and (3) the installation of outside telephones. E.g., see *Rhem II, supra*. Generally, detainees have a right to participate in training or educational programs offered other prisoners.

Wilson v. *Beame*, 380 F. Supp. 1232 (E.D.N.Y. 1974). And one recent case has held that a pretrial detainee participating in a State-approved, medically supervised (methadone) drug treatment program prior to arrest is entitled to continue the prescribed course of treatment, and could not be subjected to forced (withdrawal) detoxification even though medically supervised. *Cuknik* v. *Kreiger*, 3 Pris. L. Rep. 221 (E.D. Ohio, July 16, 1974).

After obtaining the general information from nationwide sources concerning local jails, Mr. Davis and his auditors then contacted the council member in charge of public safety to obtain information she could provide concerning the local jails. Through her, from the files of the Commissioner of Public Safety, the auditors obtained the following information, including the data in the table.

The local ordinances provided that the local jails be under the supervision of the Captain in charge of the local precinct. There were five precincts and five local jails. The Commissioner of Public Safety, the Council Member, only had general supervision of the activities of the local jails. Her primary objective was to help the captain in the adoption of budgets, communicate any extraordinary needs to the council as a whole, and in general represent the problems of public safety.

The ordinance also said that the jails were to be used for committing persons who are awaiting trial, who have been sentenced to less than one year, and who are to be held longer than 48 hours. Under 48 hours, the person can be held in temporary lockups. Over one year, state law requires that the inmate be held in a state penitentiary.

The city attorney had recently ruled that "committing" meant more than just a place to stay. According to him, recent court cases implied that while housed physically in a jail, the inmate is entitled to other requirements than just a roof over his head. Some of these other requirements include such things as both sanitary, secure, and private physical facilities, as well as social, recreational, and educational services.

AUDIT SCENARIO 2

The Review and Testing of Management Control

Required

1. Develop a firm audit objective with criteria that are acceptable and measurable, with causes that can be pinpointed in order to make recommendations, and with effects that are significant. Consider such factors in the criteria as the ability to measure the effects, as well as the acceptance of the

Valley City, Data on City Jails, 1976

Characteristics	Jail by precinct number				
	1	2	3	4	5
General					
Year built	1974	1931	1910	1893	1938
Current capacity	31	39	36	45	19
Number of employees	4	5	5	5	3
Annual budget	$65,500	$60,000	$55,500	$62,500	$32,500
			Percentages		
Type of stay					
Awaiting trial	68.2	60.0	85.6	64.9	95.5
Serving sentence	31.8	17.5	8.5	31.4	4.5
Other	–	22.5	5.9	3.7	–
Type of offense					
Alcohol related	25.0	10.0	35.9	45.5	40.0
Traffic related	20.5	–	2.0	14.2	20.0
Subtotal	45.5	10.0	37.9	59.7	60.0
Other felonies and misdemeanors	54.5	70.0	51.0	40.3	38.0
Other		20.0	11.1	–	2.0
Length of stay					
Less than a day	47.7	32.5	26.8	42.5	37.8
1–2 days	34.1	30.0	34.0	21.7	46.7
3–6 days	6.8	25.0	22.9	26.1	4.4
Subtotal	88.6	87.5	83.7	90.3	88.9
7–30 days	11.4	10.0	15.7	5.2	4.4
31–90 days	–	2.5	0.6	3.7	4.4
Over 91 days	–	–	–	0.8	7.3
Average length of stay (in days)	3.0	4.0	4.0	4.5	7.0
Sex					
Male	93.2	85.0	91.5	93.3	84.4
Female	6.8	15.0	8.5	6.7	15.6
Age					
Under 18	6.8	17.5	17.0	1.5	6.7
18 through 29 years	70.5	20.0	54.9	56.0	37.8
30 years and over	11.4	30.0	25.5	42.5	53.5
Unknown	11.3	32.5	2.6	–	2.2
Residence					
Within city	77.3	90.0	75.8	51.1	40.0
Neighboring	4.5	5.0	1.3	14.3	22.2
Other	18.2	5.0	22.9	34.9	37.8

criteria by the mayor and city council. Consider the causes at the various levels, not only within the jail operations, but also outside of them. Likewise, consider whether you would plan to measure the effects from a cost-benefit relationship or would you merely determine whether the jail operations are effective or ineffective?

2. Develop an audit program for the detailed examination.

The auditors now had sufficient information from the preliminary survey to come up with an audit objective somewhat as follows:

Has Valley City, through its various police precincts, administered (causes) in an effective manner its local jail program for committing persons who are awaiting trial, who have been sentenced to less than one year, or who are being held for more than 48 hours (effects) by providing adequate physical facilities and adequate rehabilitation services (criteria)?

Obviously, the terms "adequate physical facilities" and "adequate rehabilitation services" would have to be defined before the auditors could use them as a basis for measuring the effectiveness of the programs, and therefore they would have to obtain sufficient evidence to convince themselves that the criteria are adequate for measuring the results of the program.

Additional Background Data

In order to obtain a desirable standard for measuring the program's goals, the auditors inquired of the safety commissioner whether she had standards for evaluation of the conditions of the local jails. She replied that she had none and knew of no other standards that were generally accepted nationally. She did say, however, that several associations or groups had issued advisory standards or had discussed characteristics for local jails. After obtaining this material, the auditors decided that there were two major classifications of standards: physical conditions, and inmate assistance. Under physical conditions, they found that there were four classifications: inmate security and safety, sanitary conditions, inmate comfort and rehabilitation, and privacy.

Under the category of inmate security and safety, they determined that they must assess whether the jails had populations not exceeding capacity; single-occupancy cells only; adequate segregation of offenders by sex, age, and degree of violence; operable emergency exits and fire extinguishers; operable cell doors; matrons present for female offenders; and no drunk tanks.

To assess the sanitary conditions, the auditors considered whether cells had operable toilets and wash basins and whether showers were clean and worked. They also considered the availability of such personal items as soap and toothpaste, and the cleanliness of such things as blankets, sheets, and towels. To assess inmate comfort and rehabilitation, they considered whether dining facilities were separate from the cell blocks, and whether such things as recreation facilities, ventilation, and lighting were adequate. Regarding privacy, the auditors felt they must assess such things as whether visiting space was separate from the cells, and whether there was a private area where the prisoners were searched when first imprisoned.

For inmate assistance, the auditors decided to use the National Advisory Commission's standards: local correctional facilities should provide activities oriented to the inmates' individual needs, personal problem solving, socialization, and skill development. The commission recommended that these activities include:

- Education programs available to all residents in cooperation with the local school district,
- Vocational programs provided by an appropriate state agency,
- A job-placement program operated by state employment agencies and local groups representing employers and local unions, and
- Counseling.

Testing Management Control

The auditors decided that they must follow through on one individual from arrest to trial, to sentencing, and then to incarceration, in order to see the actual conditions of the operations of the management control system. The person selected happened to be a young woman arrested on a drug charge and held in the 5th precinct jail. In this small jail, there were no separate facilities for males and females, no matron on duty during the arrest, and the cells were of the multiple-occupancy type. Neither sheets nor pillow cases were issued, and the blankets issued were not cleaned before reissuance. Likewise, prisoners had no privacy for search on entry, no space for private conversations, and visitors were brought to the cell to visit since they had no private visitors area. The woman was held in these conditions for 48 hours before the judge released her on bail.

Mr. Davis and his team decided that they would not wait for this case to go to trial and possible sentencing, since the conditions in the jail would not change.

CASE 2

The Mass-transit Grant[6]

AUDIT SCENARIO 1
The Preliminary Survey

Required

1. Determine whether or not you have been provided sufficient information to come up with a firm audit objective for this program.
2. If so, state the audit objective for the program, including a firm criteria, who caused the results, and the possible results.
3. If you believe you do not have sufficient information for a firm objective, state the procedures you would follow to obtain sufficient evidence to come up with one.

During the past 20 years, grant programs have become increasingly important for federal, state and local government financing. One of those programs is mass-transit grants.

Mass transit has long suffered from insufficient capital needed to maintain and increase the effectiveness of the industry. The Congress recognized this as a national problem in passing the Urban Mass Transportation Act of 1964 (49 U.S.C. 1601) and subsequent amendments to increase the funding authority and scope of federal assistance. In 1968, the Urban Mass Transportation Administration (UMTA), Department of Transportation, was given the responsibility of providing federal assistance for developing efficient and coordinated mass-transportation systems in urban areas.

Several programs were established to carry out the purpose of the act, the largest being capital-facilities grants to state and local public bodies, which could be used to acquire and/or improve existing transit systems or to build new transit systems. Since July 1, 1973, federal financial assistance has been set at a mandatory 80 percent level of net project costs—those costs that could not be reasonably financed from revenues. Prior assistance was limited to two-thirds of the net project costs.

Capital assistance for transit systems was approved in the amount of $4.3 billion through June 30, 1975. As the table below shows, rail projects made up over 60 percent of this amount.

UMTA also sponsors a research, development, and demonstration program directed toward providing knowledge about alternative technologies that can be used to improve mass-transportation service. Through June 30, 1975, UMTA obligated $362.5 million in this program. Major projects in the areas of bus and rail technology, new systems, and automation were undertaken.

The development and purchase of rail equipment is inherently more capital intensive than similar efforts for other existing mass-transit modes, such as bus systems. UMTA's funding commitments to rail-transit systems reflect this characteristic and are aimed at enabling the nation's larger cities to provide better mass-transit systems through capital outlays for constructing, extending, maintaining, or rehabilitating rail-transit systems. In 1975, these systems operated in 12 cities in the United States, and together carried over one fourth of the

Number of Federal Grants and Amount of Grants, by Category, 1968–75

Category	Number of grants	Amount of grants (000,000 omitted)
Bus	492	$1,473
Rail	92	2,680
Other	7	157
Total	591	$4,310

nation's mass-transit passengers. In addition, many cities were constructing or planning new or expanded rail services.

Capital grants totaling $2.7 billion were awarded to rapid-transit systems and commuter railroads through June 30, 1975, to assist in purchasing 2,360 rapid-transit cars, 275 light rail cars, and 1,364 commuter railroad cars; modernizing rail station in 5 cities; constructing completely new systems in 2 cities; and constructing maintenance and garage facilities.

In the research and development (R&D) activity, UMTA sponsors rail transit R&D in four areas: rapid rail, commuter rail, light rail, and rail supporting technology. UMTA's efforts in R&D through June 30, 1975, totaled about $41 million for rapid transit, $20 million for commuter and light rail, and $36 million for supporting technology.

Approximately $745 million, or 28 percent of the $2.7 billion in federal capital assistance for rail transit, has been granted to the Metropolitan Transportation Authority (MTA), an independent authority created by the state of New York to develop and improve public transportation in the 12-county New York metropolitan commuter district. Transportation facilities under MTA's jurisdiction include rapid transit, commuter railroads, buses, vehicular bridges, tunnels, airports, parking, and other facilities.

MTA's rapid-transit systems include the New York City Transit Authority (NYCTA), the world's largest rapid-transit system, and the Staten Island rapid-transit line. MTA's commuter railroad systems include the wholly owned Long Island Railroad, the nation's largest commuter railroad; 3 lines leased from Penn Central Railroad Company; the New Haven, and the Harlem and Hudson commuter service lines; and a segment of the Erie-Lackawanna Railway. As of June 30, 1975, MTA had a combined fleet of 8,475 rail cars, including 6,734 rapid-transit and 1,741 commuter rail cars. Another 854 rail cars were on order—100 commuter rail cars and 754 rapid-transit cars.

UMTA assisted in purchasing 1,778 cars either in service or on order; of these, 745 R-46 rapid-transit cars and 633 M-1 and M-2 commuter rail cars had modern high-performance features such as automatic train control (ATC); 400 did not. (ATC is the designation applied to a broad range of equipment used for such functions as collision protection, overspeed prevention, station stopping, and schedule design.)

NYCTA, which has received most of the federal rail-transit assistance to MTA, has both a rapid-transit division and a surface-bus division, and lies entirely within the limits of New York City. As of June 30, 1975, NYCTA has been granted $573 million for the rapid-transit division, which has 714 miles of track, 462 stations, and 7,000 passenger cars. Since March 1, 1968, NYCTA has had, by state statute, the same governing board as the MTA.

AUDIT SCENARIO 2

Additional Data on Management Control

Required

1. State an acceptable audit objective as it would apply to the NYCTA to determine the effectiveness of the mass-transit grant program.
2. Outline the procedures you must use to obtain sufficient evidence to thoroughly convince the reader of your report as to whether the mass-transit grants program is being conducted effectively in grants made to NYCTA.

The additional data on management control in this scenario concern a grant of $140 million committed for new rail cars in New York City before similar cars had been proved in service.

In 1970, NYCTA purchased 352 rapid transit cars, referred to as R-44 cars, with city and state funds. These cars represented a new concept in car design for NYCTA.

In 1971, before the R-44 cars were delivered, NYCTA discussed with UMTA the possibility of getting federal assistance to purchase 745 modified R-44 cars, referred to as R-46 cars. NYCTA wanted the R-46 cars, which were substantially the same as the R-44 cars, to replace 1,000 35- to 40-year-old cars. It has been NYCTA's policy for approximately 25 years to replace cars after they have reached 35 years of age.

In April 1972, when the first of the R-44 cars were placed in service, NYCTA submitted a formal application for $142 million of UMTA assistance to purchase the R-46 cars. In June 1972, UMTA approved a $63 million grant to assist in purchasing 320 of these cars. UMTA approved the grant without obtaining and evaluating performance data on the R-44 cars, which subsequently proved to be a problem: The cars broke down more often than less complex cars and were subject to undefinable problems; they were out of service more frequently than the older cars that the R-46 cars were scheduled to replace.

Although the R-44 performance data for the most part were not known before UMTA approved the original R-46 grant in June 1972, there were indications that should have alerted UMTA to the R-44 problems and potential R-46 problems. For example, before UMTA approved the grant, public hearings were held by NYCTA, to get the public's view on the need for, and desirability of, the new cars. Charges were made at these hearings that the facts presented in the NYCTA grant application to UMTA relative to the performance of the R-44 cars, were untrue; and questions were raised about the reliability and safety of the R-44 cars, such as the structural adequacy of the cars during general use and the safety implications of locked end doors, which limit the passage of passengers and train crews between cars.

A UMTA representative told auditors that since the people commenting at public hearings were not experts, their comments had no substance and therefore did not require any action by NYCTA or UMTA. The auditors noted, however, that one of the individuals was an electrical engineer. In addition, records show that NYCTA knew about certain R-44 structural defects from early tests made of the first R-44 cars before delivery in April 1972.

CHAPTER 7

Understanding Management Control

After you have read this chapter, studied the review questions, and worked through the cases, you will understand:

- The meaning and scope of management control.
- Selected standards for management control.
- How to review management control, including how to develop questionnaires and flow charts, and how to test transactions.

Introduction to Management Control

Internal control as related to a financial-statement examination, and management control as related to a performance audit, have similar characteristics but somewhat different purposes. Accountants who make financial-statement examinations understand that internal control relates to the competency of evidence needed for such examinations. In Chapter 2, which dealt with the phases of the audit function, we stated that there were two purposes for the review and testing of management control: One was to test the management control to develop evidence to determine if the tentative objective could be developed into a firm audit objective; and the other was to determine the competency of evidence obtained from the system of internal management control.

This second purpose relates strongly to review of internal control for a financial-statement examination. The auditor determines the competency of information obtained from the system of internal accounting control to determine whether he can rely on it for guidance as to the extent of the tests he must make in the detailed examination.

The auditor who is new in performance auditing must clearly understand the purposes of management control and just how these differ from his experience in making financial-statement audits. Management control in performance auditing, he will find, encompasses both internal and external control. Let us start, then, by defining internal control and management control.

Meanings of Internal Control and of Management Control

Concerning the meaning of internal control for financial-statement examinations, the American Institute of Certified Public Accountants (AICPA) states:

Internal control, in the broad sense includes ... controls which may be characterized as either accounting or administrative as follows:

.27 *Administrative control* includes, but is not limited to, the plan of organization and the procedures and records that are concerned with the decision processes leading to management's authorization of transactions.... Such authorization is a management function directly associated with the responsibility of achieving the objectives of the organization and is the starting point for establishing accounting control of transactions.

.28 *Accounting control* comprises the plan of organization and the procedures and records that are concerned with the safeguarding of assets and the reliability of financial records and consequently are designed to provide reasonable assurance that:
   a. Transactions are executed in accordance with management's general or specific authorization.
   b. Transactions are recorded as necessary (1) to permit preparation of financial statements in conformity with generally accepted accounting principles or any other criteria applicable to such statements and (2) to maintain accountability for assets.
   c. Access to assets is permitted only in accordance with management's authorization.
   d. The recorded accountability for assets is compared with the existing assets at reasonable intervals and appropriate action is taken with respect to any differences.[1]

Based upon this description of internal control, the AICPA discusses the characteristics of a good internal accounting control system, as follows:

1. Reasonable assurance that the objectives of accounting control are achieved depends on the competence and integrity of personnel, the independence of their assigned functions, and their understanding of the prescribed procedures.
2. Functions are adequately segregated. Incompatible functions for accounting control purposes are those that place any person in a position both to perpetrate and to conceal errors or irregularities in the normal course of his duties.
3. Obtaining reasonable assurance that transactions are executed as authorized requires independent evidence that authorizations are issued by persons acting within the scope of their authority and that transactions conform with the terms of the authorization.
4. In respect to the recording of transactions, they should be recorded at the amounts and in the accounting periods in which they were executed and be classified in appropriate accounts.
5. Access to assets should be limited to authorized personnel.
6. Actual assets should be compared with recorded accountability.[2]

Standards for internal accounting control are thus readily available, even though sometimes they are not accepted and used as a basis for verification by comparison with actual operations. For management control, however, a field that embraces all activities inside and outside of the organization that pertain to the operation of the organization and its internal administrative control, standards are not as readily available. Many have never been developed; or if developed, they apply to the specific organization only. These standards would include strategic plans, operating plans, organization plans, personnel requirements, resource requirements, and all other planning and operating needs of the organization. When these management and administrative controls have not been developed or are not appropriate to the activities of the organization, there is a possibility of inefficient, uneconomical, or ineffective operations.

In addition, many transactions have a direct bearing on the operations of an organization that do not take place exclusively within the organization. The law, for example, determines what a corporation can do, and society often regulates that corporation by comparison with the law: regulatory agencies determine for the organization such environmental considerations as equal employment opportunity, air pollution, and water pollution. Market conditions, borrowing conditions, and technological considerations are all activities outside an organization that can affect its internal operations. The parent corporation, also, may impose outside restraints on divisions; profit controls and pricing controls are examples.

Today in our country we see that more and more activities are being controlled by external standards. Almost all government social programs are carried out by organizations other than the ones originally given the responsibility. Health programs, for instance, are carried out by local organizations, including hospitals; research programs are carried out by universities or local research groups; energy programs are carried out by many individuals and organizations. Almost all military procurement, moreover, is accomplished through defense contractors; even space vehicles have been obtained through independent contractors.

In the field of private enterprise as well, large corporations are now using independent contractors for making many of the products they use or sell. Independent contractors, for example, make engines for automobiles, refrigerators for other corporations to sell, and railroad trains to carry specific types of passengers or freight.

Some verification for each of these activities must take place if management is to be assured that its employees comply with given standards. To assure compliance with both the external as well as the internal standards, management, then, will always have some sort of a management control system—good or bad.

We see, thus, that as we stated at the beginning of this chapter, management control will encompass not only internal but external control. Restricted to internal activities, however, management control and internal administrative control mean exactly the same thing.

Now let us define management control as we are using it in performance auditing and list some of the characteristics of good management control:

> Management control is the plan of organization and all other plans, policies, procedures, and practices needed by personnel and other resources to achieve the objectives of the entity.

The objectives of the entity should include not only the stated results expected from the production of goods or the rendering of services, but also a statement of the responsibility of management for the safeguarding of the resources and the accountability for the results.

A good system of management control would include the following:

1. A statement of the objectives of the entity,
2. A plan of organization for accomplishing the objectives,
3. Personnel of a quality and quantity commensurate with their responsibilities, with adequately segregated functions,
4. An established system of appropriate policies and practices for each department or entity, and
5. An effective system of review at all levels of activity to assure the carrying out of the established system of appropriate policies and practices.

Distinctions and Similarities Between Internal Control and Management Control

There are many similarities between management control and internal control, and yet there are important distinctions—principally in three areas:

1. increased emphasis on the need for a statement of objectives for the entity and the tie-in of management control to that statement of objectives,
2. increased emphasis on external control as compared to internal control, and
3. the expansion of control to include all activities of management, such as production, transportation, and research, rather than emphasis only on accounting activities.

Objectives of the Entity

Seldom can an organization be effective unless it knows what it is supposed to do. Efficient and economical practices are rather meaningless unless the practices produce a meaningful product or service. A saying rather common a few years ago was that the most efficient producer of buggy whips in the world went out of business because the end result was that there was no demand for buggy whips.

Yet, many governmental and private organizations still operate on the principle of *how* something is done rather than *what* is to be done or *why*. It has only been within this century that the legislative bodies of most governmental units have tried to tell the executive branch what they want and leave it to the executive branch to determine how to do it. In many private corporations too, the chief executive may have known what was wanted, but seldom did anyone under him know. Their responsibility was to carry out what they were told to do. Most government agency and private organization officials were administrators rather than managers, administering laws, regulations, policies, and procedures. Their responsibility did not include the development of what should be done and why it should be done.

Today, however, most well-managed organizations, both public and private, profit and nonprofit, understand the need for communicating the basic objectives of the organization to all levels of operations. We are using the term objectives here to mean the long-range, fairly broad statements of what the organization desires to achieve. Goals, strategies, and results desired are terms used for a shorter range, more specific desired achievement. Both concerns need to be well stated in order to develop operating plans and procedures that will achieve them in the best manner possible. An organization is effective when it achieves its objectives. It is economical and efficient when its methods of achieving its goals and objectives accomplish the results in the best manner possible under the circumstances.

M-audits for efficient and economical practices are often made without any reference to the objectives of the organization, particularly when the audit is for determining the compliance with a law, regulation, policy, or stated procedure by the employees or management. Yet, when the management of a firm is audited to determine whether the methods and activities they carry out are related to the objective of the entity, an M-audit becomes genuinely helpful as a way to improve the management rather than merely to improve the administration of a particular standard.

Plan of Organization

After considering the objectives of an entity, the next step an auditor should take in evaluating management control is to see that the entity is properly organized to carry out its objectives. He should see that responsibilities are properly divided, that each executive has been given authority commensurate with his responsibilities, and that no one person has control of all phases of an operation. He should also see that each person is accountable to some third party for his actions and that each accountable person's actions are reviewed to determine that his assignments are properly carried out. A properly designed organization chart will give some of this information.

Organization Charts — Figure 7.1 represents a typical organization chart for an industrial company—although an auditor would need more information than is here presented, such as a statement of the responsibilities for major executives, for instance.

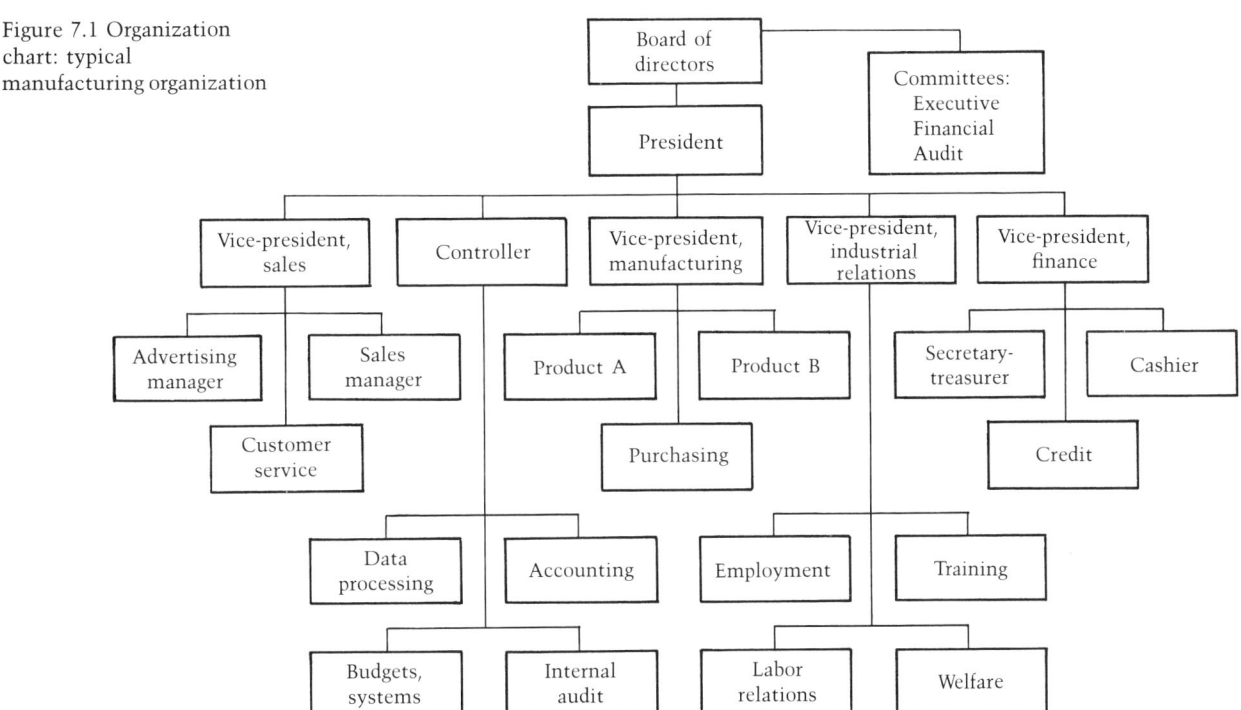

Figure 7.1 Organization chart: typical manufacturing organization

Organization charts vary somewhat in accordance with the objectives and responsibilities of the organizations. Another typical organization chart is that for the state agency responsible for state cars, discussed as Case 1 in Chapter 3, and illustrated here in Figure 7.2 The auditor in this case would also have to consider the organization charts for any agency he audits on the activity of buying gasoline for state cars. For example, he might audit a state university for this activity; he would have to know which departments granted other departments in the university the right to use state-owned automobiles for state travel, whether the automobiles were leased or bought, whether the department instructed the drivers of the vehicles where they should buy gasoline, and other information needed by the driver of the car.

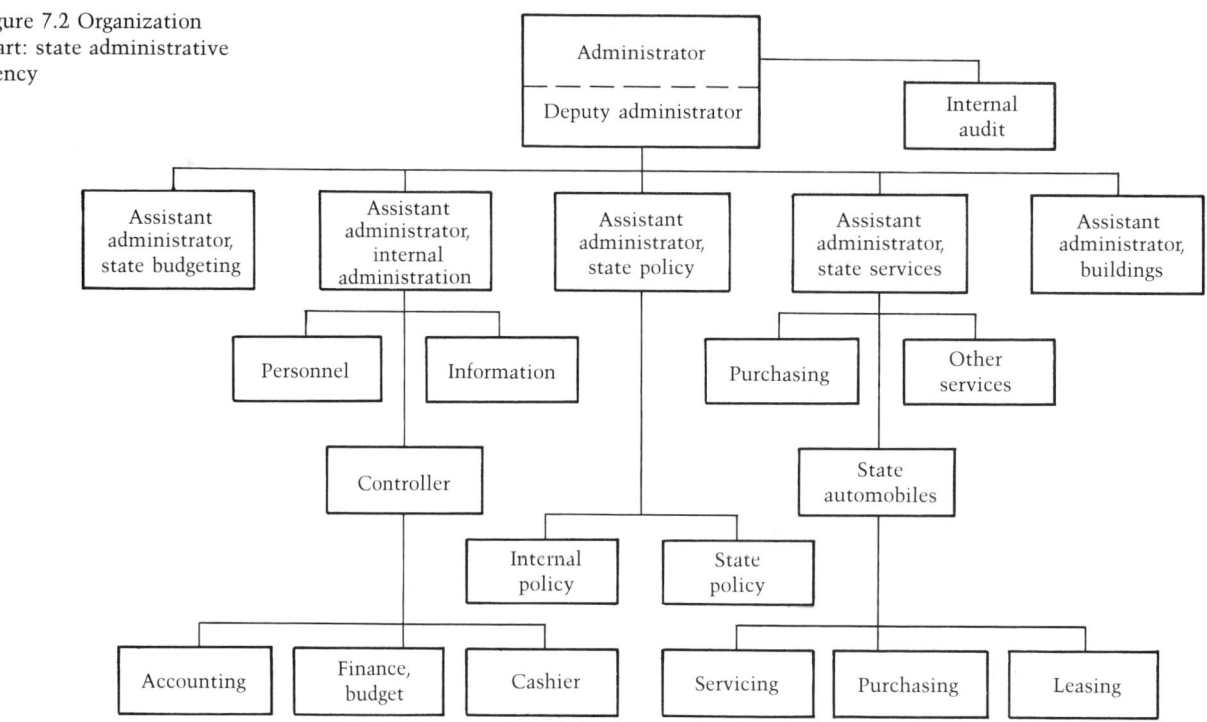

Figure 7.2 Organization chart: state administrative agency

From this example, the auditor can begin to see the complexities of external management control in an M-audit—the audit for efficiency and economy. The most complex organizations, however, are those that deal with programs. Figure 7.3 shows just how complex an organization chart can become when it reflects the interrelationships of a program among organizations.

Flow Charts

A plan of organization as reflected in an organization chart does not show the flow of transactions between organizations. The visualization of this flow is best seen in a flow chart, and standard symbols have been developed to show this flow in an electronic data-processing system. However, since the flow of many transactions in a performance audit is for manual transactions as well as for electronic transactions and may take the auditor outside of the organization in which he normally works, he may want to adapt the standard flow-chart symbols to meet his need. If he does change the symbols, he must identify them clearly so that anyone reading the flow chart can understand it.

Figure 7.4 shows the most common standard symbols used in flow-charting an electronic data-processing system; symbols used for flow-charting a particular activity are given in Figure 7.5, which illustrates material in Case 1 of this chapter.

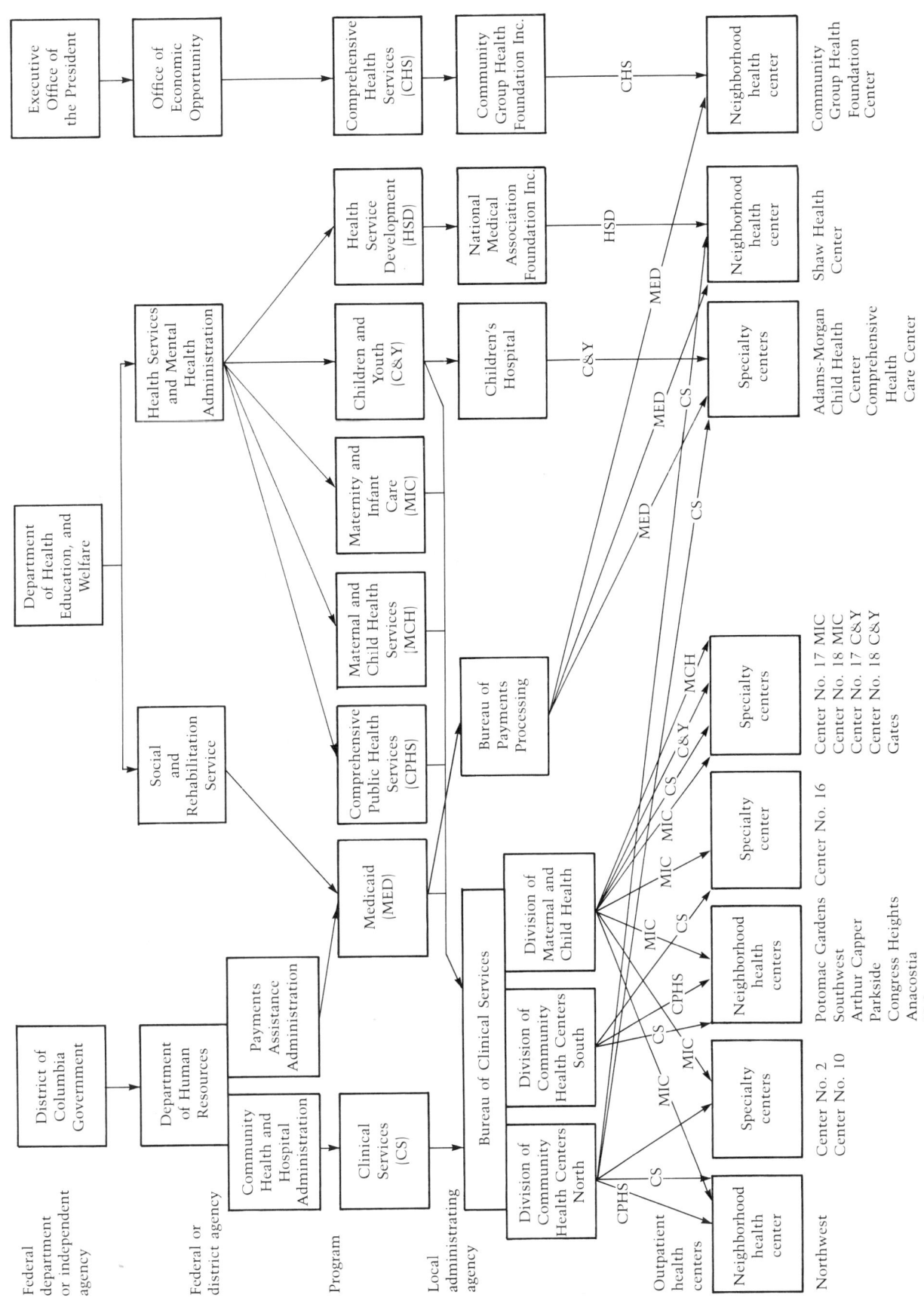

Figure 7.3 Programs funding health services in outpatient health centers in the District of Columbia, fiscal year 1972

127

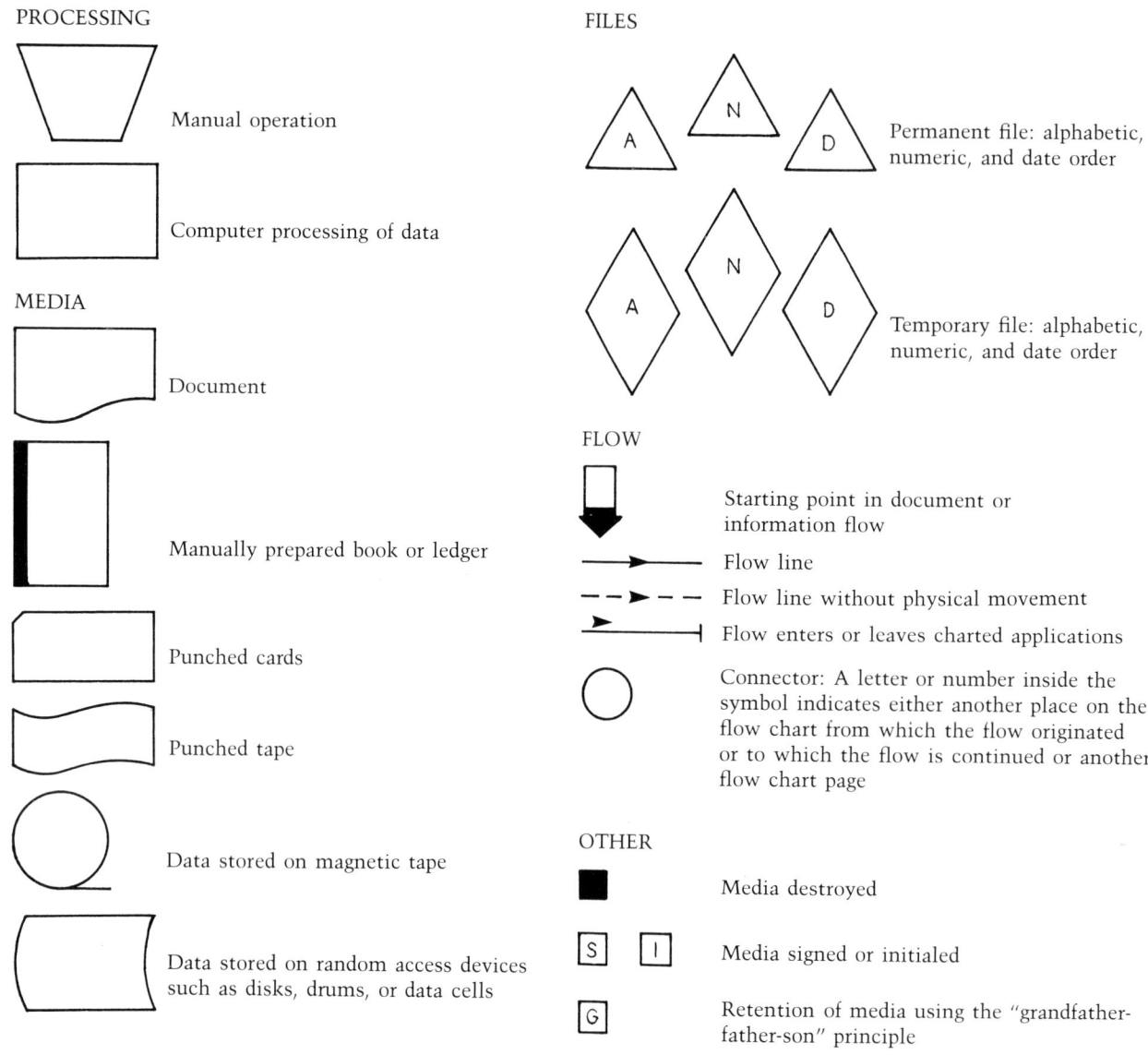

Figure 7.4 Commonly used flow-charting symbols

The auditor normally will make a rough draft of the flow of transactions when he is interviewing selected officials and employees or observing actions of these individuals during the preliminary survey and review phases of the audit. It may be noticed, too, that in flow-charting a performance audit transaction, more descriptive information is often placed in the chart as in figures 7.5 and 7.6.

Personnel and Their Functions

No organization can expect to operate satisfactorily unless duties and responsibilities are adequately separated, and persons are provided in the organization who are capable of carrying them out.

In looking over the requirements for a good management control system pertaining to personnel, the auditor would ask the following kinds of questions:

1. Have the requirements of the job been adequately stated?
2. Are personnel recruited who are qualified to fill the responsibilities of the job?

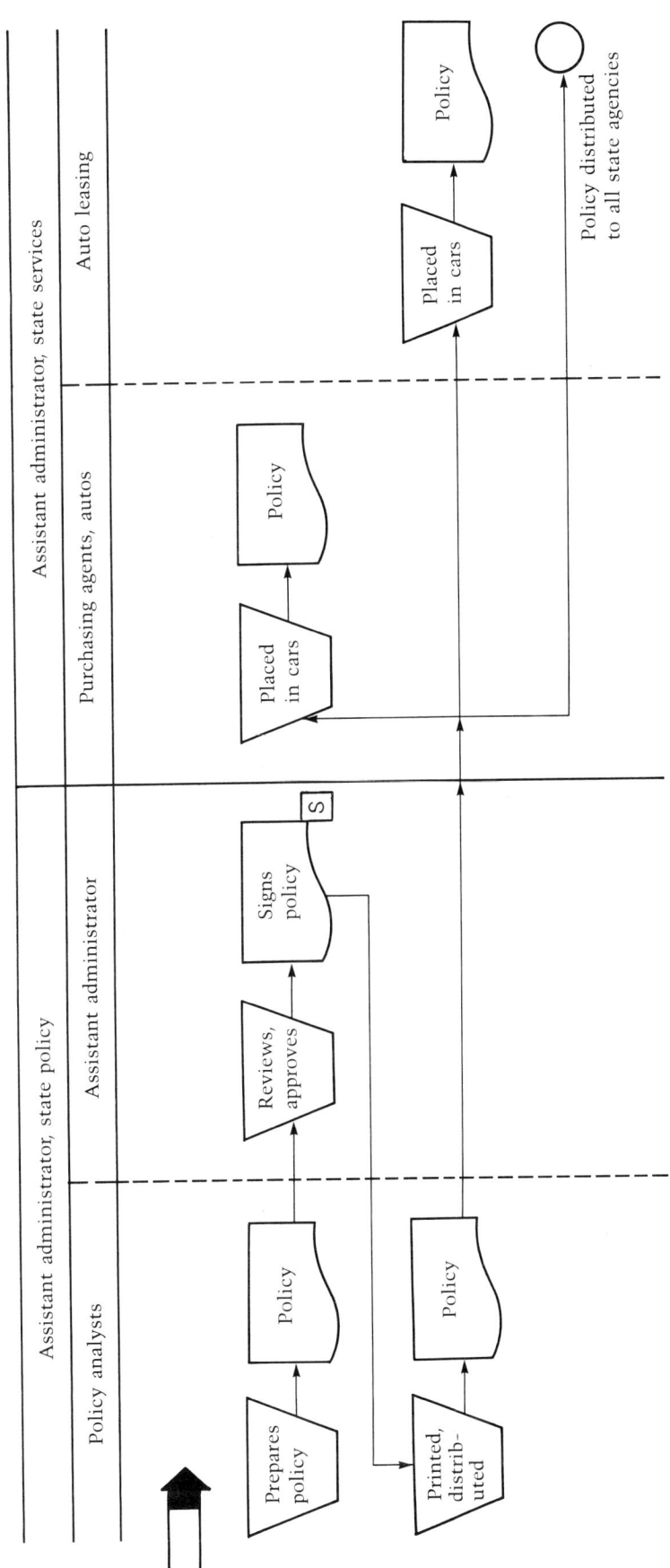

Figure 7.5 Flow chart: policy for use of cars, state administrative agency

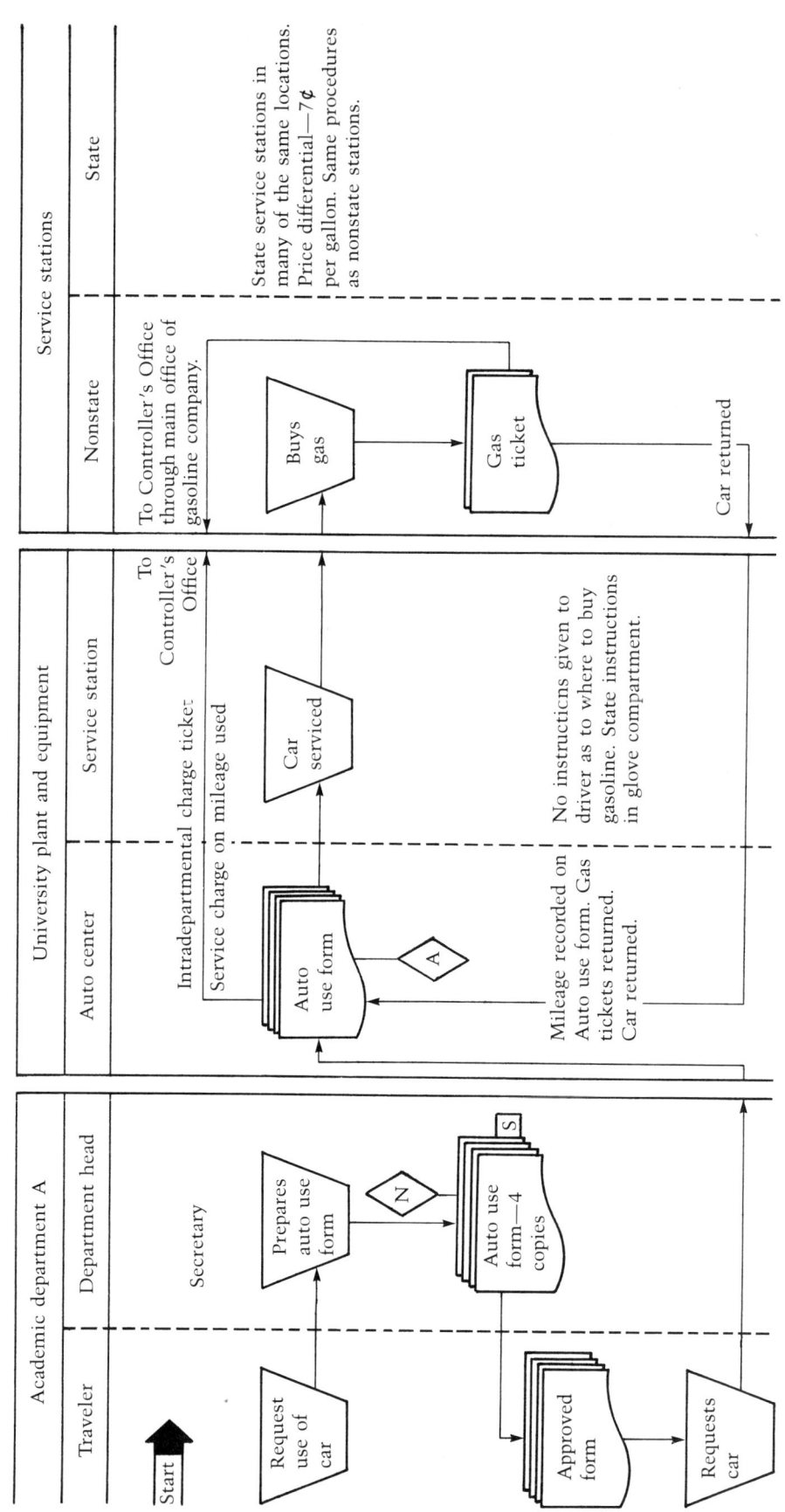

Figure 7.6 Flow of selected transactions: use of gasoline in state-owned cars, state university

3. Are there sufficient personnel available to accomplish the work?
4. Is training given to improve the quality of work performed?
5. Is there proper supervision?
6. Do employees understand not only what they are doing but why they are doing it?

Auditors who make financial-statement examinations have been concerned with people and their accounting functions for a long time, especially the adequate separation of functions. Now, the responsibility of the performance auditor extends to personnel of all types. It is just as important that the person who leases automobiles knows his responsibilities and is able to achieve those responsibilities as it is for a person who keeps records of accounts receivables and inventories to do his job properly.

When the audit involves different levels of the organization(s), the responsibility for communication between the levels must be specifically determined. Unless the lower levels know and understand what is wanted from the higher levels, it is difficult or impossible to achieve what is wanted.

In government, laws and regulations are often the controlling standards for personnel. When the quality of personnel is incapable of achieving effectiveness in a government program and that quality is the result of archaic laws or wrong interpretations, there should be some consideration for change; and the auditor will find it necessary to so indicate to the proper level of government.

Appropriate Policies and Practices

Appropriate policies and practices result from adequate long- and short-range planning, and such planning comes about more often than not when the organization has well-defined objectives. What is wanted by the organization, as well as what is wanted from the individual, should be appropriately communicated if efficient, economical, and effective operations are desired. Policies are usually communicated in the form of policy manuals. However, what is in the policy manual might or might not be what is actually being done, and it is this the auditor must discover rather than merely reading the policy and procedures manuals.

A System of Review

Effective management of any activity requires advance planning in terms of a specific standard for operations, actions, or transactions. Management must also plan for resources in the form of personnel, materials, and funds. Further, they should prescribe or suggest schedules or targets for accomplishment and where practicable, use standards for measuring efficiency of performance.

The auditor should examine these existing plans in whatever form they are used when he surveys an activity. He should also inquire into the methods followed by management itself when comparing actual performance with planned operations. This technique will provide the auditor with direct insight into the relative strength and weakness of the entire system of management control. It can also help him identify those problems warranting his particular attention and more comprehensive examination.

Furthermore, the auditor should ascertain how supervisory officials determine the following: whether (1) prescribed policies are being followed, (2) the procedures are being followed in an efficient and economical manner, and (3) authorized and prescribed procedures are effective.

Management should also be using internal reporting and internal audit methods, and the auditor should obtain complete information as to these functions. He should consider the nature and effectiveness of internal review and reporting methods in relation to each activity under review.

Direct supervision is another important review element in a good system of management control, since supervisory methods are crucial in determining causes of deficient operations.

When the auditor of financial statements prepares to review the internal control of an organization, he has three different approaches: questionnaires, usually somewhat uniform; flow charts; and testing transactions. When the performance auditor, however, approaches the review of management control of an organization or program, he usually has two ways only to begin his evaluation: flow charts, and testing transactions.

No activity has been reviewed sufficiently to develop standardized questionnaires for the review of management control of that activity, and therefore the performance auditor does not have such questionnaires he can use. However, the auditor *will* ask certain types of questions concerning the management control when testing specific transactions or items. This review should be in sufficient depth to enable him to obtain practical working information. The following types of questions are useful in order to obtain the evidence an auditor will need either to firm up his tentative objective or to determine whether information from the management control system is competent:

1. How are the operations actually carried out?
2. Are the various steps in the processing of transactions needed or useful?
3. Are the results of the transactions accomplished in terms of agency objectives, legal requirements, and common-sense practices?
4. What is the effectiveness of the control provided?
5. Does the system provide satisfactory control over costs, expenditures, receipts, revenues, and resources?
6. Do the organization's practices protect the interests of third parties, such as taxpayers, stockholders, or higher levels of management?
7. Is there duplication of effort?
8. Are available funds used properly and wisely?
9. Does management accept proper responsibility?
10. Does management control funds or activities?
11. Is there a cumbersome or extravagant organizational pattern?
12. Are the personnel capable of doing the work?
13. Are both personnel and physical resources used effectively?
14. Is there a genuine need for various operating and service units in relation to the costs of maintaining them?
15. Is there an effort to overcome any backlog?
16. Are standards established and being used by officials in judging factors requiring management appraisals?
17. Are written procedures and policies clear, or are there differing or inconsistent interpretations by various people?

If the auditor obtains appropriate answers to these kinds of questions, he will obtain a basic and a thorough knowledge as to how the operations being reviewed are actually carried out. He will obtain as well an insight into the effectiveness of the system of management control. Such knowledge is essential as a basis for planning the further work necessary to examine the efficiency, economy, and effectiveness of the controls provided by the organization's system of planning and practices.

This type of testing will also allow the auditor to obtain evidence on all three elements of the tentative audit objective—criteria, causes, and effects, which he can then consider along with such evidence found in organization manuals.

Examining management reports and internal audit reports, inspecting activities involved, and conducting discussions with responsible officials and personnel, can further help the auditor to obtain evidence on the tentative audit objective concerning the weaknesses in the management control system of the organization. The particular circumstances encountered and the specific objectives established for each assignment need to be given appropriate consideration in determining the nature and the extent of the work necessary in a given instance.

No hard and fast rules can be established as to the amount or type of work to be done, or the techniques to be used, in testing management control. The judgment and ingenuity of the audit staff play a large part: their approach should be tailor-made in each situation. It is important, nevertheless, that the auditor actually test a certain number of transactions so that he can determine the actual procedures followed and the actual policies applied by the entity, as well as identify some evidence on the three elements of the tentative audit objective.

The actions or transactions selected for review will depend upon the nature of the organization's activities or programs, along with the preliminary review analysis that the auditor made concerning the specific components to be considered for examination. The actions or transactions will represent actual steps, acts, or processes applied in carrying out an operation for the specific component.

When selecting transactions for testing, the auditor should consider those representative of the activity and should include any important or unusual items that are known. The number of transactions or actions selected for testing, therefore, is less important than their representative character. (For reference, illustrations of the steps to take in the review and testing of management control of actual transactions are given in Chapter 3.)

REVIEW QUESTIONS

1. What does internal control mean to you as it relates to financial-statement examinations? (See pp. 121–22.)

2. Standards for internal accounting control have been developed and are readily available. Can you contrast the status of management control standards with those of internal control standards? What are the implications of this status for the activities of an organization? (See pp. 122–23.)

3. What is meant by the following statements: Management control encompasses not only internal control but also external control. Management control and internal control are exactly the same when restricted to internal activities pertaining to a financial-statement examination. (See p. 123.)

4. Do you understand what management control is and can you list the characteristics of a good management control system? (See pp. 123–24.)

5. Can you distinguish between a plan of organization for entities having many levels both inside and outside of the entity and one for an organization having several levels, all of which are within the entity? (See pp. 125–26.)

6. What does the auditor normally do to get ready to prepare a flow chart? (See p. 128.)

7. All organizations are operated by people. What types of questions are asked to obtain the information concerning the jobs in an organization and the matching of the people to the jobs? (See pp. 128, 131.)

8. How does the auditor usually find the stated policies of an organization? (See p. 131.)

9. What procedures are used for testing the nature, effectiveness, and the usefulness of management control? Do these procedures allow the auditor to identify some evidence on all three elements of the audit objective? (See pp. 131–33.)

10. The auditor should obtain adequate information as to the policies, procedures, and practices employed by management in accounting for its activities. Why is it important for an auditor to have a thorough understanding of the operations and related procedures of the firm being audited? (See pp. 132–33.)

11. Can hard and fast rules be established as to the amount or type of work to be done in evaluating management control? (See p. 133.)

CASE 1

The City Garage: Management Control in an M-audit

This case is based on the information in Audit Scenarios 1 and 2 of Case 1 in Chapter 3. The reader should review pp. 46–47.

AUDIT SCENARIO 1
Plan of Organization of Large City Garage

Required

Insofar as possible, prepare an organization chart reflecting the plan of organization for the large city garage.

AUDIT SCENARIO 2
Flow Chart of Transactions Concerning Usage of Spark Plugs

Required

Prepare a flow chart of the information and transactions concerning the usage of spark plugs during the servicing of automobiles at the large city garage.

AUDIT SCENARIO 3
Acceptable Standards of Management Control

Required

Analyze Case 1 in Chapter 3 to determine the following:

1. What are acceptable standards of management control for
   a) Determining requirements for spark plugs,
   b) Purchasing fine-wire spark plugs,
   c) Replacing the fine-wire spark plugs by mechanics, and
   d) Disposing of spark plugs.
2. Were the standards you considered acceptable carried out by the organization?
3. What would need to be done to assure management that the standards were being carried out in a satisfactory manner?

AUDIT SCENARIO 4
Starting an Audit

The audit we are reviewing started because the mayor and city council talked to the head of the audit department of the city. They requested that he examine the conditions at the garage and report back to them any indications of what could be causing the costs to be so high at the garage.

Required

Assuming you had the responsibility for the garage as one of your audit responsibilities, respond to the following:

1. Should you have found the conditions at the garage before being requested to do so by the mayor and city council?
2. Indicate how you would have approached this examination if you were to do it on your own rather than being pushed into it.
3. Would your knowledge of the management controls of the organization have had any effect on your decision as to whether or not to make an audit?

136 / *Getting Started*

CASE 2

The Nursing Homes: Management Control in a P-audit

This case is based on the information in Audit Scenarios 1 and 2 of Case 2 in Chapter 3. The reader should review pp. 49–55.

AUDIT SCENARIO 1
Plan of Organization for Nursing Homes

Required

Insofar as possible, draw the various organizations that provide management control for nursing homes. The organization chart should be patterned after Figure 7.3 in this chapter.

AUDIT SCENARIO 2
Flow Chart of Fire-Prevention Program at Alpha Nursing Home

Required

Prepare a flow chart of information and actions concerning the prevention of fires at Alpha Nursing Home.

AUDIT SCENARIO 3
Standards for Fire Prevention

Required

1. Are the standards for preventing fires in nursing homes internally or externally imposed? List the standards by those externally imposed and then those internally imposed.
2. Are the current standards for fire prevention acceptable or would you consider developing new standards?

AUDIT SCENARIO 4
Testing Transactions

We have suggested that the auditor review a transaction from beginning to end to determine the quality of management control.

Required

From Case 2 in Chapter 3, review a transaction concerning management control as related to fire prevention completely through the control cycle and list what you would find at each step of the transaction.

CASE 3

Nonresident Tuition in the Fernwood Schools

Required
1. Analyze this case in terms of management control. Be sure to include external as well as internal factors.
2. Write a letter to the Fernwood Board of Education outlining your recommendations concerning problems identified in your analysis.

In 1971, the city of Fernwood adopted a nonresident tuition regulation requiring payment of tuition for any student enrolled in Fernwood schools but residing outside the city. The regulation called for the automatic dismissal of any student for whom the appropriate tuition had not been paid within 30 days of the beginning of any school term.

In August 1977, following an internal control audit, a report prepared for the Fernwood Board of Education showed about $281,000 in uncollected tuition for students enrolled from January 1971 through June 1977. For the 1976–77 school year alone, the following facts were reported: Tuition had not been collected for 61 nonresident students who had been permitted to continue in attendance all or part of the school year; tuition had not been collected for an additional 82 nonresident students for periods prior to their withdrawal or dismissal from school, and tuition had been suspended for 108 nonresident students pending consideration of claims for exemptions.

It was discovered subsequently that bills had not been issued promptly, that prescribed procedures for reporting delinquent cases for further collection action and for dismissal of nonresident students for nonpayment of tuition had not been followed, and that a central source of data needed for proper control did not exist.

At a September 1977 meeting of school board members and city officials, it was pointed out that since the students involved resided outside the city of Fernwood, the collection of past-due accounts posed certain legal questions.

CASE 4

Collections at the Local Church[4]

Required
1. Identify several of the tentative audit objectives that you could develop from the background data presented below.
2. What other types of information would you want to obtain in the preliminary survey phase in order to firm up the tentative audit objective?
3. From the information presented, what conclusion could you make in the review phase on the tentative objectives found in the preliminary survey phase?
4. Describe the weaknesses and recommend improvements in procedures for
    a) collections made at weekly services, and
    b) record-keeping for members' pledges and contributions.
5. From the conclusion you arrived at in the review phase, identify a possible detailed examination objective.
6. Give examples of the types of evidence you would want to obtain in the examination phase before an opinion or conclusion could be formed on the examination objective.

You have been asked by the board of trustees of a local church to review its internal control procedures. As a part of this review, you have prepared the following information relating to the collections made at weekly services and the record-keeping for members' pledges and contributions:

The church's board of trustees has delegated responsibility for financial management and audit of the financial records to the finance committee. This group prepares the annual budget and approves major disbursements but is not involved in collections or record-keeping. No audit has been considered necessary in recent years because the same trusted employee has kept church records and served as financial secretary for 15 years.

The collection at the weekly service is taken by a team of ushers. The head usher counts the collection in the church office following each service. He then places the collection, and a notation of the amount counted, in the church safe. The next morning, the financial secretary opens the safe and recounts the collection. He withholds about $100 to meet cash expenditures during the coming week and deposits the remainder intact. In order to facilitate the deposit, members who contribute by check are asked to draw their checks to "cash."

At their request a few members are furnished prenumbered, predated envelopes in which to insert their weekly contributions. The head usher removes the cash from the envelopes to be counted with the loose cash included in the collection and discards the envelopes. No record is maintained of issuance or return of the envelopes, and the envelope system is not encouraged.

Each member is asked to prepare a contribution pledge card annually. The pledge is regarded as a moral commitment by the member to contribute a stated weekly amount. Based upon the amounts shown on the pledge cards, the financial secretary furnishes a letter to requesting members to support the tax deductibility of their contributions.

PART Three

Making the Detailed Examination

Part 3 consists of chapters 8 through 11 and is concerned with the principles and procedures, illustrated with current practices, for the detailed examination of a performance audit.

After studying each chapter, reviewing the questions, analyzing the illustrations to be sure you understand how the basic principles of performance auditing are applied, and working the cases, you should be able to accomplish the specific objectives listed at the beginning of each chapter.

Each chapter's heading is self-explanatory of the material in that chapter. Chapter 8, concerned with evidence, invites you to learn the theory and practice of evidence as applied to performance auditing. Chapter 9 lets you apply that theory and practice to gathering evidence and recording it in working papers. Chapters 10 and 11 show you how to apply the principles and practices of gathering evidence on an audit objective in specifically illustrated working papers for an M-audit and a P-audit.

CHAPTER 8

Obtaining Evidence in Performance Auditing

After you have read this chapter, studied the review questions, and worked through the cases, you will understand:

- The various rules that will help you determine how much evidence is needed to come to a conclusion on an audit objective, whether the evidence is good or bad, and how the auditor uses evidence.
- That these rules include such items as direct and circumstantial evidence; best and secondary evidence; relevant, material, and competent evidence; and the various sources that provide competent evidence.
- That relevant evidence is related to the criteria of the audit objective; material evidence is related to the weight of influence each piece of evidence has on the auditor's mind; and competent evidence pertains to the source.
- How to determine whether evidence is competent when it comes from various sources, such as records; or testimony, such as interviews, letters, confirmations; or analyses; or observations.
- How to determine the sufficiency of evidence needed to come to a conclusion on the audit objective.

According to its word root, evidence is something "seen out of" or "clear"—something, thus, perceived by our senses; in other words, facts and information. With the more modern inventions for extending our sense perceptions of seeing, hearing, smelling, tasting, and feeling, what can be used as evidence now has been extended far beyond what it was in the past: Microscopes, electricity, electronic devices, laser beams, cameras, computers, and many other modern techniques and instruments, have widened the possibilities of what can and should be used as evidence by the auditor today. The computer model of a river basin that we discussed in Chapter 3, used to determine the extent of water pollution from various sources, is a good example. What a difference there is between using evidence from a computer model and trying to obtain information directly from the river.

Facts and Information as Evidence

As stated in Chapter 2, evidence is the facts and information used to come to a conclusion on an audit objective; and these must be planned for, gathered, and analyzed before any conclusion can be determined. Furthermore, they must be related to the criteria of the audit objective (relevant) and must be significant (material) before they can be used as evidence.

Some facts and information, needed as descriptive background data for the audit, are not necessarily used for coming to a conclusion on the objective.

Ordinarily this type of information is not evidence. For example, the facts that the Continental Company sold various types of goods and its headquarters was located in Salt Lake City may be pertinent to the audit but not have anything to do with whether the company followed generally accepted sales or production principles.

Many of our readers, having some background in financial-statement examinations, understand that their main sources of facts and information come from accounting transactions, accounts, and financial statements. When an auditor begins to make M-audits and P-audits, however, his sources of information expand dramatically. In addition to accounting-related facts and information obtained from financial management, the auditor of an M-audit might go to personnel, research, production, planning, administration, or other types of management for his facts and information. The auditor of a P-audit, on the other hand, might go to such areas as the environment, welfare, health, equal-employment opportunity, energy, tax bases, information systems, and other types of programs. It would be impossible for one performance auditor to understand enough about each of these areas to know when the facts and information were reliable, significant, and related to the audit objective; but he can gain competence by understanding clearly the various kinds of evidence.

Analytical Evidence

Evidence must be related to reality. Whatever is used as a basis for coming to a conclusion on an audit objective must have been, or must be, a part of the real world. It must have substance; it may not exist as fantasy in someone's mind. There is one case, however, when evidence really appears to come from an unreal situation: when an expert witness testifies as to what he or she knows. This conclusion or opinion, based on evidence on an objective, does in fact come from the mind of a person, but the knowledge that person uses must come from the real world and is in direct contrast to information any person other than an expert might have concerning a subject. This type of evidence, which we have called analytical, is quite common when evidence on a subobjective produces a conclusion that the auditor uses as evidence on the primary objective.

Direct Evidence

Coming to a conclusion on an audit objective is determined by the types of evidence obtained. If the auditor's subobjective is to determine the legal ownership of a building by a given company, then all he would have to do is go to the courthouse and look at the recorded deed. The deed would be called *direct evidence*; it allows the auditor to come to a conclusion on his audit objective without obtaining further evidence. Other examples of direct evidence, usually obtained on a subobjective, are the determination of the cost of an item by looking at the original invoice, the guilt of a person for a particular act by that person's admission, or the testimony of a particular individual who actually saw the commission of an act in question.

Circumstantial, or Indirect, Evidence

There are many times when it is impossible to come to a conclusion on an audit objective without building up a case through many pieces or circumstances of evidence. Seldom does only one piece of evidence directly affect the opinion. This type of evidence is called *circumstantial, or indirect, evidence*. For example, to prove that a machine was overhauled and needs to be recapitalized, the information in an invoice may show the cost of the overhaul. The records may show that the machine is still a part of the fixed assets, but to assure himself that the machine is still in useful condition and that a major overhaul was accomplished, the auditor might have to observe its operation and talk about it to knowledgeable people. All of these circumstances could convince him that the machine should be recapitalized on the records of the company.

Best and Secondary Evidence

While the concepts of direct and circumstantial evidence are important to the auditor, just as important is an understanding of best and secondary evidence. *Best, or primary, evidence* is that which under all circumstances should be used before any other evidence is considered. For example, the best evidence of a contract is the original contract itself. The best evidence of a bank confirmation is the original confirmation letter. If the original contract cannot be produced, then copies of the contract could be used; these would constitute *secondary evidence*. If used, however, it is extremely important for the auditor to assure himself that the contents of the copies are exactly the same as those of the original.

It is easier probably to see the distinction between *best evidence*, the original contract, and *secondary evidence*, a copy of the contract, if we consider what happens to letters. The original, which goes to an outsider, may have a postscript or penwritten notations on it that change the original contents so that it is different from the copy kept in the files. Similarly, consider what happens from the draft to the final document: The draft may be changed several times before the final product is released; and thus, using a draft document as evidence can often cause serious embarrassment to the auditor because it is *not* the best evidence. It should be used only if the final copy cannot be obtained; and only then, if the contents of the draft can be proved to be the same as the final.

Quality and Reliability of Evidence

In the trial of an issue before a court, various rules have been developed to determine whether records, testimony of witnesses, or actual physical objects can be allowed as evidence. In this way, policemen can determine if there is an issue and can then gather the evidence; the prosecuting and defense attorneys can present the evidence; and the jury and the judge can come to a conclusion on the point at issue from the evidence.

In auditing, there is no policeman, no prosecuting attorney, no defense attorney, no jury or judge. The auditor must place himself in all of these positions. He must determine whether there is an audit objective on which there is a need to gather evidence; and if there is, he must gather the evidence, as does the policeman. He must look at it from the side that agrees and, as well, from the side that disagrees to the objective of the audit, just as do the prosecuting attorney and the defense attorney. He must determine which evidence should or should not be considered and admitted, as does the judge. He must weigh the evidence from both sides, the side that assents and the side that dissents, and come to a conclusion he considers is probably right, as does the jury.

In addition, no judge, with rules of evidence to guide him, restricts the auditor in either obtaining or selecting which evidence can be considered. No judge says to the auditor, "That evidence is immaterial, irrelevant, and incompetent," or "That evidence is hearsay," or "I will take judicial notice of that evidence." The auditor, thus, must develop his own conceptual rules to guide him as to what is evidence, what is not evidence, what evidence should be included or excluded, and what evidence should be relied upon more than other evidence.

As we stated earlier, legal rules on the admissibility of legal evidence can provide a basis for developing conceptual rules for the admissibility of audit evidence. Some of them will be used; but these conceptual rules, while valuable to the auditor as a guide, will not restrict him in practice, because no one except the auditor himself acts in the capacity of a judge to make those restrictions. The auditor alone, then, is the one who accepts the burden of what is acceptable evidence, what is unacceptable; and what is reliable evidence, what is unreliable. Small wonder he needs the best guidelines he can find.

Our discussion of a concept the auditor can use to determine the acceptability and reliability of audit evidence will come under four basic headings: relevancy, materiality, competency, and sufficiency.

Sufficient competent evidence that is relevant and material supports the opinions or conclusions on the objective of the audit. Relevancy and materiality pertain to the quality of that support. Competency pertains to the reliability of the source of the evidence used as support. Sufficiency pertains to the weight of the support—to the quantity, as well as to the quality and reliability.

Conceptually, the auditor must at all times consider all four categories—relevancy, materiality, competency, and sufficiency—for all evidence used. Does the information relate to the audit objective? Is it significant enough to be used? Is it from a reliable source? Is there enough to convince a prudent and reasonable person? If these questions are answered in the affirmative, then the auditor will know the evidence used in developing an opinion or a conclusion to his audit objective is acceptable, reliable, and sufficient to convince him that his conclusion or opinion is the proper one.

Relevancy of Evidence

Relevancy means that the information used as evidence must have some logical relationship to the criteria of the audit objective. Let us illustrate with an M-audit such as one in which the objective relates to recapping tires: If the criteria were the policy of recapping tires after 20,000 miles of wear instead of buying new tires, then evidence to show that steel-belted radials would last longer than regular tires would be irrelevant.

Materiality of Evidence

Materiality of evidence pertains to the weight each piece of evidence plays in influencing the auditor's mind concerning the conclusion to the audit objective.

As an illustration, if we consider a fire burning 5 reams of paper, valued at $5, out of a $100,000 inventory, we can see that the $5 out of a $100,000 inventory would be rather insignificant. It would not affect our conclusion concerning the inventory to any great extent.

Materiality of evidence is a subjective quality because materiality is the amount the evidence influences the mind of the auditor towards his rendering a conclusion on the audit objective. Material evidence influences the auditor towards coming to a conclusion; immaterial evidence does not, so it is excluded. To weigh heavily on the minds of others, however, the materiality of evidence must be judged by standards that influence them in the same way as they influence the auditor.

Competency of Evidence

While relevancy and materiality pertain to the quality of the evidence that supports a conclusion on the objective of the audit, competency pertains to the source of the evidence that provides support. Competency is the reliability one places on the source of information used as evidence. To be competent, evidence must be obtained from a reliable source and must be accurate.

The following are good guides to determine competent evidence:

- Evidence obtained from an independent source provides greater assurance of reliability than that secured from the audited organization.
- Evidence developed under a good system of internal control is more likely to be reliable than that obtained where such control is weak or unsatisfactory.
- Evidence obtained by the auditor through physical examination, observation, computation, and inspection is more reliable than evidence obtained indirectly.
- Original documents are more reliable than copies.[1]

The procedures used for obtaining evidence to determine competency are most important. For example, the auditor looks at information recorded as evidence in working papers differently if it is actually taken from books and records than if it is dreamed up in someone's mind. Information placed in working papers often is shown as evidence when the reviewer cannot tell whether the information has come from records, from interviews, or from observations—or whether it has been obtained from any source at all. Evidence, then, must be developed to show the answer to the objective of competency, as well as to arrive at a conclusion on the primary audit objective.

Sufficiency of Evidence

A performance auditor is placed in several positions in regard to evidence—the positions of the policeman, the prosecuting attorney, the defense attorney, the judge, and the jury. For each of these positions he represents, the auditor needs to know how much evidence is needed to come to a conclusion on the audit objective. In the discussion of relevancy, materiality, and competency, we conceptually determined what evidence was. Now, from a performance auditor's standpoint, we need to know how to judge how much evidence is needed to come to a conclusion on the audit objective. The "how much" of evidence is often called *the weight of evidence.*

Two terms used in law to define the weight of evidence are *preponderance* and *proof beyond a reasonable doubt.* A preponderance of evidence is "that evidence which clearly and convincingly outweighs the opposing evidence in the mind of the person reaching the conclusion." It does not have to be of sufficient weight to prove or disprove the auditor's position beyond any question; but, it must be sufficiently superior to clearly and convincingly outweigh that of the opposing evidence.

Proof beyond a reasonable doubt is "that evidence which goes far beyond preponderance or being just clear and convincing." Its superiority over the opposing side must leave no reasonable question in the mind of the person reaching the conclusion on the audit objective.

Some auditors use the terms convincing, sufficiency, and reasonable in much the same manner as lawyers use preponderance. Others use these same words to mean proof beyond a reasonable doubt. Let us try to make a clearer distinction between the two terms.

Obviously, there could be a third term to mean that evidence on one side practically balances that of the opposing side. This term is unnecessary, however, if we consider that certain sides have the responsibility for proving the issue, either with a preponderance of evidence or with evidence beyond a reasonable doubt. In other words, the burden of proof is on either the assenting or dissenting side, so a stalemate would not be considered.

In some cases the burden of furnishing sufficient weight of evidence to prove the issue may be the responsibility of the one defending himself. In other words, he may be guilty until he proves himself innocent. This is the case whenever the Internal Revenue Service (IRS) questions your tax return. In most legal cases in our society, however, the burden of proving the issue, or as a minimum, of providing a preponderance of evidence, is on the side that alleges or affirms the point at issue. Stated another way, a person is innocent until proved guilty with at least a preponderance of evidence.

In all performance audit cases, the burden of proof (or the providing as a minimum, a preponderance of evidence) is on the auditor. He is the one stating the audit objective. This holds true whether the objective deals with efficiencies or deficiencies, effectiveness or ineffectiveness, or economies or lack of economies. In some instances, moreover, the weight of the evidence used to come to a conclusion on some audit objectives must be beyond a reasonable doubt, rather than only a mere preponderance. Especially is this true when the evidence pertains to causes of an audit objective. Causes pertain to individuals, and individuals may be damaged or materially harmed. Thus, when there is any question of damage or material harm to an individual, more weight of evidence than a mere preponderance is necessary.

Sources of Audit Evidence

Competency of audit evidence is related to the source. The source, in turn, is related (1) to that which one perceives, (2) to that which comes from the real world. Then, any conceptual classification of evidence-gathering techniques must be concerned with these two properties: being related to perceptions, and being related to the real world. Based on these requirements, audit evidence, therefore, can only come from three sources. The first is what the auditor perceived himself that is related to the real world; we will call this *observation evidence*. The second is what someone else perceives that is related to the real world and tells the auditor; we will call this *testimonial evidence*. The third is the particular characteristics of an item related to reality that can be perceived by anyone. In auditing, whatever one perceives in this third source is usually recorded in some form, so the auditor has access to this information from some written source. We will call this *records evidence*. Let us discuss these three sources. (A fourth source is sometimes identified as analytical evidence; however, we have classified this kind of evidence as testimonial, since the auditor in most cases is testifying as an expert witness when he comes to a conclusion on a subobjective.)

Records Evidence

As a general statement, the most important single source of facts and information that the auditor uses as evidence is records. Records include all written information—accounting records, contracts, letters, courthouse records, and documents of all types.

Courts allow accounting records to be accepted as legal evidence if they are kept in the normal course of the business and if the original purpose of the records is relevant to the point of issue. Those accounting records not kept in the normal course of the business are usually not admissible as evidence. This rule, with adaptations, is a good rule for the performance auditor to follow in evaluating the competency of audit evidence from any records source. Special studies, outside of the normal daily record keeping, would not fall within the scope of this rule.

Since auditors deal with records more than with other sources of information, they can develop a tendency to believe that anything written is accurate. This is not necessarily so. Copies of documents are often not the same as the original. Pen-and-ink changes can be made in typewritten copy; a copy of a draft in the files may not be a copy of the document mailed. The auditor should assure himself that the copy contains the same information as the original if he expects the information he uses to be competent.

In the past, the auditor has been required to obtain information from records through touch and sight. With the advent of the computer, some auditors have expressed the fear that the competency of these records may suffer; they fear that they will lose control of the information within the computer because the records cannot always be seen or touched. By understanding competency, the auditor should know when he is provided competent information, even from the computer.

Competency in a computer is related to the degree of control built into the operations of the computer system. If the computer system has good internal control, the information from that system can be just as competent as that from visual records. Good controls must be built into the system at the source of the information. Likewise, good controls must be built into the actual processing of the information, must be built into the environment of the system, and must be a part of the system when the information comes out.

The auditor may not have direct evidence on the objective as to the correctness of the information from the computer, but he can use circumstantial evidence to convince himself that the information, when handled properly, is correct and competent. This would be true even though he is unable to see and feel the records. (Computer use is treated in depth in Chapter 14.)

The procedures for obtaining evidence are important for convincing others that the evidence is competent; this is especially true for the procedures for determining the competency of evidence from computers. To convince others that the computer information is reliable, these procedures often are shown as evidence in the report.

Testimonial Evidence

A testimony often connotes only oral information obtained from the perceptions of others. Our definition of testimonial evidence, however, will be any information received from others, or ourselves, acting as expert witnesses as a result of a direct request. The request for such information can be written, oral, or analytical. Therefore, a standard bank-confirmation form replying to our written request for confirmation of a bank balance would be testimonial evidence. A letter obtained from the files would not; it would be records evidence. A conclusion by the auditor on the analysis of the savings obtained by using recapped tires instead of new tires would be testimonial evidence (analytical). An invoice showing the price of the new tires would not; it would be records evidence.

We can classify the requests for testimonial evidence, then, as follows: personal interviews, letter requests and confirmations, and analytical evidence.

Personal Interview Evidence. The auditor receives some of his most reliable evidence through in-depth interviews of another person who has knowledge of the subject. He should realize, however, that the person being interviewed may have personal goals that conflict with the objectives of the interview. Immaterial, irrelevant, and incorrect information oftentimes may be given to the auditor unless the motives of the interviewee are considered. The auditor should understand all of these factors in developing his interviewing techniques.

The auditor should also realize that when requesting information from a person, he should be sure that person has current knowledge of the information he is giving, or have some means of refreshing his memory. As we know, memory is often fleeting; the criminal investigator is trained to make notes immediately and keep those notes available to refresh his memory in case he has to testify in court.

To be competent, the information should be from the personal knowledge of the one being interviewed, and not secondhand or hearsay. While secondhand information may be used as a lead to other evidence, it should not, (unless supported from some other source) be used as evidence to support a conclusion on an audit objective. The person providing that information would be incompetent unless he had personal knowledge. When possible, the auditor should go to the original source to obtain the most reliable information.

Letter and Confirmation Evidence. Information used as evidence in an audit report is often obtained through letters and confirmations. When requesting specific information by letter, the auditor should state the questions as clearly as possible so that the responder will not misunderstand what is wanted. Under present auditing standards, confirmations are required from several sources.

Analytical Evidence. We said in the section concerning audit objectives that the conclusion on a subobjective was used as analytical evidence. Most of the detail results from the auditor making his own evaluation or analysis. This analysis by the auditor can be used as evidence—analytical evidence. Directly related to analytical evidence is evidence that the auditor obtains from other expert witnesses. A handwriting expert, a computer expert, and an inventory expert, all go through an analytical process that produces a result used by the auditor to provide evidence to come to a conclusion on a particular objective.

Observations Evidence

The auditor obtains substantial amounts of evidence through his own personal senses of seeing and feeling: He observes buildings and lands; he looks at and counts cash; he sees roads being constructed, engines being repaired, and training classes being conducted. Observation evidence is an important source of information for M-audits and P-audits.

Observations evidence must come from one who has trained himself to be observant. Poor observational habits may stem from the auditor's lack of interest or desire, from his physical condition, from his psychological condition, or from his inability to understand what he is observing. Since he is the source, the auditor must develop good observational habits to convince others that what he has seen is accurate and reliable. In addition, in his working papers he should state the conditions of his observation so that if required, others will be able to know the competency of the evidence. Often, too, it is wise for the auditor to photograph the observation; a photograph will show competency much better than a written statement.

We should notice the difference between the concepts of relevancy and materiality and the concept of competency. Relevant and material evidence are so because of the facts themselves. No additional information is usually needed to show that the evidence is relevant and material, but that is not so with competency. Even the procedures of gathering the evidence will determine its competency. Ordinarily you do not have to have evidence to prove materiality or relevancy, but you *do* have to have evidence to prove competency.

The reasoning behind the review of internal control is to prove the competency of the evidence obtained in both financial examinations and performance audits. It would be almost impossible to accept evidence from a computer unless additional evidence was gathered to prove it was competent. Therefore, we state that sufficient relevant, material, and competent evidence must be planned for, gathered, and analyzed to come to an opinion or conclusion on the objective of whether the evidence is competent.

Sampling for Audit Evidence

Much of the information from records, testimonies, or observations used as evidence can be obtained through the process of sampling instead of looking at every record, gathering testimonies from every person concerned, or observing every happening. This subject is important enough to discuss in depth and will be considered in Chapter 13.

Further Considerations on Evidence

There are five further points on evidence that an auditor should consider, and we will identify each briefly.

Evidence Needed on Both Sides of Objective

In law, both sides—the defense and prosecution—have an opportunity to present their sides in court concerning their positions. Then the judge and jury can come to a judgment. In performance auditing, it is the responsibility of the auditor to make sure that the evidence on both sides is gathered and weighed to determine that his conclusion on the audit objective is the proper one.

Always, there are two sides to any audit objective. The auditor must assure himself that both sides are examined.

No Absolute Certainty to Conclusion on Audit Objective

When an auditor deals with evidence on an audit objective, he should thoroughly understand that there can be no absolute certainty as to the conclusion on that objective. One additional piece of evidence, on one side or the other, might completely change the conclusion. Each auditor, therefore, will have to determine to his own satisfaction how much evidence, as well as the quality and reliability of the evidence, he must have. If others are concerned, as they generally are in performance audits, he must also determine how much evidence they will require to be able to accept his conclusion.

Judicial Notice

The auditor must recognize also that there is no need to prove over and over what has previously been proved. Lawyers use the term *judicial notice* to refer to something previously proved. For example, no one needs to prove the existence of the Declaration of Independence or the Constitution of the United States; everyone knows they exist. Auditors often gather a great deal of evidence to prove problems that have already been proved, when all they need is a reference to the prior proof.

Recording and Evaluating Evidence

A discussion concerning recording and evaluating evidence is of sufficient importance to provide a separate chapter—Chapter 9.

Presenting Evidence in the Report

Similarly, a discussion of presenting evidence in the report is of sufficient importance to provide a separate chapter—Chapter 16.

REVIEW QUESTIONS

1. Evidence is the facts and informations used to formulate a conclusion on an audit objective. What characteristics determine whether facts and information are evidence? (See pp. 141–42.)

2. An auditor obtains direct and indirect evidence on the audit objective. What do you think direct audit evidence means? (See p. 142.)

3. The conclusion on a performance audit objective is determined by the types of evidence obtained. Two types of evidence are direct evidence and circumstantial evidence. Distinguish between the amount of evidence needed for direct evidence as compared to the quantity needed for circumstantial evidence. (See p. 142.)

4. Best, or primary, evidence should be used before any other evidence is considered. Give an example showing circumstances under which secondary evidence must be used in place of primary evidence. (See p. 143.)

5. The auditor must place himself in the position of policeman, prosecuting attorney, defense attorney, jury, and judge. What is implied in this statement? (See pp. 143–44.)

6. Conceptually, the auditor must consider four categories for each piece of evidence used to develop an acceptable conclusion to his audit objective. Identify and define these four categories. (See p. 144.)

7. Some authorities feel that there is a fourth source of audit evidence, analytical evidence. How does analytical evidence relate to testimonial evidence? (See pp. 146, 148.)

8. The auditor obtains information from many different sources. What is the single most important source of information? Give illustrations of the above source. (See p. 146.)

9. Auditors sometimes have a tendency to believe that anything written is accurate and, therefore, copies of records are in most cases the same as the original. Is this statement valid? (See p. 146.)

10. A term used in law to define the weight of evidence is "preponderance." Discuss how this term applies to audit evidence. (See p. 145.)

11. Another term used in law to define the weight of evidence needed to form a judgment is "proof beyond a reasonable doubt." Define this term as it relates to auditing and give a brief description of it. (See p. 145.)

12. Can you be absolutely certain of a conclusion on an audit objective when you gather evidence on that objective? (See p. 149.)

CASE 1

The School Voucher Project at Alum Rock[2]

The following case comes from a report made by HEW auditors.

Required

From the information provided on this case, identify:
1. Background information not used as evidence.
2. The various conclusions to the audit objective, based on the evidence given.
3. The evidence on criteria, causes, and effects of the audit objective.
4. The types of evidence provided and the sources from which the evidence is obtained.

Background

On April 16, 1972, the Office of Economic Opportunity (OEO) initially awarded a grant to the Alum Rock Union Elementary School District (Alum Rock) of San Jose, California, to conduct a voucher demonstration project (project). The grant was made under the authority of the Economic Opportunity Act of 1964, Public Law 88-452 and was based on a proposal to OEO by Alum Rock entitled "Transition Model Voucher Proposal" for funds to support a 2-year demonstration. The proposal and grant were preceded by a feasibility study of the project at Alum Rock. Under the provisions of Public Law 92-318, administration of the grant was transferred to the National Institute of Education (NIE) on September 17, 1973.

Alum Rock was established in 1930 as one of 11 school districts serving San Jose, a city of approximately 500,000 located south of San Francisco in the Santa Clara Valley. During the 1974–75 school year, Alum Rock operated 26 schools with an enrollment of over 15,000 students from preschool through the 8th grade. In the initial year of the project, 1972–73, six schools participated, offering 22 educational programs referred to as "minischools." During the 1974–75 school year, 14 schools participated in the project with a total of 66 minischools. Grant awards for the period April 1, 1972, through June 30, 1975, totaled $7,007,570. The project was scheduled to terminate at the end of the 1976–77 school year.

The voucher concept represents a radical departure from traditional methods of financing public education. Its purpose, as stated in the proposal, is "... to improve the quality of a student's education by making schools more responsive to student needs and accountable for educational performance." Parents of students were to be issued vouchers equivalent to the cost of 1 year's education. The parents would then select a minischool from the alternatives available; and these, in turn, would receive their financial support through the vouchers turned in by the parents of students enrolled. Since the financial resources available to minischools would be determined by the selections made by parents, minischools with programs not attracting students would continue to lose resources until they responded to the needs perceived by parents.

The proposal stated five goals of the project:

1. To offer all parents in the demonstration area a range of choices for the education of their children. In particular, it is hoped that the right of educational choice presently available only to the affluent will be extended to the poor and middle income sectors of the community.
2. To allow schools to become more responsive to the needs of their communities and to involve parents more meaningfully in their decision-making processes as a consequence of this revised procedure for allocating educational resources.
3. To stimulate parents to take a more active interest and become more involved in the education of their children.

4. To improve the educational achievement of the participating students.
5. To increase the level of parental satisfaction with their schools.

Furthermore, the following section of the proposal was incorporated into the grant award:

> A thorough program of informing the parents about the nature of the voucher mechanism and the educational alternatives available is essential for the effective operation of this pilot project.

The proposal also made the following information for parents required: philosophy and program; staff profiles; budgets; class size; methods of student, teacher, and program evaluations; communications; and any other information needed to respond to requests from parents or suggestions from participating schools.

Findings: Information Provided Parents

Alum Rock provided parents of project students with considerable information for their use in selecting schools. Data were provided on student feelings on friendship, involvement, teacher support, and teacher control. In addition, parents were furnished with some data on the academic achievements of the minischools. They were advised on whether the students met, exceeded, or did not meet, their prior learning progress in reading and math. However, auditors noted that Alum Rock did not provide information that parents could use to compare the accomplishments of each school in relation to the description of the intent of their programs. Also, parents were not informed of a key indicator on the academic status of the minischool—namely, statistics were not made available on the average grade levels at which students were reading and performing mathematics. In addition, Alum Rock did not give parents staff profiles, although such information was required by the terms of the grant.

Since parents lacked some essential information that would have enabled them to make informed school selections, it seemed evident that the project would not be able to meet an important goal: to determine the full effect of parental selection of educational programs.

Research studies made before this grant was awarded stressed the importance of having well-informed parents select the schools in which their children would be enrolled. Sections from two studies that were most closely related to the project are discussed below:

CSPP Study. A study entitled, "A Report on Financing Elementary Education by Grants to Parents," proposed by the Center for the Study of Public Policy (CSPP) in December 1970, was the theoretical model to which Alum Rock addressed itself in its application for an OEO project grant. The report indicated that voucher-program parents should have specific kinds of information about alternatives available at voucher schools:

> A voucher program depends on parents intelligently choosing the right school for their child. Therefore, two things must be provided as part of any voucher program.
> - Parents must be informed of all available alternatives.
> - Parents must be able to obtain accurate, relevant, and comprehensive information about the advantages and disadvantages of each alternative.
>
> ... Such information would fall into two categories: information that facilitated comparison of schools with one another, and comprehensive information about the advantages and disadvantages of each alternative.

The report further stated that an independent agency should collect, verify, and distribute information that would enable parents to identify the effective from the less-effective minischool. The CSPP Report suggested that the easiest way to insure that needed information be made available by the school was ". . . to make the provision of information a requirement for cashing vouchers."

Feasibility Study. "The Alum Rock Union Elementary School District Voucher Feasibility Study" made by Alum Rock officials also stressed the necessity of supplying any and all information parents might need, stating that "complete and accurate information about all phases of the voucher program is a must." The feasibility study foresaw a potential conflict between the minischools and a central information office at the school district. It therefore recommended that a central information office be established that

> ... should have the authority . . . to request that all schools, as a condition to their participation, agree to supplying the information in the form and at the times needed, unless this conflicts with their philosophy and they have submitted an acceptable

substitute statement, and that the information presented be subject to verification.

In attempting to comply with grant instructions, minischools participating in the project and the school district's evaluation department compiled information each year on the programs for parents to use in selecting schools for their children. In the 1972–73 school year, Alum Rock provided parents with a booklet they could use to compare descriptions of the programs offered by all minischools for that year. In the 1973–74 school year, in addition to descriptions of the programs offered for the year, Alum Rock published a booklet that described to parents how they could become involved in their children's schools, and also provided parents with some information on student achievement in reading and math. This information, however, was not related to each minischool's stated objectives and gave data only for the minischool in which each child was enrolled.

In the 1974–75 school year, Alum Rock provided parents with similar information but it was not available to parents until the end of September so that it could not be used for making enrollment selections for that year. In the 1975–76 school year, Alum Rock completely revised its presentation of minischool descriptions and achievement information in a manner that should have enabled parents to make relatively well-informed selections of schools for the year; there were two newspaperlike booklets distributed in April so that parents would have a chance to study the material before making their selections by the end of May.

Besides these efforts to reach parents, other basic information, such as the methods most teachers planned to use to teach reading, was gathered and summarized by district staff members. Additional descriptive information was prepared by minischool staff members and students, and material from these three sources was published under one cover in newspaper format. In addition, an evaluation reported how minischools budgeted their money, including statistical data for each minischool that showed the number of students, teachers and teacher aides, the ratio of adults to students in the reading and math classes, and the grade span covered—all presented in simple language with many illustrations and an easy-to-read format.

Finally, in order to further help parents, Alum Rock prepared and distributed a booklet entitled, "How to Choose a Mini-School," which gave step-by-step instructions on how to use the information provided. Still another booklet, entitled "How to Make a School Visit," was available to serve as a guide in making an on-site evaluation of a minischool.

Additional Information Needed by Parents

Although the evidence shows that parents of voucher-project students received a significant amount of comparative information they needed to make minischool selections, the auditors believed that additional types of information should have been provided. For instance, in addition to information parents received for the 1975–76 school year selections, Alum Rock should have shown, as a measure of effectiveness, whether or not each minischool performed the services described in the booklets used by parents to make their selections for the preceding years. Further, Alum Rock should have provided, for each grade, data on the average grade levels at which voucher-project students were achieving in reading and math, and this information should have been in addition to the rate of improvement in reading and math that parents had been given. And finally, minischool staff profiles should have been provided to parents.

Reporting Services Provided. Alum Rock did not report on an overall basis for each school whether the activities and services described in parent booklets were actually provided in the classroom. Furthermore, parents were informed through conferences with teachers as to how well their children were doing, but they were not given information they could use to compare how well individual schools were doing in executing described programs. Thus, parents were not able to evaluate the descriptions of minischool programs in terms of actual performance in prior years and instead, had to rely mainly on the minischools' descriptions.

In at least one example, a minischool did not conduct its own described program, as the minutes of the Educational Voucher Advisory Committee of January 8, 1973, attest. One parent complained that

> ... She had enrolled her child in a particular voucher program on the basis of the program's original description. During the year the program went through a major change, but parents were not informed of this change. It was only by chance that

she finally learned about this modification. She felt strongly that a voucher minischool has an obligation to keep parents informed about major program changes.

The auditors stated that information as to whether minischools provided the services they described should be given to parents as part of the information they received for evaluating minischools for future enrollment.

Grade-Equivalency Data. The evaluation report given to parents for use in selecting minischools for the 1975–76 school year showed the percentage of students in each school who met, exceeded, or did not meet, expectations for learning progress in reading and math, the data being based on the relationship of each student's percentile score on a nationwide pretest given in the fall with a posttest given in the spring. The evaluation report, however, did not state what the average percentile scores were for the minischools, nor did it show the grade level at which students were learning. The auditors believed that parents should have received this information, as well as information on progress in reading and math.

Parents needed this grade-equivalency information, based on the same test results used to determine percentile data, to give balance to the achievement data provided in the evaluation report. Without grade-equivalency data, for instance, a school that showed a high percentage of its students improved in reading and math at a rate exceeding expectations would appear to be a highly successful school. It might not be an acceptable choice to some parents, however, if the grade-equivalency data showed that the school's students were achieving below the grade level of the class.

Data showing the learning progress and grade equivalency of minischools by grade were available, published in booklets or shown in line graphs. The auditors recommended that Alum Rock make learning progress and grade-equivalency information for each grade level of each minischool available for review by parents.

Staff Profiles. Alum Rock did not include staff profiles in any of the booklets furnished to parents, although these profiles, which were to describe the teaching and administrative staff, including years of service, education background, specialties, and so on, were required by the proposal. They were not distributed because principals and teachers objected to such information being provided to the voucher community, on the basis that it was not a relevant indicator of the quality of education. Alum Rock agreed with their objections.

The information could prove important to parents for reasons other than determining the quality of education. For instance, parents might be interested in teachers who have specialized training that they feel could be beneficial to their children. The auditors believed that Alum Rock should have provided parents with staff profiles as stated in the grant proposal.

Parental Decision Making

A Rand Corporation report, entitled "Family Choice in Schooling," stated that the educationally disadvantaged—the population segment that was supposed to benefit most from increased choice in schooling—were least equipped to negotiate the voucher system and therefore were unable to realize the full potential of having a school system that was responsive to their needs. In addition, the Rand Report stated that parents would not be completely educated by learning a set of facts about schools, but rather would have to constantly monitor the operation and administration of the minischool by making their own evaluations of teachers and programs. The report concluded that since relatively disadvantaged households were less effective gatherers and processors of information, they would be less able to identify and select superior minischools or to monitor their child's school over a period of time.

Responding to the Rand report, the Voucher Demonstration Project included the following statement as one of its goals:

> To allow schools to become more responsive to the needs of their communities and to involve parents more meaningfully in their decision-making processes as a consequence of this revised procedure for allocating educational resources.

To meet this goal, it would be necessary to inform parents about all aspects of the educational alternatives available to them, including descriptions of services promised for prior school years and actually provided, services planned for the coming year, grade-equivalency data, staff profiles, and detailed information that would allow comparisons of minischools by grade level. The auditors believed that the addition of such information to the type of information given to parents would help them to make better decisions and would help to increase their level of involvement in the project.

Release of Information

Teachers and principals of some minischools were reluctant to have comparative information concerning the performance of their schools released to the public. Another Rand report entitled "A Public School Voucher Demonstration: The First Year at Alum Rock," published in June 1974, discussed this position as follows:

> To begin with, the teachers and principals had no objections to distributing individual program descriptions, as they had already done the previous spring.
> The staffs strongly opposed the use of standardized achievement tests for the comparative evaluation of mini-schools. They were regarded as virtually useless in diagnosing specific learning problems, and many teachers and parents considered the tests culturally biased against poor and minority children . . .
> Acting upon these considerations, the principals pressed the superintendent for a change in the original evaluation plan. They secured a compromise in which achievement test scores would not be made public, on a program-by-program basis, until June 1974. They urged that each mini-school be allowed to develop individual measures of its own performance, tailored to the goals and objectives that had been conveyed to parents in the program descriptions.

The auditors found, however, that minischools had not yet provided grade-equivalency data derived from achievement tests or developed individual measures of performance tailored to the goals and objectives conveyed to parents in program descriptions, although the CSPP study (discussed earlier) pointed out that providing parents with such information was essential to an effective voucher program. Therefore, auditors believed that Alum Rock should require minischools to provide information on grade equivalency and individual minischool performance.

CASE 2

The Workplace Inspection Program[3]

Required

1. State the audit objective for this audit.
2. Identify the particular types of evidence—direct or circumstantial—used to come to this conclusion.
3. Identify the source of the evidence used—for example, records evidence, interview evidence, analytical evidence, and observations.

The following is the conclusion to a GAO audit objective, based on particular types of evidence.

Conclusion

- Worksite hazards that could cause death or serious injury were sometimes not identified during inspections. Detecting hazards could be improved if Labor [the Department of Labor] and the states provided better guidance on what to look for during inspections, better-evaluated inspection reports, and better-monitored compliance officers' performance at workplaces.
- Many serious hazards were not being cited

and were probably not being corrected because compliance officers were unaware of the applicability of some standards and believed others were unenforceable. Although Labor was aware of these problems, it had not acted to solve them.

- Required followup inspections to assure elimination of serious hazards sometimes were not made and often, when made, were untimely.
- Citations for some serious hazards were withdrawn, sometimes without good cause or discussion with the compliance officer who had cited the hazard. No review was made to assure that withdrawals were justified. When citations were withdrawn because of inadequate inspections, reinspections were not performed.
- Many serious hazards were cited as nonserious violations. Consequently, followup inspections were not made.
- Requests for additional time to correct hazards were routinely approved without determining that employers tried to correct hazards and that correction efforts would result in compliance with standards.

Evidence: Serious Hazards Not Detected and Citations Not Issued

It is impossible to determine how frequently compliance officers overlook serious hazards. Our review of OSHA monitoring reports of state inspections, inspection case files, and reinspections to determine if prior inspections covered all hazards, showed that compliance officers missed many hazards that could cause serious physical harm or death.

Review of OSHA Monitoring of State Inspections. The Occupational Safety and Health Act of 1970 requires the Secretary of Labor to evaluate continually each State's implementation of its plan. OSHA's monitoring of State safety and health operations includes spot-check inspections and on-the-job evaluations to determine the quality and effectiveness of State-enforcement programs. A spot-check inspection involves reinspecting a worksite inspected by the State. In an on-the-job evaluation, OSHA assesses the State compliance officer's performance during the State inspection.

OSHA's monitoring of the States of Maryland and South Carolina in fiscal year 1976 showed that State compliance officers missed many hazards, as shown below.

The OSHA semiannual monitoring reports for Colorado for the same period did not show the number of hazards missed by state compliance officers. However, our review of 20 randomly selected files for inspections monitored by OSHA showed 72 hazards missed on 13 spot-check inspections and 23 hazards missed on 7 on-the-job evaluations.

Although most hazards missed in the three states were classified as nonserious violations, some of these "nonserious" violations could cause serious harm to employees. For example,

- mechanical power press points of operation were unguarded;
- rip saws, radial saws, and a wood shaper were unguarded;
- a guillotine papercutter was unguarded;
- protective clothing was not provided for handling molten metal; and

	Inspections evaluated	Hazards missed
Spot checks		
Maryland	185	662
South Carolina	143	504
Total	328	1,166
On-the-job evaluations		
Maryland	87	339
South Carolina	81	*
Total	168	339

*The OSHA semiannual monitoring reports did not show the number of hazards missed. However, OSHA noted that the average violations cited per state inspection was 3.3 compared to 11.25 average violations cited in 56 State inspections during which OSHA accompanied the State compliance officers.

- wires were exposed on an open-face electrical box.

Problems in properly classifying serious hazards as serious violations are discussed later.

Review of Inspection-case Files. OSHA and the States maintain inspection-case files. The files include inspection reports, documents, and forms supporting proposed citations, photographs, and inspectors' notes.

We reviewed hundreds of inspection files in five federal and three state offices. Generally, the files did not contain enough information to enable us to determine if all serious hazards had been identified and cited. The files usually showed only information on worksite hazards the compliance officer believed should be cited.* They contained a description of the alleged violations and a designation of the specific standards violated. In many instances, the case files did not contain the compliance officers' original inspection notes.

In some cases, photographs in the file showed that hazards existed, but employers were not cited, and no explanation was evident for why a citation had not been issued. Despite the limited information in the case files, we identified serious hazards that were missed and serious hazards that were identified but not cited. For example:

- In February 1976, an employee in Maryland lost part of a finger while operating a power-press brake. A state compliance officer investigated the accident in April 1976 and cited the employer for violating a standard which requires that the machine point-of-operation be guarded to keep an operator's body out of the danger zone during the operating cycle.

  Since the machine involved in the accident was not operating during the investigation, the compliance officer took pictures of two other operating, unguarded press brakes to document the safety violation that caused the accident. However, the compliance officer did not cite the two unguarded machines because he was investigating an accident and was concerned only with the machine involved in that accident.

- In November 1975, OSHA investigated an accident involving an elevated platform at a sawing operation and cited the platform flooring and guardrail hazards as safety violations. The standards require the employer to maintain a log deck-platform flooring in good repair and to provide standard railing for a platform 4 feet or more above ground level. The sawmill involved had been inspected in April 1975, and 13 nonserious violations, none of which involved the elevated platform, were cited by OSHA.

  The investigation revealed that about 6 weeks after the April 1975 inspection a worker fell through a hole in the platform, sustained serious injuries, and was unable to work for 11 weeks. This worker told the OSHA investigator that he had asked the OSHA compliance officer in April 1975 to have the employer fix the post that was guarding the cutoff saw. He also stated that on several occasions he had lost his balance on the ramp near the saw due to the faulty platform flooring and, at least once, would have fallen into the cutoff saw if he had not grabbed a wire supporting a board that was being used for a saw guard. An OSHA official told us that the company should have been cited for the platform hazards during that inspection.

Reinspection of Worksites. Because we could not determine the extent of serious hazards overlooked by reviewing case files, we accompanied OSHA compliance officers on eight inspections to determine if serious hazards had been missed before. In six, previously overlooked hazards were found. Three of the six involved serious violations. Also, while accompanying OSHA on two followup inspections to determine if hazards cited during previous inspections had been corrected, we noted that additional serious hazards were identified that had been previously missed.

These 10 inspections disclosed 58 previously undetected violations, including 21 that OSHA classified as serious. Some examples of these overlooked hazards include:

- In November 1976, OSHA inspected a manufacturer in Pittsburgh. The compliance

---

* The compliance officer can only recommend citations; the decision to cite is made by the area director.

officer cited the employer for one serious violation—lack of guarding of a power press—and four nonserious violations, including a dirty restroom and lunchroom. We accompanied a different OSHA compliance officer to reinspect this workplace in December 1976. He found four additional power presses, one press brake, and one radial saw without required guarding. Because of the severity of these hazards, the compliance officer cited them as serious violations. Injuries from power presses and press brakes usually result in amputations or crushed bones. The November 1976 inspection record did not mention these hazards. The compliance officer we accompanied determined that the violations existed in November 1976, and he did not know why they had not been cited then. Abatement had not been completed at the end of our review.

- In August 1975, OSHA inspected a manufacturer in Georgia and cited 15 nonserious violations. However, OSHA officials told us that several hazards should have been cited as serious violations. We accompanied a different OSHA compliance officer to reinspect this workplace in November 1976. He found seven press brakes for bending sheets of steel without machine guarding and cited them as serious violations. One of the press brakes was cited as a nonserious violation on the previous inspection. The machines' point of operation was not guarded to keep operators out of the danger zone during operation. The machines were handfed, and employees' hands were within several inches of the bending area. The employer said that these machines were unguarded during the previous inspection. We could not determine why they had not been cited as violations. OSHA conducted a followup inspection in April 1977 and found the employer had corrected the hazards.
- In December 1976, OSHA inspected a Philadelphia area manufacturer. The compliance officer cited the employer for two nonserious violations—lack of guarding on a bandsaw blade and horizontal belts of a drill press. We accompanied a different OSHA compliance officer in reinspecting the same worksite in March 1977. He found an unguarded press brake and an unguarded blade on a radial saw which he cited as serious violations. The December 1976 inspection record did not show these hazards, although the second compliance officer determined that they existed at that time. The employer contested the citation and the penalty. Final settlement was still pending at the end of the review in September 1977.

Improvements Needed in Inspection Program

OSHA has not established management controls to assure that compliance officers look for and cite serious hazards. Preinspection information is not provided on specific plant operations, processes, or equipment that are likely to be present and pose a serious danger to workers at a particular worksite. Compliance officers do not record information in case files on what they looked for and the methods employers used to comply with standards. Major emphasis is placed on assuring that detected violations can be proved, with little emphasis on assuring that all serious hazards are detected.

OSHA has not issued specific instructions or guidelines to field offices requiring them to evaluate compliance officers' performance—either by accompanying them on inspections or visiting recently inspected workplaces. OSHA does monitor State compliance officers' performance by these methods.

Also, some serious hazards were noted but were not cited because

- Poor wording of many standards made enforcement questionable.
- Compliance officers mistakenly believed that some hazards were not covered by standards, and they were not told otherwise.

Planning and Review. In all six States visited, we found a need for (1) better guidance to compliance officers on serious hazards likely to be found at a worksite, and (2) better supervisory review of inspection results.

OSHA procedures recommend that compliance officers "familiarize" themselves with an establishment's operation and determine which OSHA standards are pertinent to the worksite. Information obtained from discussions with compliance officers showed that these procedures were not always followed. Consequently, a compliance officer might not always be properly prepared as to the hazards to look for during inspection.

As previously mentioned, case files

frequently did not include complete information on what potentially serious hazards were likely to be found at the workplace, if and how the compliance officer checked for compliance, and if and how the employer was in compliance.

Supervisory review of inspection results emphasized compliance officers' adequate documentation of violations that were included in proposed citations. Generally, such review covered the adequacy of documentation, applicability of the standard cited, wording of the citation, abatement date, and need for followup inspection. Little attention was directed to assuring that compliance officers adequately checked for compliance with standards for serious hazards likely to be found at a particular worksite.

Because compliance officers are not required to record complete information on what they looked for and supervisory reviews are limited to assuring the adequacy of documentation for proposed citations, little control exists over the quality and completeness of inspections.

Monitoring Inspections. OSHA and the States do not formally monitor the quality of their inspections. OSHA's monitoring of its enforcement program consists of (1) regional planning, (2) field performance evaluation, and (3) field observation. Such monitoring, however, does not evaluate the quality of inspections.

Regional planning helps to gauge the effectiveness of the region's resources' allocation to meet regional program objectives. Field performance evaluation and field observation determine if enforcement procedures are being applied and are timely and if case files include required data. An OSHA official said that none of these monitoring efforts assure that worksite hazards are identified, cited, and corrected.

We believe that OSHA and the States should perform spot checks and on-the-job evaluations of their compliance officers to evaluate the effectiveness of inspection procedures and the performance of individual compliance officers so that appropriate action can be taken on identified weaknesses. Spot-check monitoring visits could provide information on which to judge the quality of inspections. On-the-job evaluations could provide a method for evaluating the adequacy of training, supervision, and enforcement procedures and to determine whether individual compliance officers are capable of performing satisfactory inspections.

Hazards Not Cited When Standards Are Considered Nonexistent. Many hazards were not cited because compliance officers were unaware of the standards covering them. In many instances, OSHA and the states knew of this problem but took no corrective action.

For detected hazards not covered by standards, compliance officers should process an OSHA-9 Form recommending development of new or modified standards. States operating under approved plans use a similar State form. Since September 1971, OSHA and states have received thousands of such forms but generally have done little with them.

According to OSHA Headquarters officials, OSHA-9s received by the Headquarters Office are filed. Although some studies have been made, they said staff resources are directed to higher priority work, and little action has been taken by the Office on the forms. In Colorado and South Carolina completed forms were placed in the case files, and no further action was taken. In Maryland, the forms were reviewed, and significant ones were forwarded to the OSHA Headquarters Office, but no further action was taken by State compliance officials. At the end of fiscal year 1974, Maryland officials stopped sending the forms to OSHA because OSHA had done nothing with the forms.

Studies by OSHA showed that many OSHA-9s covered hazards already included under existing standards. OSHA officials said a 1973 study showed that about one-half of 500 OSHA-9s reviewed were for hazards covered by standards and another study concluded the same year showed similar results. OSHA took no action on these studies.

Our review in the Federal and State offices also showed that some supervisors neither reviewed the OSHA-9s or the State forms submitted to determine if a standard already existed for the hazard noted nor provided necessary feedback to compliance officers. This lack of feedback caused many hazards to be identified but not cited, and some compliance officers have stopped reporting hazards that they believe are not covered by standards.

An example of such a hazard not cited by the compliance officer follows:

> An OSHA compliance officer inspected a construction site in Pittsburgh in January 1976. He observed a gasoline-powered abrasive saw with no guard covering the lower half of the blade. Employees were exposed to the cutting edge of the

saw and to sparks and debris emitted from the blade. The compliance officer did not cite the employer for the hazard because he believed OSHA standards did not cover portable gasoline-powered abrasive saws. He submitted an OSHA-9 in January 1976 to establish a standard for this hazard.

We discussed the OSHA-9 with a safety standards official at OSHA Headquarters. He said that the hazard should have been cited under OSHA Standard 1910.212 covering general requirements for machine guarding. The standard requires all machines to be guarded to protect the operator and other employees in the machine area from hazards such as those created by the point of operation, rotating parts, flying chips, and sparks. The compliance officer who performed the inspection was not told that the hazard could have been cited under an existing standard, and no further action was taken.

Inspectors Not Enforcing Some Safety Standards. Some potentially serious hazards are not cited because they fall under "should" standards that OSHA and state compliance officials consider unenforceable.

In developing its standards, OSHA adopted some national consensus standards already established for various industries. These standards included the word "should" in some instances and the word "shall" in others. The Secretary of Labor promulgated these standards as mandatory for enforcement regardless of the wording.

Officials from Labor's Office of the Solicitor, which renders legal interpretations of standards, told us that they consider "should" standards mandatory and enforceable. However, OSHA compliance and standards-development officials contend such standards are advisory and are thus unenforceable. Compliance officials have not given field offices guidance on citing the "should" standards because they do not agree with this legal interpretation.

We found that OSHA and state compliance officers did not cite some potentially serious hazards because they believed the "should" standards that covered them were not enforceable. For example, an OSHA compliance officer inspected a contractor in Pittsburgh and found that terminal leads on a 260/280 volt welding machine were not protected from accidental contact by employees. Contact with the terminals could result in serious injury or death. He did not cite the violation because the standard provided that terminals "should" be protected from accidental contact by personnel or by metal objects.

An OSHA survey of 11 area offices in February 1977 showed that 6 of them cited "should" standards, and the remaining 5 did not. None of the five area offices we visited cited "should" standards. We also found a similar enforcement problem in State-administered programs. Compliance officials in Colorado and South Carolina did not cite "should" standards because they believed such standards were advisory instead of mandatory. Officials in Maryland cited them but did not assess penalties for violations because they believed they could not penalize an employer for violating a "recommendation" standard.

While OSHA has been aware of the enforcement problem on "should" standards, OSHA has been unable to resolve it. Hazards involving "should" standards will continue unless OSHA directs Federal and State compliance officials to enforce such standards.

CHAPTER 9

Understanding Working Papers

After you have read this chapter, studied the review questions, and worked through the cases, you will understand:

- The various reasons for preparing working papers.
- The best means of recording and analyzing evidence in the working papers.
- The way to use working papers and working-paper summaries in developing a report.

What Working Papers Are

Working papers are the records of the information obtained and the evidence gathered during the examination on the audit objective. For the preliminary survey, most of the information obtained and placed in the working papers is descriptive. By analyzing this descriptive information, the auditor determines that some of it could be evidence on all three elements—criteria, causes, and effects—of the tentative objective. However, if the auditor obtains evidence on all three elements of the tentative objective during the preliminary survey, he would not have to go through another phase to obtain evidence, since the working papers would show what information has been obtained, what information has been considered evidence, and what additional evidence is needed to convert the tentative objective to a firm objective.

The evidence gathered during the preliminary survey on the tentative objective is relevant and material, but at this point it is not necessarily sufficient or competent. In the phase pertaining to the review and testing of management and internal control, all that is needed is enough evidence to convince the auditor to continue the examination; he does not need enough to come to a conclusion on the objective, only enough to convince himself that his objective is proper. And he also needs, in this phase, to obtain sufficient evidence to determine whether any evidence he obtains from the system is competent. To determine how reliable the evidence is, the auditor must gather sufficient relevant, material, and competent evidence from the system to show that reliability.

The working papers on the review and testing of management controls for an M-audit or a P-audit must show that the auditor obtained relevant and material evidence from the management control system on two objectives: (1) to determine the acceptability and appropriateness of the tentative audit objective, and (2) to determine the reliability of the information from within the organization's management control system. As Chapter 7 emphasized, much of the information on management control often comes from outside of the organization as well as inside. For example, if the auditor is determining the standards for the usage of airplane tires for the Air Force, he might contact the commercial airlines as one place that has the same type of activity and therefore might have an acceptable standard for airplane tire usage. He must at the same time show the competency of the commercial airline information used as evidence. However, he would not obtain this information from internal management controls. Often, the evidence recorded in working papers from within the organization is on causes. Thus, the review of the internal management control system can determine how reliable or competent the evidence is.

Only when the auditor tests the system of management control will he know that acceptable policies have been set or not set, that the policies have been appropriately or inappropriately carried out, or that there is some acceptable means of evaluating the actions against the policies. Furthermore, only when he has this information recorded in the working papers will the auditor be able to summarize the information and evidence to assure himself that the objective is a good one and that he can obtain reliable information from within the organization, or that he must also go outside to obtain additional information.

The Purposes of Working Papers

Working papers for the detailed examination must show that sufficient evidence has been obtained on the audit objective for the auditor to come to an opinion or conclusion on that objective. The working papers must also show that the evidence is relevant, material, and competent, as defined in Chapter 8. The information and evidence from the working papers is further used both to prepare the report and to serve as a record in case of litigation either against the client or against the auditor. Likewise, the information in the working papers becomes the best defense available whenever the professional integrity of the auditor is questioned.

Working papers, needless to say, must be in written form. Since the human memory tends to forget important events, any information gathered during each of the phases of the examination should be put immediately into writing. Whether the information is written in pencil, pen, or typewriter makes no difference as long as it is neat, legible, concise, well written, and clearly stated. Information that is illegible, poorly stated, rambling, and irrelevant is almost as bad as no information at all.

The most important single process in an audit is the development of the objective through the detailed examination in order to come to a conclusion to report to a third party. The conclusion should be based on information and evidence in the working papers and it should be accurate.

Some important considerations the auditor should make when gathering evidence on an objective, analyzing that evidence, recording the evidence in his working papers, and coming to a proper conclusion on his audit objective are the following:

1. He must thoroughly develop the subject so that he can clearly and convincingly demonstrate to others the reasons for his conclusions.
2. He should consider the conditions at the time the happenings took place rather than at the time he is making the audit.
3. He should remember that the burden of proof is on the auditor and not on the persons being audited.
4. He should remember that even he is not perfect and therefore he should not expect perfection from others. Improvements in performance do not mean perfection. He should reflect mature and realistic judgment on the findings he makes.

5. He should subject his potential conclusion to others for critical analysis for flaws and illogical reasoning before considering it as a final conclusion. Reviews by other auditors may protect him from a serious mistake in his audit work or reasoning.
6. He must understand that he will use newer and different techniques for evidence gathering than he has previously learned. One of the more important in performance audits is interviewing; Chapter 13 gives some useful approaches to this subject. In addition, the auditor may use consultants in areas where his expertise is limited. Mathematical methods are also an important consideration for most P-audits and these techniques are discussed in Chapter 15.

The main purposes of working papers, then, are:

1. To provide a record of information and evidence on the objective of each phase of the examination.
2. To provide a record of evidence on the competency of the evidence gathered on the audit objective.
3. To provide the basis for:
   a. the audit program for the review and testing of management control from the preliminary survey working papers,
   b. the audit program for the detailed examination from the review and testing of management control working papers, and,
   c. the final report from the detailed examination working papers.

Other purposes of working papers are to provide a tool for the supervisor to manage the assignment, to provide a tool for the auditor to use in making the audit, to provide a record for future use, to provide a source of teaching material for new auditors, and to provide a protection against questioning the integrity of the auditor.

Working Papers as a Record of Evidence on the Objective

Working papers provide a record of information and evidence obtained and developed in support of the conclusion on the audit objective. As a record, the most reliable evidence is that which is recorded as soon as it is observed, heard, or analyzed. The auditor should never defer this recording until the report phase.

An audit contemplates that when it is completed the results will be reported to a third party. Adequately developing a finding requires that the auditor accumulate all appropriate information necessary for proper reporting. If he knows that he is to report on his conclusions at the time he is developing his audit objective and gathering and analyzing evidence on the objective, the auditor will come out with a better report.

When the auditor has established a firm audit objective on an apparent weakness or deficiency in the manner in which an operation or program is carried out, and has constructed an audit program for the development of the audit, he should then properly and promptly develop and record all pertinent evidence and information concerning the audit objective. The process for carrying out this development can be considered in terms of criteria, causes, and effects, as presented in Chapter 2.

In Terms of Criteria   Acceptable criteria can be those established by law, regulations, policy, or desirable practice. If no acceptable criteria have been established, the auditor will have to develop criteria of his own. It should make no difference to the performance auditor whether the criteria are established or whether he has to gather evidence to develop his own, although with established criteria, it is of course easier for the auditor to gather and record evidence. To develop his own, he often has to gather more evidence than he would with established criteria.

The process of developing the finding includes comparing actual operations with the criteria. It includes comparing actual operations with laws, regulations, performance standards, operating budgets, or an appropriately developed standard. The auditor, moreover, should reach agreement with the appropriate officials concerning the acceptability of the standard he is using.

In Terms of Causes

If the auditor is to audit properly, report effectively, and prepare appropriate recommendations, he must identify and understand the causes of the deficiency in the operations or program.

Causes, as we stated in Chapter 2, pertain to the actions of people. The auditor needs to identify persons responsible for the operations, as well as persons at higher levels of responsibility who should be controlling the operations or program. Usually, the most important cause is a management control weakness that permitted the deficiency in the activity or program to occur. Effective management control over operations or programs requires clear assignment of responsibility, with appropriate authority to carry it out.

By identifying the actions of persons who caused the deficiency, the auditor can find out why the deficiency occurred, why it continued, and whether internal procedures have been established to prevent the continuation of the deficiency. And, the cause of one deficiency may lead to the causes of other deficiencies.

Since causes pertain to people, the auditor should allow the people who may be adversely affected to make written or oral comments concerning his conclusions or recommendations before the report is released to the third party. These comments should be included as evidence, to the extent appropriate, in the final report.

In Terms of Effects

Effects can often be measured in terms of financial loss. However, the inability of the auditor to measure or estimate the financial loss is no reason for the auditor not to report on the deficiency or ineffectiveness of the program. Unsafe buildings, inadequate health care, polluted streams, if significant, are just as important to report as dollar loss.

While immediate loss or results are important, just as important are long-range results. Also, potential losses are as important as real losses. When the significance of the deficiency or the ineffectiveness is represented by a potential loss, the auditor should bring out this fact clearly and convincingly.

As a general rule, the auditor should state the effects as a dollar value. When unable to, however, he should state the probable loss, or possible loss of one kind or another. The auditor should also consider whether the deficiency is widespread or an isolated instance. The level of reporting is often determined by the significance of the finding.

In Terms of Recommendations

The auditor's responsibility should be discharged when he brings the results of his audit to responsible officials. Management should then assume responsibility for instituting corrective action or preventive measures. However, the auditor should always be in a good position to make recommendations to the responsible officials for correcting deficiencies or preventing their recurrence.

Recording Evidence in Working Papers

Evidence almost always comes in individual pieces. Interviews, for instance, are usually held with one person at a time; records observation is that of a particular record. To organize the evidence properly, therefore, a separate sheet of paper should be used for each item on each objective or subobjective.

Ordinarily, a separate classification and indexing system must be developed specifically for each audit, and the auditor should always remember the purpose of evidence: to support the opinion or conclusion on the primary audit objective. In an M-audit or a P-audit, the information on criteria, causes, and effects must be specifically shown or the auditor would be unable to tell exactly what type of audit he is making, or what activity he is evaluating.

The following exhibits, Figure 9.1 and Figure 9.2, show the organization of working papers for an M-audit and a P-audit.

Notice that the organization of the evidence in the illustrated working papers follows a logical order. The final product, a summary showing the conclusion or opinion, should always be on the top of the papers—that is, the criteria, with the evidence under them; the effects, with the evidence under them; and the causes, with all of their evidential detail, under them.

Furthermore, for each major objective or subobjective, a summary schedule is prepared. This brings together the conclusion on the objective with the criteria, the causes, and the effects of the objective, and includes the evidence summarized for each element. Each summary, then, should state somewhere just what the objective is. Many major public accounting firms are now requiring that the auditor state his objective for each working paper he prepares. Note that he would then have a reason for each piece of paper in his files; and also, he would have cause to reflect on the reason for preparing each. For example, one objective seldom shown for obtaining a direct bank confirmation is to confirm independently from the bank (causes) that the bank statement is in exact agreement (effects) with the amount shown on the confirmation form (criteria).

Working Papers as a Record of Competency of Evidence

As we have learned, in an M-audit and a P-audit much of the information comes from outside of the organization. The competency of such audit evidence is often built into the way a statement is made about the interview, the records examined, or the people or things observed. For example, let us consider the competency of a statement being used as evidence on an agency's policy, which had been adopted but not printed. The statement as evidence, would be made as follows:

> At 3:00 P.M. on January 21, 1977, in his office, Room 555, Executive Office Building, Mr. John Jones, the general counsel of Zed Agency, told me in the presence of Harry Smith, my senior assistant, that Zed Agency's executive order #123, pertaining to the legal requirement for purchasing advertising, was adopted by the agency on January 5, 1977. He gave me a copy of order 123, which reads as follows: (Quote whatever the order says). He also said that the order was sent throughout the office on January 6, and went into effect on January 10, 1977. He also gave me a copy of the transmitted memo, which reads as follows: (Quote what the memo says).

166 / *Making the Detailed Examination*

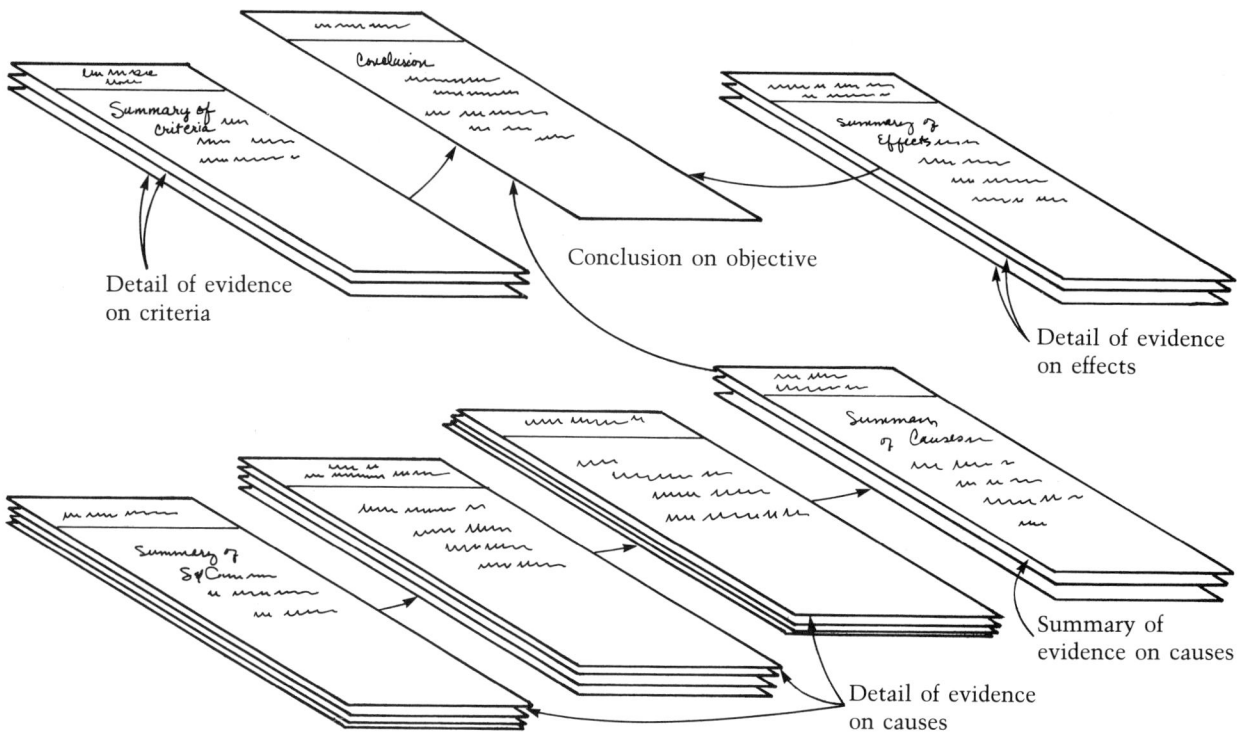

Figure 9.1 Illustration of organization of working papers — an M-audit

From the way the interview memo is written, you can see that the information comes from a reliable source and is competent. Often, however, in obtaining evidence from interviews, it is easy to misinterpret what the interviewee says and means. In order to assure himself that the statement he writes up as evidence is competent, the auditor should ask the interviewee to read the record, sign or initial it, and date the memo. (Of course, the interview must be properly planned: If it takes two or three visits to obtain the information from the interviewee, then the different dates and statements made may bring about some question in the mind of a reviewer as to the reliability of that information.)

If a person will not sign an interview memorandum, then the auditor should, in the presence of another person informally read the memo to the interviewee. They both should sign the document as being what was read to the interviewee with any corrections the interviewee may want made.

To assure the competency of the evidence the auditor obtains from records, he should state exactly where and when the information was obtained. Often it is easy to obtain a photocopy of the record so that there will be no question as to the accuracy of transcribing. However, the auditor should in all cases assure himself that the document is exactly the same as the original.

Auditors have developed special signs, called *tick marks,* to signify the competency of the evidence they obtain during a detailed examination. These signs—such as a check (√), a reverse check (\\), a double or triple mark on the stem of the check (≠), a dot or period (.), an (×), a circle (○), or any of many other types of signals—can be used in one or many colors to signify different meanings. The meaning of each tick mark may be perfectly clear to the auditor when he originally uses them, but he should under all circumstances prepare a list of the specific meanings wherever they are used, as shown in the example below.

√—Confirmation notice sent
\\—Confirmation advice received

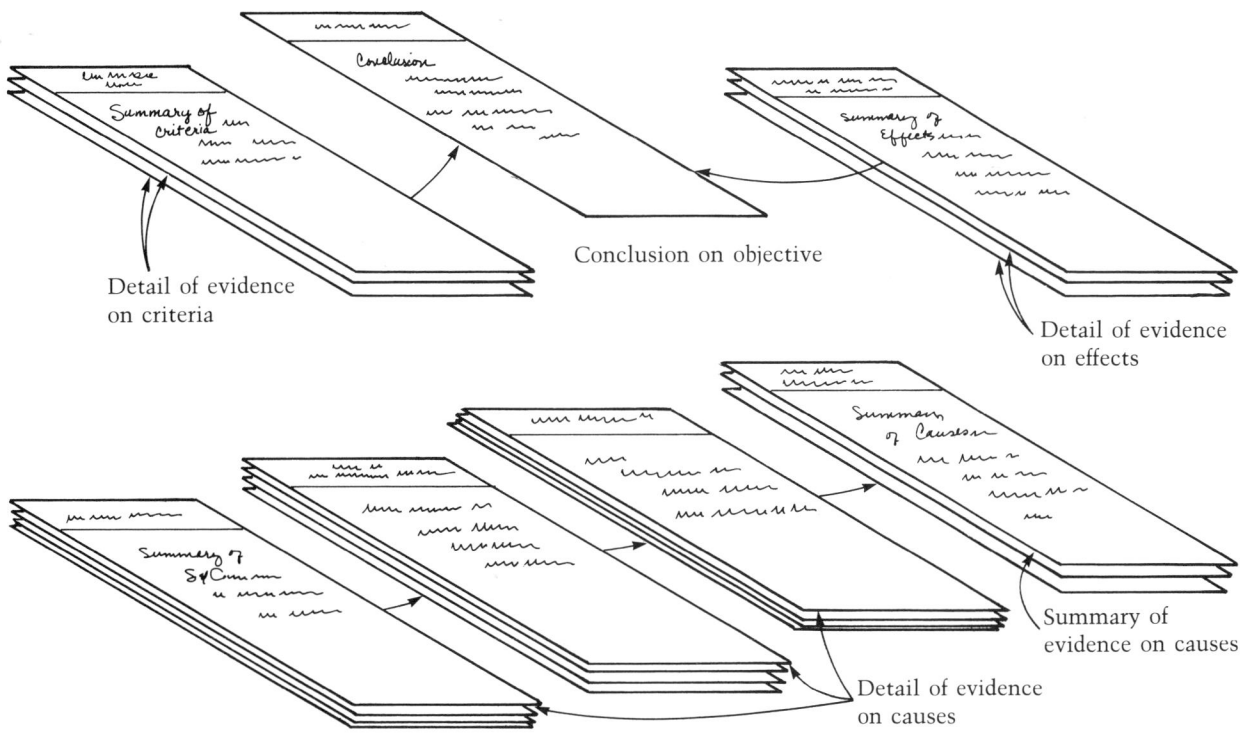

Figure 9.2 Illustration of organization of working papers — a P-audit

· —Checked from trial balance to ledger account
×—Personally counted petty cash
o—Totaled

As for observations and their competency as evidence, since the human mind often plays tricks, it is best that two people see the same thing. Also, where possible, the use of modern photography allows the auditor to obtain pictures of what he has observed. If there is any possibility of the information being used in legal cases, the auditor should follow the picture from the taking, to the developing, to the printing, and even then retain all copies, including the negative. And a final point worth noting is that graphs and charts often bring out the quality of the information better than the written or table detail. In all tables, graphs, and charts, the auditor should always show the source of the information.

Working Papers as the Basis for the Report

When the auditor comes to a conclusion on the audit objective, he should have in the working papers all of the evidence he needs to support his opinion or conclusion. The opinion or conclusion on the audit objective, with the evidence and any background data needed, becomes the basis for the report.

In an M-audit and a P-audit, the auditor should organize the working papers into such a form that the conclusion, with evidence to support it, is shown in the working papers. Most performance auditors use the draft report as the final step in the working papers. All that has to be done then is to have a supervisory auditor and an editor review the report before the final typing and presentation to the third party.

Auditors should remember that some reviewers actually change the objective of the audit during the review process. This should never be done: A change in the objective would obviously change the type of evidence required.

There is nothing, of course, that says an audit objective cannot be changed; but the change should be made while the audit is in progress, not after it is completed.

There is a further point to be made here on the report: Many audit managers complain of the inability of auditors to write clearly, logically, and concisely. Our experience indicates, however, that it is not a lack of writing skills that produces poor results: It is usually the inability of the auditor to do a good job of auditing—to state an appropriate audit objective; to gather, summarize, and evaluate the evidence on that objective; and to come to the proper conclusion on the objective. The report is rather easy to write if the audit and the working papers have been properly done.

Other Uses of Working Papers

While the primary purpose of working papers is related to the recording of evidence, there are many other valuable uses. The standards for examination demand that the subordinate is properly supervised. Each working paper should be properly and adequately reviewed by the supervisor to determine whether the assistant knows the objective, is obtaining the proper information and recording it properly, and coming to the right conclusion.

Coming to a conclusion on an objective is not an absolute science. The background and experience of the auditor often lead him to a conclusion different from that of another auditor, even though they have the same evidence. This is seen particularly in legal cases, when the prosecution and defense conclusions are quite different from each other and even from those of the judge or jury.

The information in the working papers can be invaluable to the new auditor in learning what results are expected from certain types of information, and also in showing him the meaning of relevancy, competency, and materiality. No textbook, for instance, can adequately define materiality; yet one or two illustrations from working papers easily impress on the auditor the particular meaning of this term in auditing.

We have referred several times to permanent files and current files. The auditor needs to retain much information in permanent files as a record for future use. Some of this information, along with that from discussion with the client, can be used as evidence to determine exactly what type of audit objective the auditor will use in his current examination. In M-audits and P-audits, much of the information in permanent files only needs updating to round out a preliminary survey. Also, a trained auditor can often review these permanent files and come up with a tentative audit objective without even going out of the office.

Finally, working papers can be an invaluable tool for on-the-job-training and classroom training. Most of the usage of working papers for training is in practicing firms; yet they would be extremely valuable, as situational cases, for university education and research.

REVIEW QUESTIONS

1. Briefly describe auditor's working papers and the types of information that should be included in them. (See pp. 161–62.)

2. Work papers are the records of the information obtained and the evidence gathered on the audit objective during the examination. Discuss what information the auditor would include in his work papers on his review and testing of management controls. (See pp. 161–62.)

3. In developing evidence in accordance with his program for the performance audit, list six important considerations the auditor should make. Discuss each consideration briefly. (See pp. 162–63.)

4. The auditor normally records all information obtained in the detailed examination in his working papers. Discuss the purposes of working papers. (See p. 163.)

5. Why must information and evidence on the criteria, causes, and effects of a performance audit be specifically shown? (See pp. 163–64.)

6. Properly recording information and evidence in the working papers is an important requirement. Describe some of the important considerations in organizing working papers. (See p. 165.)

7. To assure the competency of evidence obtained from records, the auditor should state exactly where and when the information was obtained. What is the importance of tick marks in showing competency of evidence in an M-audit or a P-audit? (See pp. 166–67.)

8. The opinion or conclusion on the audit objective, along with the evidence and any background data needed, becomes the basis for the report. How can the auditor organize his working papers to aid in the preparation of the reports for M-audits or P-audits? (See pp. 165, 167–68.)

9. The primary purpose of working papers is to record the evidence obtained during the audit. Discuss some other uses for the auditor's working papers. (See p. 168.)

10. The auditor needs to retain a great deal of information from his current files in the permanent files of his working papers. How can an auditor use his permanent file information in an audit for the same organization but for different activities? (See p. 168.)

CASE 1

The City Garage: Audit Working Papers for an M-audit

Required

Reread Case 1 in Chapter 3, pp. 46–48, and then complete the following:

1. Write up in working-paper form the analytical evidence that the auditor would need to show that there was a significant effect, Audit Scenario 3.
2. Write up in working-paper form a summary of all information used as evidence on the criteria of the objective of the case.

CASE 2

The Nursing Homes: Audit Working Papers for a P-audit

Required

Reread Case 2 in Chapter 3, pp. 49–59, and then complete the following:

1. Explain how you would arrange, in working-paper form, the material in the Preliminary Information section of this case.
2. In summary form, as you would place it in a working paper, bring together all the evidence concerning the criteria of the audit objective.
3. Prepare the summary working paper for the entire audit of this case. Organize your summary in terms of criteria, causes, and effects.

CHAPTER 10

Illustrative Working Papers: The Detailed Examination for a Management Audit

After you have read this chapter, studied the review questions, and worked through the cases, you will understand:

- The basic principles and practices for making an M-audit.
- How to gather evidence for an M-audit in accordance with the audit program.
- How to prepare working papers in accordance with policies suggested by your organization or with those suggested in the chapter.
- How to summarize working papers into properly prepared summaries that can be used as the basis for the report.

When the auditor reaches the detailed examination phase, he should have his audit objective well in mind and well stated, because in an M-audit, each audit deals with a different subject matter so that there is seldom a repetitive audit. Most M-audits, in fact, are one-time audits; therefore, no such comparability of data is found among M-audits as is found among financial-statement audits. The auditor must accept the exciting concept that the universe for determining objectives and gathering evidence for performance audits is almost limitless.

Conceptually, however, gathering evidence on the objective, recording that evidence, analyzing it, coming to a conclusion, and reporting the results is basically the same for all types of audits, even though the procedures for gathering and analyzing evidence are quite different. This chapter will illustrate the gathering of evidence for the detailed examination of an M-audit, along with the recording of that evidence in the working papers. No such working-paper technique as debits and credits is available for performance-audit working papers. Gathering quantitative information does, however, have a logical base, and this is demonstrated in the working papers herein presented. Most large audit organizations have particular policies pertaining to working papers, as is so in our selected case, and these will be given as a base for illustrating specific characteristics of working papers.

GAO Standards for Work-paper Preparation

Since these illustrative working papers were gathered by GAO auditors, they follow the particular standards of that organization, as follows.[1]

1. Completeness and Accuracy

Working papers must be complete and accurate in order to provide proper support for conclusions and recommendations and to enable demonstration of the nature and scope of the examination work, when necessary.

2. Clarity and Understandability

Working papers should be clear and understandable without supplementary oral explanations. The information they reveal should be clear, complete, and yet concise. Anyone using the working papers should be able to readily determine their purpose, scope of the work done, and the staff member's conclusions. Conciseness is important but clarity and completeness should not be sacrificed just to save time or paper.

3. Legibility and Neatness

Working papers must be legible and as neat as practicable. Otherwise, time will be wasted in reviewing them, and in preparing and referencing reports. Sloppy working papers may lose their worth as evidence. Crowding and writing between lines should be avoided by anticipating space needs and arrangement before writing.

4. Relevance

The information contained in working papers should be restricted to matters that are materially important, relevant, and useful with reference to the objectives established for the assignment. There is no substitute for a working understanding of the specific objectives of the audit, the reasons for performing a specific task, and their relation to approved objectives. This knowledge comes from well-planned and well-organized work programs and effective instructions by supervisors.

The practice of having all working papers contain a clear statement of purpose is very helpful in assuring that information accumulated is properly tied to audit objectives and reporting.

5. Avoidance of Excessive Detail

Avoid excessive detail in working papers. For example, involved descriptions of procedures should not ordinarily be necessary. Summaries and brief descriptions of audit steps performed, extent of work, and findings and conclusions are much more important and informative.

6. Review of Work Papers

A primary standard applicable to all audit work is that the evidence of work performed is to be reviewed by a responsible supervisor. The review of all working papers by audit seniors and supervisors and their satisfaction with the work performed and agreement with the conclusions recorded should be signified by their name on each worksheet or group of worksheets. Questions arising from these reviews and answers thereto should be included with each group or file of working papers.

In the review of working papers, due regard must be given to such factors as:

a) Compliance with the work program and any specific instructions given.
b) Accuracy, reliability, and adequacy of the work performed and the acceptability of the related working papers as evidence of such work and the results achieved.
c) Validity and reasonableness of conclusions reached.
d) Nature and extent of review by the organization audited and their consideration of the findings and conclusions.

Working papers should be reviewed by the site supervisors promptly after performance of the work. Prompt review permits efficient continuation of the work to clear up on open questions. It also avoids the disruption caused by reviewing work on problems after the staff members involved have been reassigned for work on other phases of the assignment.

7. Other Standards

a) Working papers may be prepared with pencil or pen. Pencil is preferable for schedules containing figures that might be changed. Narrative comments and permanent file memoranda and schedules are neater and more legible when written in ink or typed.

b) To save time, handwritten copy work from reference material should be minimized by using stenographic assistance, extra copies of printed matter, or available reproducing equipment. However, care must be exercised to assure that the availability of such equipment does not result in making more copies than are actually needed.

c) Sources of information appearing on a worksheet should be clearly and specifically identified. Where a document is prepared by others, the worksheet should state why and by whom the document was prepared, if not apparent from the document itself.

d) A legend for all tick marks or symbols used to denote the work done or sources of information should appear on each worksheet or top worksheet of a group.

e) To facilitate later insertions and revisions and improve legibility, all narrative comments in the working papers should be double- or even triple-spaced.

f) To the extent practicable, worksheets should be cross-referenced to other related working papers. Also, they should be cross-referenced to the work program. Effective cross-referencing often reduces the need for duplication of data.

g) To avoid confusion and complications in filing, only one subject generally should be dealt with on a worksheet.

h) Worksheets should be prepared on one side only. If it is absolutely necessary to write on the back, make an appropriate cross-reference and write the information so that the reader does not have to turn the file upside down to read it.

i) Extra copies of material such as superseded report drafts and work programs should not be kept in working paper files. If they are, the reasons for keeping them should be stated in the file.

j) The purpose of each working paper should be clearly stated either in the working paper or by reference to the program.

k) The cover of each file should show clearly such identification as:

- Assignment name.
- Name and location of organization audited.
- Subject matter.
- Audit period or other applicable date.
- Responsible office.

l) A simple system of indexing should be established for each audit.

The Importance of Summaries

Since the summary is such an important part of the working papers and the summaries given in the illustrative working papers follow GAO standards, the following policy regarding summaries is given, with minor and appropriate adaptations.[2]

Preparation of Summaries

The nature and result of the work on each segment of an assignment should, as a matter of systematic operation and good workmanship, be summarized in a clear and concise manner in the working papers. A segment may be considered as referring to a primary objective or subobjective of the audit.

Audits result in the accumulation of numerous working papers containing a variety of information in various forms—for example, copies of laws, policies and procedures, correspondence, records of interviews, and an assortment of charts and schedules—relating to one or more phases of an assignment. Although this information may be interesting, useful, and pertinent, it is of little value unless analyzed, logically organized and collated, and interrelated. In most cases, this can be accomplished most effectively through the preparation of working paper summaries.

The purpose of these summaries, as the name implies, is to sum up in a clear, concise, and convincing manner and to bring to the forefront the essence of the work performed, the results achieved, the conclusions reached, and any recommendations, as reflected in the supporting working papers.

Properly conceived and tailored to the peculiar circumstances of an assignment, working-paper summaries have a very important and special place in audit work. Such summaries serve two fundamental and interrelated purposes:

1. They force a timely and critical analysis of the evidence obtained and work done, help identify additional requirements, and serve as a basis for decisions as to the disposition of the results of the work.
2. They make possible the drafting of the report as an integral part of the fieldwork.

Summaries are also beneficial in that:

- in tying together groups of working papers relating to a particular point, they provide an orderly and logical flow to the papers and facilitate supervisory or other reviews of particular work segments.
- when appropriately indexed and cross-referenced, they become the focal point in the working papers for any particular work segment and provide a mechanical control over the underlying working papers. Depending upon their depth and coverage, they can also be useful in resolving any later questions that may present themselves after completion of the audit.
- they afford newer staff members opportunities to become acquainted with the exactness and preciseness required in the analysis of information and in the clarity, conciseness, readability, and organization required in the preparation of draft reports. Furthermore summaries, in many instances, present the underlying rationale and the original thinking leading to positions taken in reports. Therefore, the experience of preparing them provides very valuable training for staff members in developing analytical and writing skills.

Because of the diverse nature and scope of management and program audits, as contrasted to financial statement examinations, there is a need for flexibility in the design and preparation of summaries. Each summary should be tailormade to the needs of the work segment. A summary should be recognized as an internal working tool—a means to an end rather than an end in itself. It should be designed to assist the auditor in the orderly and timely progression and completion of his audit assignments. Therefore, the precise form and content of summaries must be left to his discretion. However, the following paragraphs outline some of the concepts that should be considered in preparing summaries.

In preparing audit programs and otherwise planning for an assignment, the auditor should recognize the need for preparing suitable summaries of individual segments or groups of segments of work performed. From time to time during an audit, he should insure that such summaries are compatible with and lend themselves to the ultimate purpose—that of preparing the report draft—and adjust the plan as appropriate on the basis of the information developed. The design and preparation of meaningful and useful summaries that meet this objective is an art which an auditor should strive to develop and refine.

The basic elements of an audit summary are as follows:

1. *Objective*—This section should provide a clear statement of the purpose of the audit work, an explanation of why it was undertaken, and what the audit is trying to accomplish.
2. *Work performed*—This section should state concisely what has been done relative to what was intended. If certain work that was intended was not done, this fact should be set out with the reasons therefor.
3. *Results achieved*—This section should provide a factual summary of the evidence obtained in relation to the objective. It should not include conclusions. The evidence itself should be presented as a factual summary thereof, rather than the conclusions the auditor has drawn from the facts. This section of the summary should contain the evidence, not an interpretation of it.
4. *Conclusions*—Although frequently apparent from the evidence, conclusions should be stated in relation to the objectives. The rationale for the conclusions should be presented and be relatable to the work performed and results obtained or information developed.
5. *Recommendations*—Any recommendations for corrective action should follow logically.

The narrative portions of summaries should be written with due regard to the standards of well written English composition. Carelessly prepared summaries should not be accepted. They should be reworked (by the assigned staff member) until they are satisfactory. At the same time, summaries do not constitute reports, are not directed to outsiders or laymen, and therefore need not be prepared with the same attention to polished language, style, and detailed explanation of terms and concepts necessary for reports going to a third party. It will be necessary, however, to attempt to strike a balance whereby summaries need not be up to formal report standards in terms of literary merit yet serve their purposes as to clarity, essentiality, and the underlying bases for the report.

When appropriate, sections of the summary need not be in strict narrative form. For example, where the staff member is summarizing a series of facts, it would be acceptable to say: "Mr. X (title) told us: 1. _____ , 2. _____ , and 3. _____ ," rather than going through the exercise of writing: "Mr. X told us _____ . He also said _____ . Then he said _____ ." Grammatical polish is less important, in a summary, than a clear statement of the facts.

The information contained in the summary should include identification of its source—such as "We were informed by Mr. X (title)" or "The flight log for aircraft 102 showed." This technique provides precise knowledge of the nature and source of the information and thus an indication of the probable competency of the evidence.

176 / *Making the Detailed Examination*

Levels of Summaries

There are essentially two levels of summaries:

Level I—Basic underlying summaries (subobjective summaries) tying together related pieces of information in the working papers—normally confined to a subobjective or some such aspect of a subject.

Level II—Summaries resulting from a critical analysis of information contained in Level I summaries and other information, as appropriate, to tie together an audit conclusion on the primary objective.

Level I summaries are basic, and should ordinarily be the most common summaries in the working papers. They represent a tying together of all the related items of evidence—whenever a logical need arises in working papers—to fulfill a particular work step, to support a basic point, or to clarify or complete a subobjective assignment. Such summaries should include the significant information developed in the audit work and needed to support the conclusion reached. For a relatively simple assignment, Level I summaries may be all that are required.

As a general rule, these summaries are narrative presentations marshalling evidence, in its most basic form, and stating the conclusions justified by the evidence. They should not be lengthy dissertations involving several or many complex issues as they are more manageable and meaningful when confined to one basic point or aspect of an audit. They should treat in appropriate depth all pertinent facts, deal with pro and con positions, and lead to a convincing and enduring conclusion on the subject matter. Such summaries should remain with the working papers as demonstrative evidence for later referral or follow-up and may be used as a basis for a position or statement in the report draft.

The Level II summary, stemming logically from a foundation of Level I summaries, brings together all essential information relating to the primary audit objective. This type of summary represents the final effort to tie together—in the working papers—all related evidence and the related conclusions and recommendations for a particular audit objective.

Although no specific format or style is prescribed for such a summary, it should lend itself, to the maximum extent appropriate, to the preparation of the overall report draft. The summarization and report drafting should be an inseparable function at this stage, enabling the timely and efficient report drafting as a normal part of field work.

In effect, the report draft is the ultimate summary. It should be the most refined, succinct, and convincing presentation of all. With a foundation of well-prepared, lower-level summaries, the report drafting should be a smooth and logical writing process.

Suggestions for Preparation

The writer and reviewer should critically analyze summaries to insure that all significant areas have been covered and that data needed for effective report presentation is complete and cross-referenced to the underlying details and that the logic followed is sound. All data gaps and inconsistencies in the evidence should be explored, revised, or explained, as appropriate.

Among other things, the writer and reviewer should check for:

- Consideration of internal audit coverage in the area.
- Favorable comments where warranted.
- Avoidance of exaggeration, overly categorical positions, overreaching on technical subjects, overly broad endorsement, and presentation of opinions as facts.

- Consideration of corrective action needed.
- Resolution of legal issues.
- Need for perspective.

Note sentence structure, paragraph usage, flow, etc.—if any part does not fairly and convincingly present the facts, it should be reworked.

Supervisors should remember that major reporting problems frequently stem from the manner in which underlying evidence in the working papers is analyzed and summarized. They should insure orderly and timely progress, carefully review such summaries, and instill a need for compliance with the highest practicable standards of preparation.

Illustrative Working Papers: The Case of the Overseas Flights— The Detailed Examination

These illustrative working papers are organized assuming that the work has been completed and the papers are ready for review and development of the report. A draft report has not been prepared at this stage of the audit. However, summaries of the overall audit have been made. As background for the detailed examination, reread "The Case of the Overseas Flights," Chapter 5, pp. 81–85.

When an auditor starts on an M-audit, the only basis he has for organizing his working papers is his audit objective, which in this case was stated as follows on p. 83:

> Would the Department of Defense by diverting passengers (causes) from charter flights operated by U.S. international air carriers to regularly scheduled flights of the same carriers and at the charter flight rate (criteria), (1) reduce annual operating costs by several millions of dollars, (2) save a great many millions of gallons of jet fuel, (3) reduce annual balance of payments by as much as the fuel would cost if it had to be procured overseas, and (4) improve the financially ailing condition of the U.S. international airlines by many millions of dollars (effects)?

The organization of the working papers around the criteria and the causes will not be illustrated, since sufficient evidence has been shown in the preliminary phases to affirm that the criteria have been tried and proved acceptable.

In many audits, very little work has to be done on either the criteria or the causes during the detailed-examination phase. Once they are accepted—usually during the review and testing of management control phase—the major effort must then be in gathering evidence to prove the significance of the effects. That is the case in this illustration: Little additional evidence must be obtained on the criteria and the causes, but the majority of the evidence will have to be gathered on the effects.

For example, in considering causes, various levels of the DOD along with the CAB, which sets the rate structure, could be the major causes for the DOD's failure to realize savings by diverting passengers from one type of flight to another. If the airlines were not in agreement with the change, they also could be one of the causes.

Since the effects are the principal worry to the auditors in this case, then, our illustrative working papers should be organized around them. Four different possible effects are stated in the objective: (1) reduce annual operating costs by several millions of dollars, (2) save a great many millions of gallons of jet fuel, (3) reduce annual balance of payments by as much as the fuel bought overseas would have cost, and (4) improve the financially ailing condition of the U.S. international airlines by many millions of dollars.

Because we are considering this illustration after the gathering of the evidence, we will show the working papers in the order they would be presented to a supervisor—a Level II summary first; the information refers back to the particular work paper from which the original information came.

Example: Level II Summary

Objective

The objective of this examination was to determine whether the Department of Defense would significantly reduce annual operating costs, save a substantial amount of jet fuel, reduce by a significant amount the annual balance of payments by reducing the amount of fuel purchased overseas, and improve the ailing financial condition of the U.S. international airlines by using regularly scheduled flights of the same air carriers rather than using chartered flights.

Work Performed

Information was obtained from the three international air carriers (TWA, PAA, and NWA), as well as from the Military Airlift Command at Scott AFB, Illinois, and the 21st and 22nd Air Forces at McGuire AFB, New Jersey, and Travis AFB, California. Use of regularly scheduled flights is designated as Category Y flights. Use of charter flights is designated as Category B flights.

Conclusion on Objective

Rerouting DOD passengers from chartered to scheduled overseas flights by U.S. international air carriers that fly parallel routes could (1) save about 48 million gallons of jet fuel annually (Q–1/12–1,2*), (2) reduce annual costs to DOD by about $3.5 million through better utilization of aircraft seats (Q–1/12–3), (3) improve balance of payments to the extent jet fuel is procured from foreign sources (work papers not shown), and (4) allow the financially ailing U.S. international air carriers to reduce their annual expenses by about $38 million (Q–1/12–4,5).

These savings could be accomplished by converting selected Category B flights on 13 channels, which parallel commercial overseas routes, to a Category Y system (Q–1/12–1–5). Briefly, the Category Y concept calls for converting selected Pan American World Airways, Northwest Airlines, and Trans World Airlines Category B charter flights to Category Y. Under this concept, DOD would have the option to move its passengers in groups of 20 or more on the carriers' regularly scheduled flights through commercial facilities at the Category B round-trip rate. Revenues of other commercial carriers serving MAC would not be adversely affected because the three participating airlines would be converting only their own charter flights (work papers not shown).

The carriers are willing to accept this system because their regularly scheduled flights have low occupancy rates. For example, in calendar year 1974 passenger occupancy ranged from about 37 to 66 percent. The DOD passengers would occupy otherwise vacant seats on these flights (work papers not shown).

Results Achieved

Conservation of Fuel Through Reduction of Charter Flights. Adoption of a Category Y system could reduce annual consumption of jet fuel by about 48 million gallons. These fuel savings could be achieved through conversion of Category B charter flights on 13 channels flown by Pan American Airways, Northwest Airlines, and Trans World Airlines to Category Y.

*These numbers refer to pages from the illustrative working papers.

The Boeing 707 aircraft used by the airlines on Category B charter routes consumes an average of 2,063 gallons of jet fuel per hour. Our calculations of potential fuel savings were based on an annual reduction of 969 flights using this fuel consumption rate and average flying time by channel (Q–1/12–1,2).

The carriers have already achieved significant fuel savings in temporary periods of Category Y operations. During the February through June 1974 period of Category Y operations, DOD converted 152 Northwest Airlines, Pan American World Airways, and Trans World Airlines Category B charter flights on the following three channels:

McGuire AFB—Rhein-Main Air Base (AB), Germany
Travis AFB—Yokata AB, Japan
Travis AFB—Osan AB, Korea

These conversions saved about 6.2 million gallons of jet fuel. In addition, conversions of 96 Category B charter flights during the January through March 1975 period of Category Y operations should result in further savings of about 4.2 million gallons of jet fuel (work papers not shown).

Improvement in Balance of Payments. A further benefit from reduction of jet fuel consumption would be an improvement in the United States balance of payments. Petroleum imports have been identified as a major factor contributing to the U.S. trade deficit. These imports could be reduced to the extent the jet fuel would have been procured from foreign sources. [Note: No evidence or calculations are necessary to support the effect of savings in foreign exchange. This is a good illustration of the concept of judicial notice in evidence. It is obvious to anyone, and it would not have to be proved by evidence gathering, that if fuel is bought overseas by the American carriers or is obtained from overseas for American usage, the payments would affect the foreign exchange of the United States.]

Savings Through Better Utilization of the Aircraft. Currently, DOD charters entire aircraft for passenger transportation to overseas locations, paying for all seats, whether used or not. DOD is now experiencing a seat-utilization rate of 92.3 percent on these flights. We estimate that DOD pays about $3.5 million a year for unused seats which could be avoided under Category Y (Q–1/12–3).

Category Y operations offer the potential for 100 percent seat utilization. The difference in utilization stems from different options available to MAC in treating no-shows or last-minute cancellations by passengers. If duty-status passengers do not show up for Category B charter flights, MAC can only fill the seats with space-available passengers who are not on duty or allow the flight to leave with empty seats.

Under Category Y, however, MAC can reschedule up to 15 percent of the seats booked if passengers do not show up for flights. In the 1974 Category Y operation, the Military Traffic Management Command reported a no-show rate of 10.9 percent, well within the 15 percent limitation. Therefore, DOD would no longer be paying for unused seats.

Savings Through Decreased Workloads at Military Aerial Ports. Conversion of Category B flights to Category Y will decrease the workload at MAC aerial ports, as Category Y flights are processed through the commercial terminals. By applying the applicable MAC manning standards to this decreased workload, we estimate a reduction of 125 personnel authorizations, representing about a $1.2 million savings per year (work papers not shown).

Reduction in Cost to Commercial Carriers. U.S. international air carriers could reduce annual expenses by about $38 million through adoption of a Category Y system on the 13 selected channels (Q–1/12–4,5).

These savings would accrue through canceling 969 Category B charter flights and transporting the passengers using otherwise vacant seats on their regularly scheduled commercial flights that parallel the charter routes. Although the charter flights would be cancelled, carriers would receive the same revenue from DOD.

The benefits to the carriers are of consequence to the government because the carriers are reporting financial difficulties that affect the economy. One carrier has requested a government subsidy and Pan American World Airways and Trans World Airlines have recently restructured certain routes to reduce expenses (work papers not shown).

Analysis of the Work Papers

The reader can follow the information from the Level I summaries to the Level II summary given above. However, it is just as important to know how the information on the objective is gathered in detail before it is summarized. By following the references in the work-paper summaries back to the detail work papers, the reader can see how the information was first gathered on the objective.

The reader should note, too, that while the Level I summaries are normal arithmetic work sheets, the Level II summary illustrates the need for the auditor in M-audits and P-audits to use the English language properly.

Illustrative Working Papers

MAC CHARTERS VS. COMMERCIAL SERVICE
CODE 245229
SUMMARY OF FUEL SAVINGS

J. Kennedy
3/24/75

	Average per Flight [1]		No. of Flights Converted	Total Gallons (000) [3]
	Flight Time	Gallons of Fuel Used [2]		
21st Air Force				
McGuire/Charleston — Rhein-Main	16.74	34535	270	9324
McGuire — Meldenhall	14.43	29769	21	625
McGuire — Torrejon	15.86	32719	3	98
McGuire — Rhein-Main/Meldenhall	17.13	35339	12	424
McGuire — Rhein-Main/Torrejon	18.62	38413	12	691
Subtotal			324	11162
22nd Air Force				
Travis/Norton — Hickam	11.38	23471	40.5	951
Travis/Norton — Padona				
Mid Pac route	31.65	65294	102	6666
North Pac route	27.44	56609	54	3057
Travis — Yokota				
Mid Pac	25.44	52483	129	6770
North Pac	21.42	44189	6	265
Travis — Osan				
Mid Pac	29.83	59476	24	1427
North Pac	25.74	53100	90	4774

J. Kennedy
3/24/75

SUMMARY OF FUEL SAVINGS (CONT.)

Channel	Average per Flight[1] Flight Time	Average per Flight[1] Gallons of Fuel Used[2]	No. of Flights Converted[1]	Total Gallons (000)[3]
Travis — Taipei	27.06	55825	27	1527
Travis — Guam	24.71	50977	70.5	3594
Travis — Bangkok	38.27	78951	79.5	6277
Travis — Philippines	29.50	60859	22.5	1369
Subtotal			645	36656
Total Channel			969	47818

[1] Based on our analysis of Category B charter flights of NWA, PAA, and TWA during four representative months. One-way flights converted to round-trip basis.

[2] Based on average consumption of a Boeing 707 of 2,063 gallons per hour. NWA, PAA, and TWA use 707s in A and B missions ($\frac{M-1R}{3-6}$).

[3] Col. 5 × Col. 6.

Note: Differences with prior schedules due to rounding.

Source: P $\frac{D-1}{13}$, $\frac{Q-1}{8-2}$ to 8-9

United States General Accounting Office
Form 215 (Rev. 12-66) Code 943229

P D-1/13
HCP 12/12/74

COMPUTATION OF FUEL SAVINGS (GALLONS AND $ VALUES) FOR A 12-MONTH (1-YEAR) PERIOD BASED ON PAA/TWA CAT. B FLIGHTS OVER ALL SELECTED CHANNELS DURING A 4-MONTH PERIOD, THAT COULD BE CONVERTED TO CAT. Y

	1	2	3	4	5	6	No. of Flights During 4 Sample Months	
			Channels				R/T	O/W
3	McGuire		Frankfurt		McGuire		64	7
5	Charleston		Frankfurt		Charleston		9	5
7	Charleston		Frankfurt – McGuire		Charleston		3	
9	Charleston – McGuire		Frankfurt		McGuire		2	
11	McGuire		Frankfurt		Charleston		1	
13	Charleston		Frankfurt		McGuire		5	
15			Subtotal Channel no. 1				84	12
17	McGuire		Meldenhall		McGuire		7	
19	McGuire – Frankfurt – Meldenhall				McGuire		1	
21	McGuire		Meldenhall – Frankfurt – McGuire				3	
							4	
23	McGuire		Torrejon – Sp.		McGuire		1	
25	McGuire – Frankfurt – Torrejon-Sp.				McGuire		3	
27	McGuire		Torrejon-Sp. – Frankfurt – McGuire				3	
							6	
29			Subtotal other than Channel no. 1				18	0
31							102	12

Note: For purposes of computations for O/W flights, the average fly times for outbound and inbound flights (W/P D-1/14 lines 3 and 22) were used.

Sources:
Columns 7 and 8: W/P C-1/2-8
Columns 9 and 10: W/P D-1/19
Column 11: Columns 9 + 10 times 2063 gal per hour for R.
Column 12: Column 8 times Columns 9 and 10
Column 13: Column 12 times 2063
Column 14: Column 13 times 35.4 cents per gal. (See W/P A-1/3)
Columns 8ff, lower portion – as explained

Converted No. of Flights Per Year		No. of Average Hours (Tentative) per Flight R/T	%	Average No. of Gal. Fuel for One Flight (2063 × Col.9)	Total No. of Flight Hours per Year	Gallons of Fuel Consumed per Year	Fuel Cost per Year
R/T	O/W						
					3143.04	6484092	$2295368
192	21	16.37	8.185		171.89	354609	125532
27	15	18.09	9.045		488.43	1007638	356701
					135.68	279908	99087
9		18.82			169.38	349431	123698
6		17.93			107.53	221938	78566
3		17.68			51.84	106946	37859
15		17.18			257.7	531635	188199
					4217.97	8701673	$3080392
252	36	16.74		34535	307.57	634517	224619
						9336190	$3305011
21		14.43		29769	303.03	625151	$221303
3		16.83			50.49	104161	36873
9		17.23			155.07	319909	113248
12		17.13		35339		424070	150121
3		15.86		32719	47.58	98158	34748
9		17.86			160.74	331607	117389
9		19.37			174.33	359643	127314
18		18.62		38413		691250	244703
54	0				5109.21	1838628	650875
					307.57	1040302	3731267
306	36				5416.78	634517	224619
						1174819	$3955886

Average fuel consumed and cost for one flight over Frankfurt channel.
  Total number of R/T flight hours over all variations of Frankfurt channel
    = 4,217.97 per year.
  Total number of R/T flights over all variations of Frankfurt channel
    = 252 per year.
  $\frac{4,217.97}{252}$ = 16.735 hours per R/T flight.
  16.735 hours × 2063 gal. = 34,524.
  16.74 × 2063 = 34,535 gal. per flight.
  34,524 gal. × 35.4¢ = $12,221.09 per flight.

United States General Accounting Office Form 214 (Rev. 12-66)

MAC CHARTERS VERSUS COMMERCIAL SERVICE
CODE 943229

Q-1 / 8-1
1 of 9

SUMMARY SCHEDULE OF TOTAL NUMBER OF FLIGHTS AND FUEL CONSUMPTION BY SCHEDULED AIR CARRIERS (PAA & NWA) FOR A 12-MONTH PERIOD ON EIGHT SELECTED CHANNELS

J. Battista
12/4/74

Channel Travis to:	No. [5] of Flights [6] Round trip	Other	Fuel Consumption (Gallons)
Yokota	135 ✓	0 ✓	7034910 ✓
Osan	111 ✓	6 ✓	6205338 ✓
Subtotal	246 ✓	6 ✓	13240248 ✓
Hickam (includes Norton flights)	36 ✓	9 ✓	954222 ✓
Taipei	24 ✓	6 ✓	1487217 ✓
Guam	69 ✓	3 ✓	3595377 ✓
Clark	15 ✓	15 ✓	1359357 ✓
Bangkok	15 ✓	9 ✓	6252195 ✓
Kadena (includes Norton flights)	183 ✓	6 ✓	9734430 ✓
Totals [1]	618 ✓	54 ✓	36623046 ✓

[1] Subtotal of above six channels, not including Osan and Yokota. — 372 ✓ 48 ✓ 23382798 ✓

✓ Independently verified, PKT 1/27/75

Purpose: See Title

Sources: See W/P Q-1/8-2 to Q-1/8-9

Huck 1/18/75

UNITED STATES GENERAL ACCOUNTING OFFICE
Form 215 (Rev. 12-66)

CODE 943229

TOTAL NO. OF FLIGHTS AND FUEL CONSUMED BY SCHEDULED AIR CARRIERS (PAA & NWA) FOR A 12-MONTH PERIOD ON THE TRAVIS-YOKOTA CHANNEL

2 of 9   O-1 / 8-2

J. Battista
12/2/74

Channel	Month	Round Trip (R/T) Flights – Mid Pac		
		No. Flown[2] Mid Pac	Average[2] Hours Fly Time	Total Fuel[3] Consumption (gallons)
Travis – Yokota				
	Oct. 1973	13	25.00	670475 ✓
	Nov. 1973[4]	12	25.58	633258 ✓
	Aug. 1974	9	25.60	475315 ✓
	Sept. 1974	9	25.72	477543 ✓
4-month total		43	25.44	2256591 ✓
12-month total[5]		129	25.44	6769773 ✓

Average (North Pac and Mid Pac) = (43 × 25.44)(2 × 21.42)/45
= 25.26 hours

Fuel consumption for 12 months (Cat. 5 + 7a) = 7,034,910 gallons

Average consumption of fuel per flight (Mid Pac) = (25.44 hours × 2063 gallons) = 52,483 gallons

Average consumption of fuel per flight (North Pac) = (21.42 hours × 2063 gallons) = 44,189 gallons

✓ Independently verified, PKT 1/27/75

Purpose: See title.

Source: See notes.

O-1
8-2
2 of 9

Round Trip (R/T)[8] Flights[9] - North Pac[10]		
No Flown[1] North Pac	Average[2] Hours Fly Time	Total Fuel[3] Consumption (gallons)
2	21.42	88379 ✓
2	21.42	88379 ✓
6	21.42	265137 ✓

Average consumption per flight = 7,034,910/135 = 52,110 gallons

Notes:
1. Source: "MAC Passenger Schedules," Oct.-Nov. 1973 and Aug.-Sept. 1974, available from Contract Airlift Management Office, HQMAC, Travis AFB, and Passenger Division, Directorate of Transportation, Travis AFB.
2. Statistic is developed by adding together the fly time for all flights for the month and then dividing by the number of flights flown for the month. Data is from MAC PAX schedules at Travis.
3. Statistic is developed by multiplying the number of flights times the average fly time times 2063 gallons per hour (see WIP M-1/3-6), the average number of gallons consumed per hour by a B-707.
4. There were 11 actual R/T flights and 2 O/W flights. The O/W flights (one each way) were ferried to the appropriate aerial port. Since the O/W rate is not charged in this circumstance, we counted the 2 O/W's as one R/T for a total of 12 R/T flights.
5. 4-month total times 3.

Huck
1/18/75

United States General Accounting Office
Form 215 (Rev. 12-66)
CODE 943229
3 of 9   Q-1/8-3

TOTAL NO. OF FLIGHTS AND FUEL CONSUMED BY SCHEDULED AIR CARRIERS (PAA & NWA) FOR A 12-MONTH PERIOD ON THE TRAVIS – OSAN CHANNEL

J. Battista
12/2/74

Month	Round Trip Flights – Mid Pac		
	No.^{1} per Month	Average Hours^2 Fly Time	Total Fuel^3 Consumption (gallons)
Oct. 1973			
Nov. 1973			
Aug. 1974	4	28.83	237905 ✓
Sept. 1974	4	28.83	237905 ✓
4-month total	8 ✓	28.83 ✓	475810 ✓
12-month total	24 ✓	28.83 ✓	1427430 ✓

Average (North Pac and Mid Pac) = $(8 \times 28.83) + (29 \times 25.74)/37$
= 26.41 hours

Fuel consumption for 12 months (Cols. 6 + 10 + 14) = 6,205,338 gallons

Consumption per flight: North Pac – $25.74 \times 2063 = 53,102$ ✓ gallons
  Mid Pac – $28.83 \times 2063 = 59,476$ ✓ gallons

✓ Independently verified, RKT 1/27/75

Purpose: } See W/P Q-1/8-2
Source: }

Round Trip Flights — North Pac				Other Flights (One ways, Ferries, etc.)		
No.[1] per Month	Average[2] Hours Fly Time	Total Fuel[3] Consumption (gallons)	11	No. per Month	Total Hours Fly Time	Total Fuel Consumption (gallons)
10	25.64	528953 ✓				
10	26.07	537824 ✓		1[4]	11.83	24405 ✓
4	25.03	206548 ✓		1[5]	13.75	28366 ✓
5	25.84	266540 ✓				
29 ✓	25.74 ✓	1539865 ✓		2 ✓	25.58 ✓	52771 ✓
87 ✓	25.74 ✓	4619595 ✓		6 ✓	76.74 ✓	158313 ✓

Notes:
1, 2, 3 See W/P Q-1/8-2.
4 This is a one way flight from Osan to Soo via the North Pac route.
5 Ferry mission flight originates at Travis and terminates at Osan (North Pac), and then is ferried to Guam for return flight.
6 Multiply 4-month total by 3.
7 6 one-ways being considered 3 round-trips.

Husk
1/18/75

Q-1/8-3

United States General Accounting Office
Form 215 (Rev. 12-66)

CODE 943229

4 of 9   Q-1 / 8-4

TOTAL NO. OF FLIGHTS AND FUEL CONSUMED BY SCHEDULED AIR CARRIERS (PAA & NWA) FOR A 12-MONTH PERIOD ON THE TRAVIS/NORTON — HICKAM CHANNELS

J. Battista
12/4/74

Month	Round-trip Flights - Mid Pac			Other Flights (One-ways, Ferries)		
	No. per Month[1]	Avg. Hrs. Fly Time[2]	Total Fuel Consumption (gallons)[3]	No. per Month[1]	Total Hrs. Fly Time[2]	Total Fuel Consumption (gallons)[3]
Oct. 1973	3	11.55	71483 ✓			
Nov. 1973	3	10.89	67398 ✓			
Aug. 1974	2	10.88	44891 ✓	3[4]	17.58	36268
Sept. 1974	4	11.88	98034 ✓	—	—	—
4-month total	12	11.38	281806 ✓	3 ✓	17.58 ✓	36268 ✓
12-month total	36	11.38 ✓	845418	9[6] ✓	52.74 ✓	108804 ✓

Fuel consumption for 12 months (Cols. 4 & 7) = 954,227 gallons.

Average fuel consumption per flight (11.38 × 2063) = 23,476 gallons.

✓ Independently verified, PKT 1/27/75

Purpose: } See W/P Q-1/8-2
Source: }

8	9	10	11	12	13	14
	Actual Miles Traveled [5]					
	Round-trip		One-way			
	Total Miles	No. of Flights	Total Miles	No. of Flights		
	16133	3				
	15755	3				
	10507	2	8272	3		
	16436	3				
	58831 ✓	11	8272	3		
Avg. miles per flight	5348 ✓		2757			

Notes:
1, 2, 3 See W/P Q-1/8-2.
4 Three one-ways outgoing.
5 Because of the variety of routes a mission can fly over the Hickam channel, an average number of miles per flight is developed for consistency. The Hickam channel operates as a triangle between Norton, Travis, and Honolulu. The average is developed by adding together the miles flown for the 4-month period and dividing by the number of flights. A distinction is made between R/T and O/W flights because most one-way flights travel over 2 legs (e.g., Travis → Norton → Hickam).
6 Nine one-way flights considered as 5 round-trips.

Hwok
1/18/75

United States General Accounting Office Form 215 (Rev. 12-66)

CODE 943229   5 of 9   Q-1 / 8-5

TOTAL NO. OF FLIGHTS AND FUEL CONSUMED BY SCHEDULED AIR CARRIERS (PAA & NWA) FOR A 12-MONTH PERIOD ON THE TRAVIS-TAIPEI CHANNEL

J. Battista 12/3/74

Month	Round-trip Flights - North Pac			Other Flights (One-way)		
	No. per Month [1]	Avg. Hrs. Fly Time [2]	Total Fuel Consumption (gallons) [3]	No. per Month [1]	Total Hrs. Fly Time [2]	Total Fuel Consumption (gallons) [3]
Oct. 1973	3 [4]	25.08	155220 ✓	1 [5]	11.50	23725 ✓
Nov. 1973	2 [6]	29.24	120644 ✓			
Aug. 1974	2 [7]	27.21	112268 ✓	1 [8]	12.33	25437 ✓
Sept. 1974	1 [9]	28.33	58445 ✓			
4-month total	8 ✓	27.06 ✓	446577 ✓	2 ✓	23.83 ✓	49162 ✓
12-month total	24 ✓	27.06 ✓	1339731 ✓	6 [10]	71.49 ✓	147486 ✓

Fuel consumption for 12 months (cols. 4 & 7) = 1,487,217 gallons.
Fuel consumption per flight = 2063 × 27.06 = 55,824.78
✓ Independently verified, PKT 1/27/75

Notes:
1, 2, 3 See W/P Q-1/8-2
4 Two flights via Tacoma, Yokota, Taipei, Yokota, Tacoma. One flight via Tacoma, Anchorage, Yokota, Taipei, Yokota, Tacoma. Cat B flights no longer originate at Tacoma, so for the 12-month total, assume all flights on the channel originate at Travis. (Information from Louise Thompson, Pax Payment, 22 AC.)
5 One-way flight via Taipei, Yokota, Tacoma.
6 Both flights via Travis, Seattle, Yokota, Kadena, Taipei, and return same.
7 One flight via Travis, McChord, Yokota, Tokyo, Taipei, Yokota, Travis. The other flight via Travis, Anchorage, Yokota, Taipei, Yokota, Travis.
8 One-way flight Taipei, Yokota, Travis.
9 Flight flown via Travis, Seattle, Yokota, Osan, Taipei, Yokota, Travis.
10 Consider as 3 round-trips.

Purpose: } See W/P Q-1/8-2
Source: }

HWPK 1/18/75

CODE 943229   6 of 9   Q-1/8-6

TOTAL NO. OF FLIGHTS AND FUEL CONSUMED BY SCHEDULED AIR CARRIERS (PAA & NWA) FOR A 12-MONTH PERIOD ON THE TRAVIS-GUAM CHANNEL

J. Battista
12/3/74

Month	Round-trip Flights - Mid Pac[2]			Other Flights (One-way Ferries)[5,6]		
	No. per Month[1]	Avg. Hrs. Fly Time[2]	Total Fuel Consumption (gallons)[3]	No. per Month[1]	Total Hrs. Fly Time[2]	Total Fuel Consumption (gallons)[3]
Oct. 1973	5	24.71	254884 ✓	1[4]	12.66	26118 ✓
Nov. 1973	5	24.66	254368 ✓			
Aug. 1974	7[5]	24.18	357848 ✓			
Sept. 1974	6	24.66	305241 ✓	—	—	—
4-month total	23 ✓	24.71 ✓	1172341 ✓	1 ✓	12.66 ✓	26118 ✓
12-month total	69 ✓	24.71 ✓	3517023 ✓	3 ✓	31.98 ✓	18354 ✓

Fuel consumption for 12 months (Cols. 4 & 7) = 3,595,377 ✓ gallons

Fuel consumption per flight = 24.71 × 2063 = 50,976.73

✓ Independently verified. PKT 1/27/75

Notes:
1,2,3 See W/P Q-1/8-2.
4 Flight flew Travis to Guam and was then ferried to another location.
5 One flight returned North Pac because NWA requested a crew change at Yokota per Lt. Goodson, PAXDIN, 22nd AF. Because of the unusual circumstances surrounding this flight, we will consider it a normal Mid Pac flight.

Purpose: } See W/P Q-1/8-2
Source: }

Husk
1/18/75

United States General Accounting Office Form 214 (Rev. 12-66)

CODE 943229   1 of 9   Q-1 / 8-7

TOTAL NO. OF FLIGHTS AND FUEL CONSUMED BY SCHEDULED AIR CARRIERS (PAA & NWA), FOR A 12-MONTH PERIOD ON THE TRAVIS-CLARK CHANNEL   J. Battista 12/3/74

Month	Round-trip Flights — North Pac			Other Flights (One-way Ferries)		
	No. per Month[1]	Avg. Hrs. Fly Time[2]	Total Fuel Consumption (gallons)[3]	No. per Month[1]	Total Hrs. Fly Time[2]	Total Fuel Consumption (gallons)[3]
Oct. 1973	3	29.66	183566 ✓	2[4]	28.58	58961 ✓
Nov. 1973				1[5]	16.50	34040 ✓
Aug. 1974	1[6]	29.25	60343 ✓	1[7]	13.42	27685 ✓
Sept. 1974	1[8]	29.25	60343 ✓	1[7]	13.66	28181 ✓
4-month total	5 ✓	29.50 ✓	304252 ✓	5 ✓	72.16 ✓	148867 ✓
12-month total	15	29.50 ✓	912756 ✓	15 ✓	216.48 ✓	446601 ✓

Fuel consumption for 12 months (Cols. 4 & 7) = 1,359,357 ✓ gallons.

Fuel consumption per flight = 2063 × 29.50 = 60,858.5

✓ Independently verified, RKT 1/27/75

Notes:
1, 2, 3 See W/P Q-1/8-2.
4 Both flights are results of ferry missions and are inbound from Clark (1-CRK-OKO-SOO, 1-CRK-OKO-SEA-SOO).
5 Via Travis, Anchorage, Yokota, Clark (one-way).
6 Via Travis, McChord, Yokota, Clark, Yokota, Travis.
7 Via Clark, Yokota, Travis (one-way).
8 Via Travis, Seattle, Yokota, Clark, Yokota, Travis.

Purpose: } See W/P Q-1/8-2
Source: }

Huck 1/17/75

UNITED STATES GENERAL ACCOUNTING OFFICE — Form 215 (Rev. 12-66)

CODE 943229　　　　8 of 9　　Q-1 / 8-8

TOTAL NO. OF FLIGHTS AND FUEL CONSUMED BY SCHEDULED AIR CARRIERS (PAA & NWA) FOR A 12-MONTH PERIOD ON THE TRAVIS–BANGKOK CHANNEL

G. Battista 12/3/74

Month	Round-trip Flights – Mid Pac			Other Flights (One-way, Ferries)		
	No. per Month [1]	Avg. Hrs. Fly Time [2]	Total Fuel Consumption (gallons)[3]	No. per Month [1]	Total Hrs. Fly Time [2]	Total Fuel Consumption (gallons)[3]
Oct. 1973	7 [4]	38.33	553524 ✓	1 [5]	19.50	40229 ✓
Nov. 1973	5 [6]	38.56	397746 ✓	1 [7]	18.50	38166 ✓
Aug. 1974	6 [8]	37.38	462690 ✓	1 [9]	15.50	31977 ✓
Sept. 1974	7 [10]	38.76	559133 ✓			
4-month total	25 ✓	38.27 ✓	1973693 ✓	3 ✓	53.50 ✓	110372 ✓
12-month total	75 ✓	38.27 ✓	5921079 ✓	9 ✓	160.50 ✓	331116 ✓

Fuel consumption for 12 months (Cols. 4 & 7) = 6,252,195 ✓ gallons

Fuel consumption per flight = 2063 × 38.27 = 78,951.01

✓ Independently verified, PKT 1/27/75

Purpose: } See W/P Q-1/8-2
Source: }

	8	9	10	11	12	13	14
		\multicolumn{4}{c}{Actual Aircraft Miles Traveled 11}		

	Round-trip		One-way	
	No. of Miles	No. of Flights	No. of Miles	No. of Flights
	129206	7	8630 (North Pac)	1
	92290	5	9123 (Mid Pac)	1
	110324	6	8337 (North Pac)	1
	128782	7		
	460602 ✓	25 ✓	26090 ✓	3 ✓

Avg. Miles per Flight 18424 ✓

Notes:
1, 2, 3 See W/P Q-1/8-2.
4 Five flights via Travis, Honolulu, Guam, Clark, Saigon, Bangkok, and return same. The other two flights bypass Guam.
5 Flight via Travis, Seattle, Yokota, Kadena, Clark, Bangkok, and then ferried to Osan.
6 See first sentence of note 4.
7 Via Travis, Honolulu, Clark, Bangkok.
8 Four flights via first sentence of note 4. The other flights bypass Saigon going both ways.
9 One-way flights via Bangkok, Yokota, Travis.
10 Five flights via first sentence of note 4. The other two flights bypass Saigon going both ways.
11 Same as note 5 on W/P Q-1/8-4.

Huak
1/17/75

UNITED STATES GENERAL ACCOUNTING OFFICE
Form 215 (Rev. 12-66)

CODE 943229

9 of 9   Q-1/8-9

Total No. of Flights and Fuel Consumed by Scheduled Air Carriers (PAA & NWA) for a 12-Month Period on the Travis/Norton - Kadena Channel

J. Battista 12/4/74

Month	Round-trip Flights – Mid Pac			Round-trip Flights – North Pac		
	No. per Month[1]	Avg. Hrs. Fly Time[2]	Total Fuel Consumption (gallons)[3]	No. per Month[1]	Avg. Hrs. Fly Time[2]	Total Fuel Consumption (gallons)[3]
Oct. 1973	9[4]	31.14	578176 ✓	4[5]	27.34	225610 ✓
Nov. 1973	8[7]	31.61	521691 ✓	5[5]	27.34	282012 ✓
Aug. 1974	9[9]	31.92	592659 ✓	5[10]	27.82	286963 ✓
Sept. 1974	8[11]	31.98	527798 ✓	3[12]	27.12	167846 ✓
4-month total	34 ✓	31.65 ✓	2220324 ✓	17 ✓	27.44 ✓	962431 ✓
12-month total	102 ✓	31.65 ✓	6660972 ✓	51 ✓	27.44 ✓	2887293 ✓

Fuel consumption for 12 months (cols. 4 + 7 + 10) = 9,134,430 gallons
Fuel consumption per flight via North Pac = 2063 × 27.44 = 56,608.72
Fuel consumption per flight via Mid Pac = 2063 × 31.65 = 65,293.95

✓ Independently verified. PKT 1/27/75

Notes:
1, 2, 3 See W/P Q-1/8-2.
4 Five flights via Norton, Honolulu, Guam, Kadena, and return. The other 4 flights originate and terminate Travis and fly same route.
5 All flights via Norton, Anchorage, Yokota, Kadena, Yokota, Norton.
6 Via Norton, Seattle, Yokota, Kadena, and then ferried to Thailand – North Pac.

Purpose: } See W/P Q-1/8-2
Source: }

Other Flights (One-way, Ferries)[8]		[10]	[11] Actual [12] Aircraft Miles Traveled [14][13]			
No. per Month[1]	Total Hrs. Fly Time[2]	Total Fuel Consumption (gallons)[3]	R/T – mid Pac		R/T – North Pac	
			No. of Miles	No. of Flights	No. of Miles	No. of Flights
1[6]	15.33	31626 ✓	132426	9	54224	4
1[8]	14.75	30429 ✓	117544	8	67780	5
			131859	9	68540	5
			117355	8	40220	3
2 ✓	30.08 ✓	62055 ✓	499184 ✓	34 ✓	230764 ✓	17 ✓
6 ✓	90.24 ✓	186165 ✓	14682 ← Avg. Miles per Flight → 13574			

Notes (cont):
7. See footnote 4 (only 4 flights over first route).
8. Via Norton, Travis, Anchorage, Yokota, Kadena, and ferried to Osan – North Pac.
9. Three flights via Norton, Honolulu, Guam, Kadena, and return. Five flights originate and terminate Travis and fly same route. One flight via Travis, Norton, Honolulu, Guam, Kadena, Guam, Honolulu, Norton.
10. All flights via Norton, McChord, Yokota, Iwakuni, Kadena, Iwakuni, Yokota, Norton.
11. Same as footnote 9, except only 4 flights originate at Travis.
12. One flight via Travis, Seattle, Yokota, Kadena, Yokota, Travis. Other two flights same as footnote 10.
13. Determined with aid of mileages found in W/P Q-2/1-10.

Hueck
1/19/75

United States General Accounting Office Form 214 (Rev. 12-66)

MAC Charters vs. Commercial Service
Code 943229

Q-1 / 12-3

Summary Schedule of Utilization Savings

J. Kennedy
3/21/75

1 Channel	2	3 Passenger Miles Available $P\frac{C-1}{3-2} + \frac{Q-1}{7-1}$	4 Passenger Miles Used Col. 3 − Col. 5	5 Passenger Miles Unused $P\frac{C-1}{3-2}, \frac{Q-1}{7-1}$	Computed Utilization Percentage (Col. 4 ÷ Col. 3)	Cost of Unused Passenger Miles¹ (000)
		(── in millions ──)				
21st Air Force						
McGuire/Charleston− Rhein-main		358.42	352.02	6.40	98.2	$ 157
McGuire − Rhein-main/Mildenhall		15.56	15.14	.42	97.3	10
McGuire − Mildenhall		24.47	24.26	.21	99.1	5
McGuire − Torrejon		3.53	3.20	.33	90.7	8
McGuire − Rhein-main/Torrejon		24.75	22.93	1.82	92.7	45
Subtotal		426.73	417.55	9.18	97.9	$ 225
22nd Air Force						
Travis/Norton − Hickam		35.86	26.93	8.93	75.1	$ 219
Travis/Norton − Kadena		354.42	333.86	20.56	94.2	504
Travis − Yokota		297.99	267.00	30.99	89.6	760
Travis − Osan		231.81	224.22	15.59	93.5	382
Travis − Guam		144.87	130.67	14.20	90.2	348
Travis − Philippines		54.14	48.89	5.25	90.3	129
Travis − Taipei		60.13	53.52	6.61	89.0	162
Travis − Bangkok		240.91	208.63	32.28	86.6	792
Subtotal		1428.13	1293.73	134.41	96.6	$ 3296
Total		1854.86	1711.27	143.59	92.3	$ 3521

¹ Based on col. 5 × $.02452 per mile   W/P Q-1/7-1.

Note: Differences with prior schedules due to rounding.

Source: As indicated

United States General Accounting Office Form 214 (Rev. 12-66)

McGuire A.F.B. NJ 08641   P C-1 / 3-2

Yearly Projection of (1) Number and (2) Dollar Value of Unused Passenger Miles (Based on 4 Sample Months). Selected Channels (Variations) Consolidated into 5 Channels.

GAO Channel	Five Consolidated Channels	Cat. B[3] Utilization Rate on Selected GAO Channel	Unused[4] 4 Sample Months C-1/3-1	per Year[5] Projection Avg. 1 Yr. (Col. 4 × 3)	Possible[6] Passenger Miles	Actual[1] Unused Passenger Miles per Yr.
I	Frankfurt Channel					
	Variations:					
	WRI - EDAF - WRI		975331	2926002		71746
	WRI - EDAF - WRI		0	0		0
	CHS - EDAF - WRI		456144	1368432		33554
	CHS - EDAF - WRI		277883	833649	119474424	20441
	CHS - EDAF - WRI - CHS		394395	1183185	× 3	27012
	CHS - WRI - EDAF - WRI		29427	88281		2165
	Subtotal	98.2%	2133183	6399549	358423272	154918
II	Meldenhall Channel				8156610	
	WRI - EGON	99.1%	70620	211860	× 3	5195
					24469830	
III	Torryon Channel				1175130	
	WRI - LETO - WRI	90.5%	110391	331173	× 3	8120
					3525390	
IV	Frankfurt/Meldenhall					
	Variations:					
	WRI - EDAF - EGON - WRI		31279	93837	5185290	2301
	WRI - EGON - EDAF - WRI		109885	329655	× 3	8083
		97.2%	141164	423492	15555870	10384
V	Frankfurt/Torryon					
	Variations:					
	WRI - EDAF - LETO - WRI		349243	1047729	8249346	25690
	WRI - LETO - EDAF - WRI		256960	770880	× 3	18902
		92.6%	606203	1818609	24741038	44592
	Subtotal all channels other than FRA Channel		928378	2785134		$ 68291
	Totals Five Channels	97.8%	3061561	9184683 ✓		225209

Cost of unused Pax miles for 12-month period was adjusted as follows: ① Unused Pax miles for 4 months was multiplied by 3 to project 12 months or 1-year totals; ② projected 12 months unused Pax miles multiplied by round-trip CAT B rate, .02452 (W/P A-1/2) to obtain cost of unused CAT B Pax miles for 12-month period.

Source: C-1/3-1

United States General Accounting Office — Form 215 (Rev. 12-66)

MAC CHARTERS VS. COMMERCIAL SERVICE
CODE 943229
1 of 3   Q-1 / 7-1

Summary Schedule of Cost of Unused Passenger Miles for a 12-Month Period

J. Battista 12/6/74

	Channel	Utilization (W/P Q-1/5-12,13)	Estimated No. of Flights for the 12 Months [1] Round-trip (R/T)		Other (One-ways, Ferries)	
			North Pac	Mid Pac	North Pac	Mid Pac
3	Travis — Yokota	89.6%	6 ✓	129 ✓		
5	Travis — Osan	93.5%	87 ✓	24 ✓	6 ✓	
7	Travis/Norton — Hickam	75.1%		36 ✓		9 ✓
9	Travis — Taipei	89.0%	24 ✓		6 ✓	
11	Travis — Guam	90.2%		69 ✓		3 ✓
13	Travis — Clark	90.3%	15 ✓		15 ✓	
15	Travis — Bangkok	86.6%		75 ✓	6 ✓	3 ✓
17	Travis/Norton — Kadena	94.2%	51 ✓	102 ✓	6 ✓	
19	Totals		183 ✓	435 ✓	39 ✓	15 ✓

✓ Independently verified, PKT 1/27/75

Notes:
1. See W/P Q-1/8-1 to 9.
2. See W/P Q-1/7-2.
3. Col. 8 — (Col. 3 × 8).
4. Based on rate effective August 1974 with surcharge (see W/P Q-2/1-1, Q-2/2-2). The rate for a round-trip flight during this period is $.02197 + a fuel tax surcharge of 11.60%, for a total of $.02452 per passenger mile. The probable unused passenger miles also includes one-way flights, which are more expensive ($.04612 per passenger mile), but is not included in the costs (col. 10).

Purpose: To show the cost to the Government for unused passenger miles.
Source: W/P's as indicated.

Estimated² Passenger Miles for 12 Months (millions)	Probable³ Unused Passenger Miles (millions)	Cost⁴ of Unused Passenger Miles
297.99 ✓	30.99 ✓	$158875 ✓
239.81 ✓	15.59 ✓	382267 ✓
35.86 ✓	8.93 ✓	218964 ✓
60.13 ✓	6.61 ✓	162077 ✓
144.87 ✓	14.20 ✓	348184 ✓
54.14 ✓	5.25 ✓	128730 ✓
240.91 ✓	32.28 ✓	791506 ✓
354.42 ✓	20.56 ✓	504131 ✓
1428.13 ✓	134.41 ✓	$3295734 ✓

Huck
1/18/75

United States General Accounting Office Form 214 (Rev. 12-66)

MAC CHARTERS vs. COMMERCIAL SERVICE
CODE 943229

Q-1
1 of 2   12-4

SUMMARY OF REDUCTIONS TO COMMERCIAL CARRIERS

J. Kennedy
3/24/75

		Channel	Gallons of Jet Fuel Saved (000) [3]	Total Cost Reduction [2] (000) [4]	No. of Flights Converted [5]	Operating Expense Reduction [1] (000)	Total Cost Reduction (000)
		21st Air Force					
		McGuire/Charleston – Rhein-Main	9324	$ 3478	270	$ 3180	$ 7258
		McGuire – Rhein-Main/Mildenhall	424	158	12	168	326
		McGuire – Mildenhall	625	238	21	294	527
		McGuire – Torrejon	98	37	3	42	79
		McGuire – Rhein-Main/Torrejon	691	258	18	252	516
		Subtotal	11162	$ 4164 [3]	324	$ 4536	$ 8700
		22nd Air Force					
		Travis/Norton – Hickam	951	$ 355	40.5	$ 1013	$ 1368
		Travis/Norton – Kadena					
		Mid Pac	6666	2484	102	2550	5034
		North Pac	3057	1140	54	1350	2490
		Travis – Yokota					
		Mid Pac	6770	2525	129	3225	5750
		North Pac	265	99	6	150	249
		Travis – Osan					
		Mid Pac	1427	532	24	600	1132
		North Pac	4779	1783	90	2250	4033

Footnotes: } See next page
Source: }

United States
General Accounting Office
Form 214 (Rev. 12-66)

2 of 2   Q-1 / 12-5

Summary of Reductions to Commercial Carriers
(Continued)

J. Kennedy
3/24/75

1	2 Channel	Gallons[3] of Jet Fuel Saved (000)	Total[4] Cost Reduction[2] (000)	No.[5] of Flights Converted	Operating Expense Reduction[1] (000)	Total[7] Cost Reduction (000)
	Travis – Guam	3594	$ 1341	70.5	$ 1763	$ 3104
	Travis – Philippines	1369	511	22.5	563	1074
	Travis – Taipei	1527	562	27	675	1237
	Travis – Bangkok	6227	2341	79.5	1988	4329
	Subtotal	36656	$ 13673	645	$ 16127[3]	$ 29800
	Total	47818	$ 17837[3]	969	$ 20663	$ 38500

Notes:

1. Based on airline estimates of $14,000 and $25,000 costs for Cat. B transAtlantic and transPacific flights. Excludes fuel and cost of ownership costs. W/P P-18 Ⓐ
2. Based on 37.3¢ per gallon. W/P M-1/1-4.
3. Added and computed totals differ because of rounding.

Note: Differences with prior schedules due to rounding.

Source: Q-1 / 12-1, 2

☆ U.S. Government Printing Office: 1974 — 553-629

Peer and Supervisory Review

The reader will notice from the working papers that there are often several levels of review, noted on the papers through the initials of the reviewer. Some of these are peer reviews as well as supervisory reviews. It is often beneficial for an auditor to allow one of his peers to review his working papers before the supervisor reviews them, for many of the errors and inconsistencies in logic can be caught and corrected in this way before the papers go on for higher review.

REVIEW QUESTIONS

1. Gathering evidence on the objective, recording that evidence, analyzing it, coming to a conclusion, and reporting the results differ procedurally between types of audits. Explain these differences. (See p. 171.)

2. A good standard for work-paper preparation is to avoid excessive detail. Why? (See p. 172.)

3. Sources of information appearing in working papers should be clear and specific. Indicate some of the methods of clearly identifying the sources of information on a work sheet. (See p. 173.)

4. GAO suggests that the purpose of each working paper should be clearly stated, either in the working paper or by reference to the audit program. Why is this a good idea? (See pp. 172–73.)

5. Summaries are very important parts of working papers. Discuss the reason for summaries (p. 174), and list and discuss the basic elements of an audit summary. (See p. 175.)

6. There are essentially two levels of summaries. Describe each. (See p. 176.)

7. Discuss the following statement: "Major reporting problems frequently stem from the manner in which underlying evidence in the working papers is analyzed and summarized." (See pp. 176–77.)

8. In the illustrative summary, the auditor places his conclusion before his section on the results achieved. Which method would you consider the better method? (See pp. 178–79.)

9. In the illustrative audit, the auditor references each statement he makes in the summary to the appropriate working paper. Would you consider this a proper policy for each audit organization to have? Why? (See pp. 178–80.)

10. In showing the source of the information in the "Summary of Fuel Savings" worksheet Q–1/12–1, the auditor refers to work sheets PD–1/13 and worksheets Q–1/8–1 to 8–9. What is the detail in worksheet PD–1/13 that is summarized in worksheet Q–1/12–1? What is the detail in worksheets Q–1/8–2 to 8–9 that is summarized in worksheet Q–1/12–1? (See pp. 182–83, 184–85, and 188–201.)

CASE 1

State Self-assessment Taxes: The Detailed Examination for an M-audit

Required

For this work, review Case 1 in Chapter 5, pp. 87–92, and then respond to the following:

1. From the evidence developed on the stated objective, can you conclude:
   a) That the revenue picture of the state could be improved by at least $5 million by following the stated criteria?
   b) That you could recommend future actions that would, if carried out, increase the revenues of the state?
2. Write a Level II summary comparable to the one illustrated in this chapter that could be used for developing your draft report.
3. Write a draft report from the summary.

In this case the auditor, after testing the management control of the Department of Revenue, could refine his possible audit objective into a fairly firm audit objective. He might want to add additional criteria to improve the original tentative objective.

A possible objective would be stated somewhat as follows:

Has the Department of Revenue of Piedmont collected (causes) within $5 million of the maximum revenue that should have been collected (effects) by:

1. Having made it easy for a taxpayer to file income or sales tax returns through
   a) Revised state income tax forms that tie into federal income tax forms,
   b) Properly communicated information on tax laws and requirements concerning: (1) resident taxpayers, (2) nonresident taxpayers, (3) individual taxpayers, (4) corporate taxpayers, (5) unincorporated business taxpayers, and (6) sales tax taxpayers, and
   c) Adequately provided help for taxpayers in filing their returns, as in giving instructions on forms.
2. Having made it difficult for a taxpayer not to file or accurately assess taxes due either for sales or income taxes:
   a) By having developed computerized lists of taxpayers who have had income tax withheld and
      (1) Relating list to federal returns when possible,
      (2) Identifying and following up nonfilers,
   b) By having developed computerized lists of sales tax taxpayers and matching returns with list.
   c) By having developed lists from inside and outside the department of sources of possible taxpayers who are presently not paying any of these taxes,
   d) By having promptly determined whether a business is nonprofit and therefore exempt from income taxes, but not sales taxes or profit, and liable for both sales and income taxes,
   e) By having field-audited returns selected by computer from standards that determine the possibility of maximum benefits for dollars invested,
   f) By having desk-audited selected random returns and notifying taxpayers that their returns have been audited and accepted as correct or additional tax is due, and,
   g) By having immediately started collection procedures when a tax becomes delinquent (criteria).

Evidence Gathering, Analyzing, and Summarizing

Tying in to Federal Returns. The auditors obtained a special report prepared for the Commissioner of Revenue by a committee, which recommended that the state adopt a program that would relate the state income tax law directly to the federal income tax law, although this would make it necessary to revise the current state law.

The report estimated that from taxpayers currently filing returns, there would be no direct increase in revenue by amending the law and making the state income tax provisions comparable with the federal provisions. It did estimate, however, that because of the ease of preparation of the returns using the revised forms, taxpayers who at present did not file because of the complicated tax returns and instructions would pay an additional $500,000 per year.

Properly Communicating Information and Assisting Taxpayers. As was found in the preliminary survey, any self-assessing tax system demands that the taxpayer understand the purpose behind the tax law and the procedures for accomplishing it. The measure of success is voluntary compliance, and this will depend upon the taxpayer's knowledge of the law, regulations, and enforcement procedures of the taxing system.

A department self study made approximately five years previously when the assistance program was first started, showed that the revenue of the state would increase a minimum of 3 percent if the information concerning taxes and the tax law was widely distributed, if the laws and regulations were thoroughly understood, and if the forms and instructions were understandable and not too complicated. A limited review of the forms and instructions showed that almost any high school graduate and most college graduates had difficulty in understanding the instructions and preparing the returns.

The auditor found the department had done very little in the way of

1. Preparing and distributing information that communications and news media could use to publicize the individual income tax, the sales tax, and the availability of tax assistance from the department,
2. Providing instructions and training to selected state, city, and industry employees to enable them to help their fellow employees prepare tax returns,
3. Discussing tax matters before trade associations and professional groups, and
4. Ruling on technical interpretations of tax laws.

Additional information obtained by the auditor from the department employees showed that the department's program of public assistance was almost entirely given to individual taxpayers—75 percent on income taxes and 25 percent on sales taxes—with little information provided to the general public concerning who should file, when, and what was being done to improve the ease of filing and computing taxes, except as found in the instructions on the returns themselves; furthermore, very little information other than in the forms was available to the businesses that collected and filed sales tax returns, even though approximately 35 percent of the revenue came from sales taxes.

The employees who conducted this limited assistance program said that the questions coming to them were almost always the same ones, and they suggested that the department make available to the public the answers to the questions most often asked. The tax auditors auditing returns also said the errors they found were almost always of the same type. They asked, "Why can't this information be distributed to the taxpayers and stop all of this need for us to catch it on an audit? It would increase the efficiency of the department and in most cases would increase the revenues to the state."

Based on the analytical techniques used in the report to the commissioner, the auditors made an analysis showing that if the department increased the information and taxpayer assistance program of the state, without any additional increase in costs, there was a good probability of immediately increasing revenues by an additional 1 percent, instead of the 3 percent suggested by the study group. This amount would be in addition to any obtained as a result of better enforcement procedures.

Computer Operations. The auditors obtained information from several states and from the IRS that showed all tax data and related information was placed in the computer files, which thus contained a continuously updated record of each taxpayer's account. These sources said that all settlements with taxpayers are made by computer processing of the master-file accounts. The data are used for accounting records and for issuing refund checks, bills, or notices; answering inquiries; classifying returns for audit; preparing reports; and other processing and enforcement activities. Other uses are subtracting delinquent taxes from refund claims, subtracting unincorporated business taxes due from persons who claim refunds on their individual income tax returns, using the addresses as a current mailout list, and retrieving information for audit and other compliance action.

Several states reported that their costs for such a system had been paid for many times over by identifying nonfilers and collecting taxes from them along with improving revenues. The estimate for the benefits from this activity was an immediate $5 million per year increase.

The head of the state Data Systems Division said that if she were given permission and the loan of a few high-class clerical personnel for six months, she could program the computer to accomplish such activities with very little additional cost.

Developing Lists from Inside and Outside of the Department of Revenue on Possible Business Tax Nonfilers. The department maintains a separate index file of businesses that complied with the personal property tax, a tax levied only on business property, which businesses declare each year. On the basis of these declarations, the department makes tax assessments. The index for the personal property tax, arranged by county, city, and street address, accounts for every business address in the state.

From the index file on personal property tax and the various telephone directories, the auditors selected 100 businesses and, with the help of the department's personnel, ascertained if these firms were registered for applicable sales, withholding, and franchise taxes. The results of the tests are shown in the table below.

in the personal property tax records and could not be located,
- Three were unincorporated businesses and claimed they did not gross $5,000 (minimum for filing), and
- One appeared liable for tax and was so advised.

Personal property tax records indicated that most of the 13 businesses were small firms that had been in operation from 3 to 8 years, during which most had paid personal property tax only to the state.

The procedures for identifying new businesses and obtaining their compliance with personal property tax did not include taking steps to make sure that the businesses also registered for other taxes. Similarly, businesses that registered for sales, withholding, or franchise taxes were not made specifically aware of personal property tax requirements, because the registration form did not include personal property information.

At the auditor's request, revenue department officials experienced with following up on nonfilers listed the reasons for nonfiling in what they believed to be the order of frequency, from most to least frequent, as follows:

1. Worked outside the state and the employer did not withhold tax; the filer did not understand procedures requiring the filing of a declaration.
2. Did not realize a tax return should have been filed at the end of the year, because tax was withheld or a declaration was filed.

	Number and percent
Registered for all applicable taxes	84
Unregistered for one or more taxes	13
Claimed exemption from franchise tax but had no application on file	3
	100

Of the 13 businesses not registered for one or more taxes:

- None had paid the taxes in question,
- Nine had moved from the addresses shown

3. Did not know there was a state income tax.
4. Were employed by a nonprofit group, such as a church, and thus thought they were exempt.
5. Were employed in the state but thought

they were exempt because of living and paying taxes in another state.
6. Maintained a permanent legal residence in the state but lived outside of the state.

An analysis by the auditors showed that better coordination of the tax collection activities in identifying nonfilers would net the state an additional one-half of 1 percent of revenue.

The auditors also made an analysis from city and county offices concerning such items as occupancy permits, construction contracts, and firms incorporating. They also reviewed the yellow pages of the telephone book and other sources of construction contracts to see if new businesses were coming in to the taxing system, which at present were not paying either sales or other business taxes.

Figures showed that about 2 out of every 100 reviewed were not on the tax lists. The auditors estimated an increase of 1 percent in sales or business taxes if this source of nonfilers was fully exploited.

From the above review, they also found that about 50 percent of the nonprofit organizations were not in the records as being exempt from either sales or income taxes. Although they made no analysis of the possibility of additional revenue, they knew it would be considerable, especially in the area of the sales tax.

Auditing Returns

As was found in the review and testing of management and internal controls, the department was doing a fairly good job on what they were doing. Yet they had no program tied into the desk-auditing of returns for the "policeman-on-the-beat" purpose of letting the taxpayers know that someone was looking at their returns, nor any program for determining the best type of return to examine to obtain the maximum benefits for dollar expended. The Commissioner of Revenue stated that he planned to adopt a new program, tied into the computer, to select the type of returns that would provide the maximum benefit, but he did not know exactly when it would get started.

While no means were available to estimate accurately the increase in revenue from this new program, or if there would in fact be any increase, the auditors, from a statement by the commissioner, estimated that about $1 million a year additionally could be collected.

Delinquent Taxes

The commissioner said that the collection of unpaid taxes was the ultimate enforcement action taken to administer equitably the state tax system: it was the teeth of the system.

The unpaid sales and income taxes for the past two years were as shown in the following table.

Delinquent Tax Accounts Receivable*

Tax	June 30, 1977 Number	Amount	June 30, 1978 Number	Amount
Individual income	85,000	$11,900,000	90,000	$9,000,000
Sales	16,000	6,000,000	16,000	5,000,000
Employee withholding	9,600	2,500,000	8,500	1,800,000
Unincorporated	5,500	600,000	3,000	400,000
Corporation	5,000	1,100,000	2,500	850,000

*Numbers are rounded to nearest 100, amounts to nearest $100,000.

When delinquent tax accounts are referred to revenue officers, their actions include: the use of dunning notices; telephone or field contacts with the delinquents; legal attachment of salaries, wages, bank accounts, and property; and referral to the general counsel for prosecution. At his discretion, a revenue officer may take these actions successively or selectively, depending on his evaluation of the individual or business tax-paying record.

From the auditors' analysis of the above information and the information on delinquent taxes in the preliminary review of management control, they decided that the principal problem of delinquent taxes was the backlog of cases. The collection effort was relatively successful once undertaken; for every dollar of delinquent taxes written off during the past fiscal year, $9 were collected.

In discussing this information with the

revenue officers, the auditors pointed out that earlier contact could result in fewer writeoffs and prompter collection of taxes, since many writeoffs occurred because the delinquent could not be located or had no remaining assets by the time the revenue officer initated action. The revenue officers also stated that from an analysis made two years previously, $2 million in income taxes were refunded to individuals who owed the state $1,800,000 in taxes for prior years.

CASE 2

City Welfare: The Detailed Examination for an M-audit

Required:
This case is a continuation of Case 2 in Chapter 5, pp. 93–95.
1. Prepare a conclusion on the audit objective from the evidence that follows.
2. Write a Level II summary as illustrated in this chapter.
3. Write a draft report using the summary developed as the basis for the draft report.

A possible audit objective for the detailed examination in this case would be stated somewhat as follows:

> Could the Department of Human Resources stop making potential welfare overpayments (causes) of at least $12.5 million dollars (effects) by eliminating the number of (1) potential willful misrepresentation cases on the welfare rolls, (2) recipients who may receive benefits under food stamp programs who are ineligible, and (3) recipients who may receive Medicaid payments who are ineligible (criteria).

Summary of Potential Willful Misrepresentation Cases

DHR did not effectively reduce or eliminate the number of potential willful misrepresentation cases on the welfare rolls. As a result, DHR made potential welfare overpayments of at least $26.6 million from October 1970 through December 1975. Because such misrepresentation reduces money available for the truly needy, DHR should have made a concerted effort as early as 1971 to identify these cases, as well as other cases of ineligibility or incorrect payment. (See worksheets 1 and 2, this case.)

In calendar year 1975, the Quality Control Group of DHR reported that 740 of the total cases reviewed were in error. Of these, 226 indicated willful misrepresentation by the recipient. By projecting the results of the 1975 review, the auditors estimated that an average of 4,244 potential willful misrepresentation cases were on the welfare rolls during each month in 1975. For 2,330 of these, the recipients would be ineligible for welfare payments; and for 1,914, they would be ineligible for part of the payment. Based on the average monthly payment made in error on indicated willful misrepresentation cases, DHR incurred potential welfare overpayments of about $8.7 million on such cases in calendar year 1975. For each month's delay, beginning in January 1976, in identifying and correcting these cases, DHR could incur an additional $725,000 in potential welfare overpayments.

Source of Data and Methodology for Computing Overpayments on Potential Willful Misrepresentation Cases for Worksheet 1

All data used in computing the amount of welfare overpayments made to recipients where willful misrepresentation might be involved were obtained from the Quality Control Group. This data included the number of cases the group

WORKSHEET 1

COMPUTATION OF ESTIMATED OVERPAYMENTS TO POTENTIAL WILLFUL MISREPRESENTATION CASES IN AFDC CASELOAD FOR CALENDAR YEAR 1975[a]

Month (1975)	AFDC cases reviewed	Willful misrepresentation cases	Percent of willful misrepresentation cases	Average monthly payment in error per willful misrepresentation case	AFDC caseload	Potential willful misrepresentation cases in AFDC caseload	Overpayments potential willful misrepresentation cases[b]
Jan.	137	15	10.9	$182.73	33,793	3,683	$ 672,995
Feb.	141	17	12.1	153.06	29,872	3,615	553,312
Mar.	137	19	13.9	179.89	32,851	4,566	821,378
Apr.	139	27	19.4	136.78	31,521	6,115	836,410
May	143	24	16.8	152.83	30,867	5,186	792,576
June	142	18	12.7	186.78	27,645	3,511	655,785
July	138	19	13.8	170.79	31,022	4,281	731,152
Aug.	136	18	13.2	162.06	32,406	4,278	693,293
Sept.	143	20	14.0	180.65	30,676	4,295	775,892
Oct.	141	16	11.3	166.25	30,682	3,467	576,389
Nov.	140	14	10.0	214.93	32,867	3,287	706,475
Dec.	135	19	14.1	191.53	32,926	4,643	889,274
Total	1,672	226				4,244[c]	$8,704,931[d]

[a] Computed based on cases reviewed each month by DHR's Quality Control Group. The cases are randomly sampled and statistically representative of all AFDC cases. The computation results in a 95 percent confidence plus or minus $640,000.

[b] Any adjustments to quality control data by BED on those cases that they have resolved are not reflected in these totals but, if considered, would result in a net increase in overpayment.

[c] An average of 4,244 cases per month.

[d] An average of about $725,000 in potential overpayments per month.

reviewed, the number they identified where willful misrepresentation might have been involved, and the amount of money paid in error to each of these cases. The cases identified as containing willful misrepresentation were not duplicated in any of the 12 months. Using this data, the auditors made the estimates shown on Worksheet 1.

The total potential number of willful misrepresentation cases—column 7—was computed by multiplying the average number of AFDC cases—column 6—with the percent of indicated willful misrepresentation cases—column 4. The estimated overpayments were computed by multiplying the number of potential willful misrepresentation cases—column 7—by the average amount paid in error to identified indicated willfull misrepresentation cases—column 5.

The Quality Control Group review was based on a random sample of cases; and thus, projection of sample results to the total universe would be statistically valid. Based on the size of the group's sample, the computed amount of overpayments is within a 95-percent confidence level plus or minus $640,000.

Summary of Potential Food Stamp Overpayments

AFDC recipients may receive benefits under the federal government's food stamp program. The welfare recipient can purchase, based on certain eligibility requirements such as the amount of income, food stamps at less than face value; the Department of Agriculture pays the difference. Actions resulting in a loss of welfare eligibility could result in a loss of eligibility for food stamps.

Of the 124 willful misrepresentation cases identified by the Quality Control Group in calendar year 1975, 94 received food stamps. As of March 1, 1976, BED resolved and terminated the welfare payments for 68 of these 94 cases. (Nineteen cases were unresolved and for the remaining cases, payments were either adjusted or remained the same at the time of the audit review.) Food stamp benefits were also terminated for the 68 cases.

The auditors reviewed the food stamp records to determine if the terminated AFDC recipients reapplied and were approved to receive food stamps as a non-public-assistance case, and they analyzed the monthly food stamp records covering the period of time that the cases were terminated for welfare through March 1, 1976. For those terminated from January to March 1976, they also examined the food stamp records through June 1976. Analysis showed that 8 recipients had reapplied and were approved to receive food stamps as non-public-assistance recipients, and 2 reapplied and were approved to receive both welfare and food stamp benefits. One of the 8 receiving food stamps as a non-public-assistance recipient received welfare benefits after receiving food stamps for 3 months.

The auditors estimated that the annual overpayment of food stamps to potentially ineligible willful misrepresentation cases could have been about $1.3 million in calendar year 1975. (See Worksheet 3.)

Summary of Potential Medicaid Overpayments

The Medicaid program covers the cost of medical expenses of eligible recipients. An individual or family approved to receive benefits under the AFDC welfare program is automatically eligible to receive Medicaid. Conversely, recipients found to be ineligible for welfare could be ineligible for Medicaid. HEW regulations generally provide, however, that recipients who become ineligible for AFDC welfare benefits because of increased earnings or hours of employment can continue to receive Medicaid benefits for a period of 4 months. Because of this requirement, the auditors, in determining the amount of potential Medicaid overpayments, excluded 14 of the 124 ineligible indicated willful misrepresentation cases to eliminate Medicaid payments outside the control of DHR.

Of the 226 cases identified by the Quality Control Group in the 1975 calendar year, 110, or 48.7 percent, were found to be ineligible for welfare payments, excluding the 14 cases referred to above. Thus, the 110 cases could also have been ineligible for Medicaid. Projecting this percentage to the estimated 4,244 potential willful misrepresentation cases on the welfare rolls during each month in calendar year 1975, about 2,067 such cases could be ineligible for Medicaid.

Information obtained for the 226 cases showed that on the average, each had 1 adult and about 2.4 children. Applying this data to the 2,067 cases that could be ineligible for Medicaid, 2,067

WORKSHEET 2

COMPUTATION OF ESTIMATED OVERPAYMENTS TO POTENTIAL WILLFUL MISREPRESENTATION CASES
FROM OCTOBER 1970 THROUGH DECEMBER 1974

Period of review	Cases reviewed	Ineligible willful misrepresentation cases	Percent of ineligible willful misrepresentation cases	Overpaid willful misrepresentation cases	Percent of overpaid willful misrepresentation cases	Average monthly caseload	Average monthly potential ineligible willful misrepresentation cases	Average monthly potential overpaid willful misrepresentation cases	Average monthly overpayment per ineligible case[a]	Average monthly overpayment per overpaid case[a]	Overpayment to ineligible willful misrepresentation cases[b]	Overpayment to overpaid willful misrepresentation cases[b]
Jan.–June 1974	823	62	7.5	42	5.1	29,959	2,247	1,528	$207.44	$73.39	$2,796,706	$ 672,840
July–Dec. 1974	811	51	6.3	37	4.6	30,406	1,196	1,399	197.26	74.16	2,267,701	622,499
Apr.–Aug. 1973	800	45	5.6	40	5.0	29,673	1,662	1,484	192.11	65.84	3,831,442	1,172,479
Jan.–June 1972	596	38	6.4	24	4.0	25,525	1,634	1,021	171.88	51.44	1,685,112	315,121
July–Dec. 1972	830	52	6.3	29	3.5	27,866	1,756	975	168.78	56.18	1,778,266	328,653
Apr.–June 1971	533	21	3.9	21	3.9	19,497	760	760	168.24	46.15	383,587	105,222
July–Dec. 1971	547	20	3.7	19	3.5	23,110	855	809	173.25	46.52	888,773	225,808
Jan.–Mar. 1971	521	22	4.2	23	4.4	17,253	725	759	182.20	40.03	396,285	91,148
Oct.–Dec. 1970	351	10[c]	2.8	9[c]	2.6	15,610	437	406	190.00[c]	45.00[c]	249,090	54,810
										Total Overpayments:	$14,276,962	$3,588,580

[a] Based on an average overpayment for all ineligible and overpaid cases identified by the Quality Control Group. Information was not available on the amount of overpayment for ineligible and overpaid misrepresentation cases.

[b] Computed by multiplying the average number of cases by the average cost per case times the number of months covered by the review period except for the 1973 review period which was multiplied by 12.

[c] Quality Control Group report was not available for this period. Information was obtained orally from a Quality Control Group official.

WORKSHEET 3

COMPUTATION OF ESTIMATED FOOD STAMP OVERPAYMENTS TO POTENTIAL INELIGIBLE WILLFUL MISREPRESENTATION CASES
IN AFDC CASELOAD FOR CALENDAR YEAR 1975

Month (1975)	Willful misrepresentation cases identified by quality control	Ineligible willful misrepresentation cases	Percent of ineligible willful misrepresentation cases	Ineligible willful misrepresentation cases receiving food stamps	Percent receiving food stamps	Potential ineligible willful misrepresentation cases[a]	Potential ineligible willful misrepresentation cases receiving food stamps	Cost of food stamps[b]	Total food stamp overpayments
Jan.	15	9	60.0	7	77.8	2,210	1,719	$56.71	$ 97,484
Feb.	17	8	47.1	6	75.0	1,703	1,277	51.17	65,344
Mar.	19	13	68.4	11	84.6	3,123	2,642	58.27	153,949
Apr.	27	13	48.1	10	76.9	2,941	2,262	50.00	113,100
May	24	11	45.8	9	81.8	2,375	1,943	71.22	138,380
June	18	14	77.8	12	85.7	2,732	2,341	48.75	114,124
July	19	7	36.8	6	85.7	1,575	1,350	74.00	99,900
Aug.	18	7	38.9	5	71.4	1,664	1,188	81.00	96,228
Sept.	20	13	65.0	9	69.2	2,792	1,932	66.22	127,937
Oct.	16	9	56.3	6	66.7	1,952	1,302	64.50	83,979
Nov.	14	7	50.0	4	57.1	1,664	939	72.25	67,843
Dec.	19	13	68.4	9	69.2	3,176	2,198	59.33	130,407
	226	124		94			1,758[c]		$1,288,675

[a] Computed by multiplying the number of potential willful misrepresentation cases in AFDC caseload (see Worksheet 2) by column 4.

[b] Represents the average cost of food stamps to the Department of Agriculture for each ineligible case.

[c] Monthly average 1,758.

218

adults and 4,960 children could have been on the rolls who were not entitled to Medicaid in calendar year 1975.

Based on information provided by DHR officials, about 71 percent of AFDC recipients received Medicaid benefits in fiscal year 1975 with an average annual payment of $755 for each adult and $310 for each child. Using this data, as shown in the following table, the city could have paid about $2.2 million in calendar year 1975 in Medicaid payments to potential ineligible willful misrepresentation cases who could also be ineligible to receive Medicaid.

The director, DHR, said that if a case was in fact ineligible and remained on the roll, there might be some overpayment in food stamps and Medicaid; however, a recipient's ineligibility for AFDC does not render that person ineligible for such benefits. The director said a separate determination of eligibility as a non-public-assistance case for these two programs must be made before overpayment statistics can be gathered.

The auditors recognized that an ineligible AFDC recipient could continue to receive Medicaid and food stamps as a non-public-assistance case and that this would affect the estimated overpayments. As indicated by an analysis of food stamp records, however, only 10 of the 68 cases auditors looked at applied and were approved for food stamps after welfare benefits were terminated. Thus, it would appear than ineligible AFDC recipients who can qualify for continued food stamp benefits would not materially affect the estimate of overpayments.

Records were not available to readily determine the extent to which ineligible AFDC recipients reapplied and were determined to qualify for continued Medicaid. To the extent that such cases exist the estimate would change.

Computation of Potential Medicaid Overpayments on Potential Willful Misrepresentation Cases

Potential ineligible recipients	Estimated percent using Medicaid	Estimated number using Medicaid	Average annual cost-per-person	Amount of potential overpayments
2,067 adults	71	1,468	$755	$1,108,340
4,960 children	71	3,522	310	1,091,820
Total				$2,200,160

CHAPTER **11**

Illustrative Working Papers: The Detailed Examination for a Program Audit

After you have read this chapter, studied the review questions, and worked through the cases, you will understand:

- The basic principles and practices used in making a P-audit.
- How to gather evidence for a P-audit in accordance with the audit program.
- How to prepare working papers in accordance with policies suggested by your organization or with those suggested in the chapter.
- How to summarize the working papers into properly prepared summaries, which can then be used as the basis for preparing the report.

The same principles of work-paper preparation shown in Chapter 10 for an M-audit apply to a P-audit. Summaries are just as important, although they can be prepared in a different manner for various types of audits. For example, in this illustration—based on the preliminary phase of the Indian Education audit in Chapter 6—the summary is a categorization of the answers to the questions required in the audit program. Since this audit was made by the GAO, policy standards pertaining to their work for a P-audit should be available to the reader and are presented in this book as Appendix VI; they can serve as a reference guide for practices used in this chapter's working papers.

Illustrative Working Papers: The Indian Education Case—The Detailed Examination

Background Data   These illustrative working papers for the P-audit of the Indian Education Program come from an audit made by the GAO, which officials of that office have kindly made available, and the working papers shown are actual working papers taken from their files for that audit. (Some are shown in typed form, instead of the original handwritten form in order to make them easier to read and understand.)

The reader may notice that most of the illustrative material shown is evidence recorded on the subobjectives for causes in the form of interviews. Some records evidence was gathered, obviously; the program memoranda used as the criteria and the results of the achievement tests are examples. But the majority of the evidence shown on causes came from interviews with responsible officials. Interviewing, in fact, is such an important technique in both M-audits and P-audits that material developed by the GAO on both interviewing and questionnaires is presented in Chapter 13.

A draft report, which can be referenced to the working papers, is always prepared from the summary. Since this summary is somewhat different from those usually prepared, no illustration is given of a draft report for the entire audit; but the Mt. Edgecumbe School draft report, used to summarize the evidence on this one subobjective, is illustrative of reviewing and referencing techniques for a P-audit. Also, no detailed evidence is given in the illustration on the evidence on the criteria: Since this information comes from the Program Memoranda for 1971-72, they would be the basic source of the evidence on the criteria.

Often in a P-audit, the basic objective of the entity, which the auditor might possibly use as the basis for the criteria, has never been developed or stated by the entity itself. The auditor, thus, must himself develop a measurable objective to be used. This often requires that he use experts and consultants to help him come up with a standard acceptable both to himself and to the entity, and one that can be used as the criteria for the audit. For this audit, however, the objective has been well stated by the entity.

Because of the volume, most of the working papers for this audit are not shown; instead, we will present selected papers that illustrate specific points. Even then, the papers have been condensed to delete duplicate information. The summary schedule, thus, is a limited representation only of the total information originally summarized in that schedule. Also, limited detailed information is provided for the schools represented, except for the Intermountain Boarding School, where the reader can trace back in detail the evidence summarized in the summary schedule.

Audit Objective

All the evidence has been gathered on the audit objective, and the audit objective given in Chapter 6 in the audit program was stated somewhat as follows:

> Are the Bureau of Indian Affairs and the schools that come under its jurisdiction in the process (causes) of accomplishing their objective (effects) of having the achievement level of Indian students at least equal to that for non-Indian youth by 1976 (criteria)?

As was stated in the audit program, there were many levels of causes, broken down in the audit areas of (1) officials having a good management system, (2) officials testing for achievement or I.Q., (3) officials providing remedial reading, (4) officials providing for special education, (5) officials providing for substitute teaching, and (6) officials providing for and properly using the results of counseling.

Since the criteria of the primary objective was acceptable, appropriate, and measurable, the above causes, which will be the basis for most of the illustrative detailed examination work, will enable the auditor to see whether:

1. The officials responsible have properly communicated the entity's objective, and when they have, have lower levels of management accepted the objective,
2. All levels of officials have the capability of measuring the results of accomplishing the objective, and
3. All levels of officials have provided the means for accomplishing the objective.

With the information given on the illustrative papers that make up the remainder of this chapter, the reader should be able to move directly to the summary schedule, presented on pp. 224–25 as Figure 11.1.

INDIAN EDUCATION PROGRAM
Code 14553
Summary Schedule of Responses by School Officials to Key Questions

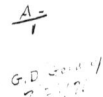

Audit Areas and Key Questions	PHOENIX AREA	
	Phoenix Boarding	Other Schools

I. <u>MANAGEMENT SYSTEMS</u>

   1. Are school administrators aware of Central Office Objectives as set forth in the 1971-72 Program Memorandums?   Yes ∧ G-2/2

   2. Is the school's education program designed to accomplish the P.M. objectives by 1976, including the establishment of objectives, identifying all restraints, developing programs to overcome all restraints, periodic milestones, and periodic evaluations?   No ∧ G-2/2

  10. What criteria has been established for measuring progress relative to accomplishment of:

     a. Central Office Objectives?   None ∧ G-2/3

     b. School Objectives?   How well the student does after finishing school. ∧ G-2/3

II. <u>TESTING</u>

   3. Does the school use the achievement and I.Q. test results for placement, identification of student needs, curriculum development, evaluating program results, and identification of weaknesses in the quality of education being provided?   Used partially for placement and considered in curriculum development. ∧ G-2/4&5

   4. Are the following tests administered:

     a. Academic achievement tests to all new entering students?   Yes ∧ G-2/4,5

     b. Academic achievement tests to all students annually at about the same time each year?   Yes ∧ G-2/4,5

     c. I.Q. tests (organized programs, not isolated tests here and there)?   No ∧ G-2/4,5

     d. Are the same or comparable academic achievement tests given from year to year?   Yes ∧ G-2/4,5

III. <u>REMEDIAL READING</u>

   1. Do school officials believe that one of the student's primary restraints to academic achievement at national norms is their inability to communicate (read, write, speak effectively in the English Language?   Yes ∧ G-3/12 (2)

IV. <u>SPECIAL EDUCATION</u>

   1. Do school officials believe there is a need for special education for students at their school (Students with physical, sensory, mental or emotional hangups)?   Yes ∧ G-2/6,9

V. <u>SUBSTITUTE TEACHING</u>   -----

VI. <u>COUNSELING</u>

   1. Is counseling provided?   Yes ∧ C-2/3-1

   3. Are counselors involved in student placement or curriculum development?   Yes ∧ G-2/3-1

   4. Do counselors give standardized I.Q. and academic achievement tests and use the data to identify student and curriculum needs?   Yes ∧ C-2/2 (1, 6 &7)

Information from 4 other schools was a part of this worksheet, but is not illustrated.

Questions 3 through 9 and 11 through 15 in Audit Area I; questions 1, 2, and 5 in Audit Area II; questions 2, 3, and 4 in Audit Area III; questions 2 and 3 in Audit Area IV; questions 1 through 3 in Audit Area V: and Questions 2, 5, and 6 in Audit Area VI are not shown in this illustration.

∧ traced to source and verified. Source as indicated. Purpose: to summarize key questions to audit objectives.

Figure 11.1

←---------- NAVAJO AREA ----------→			←---------- ALASKA AREA ----------→	
Fort Wingate Boarding H.S.	Intermountain Boarding H.S.	Other Schools	Mt. Edgcombe Boarding School	Kotzebue Day School
I.				
1. No $\frac{OD-1}{4}$	Yes $\frac{PA-3}{13}$		No $\frac{SM-3}{1-13}$	No $\frac{SK-3}{1-1}$
2. No $\frac{OQ-2}{5}$	No $\frac{PA-3}{1}$		No $\frac{SA-3}{1-1}$	No $\frac{SK-3}{1-3}$
10.		Information from other schools is not shown.		
a. None Academic Program Self Evaluation	None $\frac{PC-2}{1-2}$		None $\frac{SM-1}{1-1}$	None $\frac{SK-3}{1-1}$
b. $\frac{OC-2}{1-2}$ $\frac{OC-3}{5}$	None $\frac{PC-2}{1-2}$		None "	None "
II.				
3. No $\frac{OE-2}{1-2}$	Yes $\frac{PE-2}{4}$		No $\frac{S-1}{1-1}$	No $\frac{S-1}{1-1}$
a. No $\frac{OE-2}{1,2}$	No Yearly reading part $\frac{PE-2}{}$		Yes $\frac{SJ-7}{1-1}$	No $\frac{SK-7}{1-1}$
b. No "	Yes $\frac{PE-2}{4}$ 5		Yes "	No "
c. No "	Yes $\frac{PE-2}{5}$		Yes $\frac{S-1}{1-1}$	No $\frac{S-1}{1-1}$
d. No "	Yes $\frac{PE-2}{4}$		Yes ", 1-15	Yes "
III.				
1. Yes $\frac{OG-2}{3,7}$ $\frac{OA-2}{1,3,4}$	Yes $\frac{PG-2}{3,4,11,15}$		Yes $\frac{S-1}{1-1}$ $\frac{SA-9}{3-3}$	Yes $\frac{SK-8}{1-8}$ (p.9)
IV.				
1. Yes $\frac{OG-2}{5}$	Yes $\frac{PG-2}{8-9}$		Yes $\frac{S-1}{1-1}$	Yes $\frac{S-1}{1-1}$ (22)
V.				
VI.				
1. Yes $\frac{OH-2}{3}$	Yes $\frac{PH-2}{2}$		Yes $\frac{S-12}{1-1}$	Yes $\frac{S-12}{1-5}$
3. Placement, Yes: Curriculum Dev. not asked $\frac{OH-2}{2}$	No $\frac{PH-2}{2-3}$		Yes $\frac{SM-12}{2-1}$	Placement, No: Curriculum Dev. not asked $\frac{SK-12}{2-1}$
4. No $\frac{OH-2}{4}$	No $\frac{PH-2}{4}$		Yes $\frac{SM-1}{2-1}$	No $\frac{SK-13}{2-1}$
	Supporting schedules for this summary not given)			

Figure 11.1 (continued)

The Summary Schedule of Responses by School Officials to Key Questions

This summary schedule, which follows immediately, illustrates beautifully how information in the detailed schedules flows to the summary schedules. The reader may want to follow the flow of information from at least one of the detailed sets of working papers to the summary columns. For example, the answers to questions 1 and 2 for the Phoenix Boarding School can be referenced back to working papers G-2/2, and the answers to the other questions can be referenced back to a specific working paper.

In referencing back to the summary schedule from Alaska, the reader may note that the auditors prepared a summary report somewhat similar to a final report. Notice in this schedule how the referencer shows that every word or thought has the detail shown in another working paper. Having sufficient evidence to support every aspect of the audit objective makes the difference of having a good audit or a mediocre one. Fortunately, preparing an audit report from this type of summary and working papers becomes rather easy with practice.

Review of Indian Education
Code 14553

G-2 / 1

R Krogh
3/05/71

RECORD OF DISCUSSION

Date: March 3, 1971

Place: Administration Office,
Phoenix Indian High School (Off reservation boarding)
Phoenix, Arizona

Participants:

    Mr. Vincent Little, Superintendent, Phoenix Indian High School, (PIHS)
    Mr. M. Bollinger, Principal, PIHS
    Mr. D. Ellis, Asst. Principal (Instruction), PIHS
    Miss G. Davenport, Education Specialist (Guidance and Counseling), PIHS
    Mr. C. Crawford, Education Specialist, Phoenix Area Office (Education), Bureau of Indian Affairs (BIA)
    Mr. R. Krogh, GAO Supervisory Auditor
    Mr. T. McGonagill, GAO Supervisory Auditor

Purpose:

To obtain from the officials of the PIHS certain information of the operation of the PIHS.

Discussion:

Regarding the objectives of Indian education, I asked the PIHS officials what they considered to be the basic objective of PIHS in education. All agreed that the basic objective of PIHS was to develop an educational program which responded to the needs of the Indians, as the Indian students saw these needs, and that was geared to the pace which the students wanted and could handle. They explained that that did not necessarily mean, and in fact did not result in, a program which had as its objective an education for all students equal to what the average American received in the average high school. The

G-2
2

superintendent gave us copies of the 69-70 school year and the 70-71 school year philosophy and major objective established for PIHS (see work paper G-3/2, 2A). I told them that such objective did not appear to be entirely in line with the broad objectives stated by the BIA in several of the recent years' program memorandums (FY 69 through 72), and a fiscal year 72 issue support paper on education developed by the BIA. I explained that these documents contained such objectives as: (1) By 1976, 90% of all Indian youth graduating from high school, 50% of these going on to college, while the remainder either employed or going into further vocational education, (2) by 1980, elimination of the education gap at high school graduation between Indian youth and non-Indian youth. All present said that they were aware of these objectives stated by the BIA, however, they said that (1) no further guidance had ever been received at the school from either the Area Office or the Central Office as to how to implement programs which would achieve these objectives, (2) objectives of this nature, stated in planning documents for fiscal years two years or so ahead, were never communicated to them as the actual objective when the fiscal year arrived, (3) as far as they were concerned these objectives stated by the BIA were totally unrealistic and unobtainable, and they were ignored by the school officials. Regarding the latter point, they explained that they did not believe that it should be the objective of the Bureau's education system to provide a

G-2

3

normal high school academic-type education to all Indian students, considering the attitude of Indians, and the inadequate educational attainment of the students when they arrive at the off-reservation boarding high schools. Mr. Ellis said that in his opinion the Bureau should not tie itself down to stated objectives, but rather it should be concerned with taking the student from where he is when he enters school to as far as he is capable of reaching by the time he leaves school.

I asked the PIHS school official what ways they use to measure the results of their program in relation to established objectives. They said that the primary measurement of the results of their program as far as they were concerned was how well the student does after he leaves school. They said that they annually prepare a document which shows what the last three years' graduates are doing. They said that they felt that if this document showed that the majority were going on to college, were gainfully employed, or were involved in some other constructive activity, they would consider the program very successful. They said that they do not consider achievement test results, compared to the national norm, as the indicator of program results. They felt that such an indicator was unfair considering the various problems which their students have, such as learning English as a second language, and their educational attainment before they arrive at high school. They felt that a

G-2/4

measurement of what the student gains during his school year is a more accurate indicator of program results. Regarding the results of the current program, Mr. Ellis said that they had found that about 33% of last year's graduates went on to college.

Regarding the school's testing program, we were told that the PIHS administers entrance tests, including the California Mental Maturity Test and the California Achievement Test, to all new students at the beginning of the year. They said that the California Achievement Test is also administered to the student body in the Spring of each year. They said they received the Area Office testing policy -- W/P CU/3. They said that the Southwest Cooperative Educational Laboratory administered the test for the PIHS up until last year, but that the PIHS is administering their own tests this year. They said that all students are given the Spring testing generally, but that last year most sophomores did not receive the tests. They did no Know why this happened. (See discussion with Counselors on work paper C-2/2 for a further explanation of the testing program). The PIHS officials said that the test results were used by the counselors for various purposes such as grade placement, class placement, vocation guidance, special education needs, etc. The PIHS officials also said that the test result data was one of the things which was considered by the school's curriculum committee in establishing the school programs.

I asked the PIHS officials what the gap was between the education achievement of the PIHS students and national norms at

G-2
5

graduation from high school. Mr. Ellis made a big point, and the others tended to agree, of the fact that the education gap which I was speaking of was ignored by him because he thought it was irrelevant. He felt that it was ridiculous to compare the education achievement of Indians to national norms, considering the fact that the Indians learning English as a second language, they come to the high school with lagging achievement levels, their interests are different than the typical high school student, etc. Mis Davenport commented that the achievement tests given at PIHS indicate that the students are about two years or more behind the national norms at graduation. Several of the PIHS officials commented they they felt that the achievement tests were not valid for Indian students because of the different language and culture of the Indian students compared to the typical English language and middle class culture upon which the tests are based. However, after some discussion on this matter they generally agreed that the standard achievement tests are a valid measure of how well the student has learned the various subjects in which they are tested in the language and culture of the society in which they will generally have to live if they are going to get normal jobs enjoyed by average Americans.

I asked the PIHS officials what level their freshman read at at entrance, pointing out that we had noted that at Sherman Indian High School the reading level of about half of the freshman students was below the fifth grade level, and that only three freshman read the 9.0 grade level or better. Mr Ellis responded that he was not

G-2/6

sure of the reading level of the students at Phoenix Indian High School offhand, but that he felt that it was not as bad as the figures I indicated from Sherman. However, Miss Davenport injected that she also wasn't sure but that she thought that the PIHS students' reading level grade placement was probably pretty similar to what I had indicated. I asked the PIHS officials how they attack the reading problem of their students. They said that the students are assigned to a reading laboratory, funded under Title I, on the basis of need--i.e. since it isn't large enough for all that need it, the worst are assigned first. They explained that the students are assigned to the lab for nine-week courses. They said that experience has shown that after a nine-week session in the reading lab one hour a day, the students can handle the regular school program without difficulty caused by reading problems in terms of PIHS objectives, which did not include achievement tests. I asked the PIHS officials whether ability to read was a key to learning other subjects. Mr. Little said, and the others agreed, that it is a well known fact that if a student doesn't have adequate reading skill he will be hindered in all of his academic work. (See D-2/3 for discussion with reading teachers).

 I asked the PIHS officials what the responsibilities were of the counselors at the school. They said that there are four counselors at PIHS funded under the regular program, who are responsible for the school's testing program, assignment of students to classes, periodic development counseling including vocational guidance, personal guidance, and "crisis" counseling. In addition, they said that there are four other counselors that work in the afternoons and evenings in the dorms and are responsible for dorm administration and generally performing normal parental responsibilities in the dorm. They also said there are two counselors in the special Title I model dorm program, they are not too sure of their responsibilities. They said that all new students are placed in classes by the counselors based on the results of the achievement tests which are administered to the new students as soon as they arrive at the school. They said that because of the large number of students who must be placed immediately at this time, the students are not interviewed on an individual basis in this process. They said that students are placed in classes in each subsequent term based on decisions made by the counselors after discussing with the students their aims, evaluating the students, considering test results, etc. Miss Davenport said that each counselor has an assigned group of students for which he is responsible, and that the students are seen periodically on a scheduled basis, or unscheduled basis which the students may desire. She said that each counselor uses a standard record of consultation for for each visit with a student. She said that these forms are filed and maintained by each individual counselor.

I asked the PIHS officials how they project student enrollment for future years at the high school. Mr. Ellis said that these "projections" which appear in the Area's program memorandums are not projections at all. He said that they do not have data available at the school on which to develop projections, and that they simply use

G-2/8

capacity figures for these "projections". Mr. Crawford agrees that this is the case for all of the off-reservation high schools in the Phoenix Area.

I asked the PIHS officials how they handled substitute teaching at the school when regular teachers are absent. They said that they have authorized four positions for substitute teachers, but that because of personnel ceilings they are only allowed to fill two of them at the present and do not budget for more. They said that the two substitute teachers they use are not hired full time, as is done at Sherman. They said that these two teachers are hired for a ten-month period within which they are used as needed, and that they must be rehired each year. They said that these teachers are not allowed to teach for more than thirty days in a row at one time. They said that the two substitute teachers which they have are not enough to handle their needs. They said that they often have need for more than two substitute teachers at a time, and that in these cases they either get another regular teacher to give up his planning time to take over a class, or they assign a student responsibility for supervising the class. They said that consideration has been given in the past to contracting with some organization to provide substitute teachers on an as-needed basis. However, Mr. Ellis said, and Mr. Crawford agreed, that the Area personnel section would not allow this, saying that it was a circumvention of the personnel ceilings.

Mr. Ellis said that starting with the 70-71 school year, the school uses an ungraded system for its junior high (7th, 8th, and 9th grades) program, and a structured 10th, 11th, and 12th grade

G-2
9

system for its senior high school. He said that it is his hope that the school will eventually move to an entirely non-structured type of program concentrating on individual-like instruction and extensive use of counseling. However, he pointed out that there has been no commitment to this end at this time.

The PIHS officials said that PIHS has two special education teachers, each handling a special education class of about ten or eleven students funded under regular program (1740) BIA funding. They said that students are assigned to these special education classes based on those who are the most needy. They said that most of the students who are assigned to these special ed classes are there full time, although they also said there are a few students who are in the regular program part of the day and in the special ed program the remainder of the day. They said this is adequate to meet their needs. He also said that there is a mathematic laboratory used for remedial math work at the school.

Miss Davenport said that the school has two psychiatrists under contract who work parttime at the school handling referral cases.

Regarding the staffing in the dormitories, the principal, Mr. Bollinger, said that he felt that the current staffing in the dorms was not adequate to handle the student's needs. He explained that there are now four dorm counselors handling the five regualr dormitories (not including the Title I dorm), and that in his opinion there should be two professional counselors per dormitory to adequately handle the student's needs. He pointed out that the current dorm counselors are sometimes overwhelmed with administrative duties.

$\frac{G-2}{10}$

He also pointed out that there was only one dorm aide responsible for handling the entire dormitory system during the night.

I asked the PIHS officials <u>how they developed their budgets for future years</u>. They said that their budgets were not developed based on needs. They said that the Area Office tells them each year how much money they can spend, and that they simply spread this amount among the various line items as best they can. He pointed out that for example in the case of the current budget which they are pre-preparing for fiscal year 1973, they have been told by the Area Office that they are to develop a budget exceeding the prior year's budget by 5%. Mr Ellis said that this system was totally inadequate if the school was to respond to the student's needs, they said that there was nothing they could do about it on the local level. Mr. Crawford agreed that this was the case, and pointed out that these restrictions were established by the Central Office, and simply passed on by the Area Office.

104/1 S-1 / 1-1

SUMMARY OF RESULTS
OF
REVIEW OF THE PROGRESS
IN MEETING OBJECTIVES
OF THE INDIAN EDUCATION
PROGRAM

BUREAU OF INDIAN AFFAIRS
JUNEAU AREA
STATE OF ALASKA

CODE 14553

104/2   S-1
         1-1

Contents

                                                              Page

REVIEW OBJECTIVES

SCOPE OF REVIEW

BACKGROUND

RESULTS OF REVIEW
    Consistency of education objectives at
    management and operating levels
    Need to establish criteria for measuring
    program results in terms of objectives
    Need for an improved management
    information system
    Need for Bureauwide academic and
    intelligence testing program
    Need for curriculum to be more responsive
    to students' needs
    Need for an improved counseling function
    Substitute teachers
    Personnel ceilings

} Not illustrated

REVIEW OBJECTIVES

The objectives of our review were to evaluate the degree to which the Bureau of Indian Affairs (Bureau) is achieving its stated objective of providing Alaskan native children with an educational achievement level at least equal to that of the non-native population, to evaluate the management methods used to meet this objective and if appropriate, to offer suggestions for improving the management of the Bureau's education program.

104/4   S-1 / 1-1

SCOPE OF REVIEW

Our review of the Bureau's educational program in the State of Alaska was conducted at the Juneau Area Office, the Nome Agency, Mt. Edgecumbe boarding school and the Kotzebue day school. We also contacted the Alaska Department of Education and several native groups. The review was accomplished in accordance with the audit program provided by the Los Angeles Regional Office.

(2)

104/5

BACKGROUND

JUNEAU AREA OFFICE

The Juneau Area Office (JAO) is one of the Bureau's 11 administrative field offices within the United States. Each area office is responsible for all Bureau activities in its designated area. The Juneau Area has five ~~subordinate~~ agency offices within its geographical boundaries of the State of Alaska. We were advised that the 1970 census reported that there were about 59,000 Alaska natives in the State of Alaska.

As of December 31, 1970, the Juneau Area operated 53 day schools with an enrollment of 4903 pupils and the boarding schools with 750 native pupils enrolled. In addition, during school year 1970-71 an estimated 583 Alaska natives were ~~attending~~ enrolled in boarding schools in Oregon and Oklahoma.

Approximately $17.1 million was allocated to the Juneau Area for the 1970-71 education program.

MT. EDGECUMBE

Mt. Edgecumbe boarding school is located on an island across a narrow channel from Sitka, Alaska. The school has an authorized enrollment of 650 students and is operated ~~for the purpose~~ to provide high school and vocational training to native students from all areas of Alaska where no high school facilities exist.

The physical plant of Mt. Edgecumbe dates back to the 1939-46 period when the facilities were part of the Sitka Naval Air Station. According to Simon Conrardy, ~~Except~~

(3)

the only main new construction at Mt. Edgecumbe has been the sign of converting the existing facilities into dormitories and classrooms. ~~there has been no major new construction at Mt. Edgecumbe.~~ The school opened its doors for the 1947-48 school year with about 600 students in grades 5 through 12. In the ensuing years the lower grades were dropped. In 1958 the school limited its operation to a 4-year high school with grades 9 through 12. In May 1971 there were 627 students enrolled at Mt. Edgecumbe.

The school, under the direction of a superintendent, administrative officer, and principal, reports directly to the JAO. At the start of the 1970-71 school year, there were 57 professional staff members and 140 support personnel.

Approximately $2,800,000 was allocated to the school to operate its 1970-71 school program.

NOME AGENCY

The Nome Agency, one of five agency offices in the Juneau Area, is under the direction of the Nome Agency Superintendent. He is responsible to the Area Director for Bureau activities, including education, in the Nome geographical area.

The professional educational positions at the Nome Agency provide for an educational program administrator and an educational specialist.

The Nome Agency is responsible for the operation of 12 day schools with a total enrollment of 1420. One of these schools is the Kotzebue day school.

(4)

KOTZEBUE DAY SCHOOL

Kotzebue day school is located in the native village of Kotzebue which is about 26 miles north of the Arctic Circle. The 1970 census disclosed that Kotzebue has grown from a village of 623 persons in 1950 to approximately 2000 persons in 1970. Except for Government service organizations there is little year-round employment and many families till rely on hunting and fishing to meet part of their family needs.

The Federal Government has financed native education at Kotzebue since 1897. The school has progressed from an ungraded mission school to a school with classes ranging from kindergarten through the 12th grade. School year 1970-71 was the first year Kotzebue offered a complete high school program. Enrollment during April 1971 was 703 pupils which included 638 natives and 65 non-native students.

The school facilities at Kotzebue are modern, with the oldest structure dating back only to 1958. In addition, to the 39 regular classrooms, the school includes such other areas as a library, dining room, kitchen, gym, and shop.

At the beginning of the school year 1970-71 Kotzebue had 43 professional staff members and 30 support personnel. The school is under the administration of the principal.

For school year 1970-71, approximately $900,000 was allocated to Kotzebue to conduct its education program.

(5)

104/8

RESULTS OF REVIEW

CONSISTENCY OF EDUCATION OBJECTIVES AT MANAGEMENT AND OPERATING LEVELS

The Bureau has not effectively communicated its educational objectives to responsible officials of the Juneau Area or the administrators of the schools we visited. These objectives call for academic achievement levels for Indian youth that are equal to non-Indian youth. The educational objectives used by the Juneau Area and the schools while not in conflict with the Bureau's objectives did not specify equal academic achievement for native students. Accordingly, the Juneau Area educational program may not be fully responsive to the accomplishment of the Bureau's educational objectives.

The Bureau's educational objectives included in the Program Memorandums for fiscal years 1969 through 1973 called for equal educational achievement and/or attainment of Indian youth with the levels of non-Indian youth. For fiscal years 1971 and 1972 these objectives were as follows:

"Graduation from high school for 90 percent of all Indian youth with achievement levels at least equal to those for non-Indian youth by 1976; 50 percent of those graduating entering college with the remainder either employed or enrolled in technical training."

The fiscal year 1973 objectives again called for equal achievement for Indian youth but did not specify percentage goals or a time period for attainment.

We found that although the Bureau's FY 1972 Program Memorandum had been provided to the SAO's Agency Offices, the responsible education officials at

(6)

the JAO, the Nome Agency and the two schools visited were not aware of the Bureau's objectives.

The educational objectives of the JAO, the Nome Agency and Mt. Edgecumbe are the same as those included in the Bureau's Indian Affairs Manual. These objectives are dated December 8, 1953, and stress such items as:

--to assure adequate educational opportunities for Indian children,

--to prepare Indians for successful living, and

--to retain valuable elements of Indian life and strengthen the pride of the Indian groups.

While these objectives are not in conflict with the Bureau's objectives, there is no mention of equal academic achievement with non-native youth or the establishment of a definite period for accomplishment.

The Kotzebue educational objectives are those of the Kotzebue Advisory School Board. These objectives stress the development of the native child's abilities but again there is no mention of equal achievement with non-native youth. The Principal at Kotzebue stated that because the objectives in the Bureau's manual were so broad he did not expect any conflict between Kotzebue's objectives and those included in the Bureau's Manual.

Although the stated educational objectives of the JAO and the schools contacted do not stress equal academic achievement between native and non-native youth, Juneau Area educational officials at each level

(7)

stated that their program was directed more toward academic programs than instead of the social adjustment phase. All of the officials felt that equal academic achievement between native and non-native youth, as defined by the 1972 Program Memorandum, was a reasonable goal. However, most of the officials did not believe that this goal could be reached by 1976.

The three native groups we contacted, including the Kotzebue Advisory School Board, felt that the education of native youth should be so directed that the native youth will be on an equal competitive basis with non-native youth. They were of the opinion that equal academic achievement for non-native youth equal to non-native youth should be the objective of the Bureau's education program.

We were informed by the Juneau Area Director and Assistant Area Director (Education) that the educational objectives of the Bureau, which call for equal achievement between native and non-native youth, will be communicated to the agencies and schools in the Juneau Area. They were of the opinion that every native has the right to an education that will place him on the same level as his non-native neighbor.

Conclusion

The establishment of objectives is essential for the effective management of any program. However, if these objectives are not fully communicated to and understood by the operating levels of the organization, we believe that program direction, emphasis and resources may not be fully responsive to the accomplishment of these objectives.

104/11

Recommendation

To assure consistency in program direction, we recommend that the Bureau communicate its educational objectives to all levels within the Bureau's educational organization.

NEED TO ESTABLISH CRITERIA FOR MEASURING PROGRAM RESULTS IN TERMS OF OBJECTIVES

Criteria and guidelines for measuring the education program accomplishment of the Bureau's education program in relation to the stated objectives have not been established by either the Bureau or the Juneau Area. Accordingly, neither the Bureau nor the Juneau Area have any systematic means of measuring the progress being made towards meeting the objectives of the Bureau's education program.

For the effective management of its education program and the accomplishment of the quality educational objectives, the Bureau should have the necessary information to evaluate program results in terms of the established objectives. We believe Information should be available at the Bureau, area, agency and school level to show the progress being made towards meeting th education program objectives.

We were informed by officials at all levels visited in the Juneau Area that neither the Bureau nor the Juneau Area have provided any guidelines for implementing a program that will measure the area, agency and school's educational accomplishment relative to the Bureau's quality educational objectives. In addition, we found that there is presently no systematic program within the Juneau Area to measure how well the schools are progressing.

(9)

REVIEW QUESTIONS

1. Do the same principles of work-paper preparation apply to P-audits as they do to M-audits? (See p. 221.)

2. Do all summaries have to be prepared in exactly the same manner? Explain. (See p. 222.)

3. As in M-audits, does the program auditor often have to develop a criteria for his audit? Explain. (See p. 222.)

4. What is the audit objective for the illustrative audit in this chapter? (See p. 222.)

5. From which working paper does the answer to question II-3 for the Phoenix Boarding School come? State the detailed information that provides the answer to this question. (See pp. 224, 230–31.)

6. From which working paper does the answer to question VI-1 for the Mt. Edgecumbe School come from? (See p. 225.)

7. What is the meaning of the reference numbers "S-1/3-1 p. 5" given in the left margin of working paper S-1/1-1, p. 239?

8. Reviewers and references not only refer back to the original source of the information in a report, but they also check the exact spelling as well as the exact names of individuals or organizations. Refer to working paper S-1/1-1 p. 5, p. 243. Notice the check mark over the word Kotzebue. What does this check mark mean?

CASE 1

The Valley City Jails: The Detailed Examination

Required

After studying the material that follows and reviewing Case 1 in Chapter 6, pp. 111–16, respond to the following:

1. What is the conclusion you would draw concerning whether Valley City is effectively accomplishing its goal of providing local jails in which to commit persons for longer than 48 hours, to hold persons awaiting trial, or to commit sentenced prisoners for up to one year? In coming up with your conclusion, consider what the district attorney said concerning "local jails in which to commit persons."
2. Write a summary report concerning your local jail's P-audit.
3. What would be your recommendation to the mayor and city council?
4. What effect would your recommendation have upon the financial conditions of the city? Are there sources of revenue that could be obtained to carry out your recommendations?

The reader should have been able to come up with an objective for the detailed examination somewhat as follows:

> Has Valley City, including the mayor and city council, the local jail administrators, and other paid or nonpaid participating groups, in carrying out their responsibilities for providing local jails in which to commit persons for longer than 48 hours, to hold persons awaiting trial, or to commit sentenced prisoners for up to one year (causes) been ineffective (effects) because they have not provided adequate physical conditions and inmate assistance (criteria)? Adequate physical conditions and inmate assistance are further defined as follows:

A. Adequate physical conditions should include:
1. Inmate security and safety
   a) Populations not exceeding capacity,
   b) Single occupancy cells only,
   c) No drunk tank,
   d) Adequate segregation of offenders by sex, age, and degree of violence,
   e) 24-hour matron,
   f) Operable emergency exits,
   g) Fire extinguishers
   h) Operable individual cell doors.
2. Sanitary conditions
   a) Operable toilets in cells, clean and workable washbasins and showers, and
   b) Availability of such personal items as soap and toothpaste and the cleanliness of such things as blankets, sheets, and towels.
3. Inmate comfort and rehabilitation
   a) Separate dining facilities from cell block and not in view of toilets, and
   b) Adequate recreation facilities, ventilation, and lighting.
4. Privacy
   a) Visiting space separate from cells,
   b) Space for private conversations, and
   c) Private area where prisoners searched when first imprisoned.

B. Adequate inmate assistance should be oriented to individual needs, personal problem solving, socialization, and skill development, and should include:
1. Furloughs, work-release, and educational-release programs,
2. Vocational counseling and training,
3. Job placement, preferably operated by state employment agencies and local groups representing employers and local unions,
4. Alcohol, drug abuse, and social-service counseling, and
5. Right to practice own religion.

Summary of Evidence on the Detailed Examination

Below is a summary of the information the auditor gathered by looking at the records, by interviewing, and by actual observation of conditions at the local jails. (Note to reader: Much of the general information needed for the audit has, of course, already been obtained in evidence gathered by Mr. Davis and his audit team during the preliminary survey and the review and testing of management control).

Summary of Conditions at Five Local Jails in Relation to Desirable Characteristics

Conditions (Yes = acceptable - No = unacceptable)	Precinct 1	2	3	4	5	% Yes
I Physical Conditions						
A. Inmate Security and Safety:						
Designed Capacity Not Exceeded	yes	yes	yes	yes	yes	100
Single Occupancy Cells	no	no	no	no	no	0
No Drunk Tank	no	yes	yes	yes	yes	80
Segregation Adequate for						
Male/Female	yes	no	yes	yes	no	60
Adult/Juvenile	no	no	yes	no	yes	40
Offenders Classes held	no	no	no	no	no	0
24 Hour Matron	yes	no	no	yes	no	40
Operable Emergency Exists	yes	no	yes	no	no	40
Fire Extinguishers	yes	yes	yes	yes	yes	100
Operable Individual Cell Doors	yes	yes	yes	no	yes	80
Percent Yes	60	40	72	50	50	54
B. Sanitation:						
Operable in Cells:						
Toilets	yes	yes	yes	yes	yes	100
Washbasins	yes	yes	yes	yes	yes	100
Sanitary Showers	yes	no	yes	yes	yes	80
Laundry for Personal Clothing	yes	no	yes	no	yes	60
Items Issued:						
Soap	yes	yes	yes	yes	yes	100
Toothpaste	yes	NI	NI	NI	NI	20
Razor	yes	NI	NI	NI	yes	40
Uniforms	yes	NI	NI	NI	yes	40
Mattress	yes	yes	yes	yes	NI	80
Pillow	NI	NI	yes	NI	NI	20
Items Issued & Cleaned before Issuance						
Blanket	yes	yes	no	yes	no	60
Sheet	NI	NI	no	yes	NI	20
Pillowcase	NI	NI	no	NI	NI	0
Towel	yes	NI	yes	yes	yes	80
Percent Yes	79	36	57	57	57	57.8

C. Inmate Comfort and Rehabilitation						
Toilets Not in View of Dining Area	no	no	no	no	no	0
Recreation Facilities Indoor	no	no	no	no	no	0
Outdoor	no	no	no	no	no	0
Library	no	no	no	no	no	0
In-house Medical Facilities	no	no	no	no	no	0
Ventilation	yes	yes	yes	yes	yes	100
Lighting in Cells						
Artificial	yes	yes	yes	yes	no	80
Natural	yes	yes	no	no	yes	60
No Guard in Corridor	no	no	yes	no	no	20
Space for Programs	yes	no	no	no	no	20
Percent Yes	40	30	30	20	20	28

D. Privacy						
Visiting Space						
Separate from Cell Area	yes	no	no	no	no	20
Space for Private Conversations	no	no	no	no	no	0
Privacy for Search as Entry	yes	no	yes	yes	no	60
No Closet Circuit in Living Area	yes	yes	yes	yes	yes	100
Percent Yes	75	25	50	50	25	45

E. Inmate Assistance						
Work Release	yes	no	no	no	no	20
Furlough	no	no	no	no	no	0
Educational Release	no	no	no	no	no	0
Vocational Training	no	no	no	no	no	0
Vocational Counseling	no	no	no	no	no	0
Job Placement	no	no	no	no	no	0
Education	no	no	no	no	no	0
Alcoholic	yes	no	yes	no	no	40
Drug Abuse	no	no	yes	no	no	20
Religious	yes	no	yes	yes	no	60
Social Service Counseling	no	no	no	yes	no	20
Percent Yes	27	0	27	18	0	15

NI = Not Issued

The auditors also visited the state penitentiary and found the percentage of desirable features pertaining to physical conditions to be as shown in the following table.

Desirable features available (average)	Percentage of desirable features found in state penitentiary
Inmate security and safety	79
Sanitation	89
Inmate comfort and rehabilitation	98
Privacy	100
Total average	92

Because of the low percentage of inmate assistance, the auditors decided to check into the availability of assistance through other limited cost sources, such as other tax-supported institutions, self-supported volunteer programs, or volunteer programs that would need only a limited amount of financial assistance. The organizations contacted included school boards, alcoholic programs, employment services, ministerial societies, and public welfare agencies.

The auditors found that resources were available in various precincts, and organizations, too, were willing to provide some services. However, 63 percent of the organizations visited had not been contacted at all by jail administrators, and another 23 percent only infrequently. For example, representatives of both Alcoholics Anonymous and the state employment service indicated they provided limited services and were willing to continue with no additional financial resources. The superintendent of schools and members of the council of ministers had not been contacted by the jail administration but would be willing to provide services. The superintendent of schools indicated that additional funding would be needed. A representative of the Department of Public Welfare stated the department could provide assistance only to inmates' families. The auditors found that educational and vocational programs were available to both sentenced and pretrial inmates, but the programs were limited.

The table below is a summary of the auditors' requests concerning inmates' assistance from voluntary and state offices:

Number of organizations contacted	23
Contacted by jail officials to provide services (percentages given)	
No contact	63
Informal and/or infrequent contact	33
Currently providing services	4
Organization's attitude toward providing services	
Willing to provide services	62
Unable to provide services	13
Unwilling to provide services	21
Currently providing services	4
Restrictions to providing services	
No restrictions	23
Inadequate resources	46
Miscellaneous	31

Concerning volunteer programs, the following information was also obtained:

Criminal justice experts believe that volunteers are a viable resource for rehabilitative programs. They also point out that volunteers can serve a secondary purpose of communicating to citizens an awareness of the conditions of jails and possibly exert community pressure to improve the jail.

An LEAA-funded study* concluded that between 60-to-70 percent of the criminal justice agencies surveyed had volunteer programs. Literature includes examples of successful programs using volunteers such as:

- In a Royal Oak, Michigan, program volunteers are a major element in an extensive program for misdemeanants that offers individual and group counseling, job-placement assistance, and aid with family problems. Partial pay is provided for some participants, but many other citizens serve without pay.
- The objective of a project in Westchester County, New York, was to demonstrate how citizen volunteers could effectively enrich the activities program in a short-term institution. Forty-one volunteers with various professional backgrounds, but without any prior experience working with offenders, were recruited and trained in the special requirements governing work in a correctional institution. Courses in needlecraft, typing and shorthand, personal grooming, nursing, and arts and crafts were organized. The results showed that citizen volunteers can enrich the activities program in a short-term correctional institution.
- Charlottesville, Virginia, has a program involving

* "Guidelines and Standards for the Use of Volunteers in Correctional Programs," National Institute for Law Enforcement and Criminal Justice, Law Enforcement Assistance Administration, August 1972.

about 100 volunteers working with individual inmates at the county jail. A broad range of inmate programs operate in the jail including work release; alcoholism counseling; remedial educational, art, and hobby programs; and limited indoor recreation. All are conducted without cost to the jail.

On the basis of the above information, jail administrators apparently actively sought and used community resources.

In the local jails visited, however, administrators said they made little effort to contact the community to obtain any services for the inmates. One reason for their lack of action, they said, was the pressing need to attend to other duties. Criminal justice experts indicate that one way to ease this problem is for each jail to have a city or county social service worker, a volunteer, or someone hired specifically to act as a resource person and counselor to inmates in the jails, to encourage the inmates to use available community resources. Such an approach is a relatively effortless and inexpensive way for small jails at least to begin to address the needs of offenders.

CASE 2

The Mass-transit Grant: The Detailed Examination

Required:

After studying the material that follows and reviewing Case 2 in Chapter 6, pp. 117–19, respond to the following:

1. From the summaries of evidence concerning the grants for the mass-transit system, what would be your conclusion as to the effectiveness of the mass-transit-system grants program? Write a summary report for the overall audit from your working papers, including your conclusion.
2. What would be your recommendations to the authorities making the grants, and the agencies receiving the grants?

Summary of the Evidence
Concerning the Problems with the
R-44 Rail Cars in New York

From the records and by observations, the auditors noted that NYCTA was experiencing a large number of problems with the reliability of the R-44 rail cars, even after 3 years of service. Although these cars represented only about 4 percent of the total fleet, they accounted for 10 percent of all delays attributed to car failure.

NYCTA officials stated that it was not unusual for new equipment to experience break-in problems; nevertheless, the R-44 car had had considerably more failures than its predecessor R-42 car. After their first full year of service, the R-42 cars experienced breakdowns on the average of once every 40,000 miles, while the R-44 cars had averaged a breakdown every 7,500 miles.

NYCTA officials stated that they believed that direct comparisons between R-44 cars and older cars should not be made because new standards of measurement were needed for cars designed for high-speed automated operation requiring more sophisticated equipment than older cars. According to NYCTA, the relatively new additional equipment necessary for high-speed automated operation was responsible for the higher rate of failure.

Recognizing that the equipment on the R-44 cars and R-46 cars was more sophisticated than on predecessor cars and that this new equipment was a major cause of the failures, the experts auditors consulted did not agree that comparisons should not be made. They demonstrated that the R-44 cars did not perform as well as older cars because of this new sophisticated equipment, pointing to (1) the need to test and perfect such technology before mass production of rapid-transit cars began and (2) the need to recognize an area in which UMTA should consider its role in helping to solve current transit problems.

Records also showed that the R-44 cars did not compare well with other cars in NYCTA's fleet: They failed about twice as often as cars 35- to 40-years-old. They do not compare favorably with the entire balance of the fleet, either: During their best month of operation, the R-44 cars averaged 12,000 miles between failures, while the rest of the fleet averaged 18,000 miles. During their worst month, the R-44 cars averaged 4,000 miles between failures compared to 20,000 miles for the balance of the fleet.

The effect of this poor performance is demonstrated in the availability of the R-44 cars for revenue service. During July 1974, a comparison of car availability showed that 19 percent of the 300 R-44 cars were unavailable for revenue service while only 14 percent of the 841 35- to 40-year-old cars were unavailable. Six months later, during December 1974, 22 percent of the R-44 cars were unavailable for service while 12 percent of the older cars were unavailable. Also, a sample of records of car availability for December 1974 showed that on 19 of 21 weekdays there were not enough R-44 cars after they used the available R-44 spares or backup cars.

Because of NYCTA's concern about the reliability of the R-44 cars, it formed a task force in June 1973, which investigated various problems with the brakes, including stuck brakes and brakes applied for no apparent reason. Modifications were made to the R-44 cars based on the task force's work; over 160 modifications were made to all of the cars by the end of 1974; nevertheless, the problems persisted. Ninety-eight percent of the breakdowns of the R-44 cars were due to failures of the air brakes, car body components (especially car doors), electrical components (especially traction motors), and miscellaneous electrical parts.

Even though the brake used on earlier cars had proved reliable, a different type of air brake was installed in the R-44 cars. Transit officials said that the new brake could be used with ATC while the earlier brake could not and that the circuitry for the air brake on the new R-46 cars and the modified R-44 cars had been simplified; therefore, they hoped it would be less prone to problems.

NYCTA officials said that several problems had been difficult to resolve in the R-44 car because they appeared when the car was in service but could not be confirmed when the car reached the maintenance shop and was taken in for inspection. Causes for over 40 percent of the failures reported in 1974 could not be identified. These failures included those listed in the table below.

As of March 1975, the performance of the

Component	Failures without identified causes		Failures with identified causes	
	Number	Percent of total failures	Number	Percent of total failures
Electrical	74	4	318	18
Car body	260	15	460	26
Brakes	376	21	241	14
Truck	17	1	15	1
Air conditioning	–	–	5	–
Total	727	41	1,039	59

operating to meet the scheduled requirements because they were broken down and out of service. During this time, NYCTA found itself with a shortage ranging from 8 to 62 cars, even

R-44 cars had improved only marginally. With 36 months and over 35 million miles of revenue service, the cars were averaging only 7,900 miles between breakdowns.

*Summary of the Evidence Concerning
Other Indications of Rail Car Problems*

Various reports, studies, and articles in industry periodicals indicated that problems with new rail cars were also being experienced by several other transit systems, including commuter railroads with similar cars. Some of these problems involve ATC, air brakes, door openers, and electrical equipment. Such problems have caused delays and had an impact on the system's overall performance, and in addition, they have caused serious accidents, including instances of brake failure, a train overrunning its station stop because of ATC malfunction, and doors opening while trains were moving and closing on passengers as trains left the station. (None of these accidents had occurred on the NYCTA system.)

At the Long Island Railroad, officials told auditors that their new M-1 commuter rail cars were experiencing problems with the automatic train-operation equipment, brakes, air conditioners, and motor alternators, and they stated that some of these problems would continue to exist until better components were developed. On Penn Central's New Haven commuter trains, 20-year-old cars were out of service less frequently than the new high-performance M-2 cars: In 1974, for instance, about 23 percent of the M-2s was out of service on a daily basis as compared to only 11 percent for the older cars. The San Francisco Bay Area Rapid Transit system, after 1 year of operation, was experiencing a 30- to 60-percent failure rate of the vehicles placed into service during a normal day.

In their December 1975 letter, NYCTA officials stated that all new cars recently purchased throughout the United States were experiencing mechanical and electronic problems, and that new rapid-transit systems not yet in operation would likewise experience many problems; they believed that the cars NYCTA purchased had caused the least problems of any new cars bought recently by any rapid-transit system in the country.

*Summary of Industry Comments
on Current Problems*

Representatives of the mass-transit rail industry have expressed concern about the problems and breakdowns in equipment experienced by transit systems. At a rapid transit conference, sponsored by the American Public Transit Association in April 1975, industry representatives said that there were numerous problems currently facing their industry, such as:

- A need for reliable equipment,
- A need for standardized equipment,
- Too many systems using complex technology that does not work,
- New technology to be proved before going into production and use,
- A lack of accurate, dependable performance data available on today's cars, and
- A need for federal government to become a tougher reviewer of grant applications, not ignore cost-benefit studies, press for improved quality control, and press for reliable and standardized equipment.

*Summary of Evidence Concerning
UMTA's Role in Resolving
Technical Problems*

The auditors discussed the focus of UMTA's R&D program and its impact on industry problems with two responsible groups in the UMTA—the Office of Research and Development and the Office of Transit Management. ORD administers the R&D program, whose officials told auditors that many of their projects were aimed at tackling specific problems the industry was experiencing: doors, propulsion, noise, and ride quality. The advanced-concept train and the advanced-subsystems-development program were two such projects. They were long term; in other areas, the R&D program was near term and industry responsive. The energy storage car and gas turbine-electric commuter car projects, for instance, were direct responses to NYCTA's expressed needs. Research was being sponsored in such areas as noise abatement, tunneling techniques, and crashworthiness of vehicles.

The R&D officials of UMTA believed that operations were experiencing increasing problems with particular subsystem reliability; but they felt UMTA could not play the principal role in resolving such vendor-purchaser problems, which were considered to be the domain of supplier and customer. Also, R&D officials said that if UMTA were to resolve specific hardware deficiencies, it would be engaging in product improvement on behalf of the vendors involved—not a proper role for the federal government. These officials felt that insurance for better reliability upon delivery could be achieved through better written specifications by the grantee, and through requirements for adequate prototype testing prior to production.

While the auditors understood UMTA's position and agreed that better specifications and prototype testing are needed, they believed that the R&D should do more to assist in obtaining reliable equipment. This might mean resolving specific hardware deficiencies if these deficiencies represented continual problems within various transit systems. Federal funds paid for 80 percent of a grantee's railcar purchases, and therefore the customer who had to live with the product was not only the local transit authority, but also the federal government; UMTA clearly had a fiduciary responsibility to taxpayers to see that their funds were spent effectively.

R&D officials told the auditors that the current practice appeared to be for grantees to specify increasing levels of performance and reliability, but vendors were not prepared to meet such requirements. As the grantee imposed more stringent warranty requirements on the vendor, he simply increased the price of his product to cover the cost of replacing his components for the life of the warranty. In the auditors' view this was not an acceptable or prudent process.

Developing subsystems capable of achieving greater reliability is an R&D process. UMTA officials stated that only after reliability had been demonstrated should these subsystems be specified for production. The auditors agreed but felt it might be necessary for UMTA to sponsor research to improve a specific component.

The UMTA Office of Transit Management is responsible for improving local transit operations. A transit management official saw no problem with UMTA financing research to develop workable components for today's cars. It would seem to be a reasonable investment, for example, to develop a trouble-free traction motor. However, the office had no formal reporting system to keep track of current problems and had to obtain such information through informal contacts with local transit authorities and industry representatives.

In 1972, eighteen of the largest transit systems joined in establishing the Transit Development Corporation to serve as a catalyst for action, to provide a forum for conducting R&D programs, and to be a communications bridge between industry and government. The corporation's purpose was to pursue R&D projects with immediate foreseeable use, and it had been critical of UMTA's R&D efforts. In March 1975, a corporation spokesman observed that (1) UMTA reached principally for long-range, high-risk technology to develop futuristic transportation modes, and (2) a measure of UMTA funds should be channeled to unsophisticated problem areas in need of solutions at the present time. However, this same spokesman said in November 1975 that UMTA's R&D appeared to be redirecting some of its efforts to solve near-term problems. He believed UMTA was becoming more responsive to current problems.

Summary of Information on R-44 Cars Before Grant Was Committed

Additional information also was available on the performance of the R-44 cars at the time UMTA approved each grant amendment. For example, in September 1972, UMTA approved an additional $40 million to help purchase 202 R-46 cars. At that time the R-44 cars were averaging 6,900 miles between failures, while the balance of the fleet was averaging 18,000 miles between failures. In April 1973, when the second amendment was approved for $38.8 million to help purchase the remaining 223 cars, the R-44 cars were experiencing failures every 7,500 miles compared to 22,000 miles for the rest of the fleet.

UMTA officials told the auditors that little consideration was given to the performance of the R-44 railcars when UMTA approved the R-46 grant because each grant was treated separately. In their opinion, UMTA's task was to determine whether the local grantee had a legitimate need for UMTA funds, and UMTA had no direct responsibility for the soundness of the product purchased by the grantee nor did it require that the product meet certain testing requirements.

One UMTA official stated that NYCTA probably had the most competent people in the field and that their expertise was superior to that of the federal government; therefore, reliance on New York's judgment weighed heavily in approving its projects. UMTA accepted NYCTA officials' assurance that (1) the R-44 cars were not experiencing any insurmountable problems and (2) the cars had been tested and proved reliable. However, UMTA did not request or receive any detailed analysis or engineering reports.

Another official said that if UMTA had been aware of the problems with the R-44 cars and had followed sound procurement practices, the purchase of the R-46 cars would have been delayed. According to this official, UMTA did not normally find out about such problems because grantees were generally afraid of losing federal funds, and UMTA had no feedback system except for information volunteered by the grantees.

Procurement practices of the DOD, NASA, and the GSA showed that in areas involving the use of new technology, the acceptable procedure has been "fly before you buy." The military services and NASA had long-standing practices of requiring test and evaluation before production began. For unproven technology this might include building and testing a prototype, or testing the specific component using new technology on an existing system to see if engineering was correct.

The head of a task force, created by NYCTA to attempt to solve reliability problems with the R-44 cars, told the auditors that the R-44 car was experiencing problems primarily with its braking system, as the auditors had already learned. This brake system has been used in commuter rail and rapid-transit systems before, but it was totally new to NYCTA's system. If a prototype car, incorporating the new braking system along with other new components, had been tested, it might have led to a better understanding of the risks involved in applying this technology to NYCTA's rapid-transit system.

In December 1975, NYCTA officials stated that prototype testing was not required for the complete R-44 car because (1) NYCTA had satisfactorily used most of the components in prior cars, (2) most of the components were in satisfactory use elsewhere, (3) some of the newer items had been tested, and (4) a functional mockup had been made during the design review. However, NYCTA recognized the importance of prototypes in discussing why some of their older cars, such as the R-42s, were in fact more reliable. As they pointed out to the auditors, the R-42 cars benefited from the 6,000 more-or-less identical cars that had preceded them, while the R-44 cars included new equipment components that had not been on previous cars in NYCTA's system. NYCTA recognized that these new components were responsible for the higher rate of failure.

UMTA did not require grantees to test prototypes before placing an order for mass production; reliance was placed on the grantee to perform and/or require what it believed was adequate to procure sound, reliable equipment. However, R&D officials recognized the need for a better policy; and in commenting on this audit report, they said they had been trying to persuade the transit industry to recognize the value of prototype car testing.

At a rapid transit conference in April 1975, a representative of a major rail car builder said that the present procurement process for mass-transit vehicles was not geared toward the production of reliable rail cars. Specifically, he said that there was a need for prototype cars, definite reliability levels by the transit authorities, and standardization of equipment similar to that of DOD and the airline and trucking industries. Further, he said it was difficult to produce a reliable rail car when the nation's transit authorities each requested different cars developed from different specifications.

Industry predictions showed that over 4,000 new rapid-transit and commuter rail cars would be produced within the next 5 to 10 years; undoubtedly many would be purchased with UMTA assistance. If these cars followed recent trends, they would be more complex, more costly, and less reliable than existing cars. Considering the potential for large individualized rail car purchases for different systems and the trend to incorporate innovations, auditors felt UMTA should reassess its role of providing financial assistance to grantees who wish to purchase equipment with unproved components, or untried combinations of components, without first obtaining specific evidence that the rail cars are reliable.

Summary of Evidence Concerning Over $3.4 Million Approved for Equipment Not Planned for Immediate Use

An advanced feature of the R-46 cars was the ATC equipment. The auditors estimated the cost of this equipment to be about $5 million; UMTA's share was about $3.4 million.

ATC used sophisticated controls to move the train from station to station without manual operation by the motorman, who acted primarily as a safety monitor and supervisor of automatic equipment. ATC had four major functions: (1) automatic train protection—overspeed protection and collision prevention, (2) automatic train operation—speed regulation and programmed station stops, (3) automatic train supervision—direction of train movement and scheduling, and (4) communication—relaying information between the different parts of the system.

An ATC system required carborne equipment (on board the car) as well as wayside (along the track and/or at central control points) equipment. NYCTA's R-44 cars were the first in the present fleet to have any such carborne equipment; they had both automatic train-protection and automatic train-operation capabilities. For this carborne equipment to be used, companion equipment had to be installed along the wayside; NYCTA had not yet done this. NYCTA officials informed the auditors that at the time the R-44 and R-46 cars were designed, plans were underway for a Second Avenue subway, a high-speed Queens trunkline and certain extensions to existing lines that would be ATC-equipped. Also, as funds became available, NYCTA planned to purchase and install wayside ATC on existing lines. NYCTA internal plans, which had not been approved by the city at the time the R-44 and R-46 cars were ordered, called for its BMT Division to be equipped and ready for automatic operation by 1990 and the IND Division to be ready by the year 2020; there was no current plan for the third division, the IRT.*

Based on these plans, 554 cars, or 74 percent of the total, were to be used on the IND Division and therefore would not use the carborne ATC equipment until the year 2020 when the cars would be over 40 years old. Since the current estimated life of a railcar is about 35 years, ATC equipment on these cars would never be used. The other 26 percent of the cars, 191, to be assigned under the plan to the BMT Division, would use the equipment by 1990 when the cars would be about 15 years old.

During the auditors' review, NYCTA officials said that even though the ATC equipment would not be used for many years, cars with ATC were purchased so that the new cars would be compatible with the new subway lines, planned or under construction, which would be ATC-equipped. The most important expansion of service being planned was the Second Avenue subway and three other lines that were expected to be operational in the early 1980s. According to NYCTA officials, the R-44 and R-46 cars were not planned for exclusive use on these new lines since they would probably have their own new cars. Even so, the officials wanted all NYCTA's new-car purchases to be capable of interchangeable use on the new line.

*The Brooklyn Manhattan Transit (BMT), the Independent (IND), and the Interborough Rapid Transit (IRT) are more commonly referred by their initials than their full names.

UMTA officials said they relied heavily on the judgment of NYCTA personnel for approving R-46 cars with ATC equipment; further, they added that NYCTA considered it cheaper to install the equipment in the cars at the time of manufacture rather than to add it at a later date. This judgment was not based on any cost-benefit study; nevertheless, UMTA accepted NYCTA's judgment without any backup support.

In their December 1975 letter, NYCTA officials stated that new plans then existed for wayside ATC to be placed on a BMT line during 1978–80, and although the Second Avenue subway line had been postponed because of lack of funds, a new high-speed Queens line, with a new tunnel under the East River, was continuing. NYCTA officials told the auditors that the Queens fleet, which is to consist of both R-44 and R-46 cars, would be operating on the new line by 1982.

Although the auditors recognized that implementation of the new plans would allow for earlier use of the ATC equipment, such plans were made subsequent to the time UMTA gave approval to NYCTA to purchase ATC. Auditors did not question benefits and improvements that could be obtained with ATC; however, it did not appear to be the best use of federal funds to buy equipment components that might not be used soon after delivery and, in many cases, even within the expected lifetime of the cars. Therefore, UMTA needed to establish criteria to help determine when expenditures for new equipment that would not be used in the near term were appropriate.

The passage of the National Mass Transportation Assistance Act of 1974 (49 U.S.C. 1601) authorizing funds for transit systems to help meet operating expenses, and the availability of 80-percent federal funding for capital acquisitions, might encourage grantees to include equipment components that, while desirable, might not represent the most effective use of federal funds at the time. Therefore, auditors felt UMTA should review more closely the basis of each grantee's stated transit-system needs, as well as grantee decisions to procure equipment to meet such needs.

UMTA Research and Development Efforts Needed to Focus Systematically on Current Industry Problems

Auditors learned that the transit industry was having major problems with the reliability of new rapid-transit cars. Such problems could result from poorly written specifications, from the inability of manufacturers to meet the specifications, or from inadequate quality control. UMTA had no information-collection system to identify or categorize transit-car problems, nor did it believe it should resolve specific hardware deficiencies. Its R&D program had been criticized by the transit industry in the past for being too devoted to futuristic technology rather than to short-term activities.

The issue of how great an effort UMTA should make in solving current industry problems could be debated. However, the auditors believed that UMTA had to develop a system to identify these problems and categorize them to help determine if they were quality-control problems, or if they were technological problems common to many transit systems. In the latter case, the auditors believed that UMTA should help resolve the problems even if some of them related to a specific component.

PART Four

Using Specialized Techniques in Auditing the Performance of Management

Part 4 will provide the reader with an introduction to some specialized techniques useful in auditing the performance of management. While not intended to make you an expert, the information should enable you to determine when these techniques should or should not be employed.

There are four chapters in Part 4: Chapter 12, "Obtaining Audit Evidence Through Statistical Sampling"; Chapter 13, "Obtaining Evidence Through Interviews and Questionnaires"; Chapter 14, "Using the Computer as an Audit Tool: Auditing the Tool Itself"; Chapter 15, "Using Specialized Analytical Techniques: Using Experts and Consultants."

After studying each chapter, reviewing the questions, and working the cases, the reader should be able to accomplish the specific objectives at the beginning of each chapter.

CHAPTER 12

Obtaining Audit Evidence Through Statistical Sampling

After you have read this chapter, studied the review questions, and worked through the cases, you will understand:

- What statistical sampling is all about.
- How to use sampling in obtaining audit evidence, including knowing the advantages and disadvantages to sample evidence.
- How the principles of auditing and evidence relate to sampling.
- How to state an objective for an audit sample.
- What is meant by precision and confidence.
- How to determine a sample size from a formula or from a table for certain degrees of confidence and precision.
- The distinctions between attribute samples and estimation samples.
- When a universe is homogeneous and how to select a sample size from a random number table.

We have stated repeatedly that performance auditing is the process of planning for, gathering, and evaluating sufficient relevant, material, and competent evidence on an audit objective in order to come to a proper conclusion on that objective. Sufficiency of evidence, we have indicated, does not necessarily mean the number of items of evidence the auditor has obtained; it does mean the quality of each piece of evidence obtained, determined by the weight each played on the auditor's mind, convincing him that his conclusion to the audit objective is the correct one. For example, one piece of direct evidence can be of such quality that it can weigh as heavily on the auditor's mind as many pieces of circumstantial evidence.

When the auditor gathers evidence on the audit objective and comes to a conclusion, we have also said that conclusion is only probably the right one. Seldom, if ever, is he 100 percent certain that his conclusion is the right answer. Still, the probability should be very high that he does have the right conclusion, for he knows he has obtained sufficient relevant, material, and competent evidence on his audit objective to convince himself he has the correct answer. He also knows, however, that he can seldom obtain all of the evidence on both sides of the audit. Any additional evidence on one side or the other might change his conclusion dramatically to an opposite one. Many an innocent person has been hung because he was unable to present all of the proper evidence in his defense.

In order to have a high probability that his conclusion is the proper one, whether it be in a financial-statement examination, an M-audit, or a P-audit, the auditor has found, in practice, that he can use many techniques to obtain evidence, as we learned in Chapter 8. He can scan records looking for possible errors or inconsistencies; he can interview the most likely and competent person or persons who can give him the best information available; he can retrace records or actions of people; he can observe things and people; and he can reconfirm a selected group of accounts or actions.

Little Need for Auditor to Review Every Item

In only a very few of these cases does the auditor obtain evidence by reviewing every item in the records, by talking to every person, by observing all things and all people, or by confirming every account or every action. Auditors have been obtaining evidence by this type of testing, called *judgment sampling*, for many years, and they have found generally that it has produced good evidence—evidence that has worked well for them and has convinced them that their opinion or conclusion was correct.

There is good reason for this type of testing to produce good evidence. In making financial-statement examinations, the auditor has found over the years that there is a pattern of consistency in the actions found in recording information in the records. For example, records often show that the payroll is paid at the same time and for approximately the same amount each week or month, or the rent is paid and other types of obligations taken care of in a consistent pattern each month. The auditor, then, often looks for inconsistencies in the patterns by scanning the records, interviewing only a selected group of people, and observing the actions of a designated few.

In making M-audits and P-audits, the auditor has also discovered the same pattern of consistency in the carrying out of activities or programs. Operational practices, such as personnel or manufacturing practices, are consistently the same day after day, month after month, or year after year, whether the actions are good or bad. Therefore, indications of one deficiency in a management's practice often leads to a pattern of deficiencies that can be developed into a full-scale examination. In programs also, consistent use of policies not related to the accomplishment of its goal is often the cause of ineffective accomplishment of these objectives.

Thus, all of the techniques discussed in previous chapters are proper to be employed during either an M-audit or a P-audit. One additional technique, however, will help the auditor to improve his ability to obtain evidence in each of the many types of audits on the audit objective. That technique is called scientific or statistical sampling.

Statistical sampling is used in many ways. For example, it is used by the politician to determine opinions of his constituency when those opinions are negative, and to determine how to change those opinions in order to obtain their vote. And certain products, during the manufacturing process, are accepted or rejected on the basis of testing only a few; market surveys are made to determine the possibility of introducing a new product; grains are graded and sold on the basis of testing only a few out of the total lot; and the results of public opinion surveys are seen in the newspapers almost every day.

Auditors who use statistical sampling over judgmental sampling do so for several reasons, which they list as follows:

1. *Sufficiency of data collected can be measured.* It will depend upon how precise an answer the auditor wants and how reliable he wants his answer to be. He can then measure that preciseness and reliability through the number of items in his sample.
2. *Bias can be eliminated.* In random sampling, the choice of items to be

selected is done on a random basis rather than through a judgmental basis, which should eliminate unperceived bias.
3. *Inferences can be made concerning transactions not tested as well as those tested.* In statistical sampling the population as a whole must be considered as well as the items selected for testing.
4. *Sampling can be used by inexperienced as well as experienced auditors.* Experienced auditors may do well in judgmental sampling, but inexperienced auditors do not have the same background to develop the judgmental sample. Statistical sampling results should be the same for all types of auditors desiring the same preciseness and reliability, experienced or inexperienced.

Thus we can see that sampling is an important technique the auditor can use to gather evidence on his audit objective.

Sampling Principles Related to Principles of Auditing and Evidence

Several principles of sampling, related to the principles of auditing and evidence, can be stated. Using these as reference points, the auditor should be able to assure himself that the conclusion on his sample objective will provide meaningful evidence on his primary audit objective:

1. The auditor should always have an audit objective for his sample, as he does for all audits. The sample objective has the same three essential elements as do all audit objectives: criteria, causes, and effects. The criteria are related to the materiality (precision) desired and should be related to the primary audit objective. The effects are related to the reliability desired (confidence). And, the causes are the actions of the auditor.
2. The auditor should always state the materiality (precision) desired of the true value. An estimate derived from a sample obviously could not be expected to be exactly the same as the true value of the universe. The sample value, however, should have a high probability of falling somewhere in an acceptable range above or below the true value, and this range is the measure of precision the auditor uses as the standard or criteria of his audit objective. The precision would show what the auditor would consider as being an immaterial amount from the true value. Any values beyond that range would be material and would not be acceptable as the criteria for the audit. The measure can be stated either as an absolute figure or as a percentage.

    Relevancy means that the information used as evidence must be related to the criteria of the audit; so relevant evidence would also have to be related to the precision of the audit objective.
3. The auditor should know and state the reliability (confidence) he desires, or the risk he is willing to take, in his sampling for audit evidence. Confidence is a statement that the sample values will fall within the precision range a certain percentage of the time.
4. The auditor should assure himself that the universe for his sample is homogeneous. Homogeneity pertains to the source of information, and the source of information is related to the competency of the evidence. Thus, homogeneity would pertain to competency of evidence.
5. The auditor should assure himself that each item in the universe has the same chance of being selected as any other item when he takes a

sample. Since the selection pertains to the source of the information, the proper selection of the sample would be one means of determining the competency of the evidence.
6. The auditor should assure himself, through proper probability techniques, that his sample size is as small as possible but large enough to provide him the precision he desires and the confidence he expects; costs demand this. Also, sample size pertains to source and thus to competency of the evidence.
7. A performance auditor samples many types of universes. Most of these universes fall within the normal curve relationship. The techniques concerned with these normal curve relationships will be used to explain the basic techniques of sampling and will be discussed below under the heading, "Confidence."

Sample Objectives

Since the information from a sample will be used as evidence and since all evidence is gathered on an audit objective, then the first step in any sampling plan is to state its objective. In many cases, the objective of the audit sample will be a subobjective of the audit, rather than the primary audit objective. The auditor must then assure himself that the criteria of the subobjective is directly related to the criteria of the primary audit objective. In some cases, however, especially in M-audits or P-audits, the information obtained from the audit sample will be the evidence on the primary audit objective; but this will be the exception rather than the rule.

The following illustration is a sample objective, concerned with the determination of the value of low-value items in an M-audit of inventories containing both low-value and high-value items:

> In determining the sample size in order to compare the audit value from the sample of an inventory of low-value items for the Able Company to that of the true value of the inventory, can we be (causes—the auditor's actions) confident that our sample estimate has a 90 percent probability of falling (effects—the confidence desired) within the acceptable limits of + or − $25,000 of the recorded value of $1.5 million for the total inventory of 50,000 low-value items (criteria—the precision desired)?

The reader can see that the criteria of the sample objective pertain to the precision desired, the effects to the confidence expected, and the causes to the auditor's actions. Precision and confidence are subjective judgments. Both precision and confidence estimates should be made, however, if the auditor is to determine objectively the appropriate sample size.

Precision

Whether the auditor makes a statistical sample or a judgmental sample, he should first know how much variation he will allow from a known figure in order to have a standard for measuring results. This variation is a judgment of the amount that he would consider as being immaterial.

Using the illustration of an audit objective above as an example, even if the auditor counts every item in the low-value inventory, he would more likely than not find that the inventory figure does not exactly equal $1.5 million. His question then is: "How much variation from the $1.5 million will I allow before I begin to question whether the figure has been accurately recorded?" Precision, thus, becomes the standard for measuring the accuracy of the results; any deviation beyond the precision stated would be a material amount. In most cases, however, some allowance can be made from the true value without affecting the auditor's acceptance of the amount as being correct.

In his concern to have the probability of his sample fall within the precision limits, the auditor conveniently converts his total to an average, and his precision to an average precision. For example, if the recorded value of the inventory is $1.5 million and there are 50,000 items in the inventory, then the arithmetic mean of the inventory is $30.00 ($1,500,000 ÷ 50,000 = $30.00). The average precision would be $0.50 ($25,000 ÷ 50,000 = $.50).

Confidence and Risk

Risk is the percentage figure concerning the chance that sample values will not represent the universe within the precision limits. For example, would the auditor accept the risk that his sample mean in the above illustration would not fall somewhere between $29.50 and $30.50 ($30.00 ± $0.50)? How many times out of a hundred would he risk that chance—five out of a hundred, or 5 percent? One out of a hundred, or 1 percent? Or ten out of a hundred, or 10 percent of the times?

Most auditors are more concerned with the confidence they have that samples will fall within the precision limits than the risk they take that samples will not fall within the precision limits. Thus, instead of saying that he will take a chance that 5 percent of the time his sample figure will not fall within the acceptable precision limits, the auditor would say that he is confidence that 95 percent of the time it will.

Confidence can be considered, then, to be the number of times out of a 100, or the percentage, that a sample value randomly drawn will fall within the precision limits of the true value.

In obtaining sample estimates, the auditor's confidence level is determined through the use of the standard deviation—the measure of the variation of the various items from the arithmetic mean. It is the square root of the average amount obtained by squaring the difference between each of the various items in a distribution from the arithmetic mean of the distribution.

Stated in mathematical terms, the arithmetic mean and the standard deviation are

$$\text{mean} = \frac{\text{sum of all items in the distribution}}{\text{number of items in the distribution}}$$

$$\overline{X} = \frac{\Sigma x}{N}$$

where $\overline{X}$ = mean
Σ = sum of
x = value of individual item
N = number of items

$$\text{standard deviation} = \sqrt{\frac{(\text{sum of the value of each individual item subtracted from the mean})^2}{\text{number of individual items}}}$$

$$\sigma = \sqrt{\frac{\Sigma (\overline{X} - x)^2}{N}}$$

where σ = standard deviation (Greek letter sigma)
x = value of individual item
X̄ = mean
Σ = sum of

Under a normal curve, the standard deviations fall within a fixed set of area values from the mean. This relationship can be seen in the graph of a normal curve, as shown in Figure 12.1.

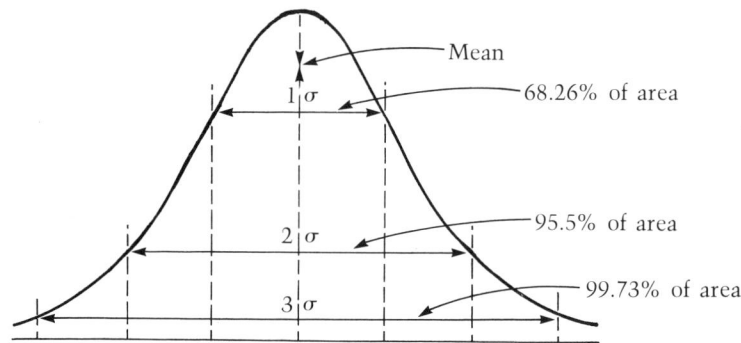

Figure 12.1 Illustration of normal curve relationships

The number of standard deviations that include the percentage of values under the curve can be stated as a table of values. For example, Table 12.1 shows the table of values for the percentages of one or more standard deviations from both sides of the mean.

Table 12.1 Selected Values of Standard Deviations from the Mean

Standard deviations from both sides of the arithmetic mean (confidence coefficient)	Percentage of items included (confidence)
+ and − .67	50.00
1.00	68.26
1.15	75.00
1.28	80.00
1.45	85.00
1.65	90.00
1.96	95.00
2.00	95.50
2.06	96.00
2.33	98.00
2.50	98.75
2.58	99.00
3.00	99.73
3.30	99.90

Using Table 12.1, we find that when a group of items forms a normal distribution and the distribution has an arithmetic mean of $150.00, with a standard deviation of $15.00, then 95 percent of the items in the distribution will fall within the range of $120.60 and $179.40. This value is determined by taking the mean of $150.00 and adding and subtracting 1.96 times the standard deviation of $15.00—1.96 times $15.00 = $29.40; $150.00 + $29.40 = $179.40; $150.00 − $29.40 = $120.60. The amount of $29.40 would be the one-sided precision (P) desired. Thus, the formula for obtaining this amount would be $P = c(\sigma)$.

These relationships can be stated in another way. If a random sample is drawn from items forming a normal distribution, there are 95 chances in 100, or 95 percent probability, that sample values so drawn will fall within the range of the arithmetic mean plus and minus 1.96 times the standard deviation. In other words, there is 95 percent confidence that sample figures fall within the precision limits if the precision limits are + and − 1.96 standard deviations from the mean. The above illustration, then, shows a 95 percent confidence that the sample figure falls within the precision limits of $120.60 and $179.40.

Confidence, we see, can be measured objectively to give the auditor assurance of the chances he will be taking for any desired precision he uses as his criteria limits.

Statisticians have also found that the means of numerous sample values follow a normal curve. Therefore, the standard deviations of the sample means would also fall within the precise limits as shown in Table 12.1. The standard deviation of the sample means is called the standard error.

From the information in this table, it is fairly easy to convert precision figures to standard deviations. Using a 95 percent confidence factor, the confidence coefficient is 1.96. If the inventory value of 2,000 items is $750,000, then the average inventory is $375. If the precision expected is + or − $50,000, then the average precision is $25. If the confidence desired is 95 percent, then the needed standard deviation is

$$\frac{\$25.00}{1.96} \text{ or } \$12.76$$

In formula form, this information would be shown as

$$\text{standard deviation } (\sigma) = \frac{\text{precision } (P)}{\text{confidence coefficient } (c)}$$

Or, stated in another way:

$$\text{precision } (P) = \text{confidence coefficient } (c) \cdot \text{standard deviation } (\sigma)$$

As we have explained, the standard deviation is usually computed from a sample mean, and is the usual known figure in sampling plans. Since the standard deviation from a sample is the standard error rather than the standard deviation, then the formula would be

$$\text{precision} = \text{confidence coefficient} \times \text{standard error}$$

Statisticians have found a direct relationship between the standard error of the sample and the standard deviation of the population. This relationship expressed in a formula is as follows:

$$\text{standard error } (SE) = \frac{\sigma}{\sqrt{n}}$$

where n = number of items in sample

Therefore, if precision (P) = confidence coefficient (c) times standard error, and standard error = $\sigma/\sqrt{n}$, then

$$P = (c)\frac{\sigma}{\sqrt{n}} \quad \text{and} \quad n = (c)^2 \left(\frac{\sigma}{P}\right)^2$$

From this basic formula, the size of a sample can be determined, if the standard deviation and the precision are known. In addition, tables for any confidence level can be determined by making ratios out of the standard deviation and the precision.

The Size of the Sample from a Formula

The criteria of the sample objective will state the range of values from which the auditor can be assured that he will find in the sample the true value a certain proportion of the time; and the confidence that the auditor's sample value will fall within the precision interval is found through the mean, the standard deviation, and the standard deviation converted to confidence coefficients. Clearly, the auditor must have some means of obtaining the mean and the standard deviation.

Often he can obtain the values by reference to previous experience, or he can obtain them by computing his mean and standard deviation from the universe. Also, he can obtain them by computing his mean and standard deviation from a small sample of items from the universe. Furthermore, if the auditor has an indication of the range of values from the mean, he can use the information from Table 12.1 to determine the standard deviation. For example, if the range of values is approximately $60 from each side of the mean of the inventory of $200, then, since the maximum range of standard deviations is 4, the standard deviation would be ¼ of this range, or $15.

To compute the sample size, the auditor, then, must know:

1. The required precision. This will be the criteria of his sample objective.
2. The percentage of confidence he desires that the true value falls within the range of precision stated. This will be the effects of his sample objective.
3. The standard deviation of the universe, the standard deviation of a sample of the universe, or an estimation of the standard deviation taken from a limited sample, or from the range from the mean.
4. Precision per unit. This will be the average precision desired, so the size of the universe must be known.
5. A ratio of the standard deviation to the precision per unit. This is obtained by dividing the standard deviation by the precision per unit.

To illustrate the computation of a sample size, let us assume the following sample objective:

In determining the sample size in order to compare the audit value from a sample of an inventory for the Able Company to that of the true value of the inventory, can we be confident that our sample estimate (causes—the auditor's actions) is 95 percent of the time (effects—the confidence desired) within the acceptable limits of + or − $2,500 from the total inventory of $75,000 for 2,000 items (criteria—the precision desired)?

If we follow the steps listed above, we find that the precision ($2,500) and the confidence (95 percent) are given in the sample objective. Since no standard deviation is given, the auditor must either accept one from a prior year, compute one from a sample, or estimate one. Suppose from a limited sample, the auditor computes a mean of $36 and the standard deviation (standard error) of $6.00. To obtain the precision per unit, divide $2,500 by 2,000, which gives $1.25. To obtain the ratio of the standard deviation to the precision per unit, divide the $6.00 by $1.25, which equals 4.8.

Our equation then reads

$$n = (c)^2 \cdot \left(\frac{\sigma}{P}\right)^2$$

$$n = (1.96)^2 \left(\frac{6}{1.25}\right)^2$$

$$n = (1.96)^2 (4.8)^2$$

$$n = 3.8416 \cdot 23.04$$

$$n = 89$$

The Size of a Sample from a Table

Many organizations have developed tables from which they can immediately determine sample size. From the basic equation we have given, tables of sample sizes can be computed for any confidence coefficient if the standard deviation and the precision are known. Since for a table, the standard deviation and the precision would be unknown, they are converted to ratios pertaining to any precision or any standard deviation.

Table 12.2 shows the sample sizes for selected ratios from 2.5 to 40.00 and is a table that will work very well for universes above 1,000. The sample size derived from Table 12.2 is exactly the same as that derived from the formula above—89.

The reader can see now that the wider the precision limits the auditor sets in his criteria for his objective, the greater the confidence he will have that his sample figure will fall within those limits. The narrower the precision limits, the less confidence he will have; thus, for the same confidence, the narrower these limits, the greater the sample size the auditor will need.

Another problem for the auditor is the use of a finite universe. The formula given on p. 269 and Table 12.2 constructed from that formula were based on the assumption of an infinite universe. A finite correction factor, which can be found in most sampling books, can be built into the formula and the table in order to take care of most finite universes the auditor may encounter.

Based on this correction factor, the new formula would then be

$$n = \frac{N}{1 + \dfrac{N(P)^2}{(c)^2(\sigma)^2}}$$

Using the information given in the preceding illustration concerning the size of a sample for an inventory, we find

$$n = \frac{2{,}000}{1 + \dfrac{2{,}000\,(1.25)^2}{(1.96)^2(6)^2}}$$

$$n = \frac{2{,}000}{1 + \dfrac{2{,}000\,(1.5625)}{3.8416 \cdot 36}}$$

$$n = \frac{2{,}000}{1 + \dfrac{3125}{138.2976}} = \frac{2{,}000}{1 + 22.5962}$$

$$n = 84.76,\ \text{or}\ 85$$

Table 12.2 Sample Sizes for 90, 95, and 99 Percent Confidence*

Sample size for each confidence			Ratio	
(1)	(2)	(3)	(4)	(5)
90%	95%	99%	$\dfrac{\sigma}{P}$	$\dfrac{\sigma^2}{P}$
		42	2.50	6.25
		51	2.75	7.56
	35	60	3.00	9.00
35	48	82	3.50	12.25
40	55	94	3.75	14.06
46	62	107	4.00	16.00
50	68	118	4.20	17.64
55	75	129	4.40	19.36
60	82	141	4.60	21.16
66	89	154	4.80	23.04
71	97	166	5.00	25.00
77	104	180	5.20	27.04
63	113	195	5.40	29.16
89	121	209	5.60	31.36
95	129	224	5.80	33.64
102	139	240	6.00	36.00
109	148	256	6.20	38.44
116	158	273	6.40	40.96
123	168	290	6.60	43.56
131	178	308	6.80	46.24
139	189	327	7.00	49.00
147	200	346	7.20	51.84
155	211	365	7.40	54.76
164	222	385	7.60	57.76
172	234	405	7.80	60.84
181	246	426	8.00	64.00
204	278	481	8.50	72.25
229	312	540	9.00	81.00
255	347	601	9.50	90.25
283	385	666	10.00	100.00
312	424	734	10.50	110.25
342	465	806	11.00	121.00
374	509	881	11.50	132.25
407	554	959	12.00	144.00
441	601	1041	12.50	156.25
478	650	1125	13.00	169.00
554	753	1305	14.00	196.00
636	865	1498	15.00	225.00
723	984	1705	16.00	256.00
816	1111	1924	17.00	289.00
915	1245	2157	18.00	324.00
1019	1389	2403	19.00	361.00
1129	1537	2663	20.00	400.00
1367	1860	3222	22.00	484.00
1626	2213	3835	24.00	576.00
1908	2597	4500	26.00	676.00
2213	3012	5219	28.00	784.00
2541	3458	5991	30.00	900.00
3458	4706	8155	35.00	1225.00
4516	6147	10651	40.00	1600.00

*Sample sizes are computed from the formula $n = (c)^2 \times (\sigma/P)^2$. For 90% confidence, $c^2 = 2.8824$, or $(1.65)^2$. For 95% confidence, $c^2 = 3.8416$, or $(1.96)^2$. For 99% confidence, $c^2 = 6.6564$, or $(2.58)^2$. Selected ratios of σ/P from 2.5 to 40.00 are given in column 4. These ratios are squared in column 5. From the table, the sample sizes should exceed 30. If the universe characteristics do not appear to be normal, sample size should exceed 100.

This amount, 85, for a finite universe, compares favorably with the amount determined from the formula and the table, 89, for an infinite universe.

If from the sample, the auditor determined an average value of $36.50, he could determine the total inventory value by multiplying by 2,000. The computed inventory would then be $73,000, well within the limits of precision required ($75,000 ± $2,500, or $72,500 to $77,500).

A great deal of the work in performance auditing, especially M-auditing, concerns the estimating of a figure, as we have done in the preceding illustrations. However, some of the work of the auditor is concerned with determining whether specific characteristics are being met. For example, in our early illustration of an M-audit concerning the use of private automobiles in lieu of government-owned cars, the auditor would be interested not only in how much was spent, but also in how many times private cars were used in place of government cars. The only answer would be a yes or no.

In all cases where there are only two answers—right or wrong, yes or no, male or female—*attribute sampling* can be used.

Attribute Sampling

Attribute sampling is used when the auditor wants to determine the smallest number of items he needs to examine from a total universe to determine the number or percentage of specific characteristics in the total universe and still feel reasonably confident that the characteristics do not exceed a determined precision.

Thus, we can see that compared to estimation sampling, attribute sampling also uses the principles of *precision* and *confidence*. Precision, of course, would have to be related to the degree of assurance that the number of attributes in the sample would relate to the total number in the universe. Confidence would relate to the percentage of times the attributes determined from samples would fall within the preciseness needed.

One other item is needed for our formula in order to determine the sample size: the standard deviation. Since the standard deviation is concerned with deviation from a normal distribution, and since attributes are concerned with only two items, or a binomial distribution, then the formula for the proportion equivalent to that for a standard deviation of a normal distribution is $\sqrt{e(1-e)}$, where e is the ratio of errors assumed to be in the population.

As we have said, the standard error is equal to the standard deviation divided by the square root of n. Converting this formula to the above equivalent, the new formula for determining the size of an attribute sample would be

$$n = (c)^2 \left[\frac{e(1-e)}{P^2} \right]$$

where $(c)^2$ = confidence coefficient squared

n = number of items in the sample

$e(1-e)$ = equivalent of standard deviation for the proportion

P^2 = precision squared

Let us assume that in our illustration of use of private cars compared to company-owned cars, we can expect an error rate of 5 percent. That is, transportation clerks will allow employees to use their own cars when they should have used a company car. That would be the normal error rate expected of the employees preparing travel vouchers. The auditor will allow an additional 3 percent as his precision. Thus, any amount of error up to 8 percent will be allowable; anything more than 8 percent would be the equivalent of transportation clerks granting the employees the right to use their own cars when they should be using company cars. The auditor believes he should have a 95 percent confidence in his sample results. The question is, "What should be his sample size?"

Using the formula, we would have

$$n = (c)^2 \left[\frac{e(1-e)}{p^2} \right]$$

$$n = (1.96)^2 \cdot \left[\frac{.05(1-.05)}{(.03)^2} \right]$$

$$n = 3.8416 \cdot \left[\frac{(.05 \cdot .95)}{.0009} \right]$$

$$n = 3.8416 \cdot \frac{.0475}{.0009}$$

$$n = 3.8416 \cdot 52.7778$$

$$n = 203$$

Tables based on this formula, with a finite correction factor, along with other correction factors, are available in most audit organizations, which in addition usually have programmed into their computers either the formula or the tables in order to determine the sample size, so that there is no reason to provide a table, such as that illustrated for estimation sampling, for attribute sampling.

To illustrate the differences in the sample size, either from a formula or from a table, based on the finite correction factor, suppose we start with the formula from page 271:

$$n = \frac{N}{1 + \frac{N(P)^2}{(c)^2(\sigma)^2}}$$

If we use for the standard deviation, $\sqrt{e(1-e)}$, as suggested above, then $\sigma^2 = e(1-e)$. By substituting in the above equation, we have

$$n = \frac{N}{1 + \frac{N(P)^2}{(c)^2(e(1-e))}}$$

Assuming a universe of 2,000 for the above illustration on the use of company automobiles in lieu of private cars, then the sample size would be computed as follows:

$$n = \frac{2,000}{1 + \frac{2,000(.03)^2}{(1.96)^2(.05(1-.05))}}$$

$$n = \frac{2,000}{1 + \frac{2,000(.0009)}{(3.8416)(.0475)}}$$

$$n = \frac{2{,}000}{1 + \frac{1.8}{.182475}}$$

$$n = \frac{2{,}000}{1 + 9.86436}$$

$$n = 185$$

The sample size of 185 for the universe of 2,000 is comparable to the sample size of 203 for an infinite population.

Homogeneous Universe

In order to be certain that the information from his sample is competent, the auditor should assure himself that the items in his universe are homogeneous. To illustrate the meaning of homogeneity as applied to sampling, let us take our illustration of a sample objective concerning the inventory of low-value items. Suppose the inventory consisted of both low-value and high-value items. The high-value items often are not homogeneous with the low-value items, even though both are considered inventory. For example, if the total inventory was $4 million, made up of 500 high-value items valued at $2.5 million and 50,000 low-value items valued at $1.5 million, the auditor should have two sample objectives rather than one in order to obtain homogeneity in his universes so that the sources of his information would be competent: One sample objective would be for the low-value items and one would be for the high-value items.

Unless there is homogeneity in the universe the auditor might have great difficulty in setting the limits in his criteria of the audit objective. For instance, the precision needed for the high-value items in the above inventory, where the average value for each item was $5,000, would differ greatly from that needed for the low-value items, where the average value was $30, or a combination of both high- and low-value items, where the average value is $79.21.

If the auditor has difficulty in setting the precision limits in his sample objective, then he can surmise that the source of his information may not be as competent as he would like and he had better determine whether the data in the universe are homogeneous. If they are not homogeneous, then it would be easier for him, in most instances, to have more than one objective and thus more than one sample.

One method of breaking down a very large group of apparently unrelated items into more homogeneous universes is called *stratified sampling*. Stratification usually increases the reliability of the estimates the auditor makes from the sample because of his ability to develop proper precision in his criteria. Any gain in reliability, however, depends upon the effectiveness of the stratification; techniques for determining proper stratification can be found in most advanced sampling textbooks. They are more often needed when making M-audits and P-audits than when making financial-statement examinations.

Random Selection

In most instances of sample selection for an audit, each item in the universe should have the same chance of being selected as every other item. In order to be sure that the auditor does not subjectively choose the items in his sample,

Table 12.3 Page from a Table of Random Numbers

Line	Column						
	(1)	(2)	(3)	(4)	(5)	(6)	(7)
801	33993	51249	76123	16507	57399	77922	36198
802	39041	05779	74278	75301	01779	60768	22023
803	56011	26839	38501	03321	43259	73148	43615
804	07397	95853	45764	43803	76659	57736	44801
805	74998	53337	13860	89430	95825	65893	96572
806	59572	95893	69765	43597	90570	60909	06478
807	74645	13940	28640	00127	04261	17650	34050
808	42765	23855	38451	11482	32671	52126	23800
809	66561	56130	30356	54034	53996	98874	78001
810	50670	13172	31460	20224	34293	59458	24410
811	53971	08701	38356	36149	10891	05178	55653
812	47177	03085	37432	94053	87057	61859	97943
813	41494	89270	48063	12253	00383	96010	41457
814	07409	32874	03514	84943	74421	86708	34267
815	03097	12212	43093	46224	14431	15065	18267
816	34728	88896	59205	18004	96431	41366	50982
817	48117	83679	52509	29339	87735	97499	42848
818	14628	89161	66972	19180	40852	91738	23920
819	61512	79376	88184	29415	50716	93393	96220
820	99954	55656	01946	57035	64418	29700	99242
821	61455	28229	82511	11622	60786	18442	36508
822	10398	50239	70191	37585	98373	04651	67804
823	59075	81492	40669	16391	12148	38538	73873
824	91497	76797	82557	55301	61570	69577	23301
825	74619	62316	00041	53053	81252	32739	65201
826	12536	80792	44581	12616	49740	86946	41819
827	10246	49556	07610	59950	34387	70013	64460
828	92506	24397	19145	24185	24479	70118	42708
829	65745	27223	22831	39446	65808	95534	03348
830	01707	04494	48168	58480	74983	63091	81027
831	66959	80109	88908	38759	80716	36340	30082
832	79278	02746	50718	90196	28394	82035	03255
833	11343	22312	41379	22297	71703	78729	65082
834	40415	10553	65932	34938	43977	39262	95828
835	72774	25480	30264	08291	93796	22281	51434
836	75886	86543	47020	14493	38363	64238	16322
837	64628	20834	07967	46676	42907	60909	73293
838	45905	77701	98976	70056	80502	68650	24469
839	77691	00408	64191	11006	39212	26862	99863
840	39178	12024	43379	57590	45307	72206	53283
841	67120	01558	99762	79752	17139	52265	97997
842	88264	85390	92841	63011	64423	50910	38189
843	78097	59495	45090	74592	47474	56157	88287
844	41888	69798	82296	09312	04150	07616	34572
845	46618	07254	28714	18244	53214	39560	68753
846	29213	42101	25089	11881	77558	72738	57234
847	38601	25735	04726	36544	67848	93937	68745
848	92207	10011	64210	77096	00011	79218	52123
849	30610	13236	33241	68731	30956	40587	45206
850	74544	72806	62226	65605	37996	00377	59917

he should use a method of random selection such as a random number table. An example follows as Table 12.3; it is taken from the Interstate Commerce Commission's table of 105,000 random decimal digits.

The digits may be selected from the table from any direction—left to right, right to left, down to up, or up to down. The auditor should decide in advance where to start, how many digits to consider at a time, which direction to move for the next group of digits, and what to do when the end of a row or column is reached.

To illustrate, suppose you want to select a sample of 200 from a universe of 2,000 numbers between 301 and 2,300. Since numbers above 1,000 include four digits, you will have to select at least four digits at a time. Start anywhere in the table; an easy way to choose is to close your eyes and place your finger on a digit in the table. Suppose your finger landed on line 826, column five. The number in that column is 49740. If you are to choose four digits, then the first number to be selected, going from left to right, would be 4974. Since it would be too large, it would not be chosen and would be discarded. The second number would be 9740; too large, it also would be discarded. The third number would be 7408 (continuing to read from left to right), also too large, as is the next, 4086. The next number, then, 0869, would be the first to be chosen. Additional numbers chosen from that line would be 1819 and 1910. When the end of the line is reached, you can go to the first column in the next line, from which the last two digits of 1910 were chosen. The next number you would choose from this line would be 1024, then 0246. This method would continue until 200 numbers had been chosen. You would then have a random selection of 200 numbers to use as a basis for your selection of items to be examined.

Tables are also available for random letters as well as for random numbers. In addition, most large-scale computers have programmed in them a table of random digits; thus if the auditor is involved in a computer audit, the random selection of a sample can automatically be obtained from the computer.

Often the auditor has difficulty in selecting random numbers from certain types of files. For examples, file drawers may be randomly stuffed with information. In that case, the auditor may want to take a systematic selection of every fourth, tenth, or other number item in relation to the total universe. He should choose, however, some random place to start his systematic selection.

REVIEW QUESTIONS

1. Does the auditor review every record, interview every person involved in the audit, or observe every action concerned with the audit? If not, how does the auditor, in most cases, determine that the conclusion is probably right? (See p. 264.)

2. Describe judgmental sampling, and list the advantages of statistical sampling over judgmental sampling. (See pp. 264–65.)

3. List and describe the seven principles of audit sampling. (See pp. 265–66.)

4. The three elements of an audit objective are always: Criteria, causes, and effects. Describe these three elements as they apply to a sample audit objective. (See p. 266.)

5. Define precision. To which element of the audit objective does precision always relate? (See pp. 266–67.)

6. Define confidence. To which element of the audit objective does confidence always relate? (See pp. 267–69.)

7. The confidence level is determined through the use of a standard deviation. Describe how the auditor would compute a standard deviation. (See pp. 267–68, 270.)

8. If precision (P) equals the confidence coefficient (c) times the standard deviation (σ), then give the formula for the standard deviation. (See p. 269.)

9. State the formula for the sample size. Show how this formula is determined, and show how a standard deviation can be determined to fit into the formula. (See pp. 269–70.)

10. What specific items must an auditor know in order to compute a sample size from a formula? (See p. 270.)

11. Auditors often use sampling as applied to attributes as well as for estimating. Explain what is meant by attribute sampling. (See pp. 273–74.)

12. Show how sample size can be corrected for the size of the population in an attribute sample. (See pp. 274–75.)

13. Homogeneity is an important factor in selecting a sample. Explain what is meant by a homogeneous universe. (See p. 275.)

14. What is one method of breaking down a universe which is not homogeneous? (See p. 275.)

15. A random sample is necessary to prevent bias. Explain how to choose a random sample through the use of a table of random numbers. (See pp. 275–77.)

CASE 1

Estimating the Assets of Mammoth City

Preliminary Information

Mammoth City recently elected a new mayor. In her first few days in office she found that the city did not have any idea of its total resources.

She talked to the city auditor about whether the city could come up with an estimate of the various types of assets it owns. For example, the mayor said she did not know whether the city had an inventory of office supplies, or how much of an inventory it had. Likewise, she could not find a perpetual inventory of the various fixed assets of the city.

AUDIT SCENARIO 1
Estimating Asset Values in Mammoth City

Explain to the mayor how you would approach obtaining an estimated figure for the following.

The city maintains a warehouse containing several sections for all city supplies. Stored in one section of this warehouse are approximately 2,000 items, which cost from $0.25 to $5.00. The flow of the stock is on a first-in, first-out basis. Records are kept of purchases and encumbrances, but no inventory records are maintained.

The section of the warehouse where these items are maintained is under the direction of a warehouse foreman. He not only supervises these items, but has charge of another section of larger items, which cost from $5.00 to $25.00. There are approximately 10,000 items in this section.

AUDIT SCENARIO 2
Determining Adequacy of Procurement Internal Control

Explain to the mayor how you could ascertain whether the internal controls for determining requirements, purchasing, storing, warehousing, and record keeping for the above two sections of the warehouse were adequate and were being followed. Explain to her how you would use attribute sampling under these conditions.

CASE 2

Classifying Civil Servants in the State of Landia

Required
1. Show how you would approach this audit problem, both from a regular audit standpoint and from the standpoint of statistical sampling.
2. Are there different types of sampling techniques that could be used to answer both of the governor's questions?

Preliminary Information

The governor suggested to the state auditor in the state of Landia that it seemed to him many of the positions in the state civil service were overgraded; if his estimate was anywhere near right, he said, the state could be paying an excessive sum for salaries.

The governor stated that his impression on overgrading came from several of his friends in industry, who were saying that the government was an unfair competitor in the labor market. He also said that several employees had talked to him about poor morale problems in some of the agencies because certain positions were overgraded.

The governor suggested to the auditor that as a start she make an analysis of one particular classification—the secretarial-stenographic series—and let him know two answers:

- what proportion of the total in this series were improperly graded,
- how much could be saved if the employees were properly classified.

Additional Information

Information from the state Civil Service Agency showed that there were 5,271 employees classified in the secretarial-stenographic series. The grades ran from 10 to 20 in this series, with salaries starting at $5,000 for grade 10 and going up to $18,000 for grade 20. The average pay for all employees was $9,560 with a standard deviation of $1,200.

Agency rules and regulations noted the possibility of error in classification. However, they state that the normal error rate is 1 percent and no agency is allowed to have more errors than 2 percent in their classification process. The Civil Service Agency said that they had not sampled the classification system for the entire state but they had made selected reviews, agency by agency.

CHAPTER 13

Obtaining Evidence Through Interviews and Questionnaires

After you have read this chapter, studied the review questions, and worked through the cases, you will understand:

- How to plan appropriately for an interview.
- How to conduct a suitable interview.
- How to write up the interview.
- How to confirm what was said in the interview.
- How to plan for obtaining information through a questionnaire.
- How to prepare a simple questionnaire for obtaining information and evidence.
- How to analyze the evidence obtained from a questionnaire.

While the two topics of interviews and questionnaires may not apply to every audit organization, the ideas contained in this chapter are beneficial to most auditors participating in audits for improving the efficiency, economy, and effectiveness of management's performance.* The ability to interview is very important to the successful accomplishment of most of those audits. In large performance audits, to obtain sufficient reliable evidence at a reasonable cost, developing and using questionnaires also becomes a very important consideration.

Interviews: Use of Oral Information

Auditors generally are required to obtain substantial amounts of information that can be used as evidence during interviews and discussions with agency representatives and others. It is important that they fully recognize and take advantage of the benefits that can be realized by interviewing knowledgeable persons during their work. Interviews are sometimes the only means of obtaining basic information, and the information so obtained may also be used to supplement, explain, interpret, or contradict information obtained by other means. Like other activities, the art of interviewing can be improved with experience by using certain techniques that may appear obvious but nonetheless require constant awareness and application.

The auditor holds many discussions on a day-to-day basis to obtain general background information or to understand better the activities he is interested in. The information obtained from these kinds of interviews is not necessarily expected to be used as evidence in a report or to contribute directly to developing a finding. The following guidance is not, therefore, specifically

---

*This chapter is adapted with the permission of the U.S. General Accounting Office from its *Comprehensive Audit Manual*, Chapter 8, Appendix I.

directed to such discussions, although there might be circumstances under which the material in this chapter would be appropriate for them.

Oral information can ordinarily be used in reports provided (1) the information is obtained from a source that is knowledgeable and responsible, and (2) its nature is properly identified.

The source of oral information should usually be stated in the report; for example, "The Controller of Cordex Company advised us that. . . ." This identification will help to indicate the responsibility level of the interviewee, or his relationship to the subject.

If factual oral information, as opposed to an opinion, is of key importance as evidence and cannot be corroborated, it is usually desirable to indicate in the report that the auditor was unable to corroborate it and why. If oral information cannot be verified by other evidence, he should recognize the resulting uncertainty of any conclusions that are based on it. In these circumstances, extreme care in wording a report is necessary to avoid any unwarranted conclusions or implications regarding the validity of such information.

Information obtained by interview, even if confirmed in writing by the interviewee, represents merely the understanding, view, or word of the interviewee, rather than information determined to be correct. The usefulness and reliability of oral information, therefore, depends greatly upon such things as its nature and source and on whether there are other practicable means by which it can more conclusively be established or verified.

To the extent practicable, significant oral information should be supported by documentation or other means. The auditor would be subject to valid criticism if he failed to take all reasonable measures to assure himself of the reliability of the information included in his report.

Sources of Interview Information

The auditor's objective is to obtain as full and correct an understanding of subjects under audit consideration as possible. Interviews should be designed to explore fully those subjects with cognizant persons. Particular attention should be given to those aspects of the activity that appear questionable. The persons responsible for the activities should normally have information on considerations given to such aspects; the reasons for existing practices; and useful information or views as to the need for, and possible methods of, improvement. The auditor should carefully consider the interviewee's apparent knowledge of the subject, possible motives, and whether the information he gives is consistent with other available information.

The fact that an individual is in a high-level position does not insure the validity of the information furnished. That person may be new in the position, for instance, or may lack the detailed, firsthand knowledge a subordinate may have.

The auditor should not waste time interviewing someone who does not have the information he wants, even if he thinks the person should have it because of the position held. He will often find that advance notice to a prospective interviewee of the subjects to be discussed will result in his being directed to a more knowledgeable person.

Whenever practicable, findings that involve apparent deficiencies should be discussed with the officials directly responsible *during* the audit—that is, while the auditors are actually obtaining and evaluating information rather than afterwards at a final conference upon the completion of the assignment.

Level of Discussions   Management aspects and the improvements in them should be discussed with officials at an appropriately high level, who are in a position to understand

Outside Experts — Outside experts may be interviewed. Such interviews should be directed at insuring that the experts can be relied upon, and will as well add credibility to the findings.

Informants — An informant, a person who has brought a matter to the auditor's attention, may be interviewed. Such persons are referred to as confidential informants if they furnish information with the understanding that their identity will not be divulged, or if the nature of the case or the information supplied makes it desirable or necessary to protect their identity.

There is a distinction between paid informants in criminal work and those persons who believe they are morally bound to expose situations to improve the general welfare. The auditor should recognize that morally bound informants are a reality and are often good sources of information.

Planning and Preparing for Important Interviews

Interviews should be properly planned. The interviewer should know what the purpose of the interview is and what the information sought is. To intelligently conduct the interview, a person should be familiar with the previously disclosed facts of the problem. This is particularly valuable in permitting the interviewer to recognize and follow up on any inconsistencies between information obtained in the interview and information previously obtained from other sources.

In planning interviews, even the interviewer should be carefully selected in terms of the persons to be interviewed and past experience interviewing them. Some high-level officials resent, and thus react unfavorably to, being interviewed by persons other than those who occupy positions at a reasonably high level of responsibility. The auditor, then, should exercise good judgment in order to avoid mismatches between interviewer and interviewee.

Advance Notice — For the more important interviews, it will help to provide interviewees advance notice of the major topics the auditor is interested in. Advance notice avoids wasted time if interviewees should want to refer to particular documents or to familiarize themselves with the subject before the interview. Furthermore, the auditor can point out other matters that might be discussed if the need arises.

If an appointment must be postponed or canceled, the auditor should promptly notify the prospective interviewee; obviously, an official will resent the discourtesy involved if the interviewer is either late for a meeting or fails to give notification of cancellation so that the interviewee can rearrange a busy schedule.

Number of Staff Members Present — Depending on the significance of the matters to be discussed, the auditor will usually find it advisable to have two staff members present to provide a greater degree of assurance that the written record of the interview accurately reflects the information obtained. The need for written confirmation of information obtained orally is discussed below.

Beginning an Interview

The interviewer should properly introduce himself if he has not previously met the interviewee. Proper identification usually removes any doubt in the mind of the person being interviewed as to the identity of the interviewer.

The initial approach is important, especially when the auditor is meeting the interviewee for the first time. He should make an effort to put the person at ease and to establish a common ground between them. Even some brief comments about inconsequential subjects, such as the weather or a sporting event, often serve to "break the ice" and establish a cordial relationship. Again, the auditor must exercise good judgment. If, for example, he knows that the interviewee is not amenable to spending even a few minutes on matters not directly related to the subject of the interview, obviously he should immediately get down to business.

Discussing the Topic

After the introduction, the interviewer should explain the purpose of the interview so that the interviewee will understand what is desired of him. Depending on the circumstances, the person may be allowed to tell his own story or he may be questioned specifically regarding the matters on which information is desired.

The discussion should be controlled by the interviewer to the extent necessary to keep it directed toward obtaining the facts or other information pertinent to the purpose of the interview, and toward conserving time. A skilled interviewer will guard against the interviewee's discussing irrelevant matters to avoid answering questions, or providing information on painful or disturbing topics.

The interviewer's attitude should be one of seeking information rather than of engaging in an argument or debate. Insofar as practicable, it is of course desirable to promote a spirit of cooperation and a common understanding of what the actual situation and facts are, and as well—if the interview is to cover such matters—an understanding of what the causes and indicated corrective actions seem to be.

Other suggestions for discussing the topic successfully include:

1. Get all the information needed during one interview; avoid to the greatest extent possible the necessity of a second interview.
2. At the conclusion of the interview, briefly summarize the salient information obtained as retelling the story may recall additional pertinent facts to the mind of the interviewer and the interviewee.
3. Do not extend the interview beyond a reasonable period of time, which should closely approximate the time agreed upon when the appointment was made.

Using Recording Equipment or Stenographers

It is not usually necessary to use recording equipment or stenographers during the interview. If the auditor considers it necessary, an agreement should be reached with the interviewee. Transcripts obtained through such methods generally contain much information that is not significant, and their use does not eliminate the need for confirming important statements made. Also, transcripts do not permit the interviewee to correct factual errors and oversights in the discussions. However, if a written verbatim record of the interview is to be made available to the interviewee for appropriate corrections, this method may be suitable for obtaining a complete record of the entire discussion. If the interviewee makes arrangements for use of a personal stenographer or recording equipment, the interviewer should request a copy of the subsequent transcript or tape.

If the auditor uses recording equipment, the resulting tapes should become a part of the working papers and should be protected and controlled accordingly. Upon request, the interviewee may have the tape duplicated.

Written Record of Interview

Information obtained through an interview should be reduced to writing as soon as possible. In some cases the auditor will find it appropriate to take notes during the interview that can be used to prepare a more detailed memorandum after the interview is completed.

How and when to take notes will frequently depend on the circumstances of the case, the complexity of the subjects discussed, and the personality of the interviewee. In some cases, note-taking may cause the interviewee to be reluctant to talk freely; and if there is such an adverse reaction, the interviewer should stop. Auditors may expect, however, that note-taking will not be objected to inasmuch as it shows concern for recording accurately what is being said.

No special form is usually used to record an interview. It may be either typewritten or handwritten, but it should appear as a separate document in the work papers and should contain appropriate details of the discussion, including: the time and place; the ranks, positions, and names of all persons involved; and the signatures of other audit staff members present. The memorandum should also indicate why the auditor believes the interviewee is qualified to discuss the subject matter. A record of an interview should never consist of an unexplained notation on a worksheet or unsupported statements or footnotes in the working papers.

Confirmation by Interviewee

Some form of written confirmation of *significant* oral information should generally be requested from interviewees unless the information is otherwise supported and a request considered unnecessary. Even a tactful request for written confirmation of significant oral information, in some instances, might discourage an interviewee from cooperating later. Under such circumstances, it would be appropriate to request oral confirmation of the information and to note the oral confirmation in the working papers.

Written confirmation is especially important if other corroborating evidence is not available, because it insures the completeness and accuracy of the record of the oral information, impresses interviewees with the significance attached to their remarks, and protects the auditor against a later controversy over what information was given.

Whether the oral information is significant enough to warrant confirmation depends on the attending circumstances. For example, information that is essential to a report conclusion or recommendation is significant. Also, oral information that varies from documentation or that criticizes policies and practices or individuals is usually significant enough to require written confirmation—certainly if it appears possible that such information will be included in a report.

It may sometimes be advisable to request confirmation of oral information even if the information is not essential to a potential report finding. For example, information obtained during discussions on a highly technical subject, or on one that involves numerous dates, amounts, or statistics, should usually be confirmed by the interviewee even though the information is used only as background data in the report. In such instances, the risk of error in recording the information or in obtaining incomplete or erroneous information may necessitate the confirmation.

Either oral or written confirmation of significant oral information by an interviewee does not obviate the auditor's need to verify the information by other means such as observation, discussions with others, and/or review of available documentation. The auditor should note that confirmation by the interviewee is principally a means for confirming the understanding of what was said and does *not* constitute a verification of its basic validity.

While the auditor's objective is to obtain needed information from appropriate sources, he needs to be fair in using such data; and thus the interviewee should be made aware of the importance attached to the information given and of its possible use.

Form of Confirmation

Oral information by the interviewee can usually be confirmed best by the staff at the audit site. Interviewees, if asked, will usually acknowledge in writing the completeness and accuracy of an interview memorandum. Auditors should request interviewees to sign the typewritten or handwritten memorandum indicating that they concur; if requested, auditors should give them a copy of the memorandum. The following statement on the last page of the memorandum would generally be appropriate:

> I have read this memorandum of interview and I agree that it presents fairly the matters discussed and the statements made during the interview.
>
> Signature and date
of signature

Refusals to Confirm Oral Information

If an interviewee should refuse a request for written confirmation of significant oral information, the auditor should ask the person to confirm the information informally by reading, and if necessary correcting, the write-up. The confirmation should be obtained in the presence of two auditors; and the interviewer's notation of the oral confirmation, together with the signature of the other auditor, should be attached to the interview memorandum.

If an interviewee refuses to confirm the significant oral information either in writing or orally, the auditor should attach a note to this effect to the interview memorandum and indicate the interviewee's reasons for refusal.

In any case in which there is an apparent unwillingness to accept responsibility for information given, the auditor should consider the probable effects of the use of such data in the report. When practicable, the auditor should discuss the matter with other responsible officials—or use other available means such as correspondence—to corroborate the information.

Illustrative Working Papers for Interviews

In Chapter 11 we illustrated, from "The Indian Education Case," the flow of information from the detail to the final summary in the working papers for a P-audit. The following additional working papers from that audit illustrate the application of good interviewing techniques to this particular audit. (The original interviews were recorded in handwriting; copies have been typed for readability.)

Notice that the papers include such significant details as the purpose of the interview, the time, the place, the participants, and the significant detail from the interview.

The exit-conference working papers are a little different from the normal interview working paper. The auditor is there to tell the participants the result of the audit. Additional evidence, such as is shown in work papers OA-2/4-6, is often obtained from this type of interview.

REVIEW OF INDIAN EDUCATION OD-1
Code 14553   4

D. Bullock
4/23/71

RECORD OF DISCUSSION

DATE: 4/23/71

PLACE: Fort Wingate High School, Fort Wingate, New Mexico

PARTICIPANTS: Fort Wingate High School
Mr. Jerry Jaeger, Principal
Mr. Bruce Hoover, Asst. Principal

GAO
Mr. D. M. Bullock, Auditor

PURPOSE: To determine if Messrs. Jaeger & Hoover were aware of the Central Office objectives as stated in the program memorandums.

DISCUSSION:

Both Mr. Jaeger and Mr. Hoover stated that they were not aware of the Central Office educational objectives as published in the Program Memorandums (see Audit Program for objectives) and that therefore they had not specifically budgeted in terms of these objectives.

Mr. Jaeger stated that Wingate school objectives and philosophies are communicated to the area and Agency offices in the form of information copies of various booklets and handbooks that are prepared at the school. There is no direct communication with the Central Office so he can't say whether the Central Office is aware of WHS objectives.

J.C.
5/23/71

REVIEW OF INDIAN EDUCATION   OG-2
        Code 14553   3

                                     1 of 5
                                     D. Bullock
                                     4/23/71

RECORD OF DISCUSSION

DATE: 4/22/71

PLACE: Fort Wingate High School (FWHS), Fort Wingate, New Mexico

PARTICIPANTS: FWHS
  Mr. Bruce Hoover, Asst. Principal

  GAO
  Mr. D. M. Bullock, Auditor

PURPOSE: To discuss the responsiveness of the curriculum compared to student's needs.

Mr. Hoover stated the following:

He agreed that the student academic achievement levels at FWHS were probably lower, on the average, than national norms. He attributes this poor achievement to the language barrier, rather than to social, emotional, or psychological problems.

The cause of the language barrier is the home life of the student, where only Navajo is spoken by the parents.

Another reason for the Navajo student's poor achievement, he thinks, is the lack of competitiveness inherent in the Navajo's nature. He doesn't want to rise above the group in any way.

L.C.
5/23/71

REVIEW OF INDIAN EDUCATION
Code 14553

OG-2
4

2 of 5
D. Bullock

Record of Discussion, cont'd.

The written criteria for admission to FWHS is contained in the Navajo Area Office publication "School Enrollment and Guidelines."

GAO note

Basic criteria for students who may attend reservation boarding schools:

1) Cannot attend any school on a day basis and are eligible for one off the grades offered.

2) Recommended for social welfare reasons and approved by the Agency - - -

3) High School pupils may not be approved for boarding school care who reside within a mile and a half from the BIA School or bus route.

These guidelines are used by the school, although exceptions have been made with agency or area approval.

The vast majority of the students at FWHS are more than 1 1/2 miles from a bus line and there is no day school available. Although there has been no analysis of the student body in terms of the criteria for admission, he thinks that more than 95% of the students are enrolled under the criteria 1 and 3 above. The other 5% or so may be welfare cases, or transfer students who preferred Ft. Wingate for

REVIEW OF INDIAN EDUCATION
Code 14553

$\frac{OG-2}{5}$

3 of 5
D. Bullock
4/22/71

any number of reasons and whose application was approved by Agency. He knows of only two or three cases where the students are enrolled at FWHS because of social reasons. He believes that there are a number of students who need special education, but that the school does not have a program and doesn't plan to institute one in the foreseeable future.

The student body at FWHS, in his opinion, is pretty well emotionally balanced. There are some problems with the students drinking and going off campus without permission, but he doesn't think these problems are any worse than would be experienced with any group of young people in the same circumstances.

He thinks the school's present regular programs are designed to meet, and succeed in meeting, the special needs of the students, but stated that the programs are not designed to meet Central Office objectives. Each teacher is encouraged to use special materials that would more specifically meet the needs of the children. Due to the isolated

REVIEW OF INDIAN EDUCATION
Code 14553

OG-2
/6

4 of 5
D. Bullock
4/22/71

environment which most of the students grew up in, special emphasis is given to develop courses which give the children a chance to gain knowledge and experience that they have missed in their home life. By and large he thinks that these efforts have been successful.

All students that require special training due to poor achievement are identified by tests administered within the classroom. Shortly after the school year begins each teacher divides the class into 3 phases, or levels of subject knowledge. The lowest phase identifies those students who require remedial or special training. Special attention is given to all of these slow students during the year in an effort to bring them up to the next phase. Teaching aids who speak Navajo are used to teach these students the concepts that they are not able

REVIEW OF INDIAN EDUCATION
Code 14553

$\frac{OG-2}{7}$

5 of 5
D. Bullock
4/22/71

to understand in English. The slow learners are normally not segregated into separate classes. They usually receive the regular course work, but also receive extra help. Six teaching aids and a library technician have been funded under Title I, PL 89-10 to help provide this special attention to the slow learners.

He agrees that reading skills are essential to success in other academic course work.

Students with reading problems are identified at the time the 3 phases, or levels of knowledge, are determined by each teacher as discussed above (see p. 4 of 5).

He feels that FWHS needs a more vigorous reading program and better teachers in this area. He stated that a new reading center purchased through PL89 has been received and that it will be installed and operating by September 1971. Efforts are being made to teach the present staff the necessary skills and he believes that 71/72 will show real progress in this area.

REVIEW OF INDIAN EDUCATION
Code 14553

$\frac{OA-2}{4}$

1 of 3
D. Bullock
5/12/71

EXIT CONFERENCE

DATE: 5/7/71

PLACE: Fort Wingate High School, Fort Wingate, New Mexico

PARTICIPANTS: Fort Wingate High School
Mr. Jerry Jaeger, Principal
Mr. Bruce Hoover, Asst. Principal
Mrs. Verna Enyart, Guidance Supervisor

GAO
Mr. D. M. Bullock, Auditor

PURPOSE: To inform the school's administration of the results of our interview.

I briefly outlined our findings (see agenda for Exit Conference on WP $\frac{OA-2}{7}$) and asked for a discussion of the points mentioned. All persons agreed with my remarks except as discussed further below. At this point Mrs. Enyart left the meeting. Mr. Jaeger & Mr. Hoover agreed that my comments regarding the results of the review correctly reflected the situation in all areas covered. Mr. Jaeger added that he had never heard of the Central Office Program Memorandum objectives and did not believe that they were realistic as they pertained to the Navajo people. The Navajo parents were just not yet convinced that education was worthwhile and it would probably

REVIEW OF INDIAN EDUCATION
Code 14553

OA-2
5

2 of 3
D. Bullock
5/12/71

Exit Conference, cont'd.

take another generation before the objectives could be achieved.

He also stated that in his opinion Fort Wingate High School should be removed from the jurisdiction of Eastern Navajo Agency and placed directly under the Area Office. He said the Agency Education people were oriented towards Elementary School management and often failed to recognize the differences between primary and secondary schools. This caused problems in staffing because the school had to accept Agency's teacher assignment policies while believing that they could obtain higher quality personnel if they were allowed to do their own recruiting.

He also believed that Agency shortchanged the school when assigning funds for operation of the school. He said that he didn't believe they did this deliberately, but rather because they forgot that it costs more money on a per-

REVIEW OF INDIAN EDUCATION
Code 14553

$\frac{\text{OA-2}}{6}$

3 of 3
D. Bullock
5/12/71

Exit Conference, cont'd.

student basis to operate a high school than it does to operate an elementary school.

Mr. Jaeger stated that an IQ and academic achievement testing program will be initiated next year under the supervision of the Guidance Department. He stated that he had doubts about the reliability of IQ and achievement tests administered to Indian students, but that he agreed that they would probably be of some value, especially for placement counseling. Mr. Hoover agreed with that statement.

Both Mr. Jaeger and Mr. Hoover agreed that if the Central Office's PM objectives are to be met a well organized and managed program directed toward that goal is needed.

Questionnaires: Advantages and Disadvantages

Questionnaires can be useful for gathering information and evidence pertinent to all reviews. They can be submitted to those individuals, organizations, private firms, and others expected to have knowledge of the program or audit area with which the auditor is concerned. The responders may be associated with an area directly, or indirectly as beneficiaries, users, administrators, contractors, or simply as potentially knowledgeable sources of information who might help the auditor in his work.

The primary advantages of questionnaires, compared to the process of interviewing many persons, are convenience and economy in terms of cost and time. Also, the information obtained can be more easily tabulated because of its specificity and overall uniformity.

The disadvantage of a questionnaire is that it is basically inflexible; the auditor gets no more than he asks for in the absence of costly and time-consuming follow-up and verification. The information obtained through questionnaires has a very low reliability rate—clearly less than oral information. It must be used with care; and unless corroborating evidence is available, such evidence would not be adequate support for conclusions and recommendations dealing with important program matters.

Planning for Use of Questionnaires

The potential value and use of questionnaires should be considered in developing a work program. A decision whether to use this technique should be made early in the planning phase of the work. The auditor should bear in mind, however, that a questionnaire is but one way of gathering needed information and will not generally be the only way.

Design

Some basic principles to use in designing questionnaires follow:

1. Consider the educational levels and experience of potential responders. Simple and direct questions consistent with the subject matter will usually produce the best results.
2. Keep the length of the questionnaire within reasonable bounds. Screen the draft questionnaire carefully to make sure that all questions are relevant. An overly long questionnaire imposes a burden on the responder and the response may suffer.
3. Answers should be reasonably available to the responder. Although some questions may require work by the responder, such questions should be kept to a minimum and their importance should be made clear in transmitting the questionnaires.
4. Group the questions logically. The answer to one question may require a decision on which other questions should be answered or omitted. Help the responder by leaving a simple trail to follow.
5. Use multiple-choice questions whenever possible with space for "other" answers. Questions requiring narrative answers are less desirable but cannot be avoided when the needed information represents the unique experience of the responder.
6. Allow sufficient space for answers. This will help both the responder and the person who tabulates the answers. Also provide space for "any additional comments" the responder may wish to add. These may not

always be susceptible to meaningful tabulation, but they might furnish useful insights.

7. Questions should be framed to avoid defensive reactions by the responders. Try not to place responders in a position of providing potentially embarrassing answers. They will not be completely candid if they feel that their answers might harm them. A thoughtfully developed transmittal letter (see below) can help alleviate possible hesitancy over giving honest answers.

8. It may be worthwhile to test the questionnaire on a limited basis before it is sent to all potential responders. Reworking may then be necessary.

Selection of Responders and Distribution of Questionnaires

A sound statistical-sampling plan for selecting potential responders is important if the information obtained is to result in valid projections and conclusions. Controls over responses should be established, and a systematic follow-up on late responders should be provided for.

A carefully prepared letter forwarding the questionnaires to the potential responders is essential if answers are to be obtained. The tone of the letter should be cordial, should be designed to encourage response, and should emphasize the importance of the information solicited.

The letter should set a reasonable date for forwarding the response, consistent with audit requirements but nonetheless considerate of the time needed by the responder to evaluate the questionnaire and prepare answers. A self-addressed, postage-paid envelope should be part of the package.

When follow-up letters are needed after the due date, the auditor should again be cordial and friendly and should avoid the appearance of being overbearing or demanding.

Tabulating Answers

The method of tabulation—whether manual or with computer equipment—should be decided before the questionnaire design is completed. The design and proposed tabulation method should be compatible. Depending on the audit objective and the type of answers anticipated, it should be possible to set up a plan whereby completed questionnaires can be tabulated as received, rather than waiting for all responses.

Avoid interpreting answers. If a responder's answers are inconsistent, consider setting the questionnaire aside for direct confirmation. Direct personal confirmation may also be desirable for a limited sample of responses as a means of checking the basic validity of the answers.

Because it is likely that conclusions will be developed on the basis of the tabulated answers, controls should be established to insure accurate tabulations.

REVIEW QUESTIONS

1. When can oral information be used in audit reports? (See p. 282.)

2. What does the usefulness and reliability of interview information depend upon? (See p. 282.)

3. How do you determine whether the person being interviewed is a competent source? (See p. 282.)

4. What process does an auditor go through to plan properly for an interview? (See p. 283.)

5. Explain how you start an interview. (See pp. 283–84.)

6. Explain whether you should take notes, use recording equipment, or not use any outside helps to remember what should be written up as a result of the interview. (See p. 285.)

7. Should persons interviewed be given an opportunity to confirm what they have said to you? (See pp. 285–86.)

8. What is the advantage of using a questionnaire instead of an interview? What are the disadvantages? (See p. 296.)

9. List the basic principles to use in designing a questionnaire. (See pp. 296–97.)

10. Do you normally need a covering letter with a questionnaire? If so, describe some of its important characteristics. (See p. 297.)

CASE 1

Indian Education: Analyzing Information from Interviews

The record of discussion on the Review of the Indian Education Program provides an excellent illustration of group interview results and can be used both to demonstrate and to apply the information given in this chapter on interviewing.

Required

Reread these three interviews, pp. 287–95, and then respond to the following questions:

1. What were the objectives of the three interviews?
2. What procedures and guidelines did auditors have to go through before they came for the interviews?
3. How would auditors be able to keep a record of these discussions? One of them is rather lengthy.
4. Are the interviews adequately written up as evidence? Explain.

CASE 2

Computer Security: Can a Questionnaire Help?[1]

Required

1. Explain whether the questionnaire that follows would provide reliable information on an audit pertaining to whether a data processing installation is adequately protected from physical harm or from fire hazards, floods, sabotage, theft, power failures, or other types of misuse.
2. Explain how this type of questionnaire could be used when tabulating results. Would it be used for the audit of one installation or many installations? Would your answer differ if there were only one installation?
3. What additional information besides that provided from the questionnaire would be needed to answer the audit objective?
4. Are these types of questions related to the questions that need to be answered when reviewing management control?

QUESTIONNAIRE CONCERNING SECURITY AT
DATA PROCESSING INSTALLATIONS

	Installations		
	Yes	No	N/A*
Access control:			
Is the location			
—target for vandals?			
—advertised?	___	___	___
—screened from the street?	___	___	___
Are guards at entrances?	___	___	___
Are photo-badge systems used?	___	___	___
Are visitors controlled?	___	___	___
Do employees challenge unfamiliar visitors?	___	___	___
Are entrance security devices used?	___	___	___
Is access to computer limited during			
—working hours?	___	___	___
—off-shift hours?	___	___	___
Fire exposure:			
Are fire resistant/noncombustible materials used for			
—buildings?			
—partitions, walls, doors?	___	___	___
—furnishings?	___	___	___
Are smoke detectors installed?	___	___	___
Do the smoke detectors turn off air-conditioning facilities automatically?	___	___	___
Is the smoke detector system tested periodically?	___	___	___
Do fire extinguishers use			
—automatic carbon dioxide?	___	___	___
—halogenated agent?	___	___	___
—water?	___	___	___
Are personnel trained for firefighting?	___	___	___
Is smoking restricted in computer area?	___	___	___

---

*Does not apply to installation and/or installation management that was reluctant to discuss these aspects of data processing security.

	Installations		
	Yes	No	N/A

Fire exposure, cont'd.

   Are fire drills conducted regularly?

   Are emergency power switches located at exits?

   Do emergency power switches include air-conditioning system?

Flood control:

   Are computers located below water grade?

   Do overhead steam or water pipes exist?

   Does adequate drainage exist
   —under raised floors?
   —on floors above?
   —for adjacent areas?

Housekeeping:

   Are flammable materials properly stored?

   Is area under raised flooring cleaned regularly?

   Are paper and supplies stored outside computer room?

   Are tapes and disks stored outside computer room?

Electric power:

   Is electrical power supply considered reliable?

   Are voltmeters used to monitor supply?

Air conditioning:

   Is air conditioning dedicated to computer area?

   Are backup air conditioning facilities available?

| | Installations | | |
| | Yes | No | N/A |

File considerations:

  Are duplicate program files stored offsite?

  Are fire-resistant containers used for storage of program files?

  Is a current inventory of program files maintained?

  Have program files been tested on backup facilities within past 3 months?

  Are computer programming changes controlled?

  Are programming changes made on a duplicate rather than the original program file?

  Are items taken from files recorded?

  Are duplicate copies of documentation maintained?

  Are copes of documentation stored offsite?

  Is fire-resistant storage equipment used for documentation?

  Are backup copies of documentation reviewed periodically to assure applicability?

  Are all data files physically controlled by the computer center rather than the user?

  Are data files classified by degree of sensitivity?

  Are data files stored outside the computer room?

  Is the storage area for data files fire protected?

  Is access to storage area for data files specifically controlled?

  Are fire-resistant containers used for storage of data fiels?

Resource sharing considerations:

  Are remote terminals used only by selected individuals?

| | Installations | | |
	Yes	No	N/A

Personnel considerations:

Are employee background checks performed? ___ ___ ___
Are background checks updated periodically? ___ ___ ___
Is continuing education provided for security matters? ___ ___ ___
Is one person responsible for managing security? ___ ___ ___
Has security policy been developed? ___ ___ ___
Is in-house service personnel traffic
—controlled in vital areas? ___ ___ ___
—supervised? ___ ___ ___
Is a list prepared for authorized vendor service personnel? ___ ___ ___
Is positive identification required for vendor service personnel? ___ ___ ___
Are vendor service personnel supervised while on premises? ___ ___ ___
Are vendor employee background checks verified? ___ ___ ___

Hardware considerations:

Are hardware operations compared to scheduled activities? ___ ___ ___
Are meter hours correlated with reported utilization hours? ___ ___ ___
Are all periods of reported down time verified? ___ ___ ___
Is all incoming work checked against an authorized users list? ___ ___ ___
Is output spot-checked for possible misuse? ___ ___ ___
Are output distribution lists updated periodically? ___ ___ ___
Are tapes cleaned at regular intervals? ___ ___ ___
Are tape utilization records maintained? ___ ___ ___
Is magnetic detection equipment used? ___ ___ ___

	Installations		
	Yes	No	N/A

Software considerations:

Is vital software and documentation secured? ____ ____ ____

Are backup files maintained at a secondary site? ____ ____ ____

Is access to essential software restricted on a need-to-know basis? ____ ____ ____

Is multilevel access control to files provided by
—levels of security? ____ ____ ____
—breakdowns within files? ____ ____ ____
—restrictions for read-only, write-only, and update? ____ ____ ____

Are security software utilities and access codes validated periodically? ____ ____ ____

Is a monitor log maintained for those who access data banks or sensitive files? ____ ____ ____

Is a software security routine used to monitor unauthorized attempts to access files? ____ ____ ____

Are passwords utilized to identify users of terminals? ____ ____ ____

Are passwords changed frequently? ____ ____ ____

Are terminal users restricted to high-level languages? ____ ____ ____

Do operating systems have built-in protection to prevent the bypassing of other software security techniques? ____ ____ ____

Are memory bounds in operating system software tested following maintenance and program loading? ____ ____ ____

Are restart and recovery procedures used in applications programs? ____ ____ ____

Do restart procedures operate on random as well as sequential files? ____ ____ ____

Are programming changes documented and controlled? ____ ____ ____

	Installations		
	Yes	No	N/A

Resource sharing considerations, cont'd.

  Is access to remote terminals controlled by
  —locked doors?
  —posted guards?
  —other restraints?
  Are passwords used to identify specific terminals and users?
  Is password system considered tamper-proof?
  Are passwords changed frequently?
  Is access to password file restricted?
  Does system software restrict time-sharing users to specific data files?
  Is right to add, delete, or modify files limited by software controls?
  Does time-sharing software record all activity against a data file?
  Is there software protection for online operating systems and applications programs?
  Are security override procedures classified at the highest level and use of overrides monitored closely?
  Is time-sharing security system monitored and reviewed?
  Is debugging of security system closely monitored and controlled?

Contingency planning and backup:

  Does the installation have a formal written contingency plan?
  Does the installation have a contingency training program?
  Is a backup computer available?
  Is the backup computer in the same room as the operating computer?
  Can the backup facility handle the current workload?

	Installations		
	Yes	No	N/A

Contingency planning and backup, cont'd.

    If no designated backup, does center have access to another computer? ____ ____ ____

    Is an implementation plan available for use of backup installation? ____ ____ ____

CHAPTER 14

Using the Computer as an Audit Tool, and Auditing the Tool Itself

After you have read this chapter, studied the review questions, and worked through the cases, you will understand:

- How to gather background information on a computer system.
- The use of generalized audit software when utilizing the computer as a specialized audit tool.
- That the computer can be used to gather and analyze evidence.
- How to review and test the management control of the computer system for competency of evidence from the system.
- How to review and test the management control of the system for possible audit objectives.
- The standards for good management control for a computer system.
- How to determine the reliability of information that comes from a computer system, including what must be done when the information is not considered reliable.
- How to use some of the newer techniques for determining the reliability of information from computers, such as *integrated test facilities*, *simulation*, and *tracing and tagging*.

Computers, Computer Usage, and Computer Auditing

It has been only in the short period of time since about 1950 that auditors have taken notice of the computer, and only in the last few years have their concerns been strong enough for them to learn much about the intricacies of this important resource.

In most audit situations, auditors became involved with the computer as a result of making financial-statement examinations; and at first, they considered it simply as an extension of punched-card accounting, which in turn they had considered as merely an extension of hand-kept records. Auditing habits suggested that all they had to do was keep the books and records on the computer, audit those records much as they had the punched-card records, or use the computer to provide evidence for the audit much as the punched-card machine did.

Auditors felt that they could ascertain the correctness of the final statements from the computer, even if they had to go through the actual process of repeating the transactions that created the accounts that went on the final statements. This process was called *auditing around the computer,* and it continued until auditors found that the computer was more than merely an extension of punched-card and hand-kept records; it was a completely new process that could do more than just keep records: It could develop and process transactions as well as keep the records of those transactions, and it could also print out what it was commanded to—not only what the records showed.

Financial-statement auditors have probably become involved more in auditing the results of the computer's operations than any other type of auditors and have thus developed valuable standards for auditing the computer. The AICPA says:

> .10 The objectives and the essential characteristics of accounting control do not change with the method of data processing. However, organization and control procedures used in electronic data processing may differ from those used in manual or mechanical data processing. For example, electronic data processing of sales, billings, and accounts receivable may perform the ancillary function of verifying invoice totals and extensions, a control that usually is established in manual data processing through independent clerical calculations. Further, in some EDP (electronic data processing) systems (such as one using direct terminal input as the basic source of data to be processed in a payroll, cost accounting, or inventory control application) control functions that otherwise would be performed by several individuals and departments may be concentrated within the EDP activity.[1]

It was only a matter of time until auditors became concerned with computer fraud, and it became a more common occurrence when those who had the use of the computer found that auditors knew little or cared less about the workings of this new resource. With the possibility of being held liable for computer fraud if their auditing procedures were not sufficient to determine at least the most flagrant cases, auditors began to pay more attention to this useful resource. Clearly, while computers were valuable as auditing tools, they themselves—their use—had to be audited as well. We shall consider how to audit the computer later in this chapter.

By the time auditors began thoroughly to realize their need for more extensive computer knowledge, they found that computer usage consisted of at least three, possibly four, completely different types:

1. The computer was owned or leased by the company and all actions concerning its use were handled in-house, that is, within the company.
2. The computer was owned and operated by a service bureau. The service bureau usually had control of data, programs, and activities of the computer. Also, not only the client, but many other users, paid for its use.
3. The central computer was owned by another party, but the user was provided a keyboard that could be used with a telephone. The user could use the central computer through the keyboard and the telephone almost any time he wished. This method, called time sharing, allowed many customers to use the central computer at one time.
4. Another type was a kind of combination in-house and service-bureau method. An organization bought a computer but did not necessarily operate and staff it. An outside group did all the programming and processing of the information in the computer.

From the standpoint of performance auditing, each of these different types of computer operation suggests certain problems to the auditor, all of which fall within three general headings:

1. How do you use the computer to do some of the general and specialized work of the auditor?
2. How do you audit computer operations for efficiency, economy, and effectiveness?
3. How do you determine whether the information from the computer is reliable?

Using the Computer as a Specialized Audit Tool

The uses of the computer in performance auditing are limited only by the imagination of the auditor. If we recall once again that performance auditing is the gathering, recording, summarizing, and analyzing of evidence on an audit objective in order to come to a conclusion on that objective, then we begin to see that the computer can perform many of the tasks the auditor has so often done himself in the past.

Gathering, Recording, and Summarizing Evidence

Any task, quantitative or verbal, for which standards can be established, can be performed by the computer. For example, if the auditor desires to select a sample from records within the computer, most computers have programs available that will select the size of the sample, select a random group of items to meet that size, determine whether the sample size meets the criteria of the sample objective, and arrive at the estimated amount of the population derived from the sample. Another example is the way in which the computer can select respondents and address questionnaires or other requests to them.

The best illustration, however, may be the way in which needed information is provided from the computer in readily accessible form that can be used directly as evidence without further revision by the auditor. Many computers have in their files information on many of the subjects the auditor will address in his performance audit. Medical information, legal information, capital-asset information, personnel information, and many other types of information already in the computer can be provided in the form that the auditor needs.

The data can be summarized, compared with other data, and analyzed for completeness with certain types of programs available to the auditor. The auditor can request the client to prepare the program, or prepare his own program, or use a program called *generalized audit software*.

Generalized audit software packages have been defined as a set of preprogrammed subroutines that are developed for editing, operating, or output purposes to be used when auditing computer operations.

Instead of having to prepare specific programs for reviewing many operations of the computer, the auditor can use these specialized subroutines. They can accomplish a wide range of tasks: retracing transactions, scanning, recalculations, confirmations, and various analyses such as trend analysis and sample selection.

Only a limited amount of additional training is needed to prepare an auditor to use one of these packages. The additional programming is rather simple, based on a set of preprinted specifications. Several major public accounting firms, as well as other organizations, have prepared these generalized audit software packages for the use of their staff, and most have made the packages available for use by other auditors for a reasonable fee. In addition, some government agencies have developed comparable packages for their own use.

These types of programs are exceptionally valuable when the auditor needs to extend his auditing procedures directly into computer transactions. Most of the generalized audit software packages in the past have been developed for use with batch processing. Recently, however, audit programs have been developed for use with on-line, real-time computer-processing applications.

Analysis of the Evidence with a Computer

Many of the analyses the auditor previously had to make by hand can now be obtained directly from the computer or through the use of the computer; the generalized audit software programs just discussed are examples.

In addition, much of the mathematical work, such as would have to be done to determine sample size, can be done for technical data as easily as it has been done in the past for financial data. (This use will be further discussed in the next chapter.) Various models—such as a model of a river system, of a city, of an educational system—can be placed in the computer and from it the conditions can be derived that would probably come about through various changes. Evaluations of statistical data of test groups for educational or medical programs are often needed; these, too, and similar types can be accomplished through the use of a computer.

One of the major quantitative analyses that can often be done through a computer is the determination of total effects. With comparative ease, the computer can bring together many individual detailed analyses into a total amount.

Auditing Computer Operations

The AICPA sets forth the following standards for auditing the computer:

> .04 The first general auditing standard is as follows: "The examination is to be performed by a person or persons having adequate technical training and proficiency as an auditor." If a client uses EDP in its accounting system, whether the application is simple or complex, the auditor needs to understand the entire system sufficiently to enable him to identify and evaluate its essential accounting control features. Situations involving the more complex EDP applications ordinarily will require that the auditor apply specialized expertise in EDP in the performance of the necessary audit procedures.[2]

Fortunately, we have learned that auditing computer operations involves the same pattern outlined in previous chapters for auditing any operation or program, and thus consists of the following phases:

1. The preliminary survey,
2. The review and testing of management control,
3. The detailed examination, and
4. The report.

The Preliminary Survey

As is true of every examination, the auditor should obtain background information on the organization being audited. In addition, he should obtain an understanding of the computer activities in that organization, and the relationship of the computer activities to the overall management of the organization. If the auditor is using information from the computer as evidence on an audit objective for a program or activity, he should also obtain information concerning the relationship of the computer information to that activity or program.

This background data on the management control system of the computer would consist of the following types of information:

1. Plan of organization
   a) Identify key officials in the organization and their relationship to the officials of the EDP organization.
   b) Identify key officials of the EDP organization, along with size and composition of EDP staff.
   c) Determine whether organization has EDP steering committee, whether representative of top management chairs the committee, whether major users of computer information are on the committee, and whether committee sets basic EDP policy for the organization.
   d) Determine whether internal audit groups are capable of auditing and do audit the EDP function, including participation in developing the EDP system and controlling copies of audit programs.
   e) Identify principal users of the system, including the users of information pertaining to activity or program under audit. Determine whether users are satisfied with the computer operations.
   f) Determine that EDP staff are adequate and trained, that the functions of the staff are not incompatible, and that no unauthorized personnel have access to the computer.
2. Costs
   a) Determine total costs, including leased costs.
   b) Compare budgeted with actual costs for at least two years.
3. Equipment and other resources
   a) Determine the various types of equipment used (hardware, terminals, other).
   b) Determine the particular types of software used.
   c) Determine each particular system that relates to the activity or program. Show whether it is batch or on-line, programming language, hours used, other relevant data.
   d) Determine programmed controls in the computer or in the programs.
4. Application to program or activity
   Determine each application of computer to activity or program, including application by service bureau.
5. Policy and procedures
   Determine whether data center has written policy and procedure manuals for documenting all activities.
   a) Preparation of source documents manual
   b) Data/entry conversion manual
   c) Computer operations run manuals.
   d) Manual for documentation for programs
      (1) Description of programs
      (2) Specifications of programs
      (3) Format and descriptions of input, output, and master files
      (4) Operating instructions
      (5) Test data
6. Recruiting and development
   Decide whether organization has acceptable recruiting program and continuing development program, in order to have an adequately trained staff.

Many of these basic standards on background information fall under the heading of general controls as described in the AICPA auditing standards for EDP, and they become very important to other standards of operations. For example, if management is not interested in the EDP operations and does not participate in the steering committee or take interest in the overall operations, the chance of improper management of the EDP system is much greater. Also, if the functions of the staff are incompatible, the organization runs a great deal of risk of collusion in operations or loss of assets.

After reviewing the information obtained during this phase of the EDP examination, the auditor should be able to determine whether he could identify further areas warranting attention. If he does, he should then test some transactions through the computer in order to evaluate the internal controls in the computer. These controls have become fairly well standardized and will be given in the next section.

The Review and Testing of Management Control

By following two or three selected transactions through the computer, the auditor can determine whether the controls within the computer are adequate. Let us consider these controls as we follow the transactions as they would go through the computer. Ordinarily, the transactions would fall under the headings of: (1) input control transactions, (2) processing control transactions, and (3) output control transactions.

Input Control for the Transactions. In order to assure himself that the input controls for the transactions were adequate, the auditor would:

1. Be sure that all documents are promptly received and introduced into the system, and that no document goes through the system that should not.
    a) Each point of origin should prepare a list of documents,
    b) A predetermined total should be computed for each batch of documents,
    c) Each document should have a sequential number assigned and have a data and time assigned,
    d) Each document should be filed in such a manner that it can be recovered after processing,
    e) A record count should be kept of the documents, and
    f) The input department should balance control totals with the initiating department.
2. Be sure that when a procedure is developed for control purposes, it is followed.

Processing Control for the Transactions. Processing controls can be subdivided into four separate categories: (1) preparatory controls, (2) program controls, (3) processing controls, and (4) end-of-processing controls. In addition, the processing can be accomplished either by batch processing or by service bureau or other remote processing.

Preparatory Controls. During the review of the preparatory controls, the auditor should refer to the background information to assure himself that controls affecting this area have been considered. For example, the EDP department might have excellent procedure manuals, but the question is: "Are they being followed?" And do the program-run manuals define such factors as definition of input data, source, and format; program listings and changes; error correction procedures; prevention of loss of data; balancing of totals; and determination of properly authorized input only?

Another major control to consider at this time is what would happen if the processing destroyed all records. Have controls been considered that protect the overall destruction of the EDP records? Also, the auditor should consider the codes used in the actual processing and should verify those codes. And finally, he should consider the procedures to insure that data are not lost, added, or altered during the processing.

Program Controls. The programs determine the actual procedures for processing the information in the computer. The auditor should:

1. Assure himself that the programs are current,
2. Assure himself that the programs have built-in checks, such as file identification, to prevent running wrong program,
3. Assure himself that the programs have proper logic checks,
4. Assure himself that the programs are only revised after written requests approved by the users,
5. Assure himself that program testing procedures have been established,
6. Assure himself that duplicate programs are maintained at a location other than the EDP departments, and
7. Assure himself that changes in programs are adequately documented.

Processing Controls. In the processing area, the auditor should:

1. Assure himself that daily equipment operating logs are maintained, with down time explained,
2. Assure himself that error logs are maintained, with information concerning disposition of errors,
3. Assure himself that operators cannot circumvent instructions,
4. Assure himself that input controls balance with processing controls,
5. Assure himself that initiating departments check errors compiled from their data, and
6. Assure himself that run-to-run totals are verified at appropriate points in the processing to check for completeness of processing.

The auditor must obtain additional assurances if the system uses some form of remote processing. These would include assurances that:

1. Authorization codes are used and controlled to restrict unauthorized usage,
2. The computer will allow only authorized codes for particular transactions,
3. The computer program keeps a summary of all transactions, and
4. The computer provides a balanced file for all processed records daily and that master files are balanced periodically.

End-of-Processing Controls. The auditor should consider several end-of-processing controls. For example, when the computer prints out errors, what should be done with the results? Are the errors corrected before the completion of the processing, or are they placed in a suspense file?

Likewise, the auditor should have some form of audit trail. Has the system provided sufficient output during processing to provide this audit trail?

Additionally, the auditor should be assured that all processing has been accomplished. For example, are internal trailer labels containing control totals generated and tested to assure that all processing has been accomplished? And in remote processing, is the control trailer updated after each transaction?

Output Controls for the Transactions. It should be possible to trace forward all transactions from input to processing to output in the EDP system. It should be possible to balance control totals from the initiating department with the output. The auditor should thus consider the following:

1. Are output controls reconciled to input and processing controls?
2. Is output compared with source documents?
3. Is output delivered on a timely basis and only to authorized recipients?
4. Is the master file reviewed periodically?
5. Is there a schedule of documents and reports related to the activity that should be produced by the computer? Does someone review the output for completeness and acceptability?

Once the auditor has tested one or two transactions through the management control system, he should have sufficient evidence to support a firm audit objective. He then would go to the detailed examination.

The Detailed Examination

One or two illustrations are seldom sufficient to support a conclusion to an audit objective. The auditor must then have sufficient relevant, material, and competent evidence to support his conclusion.

Obviously, poor management control in a computer system can lead to fraud or to a lack of efficient, economical, or effective operations, while improvement in these controls can lead to the opposite. Improved efficiency and economy of operations of the computer might be in such areas as (1) lease versus buy, (2) use of excess capacity, (3) use of in-house computer when service bureau could provide the same service at much reduced rates or costs, and (4) excess reporting of useless data.

Each of these activities, and many more, including almost every area of management control activities, provides an opportunity for the auditor to report to management increased savings by improved operations of the computer activity.

Likewise, the computer system has an objective; quite often it does not live up to that objective and hence is not effective. A recent report by the GAO on the Defense Integrated Data System, for instance, states that the system has not achieved its performance objectives.[3]

When dealing with broad areas, such as a state, the auditor can often consolidate several computer activities into one, thus bringing about considerable savings. Also, when computers are replaced, computer programs often need to be completely redone, at a great cost in time and money. By planning for the programming aspect of the old and the new computers, substantial amounts can often be saved.

The two cases given for this chapter are illustrative of the way an EDP operation can be made more efficient, economical, or effective.

The Report

Reporting for improving the performance of computer operations would be comparable to other performance audit reports.

Relying on Information from the Computer

In Chapter 8, we stated: "Competency is the reliability one places on the source of information used as evidence"; and in Chapter 3, we stated that there were two purposes for reviewing and testing management control: (1) to obtain evidence on all three elements of the audit objective in order to have a firm audit objective, and (2) to determine that the evidence obtained from within the entity would be competent if the audit were extended into a more detailed

EDP Accounting Control Procedures

.06 Some EDP accounting control procedures relate to all EDP activities (general controls) and some relate to a specific accounting task, such as preparation of account listings or payrolls (application controls).

.07 General controls comprise (a) the plan of organization and operation of the EDP activity, (b) the procedures for documentation, reviewing, testing, and approving systems or programs and changes thereto, (c) controls built into the equipment by the manufacturer (commonly referred to as "hardware controls"), (d) controls over access to equipment and data files, and (e) other data and procedural controls affecting overall EDP operations. Weaknesses in general controls often have pervasive effects. When general controls are weak or absent, the auditor should consider the effect of such weakness or absence in the evaluation of application controls.

.08 Application controls relate to specific tasks performed by EDP. Their function is to provide reasonable assurance that the recording, processing, and reporting of data are properly performed. There is considerable choice in the particular procedures and records used to effect application controls. Application controls often are categorized as "input controls," "processing controls," and "output controls."
  a) Input controls are designed to provide reasonable assurance that data received for processing by EDP have been properly authorized, converted into machine sensible form and identified, and that data (including data transmitted over communication lines) have not been lost, suppressed, added, duplicated, or otherwise improperly changed. Input controls include controls that relate to rejection, correction, and resubmission of data that were initially incorrect.
  b) Processing controls are designed to provide reasonable assurance that electronic data processing has been performed as intended for the particular application; i.e., that all transactions are processed as authorized, that no authorized transactions are omitted, and that no unauthorized transactions are added.
  c) Output controls are designed to assure the accuracy of the processing result (such as account listings or displays, reports, magnetic files, invoices, or disbursement checks) and to assure that only authorized personnel receive the output.

.09 EDP accounting control procedures may be performed within an EDP organization, a user department, or a separate control group. The department or unit in which accounting control procedures are performed is less significant than the performance of the procedures by persons having no incompatible functions for accounting control purposes and the effectiveness of the procedures.[4]

examination. If the determination was made that the evidence was not competent after reviewing the management controls, then the auditor would need to extend his auditing procedures, and this would mean that the auditor might need to obtain evidence from alternative sources, which he should identify as the best possible.

We have said that the reliability of audit evidence is related to competency, and competency is determined by reviewing and testing internal and management control that applies to the source of the information. When the computer is the source of that information, then the way to determine the reliability of the information that comes from it is to review and test the management control of the computer.

A great deal of work has been done by the AICPA in setting standards for auditing internal controls as applied to computers that are related to financial-statement examinations. These standards, listed in the box, can be adapted readily to performance audits.

Once the auditor accepts the idea that the reliability of information from a computer system is related to that system having good management controls and carrying them out, then he can determine the reliability of the information, which he will use as evidence, by evaluating the management controls.

Extending Audit Procedures to Assure Competency of Evidence

In his evaluation of management control, the auditor has gathered background information and evidence on the various controls pertaining to EDP to determine their effectiveness. He must then analyze that evidence and information to determine the effectiveness of the particular controls so that he can judge the risk he would be taking in accepting or rejecting the information from the computer, based on whether it was competent or not.

In general, if answers to the questions or statements given in the preceding sections are in the affirmative, then there would be the indications of good internal control. That is, when the standards given in the preceding sections, which are indicative of good management control within the computer area, are carried out appropriately, then the auditor would consider the risk of using the information from the computer as competent, low or minimum risk. If not carried out properly, the auditor could consider the situation indicative of higher risk and would probably need to extend his audit procedures.

In addition to extending the audit procedures for the activity or program, the auditor can extend the audit procedures directly concerned with examination of the management controls. Various methods have been devised for extending audit procedures pertaining to the computer to determine whether the information from the computer is competent. They include:

1. Auditing computers with a test deck,
2. Auditing with generalized audit software, and
3. Auditing around the computer.

Auditing Computers with a Test Deck

A test deck can be defined as a set of simulated transactions that can be processed through a computer system to see whether proper transactions will be processed accurately and improper ones identified and rejected. One authority lists the advantages and disadvantages of auditing with test decks as follows:

Advantages:

1. A test deck can be designed for any program, system, or equipment,
2. Test results can be readily checked,

3. The test data are processed either correctly or incorrectly,
4. The auditor can choose the types and combinations of transactions or procedures to be tested,
5. The auditor can accept test results without actually tracing data through processing stages, and
6. Extensive technical knowledge of computer systems or the ability to write computer programs is not required. (However, a working knowledge of file structure, input and output formats, and data-processing procedures is necessary.)

Disadvantages:
1. A test deck is valid only for the single application or program for which it is designed,
2. It tests procedures only for a given point in time and therefore must be updated to incorporate any system or other changes that would affect the validity of the tests, such as changes in file structure, statutes, rules, or regulations,
3. It is costly and time consuming to develop a good test deck, and
4. It is impractical, if not impossible, to design a test deck to test every conceivable situation in a typical administrative or accounting-type computer system because of the virtually limitless variety of transactions and conditions that could occur.[5]

Auditing with Generalized Audit Software

Generalized audit software can be used not only for making special analyses, but also to determine the quality of the controls operating in the computer; this subject was discussed earlier in this chapter.

Auditing Around the Computer

For many years auditing around the computer was the only way the auditor determined the results of his audit. Even today, when the auditor finds he is unable adequately to extend his tests through test decks, generalized audit software, or other methods, he can retrace the transactions manually or through mechanical means. Obviously, this method is the most costly and often the least valuable of the various methods of extending audit tests. Sometimes, however, it is necessary—in certain fraud cases, for instance.

More Advanced Computer Auditing

Many of the tools and techniques for auditing the computer become almost obsolete in a few years. With online, real-time computers, the situations for auditing them, or using them for more advanced analytical purposes, become more and more complex. And with the advent of the minicomputer, more and more people and organizations are using computers for even the simplest tasks as well as for the more complex ones.

To keep up with the increasing use and complexity of the computers, several new techniques have been developed in recent years; these are used not only for auditing but also for testing computers to determine whether the machines are operating properly. Three of the newer techniques we will discuss are:

1. Integrated test facilities,
2. Simulation, and
3. Tracing and tagging.

Integrated Test Facilities

In an integrated test facility, the auditor integrates into the normal operating system a "test" person, department, or activity. Transactions will flow into the computer information system for the fictitious operation exactly as they would for a normal operation. By observing the total operations of these test data, the auditor can determine whether the computer is processing the information exactly as prescribed.

To illustrate the operation of a test facility, let us assume that it is a normal buyer, but fictitious. Orders would be placed, goods would be shipped, invoices would be prepared, and cash would be received. The auditor can easily ascertain whether the system is operating properly by following the transactions completed by the computer.

The main problem with the integrated test facility as a means of examining the operations of a computer is that all of the dummy transactions must be backed out of the computer before any usable information report is prepared. On the other hand, if the operators of the system have any inkling that this type of testing is being done, the possibility of their introducing fraud into the system is considerably reduced.

Simulation

In the integrated test facility type of evaluation of a computer's operations, the auditor sees test data used with live programs. Somewhat the reverse happens in simulation: The auditor sees the use of live data being evaluated with test programs. Since retesting the entire operations of a computer system would be rather costly, the usual pattern is to simulate a part of them only.

The auditor develops a program based on the functions to be tested. He then runs through the computer all of the transactions related to the area he is testing in order to compare the simulated results with the original processing results. In this way, any part or all of any computer application can be tested through simulation.

Tracing and Tagging

As described in Chapter 3 under the review and testing of management control, the auditor usually traces one or two relevant transactions pertaining to the particular objective he is following. He can usually follow those transactions by visual observation, or by looking at the records. Following the path of a transaction of a computer, however, cannot be done in this manner; the auditor must follow it through the program prepared, and he can do this by using a printout of the path.

A special programming option will allow the auditor to have this printout. Along with this programming option, the auditor can also tag certain types of transactions—those material to his particular audit objective—and then have a printout made of these transactions.

We see, then, that tracing and tagging both follow almost the same procedures the auditor normally follows in reviewing management control, but they are done electronically rather than manually.

Other Techniques

Many other techniques are currently available or being developed for evaluating the operations of a computer system in terms of efficiency, economy, or effectiveness; for determining the reliability of the information from the computer; or for using the computer for performing analyses. Many books and manuals are available for studying the actual operations of a computer; yet only a relatively few are available that explain the procedures necessary for auditing the computer's operations.

We know that the AICPA has played an important part in setting standards for auditing financial statements in a computer environment; and the Institute of Internal Auditors has recently issued a three-part guide on systems auditability and control, as well as other books on this important subject. The reader will find a list of current references in the bibliography of this book.

REVIEW QUESTIONS

1. Are the essential characteristics of internal control changed with the method of data processing? Explain. Would the essential characteristics of control pertaining to any management activity change with the method of data processing? (See p. 308.)

2. Describe the four different types of computer usage. (See p. 308.)

3. All problems concerning computer usage as related to performance auditing fall within three general headings. List and describe them. (See p. 309.)

4. In making any evaluation, the auditor begins by obtaining background data. Discuss the types of background data an auditor should obtain when reviewing the management controls pertaining to an EDP system, and describe specifically the information that needs to be obtained. (See pp. 310–12.)

5. List and describe the various types of internal controls within the computer. Describe the specific actions the auditor should take to be assured that these controls are meaningful controls. Describe the various input controls. List and discuss the various types of processing controls. (See pp. 312–14.)

6. When reviewing the management controls of a computer, what types of audit objectives could be found that would lead to a full-scale audit of the computer. (See p. 314.)

7. What is meant by generalized audit software? Discuss the uses of this package. (See pp. 316–17.)

8. One of the purposes of reviewing and testing management control is to determine the competency of the evidence from the management control system. Discuss this statement as it applies to obtaining information from the computer to be used as evidence. (See pp. 314–18.)

9. Some controls are considered general controls and some are considered application controls. Discuss the differences. (See p. 315.)

10. Once the auditor has made a review of the internal and management controls of the computer, he must evaluate the information he has obtained from that review. Discuss what he must do when his review discloses that the controls for the computer are not operating properly. (See pp. 316–18.)

11. List and discuss the advantages and disadvantages of using a test deck to extend the auditing procedures for the review of management control of a computer. (See pp. 316–17.)

12. What is meant by integrated test facility? By simulation? By the process of tracing and tagging? (See pp. 317–18.)

CASE 1

Analysis of a Complete Audit: Improvements Needed in Managing Automated Decision Making by Computer[6]

Required

1. What would be the reason for an audit agency to start an examination on a computer's automated decision-making applications?
2. State the objective of this audit. Earmark in your stated objective the specific criteria, the causes, and the effects.
3. Outline the steps you would take in your detailed examination program to come to a proper conclusion on the audit objective.

AUDIT SCENARIO 1
The Preliminary Phases

By now the reader surely understands the relationship among the various audit phases and understands, too, that the activities of an entity often cross organizational lines. In the state, the city, the county, or divisions of a corporation, many of the activities are present in each of the subdivisions of the organization. A good illustration of one such activity is computer operations, which are often scattered throughout the agencies, divisions, or other types of subdivisions of the primary organization.

This case is typical of situations in which a performance audit could be made for a particular activity throughout any organization—federal, state, or local.

Introduction

Many early business applications on computers involved entering, manipulating, and summarizing data, and generating reports. Most output was manually revised for correctness, and/or to decide what actions should be taken on the basis of the output report.

As more complex computer processing developed, the applications became more innovative. Computers were assigned certain repetitive decision-making work that duplicated steps people had previously taken to do the job. Since these applications have no established name, we are using the term *automated decision-making applications*.

Automated decision-making applications are computer programs that initiate action (through output) on the basis of programmable decision-making criteria established by management and incorporated in computer instruction. The distinguishing characteristic of these applications compared to other computer application programs, is that many of the computer's actions take place without manual review and evaluation.

An inventory application is an example of a computer application program. If the computer processing of a requisition for material reduces the on-hand quantity below the reorder point and if the computer issues a purchase order without anyone reviewing the proposed procurement quantity, then the application is an automated decision-making application. Some of the computer output of these applications is reviewed. In the foregoing example, for instance, the application might call for manual reviews of quantities on all orders over $5,000, while releasing all purchase orders under that amount without review.

The applications in this case were reviewed (1) because millions of dollars were involved in the unrevised actions that they initiated and (2) because there were indications that funds were being wasted as the result of incorrect actions.

Background Data

In order to obtain background data on this activity of the federal government, a questionnaire was used. Information from the questionnaire showed that there were 32 departments and agencies that used automatic decision-making applications. The applications consisted of those shown in the table below.

Function	Number of times function was cited	Function	Number of times function was cited
Controlling	12	Maintenance	7
Notification	12	Procurement	7
Fiscal	12	Diagnostic	6
Payment	12	Scheduling	5
Supply	11	Disposal	4
Billing	10	Cataloging	3
Distribution	9	Personnel	3
Eligibility	8	Safety	2

The nature of the output was as shown in the following table.

Nature of output	Number cited	Total action (000 omitted)	Total monetary impact (000,000 omitted)
Payment authorizations or checks to:			
Contractors or grantees	2	2,200	1,805
Members of the public	6	178,500	4,645
Government employees (other than payroll)	1	50	2
Bills sent to:			
Contractors	1	25	4
Government organizations	4	4,300	1,637
Members of the public	4	4,800	815
Purchase orders or supply requisitions	6	7,000	1,114
Directives to ship material	6	65,050	500*
Directives to dispose of material	3	2,000	14*
Production, repair, or rework schedules or instructions	3	48,000	285*
Notifications to members of the public	5	5,550	N/A
Other	12	111,400	N/A
Total	53	428,875	

*Represents the value of material on which these actions were taken. Information collected indicates that the transportation costs represent about 5 percent of the value of material shipped; the disposal costs about 3 percent of the material disposed of; and production, repair, or rework cost about 23 percent of the value of the material.

Adverse conditions common to several agencies, which resulted in the applications automatically initiating uneconomical or otherwise incorrect actions, can be broadly categorized as (1) software problems and/or (2) data problems.

Software Problems. Several software problems that can cause bad decisions by automated decision-making applications include:

- Designing software with incomplete or erroneous decision-making criteria. Actions have been incorrect because the decision-making logic omitted factors that could have been included. In other cases decision-making criteria included in the software were inappropriate, either at the time of design, or later due to changed circumstances.
- Failing to program the software as intended by the customer (user) or designer, resulting in logic errors often referred to as programming errors.
- Omitting needed edit checks for determining completeness in input data. Critical data elements have been left blank on many input documents; and because no checks were included, the applications processed the transaction with incomplete data.

Data Problems. Input data quality is frequently a problem. Since much of this data is an integral part of the decision-making process, its poor quality can adversely affect the computer-directed actions. Problems include:

- Incomplete data used by automated decision-making applications. Some input documents people prepared omitted entries in data elements that were critical to the application but were processed anyway. The documents were not rejected when incomplete data were being used. In other instances, data that the application needed and that should have become part of ADP files were not put into the system.
- Incorrect data used in automated decision-making application processing. People have often unintentionally introduced incorrect data into the ADP system. Incorrect data affected application decisions.

AUDIT SCENARIO 2
The Detailed Examination and the Report
Required

1. Prepare a summary work sheet, equivalent to that in Chapter 5, from the information in the table, "Summary of Causes of Software Problems" in this case.
2. The case identifies causes as being related to software problems and data problems. Are there other types of causes that should be identified?
3. Before your report would be accepted as being significant, the loss or possible loss would have to be significant.
   a) What is the significance of the effect in this case?
   b) Prepare a summary work sheet to show the significance of the effect.
4. State a conclusion to this audit.
5. State a recommendation that you would make concerning needed improvements in the operations of this activity.

Proposed Solutions: Software Problems

The following table is a summary obtained from experts concerning proposed solutions to the software problems related to automatic decision making.

- Documentation should be prepared that highlights (1) key portions of the automated decision-making criteria, (2) data elements that are critical to the decision making, and (3) the edit checks placed (or justifications for omitting them) in the software. A formalized synopsis of these items should be prepared for review and approval by top management.
- Qualified auditors or others who are independent of designers and users should review the designed application before it is placed into operation. Others could include a design team independent of the original designer and user. They would be responsible for evaluating the (1) adequacy of the decision-making criteria, (2) logic in the coded application, and (3) needs and uses of edit checks to detect incomplete data elements put into the application.
- Similar independent teams should review the operation of these applications shortly after they are implemented. The objectives would be to evaluate the adequacy of the

Summary of Evidence on Causes of Software Problems

Cause	Opinions of people answering the questionnaire— degree of cause*		Identified from contacts with officials	Cited as a cause by internal auditors
	Moderate to very large	Somewhat small or none		
Inadequate communications between the parties to software design	251	4	x	
Incorrect perceptions of the nature of actual transactions to be processed	233	22	x	x
Inadequate documentation preventing adequate reviews of software	229	28	x	x
Time constraints hampering the effectiveness of the design process	216	40	x	
Absence of written criteria or guidelines for designers to follow	204	49	x	
Detail and complexity involved in designing, coding, and reviewing software	177	79	x	x
Reliance on the expertise and experience of people doing the work (state of the art)	171	83	x	x
Undetected changes in circumstances making the application obsolete	167	90	x	x
State of the art in software testing which prevents testing all possible conditions	164	91	x	

*The questionnaire presented "some possible causes of the design conditions (problems)...," and asked that "based on your software design experience... indicate the degree to which you believe each of these causes contributes to the design condition (problems) in general." The responses allowed were to a: very large degree, somewhat large degree, moderate degree, somewhat small degree, very small degree, or not at all.

decision-making criteria in an operational environment and to provide for early detection of any bad decisions. This would allow for early correction of problems.
- Some form of cyclical system monitoring of actions initiated by operational automated decision-making applications should exist. Teams composed of (but not restricted to) designers, users, and auditors could analyze application-initiated actions to (1) see if desired results were achieved the best way, (2) identify unforeseen circumstances that would require modifying the application, (3) determine that the actions were as the user and designer intended, and (4) insure that decision making was not adversely affected by incomplete data not being screened by an edit check.
- The designer and user should be physically located in the same place during design phases to allow for constant communication. In effect, the design would be a joint effort and would help to insure that adequate decision-making criteria were contained in the application.
- Priorities should be established for software modification (changes) that are at least partially based on the cost of continuing incorrect automatic actions if no changes are made within a short time.
- The initiator of the needed software modification (for example, headquarters,

user, audit team, and/or others) should be informed about the status of the change and be provided with confirmation that the changes have been made.

Proposed Solutions: Data Problems

The following table is a summary obtained from experts concerning proposed solutions to the data problems related to automatic decision making.

- Establish follow-up procedures for insuring the (1) timely receipt of data preparation instructions and (2) use of instructions by data preparers.
- Emphasize in training the importance of complete and correct data on computer input documents.
- Make selective manual verification of key data on input documents and in ADP files with hard copy documents and with the data originator.
- Establish a single organization (data-base administrator) that could be responsible for the above steps as well as evaluating and testing internal and external data controls employed and input documents designed and used.

Illustrations of Software Problems

The following are two examples of software problems frequently experienced with automated decision-making applications.

Army Processing of Requisitions for Shipment to Overseas Locations. Several Army inventory control points provide materiel support to overseas customers who submit requisitions for materials to the control points. Automated decision-making applications are used to screen materiel availability at U.S. depots. The computer produces a directive, which is automatically issued to a depot to ship material to the overseas customer. These applications process over 100,000 overseas requisitions annually.

Early in the 1970s, the Army implemented a system designed to improve supply support to overseas customers from U.S. depots. The control

Summary of Evidence on Causes of Data Problems

Cause	Opinions of people answering the questionnaire —degree of causes*		Identified from contacts with officials of Federal agencies	Cited as a cause by internal auditors
	Moderate to very large	Somewhat small or none		
Forms designed and used for input preparation are too complex	183	21	x	
ADP files are not always adequately reviewed to assure that good data is being used	178	26	x	x
Instructions to people preparing data input are not always provided, are provided late, or are not adequate	175	30	x	x
Preparers of data input are not always adequately trained	159	46	x	x
Manual reviews of input documents are not always adequate	144	61	x	x
High volumes of transactions cause input preparers to make errors (workload pressures)	131	73	x	x

*The questionnaire presented "some possible causes of the data conditions (problems) ..." and asked that "based on your data management experience ... indicate the degree to which you believe each of these causes contributes to the data condition (problems) in general." The responses allowed were to a: very large degree, somewhat large degree, moderate degree, somewhat small degree, or very small degree, or not at all.

points were instructed to design their ADP applications so that materiel would be issued from east coast depots to satisfy European customers and from west coast depots to satisfy Pacific customers. Controls were required to prevent the software from releasing cross-country shipments without manual review.

The Army Audit Agency examined the applications in effect at 5 control points. At 4 activities it found that the applications were not adequate to insure maximum filling of requisitions from the appropriate depots. For instance, in the initial requisition processing for overseas customers, the software used by one of the high-volume control points screened stock availability at 8 depots before finding the appropriate depot. For releasing back-ordered stock requisitions, depots on the opposite coast were often selected for materiel availability. The auditors reported that, at 3 control points, controls to prevent the automatic release of materiel from the wrong depots were not implemented and material was automatically released for cross-country shipments. At least 2 control points used software that existed before the criteria for supporting overseas activities were developed.

The audit agency estimated that, because of the use of these erroneous criteria, unnecessary transportation costs of $900,000 a year were incurred. In addition, $1.3 million was incurred in increased inventory investment (pipeline) costs.

The Army Materiel Command agreed with the audit agency's assessment of the problem and promised to revise the criteria contained in Army control-point applications.

Navy Scheduling of Aircraft Equipment for Overhaul. The Navy's central manager for aircraft spare equipment and parts uses a computer to identify and schedule overhaul for reparable components needed for future use. Until April 1974, the application used was called the Navy integrated comprehensive reparable item scheduling program.

This application considered inventory on hand, requirements, and other data in ADP files to determine

- which components should be scheduled for overhaul,
- what quantities should be overhauled,
- which depots should do the work, and
- what priorities depots should give in deciding which items should be overhauled first.

Depots used punched-card output as the basis for scheduling components for induction into their overhaul facilities. Priority levels shown on the output affected the depots' decisions regarding which items and quantities would be overhauled first. (Not all the quantities the program indicated for overhaul were processed because of limited depot overhaul capacity.)

The priority levels shown in the output ranged from level 0 (zero)—highest priority—to level 3—lowest priority.

During a 1-year period,* Navy facilities spent about $145 million to overhaul aircraft components valued at about $797 million —mostly on the basis of the program's output. The Naval Audit Service, reviewing the operation, identified several major software problems, all of which resulted in overstating overhaul requirements.

- A data element used in computing priority level 1 contained data that resulted in duplications in computing levels 2 and 3. Gross overhaul requirements scheduled by the program were therefore overstated. When the program was designed, this duplication was overlooked.
- Data elements showing recurring material usage, used to compute levels 2 and 3, were greatly overstated because of two software problems:
  1. Required reductions to the materiel usage quantities were not made automatically, because certain Navy activities were leaving a data element blank on input documents sent to the central manager. Our follow-up determined that because of the designer's oversight or judgment error, no edit check was placed in the software to detect this missing data.
  2. There were no software procedures for automatically reducing recorded materiel usage quantities when customers canceled back orders and requisitions. Our follow-up disclosed that when this application was designed, the designer believed that canceled back orders and requisitions would rarely occur.

*The figures presented are for an overlapping but not identical period. The overlap is 6 months.

The audit service estimated the effect of these incorrect actions was millions of dollars in unnecessary and premature overhaul costs. Although the Navy command officials did not agree with the auditor's reported figures, they agreed that the problems identified were valid. Corrective actions have been taken or initiated.

A GAO report (B-162152, May 21, 1974) "Better Methods Needed for Canceling Orders for Materiel No Longer Required" discussed the Navy's practice of not automatically reducing recorded materiel usage when unfilled customer orders were canceled. The report stated, "We estimate that this overstatement resulted in annual unnecessary materiel buys and repairs totaling about $10 million." Of that amount, more than $3 million was for repairs initiated by this automated decision-making application.

Illustration of Data Problems

The following two examples of data problems show how bad data can adversely affect the actions directed by automated decision-making applications.

Veterans Administration Payments for Apprenticeship and Other On-job Training. The Veterans Administration (VA) uses a computer application to make monthly payments to more than 185,000 veterans in apprenticeship or other on-job training. This application is designed to make payments at a rate that decreases every 6 months, under the assumption that a veteran's pay will increase as he learns his trade.

Data put into the computer are the basis for automatically determining the rates at which the veteran will be paid. Each month, additional data are put in regarding the veteran's continuing eligibility to receive the payments.

This application is programmed to read input documents and distinguish apprenticeship and other on-job training awards from other types of education awards. When the application recognizes these on-job training awards, it refers to appropriate rate tables to determine the proper payment. The application refers to a new lower rate every 6 months and automatically initiates payments at the reduced rate. Annually, this application initiates about 1.4 million unreviewed checks for more than $225 million in apprenticeship and other on-job training awards.

Two types of input documents initiate payments for these awards. An original award document is designed to initiate payments to a veteran not previously receiving them. If the veteran has already received benefits and there is a need for (1) reentrance, (2) a supplemental award, or (3) new key data such as dependency changes, a different input document (supplemental award code sheet) is prepared. Both documents contain data elements that allow the computer to determine that it is an apprenticeship or other on-job training award and that the reducing rate table should be used.

The data entry on the supplemental award document that causes the program to build the scheduled rate reduction is code 77 in a data element called change reason.

VA internal auditors reported that 22 of 121 tested supplemental award documents for these benefits did not contain change reason code 77 on the input documents (the data problem). These documents were received from 10 different VA locations. The application accepted and processed the documents because the software did not contain an edit check to disclose and reject documents with incomplete entries in this data element (a related software problem).

Because the data was incomplete, the computer used a single rate for the entire period of training at the highest step indicated. This problem caused potential overpayments of $700,000.

Possible causes cited for processing incomplete input documents included new personnel—requiring additional training—and fatigue. The designer overlooked the needed edit check, a software problem, in preparing the detailed and complex software.

Army Processing Requisitions for Radioactive Material. The Army uses a computer to automatically process customer requisitions for commodities. One Army agency uses an application to process at least 250,000 requisitions annually for material valued at a minimum of $250 million. About 35 percent of the customer requisitions are output for manual review and evaluation for any of several reasons. The remaining 65 percent are processed without manual review.

Some commodities the agency manages contain radioactive material. The Army master data ADP file is supposed to contain a special control code (code 8) in a specific data element for commodities containing radioactive material. This code, which should be put in by item managers, prevents automatic issues. The item managers receive commodity requisitions for review and evaluation. This manual intervention is required to insure that the requisitioners are (1) authorized to receive the material, (2) aware of the radioactive content, and (3) aware of the safeguards that must be used.

The Army Audit Agency reviewed 86 radioactive commodities and managed to determine if the proper special-control item codes were contained in ADP files. The review showed that 29 of the commodities were incorrectly coded:

- Eleven commodities were coded as a regulated item (code 1) but not as radioactive. (A regulated item is one that is scarce, costly, or highly technical.)
- Eighteen commodities contained an O code in the ADP files. An O code indicates that no special controls or handling are required. Many requisitions for these commodities are processed automatically.

Most of the incorrectly coded commodities had been in the supply system from 4 to 13 years.

During the audit agency's review of 1 year's transactions, at least 38 customer requisitions were automatically filled for 18 incorrectly coded commodities. Army customers and foreign governments under military assistance programs were issued 423 units on these 38 requisitions.

Since the commodities were incorrectly coded, the item managers did not coordinate the issue of the units with the 38 customers. Consequently, there was doubt that the customers should have been issued the material or that they were aware of the radioactivity in the commodities.

Army officials cited the following possible reasons for the incorrect codes contained in ADP files:

- The item managers who prepared the input to ADP files may not have been fully aware of the requirements and procedures for coding radioactive material,
- The agency's health physicist may not have notified the item managers of the radioactivity contained in these commodities, and
- The item managers may have been notified but failed to input the correct data codes.

Army officials agreed with the agency's findings and said they would (1) correct the ADP files for all radioactive commodities, (2) reemphasize to item managers the need for assigning the proper special control item code to commodities, and (3) have a health physicist study the commodities to insure that the items could be used safely by the customers that received them automatically. The special study determined that the commodities involved could be safely used by the recipients.

CASE 2

The Computers that Were Converted in the State of New Kent[7]

Required
1. Identify the program controls that need improvement.
2. Would these controls have any effect on the quality of the information from the computers?
   a) The old computers?
   b) The new computers?

The price of the equipment was the largest part of the costs in the early days of computers. Today, however, the programs—or the software—cost considerably more than the equipment. A major expense is called conversion costs. Program conversion costs are incurred to make programs devised for one computer work on another. The effort needed to make computer programs work on a new computer varies greatly from one situation to another but in the aggregate is quite large for the reason that there is little standardization in computers. Even different models of the same computer may not run each other's program without some modification.

Considerable work is often necessary then, to make one program work on another computer. In the state of New Kent, the total cost of this conversion effort was about $100 million each year. Auditors estimated that nearly one-fourth of the total conversion costs—about $25 million—could be saved each year if proper consideration were taken toward this end.

Some of the reasons auditors found for these high conversion costs in New Kent were:

- Lack of readily available software conversion expertise in the state,
- Poor quality of the software to be converted, including unnecessary use of features peculiar to an old computer that do not work on the new one,
- Inadequate flow charts and other data (called documentation) that explain the working of the software to be converted,
- Selection of new computer equipment that required more work on conversion because equipment had not been standardized among manufacturers, and
- Lack of programmer productivity aids, or a set of tools and techniques to be used by programmers, which could reduce the amount of human effort needed in conversion.

Auditors recommended that the state Department of Administration establish a center in the state for software conversion. It would be possible, after the center was established, for them to determine the total costs of new computer purchases. Auditors also recommended that department heads develop appropriate standards for software development, including the programs and the documentation.

The state should also publish a set of programmer productivity aids for statewide use in order to improve the productivity of programmers on both the original programs and program conversion.

CHAPTER 15

Using Specialized Analytical Techniques—Using Experts and Consultants

After you have read this chapter, studied the review questions, and worked through the cases, you will understand:

- Some of the more modern quantitative tools such as probability methods, linear programming, and network analysis—and gain a working knowledge of these tools.
- The use of experimental models in performance auditing.
- The use of cost-benefit and cost-effectiveness analysis in performance auditing.
- When and how to use experts and consultants as a part of the audit team or as consultants to the audit team.

In previous chapters, we have stated that there is a difference between performance evaluation and performance auditing. Performance auditing, according to our definition, is the *independent* review of an organization's activities or programs for a third party. Performance evaluation, on the other hand, is an evaluation for management's own needs by a person not independent from management. Management, without question, should have evaluators who help them decide which standards are best for the organization. But also, they should have independent audits.

Whenever possible, the independent auditor should rely on management's standards as the basis for the criteria of his audit. But quite a few organizations have not developed or stated the standards necessary for efficient, economical, or effective management. The auditor, in those cases, does not have much choice but to develop his own standard. To do so, he must often use, as does the performance evaluator, some highly specialized techniques. These, as well as the technique of using experts and consultants to help develop the standard, are the topics we will discuss in this chapter.

Although the material presented will be essentially introductory, we should be able to show the auditor how he can use these techniques and when he should use them. Few auditors will become specialized enough in all of these techniques; however, the auditor, as an audit specialist, should know which ones he can use and when.* Further, he should know that if a particular speciality is needed, he can obtain the services of an expert in that particular area.

---

*For readers who desire to become more thoroughly acquainted with specific techniques, sufficient reference books are available on each subject for them to obtain that knowledge. As a start they may refer to the bibliography beginning on p. 463 of this book.

Specialized Analytical Techniques: Several Models

Several approaches can be used to help the auditor learn the subject of specialized analytical techniques. We will organize our topics under the following headings:

1. Probability models,
2. Experimental models,
3. Balancing models,
4. Optimizing models, and
5. Other mathematical models.

Probability Models

In Chapter 12 on sampling, we introduced one use of probability. When the auditor says he wants to be confident that his sample figures will fall within his precision limits 95 percent of the time, he is applying probability principles.

Many of the more specialized techniques that may be used in performance auditing are also based on probability principles. Network analysis, including program analysis and review techniques (PERT) and critical path methods (CPM), are additional examples discussed later in this chapter.

Probability was originally developed as a theory of chance. Today its principles can apply to almost all types of situations—business, government, auditing, and accounting—as well as to the physical and social sciences. An event can or cannot occur in almost all activities of government or business. And if probability is the ratio of the number of ways an event can occur to the total possible happenings of that event, then probability principles can be applied to almost all activities of management.

In approaching an understanding of probability, there are three different subjects a person should know: (1) the number of times an event can occur out of the total possible number of events, (2) when events should be added to obtain the probability, and (3) when the events should be multiplied to obtain the probability.

Most explanations use a simple illustration of the throw of the dice to explain probability. For example, if a person only has one die, with six sides, and each side has equal chances of occurring, then each side has a 1/6 chance of being rolled. Thus, number one has a 1/6 chance; number two has a 1/6 chance, and so on.

When two dice are rolled, there are 36 ways all of the numbers can occur, as Table 15.1 illustrates.

Using this table, we can see that a 7 has 6/36 chance of being rolled. Suppose we wanted to see the probability of throwing either a 7 or an 11. The 7 has 6/36 probability of being thrown, while the 11 has a 2/36 probability. In this sort of situation, to find the probability of the two events, the two probabilities are added. If one event is mutually exclusive from the other, then the two probabilities are added to obtain the probability of both events.

However, if we have one event that is conditional on the other event happening, then the two probabilities are multiplied. For example, when we throw one die, the chances are 1/6 that any one number will show. When we throw two dice, the chances are (1/6) (1/6), or the number of chances in 36 for any one number to show. When we throw three dice, then the chances will be (1/6) (1/6) (1/6), or the number of chances in 216 that any one number will show.

Table 15.1 Thirty-six Ways that Numbers Can Occur When Two Dice Are Rolled

Number	Times	Ways
2	1	1 and 1.
3	2	2 and 1; 1 and 2.
4	3	3 and 1; 1 and 3; 2 and 2.
5	4	4 and 1; 1 and 4; 3 and 2; 2 and 3.
6	5	5 and 1; 1 and 5; 4 and 2; 2 and 4; 3 and 3.
7	6	6 and 1; 1 and 6; 5 and 2; 2 and 5; 4 and 3; 3 and 4
8	5	6 and 2; 2 and 6; 5 and 3; 3 and 5; 4 and 4.
9	4	5 and 4; 4 and 5; 6 and 3; 3 and 6.
10	3	6 and 4; 4 and 6; 5 and 5.
11	2	6 and 5; 5 and 6.
12	1	6 and 6.
	36	

The reader may have noticed that the table shown above reflects somewhat of a normal curve pattern. Under a condition such as that described in Chapter 12 on attribute sampling, where there are only two possible answers, such as yes or no, then the curve would fit a binominal distribution and could be measured accurately. When the curve becomes one that follows a normal pattern, such as that discussed in Chapter 12 on estimation sampling, then the normal curve can be used to determine the probability.

With this limited discussion, the reader can see that the possibility of measuring any of the various events that management might encounter, in terms of the probability of that event occurring, becomes very possible, especially with the capability of the computer now at the disposal of management and the auditor.

All models are a representation of reality. Probability models are used to represent the reality management encounters in carrying out its activities and programs. Since chance is a very important element in any activity, the manager can quite often substitute probability theory instead of using hunches for the chances he takes.

Probability applications can be used not only for P-audits but are often used in production, personnel, and research activities—activities that can be audited for both economy and efficiency.

The reader will see the application of probability principles in the following discussions on each of the various models.

Experimental Models

A useful method of determining the most appropriate standards for action by management is through experimental models, which make a comparison with other activities. Often the analyst designs an experiment to compare what he has discovered through mathematical models in order to determine that his abstract mathematical model relates directly to reality. This comparison of two or more activities gives him an indication of the best method of proceeding with the problems management encounters.

The GAO offers the following good description on the use of experimental models:

Experimental methods—attempt to measure the results of the program as though everything else is held constant. This is done by measuring the difference, in terms of the measures of success, between those affected by the program and a control group which is not. This is the preferred method for evaluation of social experiments, but it can also be used for any evaluation when the essential requirements of random assignment and control are feasible. This is the approach that was used in the New Jersey Negative Income Tax experiment. In that experiment, several different amounts of monetary incentives were given to different groups of families in the same situation to see what effect the incentives had on work and spending habits. Responses were compared with the habits of families in the same situations that received no monetary incentive from the experiment during the same time.

The analytical strength of the experimental method makes it a very useful tool. This value must be balanced against other considerations, such as cost and ethical and legal constraints, before this approach is selected.

Experimental designs require that the affected group and the group not affected possess similar characteristics. This is the reason for a strict requirement that the potential participants be *randomly* assigned so that each one has the same chance of assignment to either group before the program begins. Unless randomization is achieved, there is no assurance that the results are attributable to the program.

For example, unless randomly assigned, participants might enroll because they are more perceptive and desire the benefits more than others who are eligible. This biases any comparison of the response or performance of the two groups because their motivations and other characteristics were not the same.

Nonrandom comparison group methods—are commonly used when the requirements for strict randomized control cannot be satisfied. Attempts are made to make the comparison group as similar to the experimental group as possible by matching individuals with the same sex, age, racial, or socioeconomic characteristics. The differences in results between the two groups (experimental and the matched comparison) are attributable, as in experimental designs, to the results of the program. However, without random assignment there is greater danger that the observed results are attributable to nonprogram influences. Other difficulties with the method include potential bias resulting from self-selection by participants.

Comparison of similar programs—attempts to establish measures and data with which the outcomes of two or more ongoing programs or components can be compared. Program comparisons are attractive for several reasons. They (1) provide information on effectiveness of alternatives in comparable terms and for the same time period, (2) reduce the need to rely completely on the elusive "control" of experimental methods applied to one project, (3) help generalize the results if widely distributed "representative" projects can be included, and (4) offer an opportunity to identify exceptional performance and to study what is operationally different about those projects.

Program comparisons comprehensive enough to yield the above advantages are costly and difficult to manage. For example, although "planned variations" must be carefully documented at the outset, once in operation they will seldom be free of further changes, which also must be documented. It should be noted whether such changes are "positive" (efforts to apply even better methods) or "negative" (resistance to adopting the prescribed methods).

Time series—involves a series of measurements at periodic intervals before the program begins and during the program. For example, in evaluating the safety results of Connecticut's crackdown on speeding, it was possible to use time series data collected for several years before and after this new policy change. An abrupt change in such trend data is strong evidence that the action taken caused the observed change in the trend. If measurements can also be obtained in another setting treated as a comparison group, additional insights are possible.

Careful interpretation is needed when using time series data. There may be a time lag between receipt of services and the impact of the services. The analyst should also be alert for cyclical phenomena, such as unemployment levels, which might cause part of the trend.[1]

Balancing Models

One of the more familiar models with which the accountant and auditor have dealt is the balance sheet model. While it is not considered a mathematical model, it fairly well represents reality. When the accountant says that "Assets = Liabilities + Capital + Income − Expenses," he is representing what management wants from the financial activities of the organization.

Somewhat comparable to this balancing type of model are the cost-benefit, cost-effectiveness, and cost-value analyses. These analyses are discussed by the GAO as follows:

Estimating measurable consequences. Estimates must be made of anticipated measurable consequences as well as of all costs and resource inputs under various conditions and levels of available resources. Measurable consequences include effectiveness, side effects, and distribution considerations. In making such estimates, the data on actual costs and effectiveness found in prior appraisals of similar programs should be used together with actual operating data. It may also be necessary to use well-developed causal models to make such effectiveness estimates. Although these models must adequately simulate the real situation, an existing model may serve. Experience has shown that it is costly and time consuming to develop a completely new model.

Some effort should be made to estimate side effects and their influence on resources. An estimate is needed, to the extent possible, of the differences of impact on the beneficiaries and the cost bearers (distribution considerations). Approximations may have to be used for side effects and distribution estimates, and various value judgments are involved in weighing both.

When analyzing costs that should be associated with effectiveness, various cost concepts are needed, and information on these costs is usually available. When analyzing costs that should be associated with side-effect and distribution considerations, total as well as incremental costs should be developed. Frequently such costs are incomplete. They should be checked for reasonableness and consistency with the alternatives of interest.

Information at the margin, as contrasted with information on total quantities, is very important in resource allocation decisions. Approximations of incremental costs, however, are more easily obtained than are approximations of the marginal aspects of other program consequences. A reasonable effort should be made to estimate the direction and magnitude of the variations of program consequences over relevant ranges.

Information on measurable consequences obtained from audits, evaluations, or other studies should be used. Historical and trend data may provide information concerning how the various consequences are affected by the scale of activity.

Assessing provisional orderings. Once the total and incremental consequences of the alternatives have been estimated, the alternatives should be arrayed in some order. This ordering may be based on one of several available approaches.

One approach is "cost effectiveness." This approach focuses on resources expected to be consumed and how well the objectives are achieved. Using this framework, a preferred alternative is identified as one that produces the largest achievement for a given level of costs or that minimizes resources expended for attaining a given level of effectiveness.

While the cost-effectiveness approach provides a basis for ordering competing alternatives, it does not clearly allow for comparisons of alternatives associated with multiple, possibly conflicting, objectives. Other consequences of alternatives—side effects and distribution considerations—are not an integral part of the analysis and may require separate examination.

A second approach to ordering alternatives is "cost-benefit" analysis. Side effects and distribution considerations are incorporated in this approach. Major consequences, or benefits, are measured in dollars, and differences between monetary benefits and costs provide the basis for choice among alternatives. Theoretically, cost-benefit analysis is more useful than cost-effectiveness analysis in treating differing as well as conflicting objectives. The streams of benefits and costs can be discounted to their equivalent present values, thus accounting for the effects of time. Conceptually, decisionmakers could select programs based on ranking of net present value benefits (or derivatives of this data) until the total available resources were exhausted. However, this approach requires that all measures can be converted to dollars (a difficult task at best) in a way that the decision maker understands. Because of the difficulty of quantifying side effects and distributional effects, there is often no clear distinction between cost-effectiveness and cost-benefit analysis.

Another approach is "cost-value" analysis. This is a technique for obtaining generally acceptable quantitative weights for use in comparing the value of the alternatives. In this approach, the weights assigned to various outcomes are based on decisionmakers' judgments.

The cost-value method combines elements of cost-effectiveness and cost-benefit analysis. Side effect and distribution considerations can be incorporated with effectiveness. Because the judgments of decisionmakers differ, various sets of judgments should be used and the ordering(s) of alternatives should be tested for its/their sensitivity to these differences. In such analysis both the array of consequences associated with each alternative and the ordering based on the various value systems should be presented to decisionmakers.

Each approach has both strengths and limitations, but all share certain limitations. One such limitation is uncertainty caused by such things as variations in assumptions and the quality of information on the alternatives. Because uncertainty is always present in anticipating future outcomes, undue reliance should not be placed on small differences in ordering(s) of alternatives. The quantitative analysis that has been discussed should be supplemented with an analysis of nonmeasurable consequences. A serious attempt should be made to indicate the significance of nonmeasurable consequences.[2]

Most of the analyses discussed in the preceding quotation deal with both prospective and ongoing programs. Therefore, the auditor can use many of the ideas to develop criteria for making the audit or to assess the effects of not using the appropriate standard.

Optimizing Models

In the preceding discussion on models, one concept was clearly common to all three models: they were representations of reality. In the probability model, reality was related to the chance one takes in making any decision. In the experimental models, it was related to one condition or group being held constant—the control group—while another was not. In the balancing model, cost-benefits, cost-effectiveness, and cost-values attempted to measure the reality of other types of analyses of the activity.

Optimizing models also represent reality, but in addition each of the five identified below has other concerns. After describing each briefly, we will discuss them in detail and illustrate linear programming.

1. *Linear programming models.* In any activity, where there is a linear relationship between the variables in that activity, and where there are some constraints on the use of the particular resources considered as a variable, then the maximum or minimum relationships between resources can be determined. The maximum or minimum relationships can be determined for any type of activity—production, personnel, finance, transportation, research, and so forth. Some particular activities, such as transportation, have adapted the linear programming techniques to that particular activity and given it a name—the transportation method, for example.
2. *Queuing models.* Many problems the auditor encounters are concerned with some form of waiting: The mechanic waits for airplane repair parts, the buyer waits for the seller, the hospital patient waits for

service, the person wanting to eat waits in line at the cafeteria. All are some form of queuing.

3. *Game theory models.* Game theory is used when an organization optimizes its results under competitive conditions. Any activity where there are opposing interests—that is, where others are interested in the results and would influence those results—can be analyzed with game theory models.
4. *Network analysis models.* In trying to attain an objective, an organization must follow certain steps, and these can be charted in order to determine the responsibilities to be followed. In analyzing the probabilities of accomplishing the various steps, which involve times and uncertainties, network analysis models, based on probability, can be used.
5. *Markov chain models.* In any activity or program where there are conditions of change, Markov chain models can be used to analyze those conditions of change, and arrive at the optimal solution.

Linear Programming Models

Linear programming is probably the most common of the various types of models used for maximizing or minimizing certain functions—for allocating scarce resources of a firm in the best manner possible, for instance. Three different methods may be used to determine the best allocation: (1) graphically, (2) algebraically, and (3) through the simplex method.

One problem in linear programming that many auditors might not be familiar with, shown in our illustration, is that of inequalities. The equation might state the problem in the form of being equal to or less than, or equal to or more than, rather than merely being equal to. This is a rather common form of statement especially when dealing with constraints.

Since in linear programming the organization must state its objectives in some manner that can be related in a linear way, and there are only a limited number of resources to accomplish the objective, then the proposed solutions can often be portrayed graphically. Let us use an illustration the auditor can grasp without mathematics. We will illustrate the case graphically and then show how it can be carried further.

To start with, let us assume that we have a plant that can produce either Product A or Product B. Product A has a profit of $10 per unit while Product B has a profit of $8 per unit. Of the total of 3,000 pounds of material available each week, Product A would use 20 pounds per unit and Product B the same.

At this point, it is obvious that the full amount of material, 3,000 pounds, should be used to produce 150 units of Product A in order to maximize the profits. The relationships can be shown in a graph, as Figure 15.1 illustrates.

In graphical analysis, the corner points of the graph—in the above case the 150 of Product A and the 150 of Product B—become important considerations. The corner point of Product B would be the minimum profit, and the corner point of Product A would be the maximum point. Any point in between would be above the minimum but below the maximum. For example, if we produced 75 units of Product A and 75 units of Product B we would have the following results:

	Units	Profit	Total
Product A	75	$10	$ 750
Product B	75	8	600
Total			$1,350

Figure 15.1 Linear relationships—products A and B

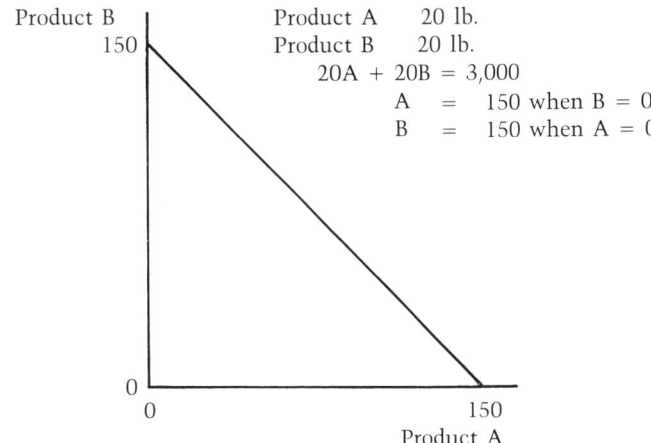

Note that the $1,350 is less than the maximum profit of $1,500 but more than the minimum profit of $1,200.

Let us add more constraints and see how they will affect the objective of maximizing the profit. First, the total facts in the case under consideration are:

- *Objective:* Maximize profit (Note: There is a distinction between maximizing profit and other objectives, such as using all of the material.)
- *Profit per unit:* Product A, $10 per unit. Product B, $8 per unit.
- *Materials:* Only 3,000 pounds of the material is available each week to produce either Product A or Product B, of which Product A needs 20 pounds of material per unit and Product B needs 20 pounds of material per unit.
- *Machine time:* Only 1,200 hours of machine time per week are available for producing both products, of which 10 hours of machine time are needed to produce a unit of Product A and only 6 hours of machine time are needed to produce a unit of Product B. (Product A must have a special insignia placed on it. There are only 100 of those insignia available each week.)

The relationships of the three constraints can be expressed in a form that can be placed on a graph as follows:

Material: $20A + 20B \leq 3{,}000$

That is, 20 pounds of material times the number of units of Product A plus 20 pounds of material times the number of units of Product B must be equal to or less than 3,000 pounds. The maximum units of A would be 150 when the production of B is zero, and the maximum units of B would be 150 when the production of A is zero.

Machine time: $10A + 6B \leq 1{,}200$

That is, 10 hours of machine time times the units produced of Product A plus 6 hours of machine time times the units produced of Product B cannot exceed the total machine time available of 1200 hours. The maximum units produced of A, when B is zero, is 120, while the maximum units of B, when A is zero, is 200.

Insignias: $A \leq 100$

There are always 100 units of A production available no matter how many units of B are produced when the insignias only are considered.

Now let us see these relationships presented in graph form:

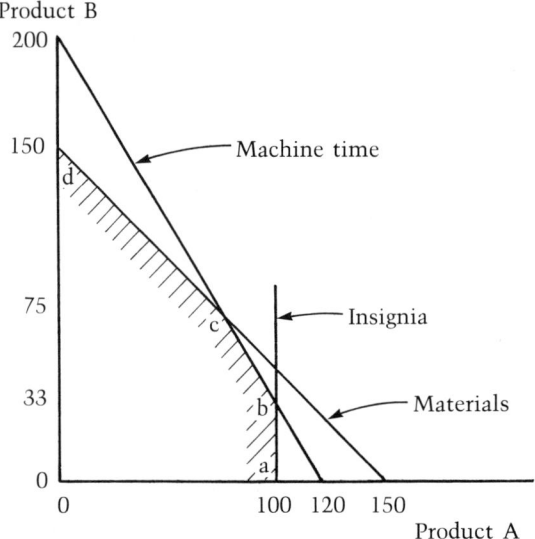

Figure 15.2 Linear relationships: three constraints.

By looking at the graph, you can see that there are only four points depicted, labeled a, b, c, and d. The constraint relationships are found in the shaded area of the chart. From these relationships we can find the maximum profit point—our objective. Let us consider the relationships at these points in the tables below.

Constraints (indicated by *)

	Materials			Machine time			Insignia	
	Units	Amount	Total	Units	Amount	Total	Units	Total
Point a								
Product A	100	20	2,000	100	10	1,000	100*	100*
Product B	—	—	—	—	—	—	—	—
	100		2,000	100		2,000	100*	100*
Point b								
Product A	100	20	2,000	100	10	1,000	100*	100*
Product B	33	20	266	33	6	198		
	133		2,666	133		1,198*	100*	100*
Point c								
Product A	75	20	1,500	75	10	750	75	75
Product B	75	20	1,500	75	6	450		
	150*		3,000*	150		1,200*	75	75
Point d								
Product A	—	—	—	—	—	—	—	—
Product B	150*	20	3,000*	150	6	900		
	150*		3,000*					

Maximum Profits (indicated by †)

Point a	100 @ $10	= $1,000	total	$1,000
Point b	100 @ $10	= $1,000		
	33 @ 8	= 264	total	$1,264
Point c	75 @ $10	= $750		
	75 @ 8	= 600	total	$1,350†
Point d	150 @ $8	= $1,200	total	$1,200

From these relationships and constraints, it is easy to see that the maximum profits can be obtained by producing 75 units of Product A and 75 units of Product B.

Once the auditor understands the basic idea of the various models given, he can obtain help to solve a particular problem. When a problem in linear relationships becomes more complex than the two-dimensional relationships shown, then of course it is necessary to go to more complex methods to solve it. The simplex method is one of these, but because of the numerous calculations involved, it would in most cases need to be worked on a computer.

Fortunately, many organizations have the formula for computing the answers to complex linear programming problems in their computer so that the simplex process—a process for repeating the equation solutions—can often be used. When several types of mixes are used in the linear programming problem, in fact, the simplex method is the only one that would satisfactorily solve the problems.

Management, in many cases, has already used linear programming methods to determine its standard for operations, and the auditor should at least be able to determine whether the standard is the most appropriate one.

Queuing Models

Queuing is waiting, as we have described. Mathematical techniques have been devised to optimize the results or minimize the costs that result from queuing. Some of these techniques are based on the probabilities discussed in the first part of this chapter.

Game Theory Models

The strategy in gaming is to win or to minimize losses in some action to be taken. War gaming is a good example. Many of the solutions to problems of this type are based on matrix algebra, so it would be valuable for an auditor to learn some of the techniques of this subject.

Network Analysis Models

In charting the responsibilities to attain an objective, management might not know the times and uncertainties in time for accomplishing the tasks, the interdependencies between responsibilities, nor the various slippages that might result because of time. In order to overcome these deficiencies in charting organizational responsibilities, certain organizations have developed mathematical techniques—Program Evaluation and Review Techniques and the Critical Path Method—that provide many answers the charts did not.

Program Evaluation and Review Techniques, called PERT, were developed to provide standards for control for the complex military weapons system, the Polaris missile on the atomic submarine, for instance. Usage of PERT is almost restricted to complicated operational systems because of the heavy reliance on mathematical methods and computer methodology.

The Critical Path Method, called CPM, is a less complex system, using visual methods as well as mathematical methods. Its usage is for less complicated operational management systems than a Polaris missile.

Both systems develop standards for planning and scheduling activities concerned with carrying out activities that are dependent upon, as well as related to, each other.

Markov Chain-analysis Models

The mathematical models described above, in most cases, are based on a relatively stable set of conditions. Markov analysis is useful when we assume change in the set of conditions.

Most chain analysis sooner or later comes to a stable condition—for example, analysis of changing conditions in high school education would come to an end when the subjects being studied graduated. Markov chain analysis is valuable to the auditor in many specific situations of the changing total environment—education, welfare, crime, and physical environment.

Other Mathematical Models

A model is a representation of reality. Sometimes it is possible to represent reality mathematically. Then through a change in the variables, it is possible to determine the results caused through that change. Several organizations have developed mathematical models of cities. By changing one of the variables, it is possible to see what results from that change.

In one audit of grants for water pollution that we considered in Chapter 3, a model of a river system was developed. The variables represented the amount of pollutants from various sources—human pollution, agricultural pollution, and industrial pollution. It was possible to show that even though all human pollution was eliminated, the agricultural and industrial pollution was so great that the river's water quality could not meet the standards required.

One of the problems of developing mathematical models is the cost. Another problem is the time needed to develop one of these models. Thus, if it seems necessary to use a mathematical model for audit purposes, the auditor should attempt to find a model already developed.

Using Experts and Consultants

Auditing, as a field, has developed primarily within the accounting profession. In most instances, therefore, the auditor is both an expert auditor as well as an expert accountant. As an expert auditor he is skilled in gathering, analyzing, and summarizing evidence on an audit objective in order to come to a conclusion on that objective, and skilled in reporting the results of his audit to a third party. Yet there are many instances when the auditor would feel much more qualified if he had additional expertise in the subject matter concerned with the audit, as the preceding section on specialized techniques illustrated.

Help in using mathematical techniques, however, is only a small part of the usage of experts. In the P-audit field, especially, the auditor can use the help of experts and consultants in such specialized areas as education, social services, welfare, industrial pollution, recreation, governmental administration, and highway construction—to name but a few.

The way to use experts and consultants depends upon the way the audit group is organized. Two separate methods of organizing for carrying out audit operations will be considered:

- The normal audit organization, and
- The task force organization.

Use of Experts and Consultants in the Normal Audit Organization

Most audit organizations are organized into groups of specialists in certain subject matters in the following manner:

- Partners or directors
- Supervisors or assistant directors
- Managers
- Seniors
- Juniors, or senior assistants

This type of organization works well since the members are organized by specialty to start with and thus become fairly familiar with the activities of the entity they will examine.

Their need for an expert will only be for specialized occasions, and they can obtain the expert on a consulting basis rather than as a member of the team. For example, if during the audit of an organization, the audit group had need of an expert in developing questionnaires, the expert would be obtained on a consulting basis for that one task only.

Many times the experts in a particular field are members of the organization being audited. They often can be used as consultants for a particular point of reference, and in such a case they are providing evidence on the audit in that particular field.

In the beginning of very complex audits, a panel of consultants can be used to help the audit team determine the direction of the audit. They can also be used to provide a background in the particular subject matter for the auditors. For example, suppose the audit team was going into the subject of air pollution. A panel of consultants in this field would give the auditors a good idea of the direction they should take in the audit, as well as provide them with a basic knowledge of the subject.

Most of these experts can be obtained from universities, on a limited consulting basis. Some private industrial organizations, as well as research organizations, will provide a few of their experts to governmental audit organizations for a limited salary in order to show that they have an interest in improved governmental administration.

Experts and consultants, then, are brought into the normal audit organization only when needed and seldom become a permanent part of the organization. Yet, if the audit organization builds up a roster of specialists in various fields, these specialists can become an important segment of the audit staff.

Use of Experts and Consultants as Members of a Task Force

In recent years, management of various organizations have found that instead of following the normal hierarchical pattern to accomplish a task they set out to do, they can accomplish it in a much better manner by using a task force. This is true especially when they are attempting to accomplish a task that involves many disciplines. One of the most successful examples of such an attempt was landing a man on the moon. Many of the tasks for that project were accomplished through task forces and project leaders rather than through the normal hierarchical organization.

A task force also works well in auditing some of the very complex programs that involve many disciplines as well as many organizations. Instead of having the audit team composed only of auditors, the task force will be composed of members concerned with each of the disciplines that may be encountered by the audit. For example, in an audit of education, the team may be composed of auditors, statisticians, education specialists, and educational administrators. In an audit of highway construction, the team may be composed of auditors, engineers, and mathematicians.

Each of these teams must be supervised by a project leader, and each member of the team must know exactly what is to be accomplished by the task force in addition to the specific task he will accomplish.

We can see that when the audit organization goes to the task force approach, they will have to have these various experts on given disciplines as permanent members of their staff. Most audits, after all, take quite some time to complete, and few specialists like to become a member of a task force for a particular task and then be relegated to the unemployment ranks.

Developing a staff of experts and consultants within the framework of an audit organization may mean the complete rearrangement of the organization. Few engineers, for instance, want to become members of the audit organization unless they can succeed in their own specialty. Similarly, few public health specialists, mathematicians, aerospace engineers, physicists, foresters, or pharmacists would like to become members of the audit organization unless they are able to use their specialty.

Most of them, however, will have to learn that they will be auditors first and specialists second. In our own field, this has happened to accountants: They have become auditors first; secondly, they are accountants. But with this understanding, most specialists can become very good auditors, with an opportunity to apply their specialty whenever the occasion arises.

REVIEW QUESTIONS

1. An auditor may not have the particular specialized capability for a particular audit. What is one solution to this dilemma? (See p. 329.)

2. If one event is mutually exclusive from another event, how do you determine the probability of both events occurring? (See p. 330.)

3. If one event is conditional on the other event happening, how do you determine the probability of both events occurring? (See p. 330.)

4. Since all models are representations of reality, are there some models that represent the chances management might take? Discuss. (See p. 331.)

5. Sometimes the results of a program are measured as if everything else is held constant. What method is this called and how is it accomplished? (See p. 332.)

6. In dealing with experimental methods the persons assigned to the groups

should be randomly assigned. When strict randomized control cannot be accomplished, what method should be used? (See p. 332.)

7. Describe cost effectiveness. What are some of the problems encountered by the auditor in using cost effectiveness? Describe cost-benefit analysis and its problems. Describe cost-value analysis and its benefits and limitations. (See p. 334.)

8. Define linear programming. What methods are used to determine the best allocation of resources under linear programming? (See pp. 334–39.)

9. What is meant by queuing? By game theory? By network analysis? When should each method be used by the auditor? (See pp. 339–40.)

10. When is the Markov chain-analysis method used? What is accomplished when this method is used? (See p. 340.)

11. Almost any situation can be represented by a mathematical model representing reality. What are some of the limitations of converting reality to a mathematical representation? (See p. 340.)

12. Discuss some of the situations in which an auditor could use experts or consultants. (See pp. 340–41.)

13. Describe two methods that can be used by auditors to receive help from consultants and experts when the audit group is under a normal audit organization. (See pp. 341–42.)

14. A task force is often described as being a circular rather than an hierarchical organization. Discuss when a task force should be used and how it is used. (See pp. 341–42.)

CASE 1

Ranges for Measuring Risk and Uncertainty in Cost Estimates[3]

Required

1. Identify the model you would use in order to come up with the effects for this audit.
2. Suggest how you could possibly come up with a better measurement basis by using a range of uncertainties rather than a point estimate.

The following is a summarized report concerned with measuring risk and uncertainty in cost estimates. The facts could have come from a federal, state, or local audit.

For many years, most agencies having long-range programs have faced the same recurring problem: Ultimate costs of the programs are often many times the estimated costs on which they were approved. Although agencies make continuous efforts to improve the reasonableness of their estimates, overoptimism still exists, inflation continues, and problems of many types plague the major programs.

Cost estimating is more an art than a science. Cost estimates are not statements of fact; rather, they are judgments of the cost to perform work under specified conditions. For programs that span years from the drawing boards to completion, economic uncertainties and technological risks are inherent. The single-point or specific-dollar estimate assumes a certainty as to cost that does not exist.

Substantial deviations between an initial program cost estimate—or point estimate—and actual or ultimate cost are not reasonable, given these inherent uncertainties. One way to assess the problems is to determine a range of potential cost by analyzing probable uncertainties and risks that can be reasonably anticipated in a developmental program.

Presenting a cost range should help decision makers assess major areas of probable risk and uncertainty and the potential cost of a program if these uncertainties occur. Questions such as the following can provide useful and valuable information:

- What significant uncertainties will drive cost to extremities of a range?
- What are the chances that an uncertain event will occur?
- What will minimize the occurrence of an uncertain or risky situation?
- What is the probability of exceeding the best estimate of cost? Of being below the best estimate? Of exceeding the upper end of the range?
- At what point in the range will the program cease to be the most cost-effective solution to meet the need?

Agencies in the executive branch continue to present early cost projections to the legislature as single-point estimates despite the fact that they are highly misleading. As programs proceed and costs vary from point estimates, requirements are not fulfilled, problems exist with what is acquired, future planning becomes unrealistic and unbalanced, program officials are often accused unjustly of mismanagement, and credibility with the legislature and the public is diminished.

Some agencies require the identification of uncertainties in major programs for decision reviews, but they do not require that a cost range be estimated to quantify the potential cost impact of the uncertainties. This is not to say that a range estimate will solve all the problems, and it should not completely replace the point estimate; but a range of probable cost should be presented in addition to the single-, most likely, point estimate, which would remain program and budget cost targets. This information can help decision makers decide whether the program is worth the stated risks—that is, whether the risks involved are greater than the need, or whether to proceed despite the risks. As the program progresses, a revised range of probable cost can be used in deciding whether to continue, revise, or hold the program until critical problems are resolved.

CASE 2

Procuring M.D.s for the Service: A Cost-effectiveness Analysis[4]

Required

1. From the following digest of a GAO report, state the advantages and disadvantages of the techniques used to develop the facts for this report.
2. Are there other techniques that could have been used?

The Uniformed Services Health Profession Revitalization Act of 1972 (Public Law 92-426) authorized the Department of Defense to procure physicians by establishing the Armed Forces Health Professions Scholarship Program (10 U.S.C. 2121) and the Uniformed Services University of the Health Sciences (10 U.S.C. 2112).

Since this legislation was enacted, several studies have been made to help the Congress determine the cost effectiveness of both programs. Studies by the House Appropriations Committee's Surveys and Investigations Staff and the Defense Manpower Commission concluded that the university program was substantially less cost effective than the scholarship program; whereas a Uniformed Services University study concluded that the university program was *more* cost effective.

The debate over which program was more cost effective continued during the fiscal year 1976 budget hearings on military construction. After $64.9 million was appropriated for building the second increment of the university's medical school facility, two senators requested GAO to ascertain which program was in fact more cost effective.

GAO's cost-effectiveness analysis differed from the previous studies in that GAO attempted to show the full costs of the department's *procuring* and *retaining* physicians; prior studies were limited to procurement costs only.

GAO's analysis specifically addressed the future uses of resources, considering only those costs directly attributable to the implementation of each alternative (i.e., incremental costs).

The department disagreed with GAO's exclusion of non-Defense federal subsidies to civilian medical schools as a cost attributable to the scholarship program. Also, the department pointed out that GAO's analysis was a cost-effectiveness rather than a cost-benefit analysis, which would recognize the intangible benefits to be derived from establishing the university.

GAO, however, did not include non-Defense federal subsidies to civilian medical schools because this federal assistance

- Was provided before and had been provided since the establishment of the scholarship program, and
- Would continue regardless of whether the scholarship program continued or was completely abandoned.

GAO performed a cost-effectiveness—rather than a cost-benefit—analysis because of the subjectivity involved in quantifying the numerous intangible benefits that could be identified in connection with either program.

GAO's primary unit of measurement was the estimated cost per staff year of expected service from graduates of each program. Interim measurement steps were also included in the analysis to show (1) the estimated educational cost per graduate from each program and (2) the estimated educational cost per staff year of expected service of each program's graduates.

University officials contended that (1) university and scholarship-program graduates differ in their ability to fulfill required military medical needs and (2) an expanded scholarship program would decrease the nation's ability to meet the civilian sector's need for physicians.

These contentions were nonquantifiable and were thus not included in GAO's cost-effectiveness analysis. GAO believed, however, that these were important concerns that must be considered along with the program's cost effectiveness.

GAO's analysis showed that in fiscal year 1984, the first full year of simultaneous operation of both programs:

- The estimated educational cost would be $36,784 for each of 988 graduates of the scholarship program and $189,980 for each of 175 university graduates.
- The estimated educational costs per staff year of expected service would be $4,362 for the scholarship-program graduates and $10,232 for university graduates.
- The total cost per staff year of expected service (including anticipated pay and retirement costs) would be $21,444 for scholarship-program graduates and $26,236 for university graduates.

The department's estimates of potential costs and expected benefits under each program are subject to change. Some of these estimates—particularly those for the university program—have already changed often. Because of these uncertainties, GAO conducted several sensitivity tests to show how changes in certain assumptions affect the two programs' cost effectiveness. For example, one test showed that, as civilian medical school tuitions increase, the cost effectiveness of the scholarship program decreases.

This GAO report should help the Congress in (1) assessing the actual cost effectiveness of each program, (2) understanding the uncertainties involved in determining cost effectiveness, and (3) deciding whether to reconsider its position on the authorization and funding of the university program.

Also, the Congress might apply the overall GAO methodology used in this report to assess the appropriateness of future requests from the DOD or other federal agencies for expanding or initiating health-profession procurement programs.

Further, in the event the Congress wished to consider alternatives to the university, GAO developed three alternatives that could produce equivalent numbers of expected staff years of physician services more cost effectively than both programs operating concurrently. Each alternative would require action by the Congress to terminate the university program and action by the Congress and/or the department to

- expand the scholarship program,
- fully sponsor any scholarship-program participant taking civilian residency training, or
- increase the initial active-duty obligation for scholarship participants.

If the university program were terminated, funds could be made available to provide grants to help expand civilian medical schools to accommodate additional scholarship-program students.

PART Five

Reporting the Results of the Audit

Part 5 will deal in depth with the primary reason for an audit—to communicate its results to a third party. To learn how to report properly the results of the audit, then, has been a fundamental objective of this book. There are two chapters in Part 5: Chapter 16, "Understanding the Principles of Reporting," and Chapter 17, "Writing a Clear, Concise, and Objective Report."

In addition to the illustrations given in the chapters in this part, other illustrations of applied principles and practices of developing, organizing, and writing an effective report are given in the appendixes.

CHAPTER 16

Understanding the Principles of Reporting

After you have read the chapter, studied the review questions, and worked through the cases, you will understand:

- How to organize your report.
- How to state background information in your report.
- How to develop the logic pertaining to the results of the audit in your report.
- How to state your conclusions and recommendations.
- How to relate the principles of reporting you have learned in financial-statement examinations to those in performance auditing.
- How information flows from the working papers into the report.
- How you can obtain benefits through peer and supervisory reviews of your report.

Auditors reporting for financial-statement examinations are quite often awed with the responsibilities they have for reporting on performance audits. They are accustomed to a great deal of uniformity in their reporting, developed over the years by committees of the American Institute of Certified Public Accountants. No comparable organization exists to fulfill this responsibility for developing more uniformity in performance audits. And yet, we may be able to use some of the standards for reporting on financial-statement examinations and governmental audits to develop a somewhat understandable structure for reporting on performance audits.

Standards of Reporting

First, let us review the standards for reporting for financial-statement examinations. The AICPA states:

1. The report shall state whether the financial statements are presented in accordance with generally accepted accounting principles.
2. The report shall state whether such principles have been consistently observed in the current period in relation to the preceding period.
3. Informative disclosures in the financial statements are to be regarded as reasonably adequate unless otherwise stated in the report.
4. The report shall either contain an expression of opinion regarding the financial statements, taken as a whole, or an assertion to the effect than an opinion cannot be expressed. When an overall opinion cannot be expressed, the reasons therefor should be stated. In all cases where an auditor's name is associated with financial statements, the report

should contain a clear-cut indication of the character of the auditor's examination, if any, and the degree of responsibility he is taking.[1]

The standard short-form report consists of two paragraphs, a scope paragraph and an opinion paragraph. The scope paragraph says:

> We have examined the balance sheet of X Company as of (at) December 31, 19XX, and the related statements of income, retained earnings, and changes in financial position for the year then ended. Our examination was made in accordance with generally accepted auditing standards and, accordingly, included such tests of the accounting records and such other auditing procedures as we considered necessary in the circumstances.

The opinion paragraph says:

> In our opinion, the financial statements referred to above present fairly the financial position of X Company as of (at) December 31, 19XX, and the results of its operations and the changes in its financial position for the year then ended, in conformity with generally accepted accounting principles applied on a basis consistent with that of the preceding year.[2]

Most departures from the standard short-form report, such as qualifications to the opinion or disclaimers, will be explained in a separate paragraph, between the scope paragraph and the opinion paragraph.

The reader should notice that there is quite a bit of good logic expressed in the development of this standard short-form report, that it is well organized as well, and that the words, sentences, and paragraphs say what is meant.

Comparable to the AICPA standards are those of the Comptroller General, which the reader may review as Appendix I. The basic ideas to be gleaned from both these statements on reporting standards can be given in terms of differences and similarities. Generally, the differences between a report for a financial-statement examination and a report for a performance audit can be identified as follows:

- The writer of a performance audit report does not express his results in the form of financial statements. His report is based on standard English usage rather than on accounting statements.
- Each report is separate and distinct from any other report. Therefore, there is no uniformity of presentation, nor a standard language.
- The reader of the report, in most circumstances, will not have a thorough understanding of the management activity or program on which the auditor is reporting. So, the auditor must describe and explain in much more detail the activity or program he has examined in his performance audit than he would have to in a financial-statement examination.

Some of the similarities between financial-statement examination reporting and performance audit reporting are the following:

- Both types of audits follow a logical approach to report writing. Reports are based specifically upon the logic followed in the examination.
- Both types of reports follow a logical organization within the report itself.
- While there is a similarity between expressing opinions on financial-statement examinations and conclusions on performance audits, performance audits also include recommendations.

Recognizing the various similarities and differences between M-audits and P-audits and financial-statement examinations will help the auditor to understand this chapter. What he already knows from his background in financial-statement auditing will be expanded upon so that he may develop the additional knowledge that will enable him to report satisfactorily on his performance audits. The structure of the chapter will then be as follows:

- Logical organization of the report.
- Background data concerning the organization, activity, program, or function.
- Reporting the results of the audit.
- Recommendations.
- Scope of the examination.

Logical Organization of the Report: Two Patterns

Two basic organizational patterns can be developed by the auditor for logically reporting the results of a performance audit:

- Follow the flow of information that goes in the report in much the same manner as it was developed in the audit.
- Follow the flow of information that goes in the report in order of importance to the reader.

Pattern 1: The Flow of Information into the Report as Developed in the Audit

Usually an auditor first gathers background information concerning the activity or program he is to examine, and from this background information he derives his audit objective.

Since he has only a tentative audit objective in the beginning, the auditor must gather some evidence from the management control system to have a firm objective. Of course, his audit objective must have evidence on all three elements—criteria, causes, and effects—before he would have a firm objective.

Then, the auditor must gather evidence that is sufficient, relevant, material, and competent, on all three elements, in order for him to come to a conclusion on that objective.

In order of development of the audit, then, the auditor follows these steps:

1. He gathers background information and tests management control,
2. He states his audit objective,
3. He gathers evidence on his objective, and then
4. He comes to a conclusion on the objective.

During this process, the auditor has been following certain procedures to assure himself that his audit is complete and objective. Often called the scope of the examination, these procedures limit the auditor in his overall approach to the audit. The AICPA, as we have seen, considers the scope of the audit important enough to place it in the first paragraph of the standard short-form report for financial-statement examinations. Yet, the overall scope cannot usually be determined until the entire examination is completed; and thus, logically, it should be placed at the end of the report.

Furthermore, the recommendations to be made cannot be determined until the audit is completed, and therefore they too should appear at the end. A recommendation quite often is considered the reverse of the objective. That is, instead of asking the question, "Did actions of individuals, based on the criteria, cause significant effects?" The auditor states the recommendation positively: "Let your actions follow the criteria and you will have good effects."

Two additional steps are needed, thus, to complete the logical organization under Pattern 1:

5. He makes recommendations, and
6. He states the scope of the audit.

This pattern of reporting, which follows the flow of information in much the same manner as it was developed in the audit, is shown in Figure 16.1 as Pattern 1.

Pattern 2: The Flow of Information into the Report in Order of Significance to the Reader

In writing to third parties, most auditors have found that the third parties are more interested in finding the results of the audit than they are in finding how the results were achieved. They want to know the results as soon as possible; and therefore the auditor, instead of writing the report in the order that the audit took place, brings out the results first, based on the objective, and then includes sufficient evidence to support the results.

In either pattern, since the third party is often not sufficiently acquainted with the activity or program, background information needs to be included in the report; it serves to introduce the subject of the audit to the third party. After this introduction, the auditor would present his conclusion on the audit objective. The conclusion is then followed with sufficient evidence to allow the reader to come to the same conclusion as the auditor.

Figure 16.1 illustrates this type of flow of information in order of importance to the reader, or third party; it appears in the figure as Pattern 2.

Either Pattern 1 or Pattern 2 will logically organize the contents of a performance audit report, but the policy of some organizations requires that one pattern or the other be followed. Since most audit agencies currently follow Pattern 2, we will use it as our basis for a more detailed study of the report. To follow this pattern, the auditor takes these steps:

1. He presents background information,
2. He gives the conclusion with sufficient evidence to support the conclusion on the audit objective,
3. He makes recommendations, and
4. He states the scope of examination.

If the organization being audited is given an opportunity to comment on the report before it is issued, and they present additional evidence that may have a bearing on the results of the report, an additional section—often called *agency comments*—may be added between the recommendations and the scope-of-examination sections.

Background Information

As we have emphasized, a third party seldom has sufficient knowledge concerning the activity or program being audited to permit the auditor to go directly to the conclusion in his report. The reader (third party) thus usually needs some introductory information about the organization, the activity, or program being audited—and in addition, may need to know something about the nature of the audit.

This background information should introduce the reader to the basic message the auditor is trying to communicate, in terms of the results achieved from the audit or the conclusion reached, along with sufficient evidence to support the conclusion.

Examination Phases

1. Background information and tests of management control provide information leading to objective for detailed examination.

2. Detailed examination objective—Did actions of individuals, based on criteria, cause significant effects?

3. Evidence—Sufficient relevant, material, and competent evidence on which the auditor can come to a conclusion on the objective. The rhetoric of presenting the evidence must be such that there is no question as to its acceptability as evidence:
   - Criteria—evidence that demonstrates that criteria are acceptable.
   - Causes—evidence that demonstrates that a person or persons at specific levels of responsibility caused actions that resulted in significant effects.
   - Effects—evidence that demonstrates resultant effects are significant.

4. Conclusion—conclusion on detailed examination objective. Based on the evidence, the conclusion would be:
   - That action or lack of action of individuals, based on acceptable criteria, caused significant effects—conclusion is ready to report.
   - That action or lack of action of individuals, based on acceptable criteria, did not cause significant effects—conclusion need not be reported.

5. Scope can be determined upon completion of audit.

Report Development Phase: Two Patterns

Pattern 1
1. Background information is the same as in the examination phases.
2. Audit objective. Same as detailed examination objective in examination phases.
3. Evidence. Same as for detailed examination. The auditor may characterize the evidence in the report in order to make it more interesting to the reader.
4. Conclusion. Same as conclusion in the detailed examination.
5. Recommendation. If action in future is carried out in accordance with appropriate plan (criteria), then the resultant effects should be good.
6. Scope of examination. Same as determined in examination phases.

Pattern 2
1. Background information. Same as in examination phases.
2. Conclusion. Same as conclusion in detailed examination.
3. Evidence on objective. Evidence on which above conclusion is reached. Same as evidence in detailed examination.
4. Recommendation. If action in future is carried out in accordance with appropriate plan (criteria) the resultant effects should be good.
5. Scope of examination. Same as determined in detailed examination.

——— Pattern 1 flow
– – – Pattern 2 flow

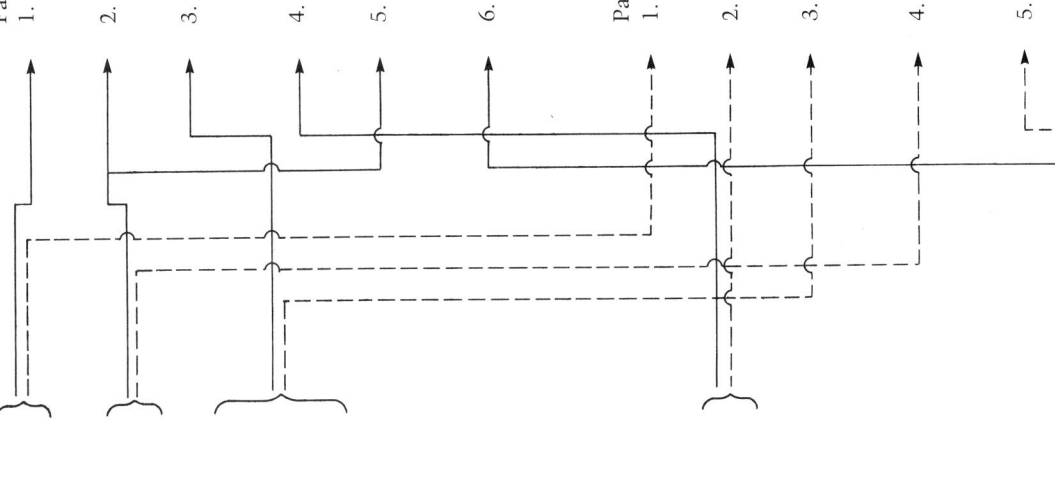

Figure 16.1 Flow of information from the examination phases to the report development phase, illustrating pattern 1 and pattern 2.

353

The auditor needs to provide answers to the following types of questions in order for the reader to be able to understand the basic message:

- When was the organization created?
- What is the purpose of the organization, activity, or program?
- What is the nature and size of the activity?
- Who has the responsibility for the organization, activity, or program?
- What is the relationship between the segment being reported on and the overall organization?
- What is the reason for making the audit?

With answers to such questions, the reader should have sufficient background information for the auditor to report the conclusion to his audit objective.

Reporting the Results of the Audit

The logic pertaining to reporting the results of the audit is much the same as the auditor uses in developing the audit itself. To start his audit, the auditor needed an audit objective, which he developed in terms of three elements—criteria, causes, and effects. He gathered evidence on each of these to come to a conclusion on that objective.

Before starting to write his report, then, the auditor should have done a good job of auditing. If he has used acceptable auditing standards, the report conclusion will follow the basic logic used to develop the audit. For example, his conclusion would be: *Based on the criteria, some individual or organization did not accept or follow the criteria, which thus resulted in a deficient effect or an ineffective result.*

All reportable results, then, will be comparable to the audit results, and will be stated in terms of criteria, causes, and effects. Thus, the auditor will state the criteria in terms of an appropriate standard for the activity or program, the causes in terms of what were the actual happenings at the time the audit took place as well as what should have been happening, and the significance of the results of not carrying out the appropriate standard.

Let us illustrate these statements for both an M-audit and a P-audit.

M-audit: Inadequate Control over State Revenues and Cash Receipts

Conclusion. A state auditor's report dealt with inadequate controls over the financial operations of recording cash receipts and using idle cash.

Criteria Used to Measure Efficiency. State regulations require collection banks to transfer moneys, including the balance of the prior period, to the treasurer's revolving fund on the 1st and 15th of each month. The regulations also require that the method of depositing and recording cash receipts accomplish full and prudent use of idle cash.

Conditions Found by the Auditor. During the state audit, the auditors found that collection banks retained state moneys for 3 to 5 weeks and longer. Since deposits in the collection banks were generally from local residents and corporations, it would take less than 5 days to clear items. It takes an additional week or more before moneys are transferred from the revolving account to the general account. Thus cash is inadequately used for 3 to 8 weeks or more. The auditors found 6 inactive bank accounts.

Also, they found excessive balances in the primary bank during the audit period.

Effects of the Conditions. The excessively long clearing period for funds remaining idle in collection banks and in the revolving fund results in loss of interest income.

Interest was also lost on balances in inactive bank accounts. The total balances in these accounts ranged from a high of $23 million in February and March 1971 to a low of about $5 million in September 1971. Two banks alone retained inactive balances totaling $8,294,420 as of March 15, 1972. There was no reason to maintain interest-free bank balances of this size.

In the primary bank, interest on balances exceeding $10 million invested in U.S. Treasury bills for 7 days at an annual 4-percent yield (not compounded) would have amounted to an additional $1,159,200 during the audit period.[3]

P-audit: Objectives of a Water Pollution Grant Not Realized

Environmental Protection Agency auditors audited a 3-year grant awarded to a state environmental service agency under the Federal Water Pollution Control Act (FWPCA) and reported that the state agency did not meet its objective. The grant required the development of a comprehensive pollution control and abatement plan for controlling water pollution in the state harbor.

Goal of the Program. Section 3 (c) of FWPCA established a program to make grants to a state or states not to exceed 50 percent of the administrative expenses of a planning agency for a period not to exceed 3 years, if such agency provides for adequate representation of appropriate state, interstate, local, or international interests in the basin, or portion thereof involved, and is capable of developing an effective, comprehensive water quality control and abatement plan for a basin.

The state agency was awarded a grant from January 1970 to January 1973 for developing a comprehensive pollution control and abatement plan to define the program to be used for controlling water pollution in the state harbor.

Condition Found by the Auditor. The review disclosed that the state agency had not accomplished grant objectives. A comprehensive pollution control and abatement plan for the state harbor had not yet been developed, although the 3-year grant period had expired.

Effect of Not Meeting the Goal. A total of $916,000 in federal funds has been paid to the state agency for developing a plan, yet none of the major objectives has been accomplished.

Cause that Contributed to Failure to Meet the Goal. In the auditors' opinion, the state agency's administration of the project was inadequate and it did not make a concerted effort to complete the project. Although the agency defined five subgoals to achieve the objectives of the grant, none of the goals were completed, nor had substantial progress been made in their completion.[4]

Notice that in the illustrations the word *condition* is used in lieu of the word *causes.* Condition is often used to mean the actual situation that caused

356 / *Reporting the Results of the Audit*

the effect. An excellent statement on developing a report, from the GAO Report Manual, is included for the reader as Appendix VII.

Recommendations

Recommendations are usually brief suggestions by the auditor as to what should be done to encourage the entity being audited to bring about improvements in performance. Recommendations are not requirements set by the auditor as to standards that should be followed by the entity. The management of the organization has the responsibility for requiring recommendations to be followed; all the auditor can do is suggest the basis for improvement.

If, during the audit, the auditor has determined the why of the causes, then the recommendation becomes rather easy to state, as the following two recommendations, adapted from the preceding two cases, will illustrate.

Auditor's Recommendations: M-audit

The auditors recommended collection banks be required to transfer moneys on Wednesday of each week directly to the general account. The amount transferred should equal the funds in the collection account as of Friday of the previous week. With each transfer, the bank should be required to report collected (cleared) and uncollected (uncleared) amounts to the treasurer and Department of Revenue and advise them of uncollected items that are over 15 days old.

The auditors recommended also that balances in inactive accounts be converted to time deposits, or invested in U.S. Government obligations, and the primary bank be responsible for insuring adequate clearing balances.

The auditors further recommended that the required daily balance in the primary bank be calculated on the basis of state cash flows and other pertinent data; excess funds should be invested for short-term periods.[5]

Auditor's Recommendations: P-audit

The appropriate program officials should take action to recover all federal funds paid to the state under the grant.[6]

Scope of the Audit

The first paragraph of the standard short-form report for financial-statement examinations is the scope of the audit paragraph. In performance audits, which are rather brief, a reference to the scope of the audit can be made in the section on background information.

Yet, in the more complex Pattern 2 audit report, where the results of the examination are its most important aspect, any reference to the scope of the audit in an early section may detract from the message being presented. Most often, then, the scope of audit is usually the last section in the report.

Peer Reviewing and Referencing

Before issuance of any audit report, it should be reviewed for accuracy and adequate support. Generally, draft reports should be reviewed and referenced by peers at the location where the report is prepared before submitting for supervisory review. During the referencing process, any statement, name, location, or computation should be referred back to the original working papers to assure that no error, either accidental or intentional, is made.

Relationship Between Work Done and the Report

The reader will notice the very close relationship between the information in the working-paper summaries—which summarized the work done in the preliminary phases and the detailed examination—and the report. If the work has been done properly, then the auditor should be able to develop his report without too much difficulty. He must, of course, polish his grammatical presentation, and to a certain extent, that comes from practice.

Before he has a final, well-polished report, he usually prepares a draft report, which he submits to the organization or organizations concerned with the audit, for their comments in order to be sure that the report is fair, complete, and objective.

Seldom is a draft report submitted to the third parties interested in the audit. Changes may be made as a result of the comments from the organizations concerned, and early submission to third parties may create more problems than it resolves. It is the final report that should be submitted to the third parties.

The Report Summary or Digest

Often, the auditor develops and presents a summary or digest of the report in order to make it easier for the reader to understand the entire report, especially if the report is fairly long. Furthermore, many readers of performance audit reports are so busy that they need a digest to help them determine whether they want to read the entire report for the information they need.

Chapters

A long report should generally be broken down into chapters. Although the chapter headings will depend upon the subject matter, they will usually follow the basic headings suggested earlier in this chapter. They include:

1. Background information (or introduction)
2. Conclusion, with evidence on the objective to support the conclusion. (The title of the chapter would relate to the subject matter on which the conclusion is drawn.)
3. Recommendations
4. The scope of the review

An excellent example of a longer report with a digest and chapters, as well as appendixes, appears in this book as Appendix VIII, the GAO report on the DOD's handling of overseas flights.

REVIEW QUESTIONS

1. Is there uniformity in reports for performance audits as there is for financial-statement examinations? (See pp. 349–50.)
2. The standard short-form report for financial-statement examinations has a scope paragraph and an opinion paragraph with a separate paragraph for

variations from the standard report. Are there scope sections and conclusion sections in a performance audit report? (See pp. 351–52, 357.)

3. The author discusses two patterns for logically organizing a report. Make a distinction between the two patterns and list the sections covered by each. (See pp. 351–52.)

4. What usually goes in the background section of the report for a performance audit? (See pp. 352, 354.)

5. Writing the conclusion section of the performance audit report, along with the evidence to support the conclusion, follows a logical organization. Is the pattern of the logic different in the report than in the audit? Discuss. (See pp. 354–56.)

6. What elements of an audit are included in the section of the report pertaining to the conclusion and the evidence to support the conclusion? (See pp. 354–56.)

7. A recommendation section is usually found in a performance audit report. Why? (See p. 356.)

8. Can a reference to the scope of the performance audit be made in the background section of the report? (See p. 356.)

9. Where is the scope section placed in a performance audit report? (See p. 356.)

Understanding the Principles of Reporting / 359

CASE 1

Organizing Two Audit Reports

AUDIT SCENARIO 1
The City Garage

Required

From Case 1 in Chapter 3, pages 46–48, complete the following:

1. In outline form, properly organize the report on the M-audit of the large city garage.
2. Include in the outline of the report chapter headings and good subheadings.

AUDIT SCENARIO 2
The Nursing Homes

Required

From Case 2 in Chapter 3, pages 49–59, complete the following:

1. In outline form, properly organize the report on the P-audit for nursing homes.
2. Include in the outline of the report chapter headings and good subheadings.

CASE 2

State Self-assessment Taxes: The Report

Required

1. Review your audit summary, which you prepared in Chapter 10, Case 1, page 211, Requirement 2, and from that summary prepare a draft report for the section concerning the conclusion and the evidence on the conclusion.
2. Write a recommendation section for your report.

Each auditor will write his summary and draft report a little differently from any other auditor. However, the basic conclusion in the summary for this case should have been stated somewhat as follows:

The state of Piedmont and the state Department of Revenue could have collected a minimum of an additional $20–25 million in sales and individual and business income taxes if they had developed and carried out the following programs:

1. Made it easier for taxpayers to file their income or sales tax returns by:
   a) Having recommended to the governor and state legislature to revise the state law so that the income tax forms and requirements would tie into the federal tax returns,
   b) Having properly communicated information on tax laws and requirements concerning:
      (1) resident taxpayers,
      (2) nonresident taxpayers,
      (3) individual taxpayers,
      (4) corporate taxpayers,
      (5) unincorporated business taxpayers, and
      (6) sales-tax taxpayers,
   c) Having adequately provided help to taxpayers in filing their returns by providing understandable instructions to forms and by providing taxpayer assistance.

360 / *Reporting the Results of the Audit*

2. Having made it difficult for taxpayers to not file and accurately assess their taxes either for sales or income taxes by:
   a) Having developed computerized lists of taxpayers who have had income taxes withheld and (1) relating to federal return when possible and (2) identifying and following up on nonfilers,
   b) Having developed a computerized list of all possible sales tax taxpayers and matching returns with the list,
   c) Having developed a list from sources both inside and outside the revenue department of possible business tax taxpayers who are not presently paying sales or income taxes,
   d) Having promptly determined whether a business is nonprofit and therefore exempt from income taxes but not sales taxes or promptly determined that the organization considered as nonprofit is really a profit business and subject to both sales and income taxes,
   e) Field-audited returns selected by computer from standards that determine possibility of maximum benefits for dollar invested,
   f) Desk-audited selected returns and notified taxpayers that their returns have been audited and accepted as correct, or audited and returned as incorrect, and
   g) Immediately started collection procedures when a tax becomes delinquent.

The auditor would also have sufficient evidence in his summary to support his conclusions as stated.

CASE 3

City Welfare: The Report

Required

1. From the material given on Case 2, Chapter 5, pages 93–95, and continued as Case 2 in Chapter 10, pages 215–20, prepare the background section of the report.
2. From the summary you were assigned to prepare in this case in Chapter 10, Requirement 2, develop the section of the report pertaining to the conclusion, with the evidence to support the conclusion.
3. Prepare a digest of the conclusion section.

CHAPTER 17

Writing a Clear, Concise, and Objective Report

After you have read this chapter, studied the review questions, and worked through the cases, you will have learned what makes a good report and how to write one. You will understand:

- The level of the reader of your audit reports.
- The style of writing.
- The level of importance of each item in a section.
- The right word.
- Sentences and paragraphs.
- Editing your writing.
- Editing the report.

When the auditor has made his audit, knows what he wants to write, has organized his report into major sections—such as the background section, the conclusion and evidence section, the recommendation section, and the scope section—then his next step is to organize each into a flow of written language that makes it clear, concise, objective, and easily readable by a third party.

What the auditor organizes in each of these sections are paragraphs, sentences, and words. First, however, he must have in mind such indicators as those listed above: the level of the reader, the style of writing needed, and the level of importance of particular items in each section.

Readers of Audit Reports

The auditor often does not stop to reason out the question: "To whom am I writing this report?" Especially, in large audit organizations, the auditor is more interested in having his supervisor approve the report than in considering that the report is to be read by someone outside the organization. Often this outside reader is not a technician and yet must read a technical report.

To communicate successfully the results of this audit, the auditor must first be sure who is considered the writer of the report: Is it the auditor himself? Or does the reader consider the writer to be the state auditor, the partner of the public accounting firm, or the city auditor, so that the auditor is serving as ghost writer? If he is writing for someone else, the auditor must remember to use the language of that writer.

Most readers of audit reports are fairly well educated in their professional or managerial positions; many are newspaper writers, business writers, or legislative or executive assistants. The best way to reach this conglomerate of readership for the auditor's report is to write as if college juniors—whose reading-level average is tenth grade—were going to read it. In other words, because he is writing about difficult or technical ideas, the auditor should write to the level of reading ability of the majority of educated Americans. He should not write at too low a level or at too high a level.

The writing, then, for this type of readership, should be a mixture of medium-length paragraphs, with a few short paragraphs interspersed for emphasis and diversity. The sentences should be the normal formations—noun-verb and noun-verb-noun with linking verbs and adverbs. Wherever possible, the active voice should be used. The writer should stay away from describing what he did and tell the results of his work. He should draw attention to the most important subjects through the use of subheadings, and yet not use so many that he loses track of the main proposition he is trying to communicate.

Style of Writing

We have mentioned the style of writing for financial-statement reports. There is just as much distinction in the style of writing for performance audit reports.

First, the performance audit report must be written in an objective style: The auditor should not exaggerate or overstate. The information presented as evidence should be genuine evidence, not incompetent or hearsay information. When possible, the auditor should write constructively, giving recognition to performance that is good as well as to performance that is bad; and when management has put forth efforts to correct the deficiencies in performance, the auditor should recognize these efforts.

Level of Importance of Each Item in the Section

Much as the auditor recognizes the importance of sections by their location in the report, so he should also recognize the importance of particular items in each section by their locations in the section. For example, the auditor considers many types of causes in his report; yet some are more important than others. The most important of the causes should be placed first in the section, with the others following in order of importance. Effects, also as an example, are of several levels of importance. The actual dollar loss, obviously, is much more important in terms of significance than possible dollar loss.

The Right Word

Words are the foundation for all writing. The choice of the right word may make the difference between being understood and not being understood. For example, the auditor may be writing about the actions of the head of the accounting department of a university. If he calls the head "a university employee," the title may be correct but too abstract; the more concrete the word can become, the easier it is for a person to understand what is meant.

Many audits of performance are technical, and converting technical terms to normal usage is often not easy. For example, a recent audit report used the title "A Narrowband Secure Voice Technique." Without a layman's definition of this term, at least as a subtitle, few individuals would understand the subject matter.

Some writers use nouns formed from verbs instead of using the verb form itself. For example, instead of saying, "The utilization rate is low," it would probably be better to say simply, "The room is used very little." Or why say "give encouragement to" instead of "encourage"?

Many auditors often use trite expressions without thinking. For example, the expression "as evidenced by" often creeps into an audit report. Other overused expressions are: "with respect to," "the extent to which," and "at the present time." Often these expressions are better said with a substitute: "about" in place of "with respect to," and "now" in place of "at the present time."

Jargon is often considered as unintelligible language because the person using it has his own meaning for the word—a meaning no one else will understand except a few persons in his own field. For example, "inquired into" has many meanings. It may mean studied, examined, asked about, or some other similar term. Why should the auditor not use the term that specifically states his meaning? Here is another phrase often seen in the recommendation section of a report: "It is recommended that consideration be given." Why not just say "We recommend"? Some of the older jargon is being replaced gradually with more exact, more intelligent words. For example, many older letters had expressions such as "Pursuant to our agreement." Now we more often see in such a letter, "As we agreed."

Many more trite and jargon expressions can be found in books about modern writing some of which are listed in the bibliography under the heading "Audit Report Writing."

Sentences and Paragraphs

A recent monograph on writing audit reports, in commenting on paragraphs, says:

> The best and quickest way for the writer to check each paragraph is to look for: coherence, logic, unity, and emphasis.
>
> *Coherence*—Do all sentences move smoothly from one to another? Are there smooth transitions from paragraph to paragraph?
>
> *Logic*—Do ideas follow in orderly sequence?
>
> *Unity*—Does each sentence contribute solely to the main idea in that paragraph?
>
> *Emphasis*—Is the main point of the paragraph clear? Is there a stated (or implied) topic sentence about which all the other sentences revolve? Does that point stick with the reader as he moves to the next paragraph?[1]

These are excellent points to consider in writing any paragraph, long or short, composed of simple sentences or complex ones.

As the points above make clear, paragraphs evolve through sentence building. There are simple sentences, compound sentences, complex sentences, and compound-complex sentences. The good writer uses each type for the building blocks of his paragraphs.

As in the paragraph, the location of the key idea is important in the sentence. In a short sentence the key idea should be at the beginning; in long complex, compound, and compound-complex sentences it is usually at the end and is normally the subject of the sentence.

A first important rule in writing good sentences and clear paragraphs is to use the active voice rather than the passive voice. The main idea then stands out immediately. If the subject is acted upon, rather than doing the acting, as is true of the passive voice, it is often difficult to determine who the subject is. For example, if we say: "No contract had been negotiated" (passive), the subject is left out completely. It is much clearer to state, "Neither the state insurance agency nor the state personnel department had negotiated a contract for health insurance with an insurance carrier in the state" (active).

Long sentences using the passive voice often cause the reader to lose his way. It is sometimes hard to distinguish who is receiving or giving the action, especially when the subject is far removed from the verb. This type of sentence can be improved (1) by using the active in place of the passive voice, (2) by moving the subject closer to the verb, and (3) by placing them both either at the front of the sentence or at the end of the sentence.

The writer can also make some sentences clearer by shortening them, perhaps by breaking down one sentence into two. Very short sentences often give emphasis; but if used too often, they can become boring. A good rule-of-thumb is to think of the best average word length for most sentences as about twenty words.

One common error of most unpracticed writers is to add one idea on top of the other without relating the various ideas. Doing this within the framework of one sentence, the writer certainly distracts the reader from the main point. Similarly, long strings of prepositional phrases are distracting. Prepositions help to distinguish important ideas from less important ideas, but when the writer hooks one prepositional phrase on top of another, he may bury his main idea.

As a class, auditors are often rather conservative, and this may be one reason that in their writing they often state the same point over and over—as if repetition will convince the reader. This redundancy, including the words it adds, often does the opposite of convince: it causes the reader to want to stop reading. A cure for wordiness of any type is to eliminate any word that does not name, show action, modify, or connect.

Other qualities of good writing that you, as the writer of the report, should always consider are:

- Do your subject and verb always agree?
- Do your sentences have variety and length, with no extremely long sentences?
- Are your paragraphs short enough so that the reader can grasp the main idea in each paragraph?
- Can the person or thing to which the pronoun refers be determined?
- Is your grammatical construction parallel where needed?
- Do you use punctuation properly?
- Do you use nouns to give action when they cannot? For example, do you say "The book discussed the subject." Can a book discuss, or is it the author who does the discussing?
- Do you have too many "it is" and "there are" sentences?
- Do you have too many repetitious words and phrases?
- Do you use abstract words instead of concrete words?
- Are your sentences too simplistic?
- Do you have faulty emphasis by misplacement of words in the sentence?

Edit the Report

Few auditors are able to write a finished report without considerable rewriting and editing. As one authority states:

> Clear writing is no accident. A report is made easy to read and understand by analyzing the sense and substance of *what* is said and *how* it is said, and then rewriting the message in standard English.[2]

So in order for you to have a well-written report that is excellently organized, concise, complete, clear, and accepted by the reader as a report he will read, you must take the time and effort to do a good job of rewriting and editing. Make sure in your editing and rewriting that:

- Your overall report is logically organized.
- Your chapter or section headings are properly stated.
- Your style of writing is such that it will be accepted by your intended audience.
- Each of your paragraphs contains only one idea; that idea is clearly understood; the idea from one paragraph flows smoothly to the idea in the next in logical order; your paragraphs vary in length, with no paragraph being so long or disconnected that the idea in it cannot be grasped by the reader; and each sentence in each paragraph contributes to the main idea in that paragraph.
- Your sentences are usually stated in the active voice; they use action verbs close enough to the subject to tell what is being acted upon; they do not have too many "it is" and "there are" constructions; they do not have dangling phrases or overly modified words; they have parallel thoughts in parallel grammatical form; they are not so long and involved as to be incomprehensible, but not too short as to be monotonous; and the subject and verb agree.
- Your words are the right words—concrete, not abstract; professional, not jargon or idioms; exact enough, not redundant words or expressions; English, not Latinized versions of English, words; verbs as action verbs, not as weak nouns, and common terms, not technical terms.
- Your punctuation is appropriate.

In conclusion, the reader's attention is invited to Appendix IX, which is made up of further selected GAO policies that set forth good standards for both content and quality in a report.

REVIEW QUESTIONS

1. This chapter contains five or more major topics concerning writing effective audit reports. Can you list them? (See p. 361.)

2. How does one determine the order of importance of items in a section of a performance audit report? (See p. 362.)

3. What do you consider the meaning of "style of writing?" (See p. 362.)

4. Illustrate how an auditor can make a report meaning clearer by using concrete instead of abstract words. (See pp. 362–63.)

5. Check the next paragraph you write to see if you have words in it that are verb forms used as nouns. See if you can convert such nouns back to verbs. Some illustrations could be: *consider* for consideration of, *enlarge* for maximization, and *limited* for limitation.

6. A paragraph can be checked quickly by looking for four characteristics. Name and describe each. (See pp. 363–64.)

7. What is one of the first rules of good writing? Give an illustration of how you can apply this rule to your writing. (See p. 363.)

8. The average number of words in a sentence written to the readers of an audit report is about twenty. Average the number of words in your next piece of writing and compare this with twenty.

9. The author lists twelve other qualities of good writing. What would you consider the one quality you most need to improve? (See p. 364.)

10. Is there another quality of good writing that you might consider just as important as those listed in the text? (See pp. 364–65.)

CASE 1

The Valley City Jails: The Report

This case is a continuation of the presentations in chapters 6 and 11, pp. 111–16 and 249–53.

Required

1. Review the conclusion, the audit evidence, and the audit objective given in Chapter 11 for this case and write a findings section of a report.
2. From the findings section, write a digest of the findings that could be included in the final report.
3. Write a conclusion and recommendations section of the report.
4. Do you believe that the precinct captains would agree with your conclusions concerning the local jails? Suppose two of the five precinct captains did not believe that inmate assistance should be provided at all by outside help. What evidence do you have in your working papers to rebut this belief? Write the agency comments section of the report.
5. In each of the pieces of written work you do for this case, attempt to follow the standards for good writing set forth in this chapter, using some of the specific techniques illustrated.

A report on an audit of the complexity of this one would be quite voluminous. The auditor would have to present evidence to support his conclusions as well as provide sufficient information of a background nature to help the reader understand the conclusions and recommendations.

In your written responses to the above requirements, you may answer in summary form rather than in great detail.

CASE 2

The Mass-transit Grant: The Report

This case is a continuation of the presentations in chapters 6 and 11, pp. 117–19 and 253–59.

Required

1. Review the conclusion, the audit evidence, and the audit objective given in Chapter 11 for this case and write a findings section of the report.
2. From the findings section, write a digest of the findings that could be included in the final report.
3. Write a conclusion and recommendations section of the report.
4. Prepare a cover for the report.

5. In each of the pieces of written work you do for this case, attempt to follow the standards for good writing set forth in this chapter, using some of the specific techniques illustrated.

You should also summarize your responses to the above written requirements rather than try to write them in great detail.

CASE 3

Indian Education: A Reaudit[2]

Required

1. Would a new audit objective have to be developed in order to make this reaudit?
2. What evidence would have to be gathered, summarized, and analyzed in order to come to a conclusion that the Bureau of Indian Affairs had not accomplished the objective as set in prior years?
3. Would your organize your working papers differently than you did for the first examination?
4. What major differences would you make in your report?
5. Considering the material set forth in this chapter, what comments, favorable or unfavorable, would you offer on the writing in the digest of this reaudit?

One of the reasons for a performance audit is to call to the attention of management whether or not a program is being carried out effectively. It is not uncommon, however, for management to pay very little attention to the audit report. The auditor can often reinforce his audit conclusions and recommendations by reauditing the activity or program. This case is based on the digest of a reaudit of the Indian Education Program, the audit we considered as an illustration in the text of chapters 6 and 11. Read the digest carefully in order to perform the required work. The interested reader may also wish to refer to the report itself, which appears in this book as Appendix X.

REPORT OF THE COMPTROLLER GENERAL OF THE UNITED STATES	CONCERNED EFFORT NEEDED TO IMPROVE INDIAN EDUCATION Bureau of Indian Affairs Department of the Interior

DIGEST

In April 1972 GAO told the Congress that the educational programs in schools operated by the Bureau of Indian Affairs needed to be improved. In its report GAO recommended that the Department of the Interior require the Commissioner of Indian Affairs to:

—Clearly apprise all operating levels of its goal of reaching a level of academic achievement for Indian students equal to the national average and the date when this was to be accomplished.

—Identify and assign priorities for dealing with all critical factors that would impede progress toward the goal.

—Develop a comprehensive education program designed to overcome obstacles that would impede progress toward the goal but flexible enough to meet the needs of students in all Bureau schools.

Interior stated in 1972 that GAO's conclusions and recommendations would constructively support the Bureau's efforts to improve its education program. However, during a current review GAO noted that the problems identified in 1972 still existed and the Bureau had not taken appropriate action to implement GAO's recommendations.

There was little evidence that the Bureau had made progress since 1972 toward improving educational achievement of Indian children. For example, the Bureau had not communicated its educational goal to its area offices and schools nor designed and implemented a specific plan for raising Indian students' academic achievement levels. The Bureau did not update the goals and objectives published in its manual in 1953 and failed to define what constitutes adequate Indian education for the 1970s.

CED-77-24

Certain factors, such as the lack of adequate special education programs for students with a higher-than-average incidence of hearing loss and other problems, impede progress in academic achievement. The Bureau did not design specific programs or provide area offices or schools with instructions for dealing with such factors.

GAO's 1972 report also recommended that the Bureau improve its management information system to provide information on academic aptitude and achievement levels of students and on program-oriented financial management reports. The Bureau had made some changes in its management information system, but it still does not provide education program managers with information they need.

Bureau officials said the 1972 recommendations had not been implemented because the Bureau's Office of Indian Education Programs had not provided adequate program direction. The officials attributed this to the constant turnover in the Director's position and to the Bureau's organizational structure which prevented the Director from dealing directly with area offices and schools.

RECOMMENDATIONS TO THE
SECRETARY OF THE INTERIOR

GAO repeats the substance of its prior recommendations that the Secretary of the Interior require the Commissioner of Indian Affairs to:

—Determine the educational needs of Indian students, so appropriate programs can be designed to meet the needs.

—Establish realistic goals and objectives for meeting such needs and communicate the goals and objectives to all operating levels in the Bureau.

—Develop a comprehensive educational program which includes specific policies and procedures for dealing with problems which impede progress in meeting established goals and objectives.

—Monitor and evaluate implementation of established educational goals and programs at all operating levels of the agency.

—Develop a management information system that will provide:

1. Meaningful and comprehensive information on the academic aptitude and achievement levels of students in the Bureau's school system.

2. Program-oriented financial management reports to meet the management needs of Bureau education program officials.

MATTERS FOR ATTENTION
BY THE CONGRESS

Since the Bureau has made no major progress over the last several years in implementing policies, procedures, and programs to insure that the educational needs of Indian students are met, the congressional committees should more intensively monitor the Bureau and, if adequate progress is not made, explore other alternatives, such as transferring responsibilities for administering Indian education programs to another government agency.

AGENCY COMMENTS

The Department of the Interior agreed with GAO's findings, conclusions, and recommendations with minor exceptions. The Department, in pointing out some new "program direction" being considered by the Bureau, stated that the role of the Bureau "in the future, as determined by the Congress and Indian communities of the country, is to support and strengthen Indian self-determination." The Department stated that "self-determination in education means that tribes should decide education issues and programs." According to the Department, the Bureau's role will be that of providing technical services, the full meaning of which is not, at this point, clearly known.

As more tribes move to determine their own educational issues and programs under self-determination agreements, the Bureau must make sure that (1) the educational needs of Indian students are clearly identified and (2) realistic goals, objectives, and programs are established which will provide educational opportunities that enable Indians to compete in the careers of their choice. Under self-determination the Bureau's monitoring and evaluating activities should be set as one of its top priorities.

APPENDIX I

GAO Standards for Audit of Governmental Organizations, Programs, Activities, and Functions

General Standards

1. The full scope of an audit of a governmental program, function, activity, or organization should encompass:
    a. An examiniation of financial transactions, accounts, and reports, including an evaluation of compliance with applicable laws and regulations.
    b. A review of efficiency and economy in the use of resources.
    c. A review to determine whether desired results are effectively achieved.

    In determining the scope for a particular audit, responsible officials should give consideration to the needs of the potential users of the results of that audit.
2. The auditors assigned to perform the audit must collectively possess adequate professional proficiency for the tasks required.
3. In all matters relating to the audit work, the audit organization and the individual auditors shall maintain an independent attitude.
4. Due professional care is to be used in conducting the audit and in preparing related reports.

Examination and Evaluation Standards

1. Work is to be adequately planned.
2. Assistants are to be properly supervised.
3. A review is to be made of compliance with legal and regulatory requirements.
4. An evaluation is to be made of the system of internal control to assess the extent it can be relied upon to ensure accurate information, to ensure compliance with laws and regulations, and to provide for efficient and effective operations.
5. Sufficient, competent, and relevant evidence is to be obtained to afford a reasonable basis for the auditor's opinions, judgments, conclusions, and recommendations.

Source: United States General Accounting Office, the Comptroller General of the United States, *Standards for Audit of Governmental Organizations, Programs, Activities, and Functions* (Washington, D.C.: U.S. Government Printing Office, 1974), pp. 6–9.

Reporting Standards

1. Written audit reports are to be submitted to the appropriate officials of the organizations requiring or arranging for the audits. Copies of the reports should be sent to other officials who may be responsible for taking action on audit findings and recommendations and to others responsible or authorized to receive such reports. Unless restricted by law or regulation, copies should also be made available for public inspection.
2. Reports are to be issued on or before the dates specified by law, regulation, or other arrangement and, in any event, as promptly as possible so as to make the information available for timely use by management and by legislative officials.
3. Each report shall:
    a. Be as concise as possible but, at the same time, clear and complete enough to be understood by the users.
    b. Present factual matter accurately, completely, and fairly.
    c. Present findings and conclusions objectively and in language as clear and simple as the subject matter permits.
    d. Include only factual information, findings, and conclusions that are adequately supported by enough evidence in the auditor's working papers to demonstrate or prove, when called upon, the bases for the matters reported and their correctness and reasonableness. Detailed supporting information should be included in the report to the extent necessary to make a convincing presentation.
    e. Include, when possible, the auditor's recommendations for actions to effect improvements in problem areas noted in his audit and to otherwise make improvements in operations. Information on underlying causes of problems reported should be included to assist in implementing or devising corrective actions.
    f. Place primary emphasis on improvement rather than on criticism of the past; critical comments should be presented in balanced perspective, recognizing any unusual

difficulties or circumstances faced by the operating officials concerned.
g. Identify and explain issues and questions needing further study and consideration by the auditor or others.
h. Include recognition of noteworthy accomplishments, particularly when management improvements in one program or activity may be applicable elsewhere.
i. Include recognition of the views of responsible officials of the organization, program, function, or activity audited on the auditor's findings, conclusions, and recommendations. Except where the possibility of fraud or other compelling reason may require different treatment, the auditor's tentative findings and conclusions should be reviewed with such officials. When possible, without undue delay, their views should be obtained in writing and objectively considered and presented in preparing the final report.
j. Clearly explain the scope and objectives of the audit.
k. State whether any significant pertinent information has been omitted because it is deemed privileged or confidential. The nature of such information should be described, and the law or other basis under which it is withheld should be stated.

4. Each audit report containing financial reports shall:
   a. Contain an expression of the auditor's opinion as to whether the information in the financial reports is presented fairly in accordance with generally accepted accounting principles (or with other specified accounting principles applicable to the organization, program, function, or activity audited), applied on a basis consistent with that of the preceding reporting period. If the auditor cannot express an opinion, the reasons therefore should be stated in the audit report.
   b. Contain appropriate supplementary explanatory information about the contents of the financial reports as may be necessary for full and informative disclosure about the financial operations of the organization, program, function, or activity audited. Violations of legal or other regulatory requirements, including instances of noncompliance, and material changes in accounting policies and procedures, along with their effect on the financial reports, shall be explained in the audit report.

APPENDIX II

Checklist Prepared by the American Institute of Certified Public Accountants

Pre-Engagement Checklist

The following checklist for expanded-scope audits involving an evaluation of economy, efficiency, or program results has been prepared to (1) assist CPAs in understanding the nature of each potential engagement, (2) guide those who issue RFPs in providing the desired information, and (3) aid the CPA in structuring a proposal and work program.

The checklist contains a series of questions which fall into four broad categories—

- *Engagement Environment.* The professional relationship between the CPA and the government entity to be evaluated.
- *Economy and Efficiency.* Elements of the engagement that will affect the CPA's proposal.
- *Program Results.* Elements of the engagement that will affect the CPA's proposal.
- *Professional Proficiency.* The CPA's qualifications to undertake a specific engagement.

Pre-Engagement Checklist

Engagement Environment

1. Who is requesting the evaluation?
2. What motivated the request?
3. Will the requester or recipient be able to implement the report recommendations?
4. Are engagement objectives and scope of work well defined and attainable?
5. Does the scope entail a constructive piece of work?
6. Is sufficient time alloted for the CPA to complete the engagement?
7. Will the applicable laws and regulations be specified in the engagement agreement?
8. Will the criteria for selecting an independent firm be based on competence as well as on price?

Economy and Efficiency

1. Is there agreement between the CPA and requester on which areas are to be reviewed (e.g., programs, departments, activities, or projects)?
2. Is there a clear understanding of which functional areas are to be reviewed (e.g., personnel utilization, data processing, procurement, financial management, warehousing, inventory management, and so forth)?
3. Have there been prior reviews (internal or external) of the same area?
4. Were any actions taken as a result of prior reviews?
5. Will prior reviews be made available to the CPA?
6. Has the requester specified any existing data and reports which may be accepted as reliable without further verification?
7. To what extent does the work to be studied lend itself to measurement?
8. Have criteria for measuring economy and efficiency been established (e.g., does the entity have existing productivity standards)?
9. Have the data related to the established criteria been accumulated?
10. Will the data be available to the CPA?
11. Is routine reporting of productivity a current or feasible practice?
12. To what extent are cost data available?

Program Results

1. Are there well-defined program objectives?
2. Are there reasonable well-defined timetables for achieving program objectives?
3. Have criteria been established for evaluating program results?
4. Are the criteria quantifiable, or at least measurable, and to what extent can the results be measured objectively?
5. Have the data related to the established criteria been accumulated?
6. Will the data be made available to the CPA?
7. Has management prepared a current assessment of the program's results?

Source: American Institute of Certified Public Accountants, *Management Advisory Services, Guideline Series Number 6. Guidelines for C.P.A. Participation in Government Audit Engagements to Evaluate Economy, Efficiency, and Program Results.* (New York: American Institute of Certified Public Accountants, 1977), pp. 16–18. Copyright © by the American Institute of Certified Public Accountants.

8. Have there been any previous external evaluations of the program?
9. Were any actions taken as a result of previous evaluations?
10. Will previous evaluations be made available to the CPA?

Professional Proficiency

1. Is the CPA familiar with the government environment (e.g., source of funding, related agencies, potential subsequent reviews, and so forth)?
2. Does the CPA understand the scope of the engagement?
3. Does the CPA possess or have access to technical skills required to review and evaluate functional areas involved?
4. Does the CPA understand the specific government program and have access to the specific skills needed to evaluate the program results?

APPENDIX III

The Proposal and Engagement Letter

One of the questions most frequently asked of the MAS division concerns the form and content of an MAS proposal or engagement letter. Little has been published on this. John R. Mitchell, director of the AICPA's MAS division, discusses his own views on the subject. They are supplemented by a brief bibliography.

An example of a proposal letter is shown in Figure A.1. Upon acceptance by the client it becomes an engagement letter. The substantive content and wording of this hypothetical proposal are relatively unimportant; the form and structure are essential. The comments which follow are related to the eight sections of a proposal, seven of which are illustrated in the exhibit.

1 Introduction

The introduction sets the tone for the entire letter. It should be formal and forthright. Note all the specifics included in the opening paragraph—the date of the visit, the subject of the study and the names of all executive and supervisory personnel encountered during the preliminary survey.

In some instances a less formal style might appear to have certain advantages. However, despite the friendship and mutual respect which you may share with your client, remember that you are asking him to spend a substantial sum for what is essentially an intangible service. This is a business proposition and it should be handled in a businesslike manner. While drafting your proposal, assume that your client will show it to someone you have never met, to ask his opinion. This will prompt you to include all the pertinent facts and to avoid the common mistake of assuming that when your client is actually making his decision he will remember all the things you told him several days earlier.

2 Basic Objectives

The statement of the engagement's basic objectives is probably the most critical section of your proposal. When you lose your reader here, you never get him back.

The objectives should be stated simply and concisely, in terms the client will immediately recognize. This section should present *his* definition of the problem or opportunity, rather than yours. (If yours happens to differ from his, you should cover this elsewhere—under either "Approach" or "Benefits.")

Concentrate here on major, fundamental objectives and ignore the less important by-products, which can be mentioned later. If this section occupies more than half a typewritten page, go back and take out the excess words. If after rewriting it is still more than half a page, go back again and take out the less important thoughts.

Wherever possible, use the client's own terminology. For example, if (as in this case) the client's personnel always refer to "invoicing" rather than "billing" you should follow this lead, regardless of your personal preferences.

3 Approach

This should be a clear, tightly organized and specific statement of your work plan. It should omit nonessential details and stress those activities which are important to the client.

Clarity and simplicity are essential—if the client cannot readily understand your proposal, he will wonder how he can ever use your recommendations.

Use of numbered and underscored steps is desirable. This emphasizes the key points, assists the reader in reviewing the proposal and stresses your program's orderly and methodical character.

4 Benefits of Proposed Program

After reading the caption, your client will expect this section to emphasize the reasons why he should approve the proposal. Do not disappoint him. Unless you state the anticipated benefits clearly and confidently, he will infer that there are doubts in your own mind, that you may not really want the assignment or that you are subtly preparing him for a marginally successful outcome. Nevertheless, it is important that you maintain your integrity, your dignity and your image as an organized and systematic professional.

Source: John R. Mitchell, *"The MAS Proposal Letter,"* The *Journal of Accountancy,* June 1975, pp. 38–45. Copyright © 1975 by the American Institute of Certified Public Accountants, Inc.

5 Staffing

This section usually presents concise and fairly formal resumes of the key personnel who will be involved. Alternatively, the resumes can be appended to the proposal letter. In some cases, particularly on large engagements or when there will be a time lag between proposal and acceptance, it is not practical to identify staff members by name. Then the resume of the person who will be in charge should be included with an illustrative description of the types of personnel who will assist him.

6 Professional Time and Fees

Although the caption does not directly imply it, this section usually contains your proposed time schedule. (If the timing is unusually critical or complex, use a separate section.)

Your proposed fee, or the basis on which it will be calculated, should be stated as specifically as possible. Special consideration should be given to whether you should quote a flat fee, or a range (as illustrated here). Where the amount of the fee is considered an important factor, a flat fee may be preferable, since with ranges clients will often, for simplicity, use just the ceiling amount, especially for comparative purposes. A range, however, is usually more realistic, and often seems more appropriate with a client with whom you have a long standing relationship of mutual confidence.

6a Professional Qualifications

Sometimes there is a separate section (not illustrated here) in which the firm presents its unique qualifications for this engagement. This is particularly helpful, for example, when a firm has special qualifications in a certain industry. It is also frequently used in proposals to government agencies.

If references are provided, they should be here. Typical wording would be:

"Should you wish to check further into our firm's professional competence, and our reputation for accomplishing the objectives of an engagement such as this, I suggest that you contact the following: . . . ." This would be followed by a list of from three to five prior MAS clients. Each client's full name, address and phone number would appear, along with the name and title of the person to contact. In some cases it may be helpful to include a brief description of the work done. When expertise in a particular industry is claimed, trade association references may also be included. Of course, all references should be authorized.

7 Conclusion

When you know the client well, it is often good practice to make the conclusion warmer and more personal than the other sections. The most important point, however, is that it should end in a positive vein, conveying your confidence and your enthusiasm for performing the engagement.

Note that no space is provided for an "acceptance" signature. Demanding such a signature could convey the impression that you lack confidence in the client's reliability. If a proper relationship is established, an acceptance signature should usually be unnecessary.

Selected Bibliography

Accountants Letter Book. Englewood Cliffs: Prentice Hall, 1966.

Documentation Guides for Administration of Management Advisory Services Engagements. New York: AICPA Committee on Management Services, 1971.

Guidelines for Administration of the Management Advisory Services Practice. New York: AICPA Committee on Management Services, 1968.

Management of an Accounting Practice Handbook. New York: AICPA Management of an Accounting Practice Committee, 1975.

Professional Practices in Management Consulting (rev ed). New York: Association of Consulting Management Engineers, 1966.

Sample Engagement Letters for an Accounting Practice. New York: AICPA, 1974, pp. 12–41, 123 et seq.

Suggestions for Preparing Proposals. New York: Association of Consulting Management Engineers, 1954.

LASALLE AND TUCKER
Independent Public Accountants
876 5th Street
Detroit, Michigan 9998

July 10, 19XX

Mr. William Packard
President
The Martin Corporation
123 4th Street
Detroit, Michigan 99999

Dear Bill:

1 Introduction

I would like to express my thanks to you for inviting me to review your order entry and invoicing operations, and for the courtesy and assistance extended to me during my visit on Tuesday, July 7. Your associates, James P. DeSoto and Frances A. Crosley, were most helpful, and I extend my thanks also to them.

In accordance with your request, we are submitting this letter of proposal based on our discussions, my brief reconnaissance of your operations and my review of the materials which you furnished to me.

2 Basic objectives

It is our understanding that you are contemplating the use of management consulting services in connection with your order entry and invoicing operations in order to accomplish the following principal objectives:

1. Update and simplify the order fulfillment procedures in order to make more effective use of existing personnel and equipment;
2. Install simple but effective supervisory controls on paper flow, scheduling, quality and productivity;
3. Improve the general caliber of customer service; and
4. Reduce the overall processing cost.

3 Approach

We are convinced that substantial and immediate improvements in customer service, supervisory controls and operating costs could be obtained if your present routines were streamlined. We therefore propose to undertake the following five phase program.

1. Conduct a _general performance analysis_ of each step in your order processing routines, and make detailed studies of those operations which appear substandard from the standpoints of cost and time required. This review would start with the receipt of orders in your incoming mail department, and cover all steps through invoice preparation, including cashiering, order editing and pricing, credit approval, typing and proofing.

Special attention will be given to the following areas: (a) departmental organization and work assignments; (b) supervisory and production control mechanisms; (c) expediting new customer order entry; (d) filing and retrieval concepts and techniques; and (e) management information requirements.

Figure A.1 Example of a proposal letter

Mr. Packard   -2-   July 10, 19XX

    2. <u>Develop an improved system</u> for the clerical fulfillment functions which would provide fundamental improvements over present practices.

    In developing new procedures and controls, consideration would be given to all applicable office engineering techniques, including: (a) total activity organization; (b) functional work assignments; (c) batching and work flow controls with exception techniques; (d) and retrieval equipment; (f) improved forms design; and (g) work simplification.

    The extent to which we would go into each facet of your operations would be dependent on the problems found in our preliminary analysis. Where conditions appear favorable we would devote our major efforts to the development of improvement programs in the areas in which our assistance would make the greatest long-term contribution.

    3. <u>Prepare a concrete report of our recommendations</u>. The substance of our findings and recommendations will be presented in very specific terms in outline form, and we would be prepared to discuss our report thoroughly with you and your associates upon its presentation. The report will include all necessary organization and flow-charts; equipment specifications; procedural outlines; illustrations of the recommended controls and reports; and a plan of action including timetable and responsibility assignments.

    4. <u>Monitor the implementation</u> of the recommended improvements. We would train your supervisors in the use and intent of all new procedures and techniques, and we would plan and assist in the re-orientation and training of operating personnel. We would assist in detailing the required conversion and operating procedures to assure that the full potential of the fundamental improvements is realized. We would participate in or review all major operating decisions during the conversion period, and we would monitor time schedule and budgetary compliance.

    5. <u>Follow up the installation</u> to assure that it is operating effectively and producing the anticipated service and control improvements and cost benefits. Our service includes a minimum of three procedural audits, professional time at our expense, in the year following completion of the installation to assure that the new procedures are operating effectively and producing the intended benefits.

<u>Benefits of proposed program</u>

    On the basis of my reconnaissance of your operation, and of the results which we have attained in other order processing engagements, we anticipate that the proposed program will produce the following principal benefits:

    1. <u>Cost reduction</u>. We are convinced that the cost of the proposed program will be offset by a substantial margin

Mr. Packard   -3-   July 10, 19XX

by the direct savings which should result in the first year, and that these savings will continue thereafter.

2. <u>Service improvement</u>. We believe that the service which you provide to your customers will be significantly improved in terms both of clerical accuracy and of your order fulfillment time cycle.

3. <u>Improved control</u>. A system of controls on quality, timeliness, security and productivity will enable the overall management of your order processing operations to be upgraded, and will provide the basis for intelligent evaluation of any further system improvements such as, ultimately, computerization.

<u>Staffing</u>

This assignment would be conducted under my personal supervision, and I would participate directly in all phases of it. Assuming that we have your authorization to proceed by August 1, I would be assisted by my associate, Richard Maxwell, who would conduct most of the field work.

As you know, Bill, I have been providing accounting and related services to your firm for over 12 years, and I feel that I am quite familiar with your objectives, your systems and your personnel. I am a certified public accountant, and a graduate of Hudson College with an MBA degree from Stanley University. Over the years I have helped dozens of clients to improve and upgrade their order processing and accounting systems. I have served on the State CPA Society's Management Advisory Services Committee, and on two occasions the Society has called on me to conduct management services training courses for its members.

Mr. Maxwell has for almost two years been a senior member of our professional staff, during which time he has helped a number of our clients to improve customer service, develop more meaningful management information, and reduce clerical costs. He has a BBA degree from Aston College, and has already taken and passed three of the four parts of the CPA exam. Before joining our staff he was a systems and methods analyst in the headquarters offices of Cord Products, Inc.

<u>Professional time and fees</u>

Our present schedule would permit us to begin this engagement on Monday, August 18, and we would expect to complete Phases 1, 2 and 3, through delivery of the report and recommendations, within three months of the day we start. It is too early now to estimate the time and resources which will be required for the implementation and follow-up services outlined under Phases 4 and 5; we shall be pleased to submit a specific proposal for these at a later date.

Our fees are based on actual hours devoted to a project.

Mr. Packard   -4-   July 10, 19XX

6 | I estimate that the total fee for Phases 1, 2 and 3 would be between $9,000 and $12,000; and under no circumstances would it exceed the latter amount. Out of pocket expenses, including report preparation and any travel outside the city, are billed additionally, at cost. Fees and expenses are billed and payable monthly.

7
Conclusion

   Bill, the problems posed by this assignment are very familiar ones to me and to members of our staff. Our firm is recognized throughout the state for its technical competence in management advisory services such as those we propose here, and for the professionalism with which we apply that competence. You can be confident that, in view of our long-standing and continuing accounting relationship, we shall do everything necessary to assure the development of a smooth, efficient and well-controlled order processing system which will enhance your operating effectiveness and your profitability for years to come.
   We therefore greatly appreciate the opportunity to submit this proposal. It would be a pleasure and an honor to work with you, Jim De Soto and Fran Crosley on an assignment of such fundamental importance to your continued progress.
   With personal regards,

                        Sincerely,

                        Paul B. Tucker, CPA
                        Partner

PBT:jd

APPENDIX IV

Illustration of Assignment Approval, with Tentative Report Digest

ASSIGNMENT AUTHORIZATION
GAO FORM 100

1. DIVISION FILE NO.	2. DPC USE ONLY	3. ASSIGNMENT TYPE	4. PHASE	5. PRIORITY	6. PRODUCT TYPES	7. PRODUCT TARGET DATES	8. ASSIGNMENT NO.
		F	R	2	1C	DRAFT: 7/76 FINAL: 11/76	01736

9. TITLE	13. GAO PROGRAM CATEGORY	15. ISSUE AREA/L.O.E. DATA
Review of Administrative Costs Associated with Federal Assistance Programs	Management Review of Economy and Efficiency	PRIMARY Primary I/A & LOE--0400 SECONDARY None

14. SOURCE OF REQUIREMENT/PROPOSED USER DATA
NAME:

10. PROGRAMMING DIVISION AND OPERATING GROUP	16. DEPARTMENT/AGENCY
GGD-IGR	OMB, HEW, Agriculture, Justice, Labor

11. COGNIZANT DIVISION AND OPERATING GROUP	TYPE: OTH	

12. ASSIGNMENT AREA	REQUEST DATE (Mo./Day/Yr.)	17. BUDGET FUNCTIONAL CATEGORY
Intergovernmental Relations Assoc.		0802

STAFFING SPECIFICATIONS

18. PERFORMING ORGANIZATION			19. AGENCY OR CONTRACTOR LOCATIONS AT WHICH WORK IS TO BE PERFORMED	20. TIMEFRAMES		21. TOTAL AUTHOR-IZATION	22. ESTIMATED STAFF-DAY EXPENDITURE		BALANCE TO COMPLETE
NAME	RESPONSIBLE FOR			MO./YR. START	MO./YR. COMPLETE		PROGRAM PERIOD		
	LEADERSHIP	WORK PROGRAM					FY76	FY77	
GGD-IGR			Federal agencies headquarters in Washington, D.C.	10/75	11/76	350	250	100	
FO-Seattle			Regional offices of Federal agencies and State and local governments in Federal region X.	10/75	7/76	600	600	-	
FGMSD-TAG-SA				10/75	11/76	50 / 1000	40 / 850	10 / 110	

PAGE 1 OF 3

ASSIGNMENT AUTHORIZATION
GAO FORM 100A CONTINUATION

	CHANGE NO. 12/6/75	ASSIGNMENT NO. 01736
	30 APPROVALS	DATE
	AUDIT MANAGER	
	TEAM LEADER	
	ASSISTANT DIRECTOR	
	ASSOCIATE DIRECTOR	
	DIVISION DIRECTOR	

31. JUSTIFICATION/TERMINATION REPORT

During the last 15 years, Federal assistance to State and Local governments has increased from $6.6 billion to an estimated $55.6 billion in fiscal year 1976. The number of Federal assistance programs has substantially increased also and now totals 1010. Concern has been expressed that this substantial increase has resulted in complex grant structures and has considerably increased the administrative burden of operating these programs at all levels of government. There is presently much speculation concerning the costs to administer and deliver Federal assistance, particularly when viewed from the standpoint of what percentage of dollars appropriated actually reach the intended beneficiaries. The prevailing opinion seems to be that too much of total spending is consumed by the Federal, State and local levels of government involved in administering and delivering Federal assistance programs.

Our survey demonstrated that reliable data on the costs and functions involved in administering and delivering Federal assistance programs is not readily available or being accumulated on a program by program basis. By using a questionnaire approach, however, along with intensive follow up efforts, we have been able to identify the costs of and functions performed by these administering levels.

Our survey data showed that administering levels consumed $9.2 million or 4.4% of a total $207.2 million in available assistance funds, or restated, it cost $9.2 million to deliver $198 million of assistance funds to project operators. Broken down by type of delivery method, administrative costs as a percentage of total funds available was 13% for block grants, 6% for formula grants, and 3% for discretionary grants. Whether these percentages are high or low is a matter of individual judgment and cannot be answered without evaluating the effectiveness of each individual program.

While we don't intend to address the effectiveness of each program, we do intend to assert that accurate cost information is essential for efficient and effective program management and control.

At present, program administrators do not have sufficient cost information readily available to determine how efficiently or effectively their programs are operating, where potential savings may be realized, or what financial control areas may need more management attention.

Our primary objective in this review will be to disclose information on the costs and functions involved in the delivery of Federal assistance programs. We believe this to be important in view of the continuing concerns and criticisms with respect to the cost of government and the amount of funds left over for the ultimate beneficiaries. As noted above we did not find administrative costs as a percentage of total costs to be significatly high and thus we may dispell or alleviate much of the concern and criticism. However, the relationship becomes more

ASSIGNMENT AUTHORIZATION
GAO FORM 100A CONTINUATION

CHANGE NO. 12/6/75	ASSIGNMENT NO. 01736	
30 APPROVALS		DATE
AUDIT MANAGER L H Eady	L. H. Eady	11/7/75
TEAM LEADER		
ASSISTANT DIRECTOR B W Thurman	BW Thurman	11/7/75
ASSOCIATE DIRECTOR A. M. Hair, Jr.	A. M. Hair, Jr.	11/19/75
DIVISION DIRECTOR V. L. Lowe	V. L. Lowe	11/28/75

31. JUSTIFICATION/TERMINATION REPORT

significant when viewed in terms of absolute dollars. Thus the need for accurate information on the cost of, and functions performed by, administering levels in the delivery of Federal assistance.

In our review we will attempt to analyze variations among programs by type of delivery method, type of organizational structure, and type of service delivered. The results of our analysis will be used to further demonstrate the need for a system to routinely monitor and assess the allocation of resources (staff and dollar) by administrative functions. Such a system may also yield information for use in developing standards on how much of staff and dollar resources should be devoted to administrative functions. Because of the time frame and staff days required, we are confining our review to Washington headquarters and one regional office for the programs included in our sample.

The Seattle Regional Office was chosen for this assignment because of their participation in the survey phase and their accumulated knowledge of the programs and activities that were included in our sample. The Seattle Office also is working with FGMSD to prepare a computer program to facilitate the analytical comparison of data by program and agency categories.

This assignment was included in the Division's 90-day tentative assignment list dated 11/4/75 and is consistent with the Division's long-range work plan.

This assignment was initiated as a survey under code 01732 in January 1975, redirected to a sampling and questionnaire approach in April 1975 with a total staff day expenditure of 637 as of October 11, 1975.

In accordance with the Comptroller General's memorandum dated May 24, 1972, concerning implementation of functional and program responsibilities of audit divisions, we plan to coordinate our audit effort with the staffs of the Manpower and Welfare Division, Resources and Economic Development Division, Financial and General Management Studies Division, and also the Office of Program Analysis.

0400--Intergovernmental Relations and Revenue Sharing
This review will be a step toward gaining an understanding of the various methods used to deliver Federal assistance as discussed in the proposed line of effort statement on "The different Federal assistance approaches: Do they make a difference?"

COMPTROLLER GENERAL'S
REPORT TO THE CONGRESS

Code 01736
OPPORTUNITIES TO IMPROVE
ADMINISTRATION OF FEDERAL
ASSISTANCE PROGRAMS
Office of Management and
Budget and other Federal
agencies
(Code 01736)

D I G E S T

Federal financial assistance to State and local governments and other non-Federal organizations has increased dramatically, from $3 billion in fiscal year 1955 to an estimated $55.6 billion in fiscal year 1976. Currently Federal domestic assistance comes through 1,010 programs administered by 54 Federal agencies. Approximately 550 of these programs involve financial assistance.

Seven Federal agencies are responsible for administering 90% of the assistance estimat-d to be provided in fiscal year 1976. These agencies employ a total of 433,400 personnel at a cost of about $7.9 billion a year.

There is presently much speculation concerning the costs to administer and deliver Federal assistance to project operators, particularly when viewed from the standpoint of what percentage of assistance funds actually reach the intended beneficiaries. In view of the speculation and congressional concern over the administration of Federal programs, GAO sought to determine the cost of, and functions performed by, administering levels in the delivery system.

Information of the type sought by GAO was not readily available. Federal agencies have no system for identifying and reporting on the costs or number of staff involved in administering a specific program or the type and degree of involvement at each administering level. As a result, the

Congress, in exercising its review and oversight responsibilities, lacks information essential to evaluate program efficiency and the adequacy of existing or proposed staffing levels of Federal agencies. Further, the Congress and Executive agencies have little basis for evaluating the impact of proposed programs on the administrative structure of the various levels of Government.

To obtain estimates on the costs and functions involved in the award and administration of funds to project operators, GAO randomly selected 83 assistance programs. Under these programs, 19 Federal agencies, using a variety of delivery methods, provided over $15 billion in Federal assistance. For each program GAO determined the type and costs of involvement by administering levels at the Federal headquarters and regional offices, States, and other organizations involved in grants administration. GAO's scope did not include an analysis of costs and functions performed by project operators; those organizations who deal with the ultimate program beneficiaries at the last level in the delivery system network.

With the use of questionnaires and laborious follow-up efforts, GAO found that:

- --the cost of Federal and non-Federal administering levels ranged from 2 to 25 percent of the total funds available for administration and grant awards.
- --of the total funds available, administering level's costs averaged 13 percent for block grants, 8 percent for formula grants, and 3 percent for discretionary grants and contracts.
- --the cost to provide funds to project operators increased as the number of administering levels increased.

--Federal assistance under as many as seven different types of delivery networks was provided to the same project operator

--the degree of involvement by Federal and non-Federal administering levels varied substantially, even for similar assistance programs.

--the ways administering levels allocated their time between functions such as planning, monitoring, technical assistance, and program evaluation varied substantially for similar assistance programs.

--administrators at all levels complain of the lack of adequate staff to perform essential administrative functions.

The methods by which Federal assistance programs are administered are varied and complex. Each has its own unique characteristics and an important role to play in providing Federal assistance. This study is only a first step toward identifying the nature of and reasons for similarities and differences in individual programs, their relative costs, advantages, and disadvantages.

Federal agencies need to devote more attention to improving program administration and maximizing program effectiveness by gaining a better understanding of the administrative networks involved, the functions performed at each level, and the related costs to administer the various types of Federal assistance programs. Accurate information on the costs and functions performed by Federal and non-Federal administering levels is essential to efficient and effective program management and control.

RECOMMENDATIONS

We recommend that the Director of the Office of Management and Budget direct each Federal agency administering Federal assistance programs to:

--establish a system for periodically reviewing each Federal assistance program to determine and analyze for each administering level, the cost to administer the program, the number of staff involved, and the level of effort the staff devotes to the various administrative functions.

--establish a system for reporting to the Congress on the results of their studies prior to or during authorization and appropriations hearings.

APPENDIX V

Illustration of Analysis Needed for Continuing Assignment Authorization: Review of Food Stamp Program Service and Administration

ASSIGNMENT AUTHORIZATION
GAO FORM 100

1. DIVISION FILE NO.	2. DPC USE ONLY	3. ASSIGNMENT TYPE	4. PHASE	5. PRIORITY	6. PRODUCT TYPES	7. PRODUCT TARGET DATES	8. ASSIGNMENT NO.
RED 6-64		F	R	1	1A	DRAFT: 11/75 FINAL: 6/76	02365

9. TITLE
Review of Food Stamp Program Service and Administration

13. GAO PROGRAM CATEGORY
Congressional Requests- Program Results

15. ISSUE AREA/L.O.E. DATA
PRIMARY: 1/A & LOE--1707
SECONDARY: 1/A & LOE--1300

10. PROGRAMMING DIVISION AND OPERATING GROUP
RED-AGRI/RD

11. COGNIZANT DIVISION AND OPERATING GROUP

14. SOURCE OF REQUIREMENT/PROPOSED USER DATA
NAME: Chairman, House Committee Agriculture
TYPE: CCO

16. DEPARTMENT/AGENCY
Agriculture
Labor (limited)

17. BUDGET FUNCTIONAL CATEGORY
0604
0505

12. ASSIGNMENT AREA
FOOD PROGRAMS

REQUEST DATE (Mo./Day/Yr.)
August 1, 1975

STAFFING SPECIFICATIONS

18. PERFORMING ORGANIZATION			19. AGENCY OR CONTRACTOR LOCATIONS AT WHICH WORK IS TO BE PERFORMED	20. TIMEFRAMES		21. TOTAL AUTHOR-IZATION	22. ESTIMATED STAFF-DAY EXPENDITURE	
NAME	LEAD-ERSHIP	WORK PROGRAM		MO./YR. START	MO./YR. COMPLETE		PROGRAM PERIOD	BALANCE TO COMPLETE
RED-AGRI/RD	S	W	Agriculture headquarters, and local Welfare office in D.C., Maryland, and Virginia	9/75	6/76	400	76 400	
FO-PHILADELPHIA			Pennsylvania State Welfare Office and local food stamp offices in Philadelphia and other locations	9/75	6/76	300	300	
FO-SAN FRANCISCO			California State Welfare Office and local food stamp offices in San Francisco and other locations	9/75	2/76	200	200	
FO-DETROIT			Michigan State Welfare Office and local food stamp offices in Detroit and other locations	9/75	2/76	200	200	

PAGE 1 OF 4

ASSIGNMENT AUTHORIZATION
GAO FORM 100(Rev. Jan. '78)

1. DIVISION FILE NO.	2. DPC USE ONLY	3. ASSIGNMENT TYPE	4. PHASE	5. PRIORITY	6. PRODUCT TYPES	7. PRODUCT TARGET DATES	8. ASSIGNMENT NO.
						DRAFT: FINAL:	02365

9. TITLE

13. GAO PROGRAM CATEGORY

15. ISSUE AREA/L.O.E. DATA

PRIMARY

14. SOURCE OF REQUIREMENT/PROPOSED USER DATA

NAME:

SECONDARY

10. PROGRAMMING DIVISION AND OPERATING GROUP

TYPE:

16. DEPARTMENT/AGENCY

11. COGNIZANT DIVISION AND OPERATING GROUP

REQUEST DATE (Mo./Day/Yr.)

12. ASSIGNMENT AREA

17. BUDGET FUNCTIONAL CATEGORY

STAFFING SPECIFICATIONS

18. PERFORMING ORGANIZATION			19. AGENCY OR CONTRACTOR LOCATIONS AT WHICH WORK IS TO BE PERFORMED	20. TIMEFRAMES		STAFF-DAY REQUIREMENTS	
NAME	RESPONSIBLE FOR			MO./YR. START	MO./YR. COMPLETE	21. TOTAL AUTHORIZATION	22. ESTIMATED STAFF-DAY EXPENDITURE
	LEADERSHIP	WORK PROGRAM					PROGRAM PERIOD / BALANCE TO COMPLETE
FO-CHICAGO			Illinois State Welfare Office and local food stamp offices in Chicago and other locations	9/75	2/76	200 / 1300	200 / 1300

PAGE 2 OF 4

ASSIGNMENT AUTHORIZATION
GAO FORM 100A CONTINUATION

31. JUSTIFICATION/TERMINATION REPORT

CHANGE NO.	ASSIGNMENT NO.
9/13/75	02365

30 APPROVALS — DATE

AUDIT MANAGER C. Grissinger — 9/28/75
TEAM LEADER
ASSISTANT DIRECTOR S. S. Sargol — 9/24/75
ASSOCIATE DIRECTOR R. J. Woods — 9/28/75
DIVISION DIRECTOR H. Eschwege — 9/14/75

The food stamp program, authorized by the Food Stamp Act of 1964, as amended (7 U.S.C. 2011, is designed to help low-income households purchase more nutritionally adequate diets by enabling them to buy subsidized food through regular grocery stores. Participating households use the money they would normally spend for food to buy food stamps of higher monetary value. The bonus value of the stamps and their price are based on household size and income. Households with no income get free stamps. The Food and Nutrition Service, Department of Agriculture, administers the program nationally and State agencies, through agreements with the Service, administer the program locally.

From inception, the program has increased dramatically both in terms of participation and cost. In the period January to March 1975, participation increased by about 1.3 million, bringing total participation to about 19 million. Estimated costs for fiscal year 1975 are in excess of $4 billion, and costs of more than $6 billion are estimated for fiscal year 1976. Because of the rapidly rising participation and costs, the Congress has been expressing increasing concern that the program be administered efficiently, that participation be limited to the truly deserving, and that adequate timely services be provided to program applicants.

The purpose of this assignment is to develop a separate report to the Chairman of the House Committee on Agriculture in response to his request of August 1, 1975 (see below), and a second report to the Congress on certain administrative aspects and program requirements that need to be modified and/or strengthened to make the program more effective. The work areas for this assignment are discussed below.

1. Analysis of extent of, and reasons for, delays in interviewing and certifying applicants and issuing them authorizations to purchase food stamps. If data available at the food stamp offices will permit, we also will provide information on the payoff that results from case workers' verifications of information given by program applicants. This work will be done on a priority basis pursuant to the August 1, 1975, request from the Chairman of the House Committee on Agriculture.

2. Analysis of actual cases to determine significance of income deductions and how they affect program eligibility and participation. We will document how, and identify which, deductions make relatively higher income households eligible for program benefits; show to what extent deductions benefit lower income households; and indicate the problems encountered in trying to verify actual deductions.

3. Review of effectiveness of the work registration requirement which is intended to keep out of the program those who voluntarily choose not to work when able to do so and employment is available. We will determine the requirement's payoff versus its cost.

PAGE 3 OF 4

ASSIGNMENT AUTHORIZATION
GAO FORM 100A CONTINUATION

CHANGE NO.	ASSIGNMENT NO.
9/13/75	02365

30 APPROVALS		DATE
AUDIT MANAGER		
TEAM LEADER		
ASSISTANT DIRECTOR		
ASSOCIATE DIRECTOR		
DIVISION DIRECTOR		

31. JUSTIFICATION/TERMINATION REPORT

4. Examination into the adequacy of efforts made to obtain repayment of improper benefits provided to participants. We will try to show how widespread this situation is and why recoveries are not greater.

In addition to providing information in response to the request of the Chairman of the House Committee on Agriculture, our work in the program aspects listed above will be of special interest and concern to Senator Buckley whose staff was told, in partial response to his March 1975 request for a GAO audit of the food stamp program, that we would give administrative costs and requirements of the program specific review attention. More recently, Congressman Cardiss Collins, in a letter to us in August 1975 expressed concern regarding the administration of the program in Illinois, one of the States in which this review will be made at the request of her office. We agreed that during our work in Illinois, we would check on some specific cases where income deductions alledgedly will not be taken into account in determining eligibility. The information we pick up on any of the cases identified for us will be furnished her office informally. Because of these factors and tight time frame, we have designated the assignment priority 1A.

This assignment will deal with the following approved issue areas and lines of effort:
1707 Food and Fiber Programs--Domestic Food Assistance Programs Designed to Promote Social Welfare.

1300 Federally Sponsored or Assisted Income Security Programs.

The review will include a consideration of the adequacy and appropriateness of recipient qualification standards as discussed in the line of effort statement on Domestic Food Assistance Programs and delays in determining eligibility and certain other aspects of program administration as contemplated under the issue area Federally Sponsored or Assisted Income Security Programs.

This assignment is included in the RED 90-day tentative assignment list for the period July through September with regional offices to be designated later. The designated regional offices will have staff available for the job.

The four field offices were selected to provide broad geographical coverage of a large program with many local variations in administrative operations and problems. Concurrent work by four staffs will shorten the calendar days necessary to provide adequate coverage of the program areas to be reviewed.

This review has been coordinated with OSP and MWD

PAGE 4 OF 4

UNITED STATES HOUSE OF REPRESENTATIVES
COMMITTEE ON AGRICULTURE
WASHINGTON, D.C. 20515

August 1, 1975

THOMAS S. FOLEY
CHAIRMAN

Dear Mr. Staats:

In recent months there has been a growing concern over the inability of the states and local projects to interview and certify applicants, and to issue them food stamps in a timely manner. There have been increasingly common accounts of persons lining up in front of food stamp offices very early in the morning and still not being certified that day; of persons waiting three and four weeks before they could apply; and of persons having to return to food stamp offices repeatedly with additional documentation to verify eligibility. In recognition of these concerns, S. 1662 has passed the Senate and H.R. 7887 has been reported out of Committee by the House Committee on Agriculture. While these bills vary in detail, the intent is to insure that people receive food stamps within a reasonable time after they apply. They would require certification and issuance of food stamps on the same day a person makes his first reasonable attempt to apply for program benefits, and eligibility would be determined on the basis of information provided in the application. Verification of this information would be made subsequently.

This Committee is quite concerned with the question of timely certification, as well as other aspects of the Food Stamp Program, and is taking steps to obtain information that will provide better understanding of a variety of program problem areas. The purpose of this letter is to confirm an informal understanding reached by a member of the Committee staff and representatives of your office that the General Accounting Office, as part of its review of the Food Stamp Program, will compile factual information on the timeliness of services provided to food stamp applicants in selected food project areas (including some in large metropolitan areas). This will involve primarily an analysis of actual recent cases to determine the extent of, and reasons for, delays in interviewing and certifying applicants and providing them the opportunity to purchase food stamps.

- 2 -

   As Sponsor of H.R. 7887, I am hopeful that it will be enacted into law. I believe the information available has demonstrated the need for this kind of emergency action. However, the action proposed is temporary in nature and therefore will need to be dealt with on a more permanent basis as the Committee looks at overall need for food stamp program revision. Also, if H.R. 7887, or something similar, is enacted into law, there is some concern that the certification procedures would result in increased program abuse. Therefore, it would be useful to have information soon after that procedure is implemented that would be helpful in assessing the extent of any additional program abuse.

   In the event that this pending legislation is not enacted, there will be continuing concern about problems of timely certification and issuance of food stamps. Therefore, information on the extent to which the problem persists during the coming months, and on the causes of the problem, will be very useful to the Committee.

   In addition, if information available at the food stamp offices permits, it would be very useful to have an assessment of the benefits that result from the verification procedures. I understand that in some offices recently visited by your representatives, certification arrangements were such that the verification procedure was not separable from the application procedure and could not be examined independently after an application was completed. If that turns out to be the case at offices your staff visits, determining the benefits from the verification requirement may not be possible. However, I would appreciate any information in this area which you can provide.

   In line with the overall schedule on the study which the Committee has under way, I would appreciate a report on these matters no later than the end of December, 1975. If your staff have questions or need additional information, please have them contact Mr. James E. Springfield, whose telephone number is 225-2171.

   Thank you for your assistance.

                                          Sincerely,

                                          Thomas S. Foley

The Honorable Elmer B. Staats
Comptroller General of the United States
441 G Street, N.W.
Washington, D. C. 20548

TSF:jsl

APPENDIX VI

Selected GAO Policies for a Program Audit

Explanation of Terms

Review of results of Government programs and activities are concerned with what program objectives have been established, what has been or is being accomplished, and the extent to which objectives established in statutes and implementing regulations are being achieved.

Although concerned primarily with accomplishments, reviews of results will, in many cases, include reviews of management policies, procedures, and practices to appraise their effects on accomplishments and achievement of objectives. This process will usually consider management efficiency and economy because program benefits stem from the consumption of resources. Generally costs should be reasonably commensurate with benefits.

Program, as we use it, is not confined to the highest level of Government, but the higher the level the more important and useful the results of our examinations should be to the Congress. For example, an evaluation where the objective is improving the health of the population would have more significance than an evaluation where the objective is increasing the number of doctors (only one of several aspects of the overall objective of improving the health of the population).

Evaluation means ascertaining the value of something by comparing accomplishment with a standard or goal.

Program evaluation goes beyond the review of program results. In its broadest sense, program evaluation involves not only appraising what is being accomplished in relation to costs but also whether the objectives of the programs are proper and suitable. Normally, our work would be limited to reviews of program results.

A *cost-benefit study* considers the relationship between the costs (inputs) incurred in achieving a program objective and the benefits or accomplishments (outputs) attained. For making a cost-benefit study we may need to consider alternative ways of achieving a program objective.

Source: Adapted from United States General Accounting Office, the Comptroller General of the United States, *Comprehensive Audit Manual* (Washington, D.C.: General Accounting Office, 1974), chap. 12.

Defining Program Objectives

It is often difficult to define program objectives. Nevertheless, obtaining statements of objectives from the performing agency and reaching agreement on them is an essential first step in measuring and evaluating progress toward meeting those objectives.

The difficulty in defining program objectives can often be traced to one or more of the following factors:

1. The enabling legislation and legislative history do not define clearly the objectives or the program.
2. Several objectives overlap or are interdependent.
3. Stated program objectives are not readily understandable by those responsible for carrying out the programs or the objectives may be confusing because they are in conflict with those of other programs.
4. Sociological factors are involved which have not been studied, researched, and analyzed to the extent necessary to be definitive.
5. The apparent intent of the Congress, that the responsible agency would define the objective, has not been followed.
6. The real program objectives have changed even though the stated objectives have remained constant.

There are no simple and clear-cut solutions to these sources of difficulty. However, to make a useful review of program results, we must do what is necessary to identify the program objectives. *It is essential that we obtain a clear understanding of those program objectives and validate such understanding through in-depth discussions with agency officials and committees of the Congress.*

When such an understanding cannot be reached, we may have to report that no concrete objectives have been established. In some instances, we may have to report that achievement of established goals is not measurable, or that those established are unrealistic or unattainable.

If outside consultants are used to assist in the review, generally it is desirable to obtain their advice or assistance in clearly identifying program objectives prior to preparing the work program.

When program objectives are being identified and studied, it is particularly important that other programs having the same or parallel objectives be considered. Several agencies may have programs with similar objectives that can be evaluated simultaneously and collectively.

When a functional area of interest is involved, we should consider whether audit coverage of more than a single agency program would be more useful to the Congress and to the agencies concerned. By taking a functional approach to a program evaluation we can, through our report, give the Congress a program area perspective that is not usually available in a more restricted evaluation, and we should be in a better position to recommend changes in organizational structures or responsibilities.

All reports on reviews of program results should include discussions of the program objectives used in our evaluations and how they were identified and established.

Factors to Consider in Reviewing Program Results

Agency management officials have the basic responsibility for continually evaluating their programs to determine the progress being made in achieving objectives. Our primary approach is to evaluate the agency's system for measuring its progress. In doing so, we should seek answers to questions such as:

- *Program effectiveness*—Is the program accomplishing the results intended, as spelled out in the legislative objectives or in the implementing directives of the agency?
- *Cost effectiveness*—Is the program succeeding within the costs anticipated at the time the legislation was enacted?
- *Compliance*—Are the program or activity being conducted and the expenditures being made in compliance with requirements of applicable laws and regulations?
- *Adequacy of information system*—Does top management have the essential and reliable information necessary to exercise supervision and controls and to ascertain direction or trends?
- *Adequacy of internal review*—Does management have adequate internal review, audit, or evaluation facilities to monitor program operations, identify program and management problems and weaknesses, and insure fiscal integrity?
- *Relationship with other programs*—Does jurisdiction overlap or are efforts duplicated for no useful purpose? Is the program coordinated with other programs aimed at similar objectives? Does it lend reasonable support to related programs? Does it cause disbenefits to other programs?
- *Cost-benefit relationship*—Are program costs reasonably commensurate with the benefits achieved?
- *Consideration of alternatives*—Have alternative programs or procedures been examined or should they be examined for potential in achieving objectives with the greatest economic efficiency? When alternatives have been considered, are studies, such as cost-benefit studies, prepared to support executive branch proposals adequate from the standpoint of analyzing costs and benefits of alternative approaches?
- *Need for program*—Is there a continuing need for the program? Legislation and regulations may not provide for program termination, and it is not unusual for a Government program to continue long after the need which it was created to meet has disappeared.
- *Appropriateness of program*—Is the program as it was designed and implemented geared to the needs of the particular target group that was used to justify the establishment of the program?
- *Clarity and consistency of objectives*—Are program objectives sufficiently clear to permit agency management to effectively accomplish the desired program results? Are the objectives of the component parts of the program consistent with overall program objectives?
- *Validity of data*—How valid was the data used to justify the program to the Congress? How valid is the pertinent data at the time of our evaluation?
- *Adequacy of information reported to the Congress*—Is the information furnished to the Congress by the agency sufficiently adequate and accurate to permit the Congress to effectively monitor program results?

Methods for Developing Information

Use of Agency and Other Studies

In accordance with our established approach to all of our audit work, we should first identify what studies have already been made by or for the agency on the management of the program or activity. During the survey phase, we should take an inventory of past, current, and planned agency and consultant studies that have a bearing on our work, including those relating to the establishment of program goals and to the measurement of progress in achieving the goals. This inventory should include studies made or sponsored by non-Federal agencies and by private organizations.

We should also inquire about any pertinent studies, and obtain copies of those reports if possible, made by or for:

- The Office of Management and Budget.
- Congressional committees.
- Agencies of State or local governments.
- Independent research organizations.

In some cases, agencies are required by law to make program evaluations and to report the results of such evaluations to the Congress. As an integral part of our program evaluation, we should determine whether there is such a requirement and, if so, how well the agency has responded to it.

We should give particular attention to legislative provisions which require a fixed percentage of program funds or a fixed dollar amount to be spent for program evaluation. Such a requirement may be unwise, particularly if an agency is not in a position to spend the money effectively. Rigid personnel regulations and scarcity of trained personnel can result in spending Federal funds for program evaluations which are not very useful.

More than one organizational unit may be involved in program evaluation. For example, departmental as well as bureau or office organizational entities may have responsibilities for reviewing the results of the program we are reviewing. We should identify and be familiar with all of these and understand how they relate to each other.

When consultants or contractors have made pertinent studies for the agency, we should examine them and inquire into the reactions of agency officials to the work and the agency's monitoring or the studies. We should also assess the usefulness of such studies to the agency and to our work.

A review of the studies prepared by the agency and by others should be helpful to us for the information they contain, the methods followed, and the assessments made. Such a review should also give us bases for drawing conclusions on the adequacy of such studies, and we should inquire into how the agency used them. We should not duplicate the timely and satisfactory work of others, but in making our review we should take full advantage of the information already developed by others and, where needed, build upon this information with studies of our own.

Most of the information that we will be considering in a program results review will have been (or should have been) considered by the agency responsible for the program. This information should greatly benefit us, and every effort should be made to obtain all significant agency information, documents, records, and reports concerning the objectives, results, and accomplishments of the program.

Use of Consultants

The complex and technical nature of some programs will make it necessary for us to use outside experts and consultants. We must do everything necessary to assure ourselves that we and the consultants fully understand and agree on the scope and objectives of the work.

The extent of our day-to-day involvement with experts and consultants in the performance of their work can vary. In most instances, it will be advantageous to assign staff to work with them or to monitor their activities and discuss problems with them. In other instances, the nature of the work may be such that limited involvement and discussions will be adequate.

The objectives of our involvement are (1) to insure that we understand (a) the nature of their work, (b) the significant assumptions they have made, (c) the reasoning underlying their analytical choices, and (d) the risks inherent in their data and analyses; (2) to make suggestions to them so that their work will be of most benefit to us; and (3) to assure ourselves that the work being done conforms to what we intended.

Obtaining Information Through Interviews and Questionnaires

Much of the data concerning the impact of Federal programs will be obtained from agency files, records, and consultant studies. In addition, interviews with those directly affected by the programs, such as intended program beneficiaries, and other persons who have direct knowledge of the programs can be valuable as a basis for gaining realistic insight into the effectiveness of the programs.

In selecting intended beneficiaries to be interviewed, we should consider persons who have completed the program, who are currently in the program, who have started and dropped out before completion, and who, although falling within the group of intended beneficiaries, have not participated at all. Care must be exercised in any attempt to project the results of interviews.

Before starting interviews on a broad scale, we might conduct pilot interviews of a small number of persons to help develop a useful questionnaire and to get an idea of the responses that can be expected from wider interviewing. The type of questions to be asked—whether calling for factual answers, opinions, or both—needs to be carefully considered. In developing specific questions, we should also consider the possible problems in collating and evaluating the likely responses.

The use of outside professional interviewing organizations may be appropriate both for developing questionnaires and for conducting actual interviews. If used, we should monitor the action to insure that the questionnaires and interviews are what we want.

If at all possible, interviews should be conducted in the survey phase or early in the review (1) to provide a basis for ascertaining probable weaknesses in the program and developing detailed review procedures and (2) to obtain valuable background on probable program effectiveness.

Depending on the type of program being examined, persons who may be indirectly affected by the program—police, school authorities, court officials—may be worthwhile sources of information regarding effectiveness.

Although oral interviews can provide us with an additional basis for evaluating program impact, this method of obtaining data from large numbers of program beneficiaries and others can be extremely time consuming and costly. Therefore we should consider obtaining the desired information through the use of questionnaires which are furnished to the persons involved with a request that they be completed and returned. However, data obtained by questionnaires is generally low-reliability evidence at best and should be verified or corroborated by other sources or methods.

Use of Analytical Techniques

It is frequently necessary to use sophisticated techniques (e.g., analysis of variance, regression analysis) in analyzing data for the purpose of measuring program results. The techniques to be used in given situations will depend on the available data and the program or activity being measured.

In those cases where we have some doubt as to the accuracy and reliability of the data used, the results of our analytical work should be subjected to sensitivity analyses. Sensitivity analyses call for the analyst or auditor to vary the value of the essential characteristic (e.g., average test scores) obtained from the data to determine what amount of error in the data would change or invalidate our conclusions. If our conclusions would change as a result of a small variance in the value of the essential characteristic, the report should point this out explicity. The report should also explain our reasons for using data which we believe may not be accurate.

Special Consideration
Cost-Benefit Studies

Cost-benefit studies (or cost-effectiveness studies where benefits cannot be quantified in dollar terms) are an important part of an assessment of program results. We should take full advantage of pertinent cost-benefit or cost-effectiveness studies prepared by the agencies and others.

If our survey work shows a need for such studies and they have not been made, or those which have been made are not adequate, we should make the studies ourselves when feasible and practicable.

Reviews of program results may be made even where quantitative measures of costs and benefits or achievements have not been developed. Although we should try, wherever practicable, to make independent cost-benefit studies in quantitative terms, the absence of historical data, "control groups," and the difficulty of measuring benefits may rule out meaningful quantitative analyses in many areas. In these cases, in making our evaluations, we must examine whatever evidence is available as to benefits achieved.

We must exercise care to insure that we only state positions or draw conclusions warranted by the facts and by our analyses. This means that we state information with great care, limit observations and conclusions to what is warranted based on our review work, and not become an advocate of any particular program.

APPENDIX VII

Developing the Report: Selected Policies from the U.S. GAO Report Manual

In planning and conducting audits, most emphasis will be placed on those aspects of an organization's operations and activities in which opportunities for improvement appear to exist. Therefore, findings normally will concern such matters as:

- Ineffectiveness.
- Inefficiency.
- Waste and extravagance.
- Improper expenditures.
- Noncompliance with laws and regulations.

Because of this emphasis, the following discussion is oriented toward reporting adverse conclusions. This does not mean, however, that only adverse conclusions are reported. On the contrary, the auditor should also appropriately recognize favorable conclusions concerning the conduct of important programs and activities.

It is most important to make sure that, before starting to write, all audit information needed to effectively communicate the message has been gathered and is available to the writer. Analysis of proposed findings according to the attributes discussed below will be useful in organizing and assessing information before the auditor has completed his audit and as he is writing his report. Such analysis will also be useful in reviewing a report, particularly when the reviewer is having difficulty in identifying specifically what is wrong with a report he intuitively is dissatisfied with.

As has been said previously, the elements of a conclusion are:

- A statement of condition (what is).
- The criteria (what should be).
- The effects (difference between what is and what should be).
- The causes (why it happened).

Comparing the Condition with the Criteria

Most audit findings originate with comparisons of "what is"—*condition*—with "what should be"—*criteria*. When the auditor identifies a difference between the two, he will have taken the first step in developing an adverse conclusion. The fact that there is *no difference* between "what is" and "what should be" often is significant—particularly when the objective is to evaluate and report on the effectiveness of a program or activity.

Professional knowledge, experience, background, and personal skills of the audit staff all play a major role in selecting the conditions to be reported as well as the criteria or standards to use in evaluating those conditions. It is important to recognize, however, the auditor assumes the burden and obligation of convincing the reader of the validity and wisdom of the criteria used. Sufficient evidence should have been gathered on it to assure its appropriateness.

Assessing the Significance

The attention that conclusions get depends largely on a demonstration that they are significant. To help demonstrate this significance, the auditor should indicate whether reported adverse conditions are isolated or widespread and the rate or frequency of occurrence.

Significance is usually judged by *effect*. Effects (either actual or potential) frequently can be stated in quantitative terms, such as dollars, time, units of production, or number of transactions. Sometimes effects, such as lowered morale, are intangible but nevertheless significant. Regardless of the terms used, the report must include sufficient information to convince the reader that the matter warrants attention.

Explaining Why the Deviation Occurred

The reasons for a deviation between "what is" and "what should be" must be identified and explained. When the auditor knows why something happened—the *cause*—he can more readily determine how to prevent its recurrence. A constructive recommendation depends on an identification of the basic management weakness that permitted a deviation to occur. In all cases, the auditor should clearly and logically present the relationship between the stated cause and any recommendation.

Source: Adapted from the United States General Accounting Office, the Comptroller General of the United States, *Report Manual* (Washington, D.C.: General Accounting Office, 1974), chap. 13.

The following is an example of the way to organize the elements of an audit conclusion.

- *Condition*—An agency's inventory quantity continually have been inaccurate and unreliable. Considerable effort is put forth by the organization to reconcile the dollar values in the quantity and dollar records, but this effort serves only to ensure the accurate transfer of data—correct or incorrect—from one record to another. It does not ensure the accuracy and reliability of inventory data used for making management decisions.
- *Criteria*—Effectively managing inventory requires reliable and accurate inventory records in both quantities and dollars.
- *Effects*—Material not needed, valued at $1,200,000, is ordered and material needed, valued at $750,000, is not available when required. Inaccurate financial data also adversely affect management decisions concerning budgetary requirements.
- *Causes*—The inventory systems do not provide for timely reconciliation of detail stock records (count documents showing the quantities received) with financial records (data from vendors' invoices) and, as a result, there is no assurance that the stock records are correct.

APPENDIX VIII

Illustrative Report, with Appendixes: Fuel Savings and Other Benefits Achieved by Diverting Department of Defense Passengers from Chartered to Scheduled Overseas Flights

Source: Report to the Congress by the Controller General of the United States, *Fuel Savings and Other Benefits Achieved by Diverting Department of Defense Passengers from Chartered to Scheduled Overseas Flights*, Department of Defense, Civil Aeronautics Board, LCD-75-231 (Washington, D.C.: General Accounting Office, 1976).

COMPTROLLER GENERAL'S
REPORT TO THE CONGRESS

FUEL SAVINGS AND OTHER BENEFITS
ACHIEVED BY DIVERTING DEPARTMENT
OF DEFENSE PASSENGERS FROM
CHARTERED TO SCHEDULED OVERSEAS
FLIGHTS
Department of Defense
Civil Aeronautics Board

D I G E S T

Expansion of a temporary arrangement for diverting Department of Defense passengers from chartered flights operated by U.S. international air carriers to occupy otherwise unoccupied seats on the regularly scheduled commercial flights of the same carriers could

--save as much as 48 million gallons of jet fuel annually (see p. 4);

--improve the U.S. balance of payments to the extent that the jet fuel saved would have been procured from foreign sources (see p. 4);

--reduce annual costs to the Department by as much as $3.5 million through better utilization of seats (see p. 5).

--allow the financially ailing U.S. international air carriers to reduce annual operating costs by as much as $38 million (see p. 5).

The Secretary of Defense should negotiate with the appropriate air carriers to expand the temporary program to all routes where certificated air carriers operate charters which parallel their commercial routes. (See p. 9.)

The Civil Aeronautics Board should evaluate extending the diversion concept for the four routes on which it has already authorized temporary service, and for other requested routes, in terms of the national interest in fuel conservation and mutual benefit to the Government and to the air carriers. (See p. 9.)

The expanded diversion would involve substituting scheduled service for selected charter

Tear Sheet. Upon removal, the report cover date should be noted hereon.

LCD-75-231

flights on a total of 13 Military Airlift Command channels. Under this concept, the passengers would move in groups of 20 or more on the carriers' regularly scheduled flights through commercial facilities at the charter rate which is much less than the regular commercial fare. (See pp. 3 and 4.)

The military passengers would occupy otherwise vacant seats on these flights. Although the affected carriers would receive less in total revenue from the Department, the savings in operating costs would greatly exceed this reduction. (See p. 5.)

The carriers are willing to accept the charter passengers at the lower rates because their regularly scheduled flights have low occupancy rates. For example, in calendar year 1974, passenger occupancy rates ranged from about 37 to 66 percent. (See p. 6.)

The Department believed the estimates of savings were somewhat overstated, but generally concurred in GAO's recommendation that the diversion concept be expanded. Although the Civil Aeronautics Board has allowed temporary diversion on several occasions, including the current test program scheduled to run through June 1976, its officials have deferred adopting a final position on the diversion concept, pending hearings on its merits. (See pp. 3 and 9.)

CHAPTER 1

INTRODUCTION

The Military Airlift Command (MAC), a major command of the U.S. Air Force, is the single operating agency for airlift services within the Department of Defense (DOD). MAC is responsible for providing overseas air transportation for military personnel and for their dependents.

MAC headquarters at Scott Air Force Base (AFB), Illinois, directs the activities of this airlift force. Operational control is vested in the 21st and 22d Air Forces at McGuire AFB, New Jersey, and Travis AFB, California, respectively. Components of these Air Forces in the United States and overseas carry out the day-to-day functions necessary to operate a global airlift service.

MAC, in addition to operating its own aircraft, contracts with commercial airlines for additional airlift. MAC procured about $170 million worth of airlift services in fiscal year 1975; about $140 million worth of this was for transportation of passengers.

Airlift procurement is divided among air carriers in proportion to their participation in the Civil Reserve Air Fleet program. This program obligates the carriers to provide specific aircraft to MAC in emergencies.

During fiscal year 1974 MAC moved over 1.1 million passengers between the United States and overseas locations. About 78 percent of these passengers traveled on chartered commercial aircraft under contract to MAC. The charter rate per passenger, established and approved by the Civil Aeronautics Board (CAB), is much less than the standard commercial fare. Under the charter arrangement, however, MAC must pay for all available seats on the aircraft, whether used or not.

Charter flights are procured both from supplemental airlines (carriers which normally do not offer regularly scheduled passenger service) and from certificated carriers (carriers which also provide regularly scheduled flights on CAB-approved routes). The charter flights usually depart from and arrive at military air bases rather than commercial facilities.

Procurement of commercial airlift is subject to CAB regulation. CAB is an independent regulatory agency with broad authority to regulate and promote civil aeronautics within the United States and between the United States and foreign countries. In carrying out these responsibilities, CAB issues regulations which have the force of law and which set forth its policies, requirements, and procedures.

In 1973, because of the fuel crisis, CAB approved applications from several certificated air carriers for authority to divert military passengers from charter flights to their regularly scheduled flights on a temporary basis. This action was to move the passengers into otherwise unoccupied space on scheduled flights, thereby eliminating the need to operate certain charter flights. Under this procedure, substitute service was scheduled several weeks in advance and DOD passengers were port called directly to a commercial airport.

Our review was made to evaluate this arrangement and to determine the benefits that could be achieved by extending and expanding the program.

CHAPTER 2

DIVERTING CHARTER PASSENGERS TO REGULARLY

SCHEDULED FLIGHTS

Diverting passengers from charter flights operated by U.S. international air carriers to regularly scheduled flights of the same air carriers could (1) save as much as 48 million gallons of jet fuel annually, (2) reduce annual costs to DOD by as much as $3.5 million through better utilization of aircraft seats, and (3) allow the financially ailing U.S. international air carriers to reduce annual expenses by as much as $38 million.

The diversion would involve substituting commercial service for selected charter flights operated by Pan American World Airways, Northwest Airlines, and Trans World Airlines. DOD would have the option of moving its charter passengers, in groups of 20 or more, on the scheduled flights through commercial facilities at the charter rate.

Under the diversion concept, DOD passengers would be routed directly into commercial airports and would occupy otherwise vacant seats on regularly scheduled flights. The corresponding charter flights would be eliminated. Although the carriers would receive less revenue from DOD, the savings in operating costs would greatly exceed this reduction.

The carriers involved are willing to accept the charter passengers at the lower charter rate because their regularly scheduled flights have low passenger occupancy rates. For example, in calendar year 1974 the passenger occupancy rates ranged from about 37 to 66 percent. Revenues of other commercial air carriers would not be adversely affected because the three airlines would be only converting their own charter flights.

CAB denied the initial petitions of the airlines for authority to transport charter passengers on regularly scheduled flights but later allowed the carriers to do so on specific routes for a 5-month period. CAB denied two subsequent petitions for authority to continue the practice but later allowed the carriers to handle the diverted passengers for a 6-month period. CAB later approved carriers' tariffs on the basis of charter rates that, in effect, permitted the diversion for another 15 months beginning April 1, 1975.

CONSERVATION OF FUEL BY
REDUCING CHARTER FLIGHTS

Diverting charter passengers on selected routes could reduce annual jet fuel consumption by as much as 48 million gallons. These savings could be achieved by substituting scheduled service for charter flights on 13 channels flown by Pan American World Airways, Northwest Airlines, and Trans World Airlines which parallel their commercial routes. We recognize that adding passengers to commercial flights will increase related fuel requirements somewhat, but this increase is insignificant when compared with the fuel that would be used on the charter flights eliminated.

The Boeing 707 aircraft generally used by these airlines on charter flights consumes an average of 2,063 gallons of jet fuel per hour. Our calculations of potential fuel savings were based on an annual reduction of 969 flights, the average fuel consumption rate, and the average time by channel. (See app. III.) The 969 flights represent our estimate of the total number of charter flights flown annually by the three carriers over 13 channels during 1973 and 1974. Potential savings would be reduced to the extent that passengers could not be absorbed on scheduled flights. For instance, we have been assured by international carriers that military requirements could be absorbed on existing scheduled flights, However, an occasional unexpected surge in either military or commercial traffic could result in MAC contracting for charter flights.

The three carriers have already achieved large fuel savings in the periods when charter passengers were diverted to scheduled flights. From February through June 1974, DOD converted 152 charter flights on the following three channels:

--McGuire AFB to Rhein-Main Air Base (AB), Germany

--Travis AFB to Yokota, Japan

--Travis AFB to Osan AB, Korea

These conversions saved about 6.2 million gallons of jet fuel. In addition, MAC estimated that conversion of 96 charter flights from January through March 1975 would result in further savings of about 4.2 million gallons of jet fuel.

The cancellation of charter flights and the diversion of passengers to scheduled flights conserves fuel, thus decreasing fuel imports, which has a beneficial effect on the U.S. trade balance.

SAVINGS BY BETTER UTILIZATION OF AIRCRAFT

Currently, DOD charters an aircraft for passenger transportation to overseas locations paying for all of the seats, whether occupied or not. DOD is now experiencing a seat occupancy rate of 92.3 percent on these flights. We estimate that DOD pays about $3.5 million a year for unoccupied seats. A large part of this cost could be avoided by diverting passengers from charter to scheduled flights. (See app. IV.)

On charter flights, if duty-status passengers do not show up, MAC can only fill the seats with "space-available" passengers 1/ or allow the flights to leave with unoccupied seats. However, under the diversion concept, if passengers do not show up for a flight, MAC can reschedule up to 15 percent of the seats booked on later flights without a penalty charge. During the 1974 diversion operation, the Military Traffic Management Command reported a no-show rate of 10.9 percent; thus MAC could reschedule passengers without a cost penalty.

REDUCTION IN COMMERCIAL CARRIERS' COSTS

U.S. international air carriers could reduce their annual operating costs by as much as $38 million and cancel as many as 969 charter flights by substituting scheduled service for charter service on 13 selected channels. (See app. V.) The charter passengers would use unoccupied seats on the same carriers' scheduled flights which parallel the charter routes. Although the carriers would receive less revenue from DOD, the savings in operating costs would greatly exceed this reduction.

The Government is interested in benefits to carriers because carriers are reporting financial difficulties. For instance, one carrier has requested a Government subsidy, and two others have recently restructured certain routes to reduce expenses.

1/Passengers traveling in a nonduty status for whom MAC is not obligated to provide transportation and receives no reimbursement.

CARRIERS WILLING AND ABLE TO HANDLE DOD CHARTER PASSENGERS

The carriers are willing to accept the charter passengers on their scheduled flights at the lower charter fares because the occupancy rate on these flights is low. During calendar year 1974, occupancy rates on international flights were as follows:

	Trans World Airlines		Pan American World Airways		Northwest Airlines
	Atlantic	Pacific	Atlantic	Pacific	Pacific
	(percent)				
January	37.6	54.1	54.0	55.7	54.8
February	37.2	48.3	42.3	48.9	51.2
March	47.0	48.9	48.3	48.1	51.3
April	49.0	48.9	50.5	42.3	40.9
May	55.8	50.8	55.7	45.1	46.2
June	57.5	57.1	52.6	46.7	49.7
July	59.7	52.7	53.9	46.0	44.8
August	55.6	60.2	52.7	52.5	65.9
September	55.8	43.1	53.3	42.9	41.8
October	56.6	40.8	48.4	44.4	45.7
November	44.5	42.7	43.1	44.2	52.2
December	50.2	45.0	48.6	43.3	43.0

Although passenger traffic was somewhat seasonable, it should be noted that even during the busier months the occupancy rates rarely reached a monthly average of 60 percent.

Accordingly, airline officials assured us that they would even be able to absorb the diverted charter passengers on their scheduled flights during the peak passenger season. In the occasional instances in which scheduled commercial space was not available, the charter flights would be flown.

CAB HAS APPROVED DIVERSION, BUT ONLY ON A TEMPORARY BASIS

In 1972 Northwest Airlines and Trans World Airlines petitioned CAB for exemption authority to divert DOD passengers from charter to scheduled flights. In 1973 Pan American World Airways filed a similar request.

The airlines, in these and subsequent petitions, contended that eliminating charter flights would not only save fuel but would also improve the U.S. balance of payments position since much of the fuel saved would otherwise be purchased from foreign sources. They also said the service would reduce their costs without diverting revenues from other MAC-contracted carriers.

CAB denied the initial petitions of the airlines as being economically unsound. However, in late 1973 it approved subsequent airline petitions because of the fuel crisis. The CAB order allowed diversion of charter passengers for only a limited time on specific routes. The diversion began in February and ended June 30, 1974. During this time charter flights were converted on three channels.

The Military Traffic Management Command, in evaluating the diversion operation in 1974, reported that, from DOD's transportation viewpoint, the service was a complete success. The Command stated that because of increased flexibility and convenience and the need to conserve fuel, DOD should vigorously support the airlines' request to extend the diversion of charter passengers through fiscal year 1975.

CAB denied two subsequent airline petitions for authority to continue handling charter passengers on scheduled flights, but in October 1974 CAB approved continuation on three selected routes for the period ended March 31, 1975. At that time it stated:

> "We also wish to make it clear that our action herein is not to be interpreted as an endorsement of a part-charter concept. Rather this action is in response to the softening of international traffic, the continued fuel crisis and its impact on our balance of payments, and the need to take whatever reasonable steps are available to assist our financially pressed international carriers."

It further stated that:

> "* * * neither the carriers nor DOD should plan on any further extensions."

Despite the warning in the CAB decision, in February 1975 Northwest Airlines and Pan American World Airways filed tariffs which provided for the transportation of charter passengers on scheduled flights at the charter rate. The tariffs covered four selected routes. On March 31, 1975, CAB approved these tariffs for a 6-month period beginning April 1, 1975. It later extended this approval through June 1976.

Trans World Airlines did not file a similar tariff. In October 1974 Trans World Airlines and Pan American World Airways applied to CAB for restructuring of their Atlantic and Pacific flights as an economy measure. CAB approved the joint application, effective January 30, 1975. Essentially, service on the Trans World Airlines routes serving Europe and Asia and paralleling MAC charter routes will be provided by Pan American World Airways.

AGENCY COMMENTS AND OUR EVALUATION

CAB

On September 19, 1974, we interviewed responsible CAB officials on the relative merits of the diversion concept. They told us that it was CAB's policy to resist mixing chartered and scheduled services. CAB believes that the carriers must have a cost-based fare structure--each passenger carried must bear a pro-rata share of the service-- if the transportation system is to be economically sound.

On February 27, 1975, we again met with CAB representatives and told them that our analysis of the diversion operations showed the potential fuel savings and other benefits discussed in this report. They told us that CAB had an open mind on diverting charter passengers to scheduled flights, but they reiterated their belief that discounted fares were not beneficial to either the air carriers or the Government.

In general, we are not differing with CAB's position. However, the Government passengers we are discussing would not have traveled in scheduled service at all if it were not for the diversion concept. As indicated earlier, diverting Government passengers clearly results in savings in carriers' operating costs.

In commenting on our report, CAB officials deferred adopting a final position on the diversion concept pending a hearing on its merits. We were told that this hearing could not be held until sometime in late 1976 or early 1977. CAB's comments are included as appendix I of this report.

DOD

DOD officials generally agreed with our recommendation that the diversion concept be expanded. They said, however, that our estimates of savings were somewhat overstated.

The complete text of DOD's comments and our evaluation of them are included as appendix II of this report.

CHAPTER 3

CONCLUSIONS AND RECOMMENDATIONS

CONCLUSIONS

Diverting charter passengers on the four routes currently authorized will result in fuel savings to the Nation and in economic benefits to DOD and the carriers. However, the potential is far greater considering the number of routes over which certificated carriers operate charter flights which parallel their regularly scheduled flights.

RECOMMENDATIONS

We recommend that the Secretary of Defense negotiate with air carriers to expand the temporary program of diverting charter passengers to regularly scheduled flights on all routes where certificated air carriers operate charters which parallel their scheduled flights.

We recommend that CAB evaluate extending the diversion concept to the four routes on which it has already authorized temporary service and to other requested routes because of the national interest in fuel conservation and because of the mutual benefit to the Government and to the participating air carriers.

We want to reiterate that the expanded diversion concept will affect only certificated carriers that operate charters which parallel their regularly scheduled flights. Carriers not involved in the diversion would continue to receive their share of MAC business.

CHAPTER 4

SCOPE OF REVIEW

We assessed the feasibility of and the potential savings and other benefits to be realized by substituting regularly scheduled service for charter service. The work was done primarily at headquarters, 22d Air Force, Travis AFB, California; headquarters, 21st Air Force, McGuire AFB, New Jersey; and headquarters, Military Airlift Command, Scott AFB, Illinois.

Estimates of potential annual savings and other benefits were based on analysis of charter flights of Pan American World Airways, Northwest Airlines, and Trans World Airlines on 13 channels during October and November 1973 and August and September 1974. These months were selected because of difficulties in extracting data on other months from MAC records. Air Force officials agreed that these months were representative periods for evaluating the current use of charter flights and the potential impact that would result from diverting charter passengers to scheduled flights.

In September 1974, before completing our field work, we obtained the views of personnel in DOD, CAB, and the commercial airlines on the diversion concept. Upon completing our fieldwork we discussed the results of our work with these agencies officials. Among the personnel contacted were:

- --Director for Transportation and Warehousing Policy, Office of the Assistant Secretary of Defense (Installations and Logistics).

- --Deputy for Transportation, Office of the Assistant Secretary of the Air Force (Installations and Logistics).

- --Managing Director, CAB.

- --Deputy Director, Bureau of Economics, CAB.

- --Vice President, Northwest Airlines.

- --Vice President, Trans World Airlines.

- --Vice President, Pan American World Airways.

- --President, Air Transport Association of America.

- --President, National Air Carriers Association.

APPENDIX I   APPENDIX I

CIVIL AERONAUTICS BOARD
WASHINGTON, D.C. 20428

IN REPLY REFER TO: B-1-66

August 18, 1975

Mr. Victor L. Lowe
Director, General Government Division
General Accounting Office
441 G Street, N. W.
Washington, D. C. 20548

Dear Mr. Lowe:

Thank you for the G.A.O. draft report on fuel savings and other economic benefits derived by diverting Department of Defense passengers from chartered to scheduled flights (Code 943229). By Order 75-7-104, July 22, 1975, the Board instituted an investigation of this matter, a self-explanatory copy of which is enclosed for your information. It is hoped that this proceeding will lead to a final determination on the merits of the military part charter service concept.

We consider the recommendations set forth in the GAO draft report to be premature, and for this reason we cannot concur at present. Rather, we suggest that these recommendations be deferred pending a final Board decision in our investigation.

We appreciate the opportunity to comment on this report in advance of your finalizing it and hope the above commentary is helpful.

Sincerely,

John E. Robson
Chairman

Enclosure

APPENDIX II   APPENDIX II

ASSISTANT SECRETARY OF DEFENSE
WASHINGTON, D.C. 20301

25 AUG 1975

INSTALLATIONS AND LOGISTICS

Mr. F. J. Shafer
Director, Logistics and Communications Division
U.S. General Accounting Office
Washington, D.C. 20548

Dear Mr. Shafer:

This is in response to your letter of June 9, 1975, to the Secretary of Defense transmitting copies of your draft report concerning "Fuel Savings And Other Benefits By Diverting Passengers From Chartered to Scheduled Overseas Flights," OSD Case #4096.

The Department of Defense supports expanded use of blocked space Category Y service under a more permanent and broader Civil Aeronautics Board (CAB) authority, as long as it is formulated on the overall mobilization base contract awards, when it is in line with the military mission requirement and in agreement with the commercial carrier concerned. Although the savings are considered to be somewhat overstated, any fuel savings that can be achieved without impacting on Defense readiness and added costs should be pursued. We, therefore, concur with the recommendations to have the Secretary of Defense negotiate with the appropriate air carriers to expand the program and for the CAB to evaluate extension of the diversion concept on the present four routes and on other requested routes when in the National interest. However, to expand the program on all routes where the certificated air carriers operate charters that parallel their commercial flights is not always consistent with the requirements of the National defense.

Specific comments regarding the findings, conclusions, and recommendations in the report are attached as Enclosure 1.

Sincerely,

PAUL H. RILEY
Acting Assistant Secretary of Defense
(Installations and Logistics)

Enclosure
a/s

12

APPENDIX II   APPENDIX II

Secretary of Defense Comments on GAO Draft Report:

"Fuel Savings and Other Benefits by Diverting Passengers from Chartered to Scheduled Overseas Flights" (OSD Case #4096)

1. Comments on the findings and conclusions:

    a. Savings of 48 million gallons of jet fuel annually could be overstated if the act of adding Category Y traffic coupled with marketing influences causes additions to scheduled service in the future that would not otherwise be required.

    b. A reduction in annual costs "by about $3.5 million through better utilization of aircraft seats" is similarly misleading. The report assumes that all DoD travel that parallels commercial routes will fall under Category Y. However, to expand the program on all of these routes is not always consistent with the requirements of the National defense or is not necessarily compatible with the GAO final recommendation that the concept not affect revenues of the other certified carriers and those of supplemental air carriers. The Military Airlift Command (MAC) international airlift contracts are awards pursuant to the authority of 10 U.S.C. 2304 (a)(16) (Mobilization Base) and, as such, each carrier's award is based directly upon the number of suitable aircraft the carrier is willing to commit to the Civil Reserve Air Fleet (CRAF). Presently NWA and PAA are the only scheduled carriers that have fixed contracts for FY 76, and the aircraft committed by NWA and PAA do not justify awards of the magnitude set forth in the GAO report. If this were arbitrarily done in the scope indicated, it would adversely impact the other (supplemental and scheduled) carriers and their continuance in the CRAF program could be in jeopardy.

    c. In addition, in stating a $3.5 million annual cost reduction, the report does not address potential added DoD costs of moving passengers from military centers, located near military charter airfields, to commercial air terminals on the scheduled routes, and vice versa. Also, the report does not address potential future cost ramifications that could increase charter rates based on added terminal services provided by the commercial carrier that is presently handled by the military at military gateways. When these services are done by the airlines, the carriers' commercial systems cost will be included in the CAB cost analysis, and might increase the Category B rate as well as the corresponding Category Y costs. Conversely, the increased profits reported by the carriers in Category Y service may offset these terminal expenses. Thus, it is not certain at

13

APPENDIX II   APPENDIX II

this time regarding the amount of savings that might be realized through expanded use of Category Y airlift.

d. The reduction of 125 positions in the aerial port was not clearly demonstrated either by methodology or rationale. Aerial port manpower needs are determined by wartime mission requirements, not peacetime workloads. The asserted reduction of certain other aerial port personnel cited in this report as having been the subject of a 13 March 1975 GAO Letter Report, was refuted by the DoD response, which emphasized this point. Detailed documentation supporting this position has been provided to the Senate Armed Services Committee, the Senate Appropriation Committee, and more recently to the GAO stating that it will be made the subject of a special examination. The 125 aerial port personnel authorizations alluded to in the current report represent vital wartime positions which in our view cannot be eliminated.

2. Comments on GAO recommendations:

a. While the draft report covers the CAB limited approvals and their reluctance to approve future applications, it does not address the limitations imposed by CAB under the present authority and how these limitations also will not permit the carrier or MAC to convert to the magnitude indicated in the GAO report. In all cases, the Air Force on behalf of DoD has filed petitions with the CAB in support of the commercial carriers' petitions for exemption to carry military charter passengers on regularly scheduled service. We have requested that the Board not impose conditions which would eliminate or reduce the flexibility needed to permit maximum negotiation and use of the authority to meet the military operational requirements. We have recommended the CAB authority be broad and provide for the transfer of full airplane charter commitments for movement in available seats on scheduled commercial flights by the same carriers over the same or similar routing, whenever the DoD and the carrier in question can reach mutual agreement on the exact transfer. It was our position and understanding that it would apply only with respect to passenger transportation services which the DoD had first ordered from those carriers as full planeload charter service under the DoD's mobilization base award program. Thus, as indicated above, the extent to which the DoD would use the authority being sought by the scheduled carriers would depend upon the amount of charter service ordered under the mobilization base program from each carrier. However, the CAB in granting the authority felt that certain limitations were necessary to provide assurance that the exemptions do not work to the disadvantage of other carriers who do not have certificated scheduled services to avail themselves under the exemptions, but who are also competitors for MAC contracts. Therefore, the CAB restricted the

14

APPENDIX II   APPENDIX II

exemptions authorized to the military charter passengers which would have **otherwise** been carried on the round-trip planeload charter missions under **MAC** fixed buy allotments.

b. Thus, the routes were not only specified but the program was also limited to the fixed commitments made to the carriers at the beginning of the fiscal year. This represents approximately 60 percent of MAC total yearly passenger buy from the commercial air industry. Expansion charters which are still part of the overall award under the mobilization base are not eligible for conversion. This limitation by itself reduces the potential yearly conversion indicated by GAO in Appendix I of the draft report by 30 percent and, of course, this means that the fuel and economic savings are also overstated under the method of computation used by the GAO. In addition, when we consider that the GAO converted all one-way missions to round trips in their computations, and did not consider such factors as military requirements that could not be met by the commercial scheduled service or the commercial oversea airport facilities, and that our charters serve both on-line and off-line scheduled points in their estimate, then the number of missions which have the potential for conversion must be further reduced. In essence, using or establishing a criteria based only on diverting passengers from charter and commercial flights is erroneous and tends to overstate the potential savings and advantages that are available through such a program.

APPENDIX II   APPENDIX II

EVALUATION OF DOD COMMENTS

ON FINDINGS AND CONCLUSIONS

1. DOD: Savings of 48 million gallons of jet fuel annually could be overstated if the act of adding Category Y 1/ traffic coupled with marketing influences causes additions to scheduled services that would not otherwise be required.

    GAO: GAO agrees that the above figure represents the maximum potential for savings and has changed the wording of the report to indicate this. The international air carriers whose charter flights would be converted to scheduled service have assured us that the military traffic could be absorbed on existing scheduled flights. However, to the extent that the military passengers could not be absorbed, charter flights (not additional scheduled flights) would be flown. Our recommendations are not intended to impede this flexibility.

2. DOD: A reduction in annual costs by about $3.5 million through better utilization of aircraft seats is similarly misleading. The report assumes that all DOD travel that parallels commercial routes will fall under Category Y. However, to expand the program on all of these routes is not always consistent with the requirements of the national defense or is not necessarily compatible with the GAO final recommendation that the concept not affect revenues of the other certified carriers and those of supplemental air carriers. The Military Airlift Command international airlift contracts are awards pursuant to the authority of 10 U.S.C. 2304 (a) (16) (Mobilization Base) and, as such, each carrier's award is based directly upon the number of suitable aircraft the carrier is willing to commit to the Civil Reserve Air Fleet (CRAF). Presently Northwest Airlines and Pan American World Airways are the only scheduled carriers that have fixed contracts for fiscal year 1976, and the aircraft committed by these carriers do not justify awards of the magnitude set forth in the GAO report. If this were arbitrarily done in the scope indicated, it would adversely impact the other (supplemental and scheduled) carriers and their continuance in the CRAF program could be in jeopardy.

1/Category Y--military passenger traffic carried on commercial flights at special CAB-established rates.

16

APPENDIX II   APPENDIX II

> GAO: The DOD personnel have apparently misunderstood our report. GAO did not assume that all DOD travel that parallels scheduled routes will fall under Category Y. Our report deals with three commercial airlines flying charters for MAC. We pointed out that the DOD personnel and dependents traveling on the chartered flights of these carriers could have traveled on regularly scheduled flights of the same airlines with large savings in fuel and overall cost. GAO suggested that use of scheduled service be extended to all charter routes where this opportunity exists. Again, the $3.5 million is a maximum and savings would be reduced to the extent that passengers could not be diverted.

3. DOD: In addition, in stating a $3.5 million annual cost reduction, the report does not address potential added DOD costs of moving passengers from military centers, located near military charter airfields, to commercial air terminals on the scheduled routes, and vice versa. Also, the report does not address potential future cost ramifications that could increase charter rates on the basis of added terminal services provided by the commercial carrier that is presently handled by the military at military gateways. When these services are done by the airlines, the carriers' commercial systems cost will be included in the CAB cost analysis and might increase the Category B rate as well as the corresponding Category Y costs. Conversely, the increased profits reported by the carriers in Category Y service may offset these terminal expenses. Thus it is not certain at this time regarding the amount of savings that might be realized through expanded use of Category Y airlift.

   GAO: The comment regarding added costs of moving passengers to and from the commercial air terminal ignores the fact that most passengers do not orginate near MAC terminals and often must use the commerical terminal anyway. Thus, the use of commerical gateways results in savings in shuttle costs to MAC aerial ports and, due to its convenience, has been applauded by the military services. Speculation about increases in charter rates ignores the fact that carriers have been providing scheduled services at fares based upon one-way charter rates (Categories A and Z) for many years with no effect on charter rates.

4. DOD: The reduction of 125 positions in the aerial port was not clearly demonstrated either by methodology or rationale. Aerial port manpower needs are determined by wartime mission requirements, not peacetime workloads.

APPENDIX II   APPENDIX II

> The asserted reduction of certain other aerial port personnel cited in this report as having been the subject of a GAO letter report, March 13, 1975, was refuted by the DOD response which emphasized this point. Detailed documentation supporting this position has been provided to the Senate Armed Services Committee, the Senate Appropriation Committee, and more recently to GAO stating that it will be made the subject of a special examination. The 125 aerial port personnel authorizations alluded to in the current report represent vital wartime positions which, in our view, cannot be eliminated.

GAO: The question of staffing aerial ports was considered in another GAO report and is presently being reevaluated at the request of the Senate Armed Services and Appropriations Committees. Consequently, we have deleted reference to staffing from this report.

5. DOD: While the report covers CAB's limited approval and its reluctance to approve future applications, the report does not address the limitations CAB imposed under its present authority and how these limitations also will not permit the carrier or MAC to convert to the magnitude indicated in the GAO report. In all cases, the Air Force, on behalf of DOD, has filed petitions with CAB in support of the commercial carriers' petitions for exemption to carry military charter passengers on regularly scheduled service. We have requested that CAB not impose conditions which would eliminate or reduce the flexibility needed to permit maximum negotiation and the use of authority to meet the military operational requirements. We have recommended the CAB authority be broad and provide for the transfer of full airplane charter commitments for movement in available seats on scheduled commercial flights by the same carriers over the same or similar routing, whenever the DOD and the carrier in question can reach mutual agreement on the exact transfer. It was our position and understanding that it would apply only with respect to passenger transportation services which DOD had first ordered from those carriers as full planeload charter service under DOD's mobilization base award program. Thus, as indicated above, the extent to which DOD would use the authority being sought by the scheduled carriers would depend upon the amount of charter service ordered under the mobilization base program from each carrier. However, CAB, in granting the authority, felt that certain limitations were necessary to provide assurance that the exemptions do not work to the disadvantage of other

APPENDIX II   APPENDIX II

carriers who do not have certificated scheduled services to avail themselves of under the exemptions, but who are also competitors for MAC contracts. Therefore, CAB restricted the exemptions authorized to the military charter passengers which would have otherwise been carried on the round-trip planeload charter missions under MAC's fixed buy allotments.

Thus, the routes were not only specified but the program was also limited to the fixed commitments made to the carriers at the beginning of the fiscal year. This represents approximately 60 percent of MAC's total yearly passenger buy from the commercial air industry. Expansion charters which are still part of the overall award under the mobilization base are not eligible for conversion. This limitation reduces the potential yearly conversion indicated by GAO in appendix III of the report by 30 percent and, of course, this means that the fuel and economic savings are also overstated under the method of computation used by the GAO. In addition, when we consider that GAO converted all one-way missions to round trips in their computations and did not consider such factors as military requirements that could not be met by the commercial scheduled service or the commercial overseas airport facilities and that our charters serve both on-line and off-line scheduled points in their estimate, then the number of missions which have the potential for conversion must be further reduced. In essence, using or establishing criteria based only on diverting passengers from charter and commercial flights is erroneous and tends to overstate the potential savings and advantages that are available through such a program.

GAO: Once again, these comments reveal a basic misunderstanding of GAO's report. GAO is aware of CAB's restrictions and has recommended that CAB approve diverting military passengers from charter flights which parallel scheduled service routes flown by the same carriers to these scheduled flights when possible. While it is true that GAO converted one-way missions to round-trip missions in its computations, this reduced the savings rather than increased the savings, as alleged by DOD, because the one-way charter rate per passenger mile is almost twice the round-trip charter rate per passenger mile. The computation using round-trip missions was done to avoid overstating potential benefits.

It is not true that GAO did not consider military requirements which could not be met by scheduled service or charters servicing off-line as well as on-line points.

19

APPENDIX II   APPENDIX II

GAO dealt only with those charters servicing on-line points which paralleled scheduled flights servicing nearby locations. Those charters transported military personnel and their dependents to areas also served by scheduled service flights.

GAO recognized that off-line points and specific military requirements would still require charter service. Such service, however, is necessarily separate from the charter flights for which diversion to scheduled service is recommended.

APPENDIX III   APPENDIX III

POTENTIAL ANNUAL JET FUEL SAVINGS BY SUBSTITUTING
SCHEDULED SERVICE FOR CHARTER SERVICE (note a)

Channel	Average per flight Round-trip flight time (hours)	Gallons of fuel consumed (note b)	Number of flights converted (note c)	Total gallons of fuel
				(000 omitted)
21st Air Force:				
McGuire AFB, New Jersey/Charleston AFB, South Carolina--Rhein-Main AB, Germany	16.74	34,535	270	9,324
McGuire AFB, New Jersey--Rhein-Main AB, Germany/Mildenhall AB, England	17.13	35,339	12	424
McGuire AFB, New Jersey--Mildenhall AB, England	14.43	29,769	21	625
McGuire AFB, New Jersey--Torrejon AB, Spain	15.86	32,719	3	98
McGuire AFB, New Jersey--Rhein-Main AB, Germany/Torrejon AB, Spain	18.62	38,413	18	691
			324	11,162
22d Air Force:				
Travis AFB/Norton AFB, California--Hickam AFB, Hawaii	11.38	23,477	40.5	951
Travis AFB/Norton AFB, California--Kadena AB, Okinawa				
Mid-Pacific route	31.65	65,294	102	6,660
North Pacific route	27.44	56,609	54	3,057
Travis AFB, California--Yokota AB, Japan				
Mid-Pacific route	25.44	52,483	129	6,770
North Pacific route	21.42	44,189	6	265
Travis AFB, California--Osan AB, Korea				
Mid-Pacific route	28.83	59,476	24	1,427
North Pacific route	25.74	53,102	90	4,779
Travis AFB, California--Anderson AFB, Guam	24.71	50,977	70.5	3,594
Travis AFB, California--Clark AB, Philippines	29.50	60,859	22.5	1,369
Travis AFB, California--Taipei International Airport, Taiwan	27.06	55,825	27	1,507
Travis AFB, California--Bangkok International Airport, Thailand	38.27	78,951	79.5	6,277
			645	36,656
Total			969	47,818

a/Based on an analysis of charter flights of Northwest Airlines, Pan American World Airways, and Trans World Airlines during 4 representative months.

b/A Boeing 707, such as those used by the carriers on MAC charters, uses an average of 2,063 gallons of fuel per hour.

c/The number of flights is shown on a round-trip basis. One-way flights were converted to round-trip flights--i.e., two one-way flights equal one round-trip flight.

APPENDIX IV   APPENDIX IV

POTENTIAL ANNUAL SAVINGS TO DOD THROUGH

IMPROVED SEAT UTILIZATION (note a)

Channel	Passenger miles (note b) Available	Used	Unused	Computed utilization percentage	Savings through use of commercial service (note c)
	————(millions)————				(000 omitted)
21st Air Force:					
McGuire AFB, New Jersey/Charleston AFB, South Carolina--Rhein-Main AB, Germany	358.42	352.02	6.40	98.2	$ 157
McGuire AFB, New Jersey--Rhein-Main AB, Germany/Mildenhall AB, England	15.56	15.14	.42	97.3	10
McGuire AFB, New Jersey--Mildenhall AB, England	24.47	24.26	.21	99.1	5
McGuire AFB, New Jersey--Torrejon AB, Spain	3.53	3.20	.33	90.7	8
McGuire AFB, New Jersey--Rhein-Main AB, Germany/Torrejon AB, Spain	24.75	22.93	1.82	92.7	45
	426.73	417.55	9.18	97.9	225
22d Air Force:					
Travis AFB/Norton AFB, California--Hickam AFB, Hawaii	35.86	26.93	8.93	75.1	219
Travis AFB/Norton AFB, California--Kadena AB, Okinawa	354.42	333.86	20.56	94.2	504
Travis AFB, California--Yokota AB, Japan (note d)	297.99	267.00	30.99	89.6	760
Travis AFB, California--Osan AB, Korea (note d)	239.81	224.22	15.59	93.5	382
Travis AFB, California--Anderson AFB, Guam	144.87	130.67	14.20	90.2	348
Travis AFB, California--Clark AB, Philippines	54.14	48.89	5.25	90.3	129
Travis AFB, California--Taipei International Airport, Taiwan	60.13	53.52	6.61	89.0	162
Travis AFB, California--Bangkok International Airport, Thailand	240.91	208.63	32.28	86.6	792
	1,428.13	1,293.72	134.41	90.6	3,296
Total	1,854.86	1,711.27	143.59	92.3	$3,521

a/Based on analysis of charter flights of Northwest Airlines, Pan American World Airways, and Trans World Airlines during 4 representative months.

b/Passenger miles equal the distance traveled multiplied by the number of passengers carried; i.e., five passengers going 1 mile equals 5-passenger miles. Under the charter system, DOD charters the entire airplane and pays for all of the available passenger miles based on the number of seats available---even those that are unoccupied. The savings derived by diverting to scheduled flights occur because DOD pays for only those passenger miles used on a particular flight (assuming that unoccupied seats do not exceed the 15-percent rescheduling provision).

c/Based on the round-trip charter rate effective August 1974. The rate during this period was 2.197 cents per passenger mile plus a fuel surcharge of 11.60 percent for a total of 2.452 cents per passenger mile. We did not segregate one-way flights even though they have a higher rate.

d/Includes available, occupied, and unoccupied passenger miles on both mid-Pacific and North Pacific routes.

APPENDIX V   APPENDIX V

POTENTIAL COST REDUCTIONS
TO COMMERICAL CARRIERS (note a)

Channel	Number of flights converted (note d)	Fuel cost reductions (note c)	Gallons of jet fuel saved (note b)	Operating expense reductions (note e)	Total cost reductions
		—————————(000 omitted)—————————			
21st Air Force:					
McGuire AFB, New Jersey/Charleston AFB, South Carolina--Rhein AB, Germany	270	$ 3,478	9,324	$ 3,780	$ 7,258
McGuire AFB, New Jersey--Rhein-Main AB, Germany/Mildenhall AB, England	12	158	424	168	326
McGuire AFB, New Jersey--Mildenhall AB, England	21	233	625	294	527
McGuire AFB, New Jersey--Torrejon AB, Spain	3	37	98	42	79
McGuire AFB, New Jersey--Rhein-Main AB, Germany/Torrejon AB, Spain	18	258	691	252	510
	324	4,164	11,162	4,536	8,700
22d Air Force:					
Travis AFB/Norton AFB, California--Hickam AFB, Hawaii	40.5	355	951	1,013	1,368
Travis AFB/Norton AFB, California--Kadena AB, Okinawa					
Mid-Pacific route	102	2,484	6,660	2,550	5,034
North Pacific route	54	1,140	3,057	1,350	2,490
Travis AFB, California--Yokota AB, Japan					
Mid-Pacific route	129	2,525	6,770	3,225	5,750
North Pacific route	6	99	265	150	249
Travis AFB, California--Osan AB, Korea					
Mid-Pacific route	24	532	1,427	600	1,132
North Pacific route	90	1,783	4,779	2,250	4,033
Travis AFB, California--Anderson AFB, Guam	70.5	1,341	3,594	1,763	3,104
Travis AFB, California--Clark AB, Philippines	22.5	511	1,369	563	1,074
Travis AFB, California--Taipei International Airport, Taiwan	27	562	1,507	675	1,237
Travis AFB, California--Bangkok International Airport, Thailand	79.5	2,341	6,277	1,988	4,329
	645	13,673	36,656	16,127	29,800
Total	969	$17,837	47,818	$20,663	$38,500

a/Based on analysis of charter flights of Northwest Airlines, Pan American World Airways, and Trans World Airlines during 4 representative months.

b/See appendix III.

c/Commercial carriers purchased fuel from DOD on the basis of a price of 37.3 cents per gallon--the DOD cost for jet fuel as of January 17, 1975. It should be noted that prior to this date, the scheduled carriers were able to purchase fuel for charter flights from DOD at a special contract price of 11.3 cents per gallon. The carriers estimated that they purchase about 60 percent of their charter fuel from DOD.

d/Includes one-way flights converted to a round-trip basis.

e/Based on the carriers' estimated costs of about $25,000 and $14,000 for typical round-trip transpacific and transatlantic flights, respectively. These estimates were exclusive of fuel and aircraft ownership costs.

APPENDIX VI   APPENDIX VI

PRINCIPAL OFFFICIALS RESPONSIBLE

FOR ACTIVITIES DISCUSSED IN THIS REPORT

	Tenure of office	
	From	To
DEPARTMENT OF DEFENSE		
SECRETARY OF DEFENSE:		
Donald H. Rumsfeld	Nov. 1975	Present
James R. Schlesinger	July 1973	Nov. 1975
William P. Clements, Jr. (acting)	Apr. 1973	July 1973
Elliot L. Richardson	Jan. 1973	Apr. 1973
Melvin R. Laird	Jan. 1969	Jan. 1973
DEPUTY SECRETARY OF DEFENSE:		
William P. Clements, Jr.	Jan. 1973	Present
Kenneth Rush	Feb. 1972	Jan. 1973
ASSISTANT SECRETARY OF DEFENSE (INSTALLATIONS AND LOGISTICS):		
Dr. John J. Bennett (acting)	Apr. 1975	Present
Arthur I. Mendolia	June 1973	Mar. 1975
Hugh McCullough (acting)	Jan. 1973	June 1973
Barry J. Shillito	Feb. 1969	Jan. 1973
DEPARTMENT OF THE AIR FORCE		
SECRETARY OF THE AIR FORCE:		
John W. Plummer (acting)	Nov. 1975	Present
Dr. John L. McLucas	July 1973	Nov. 1975
Dr. John L. McLucas (acting)	June 1973	July 1973
Dr. Robert C. Seamens, Jr.	Jan. 1969	May 1973
ASSISTANT SECRETARY OF THE AIR FORCE (INSTALLATIONS AND LOGISTICS):		
Frank A. Shrontz	Oct. 1973	Present
Richard J. Keegan (acting)	Aug. 1973	Oct. 1973
Lewis E. Turner (acting)	Jan. 1973	Aug. 1973
Philip N. Whittaker	May 1969	Jan. 1973

APPENDIX VI   APPENDIX VI

	Tenure of office	
	From	To

CIVIL AERONAUTICS BOARD

CHAIRMAN:
John E. Robson	Apr. 1975	Present
Richard J. O'Melia (acting)	Jan. 1975	Apr. 1975
Robert D. Timm	Mar. 1973	Dec. 1974
Secor D. Browne	Oct. 1969	Mar. 1973

APPENDIX IX

Writing the Report: Selected Policies from the U.S. GAO Report Manual

Significance

Significance, as applied to our reports, is a relative term and one that cannot be defined precisely to cover all situations. Significance and congressional interest are key factors influencing our decisions on the level of reporting.

The matters included in all of our reports must be of sufficient significance to justify our reporting them and to warrant the attention of those to whom the reports are directed. The usefulness—and therefore the effectiveness—of our reports is diminished by the inclusion of insignificant matters because they tend to distract the readers' attention from the truly important matters we report.

Decisions as to the significance of matters to be reported must represent a composite judgment of all the pertinent factors involved.

Usefulness and Timeliness

The preparation of our reports must be preceded by careful analyses of the purposes to be served, the intended recipients, and the kinds of information needed by the recipients to accomplish the designated purposes. We must study the information to be reported from the perspective of the recipients. Whether our purpose is to stimulate constructive action or to provide information, our reports must be structured to the interests and needs of our audience.

If the distribution of a report is expected to be limited to agency officials or others who are well acquainted with the particular activities discussed in the reports, the amount of background information and detail can be reduced. However, we should not assume such limited audiences for our reports to the Congress or to agency heads. These reports should be written so they will be clear to any reasonably intelligent, well-informed person who is not very familiar with the particular programs, activities, or even the agencies involved.

Timeliness, like usefulness, is essential to effective reporting. A carefully prepared report may be of little value if it arrives too late for the decisionmaker to fully consider the information reported in relation to any decisions he needs to make.

Problems affecting the timeliness of our reports often originate in the planning, management, and analytical phases of the work. Delays in processing reports are often traceable to unresolved or unrecognized problems that should have been solved during the finding development phase. Integration of reporting with the planning and execution phases of our work should help to highlight these problems and facilitiate their timely solution.

Findings involving such matters as unnecessary expenditures, waste of public funds, illegal transactions, and other failures to protect the Government's interests should be communicated without delay in order that prompt and decisive corrective actions may be taken.

Accuracy and Adequacy of Subject

All the prescribed report preparation, review, and processing procedures must be applied with the objective of producing reports that contain no errors of fact, logic, or reasoning.

The need for accuracy is based on the need to be fair and impartial in our reporting and to assure users and readers of our reports that what we report is reliable. One inaccuracy in a report can cast doubt on the validity of an entire report and can divert attention from the substance of the report. Also at stake is the professional reputation of the General Accounting Office.

All factual data, findings, and conclusions in our reports must be adequately supported by enough objective evidence in our files to demonstrate or prove, when we are called upon, the bases for the matters reported and their accuracy or reasonableness. Except as necessary to make convincing presentations, detailed supporting data need not be included in our reports. It must be kept in systematically maintained files and be readily available, however.

Opinions and conclusions in our reports should be clearly identified as such and must be based on enough audit work to warrant them. In most cases, one example of a deficiency cannot support a broad conclusion and a related recommendation for

---

Source: Adapted from the United States General Accounting Office, the Comptroller General of the United States, *Report Manual* (Washington, D.C.: General Accounting Office, 1974), chap. 4.

corrective action. All that it supports is the finding of the fact that there was a deviation, error, or weakness.

On some of our assignments, we are not able to do all the work necessary to completely verify the correctness of information obtained. When this occurs, we must state the source or basis of the information and include any necessary qualifications.

Convincingness

Our findings must be presented in a convincing manner, and our conclusions and recommendations must follow logically from the facts presented. The information in our reports must be sufficient to persuade the readers of the importance of our findings, the reasonableness of our conclusions, and the desirability of their accepting our recommendations. Reports designed in this manner can do much to focus the attention of responsible officials on the matters in our reports which warrant attention and to stimulate actions on them.

We must not take the approach that "It's so, because we say it's so." The burden of proof is on us, not on the agency.

Objectivity and Perspective

Each report should present our findings in an objective and unbiased manner and should include sufficient information on the subject matter to provide our readers with *proper perspective*. Our objective is to produce reports which are fair and not misleading and which, at the same time, place primary emphasis on matters needing attention. We must, however, guard against the tendency to exaggerate or overemphasize deficient performance noted during our reviews.

The information needed to provide proper report balance and perspective should be worked into the digests as well as into the other parts of our reports and should include:

1. Appropriate information as to why we made the particular examinations on which we are reporting.
2. Clear statements of the nature and scope of our examinations. *Where appropriate,* the reports should clearly show that our primary emphasis was on examining into matters apparently needing attention and that we did not undertake evaluations of the total activities or operations.
3. Information about the size and nature of the activities or programs to which our findings relate so as to provide perspective against which the significance of the findings can be judged. Where applicable, the reports should draw attention to the relative newness or experimental nature of the programs or activities so that our findings can be considered in this light.
4. Correct and fair descriptions of our findings so as to avoid misinterpretation and misunderstanding. This requires recognition of pertinent advance comments obtained and identification of all significant relevant factors even though some may be contrary to our findings. It requires also that information be included on the size of our tests and the methods of selecting items to test so that the readers may relate such information to the total activity and to our findings.
5. Information as to the satisfactory aspects, not just the deficient aspects, of operations examined into where significant and where warranted by the extent of our work. This does *not* mean, however, that when we have something bad to report we must say something good to balance it.

Clarity and Simplicity

To effectively communicate, our reports must be presented as clearly and simply as practicable. Clarity is also important because the information in our reports may be used on short notice by GAO officials who did not directly participate in the underlying work or in the preparation and review of the reports.

We should not presuppose detailed technical knowledge of the subjects by the readers. Where technical terms and unfamiliar abbreviations, and the like, must be used, they should be clearly defined. Our efforts at "style" should be aimed at making the meaning clear. Flowery, pedantic expressions and stilted language must be avoided.

Proper organization of report material and precision in stating facts, analyzing them, and drawing conclusions are essential to clarity. Many of our reports deal with complex subjects and various report sections are interrelated. This sometimes makes it difficult to avoid repetition. To the extent possible, however, each GAO report should be so organized that, except for information also included in the digest, all we have to say on a given subject is covered in one place in a report.

Visual aids (pictures, charts, graphs, maps, etc.) should be used whenever possible, to make our reports more easily understood and therefore more useful.

Conciseness

Our reports must be no longer than necessary to communicate the information we seek to report. They should not be mired down with too much detail—words, sentences, paragraphs, or sections that do not clearly tie in with the report messages. Too much detail detracts from the reports and may even conceal the real messages or confuse or discourage readers.

Although there is room for considerable judgment in determining the content of our reports, we should keep in mind that reports which are complete but still concise are more likely to receive attention. Our report audience largely comprises busy people who do not wish to be burdened with unessential details.

Completeness

Although our reports must be concise, we must remember that brevity that does not inform is not a virtue. Our reports must contain sufficient information about our findings, conclusions, and recommendations to promote adequate understandings of the matters reported and to provide convincing, but fair, presentations in proper perspective. Sufficient amounts of background information must be included to achieve these ends, and agency or contractor views must be given appropriate recognition.

Reports to the Congress must cover all matters required by law and must include such information as is necessary to keep the Congress adequately informed on the results of our audit work.

We should not expect readers to be possessed of all the same facts that we have, and therefore our reports should not be written on the bases that the bare recitals of facts make the conclusions that we have reached obvious or inescapable. If we have conclusions or opinions that we want the readers to know about, we should state them specifically rather than leave them to be inferred by the readers.

Constructiveness of Tone

In line with our basic objective of improving the administration of Government activities, the tone of our reports should be designed to encourage favorable reaction to our findings and recommendations. The titles, captions, and texts of our reports should be stated in constructive terms. Although our findings should be presented in clear forthright terms, we should keep in mind that our objective is to obtain favorable reaction and that this can best be accomplished by avoiding language which unnecessarily generates defensiveness and opposition. Although criticism of past performance often is necessary to demonstrate the need for some management improvememt, our emphasis in the reports should be on the needed improvements rather than on criticism.

APPENDIX X

Illustrative Report: Indian Education Program

Source: Report to the Congress by the Comptroller General of the United States, *Opportunity to Improve Indian Education in Schools Operated by the Bureau of Indian Affairs*, Department of the Interior, B-161468 (Washington, D.C.: General Accounting Office, 1972).

COMPTROLLER GENERAL OF THE UNITED STATES
WASHINGTON, D.C. 20548

B-161468

To the President of the Senate and the
Speaker of the House of Representatives

This is our report on the Department of the Interior's opportunity to improve Indian education in schools operated by the Bureau of Indian Affairs.

Our review was made pursuant to the Budget and Accounting Act, 1921 (31 U.S.C. 53), and the Accounting and Auditing Act of 1950 (31 U.S.C. 67).

Copies of this report are being sent to the Director, Office of Management and Budget; the Secretary of the Interior; and the Executive Director, National Council on Indian Opportunity.

Comptroller General
of the United States

Contents

		Page
DIGEST		1

CHAPTER

1 INTRODUCTION 5
    Overall perspective 6
    Background 7

2 OPPORTUNITIES FOR IMPROVING INDIAN EDUCATION 9
    Need to organize programs around established goals for Indian education 11
        Need for training to compensate for English communication handicaps 12
        Need for special education programs 15
        Need for professional counseling services in BIA schools 16
        Need to obtain substitute teachers 19
    Need to improve BIA's management information system 20
        Need for academic aptitude and achievement data 20
        Need for program-oriented financial management reports 22

3 CONCLUSIONS AND RECOMMENDATIONS 25
    Conclusions 25
    Recommendations to the Secretary of the Interior 26
    Matters for consideration by the Congress 27

4 AGENCY COMMENTS AND GAO EVALUATION 29

5 SCOPE OF REVIEW 32

APPENDIX

I Letter dated March 16, 1972, from the Director of Survey and Review, Department of the Interior, to the General Accounting Office 33

COMPTROLLER GENERAL'S
REPORT TO THE CONGRESS

OPPORTUNITY TO IMPROVE
INDIAN EDUCATION IN
SCHOOLS OPERATED BY
THE BUREAU OF INDIAN AFFAIRS
Department of the Interior
B-161468

DIGEST

WHY THE REVIEW WAS MADE

American Indians and Alaska Natives are considered to be among this country's most disadvantaged citizens, whether the scale of measurement is employment, income, housing, health, or education. It generally is recognized by Indian leaders and Government officials that education is a key element in the ultimate solution of the problems that these disadvantaged citizens face.

In recent years both the President and the Congress have focused considerable attention on the continuing problems which have beset Indian education. Senate Report 91-501, entitled "Indian Education: A National Tragedy--A National Challenge," outlined a number of serious inadequacies in the Bureau of Indian Affairs' (BIA) education program and recommended that the Federal Government set specific goals for rapid attainment of equal educational opportunity for Indian children, including parity of achievement level of Indian high school students with national norms.

During the 5-year period ended June 30, 1971, BIA expended about $500 million to operate Federal schools and dormitories having a total annual enrollment of about 50,000 Indian children. Although complete and accurate data was not available, BIA estimated, on the basis of limited data available in 1968, that Indians graduating from BIA high schools generally had only about a ninth-grade education as measured by standardized academic-achievement tests.

The General Accounting Office (GAO) made this review to evaluate the management methods used by BIA in meeting the goals set for education of Indian children in BIA-operated schools.

FINDINGS AND CONCLUSIONS

The major goal of BIA's education program is to close the education gap between Indians and other Americans by raising the academic-achievement level of Indian students up to the national average by 1976. It appears that relatively little progress has been made toward achieving this goal. (See p. 9.)

Tear Sheet

APRIL 27, 1972

In fact BIA's education programs have not been designed to achieve this goal. Officials at five of 12 schools and at one of three area offices visited told GAO that they were not even aware of the goal. Officials at the remaining schools and area offices stated that they had not made a specific effort to design their programs to reach this goal and had not received any guidelines or instructions concerning it from the BIA central office. (See p. 11.)

Certain factors which adversely affected students' ability to achieve at the national average were not fully dealt with in the established school programs. For example:

- --Inability to communicate effectively in the English language generally was recognized as a primary restraint to normal educational progress. Standardized achievement tests indicated that almost all students in the schools GAO visited had communication skills deficiencies. GAO noted, however, that the schools generally did not have adequate programs to deal with this problem. (See pp. 12 and 13.)

- --BIA officials estimated that the number of Indian children in their schools needing special education for physical, sensory, mental, or emotional handicaps was at least double that normally found in public schools and might be as high as 50 percent of total enrollment in boarding schools off the reservations. Six of the 12 schools visited by GAO, however, had not established special education programs, and some of the special education programs which had been established at several other schools were not adequate. (See pp. 15 and 16.)

- --BIA's guidance programs generally have emphasized dormitory administration in boarding schools and have not provided Indian students with a broad range of professional counseling services, including academic counseling. The counselors' activities were concerned primarily with social and personal problems of the students. (See pp. 16 to 18.)

- --Of the 12 schools visited, 10 did not have adequate provisions for obtaining substitute teachers to assume responsibility for classes when regular teachers were absent. (See p. 19.)

BIA did not have an effective management information system which would provide education program officials with data necessary for identifying educational needs of Indian children, designing programs and activities for accomplishing educational goals, allocating resources to these programs, and evaluating the costs and benefits in relation to the educational goals. (See pp. 20 to 24.)

RECOMMENDATIONS OR SUGGESTIONS

The Department of the Interior should require the Commissioner of Indian Affairs to:

--Clearly apprise all operating levels of the goal of reaching a level of academic achievement for Indian students equal to the national average and the date by which it is to be accomplished.

--Identify and assign priorities for dealing with all critical factors known to impede progress toward accomplishment of that goal.

--Develop a comprehensive educational program which is designed specifically to overcome the factors which impede progress in meeting the goal and which is flexible enough to meet the needs of students in all BIA schools.

--Establish periodic milestones, such as the amount of improvement in the academic-achievement level necessary at the end of each successive year, to accomplish the established goal.

--Periodically evaluate program results on the basis of these predetermined milestones to allow timely redirections of effort as may be necessary.

--Develop a management information system providing:

1. Meaningful and comprehensive information on the academic aptitude and achievement levels of students in the BIA school system.

2. Program-oriented financial management reports geared toward the management needs of BIA education program officials. (See pp. 26 and 27.)

AGENCY ACTIONS AND UNRESOLVED ISSUES

The Department of the Interior stated that it was in general accord with GAO's findings and that GAO's conclusions and recommendations would constructively support BIA's efforts to improve its education program.

The Department stated that it would be normal to expect that from 5 to 10 years would be required to statistically prove any increased effectiveness through student test results. The Department noted that GAO had not given due cognizance to departmental and congressional commitments and efforts to improve educational opportunity for the American Indian.

GAO agrees that it would have been desirable to obtain student academic-achievement data covering several years. Such data was not available, however, and, by necessity, GAO's evaluation of progress achieved by BIA was limited to available data.

The Department's comments on GAO's recommendations are discusssed below.

--A task force was established in March 1971 to review the goals and objectives of BIA's education program and the necessary organizational changes to achieve them. The Department did not indicate, however, what action would be taken to apprise all operating levels of the goal of reaching a level of academic achievement equal to the national average and the date by which it was to be accomplished.

--The Department outlined a number of steps to be implemented in fiscal year 1973 for identifying and assigning priorities for dealing with all critical factors known to impede progress toward accomplishment of its goal.

--Concerning GAO's recommendation for development of a comprehensive education program that would meet the needs of all students in BIA schools, the Department stated that actions were being taken to upgrade the ability of school personnel to deal with the special nature of the students served. GAO believes that, although these actions should help to improve BIA's education program, action also must be taken to ensure that the special needs of all students are identified and met.

--Regarding GAO's recommendations for establishment of milestones and for periodic evaluation of program results, the Department stated that these exercises were impractical since the BIA goal must be tempered by the reality of Indian self-determination, the special nature of the students served, and the availability of funds. GAO believes that effective management requires the development of an appropriate strategy for meeting established goals and the periodic evaluation of progress toward meeting these goals.

--Concerning GAO's recommendation for development of an education management information system, the Department outlined various activities which would be undertaken to design and implement such a system. GAO believes that effective use of information provided by the system should assist BIA in managing its schools. (See pp. 29 to 31.)

MATTERS FOR CONSIDERATION BY THE CONGRESS

In view of the concern which has been expressed by the President and by members of the Congress regarding the quality of Indian education, the Congress may wish to consider enacting legislation requiring BIA to furnish certain specific information as suggested in this report, which the Congress could use to evaluate the progress being made in improving Indian education. (See pp. 27 and 28.)

CHAPTER 1

INTRODUCTION

American Indians and Alaska Natives (hereinafter referred to as Indians) are considered to be among this country's most disadvantaged citizens, whether the scale of measurement is employment, income, housing, health, or education. It generally is recognized by various Indian leaders and Government officials that education is one of the key elements in the ultimate solution of the complex problems faced by these disadvantaged citizens.

In recent years both the President and the Congress have focused considerable attention on the continuing problems which have beset Indian education. In a July 1970 message to the Congress, the President stated that one of the saddest aspects of Indian life was the low quality of Indian education.

In November 1969 the Special Subcommittee on Indian Education, Senate Committee on Labor and Public Welfare, concluded a 2-year investigation by issuing Senate Report 91-501, entitled "Indian Education: A National Tragedy--A National Challenge." The Subcommittee outlined in its report a number of serious inadequacies in the education programs of the Bureau of Indian Affairs and concluded that "The present organization and administration of the BIA school system could hardly be worse."

The Subcommittee recommended that the Federal Government commit itself to providing Indians with an excellent education, including maximum Indian participation in, and control of, Indian education programs. In addition, the Subcommittee recommended that the Federal Government set specific goals for rapid attainment of equal educational opportunity for Indian children, including parity of achievement level of Indian high school students with national norms.

Because of the national interest in Indian education which had been expressed by the President and the Congress, the General Accounting Office undertook a review of the management of the BIA school system. Our review was concerned primarily with evaluating management methods used by BIA to meet the goals set for education of Indian children in BIA-operated schools.

OVERALL PERSPECTIVE

Each administration since 1960 has announced a policy calling for full participation by Indians in American life and a standard of living and an education equal to the national average.

BIA established certain educational goals in 1963, which were directed specifically toward closing the education gap between Indians and non-Indians by 1970. Except for a change in the target date, these goals have continued into the 1970's. The goals outlined in BIA's fiscal years 1971 and 1972 Program Memorandums,[1] dated June 1969 and May 1970, respectively, are that (1) 90 percent of all Indian youth graduate from high school, (2) by 1976 the achievement level of Indian students at least equal that for non-Indian youth, (3) 50 percent of the graduates enter college, and (4) the remaining 50 percent be either employed or enrolled in technical training.

The BIA goal of raising the academic-achievement level of Indian students at least up to that attained by non-Indian students appears to be consistent with the educational goals of the Indians themselves. For example, a private firm conducting a study of Indian education in 1969 reported that Indian students and parents, school administrators, teachers, and educational consultants were in substantial agreement that the goal of Indian education should be equal opportunity for Indian and non-Indian Americans. The study report further defined this goal as academic achievement for Indian high school and college graduates equal to that of non-Indians.

---

[1] BIA program memorandums are documents which present statements of major program issues requiring decisions in the current budget cycle and which have implications in terms of either present or future costs or the direction of a program or group of programs.

This goal was articulated by an Indian school board member during an April 1969 education conference at the Fort Apache Reservation, Arizona, as follows:

> "Our ultimate goal should be to educate our children so that their qualifications for any open position will be on an equal par with, if not better than, the non-Indians. This is the goal we should strive for."

A study of Indian education conducted by a former BIA Deputy Assistant Commissioner for Education under a grant by the Office of Education, Department of Health, Education, and Welfare, focused on the 1960's and the accomplishments during that decade. That study indicated that BIA had made progress in increasing the percentage of Indian children enrolled in school and in increasing the number of Indian high school graduates. In its 1972 Program Memorandum, however, BIA estimated that the academic-achievement level of Indian children graduating from BIA high schools was 3.3 years below the national average. We could not readily ascertain the reliability of this estimate because BIA does not accumulate achievement test data from its schools.

CHAPTER 2

OPPORTUNITIES FOR IMPROVING INDIAN EDUCATION

The major goal of BIA's education programs is to close the education gap between Indians and non-Indians by raising the academic-achievement level of Indian students up to the national average by 1976. It appears, however, that BIA has made relatively little progress toward attaining this goal, largely because BIA has not adequately communicated this goal to its area offices and schools and has not developed a specific plan for identifying and overcoming obstacles to, or for measuring progress toward, the accomplishment of this goal.

Our review of BIA records showed that they did not provide sufficient information to determine the actual progress that had been made toward raising the academic-achievement level of Indian children. As discussed in more detail on page 20, the formulation of academic achievement-testing programs was left to the discretion of the education officials at each of BIA's 11 area offices and the established testing programs differed from area to area. Also individual schools within the areas often did not follow the established programs. Further the results of tests that were administered at the schools were not compiled and evaluated on a national basis at the BIA central office. As a result the central office did not have the comprehensive academic-achievement data needed for comparing progress in attaining the goal of the education program on a school-to-school and year-to-year basis.

Academic-achievement data that was available at the 12 schools we visited showed relatively little evidence of progress from year to year. For example, the following table shows the gap between the national average and the average achievement level of Indian students at three elementary schools in the Phoenix Area, as measured by California

Achievement Tests[1] administered in the spring of 1970 and again in the spring of 1971.

Year in which tested	Achievement gap Grade							
	1	2	3	4	5	6	7	8
(years below national average)								
1970	0.7	0.8	1.4	1.2	1.3	1.6	1.3	1.9
1971	0.9	1.4	0.5	1.5	1.4	1.8	1.7	2.0

As shown above the gap between the national average and the average achievement level of Indian students shows a reduction in only the third grade.

The results of California Achievement Tests administered to students at three off-reservation secondary boarding schools located in the Navajo, Phoenix, and Juneau Areas also disclosed that there had been little evidence of progress, as shown below.

Year in which tested	Achievement gap											
	High school A Grade				High school B Grade				High school C Grade			
	9	10	11	12	9	10	11	12	9	10	11	12
(years below national average)												
1970	3.3	3.8	4.6	5.3	1.8	2.5	2.7	3.6	0.6	1.2	1.1	1.6
1971	3.5	3.7	4.5	5.3	2.9	2.8	3.4	4.4	0.7	1.3	1.9	2.1

We discussed the above academic-achievement data with various education consultants, all of whom agreed that it showed that there had been little evidence of progress.

---

[1] The California Achievement Test is one of a number of standardized tests used by educators in elementary and secondary schools to measure the academic-achievement levels of their students. Other standardized achievement tests used in BIA schools we visited included the Metropolitan Achievement Test and the Stanford Achievement Test.

NEED TO ORGANIZE PROGRAMS AROUND
ESTABLISHED GOALS FOR INDIAN EDUCATION

We found that BIA had not developed a specific plan to accomplish its goal of raising the academic-achievement level of Indian students up to the national average. Although the goal had been established and included in BIA's annual program memorandums, BIA did not plan and organize its education programs to achieve it.

Officials at BIA's central office and at the three area offices and 12 schools visited agreed that the education programs were not designed to reach the goal of raising the achievement level up to the national average by 1976. In fact officials at five schools and at one area office told us that they were not even aware of this goal. Officials at the seven other schools and two area offices told us that they had heard of the goal. They said, however, that they had not made a specific effort to design their programs to reach this goal because they had not been officially notified of it and had not received any guidelines or instructions from the central office concerning it.

The educational goals set forth in BIA's Manual, which was furnished to the schools and area offices, dated back to 1951 and were very general. These dealt primarily with such matters as physical, mental and moral development; citizenship; and health habits. The goals did not include closing the academic-achievement gap.

School officials cited a number of matters which had an adverse effect on the quality of education provided to children in BIA schools. These matters included the need for compensatory training in English communication skills, special education programs, professional counseling services, and substitute teachers. These matters, which are discussed below, are not intended to represent all the factors which have an impact on the quality of Indian education; instead, they are intended to illustrate that BIA has not organized its education program to accomplish its goal.

NEED TO IMPROVE BIA'S MANAGEMENT INFORMATION SYSTEM

An effective management information system would seem essential in developing, implementing, and evaluating an educational program. Such a system could provide education program officials with the data they need for identifying the educational needs of students, both individually and collectively; for designing programs and activities for accomplishing the desired educational goals; for budgeting and allocating resources to support these programs; and for evaluating the costs and benefits of these programs in relation to the planned educational goals. BIA officials generally agreed that they did not have an effective management information system for providing such data.

Need for academic aptitude and achievement data

Central office education officials stated that the results of standardized academic aptitude and achievement tests not only would be useful at the school level in identifying students' needs and measuring their progress but also would be needed by them in formulating and evaluating the results of programs designed to accomplish the goal of raising the academic-achievement level of Indian students to the national average.

BIA records did not contain sufficient information for determining the actual progress that had been made toward the accomplishment of this goal, nor did BIA have an overall student-testing program for obtaining such information. Education officials at each area office decided on the testing program to be followed by schools under their jurisdiction; however, test results were not compiled and evaluated at the central office. Outlined below is a brief comparison of the testing program followed in the three areas we visited.

Need for program-oriented financial management reports

The operating cost of the BIA school system for fiscal year 1971 was approximately $118.6 million. We found, however, that central office education program officials did not know by whom or for what purposes these funds had been used.

CHAPTER 3

CONCLUSIONS AND RECOMMENDATIONS

CONCLUSIONS

Improving the educational achievement level of Indian students appears to be one of the most important keys to overcoming the problems the Indians face. Information available at the schools we visited revealed relatively little evidence of progress.

Although BIA had established a goal of eliminating the disparity between educational achievement attained by Indian children and their non-Indian peers by 1976, it did not adequately communicate this goal to the operating levels nor did it develop and implement a specific plan of action by which it intended to raise Indian students' academic-achievement level. Certain constraints to improving academic achievement, such as English communication handicaps, were evident; yet established school programs did not deal with them completely and in some cases did not deal with them at all.

Considering the magnitude of the goal that was established by BIA and the obvious complexity of the problem, it appears that it is essential to have a well organized and managed program specifically designed to accomplish that goal. We believe that such a program should be formulated through a systematic analysis of (1) the program's goal and (2) the critical factors contributing to, or impeding effectiveness in, achieving that goal.

In view of the limited progress made to date in raising the academic-achievement level of Indian children to the national average, it may be necessary for BIA to evaluate the reasonableness of the 1976 target date. We believe, however, that, regardless of the target date which might be established, BIA will not achieve its goal unless the fundamental concepts of a sound management system are implemented.

We believe also that BIA should develop an effective management information system to assist the program manager in assessing the specific educational needs of the students, in identifying the major problems that must be dealt with, in devising the specific strategy for overcoming these problems, in implementing an education program responsive to the students' needs, in measuring progress toward stated goals, and in assessing the effectiveness of each responsible level within the BIA school system in achieving the established educational goals. The system should provide for comprehensive and consistent data on the students' academic aptitude and achievement levels and program-oriented financial management reports.

RECOMMENDATIONS TO THE SECRETARY OF THE INTERIOR

We recommend that the Department of the Interior require the Commissioner of Indian Affairs to:

- --Clearly apprise all operating levels of the goal of reaching a level of academic achievement for Indian students equal to the national average and the date by which it is to be accomplished.

- --Identify and assign priorities for dealing with all critical factors known to impede progress toward accomplishment of that goal.

- --Develop a comprehensive educational program which is designed specifically to overcome the factors which impede progress in meeting the goal and which is flexible enough to meet the needs of students in all BIA-operated schools.

- --Establish periodic milestones, such as the amount of improvement in the academic-achievement level necessary at the end of each successive year, to accomplish the established goal.

- --Periodically evaluate program results on the basis of these predetermined milestones to allow redirections of effort as may be necessary.

- --Develop a management information system providing:

1. Meaningful and comprehensive information on the academic aptitude and achievement levels of students in the BIA school system.

2. Program-oriented financial management reports geared toward the management needs of BIA education program officials.

Notes

Chapter 1. On Auditing the Performance of Management

1. McMickle, Peter L., and Elrod, Gene, *Auditing Public Education: The Aide Project* (Montgomery, Ala.: Alabama Department of Education, 1974), p. 32.
2. Wholey, Joseph S., Scanlon, John W., Duffy, Hugh G., Fukumoto, James S., and Vogt, Leona M., *Federal Evaluation Policy* (Washington, D.C.: The Urban Institute, 1970), p. 24.
3. Adapted from the Comptroller General of the United States, *Examples of Findings from Governmental Audits* (Washington, D.C.: U.S. General Accounting Office, 1973), p. 3.
4. Ibid., pp. 6–7.
5. Ibid., pp. 26–28.
6. Ibid., pp. 19–21.
7. Ibid., pp. 24–25.

Chapter 2. Understanding the Phases of the Audit Function

1. Comptroller General of the United States, *Standards for Audit of Governmental Organizations, Programs, Activities, and Functions* (Washington, D.C.: U.S. General Accounting Office, 1974), p. 7.
2. American Institute of Certified Public Accountants, *Management Advisory Services, Guideline Series Number 6. Guidelines for CPA Participation in Government Audit Engagements to Evaluate Economy, Efficiency, and Program Results* (New York: American Institute of Certified Public Accountants, 1977), p. 19. Copyright © by the American Institute of Certified Public Accountants.

Chapter 3. Determining Efficient, Economical, and Effective Operations

1. Adapted from an audit of the U.S. General Accounting Office, *Review of Uneconomical Utilization and Premature Disposal of Aircraft Spark Plugs by the Department of the Air Force*, B-132983 (Washington, D.C.: General Accounting Office, 1963).
2. Adapted from an audit of the U.S. General Accounting Office, *Federal Fire Safety Requirements Do Not Insure Life Safety in Nursing Home Fires—Department of Health, Education, and Welfare*, MWD-76-136 (Washington, D.C.: General Accounting Office, 1976).

Chapter 4. Planning and Programming the Audit

1. American Institute of Certified Public Accountants, *Statements on Auditing Standards* (New York: American Institute of Certified Public Accountants, 1977), p. 231. Copyright © 1977 by the American Institute of Certified Public Accountants.
2. Comptroller General of the United States, *Standards for Audit of Governmental Organizations, Programs, Activities, and Functions* (Washington, D.C.: U.S. General Accounting Office, 1974), p. 6.
3. Ibid., p. 7.
4. U.S. General Accounting Office, *Comprehensive Audit Manual* (Washington, D.C.: U.S. General Accounting Office, 1974), p. 18–2.

For references to cases, see Chapter 3 notes above.

Chapter 5. Reviewing Management Audit Principles Using Real-Life Situations

1. "The Spark Plug Case," considered a classic case in the GAO, was developed from a report to the Congress by the Comptroller General, *Review of Uneconomical Utilization and Premature Disposal of Aircraft Spark Plugs by the Department of the Air Force*, B-132983 (Washington, D.C.: U.S. Government Printing Office, 1963).
2. "The Case of the Overseas Flights" was developed from a report to the Congress by the Comptroller General, *Fuel Savings and Other Benefits Achieved by Diverting Department of Defense Passengers from Chartered to Scheduled Overseas Flights, Department of Defense, Civil Aeronautics Board*, GAO-LCD-75-231 (Washington, D.C.: General Accounting Office, 1976).
3. Adapted from an audit of the U.S. General Accounting Office, *How the District of Columbia Might Better Manage Its Tax Compliance Program*, GGD-76-46 (Washington, D.C.: General Accounting Office, 1976).
4. Adapted from an audit of the U.S. General Accounting Office, *Ineffective Management of Welfare Cases Costing Millions*, GGD-76-109 (Washington, D.C.: General Accounting Office, 1976).

Chapter 6. Applying the Principles, Policies, and Practices of Program Auditing

1. U.S. General Accounting Office, *Evaluation and Analysis to Support Decisionmaking,* PAD-76-9 (Washington, D.C.: U.S. Government Printing Office, 1976), pp. 13–15.

2. U.S. General Accounting Office, *Salmonella in Raw Meat and Poultry: An Assessment of the Problems,* Food and Drug Administration, Department of Health, Education, and Welfare, GAO MWD 74-149, prepared for the Congress (Washington, D.C.: General Accounting Office, 1974).

3. U.S. GAO, *Decisionmaking,* pp. 15–16.

4. U.S. Congress, Senate, *Indian Education: A National Tragedy,* S. Rept. 91-501, 1969.

5. Adapted from a report to the Congress by the Comptroller General, *Conditions in Local Jails Remain Inadequate Despite Federal Funding for Improvements,* Law Enforcement Assistance Administration, Department of Justice, GGD-76-36 (Washington, D.C.: General Accounting Office, 1976).

6. Adapted from a report to the Congress by the Comptroller General, *Opportunities for Improving the Effectiveness of Rapid Transit Grants,* Urban Mass Transportation Administration, Department of Transportation, RED-76-75 (Washington, D.C.: General Accounting Office, 1976).

Chapter 7. Understanding Management Control

1. American Institute of Certified Public Accountants, Codification of *Statements on Auditing Standards* (New York: American Institute of Certified Public Accountants, 1977), pp. 243, 248. Copyright © 1977 by the American Institute of Certified Public Accountants.

2. Ibid., pp. 249–53.

3. U.S. General Accounting Office, *Study of Programs for Health Services in Outpatient Health Centers in the District of Columbia,* B-118638 (Washington, D.C.: General Accounting Office, 1973), p. 36.

4. Material from the Uniform CPA Examinations, copyright © 1971, by the American Institute of Certified Public Accountants, Inc., is adapted with permission.

Chapter 8. Obtaining Evidence in Performance Auditing

1. U.S. General Accounting Office, *Standards for Audit of Governmental Organizations, Programs, Activities and Functions* (Washington, D.C.: U.S. Government Printing Office, 1974), p. 4.

2. U.S. Department of Health, Education, and Welfare, Audit Agency, *Audit of Voucher Demonstration Project, Alum Rock Union Elementary School District, San Jose, California, for the Period April 1, 1972 through June 30, 1975.* Audit Control No. 71475-09 (Washington, D.C. 1977).

3. U.S. General Accounting Office, *Workplace Inspection Program Weak in Detecting and Correcting Serious Hazards,* HRD-78-34 (Washington, D.C.: General Accounting Office, 1978).

Chapter 9. Understanding Working Papers

For references to cases, see Chapter 3 notes, above.

Chapter 10. Illustrative Working Papers: The Detailed Examination for a Management Audit

1. U.S. General Accounting Office, *Comprehensive Audit Manual, Part I,* Chapter 19 (Washington, D.C.: General Accounting Office, 1974), pp. 19:7–10, 16–17, 5–7.

2. Ibid., pp. 10–16.

For references to cases, see Chapter 3 notes, above.

Chapter 11. Illustrative Working Papers: The Detailed Examination for a Program Audit

For references to cases, see Chapter 6 notes, above.

Chapter 13. Obtaining Evidence Through Interviews and Questionnaires

1. Adapted from a report to the Congress by the Comptroller General: *Managers Need to Provide Better Protection for Federal Automated Data Processing Facilities,* FGMSD-76-40 (Washington, D.C.: General Accounting Office, 1976).

Chapter 14. Using the Computer as an Audit Tool, and Auditing the Tool Itself

1. American Institute of Certified Public Accountants, *Codification of Statements on Auditing Standards* (New York: American Institute of Certified Public Accountants, 1978), numbers 1-22, p. 310. Copyright © 1978 by the American Institute of Certified Public Accountants, Inc., New York, New York.

2. Ibid., p. 308.

3. U.S. General Accounting Office, *The Defense Integrated Data System,* LCD 77-117 (Washington, D.C.: U.S. Government Printing Office, 1977).

4. AICPA, *Auditing Standards,* p. 308.

5. U.S., General Accounting Office, *Auditing Computers with Test Decks* (Washington, D.C.: General Accounting Office, 1975).

6. Adapted from a report to the Congress by the Comptroller General, *Improvements Needed in Managing Automated Decision-making by Computers Throughout the Federal Government,* FGMSD-76-5 (Washington, D.C.: General Accounting Office, 1976).

7. Adapted from a report to the Congress by the Comptroller General, *Millions in Savings Possible in Converting Programs from One Computer to Another,* FGMSD77-34 (Washington, D.C.: General Accounting Office, 1977).

Chapter 15. Using Specialized Analytical Techniques —Using Experts and Consultants

1. U.S. General Accounting Office, *Evaluation and Analysis to Support Decisionmaking,* PAD-76-9

(Washington, D.C.: U.S. Government Printing Office, 1976), pp. 18–20.

2. Ibid., pp. 25–27.

3. Adapted from a report to the Congress by the Comptroller General, *A Range of Cost Measuring Risk and Uncertainty in Major Programs—An Aid to Decisionmaking,* PSAD-78-12 (Washington, D.C.: General Accounting Office, 1978).

4. Adapted from a report to the Congress by the Comptroller General, *Cost-Effectiveness Analysis of Two Military Physician Procurement Programs: The Scholarship Program and the University Program.* MWD—76-122 (Washington, D.C.: General Accounting Office, 1976).

Chapter 16. Understanding the Principles of Reporting

1. American Institute of Certified Public Accountants, *Statements on Auditing Standards* (New York: American Institute of Certified Public Accountants, 1977), p. 82. Copyright © 1977 by the American Institute of Certified Public Accountants.

2. Ibid., pp. 632–633.

3. U.S. General Accounting Office, *Examples of Findings from Governmental Audits* (Washington, D.C.: U.S. Government Printing Office, 1973), pp. 15–16.

4. Ibid., pp. 32–33.

5. Ibid., p. 16.

6. Ibid., p. 33.

Chapter 17. Writing a Clear, Concise, Objective Report

1. U.S. General Accounting Office, *From Auditing to Editing* (Washington, D.C.: U.S. Government Printing Office, 1974), p. 3.

2. Adapted from a report of the Comptroller General, *Concerted Effort Needed to Improve Indian Education,* Bureau of Indian Affairs, Department of the Interior, CED-77-24 (Washington, D.C.: General Accounting Office, 1977).

Glossary of Selected Terms

Accountability. That responsibility to some outside or higher level of authority by a person or group of persons in an organization.

Analytical evidence. Facts or information on an audit objective obtained from the auditor's own evaluation or analysis.

Attribute sampling. A method of statistical sampling for determining the sample size to determine the reliability of the number or percentage of specific characteristics in the total universe.

Audit evidence. Facts or information used to come to a conclusion on an audit objective of whether an entity's management, employees, or designated agents have or have not accepted and carried out appropriate accounting, management, or operational principles, policies, or standards for efficiently, economically, or effectively using its resources; and, the facts or information used to demonstrate to a third party that the conclusion reported is the correct one.

Audit objective. The question concerning operations or programs needing improvement that will be answered through evidence; and when answered will help decision makers improve the efficiency, economy, and effectiveness of their operations.

Audit planning and programming. Adequate preparation, usually in written form, for gathering information and evidence on the audit objective, and the proposed procedures to accomplish the plan.

Audit procedures. Specific directions for carrying out the examination phases of the audit. Specific acts to be performed.

Best (primary) evidence. Facts or information on an audit objective that under all circumstances should be used before any other evidence is considered.

Causes. Management or employee action or actions that took place or should have taken place and created a result by not following an appropriate standard.

Circumstantial evidence (indirect evidence). Facts or information on an audit objective used by the auditor to come to a conclusion by building up a case through many pieces or circumstances of evidence.

Competency of evidence. The reliability one places on the source of information used as evidence.

Compliance auditing. An audit to determine whether employees comply with the laws and regulation, or policies and procedures, that management has prescribed.

Conclusion to an audit objective. The results that come from the analysis of the evidence on an audit objective. It has three distinctive elements: an appropriate standard (criteria), actions of individuals or organizations that did or did not follow the standard (causes), and the results brought about by the actions either following or not following the standard (effects).

Confidence. The probable percentage that the results from samples randomly drawn will fall within the precision limits of true value.

Cost-benefit. The techniques for determining the product or service of greatest benefit for the least cost.

Cost-effectiveness analysis. The process for comparing the cost of resources expected to be consumed with how well the objectives will be achieved.

Cost-value. A technique for determining the greatest value of various alternatives compared to the costs of each alternative.

Criteria. Any particular standard, standards, or group of standards used for measuring the results caused by the actions of employees or management in any performance audit situation.

Critical Path Method (CPM). A form of network analysis.

Detailed examination. The third phase of a performance audit. This phase is normally considered the audit. The auditor gathers sufficient relevant, material, and competent evidence on the audit objective to come to a rational and logical conclusion on that objective. Often, a preliminary draft of the report is done during the detailed examination phase.

Detailed examination program. The written statement of objectives to be accomplished and the procedures for accomplishing them in the detailed examination phase of the audit. The program contains four parts: background information concerning the audit, the results expected from the audit work, the audit procedures needed to accomplish the results, and any special instructions.

Direct evidence. Facts and information on the audit

objective that allow the auditor to come to a conclusion on the objective without any other evidence being necessary.

Effects. The results obtained when management or employees carry out actions based on improper standards and those actions are measured against the appropriate standards; the results obtained by measuring the causes against the criteria.

Engagement letter. Formal letter confirming the arrangements of an audit.

Experimental methods. Techniques for measuring results of a program as though everything else is held constant. This is done by measuring the difference, in terms of the measures of success, between those affected by the program and a control group that is not.

Findings. The results of an audit, usually with evidence to support the results.

First party. The auditor. The person who examines second party's accountability to third party and attests the results to the third party. The first party should be independent of both the second and third parties.

Flow chart. A visual aid to the sequential processes in the flow of transactions in an organization. Often considered only for the flow of transactions in a computer.

Game theory. A simulation technique for optimizing the standards for action under competitive conditions and minimizing the losses on the actions to be taken.

Generalized audit software. A set of preprogrammed subroutines that have been developed for editing, operating, or output purposes when auditing computer operations.

Integrated test facility. A computer audit test whereby the auditor integrates into the normal operating system a "test" person, department, or activity; designed to determine whether the computer is processing the information exactly as prescribed.

Internal auditing. The process of determining whether management or employees adhere to prescribed policies. The auditors are employed by the organization, although independent of the operations being reviewed.

Internal control. The plan of organization and all other coordinated methods and procedures adopted to safeguard assets; to check the accuracy and reliability of accounting and operational data; to promote operational efficiency, economy, and effectiveness; and to encourage adherence to prescribed managerial policies that will accomplish the objectives of the organization. Usually considered only those controls within the organization.

Judicial notice. A term taken from the law describing evidence that needs no additional proof to determine its competency.

Letter and confirmation evidence. Facts or information on an audit objective obtained through letters or confirmation request.

Linear programming. Method for allocating scarce resources of a firm in the best manner possible.

Management auditing (M-auditing). One type of performance auditing to determine whether management has carried out the operations of an organization in an efficient or economical manner.

Management control. The plan of organization and all other plans, policies, procedures, and practices needed by an entity to assure that the objectives of the entity are achieved. Same as internal control when the controls are limited to within the organization. Management controls are both internal and external.

Materiality. The weight each piece of evidence plays in influencing the auditor's mind concerning the conclusion to the audit objective.

M-audit. One type of performance audit made to determine whether management has carried out the operations of an organization in an efficient or economical manner. A management audit.

Nonrandom comparison group methods. Techniques used in an experimental method when the requirements for strict randomized control cannot be satisfied.

Objective. The point of issue, the proposition to be proved, the results to be attained, the question to be answered, the allegation to be proved. Same as audit objective.

Observation evidence. Evidence obtained by the auditor through that individual's personal senses of seeing and feeling.

Operational auditing. A term used for both performance auditing and management auditing, but more often used for management auditing.

P-audit. One type of performance audit made to determine whether management has effectively accomplished the intended result of a program. An effectiveness audit.

Performance auditing. The setting of an audit objective by an independent auditor as to the efficiency, economy, or effectiveness of management's performance; the obtaining of evidence on that objective; the analysis of that evidence to come to a conclusion as to whether management has operated the program or activity economically, efficiently, or effectively; and the reporting of the results of the examination to a third party.

Personal interview evidence. Information received on an audit objective through in-depth discussions with another person who has knowledge of the subject.

Phases of an audit. There are four phases: (1) the preliminary survey, (2) the review and testing of management control, (3) the detailed examination, and (4) the report development.

Precision. The standard for measuring the accuracy of sample results.

Preliminary survey. The first phase of a performance audit. The process of obtaining background and general information in a relatively short period of time on all aspects of the organization, activity, program, or system being considered for examination to set a tentative audit objective.

Preponderance of evidence. That evidence which clearly and convincingly outweighs the opposing evidence in the mind of the auditor in order for the auditor to reach a conclusion on an audit objective or subobjective.

Program. A set of specified activities designed to accomplish a desired objective.

Program auditing (P-auditing). One type of performance auditing to determine whether management has effectively accomplished the intended result of a program.

Program budgeting. A financial plan wherein expenditures are based primarily on programs of work and secondarily on character and object.

Program evaluation and review techniques (PERT). A form of network analysis for complex activities.

Program evaluations. A term used by managers to describe the process for determining standards for effectively accomplishing the results of a program. Usually accomplished by employees of management.

Program results. The desired results or benefits to be achieved by a program. The objective of the program.

Proof beyond a reasonable doubt. That evidence which allows the auditor to reach a conclusion on the audit objective that goes far beyond being just clear and convincing.

Queuing. Techniques to optimize the results or minimize the costs that come from waiting.

Questionnaires. Forms used by auditors for gathering evidence from individuals when there are numerous individuals to be interviewed and the costs of personal interviews would be excessive.

Records evidence. Written information, such as accounting records, contracts, letters, reports, computer printouts, forms, courthouse records, and documents of all types used to come to a conclusion on an audit objective.

Relevancy. Information used as evidence that has a direct and logical relationship to the criteria of the audit objective.

Report. The fourth phase of a performance audit. The final work of the audit that communicates the results of the audit to a third party attesting to the accountability of the second party.

Report development. The formulation and conversion of the conclusion to the audit objective developed from evidence collected and analyzed during the detailed examination into a form that an interested third party can accept and understand.

Review and testing of management control. The second phase of a performance audit. The process where the tentative objective obtained in the preliminary survey phase is converted into a firm objective to be used in the detailed examination by obtaining limited evidence on all three elements of the audit objective. This phase is also used to determine whether the evidence obtained from the entity would be competent if the audit were extended into a more detailed examination.

Second party. The accountable entity being audited; accountable to the third party and is examined on that accountability by the first party.

Simplex method. A process for repeating a linear programming equation for obtaining an optimal solution.

Subobjectives. A breakdown of the primary audit objective into individual parts.

Test deck. A set of simulated transactions that can be processed through a computer system to see whether proper transactions will be processed accurately and improper ones identified and rejected.

Testimonial evidence. Any information received from others, or from analyses by the auditor, and used as evidence on an audit objective.

Third party. Entity requiring accountability from the second party and receiving report on that accountability, after an audit, from the first party.

Tick marks. Special signs to signify the competency of evidence obtained during an examination or actions taken during a review of working papers. Examples: a check ($\checkmark$), checked to interview; a reverse check ($\backslash$), followed to source document; a dot or period (.), added columns; and a double or triple mark on the stem of a check ($\neq$), checked to three sources.

Time series. A series of measurements at periodic intervals.

Transportation method. A linear programming method for determining the minimum costs for transporting goods from one location to another.

Working papers (work papers). Records of the information that has been obtained and of the evidence on the audit objective that has been gathered and analyzed during the audit.

Selected Bibliography

Performance Auditing

Agarwal, N. P. "Anatomy of Management Auditing Information." *Chartered Accountant* (India) 25 (1977): 769.

Beisser, Frederick G. "Operational Auditing: The Financial Auditor Must Become an Imaginative Surrogate Manager." *Michigan CPA* 29 (September–October 1977): 15–18.

Brown, Robert B. "Disclosure in Operational Audits (Accountability Auditing in the Community)." *Internal Auditor* 33 (October 1976): 79–81.

Cammann, Cartlandt. "Effects of the Use of Control Systems." *Accounting, Organizations and Society* 1 (1976): 301–331.

Caron, Paul F. "Management Audits—Will They Work in Project Management for DoD?" *Armed Forces Comptroller* 22 (February 1977): 20.

Castro, Jose F. O. "Approach to Operations Audit." *Accountant's Journal*, no. 2 (1975), pp. 22–24.

Crockett, James R. "Operational Auditing in the Classroom." *Internal Auditor* 34 (October 1977): 4–16.

Davidson, Anthony R. "Criteria-Matrix Approach to Project Selection in Operational Auditing." *Internal Auditor* 33 (August 1976): 62–64.

Davis, John O. "Vital Questions You Need to Ask." *Internal Auditor* 34 (June 1977): 54–58.

Dayton, Allan S. "Operations Auditing Answers Questions Beyond the Scope of Financial Reports." *Management Controls* 24 (September–October 1977): 21–25.

Dittenhofer, Mortimer H. "Management Economics and the Auditor." *Government Accountants Journal* 26 (Summer 1977): 63–71.

Flesher, Dale L. "Operations Auditing: For the Independent Auditor." *CPA Journal* 47 (July 1977): 17–21.

———. *Operations Auditing in Hospitals.* Lexington, Mass.: Lexington Books, 1976.

Fritzmeyer, Joe R. "Should Internal Auditing be Performed by a Staff of Generalists or by a Specialized Staff?" *Internal Auditor* 33 (August 1976): 41–51.

Goater, Hugh. "Management Auditing." *Management Accounting* (England) 54 (1976): 348–349.

Gran, Bradford H. "Evaluating Controls: Primary Responsibility of the Internal Auditor." *Internal Auditor* 34 (June 1977): 48–53.

Griffin, Richard J. "Audit of Operational Controls and Non-Financial Data (Accountability Auditing in the Community)." *Internal Auditor)* 33 (June, 1976): 73–75.

Guivastava, Guish K. "Management Audit—A New Dimension to Audit." *Management Accountant* (India) 11 (1976): 324–326.

Herzog, John P. "Operational Audit." *Journal of Systems Management* 28 (October 1977): 34–39.

Hughes, John Silvers. *Optimal Audit Planning.* Ann Arbor: University of Michigan Press, 1974.

Ives, Martin. "Operational Auditing-Accountability." *Association of Government Accountants Operational Auditing* (Arlington, Va.: Association of Government Accountants, 1976), pp. 106–20.

Jacobs, M. L. "Management Audits—the Expectations Approach." *South African Chartered Accountant* (South Africa) 13 (1977): 315–16.

Kaffer, William J. "Potential of Management Audits." *Public Utilities Fortnightly* 99 (March 1976): 31–33.

Kaill, Michael L. "Operations Auditing, Management Systems and Productivity Improvement." *Internal Auditor* 33 (June 1976): 75–77.

Khandelwol, N. M. "Audit of the Concept of Management Audits." *Chartered Accountant* (India) 26 (1977): 248–250, 258.

Knighton, Lennis T. "Practical Audit Approach." *Internal Auditor* 34 (June 1977): 40–47.

Lawerence, Gary L. "Management by Objectives & Program Evaluations." *Footnote (HEW)*, no. 9 (1977): 1–6.

Morris, Norman. "Operational Auditing in a Financial Environment." *Internal Auditor* 33 (April 1976): 20–29.

Nash, Joseph Victor. "An Experiment to Test the Efficacy of Operational Auditing as an Alternative to Financial Auditing." Thesis, University of Michigan, 1973.

Neal, Michael L. "Use of Personal and Operational Auditing." *Internal Auditor* 33 (August 1976): 26–28.

O'Keefe, Herbert A. *Performance Audits in Local Governments: Benefits, Problems, and Challenges.* Washington: International City Management Association, 1976.

Pashke, Gregory R. "Considering the Operations Audit." *CPA Journal* 47 (March 1977): 62–63.

"Performance Auditing at Work." *Public Management* 56 (February 1974): 16–19.
Salgado, Carmelita G. "Notes on Management Control Systems." *SGV Group Journal* (P.I.), nos. 3 and 4 (1975): 12–19.
Santocki, J. "Meaning and Scope of Management Audits." *Accounting and Business Research* (Engineering), no. 25 (1976) 64–70.
Sayers, John S. "Operational Auditing is Alive and Well." *Internal Auditor* 33 (October 1976): 34–41.
Scantlebury, Donald C. "Planning an Operational Audit." *Government Accountants Journal* 25 (Fall 1976): 18–23.
Solgado, Carmelita G. "Notes on Management Control Systems." *Accountants' Journal,* no. 3 (1975): 32–36.
Swanson, James B. *Accountant as Manager and Controller.* Sydney, Australia: Low Book Co., 1974.
Tierney, Cornelius E. "Behavioral Aspects of Performance Auditing: Creating a Productive Environment." *Governmental Finance* 5 (November 1976): 22–27.
U.S. General Accounting Office. "Using Auditing to Improve Efficiency and Economy: A Case Study of an Efficiency and Economy Audit of a Local Governmental Activity." Washington, D.C. *Government Printing Office, 1975.*
Vangermeersch, Richard. "Management Audit Is For You." *National Public Accountant* 21 (May 1976): 21.
Voripaieff, V. M. "Operational Auditing in Today's Environment" (Twenty-ninth Conference of Accountants, University of Tulsa, 1975). *Accounting Papers.* Tulsa, Okla., 1975, pp. 74–83.
Wilson, Paul W. "Purpose and Objectives of an Internal Audit Department." *Retail Control* 45 (January 1977): 2–19.
Wilson, Robert S. "Test Show Operational Audits Help the Editorial Department." *Newspaper Controller* 30 (June 1977): 6–12.
Woodward, June M. "Scientific Approaches to Performance Measurement in the Audit Process." *Governmental Finance* 5 (November 1976): 30–36.
Zouhea, Nicholas M. "Laboratory Analysis: An Operational Audit Technique." *GAO Review* 12 (Summer 1977) 38–44.

Social Auditing

Alet, Clark C. *Social Audit for Management.* New York: AMACOM, 1977.
Anderson, Robert H. "Social Responsibility Accounting: Time to Get Started." *CA Magazine* (Canada) 110 (February 1977): 28–31.
Berg, Janice C. "Social Auditing." *Armed Forces Comptroller* 21 (October 1976): 18–20.
Brooks, Leonard J., and Davis, William R. "Some Approaches to the Corporate Social Audit." *CA Magazine* (Canada) 110 (March 1977): 34–38, 43–45.
Gordon, Lawerence A. "Accounting and Corporate Social Responsibility." In University of Kansas Symposium, 1978.
Higgins, James M. "Proposed Social Performance Evaluation System." *Atlanta Economics Review* 27 (May–June 1977) 4–9.
Lipson, Harry A. "Current Efforts to Measure Corporate Social Performance." *Atlanta Economic Review* 25 (March–April 1975): 15–19.
Majumdar, A. K. "Society, Auditor, and the Social Audit." *Chartered Accountant* (India) 25 (1977): 471–74.
Mullins, Kate. "Program Evaluation, Public Sector Impact of Social Values" In American Accounting Association Southeast Regional Group, collected papers of the Twenty-sixth Annual Meeting, Memphis State University, 1974; pp. 241–44.
Tipgos, Manuel A. "Case Against the Social Audit." *Management Accounting (NAA)* 58 (November 1976): 23–26.

Computers and Auditing

Adams, Donald L. "Audit Applications of Flowcharting Software." *Edpacs* 4 (May 1977): 1–18.
Adams, Donald L. "Audit Uses of SMF Reporting and Analysis Software." *Edpacs* 4 (April 1977): 1.
American Institute of Certified Public Accountants. "The Auditor's Study and Evaluation of Internal Control in EDP Systems." *Audit and Study Guide.* New York: AICPA, 1977.
———, Computer Auditing Subcommittee. "Advanced EDP and the Auditor's Concerns." *Journal of Accountancy,* January 1975, pp. 66–72.
———, Computer Services Division, Auditing Advanced EDP Systems Task Force. *Management, Control and Audit of Advanced EDP Systems.* New York: AICPA, 1977.
Bently, T. J. "Auditability and Control of Computers." *Management Accounting,* (England) 55 (January 1977): 13–14.
Best, P. J. "File Recovery and the Audit Trail in an On-Line System." *Chartered Accountant in Australia,* (Australia), August 1976, pp. 25–27.
Byrne, Dan R., and Scott, George M. "Closing the Computer Audit Gap." *Internal Auditor* 31 (April 1977): 27–32.
Canadian Institute of Chartered Accountants. "Study Group on Computer Control and Audit Guidelines." "Computer Audit Guidelines; Guidelines on the Minimum Standards and Accepted Techniques Which Should be Observed in the Audit of Organizations Using a Computer." Toronto. 1975, pp. 138–318.
Computer as an Audit Tool. Palo Alto, Calif.: California Society of Certified Public Accountants, Committee on EDP, 1974.
Davis, Keagle W.; Mair, William C.; and Wood, Donald R. *Computer Control and Audit.* 2d ed. Altamonte Springs, Fla.: Institute of Internal Auditors, 1976.
Domingues, K. V. "Practical Applications in the use of Audit Software." *Interpreter* 35 (October 1976): 29–31.
Earl, Michael. "Program Auditing: A New Approach to Computer Audit." *Edpacs* 5 (December 1977): 5–14.

Gentile, E. A., and Grimes, James R. "Maintaining Internal Integrity of On-Line Data Basis." *Edpacs* 4 (February 1977): 1–14.

Grihalva, Richard A. "Auditing Load Libraries." *Edpacs* 5 (October 1977) 1–6.

Hannye, L. George. "Auditors and DP'ers Benefit from Association in the Systems Development Process. (EDP Systems)." *Internal Auditor* 34 (December 1977): 67–70.

Institute of Internal Auditors. *Auditing Computer Centers.* Orlando, Fla.: 1974.

Institute of Internal Auditors. *Systems Auditability and Control = Audit Practices.* A study conducted by the Stanford Research Institute. Institute of Internal Auditors, Orlando, Fla., 1977.

Jancura, Elise. *Computer Auditing and Control.* Florence, Ky.: Litton Educational Publishing, 1977.

Knowlton, Roger A. "Audit Software Package Evaluation." *Edpacs* 4 (August 1976): 1–4.

Lynn, Robert S. "Computer Auditing—A Broader Perspective." *Chartered Accountant,* February 1975, pp. 15–18.

Mair, William C. "Parallel Simulations—A Technique for Effective Verification of Computer Programs." *Edpacs* 2 (April 1975): 1–5.

McCosh, Andrew M., and Earl, Michael J. "Audit of Computer Programs." *Accountant's Magazine* (Scotland) 80 (1976): 253–58.

McRae, Thomas W. *Computers and Accounting.* New York: John Wiley & Sons, 1976.

Meyers, Gerald Erwin. "EDP Audit Packages ... Are They Really That Good?" *EDP Auditor,* Summer 1975, p. 6.

Miller, Timothy L. "EDP, A Matter of Definition." *Internal Auditor* 32 (July–August 1975): 31–38.

Neumann, Albrecht J. *Features of 7 Audit Software Packages, Principles and Capabilities.* U.S. Department of Commerce, National Bureau of Statistics, Washington, D.C.: U.S. Government Printing Office, 1977.

November, Robert; Foreman, Michael; and Watts, Wayne. "Quality Control for New EDP Systems." *Management Focus* 25 (January–February 1978): 51–55.

Parson, Oliver, W. "Questions for the Experts; Interview by Dr. Martin Bariff of Allan S. Loren." *EDP Auditor,* Summer 1976, pp. 28–29.

Pearson, Michael A. "Minimum Acceptable EDP Accounting Control Standards." *Massachusetts CPA Review* 51 (Nov–Dec 1977): 7.

Perry, William E. "Audit Aspects of Utility Programs." *Edpacs* 3 (October 1975): 1–8.

———. "Skills Needed to Utilize EDP Audit Practices." *Edpacs* 5 (November 1977): 1–13.

———, and Fitzgerald, Jerry. "Designing for Auditability." *Datamation,* August 1977, pp. 46–50.

Porter, W. Thomas. *EDP, Controls and Auditing.* 2d ed. Belmont, Calif.: Wadsworth Publishing Co., 1977.

Reneau, J. H. "The Computer as an Audit Tool: A Review of the State of the Art in the U.S." *Chartered Accountant in Australia* (Australia), August 1976, pp. 21–23.

Roddam, P. L. "Auditors and Computers." *Accountant* (England) 177 (1977): 168–69.

Schaller, Carol A. "Auditing and Job Accounting Data." *Journal of Accountancy,* May 1976, p. 36.

Sethna, Roy. "Blueprint for Generalized Computer Audit Systems." *CA Magazine* 109 (August 1976): 41–47.

Shell, Richard C. "Audit Control Over Computer Programs." *Edpacs* 2 (March 1975): 1–3.

Sherman, Samuel. "From Auditape to Computer Assisted Audit Techniques." *GAO Review* 11 (Winter 1976): 44–48.

Srinivasan, C. A., and Dascher, Paul E. "Computer System Security and Auditing Implications." *National Public Accountant* 23 (January 1978): 20–24.

Toellner, John. "Performance Measurement in Systems and Programming." *Infosystems* 24 (December 1977): 34–36.

Tyrnauer, Stuart. "Auditing Computer Program Maintenance (EDP Systems)." *Internal Auditor* 34 (August 1977): 68–72.

Quantitative Methods

Ahmad, Imtiary, and Khan, M. Raiz. "Using Cost Benefit to Manage Computers." *Management* (Ireland) 23 (March 1976): 19–21.

American Institute of Certified Public Accountants, MAS Division, MAS Environmental Accounting Task Force. *Environmental Cost/Benefit Studies.* New York: AICPA, 1977.

Baker, Kenneth R., and Damon, William W. "Simultaneous Planning Model for Production and Working Capital." *Decision Sciences* 8 (January 1977): 95–108.

Balderston, F. E. "Cost Analysis in Higher Education." *California Management Review* 17 (1974): 93–107.

Barkman, Arnold I. "Estimation in Accounting and Auditing Using Markov Chains." *Journal of Accountancy* 144 (December 1977): 75–79.

———. "Within-Item Variations, a Stochastic Approach to Audit Uncertainty." *Accounting Review* 52 (1977): 450–64.

Bennison, B. R. "Accounting for Industrial Disputes." *Management Accounting* (England) 54 (1976): 224–25.

Beswick, Charles A. "Allocating Selling Effort via Dynamic Programming." *Management Science* 23 (1977): 667–78.

Brown, Kenneth S., and Revelle, Jack B. *Quantitative Methods for Managerial Decisions.* Menlo Park, Calif.: Addison-Wesley Publishing Co., 1978.

Cerullo, Michael J. "PERT: A Useful Management Tool." *Management Accountant* (India) 11 (1976): 454–59.

Cirtin, Arnold. "Network Analysis—A Tool for Audit Planning and Control." Master's thesis, University of Cincinnati, 1974. Ann Arbor, Mich.: University Microfilms, 1976.

Dowling, T. J. "Application of Cost-Benefit Analysis to Educational Planning." *Accountants Review* (England) 26 (1975): 104–8.

Dunn, Marcus. "Present State of Performance Measurement for Not-for-Profit Organizations." In American Accounting Association Southeast Regional Group, collected papers of the 27th Annual Meeting, pp. 348–52 Richmond, Va: Virginia Commonwealth University, 1975.

Dyckman, Thomas R. "Some Contributions of Decision Theory to Accounting." *Journal of Contemporary Business* 4 (Autumn 1975): 68–69.

Eggleton, T. R. "Pattern, Prototypes and Predictions: An Exploratory Study." *Journal of Accounting Research* 14 (supplemental 1976): 68–158.

Falk, Haim, and Heintz, James A. "Predictability of Relative Risk Over Time." *Journal of Business Finance & Accounting* (England) 4 (Spring 1977): 5–28.

Felix, William L. "Evidence on Alternative Means of Assessing Prior Probability Distributions for Audit Decision Making." *Accounting Review* 51 (1976): 800–807.

Frost, Michael J. *How to Use Cost-Benefit Analysis in Project Appraisal.* 2d ed. New York: Holsted Press, 1975.

Geoffrion, Arthur M. "Purpose of Mathematical Programming Is Insight, Not Numbers." *Interfaces* 7 (November 1976): 81–92.

"Getting the Message Across with CPM." *Factory* 9 (August 1976): 14–42.

Gilbert, John P.; Light, Richard J.; and Mosteller, Frederick. "Assessing Social Innovations: An Empirical Base for Policy." In Zeckhauser, R. et al., eds. *Benefit-Cost and Policy Analysis*, pp. 3–65. Chicago: Aldine Publishing Co., 1975.

Glover, Fred. "Improved Linear Programming Formulations of Nonlinear Integer Problems." *Management Science*, 22 (1975): 455–60.

Goyal, S. K. "Note on a Simple CPM Time-Cost Tradeoff Algorithm (Notes)." *Management Science* 21 (1975): 718–22.

Hellerman, Herbert, and Tannen, Michael. "Optimal Manpower Programs in Local Labor Markets: A Planning Model." *Quarterly Review of Economics & Business* 16 (Winter 1976): pp. 55–68.

Jackson, Mary. "Operational Research Approach, Techniques and Applications." In Oliver, Stanley. *Accountant's Guide to Management Techniques*, pp. 545–562. Epping, England: 1975.

Kamal, M. A. "Critical Path Analysis Techniques in Budget Preparation." *Cost & Management* (Bangladesh) 1 (July–December 1974): 8–16.

Kapoor, S. S. "Cost-Benefit Analysis." *Management Accounting* (England) 55 (November 1977): 39–40.

Kim, Seung H., and Schmitz, Homer H. "Micro/Macro Cost-Benefit Analysis Prove New Data System's Value to Hospital, Community." *Hospital Financial Management* 29 (October 1975): 48–53.

Kirk, R. E. *Experimental Design: Procedures for the Behavioral Sciences.* Monterey, Calif.: Brooks/Cole Publishing Co., 1969.

Klingman, Darwin. "Finding Equivalent Network Formulations for Constrained Network Problems." *Management Science* 23 (1977): 737–44.

Koenig, Michael H. "Organizing the Large Activity Network." *Journal of Systems* 26 (June 1975): 36–37.

Kotiah, T. C. T. "On a Linear Programming Technique for the Steady-State Behavior of Some Queuing Systems." *Operations Research* 25 (1977): 289–303.

Krakowski, Martin. "PERT & Parkinson's Law." *Interfaces* 5 (November 1974): 35–40.

Krogstad, Jack C.; Grudnitski, Gary; and Bryant, David W. "PERT & PERT/Cost for Audit Planning and Control." *Journal of Accountancy* 144 (November 1977): 82–91.

Levin, Henry M. "Cost-Effectiveness Analysis in Evaluation Research." In *Evaluation Consortium*, Stanford University, 1974. Stanford, Calif.: Stanford University Press, 1974.

Levin, Richard I., and Kirkpatrick, Charles A. *Quantitative Approaches to Management.* 3d ed. New York: McGraw-Hill Book Co., 1975.

Mirvis, Philip H., and Macy, Barry A. "Accounting for the Costs and Benefits of Human Resource Development Programs: An Interdisciplinary Approach." *Accounting, Organizations and Society* 1 (1976): 179–93.

Misia, Santosh Kumar. "Using Linear Programming for Product Mix Decisions." *Management Accountant* (India) 12 (1977): 761–62.

Nickolai, Loren A. *Measurement of Corporate Environmental Activity.* New York: National Association of Accountants, 1976.

Paranka, Stephen. *Business Applications of Decision Science.* New York: Petrocelli/Charter, 1975.

Quade, Edward S. "Introduction and Overview." In Goldman, T. A. ed. *Cost-Effectiveness Analysis*, pp. 1–16. New York: Praeger Publishers, 1976.

Rabadi, A. B. "Social Cost-Benefit Analysis." In *Proceedings*, Commonwealth Conference of Accountants, vol. 1, pp. 34–40. New Delhi: Commonwealth Conference of Accountants, 1975, 1976.

Robinson, Don R. "Dynamic Programming Solution to Cost-Time Tradeoff for CPM." *Management Science* 22 (October 1975): 58–66.

Ryan, William C. "Management Practice and Research—Poles Apart." *Business Horizons* 20 (June 1977): 23–29.

Schmitt, John P. "Risk Management Justification—Cost-Benefit Considerations." *Risk Management* 24 (July 1977): 40.

Silver, Edward A. and Moore, John B. "Mixing of Markov Processes." *Decision Sciences* 7 (1976): 384–93.

Smith, Jack C. "Actual Cost-Methods Basics for CPAs." *Journal of Accountancy* 143 (February 1977): 62–66.

Smith, T. Arthur. "Cost-Benefit Analysis: The Cost Accounts." *Armed Forces Comptroller* 22 (February 1977): 17–19.

Sorensen, James E., and Grove, Hugh D. "Cost-Outcome and Cost-Effectiveness Analysis: Emerging Non-Profit Performance Evaluation Techniques." *Accounting Review* 52 (1977): 658–75.

Subrahmanyam, V. V. "Network Techniques for Cost Control." *Chartered Accountant* (India) 23 (1975): 573–76.
Sully, J. M. "Critical Path Analysis." *Accountant* (England) 172 (1975): 608–610.
Wiley, Joe M. "Just Enough Queuing Theory." *Datamation* 23 (February 1977): 87.
Wong, Paul J. "Using a Cost Benefit Analysis Approach to Support Audit Recommendations." *Internal Auditor* 34 (August 1977): 43–49.
Woolsey, Robert E. D., and Swanson, Huntington S. *Operations Research for Immediate Applications; A Quick and Dirty Manual*. New York: Harper & Row, Publishers, 1975.

Use of Specialists

"AICPA Shows How to Use Internal Auditors and Non-accounting Specialists for Independent Auditors." *SEC Accounting Report* 1 (November 1975): 1–2.
Farley, Jarvis. "Relations Between Actuaries and Independent Auditors." *Journal of Accountancy* 141 (February 1976): 70–72.
Radcliff, James R. "Pension Plans: Problems of Auditing and Accounting." *Viewpoint*, 1976, pp. 38–42.
"Statement on Auditing Standards No. 11—Using the Work of a Specialist." *Journal of Accountancy* 141 (March 1976): 67–70.
Thornton, Maxwell D. "Inter-Professional Relationships: The Case for a Joint Approach?" *Accountant* (England) 173 (1975): 551–52.
Williams, Donald M. "How to Profit from Specialized Help." *CGA Magazine* (Canada) 11 (March 1977): 4–6.

Interviewing

Collard, Albert. "Sharpening Interviewing Techniques." In *Peopleware in Systems*, Association for Systems Management, pp. 50–53. Cleveland: pub 1976.
Gildersleeve, Thomas. "Conducting Better Interviews." In *Peopleware in Systems*, Association for Systems Management, pp. 54–58. Cleveland: pub 1976.
Goodman, Steven E. "Facts are Fundamental for Successful Career Planning." *Advanced Management Journal* 41 (Autumn 1976): 61–66.
Holmes, Geoffrey. "How to Improve Your Interviewing." *Accountancy* (England) 87 (September 1976): 76.
Schoenfield, Mark K. "Art of Interviewing and Counseling (Part I)." *Practical Lawyer* 24 (1978): 67–74.

Audit Report Writing

"Annual Report High-Interest Areas Outlined in CSI Study." *Journal of Accountancy* 145 (February 1978): 8.
Baker, Sheridan. *The Practical Stylist*. New York: Thomas Y. Crowell Co., 1962.
Bromage, Mary C. "Bridging the Corporate Communications Gap." *Advanced Management Journal* 41 (Winter 1976): 44–51.
Brooks, Cleanth, and Warren, Robert Penn. *Modern Rhetoric*. New York: Harcourt, Brace & Co., 1958.
Bruner, E. C. "Effective Report Referencing." *Footnote* (HEW), no. 9 (1977), pp. 31–32.
Chase, Stuart. *The Tyranny of Words*. New York: Harcourt, Brace & Co., 1938.
Deutoch, Arnold R. "Does Your Company Practice Affirmative Action in its Communications?" *Harvard Business Review* 54 (1976): 16.
Fine, Harold R. "Removing the Gobbledygook from Governmental Prose." *GAO Review* 11 (Winter 1976): 25–34.
Fleet, A. H. "Communications Gap." *Management Accounting* (England) 55 (January 1977): 16.
Flesch, Rudolf Franz. *How to Write, Speak and Think More Effectively*. New York: Harper & Brothers, 1960.
———. *The ABC of Style: A Guide to Plain English*. New York: Harper & Row, Publishers, 1974.
Follett, Wilson. *Modern American Usage*. New York: Hill & Wang, 1966.
Gallagher, William J. *Report Writing for Management*. Reading, Mass.: Addison-Wesley Publishing Co., 1969.
Graves, Harold R., and Hoffman, Lynn S. S. *Report Writing*. 4th ed. Englewood Cliffs, N.J.: Prentice-Hall, 1965.
Harrison, R. B. "Corporate Report: A Critique." *CA Magazine* (Canada) 107 (December 1975–January 1976): 26–33.
Hayakawa, S. I. *Language in Thought and Action*. New York: Harcourt, Brace & Co., 1949.
"How to Write a Report." *Banking* 68 (June 1976): 43.
Hunter, Laura Grace. *Language of Audit Reports*. Washington, D.C.: U.S. Government Printing Office, 1957.
Hylton, Delmer C. "Are We Communicating?" *CPA Journal* 46 (December 1976): 11–15.
John, Richard C. "Improve Your Technical Writing." *Management Accounting* (NAA) 58 (September 1976): 49–52.
Klare, George R., and Buck, Byron. *Know Your Reader*. New York: Harper & Brothers, 1950.
Lesikar, Raymond V. *How to Write a Report Your Boss Will Read and Remember*. Homewood, Ill.: Dow Jones–Irwin, 1974.
Lothian, Niall. "Nature of Redundancy and Its Use in Company Reports and Accounts." *Accounting and Business Research* (England) 6 (1976): 216–227.
Maude, Barry. *Practical Communications for Managers*. London: Longman, 1974.
O'Hayre, John. *Gobbledygook Has Gotta Go*. Washington, D.C.: U.S. Government Printing Office, 1966.
Orwell, George. *Politics and The English Language*. New York: American Library,
Pei, Mario. *Words in Sheep's Clothing*. New York: Funk & Wagnalls Book Publishing, 1969.
Perlmutter, Jerome R. *A Practical Guide to Effective Writing*. New York: Random House, 1965.

Perrin, Porter G. *Writer's Guide and Index to English*. Glenview, Ill.: Scott, Foresman and Co., 1950.

"Reporting and Communication." *Journal UEC* 12 (1977): 209.

Roget's International Thesaurus. 4th ed., rev. New York: Thomas Y. Crowell Co., 1977.

Ross, Peter Burton. *Basic Technical Writing*. New York: Thomas Y. Crowell Co., 1974.

Sigband, Norman B. "Basic Principles of Effective Writing." *Risk Management* 23 (December 1976): 50–52.

Strunk, William, Jr., and White, E. B. *The Elements of Style*. New York: Macmillan Co., 1959.

Tierney, Cornelius E. "Audit Reports—Some Behavioral Aspects for Improvement." *Internal Auditor* 34 (June 1977): 74–77.

Ulman, Joseph N., Jr. *Technical Reporting*. New York: Henry Holt & Co., 1952.

U.S., Air Force. *Air Force Guide to Effective Writing*, Air Force Manual 11–3. Washington, D.C.: U.S. Government Printing Office, 1957.

U.S., General Accounting Office. *From Auditing to Editing*. Washington, D.C.: U.S. Government Printing Office, 1974.

Wasem, George. "Reading Annual Reports Can Be Fun." *Bankers Monthly* 93 (February 15, 1976): p. 26.

Wersman, Herman M. *Basic Technical Writing*. Columbus, Ohio: Charles E. Merrill Publishing Co., 1962.

AGA Bibliography on Operational Auditing

Ahart, Gregory J. "Evaluating Agency Management." *The GAO Review*, Winter 1971, p. 32.

Allen, J. R. "Managing the Operational Audit Function." *The Internal Auditor*, Fall 1966, p. 21.

"American Accounting Association Report of Committee on Managerial Decision Models." *The Accounting Review*, supp. to vol. XLIV (1969): 43.

American Institute of Certified Public Accountants. *Statement on Auditing Standards*. Reports on Internal Control. New York: American Institute of Certified Public Accountants, 1974, p. 174.

Anthony, R. N. "The Auditor's Role in Management Accounting." *The Internal Auditor*, January/February 1968, p. 39.

Ard, James H. "The Problem with Operational Auditing." *Federal Accountant* 22 (March 1973): 41.

Arrowood, H. S. "The Modern Concept of Internal Auditing." *The Internal Auditor*, Summer 1963, pp. 22–24.

"At Emery Air Freight: Positive Reinforcement Boosts Performance" *Organizational Dynamics* 1 (Winter 1973): 41.

Ballard, John R. "Approaches to Operational Auditing." *The Internal Auditor*, Spring 1962, p. 36.

———. "Better Service to Management." *The Internal Auditor*, September/October 1972, p. 10.

Bartholomew, George. "How to Maintain Practically Everything—Getting the System Under Control." *College & University Business* 54 (May 1973): 41.

Barton, Harold C. "One Approach to the Performance of a Management Audit." *Footnote, Journal of the HEW Audit Agency*, Spring 1974, p. 15.

Bell, Hassell B. "What Is the Role of the Internal Auditor?" *The GAO Review*, Spring 1967, p. 13.

Borut, Donald. "ICMA and Performance Auditing." *Public Management*, February 1974, p. 11.

Bouland, Herbert D. "Evaluating Results of Government Programs." *The GAO Review*, Fall 1973, p. 48.

Bradt, John D. "Effectively Presenting and Audit." *The Internal Auditor*, July/August 1969, pp. 43–49.

Brangaccio, F. David. "Controlling Bank Expenses Through Operational Auditing." *Magazine of Bank Administration* 49 (February 1973): 45.

Brink, Victor Z.; Cashin, James A.; Witt, Herbert. *Modern Internal Auditing: An Operational Approach*. New York: The Ronald Press Company, 1973.

Buckley, John W., and Lightner, Kevin M. "Financial and Operational Auditing." *Accounting: An Information Systems Approach*. Encino, Calif.: Dickenson Publishing Company, 1973, p. 1171.

Burton, John. "Management Auditing." *The Journal of Accountancy*, May 1968, p. 45.

Cadmus, Bradford. *Operational Auditing Handbook*. New York: The Institute of Internal Auditors, 1964, p. 1.

Campfield, William L. "Is Auditing a Sine Qua Non in the Management Process?" (University Corner). *The Internal Auditor* 30 (September/October 1973): 81.

———. "Education for Management Auditing." *The Federal Accountant*, Spring 1966, pp. 30–40.

———. "Trends in Auditing Management Plans and Operations." *The Journal of Accountancy*, July 1967, p. 41.

———. "Controversies and Opportunities in the New Management Auditing." *The Internal Auditor*, March/April 1971, p. 27.

———. "Auditing Management Performance." *Financial Executive*, January 1971, p. 24.

Caplan, Larry. "College Student's View of Internal Auditing." *The Internal Auditor* 30 (September/October 1973): 63.

Carmichael, Douglas R. "Opinions on Internal Control." *The Journal of Accountancy*, December 1970, p. 58.

Carolus, Roger N. "The Who's, Why's What's, and How's of Operational Auditing." *The Internal Auditor*, July/August 1968, p. 27.

Chartrand, Robert L. "The Governor and the Systems Approach." *Government Executive*, June 1973, p. 51.

Choi, Jong T. "Operational Auditing: Part I." *The Internal Auditor*, March/April 1971, p. 6.

———. "Operation Auditing: Part II." *The Internal Auditor*, May/June 1971, p. 37.

Source: Reprinted by permission of the Association of Governmental Accountants.

Christie, F. O. "In Support of the Financial Manager's Audit as Operational Common Sense." *Cost and Management* (Canada), February 1968, p. 43.

Churchill, Neil C. "Audit Recommendations and Management Auditing: A Case Study and Some Remarks." *1st Conference Proceedings, Empirical Research in Accounting: Selected Studies.* Chicago: University of Chicago Press, 1966, p. 128.

Churchill, Neil C., and Cyert, Richard. "An Experiment in Management Auditing." *The Journal of Accountancy*, February 1966, p. 42.

Cloutier, P. E. "The Management Audit." *The Canadian Chartered Accountant*, September 1966, p. 178.

Coburn, W. B. "An Approach to Management Auditing." *Management Accounting*, March 1966, p. 59.

Conly, George T. "Happiness Is a Management Audit." *Journal of Accountancy* 135 (March 1973): 89.

Crow, O. R., Jr. "Operational Audit—Any Business Function." *The Internal Auditor*, Spring 1967, p. 65.

Culpepper, Robert C. "A Study of Some Relationships Between Accounting and Decision Making Processes." *The Accounting Review*, April 1970, p. 322.

Defenbach, James A. "Performance and Program Evaluation Audits." Footnote[6], *Journal of the HEW Audit Agency*, Spring 1974, p. 8.

Dever, John E. "Performance Auditing in the City." *Public Management*, February 1974, p. 2.

Dittenhofer, Mortimer A. "The Use of Operational Auditing in Legislative Overview." *State Government Administration*, July/August 1973, p. 18.

———. "The Growing Role of the Auditor in Managing State Government." *State Government*, Spring 1970, p. 119.

———. "Federal Performance Auditing—Its Application to State Audit Effort." *The Federal Accountant*, March 1970, p. 60.

———. "The Case of Standards and Guidelines for State Audits." *The Internal Auditor*, July/August 1970, p. 61.

———. "Serendipity in Self-Audit." *The Federal Accountant*, June 1973, p. 48.

Dodwell, J. W. "Operational Auditing: A Part of the Basic Audit." *Journal of Accountancy*, June 1966, p. 31.

———. "Operations Auditing." *The Internal Auditor*, Fall 1961, p. 71.

Dolan, Francis X. "Audit Surveys in Operational Auditing." *The Federal Accountant*, March 1972, p. 63.

Dombrower, Denny. "Professional Accountant's Formula for Survival—Operational Auditing." *Canadian Chartered Accountant* 101 (December 1972): 53.

Dooley, Donald E. "Internal Auditing." *The Internal Auditor*, Summer 1962, p. 12.

Drucker, Meyer. "The Importance of Internal Review for Local Governments." *Governmental Finance*, Feb. 1973, p. 25.

Edds, John A. "Whatever Became of Operational Auditing?" *Canadian Chartered Accountant Magazine*, March 1975, pp. 44–48.

Efferson, C. A. "Creativity and Innovation in Management and Auditing." *The Internal Auditor*, Fall 1967, p. 63.

Evans, E. R. "Approach—The Key to Operational Auditing." *The Internal Auditor*, Spring 1966, p. 29

———. "Audit Technique." *The Internal Auditor*, Winter 1963, p. 66.

———. "Operational Auditing in Practice." *National Association of Accountants Bulletin*, June 1964, p. 16.

———. "Some Benefits of Operational Auditing." *The Internal Auditor*, March/April 1969, pp. 42–48.

Federal Government Accountants Association, Washington, D.C. chapter. *Sophisticated Auditing Techniques*, 1973. (Seminar on auditing techniques, October 16–18, 1972.)

Frawley, Daniel E. "Evaluating the Effectiveness of the Audit Operation." *The Internal Auditor* 30 (September/October 1973): 76.

Freitag, William. "On Efficiency and Responsibility in Nonprofit Organizations." *Management Controls*, May 1973, p. 106.

Fritzemeyer, Joe R., and Carmichael, D. R. "Reports on Internal Control to Grant Agencies." *The Journal of Accountancy*, January 1973, p. 78.

Glover, Mildred W. "Broadening the Scope of Auditing." *GAO Review*, Spring 1973, p. 34.

Gollihar, Charles R. "What Management Expects from a Management Audit." *The Internal Auditor*, May/June 1972, p. 33.

Green, Eric F. "Operational Auditing." *Transcript* (Harris Kerr Forster & Co.) 30 (August 1973): 1.

Gregory, Arthur J. "Operational Audit of the Engineering Function." *Management Accounting* (National Accounting Association) 55 (September 1973): 43.

Griffin, Richard J. "Atomic Energy Commission Performs Agency-wide Management Audits." *The Internal Auditor* 30 (July/August 1973): 75.

Grubel, Frederick. "Role of the Management Audit." *Hospital Accounting*, April 1967, p. 4.

Gustafson, George A. "Management Type Auditing." *The Internal Auditor*, November/December 1970, p. 36.

Hadder, Perry E. "The Operational Auditing Function and Its Place in the Company." *The Internal Auditor*, May/June 1972, p. 42.

Hagen, W. W. "Auditing Business Ethics." *The Internal Auditor*, January/February 1968, p. 45.

Hamelaran, Paul W., and Mazzie, Edward M. "Management Science: An Art of the State." *Government Executive*, May 1972, p. 70.

Harmeyer, W. James. "Operational Auditing: You, Too, Can Be a Consultant." *The Internal Auditor*, July/August 1971, p. 30.

Harris, William O. "Improving Federal Program Performance." *Government Executive*, September 1973, p. 54.

Harrison, H. H. "Improved Operations Through Operational Auditing." *Auditgram*, August 1966, p. 8.

Hatry, Harry P. "Problems in Performance Auditing of Local Services." *Public Management*, February 1974, p. 20.

Henry, Harold H. "Efficiency Is a Valid Goal: Improving the Management of Government/Industry Programs." *Management Review*, August 1973, p. 5.

Higgins, J. A. C. "The Effective Audit Report—Our Most Important Product." *The Internal Auditor*, May/June 1973, p. 44.

Hilgert, Raymond. "Managing with—Or Without—a Union." *College & University Business*, May 1973, pp. 52–53.

Hinkle, Allen O. "Increasing the Auditor's Responsibilities." *The Internal Auditor*, Spring 1962, p. 25.

Hitts, Al W., and Masschelin, Jack F. "The Controller—An Operational Audit Approach." *The Internal Auditor*, July/August 1972, p. 17.

Horngren, Charles T. "The Accounting Discipline in 1999." *The Accounting Review*, January 1971, p. 1.

Ives, Martin. "Operational Auditing Accountability." *Proceedings of the Seminar on Sophisticated Auditing*, Washington, D. C., October 1972, p. 51.

———. *Handbook for Auditors*. New York: McGraw-Hill Book Company, 1971.

———. "Operational Auditing in State Government." *The Internal Auditor*, May/June 1968, p. 51.

Keating, Stephen. "How Honeywell Management Views Operational Auditing." *The Internal Auditor*, September/October 1969, p. 43.

Knighton, Lennis M. "Performance Auditing in Better Perspective." *The Internal Auditor* 30 (March/April 1973): 40.

———. *The Performance Post-audit in State Government Bureau of Business and Economic Research*. Ann Arbor, Mich.: Michigan State University, 1957.

———. "Improving the Audit of Federal-State-Local Programs." *The Federal Accountant*, December 1968, p. 31.

Koontz, Harold. "Making Managerial Appraisal Effective." *California Management Review* 15 (Winter 1972): 46.

Langenderfer, Harold Q., and Robertson, Jack C. "A Theoretical Structure for Independent Audits of Management." *The Accounting Review*, October 1969, p. 777.

Lawson, Jack P. "Management Audit: How Much Training Is Needed to Perform It?" *Air Force Comptroller* 7 (April 1973): 14.

Leonard, Lawrence L. "Effectively Controlled Organization." In *Selected Papers*, 1972, p. 396. New York: Haskins & Sells, 1973.

Leonard, William P. *The Management Audit*. Englewood Cliffs, N.J.: Prentice-Hall, 1962.

Levitt, Arthur. "Operational Auditing in New York State." *New York CPA*, May 1964, pp. 337–41.

Limbert, G. Christian, Jr. "Evaluating Federal Poverty Programs." *The Price Waterhouse Review*, Summer/Autumn 1971, pp. 50–59.

Lindberg, Roy A., and Cohn, Theodore. "Corporation Operational Audit General Questionnaire." In *Operations Auditing*. New York: AMACOM, 1972, p. 295.

Lindemann, A. J. "Internal Auditing—With Emphasis on Operational Auditing." *The Internal Auditor*, Summer 1967, p. 64.

Linowes, David F. "The Accounting Profession and Social Progress." *The Journal of Accountancy*, July 1973, p. 32.

Lowe, E. A. "The Audit of Management Efficiency." *The Internal Auditor*, Winter 1966, p. 45.

Mandeville, R. L. "Management Auditing: Guidelines for Staffing and Implementation." *Systems and Procedures Journal*, November-December 1966, p. 45.

Mautz, R. K., and Newmann, F. L. "The Effective Corporate Audit Committee," *Harvard Business Review*, November/December 1970, p. 57.

McElyea, S. D. "Social Measurement: Who Does the Accounting?" *Federal Accountant*, September 1973, p. 42.

Meyers, E. B. "Operational Auditing." *The Internal Auditor*, Winter 1966, p. 17.

Miller, F. J., Jr. "Operational Auditing—Where Do We Go from Here?" *The Internal Auditor*, Fall 1963, p. 16.

Minkin, Max. "Some New Paths to Program Evaluation Reviews." *Federal Accountant*, March 1974, p. 51.

Mints, Frederick E. "Behavioral Patterns in Internal Audit Relationships." New York: The Institute of Internal Auditors, 1972, p. 1.

Morin, D. B. J. "Management's New Evaluation Tool—Operational Auditing Services." *The Canadian Chartered Accountant*, July 1967, p. 17.

Morse, Ellsworth H., Jr. "Auditing Government Operations." *The Internal Auditor* 30 (July/August 1973): 10.

———. "Comments on Survey of Attitudes on Management Auditing" (correspondence). *Accounting Review* 48 (January 1973): 120.

———. "The Auditor Takes on Program Evaluation." *The Federal Accountant*, June 1973, p. 4.

———. "Performance and Operational Auditing." *The Journal of Accountancy*, June 1971, p. 41.

———. "Operational Auditing and Standards for the Public Sector." *The GAO Review*, Winter 1973, p. 30.

———. "Accountants Evaluate Federal Management." *The Office*, January 1971, p. 66.

———. "Agencies Probed in New Operational Audits." *Government Executive*, April 1973, p. 46.

Mosher, Charles D. "How to Identify Management Problems." *GAO Review*, Fall 1973, p. 8.

Murray, Lawrence M. "Management Audit of Divisional Performance." *Management Accounting* (NAA) 54 (March 1973): 26.

"New Government Audit Standards." *Federal Accountant* 21 Sept. (1972): 112–19.

Norgaard, Corine T. "Operational Auditing: A Part of the Control Process." *Management Accounting*, March 1972, p. 25.

———. "The Professional Accountant's View of Operational Auditing." *The Journal of Accountancy*, December 1969, p. 45.

Osborne, Richard W. "Practical Aspects of an Operational Audit." *The Internal Auditor*, Winter 1960, pp. 28–38.

Palmer, R. R. "Operational Auditing of Maintenance Cost and Control." *The Internal Auditor*, Summer 1963, p. 66.

Pinkelman, Franklin C. "Development of Performance Auditing in Michigan." *The Florida CPA*, May 1967, p. 10.

———. "Effective Performance Auditing in Government." *The Internal Auditor*, July/August 1974, p. 41.

Pomeranz, Felix. "Auditing by Perception." *C.P.A. Journal*, October 1974, p. 41.

———. "Communications—Raw Material of the Operational Audit." *The Internal Auditor*, Winter 1961, p. 16.

Price, B. W. "Industrial Uses of the Management Audit." *The Florida CPA*, May 1967, p. 20.

Pyhrr, P. A. "Operational Auditing: New Profit Tool for Top Management." *Business Management*, September 1968, p. 87.

"Report of the Committee on Non-financial Measures of Effectiveness." *The Accounting Review*, supp. to vol. XLVI (1971): 165.

Reynolds, Allan L. "Examining Performance of Socio-economic Programs—The Criteria-Gap," Footnote[3], *Journal of the HEW Audit Agency*, Winter 1970–71, pp. 21–25.

Rigg, Frank J. "The Management Audit." *The Internal Auditor*, May/June 1968, p. 21.

Ringwood, Robert R. "Operational Auditing for Government Programs." *International Journal of Government Auditing*, January 1974, pp. 12–13.

Russell, Harold F. "Audiovisual Audit Report? Why Not—It's Mighty Effective." *The U.S. Army Audit Agency Bulletin*, Spring 1969, pp. 25–30.

Sato, Frank S. "Defense Management Auditing—Unrestricted Examination and Evaluation." *Defense Management Journal*, January 1975.

Sawyer, Lawrence B. "How Do You Get to Be an Internal Auditor, Grandfather?" *The Internal Auditor*, May/June 1971, pp. 56–60.

———. "Just What Is Management Auditing?" *The Internal Auditor* 30 (March/April 1973): 21.

———. *Practice of Modern Internal Auditing: Appraising Operations for Management*. Orlando, Fla.: The Institute of Internal Auditors, 1973, p. 531.

Sayers, John G. "Operational Auditing Is Alive and Well." *Canadian Chartered Accountant Magazine*, April 1975, pp. 28–31.

Scantlebury, D. L. "The Structure of a Management Audit Finding." *The Internal Auditor*, March/April 1972, p. 10.

———. "Using Analytical Expert in Auditing Audits." *GAO Review*, Summer 1974, p. 26.

Schneider, Aaron. "Operations Auditing in Action." In *Conference Papers*. New York: The Institute of Internal Auditors, 1966, pp. 69–76. (Twenty-fifth International Conference, June 7–10, 1966.)

———. "What Operational Auditing Is—and Isn't." *The Internal Auditor* 30 (September/October 1973): 10.

Secory, Thomas. "A CPA's Opinion on Management Performance." *The Journal of Accountancy*, July 1971, p. 53.

Seiler, R. E. "Operational Auditing and Its Contribution to Profits." *Proceedings, National Conference of Electric and Gas Utility Accountants*. St. Louis, Mo.: American Gas Association and Edison Electric Institute, 1961, p. G2.

———. "Operational Auditing and Motivating Executive Action." *The Internal Auditor*, Fall 1962, p. 54.

Simonetti, Gilbert, Jr. "Auditing Standards Established by the GAO." *The Journal of Accountancy*, January 1974, p. 14.

Smith, Charles H.; Lanier, Roy A.; and Taylor, Martin E. "Comments on Survey of Attitudes on Management Auditing: A Reply." *Accounting Review* 48 (January 1973): 123.

Snellgrove, Olin C. "The Management Audit: Organizational Guidance System." *Management Review*, March 1972, p. 41.

———. "Preventive Maintenance: A Challenge to Operational Auditors." *The Internal Auditor* 30 (September/October 1973): 51.

Sparks, Donald. "How to Audit Your Marketing Function." *Industrial Management*, February 1967, p. 11.

Staab, H. A.; Gissel, C. W.; and Neuman, B. J. "Operational Audit of a Production Control Function." *The Internal Auditor*, Spring 1967, p. 68.

Staats, Elmer B. "Protecting the Taxpayer's Dollar." *The Journal of Accountancy*, January 1968, p. 50.

———. "The Role of the General Accounting Office in Reviewing the Results of Federal Programs." *The GAO Review*, Summer 1971, p. 74.

———. "The Multipurpose Audit." *Management Review*, June 1971, p. 15.

———. "Management or Operational Auditing." *GAO Review*, Winter 1972, p. 26.

———. "Evaluating the Effectiveness of Federal Social Programs." *The GAO Review*, Fall 1973, p. 1.

———. "The GAO—How Its Work Affects Local Government." *Governmental Finance*, August 1973, p. 25.

———. "GAO Audit Standards: Development and Implementation," *Public Management*, February 1974, p. 5.

———. "Issues Facing Financial Managers in the Seventies." *The Federal Accountant*, September 1971, pp. 4–20.

Stepnick, Edward W. "Audit Findings—Their Nature and Development." Footnote[1], *Journal of the HEW Audit Agency*, 1969, p. 16.

Steven, Anton. "Operational Audits of Construction Contracts." *The Internal Auditor*, May/June 1973, p. 10.

Stewart, Dudely. "The Internal Auditor of the Future." *The Internal Auditor*, March/April 1970, p. 46.

Sullivan, Robert L. "Program Evaluation." *Management Controls*, November 1972, p. 254.

Tanimura, Clinton T. "State Approaches to Performance Auditing." *Governmental Finance*, August 1972, p. 24.

Tillman, John R. "Preventive Controls: An Approach to Internal Auditing." *The Internal Auditor* 30 (March/April 1973): 50.

Toan, Arthur B. "Is Accounting Geared to Today's Needs?" *Management Adviser*, November/December 1971, p. 17.

Towers, Elwood. "Aspects of Operational Auditing and Internal Control." *The Internal Auditor*, Winter 1963, p. 55.

Tull, T. M., Jr. "Administrative Audit of a Trust Department." *Trust and Estates*, October 1967, p. 905.

United States General Accounting Office. "Standards for Audit of Governmental Organizations, Programs, Activities, and Functions." Pamphlet 2000-00110. Washington, D.C.: U.S. Government Printing Office, 1972.

Walsh, F. J., Jr. "Operational Auditing in Internal Auditing." In *Business Policy Study No. 111*. New York: National Industrial Conference Board, 1963, p. 48.

Weiss, Allen. "Management Audits: The Development of a New Service." *LKHH Accountant* 53 (Autumn 1973): 46.

Westmeyer, Troy B. "Performance Auditing." *Governmental Finance* 1 (November 1972): 25.

Wilde, Fraxor B., and Vancil, Richard F. "Performance Audits by Outside Directors." *Harvard Business Review*, July/August 1973, p. 112.

Wilson, G. Peter. "Operational Auditing in the Canadian Federal Public Service." *The Internal Auditor*, November/December 1968, p. 45.

Witt, Herbert. "Criteria for Evaluating Effectiveness." *Footnote*[1], *Journal of the HEW Audit Agency*, 1969, p. 40.

Witte, Arthur E. "Management Auditing: The Present State of the Art." *Journal of Accountancy*, August 1967, p. 54.

INDEX

Accuracy and adequacy of subject, 433–34
Accountability, 4
Actions of individuals or organizations, 9
Active voice, 363
Administrative control, 121
Agency comments, 352
Agency and other studies, 400
Alternatives, consideration of, 400
American Institute of Certified Public Accountants checklist, 375
Analytical evidence, 23, 142, 147
Analytical techniques, 401
Application controls (computers), 315
Appropriateness:
  of background and general information, 25
  of policies and practices, 131
  of program, 400
  of standards, 6–9, 21
Asserted causes, 78–79
Asserted criteria, 78–79
Asserted effects, 78–79
Assessing significance in report, 403
Assignment approval, illustration of, 383
Attest, 4
Attesting to a third party, 101
Attribute sampling, 273–74
Audit, mission-oriented, 4
Audit evidence, 20
  statistical sampling, 263
Audit objective, 6, 8
  defined, 20
  in definition of performance auditing, 6–8
  elements, 21
  firming up of, 35
  illustration, 36, 42
  use, 20
Audit planning and programming, 63, 65
Audit procedures, 68
Audit program, 83
  for detailed examination, 67
  for preliminary survey, 65
Audit programming, 65–68
Audit summary, basic elements in, 175
Auditing, 4
  around the computer, 307, 316
  computer operations, 310
  internal, 4
  operational, 4
Auditor, 5

Background data (M-audit), 82
Background information:
  on audit, 25, 34, 68, 105
  in report, 352, 354
Balancing models, 333–35
Best evidence, 143
Bias, 264

Cases:
  Analysis of a complete audit: Improvement Needed in Managing Automated Decision Making by a Computer, 320
  Auditing the Uses of Equipment: A University, a Corporation, 31
  Big Costs that Came in Little Packages, 16
  Careless Cost Charges, Case of, 15
  City Garage: Audit Working Papers for an M-audit, 170
  City Garage: Management Control in an M-audit, 135
  City Garage: Planning an M-audit, 71
  City Welfare: The Detailed Examination for an M-audit, 215
  City Welfare: The Report, 360
  Classifying Civil Servants in the State of Landia, 279, 280
  Collections at the Local Church, 137
  Company Cars, Case of, 15
  Computer Security: Can a Questionnaire Help? 298
  Computers that Were Converted in the State of New Kent, 327
  Controlling Expenditures: A Federal Case, 14
  Employment Program that Did Not Employ, 17
  Estimating the Assets of Mammoth City, 279
  Federal Grant Funds, Case of, 12
  High Costs for Low Rents: The Public Housing Case, 13
  How They Made Copies at Sohi — and Copies and Copies, 32
  Indian Education: Analyzing Information from Interviews, 298
  Mass-transit Grant, 117
  Mass-transit Grant: The Detailed Examination, 253
  Mass-transit Grant: The Report, 367
  Nonresident Tuition in the Fernwood Schools, 136
  Nursing Homes: Audit Working Papers for a P-audit, 170
  Nursing Homes: Management Control in a P-audit, 136
  Nursing Homes: Planning a P-audit, 71
  Organizing Audit Reports: The City Garage, The Nursing Homes, 359
  Planning the Audit Program: A Case in Point, 72
  Probation in the State of Sylvania, Case of, 30
  Procuring M.D.s for the Service: Cost-effectiveness Analysis, 345
  Ranges for Measuring Risk and Uncertainty in Cost Estimates, 344
  School Voucher Project at Alum Rock, 151
  Self-assessment Taxes in the State of Piedmont: The Case of the Lost Revenues, 87
  Snow Removal Snowed Under, 16
  State Self-assessment Taxes: The Detailed Examination for an M-audit, 211
  State Self-assessment Taxes: The Report, 359
  Too Many Workers in the Production Department at Torex, Case of, 29
  Travel Advances that Advanced, 12
  Valley City Jails, 111
  Valley City Jails: The Detailed Examination, 249
  Valley City Jails: The Report, 367
  Welfare in the City: The AFDC Case in Yorktown, 93
  What Made the Nursing Homes Unsafe: Phases of a P-audit, 49
  What Went on in the City Garage: Phases of an M-audit, 46
  Who Used the Research Equipment at Texon—and When, 32
  Workplace Inspection Program, 155
Causes, 21, 74, 103
  asserted, 78–79
Combined program for the preliminary survey and review and testing of management control, 67

474

Comments, agency, 352
Comparison of similar programs, 332
Competency of evidence, 75, 144
Completeness, 435
Compliance, 400
Compliance auditing, 4, 35
Computer, 307
   application program, 320
   auditing around, 307, 316
   auditing operations, 310
   on-line, real-time processing, 310
   processing controls, end of, 313
Conciseness, 434
Conclusion, 20
   M-audit, 81
Condition, 355
   compared with criteria, 403
Confidence, 265–69, 271, 273
   coefficient, 268–69
and risk, 266
Consultants, use of, 401
Copies of documents, 146
Convincingness, 434
Cost-benefit analysis, 333, 345
Cost-benefit relationship, 400
Cost-benefit study, 399, 402
Cost-effectiveness, 333, 400
Cost-value, 333
Costs commensurate with revenue or benefit, 40
Criteria, 21, 74, 102
   asserted, 78–79
   compared with condition, 403
Critical path methods (CPM), 330, 339
Cross-referencing, 173

Data:
   sufficiency of, 264
   validity of, 400
Data processing, 308
Data problems, 322
Deficiencies in management, 74
Detailed examination, 24, 27
   for an M-audit, 36, 82
   for a P-audit, 42
Digest of report, 357
Draft report, 357

Economy and efficiency, 98, 375
Effects, 21, 74, 103
   asserted, 78–79
Effectiveness, 8, 40
   of product, 98
Electronic data processing, 308
End results, 7
Engagement environment, 375
Engagement letter, 64
Evaluation, 399
Evidence, 6, 141
   analytical, 23, 142, 147
   audit, 20, 263
   and audit objectives, 19, 22, 101

best, 143
competency of, 75, 144
gathering of, 162–63
observation, 146–47
personal interview, 146
preponderance of, 145
primary, 143
records, 146
relevancy of, 75, 144, 265
secondary, 143
sufficiency of, 75, 145
testimonial, 146
weight of, 145
Examination:
   and evaluation standards, 373
   directions to take, 34
   of financial statements, 6
Expected results, 7
Experimental models, 332–33
Experts, outside, 283
   use of, 340
Explaining why deviation occurred, 403

Facts and information, 141
Findings, 6
Finite universe, 271
First party, 4
Flow charting symbols, 127

Game theory models, 336, 339
GAO program audit, selected policies for, 399–402
GAO standards for audit of governmental organizations, programs, activities and functions, 373–75
General controls, 315
Generalized audit software, 309, 316

Homogeneity, 265, 275

Inferences, 265
Infinite universe, 271
Informant, 283
Information, obtaining with interviews and questionnaires, 400
Information system, 400
Input control transactions, 312, 315
Integrated test facilities, 307, 318
Internal auditing, 4
Internal control, 121, 124
Internal review, 400
Interviews, 281–83
   purpose of, 284
   use of recording equipment in, 284
   written records of, 283
Interviewer's attitude, 284

Jargon, 363
Judgment sampling, 264

Letter and confirmation evidence, 147

Level I summary, 176
Level II summary, 176
Linear programming, 335, 336

M-audit. *See* Management audit
Management, 6
   deficiencies in, 74
   employee actions, 21
Management audit, 4, 6–7, 33, 39
   basic principles, 74, 78
   defined, 6, 7
   detailed examination, 76
   for efficient and economical practices, 124
   preliminary survey, 75
   review and testing of management control, 75
   report development, 76
Management control, 26, 35, 97, 121, 123, 124
   and preliminary survey, 67
   for review of M-audit, 36
   system pertaining to personnel, 128
Managers, 124
Markov chain models, 336, 340
Mathematical models, 340
Mean, 267, 270
Mission-oriented audit, 4
Models:
   balancing, 333–35
   experimental, 332–33
   game theory, 336, 339
   Markov chain, 336, 340
   mathematical, 340
   network analysis, 330, 336, 339
   optimizing, 335–40
   probability, 330–31

Network analysis model, 330, 336, 339
Nonrandom comparison group methods, 332
Normal curve relationships, 266
Note taking, 285

Objectives, 7, 20, 98
   clarity and consistency of, 400
   of the organization, 124
   and perspective (reporting), 434
Observation evidence, 146–47
Operational auditing, 4
Opinion, 20
Opinion paragraph, 350
Optimizing models, 335–40
Oral information, 282
   refusal to confirm, 286
   written confirmation of, 285
Output controls, 312, 315
Outside experts, 283

P-audit. *See* Program audit
Passive voice, 363
Peer review, 210
   and referencing, 356

Performance,
    actual compared with planned operations, 131
Performance audit, 3–6
    reporting, 350
Personal interview evidence, 146
Personnel needs, 29
Phases of audit:
    detailed examination, 24, 27, 36, 42, 82, 104
    preliminary survey, 24–26, 33, 39, 40, 44–45, 79, 104
    report development, 24, 27, 65, 81, 104, 354
    review and testing of management control, 24, 26, 35, 41, 79, 104, 106
Phases of audit function:
    for M-audit, 38–39
    for P-audit, 44–45, 104
PPBS, 97
Precision, 265–66, 273
    limits, 269, 271
    per unit, 270
Pre-engagement checklist, 375
Preliminary survey:
    M-audit, 24–26, 33, 79
    P-audit, 39, 40
    purpose of, 25
    and review and testing of management control, 67
Preliminary work (audit planning), 64
Preparatory controls, 312
Probability, 330
    models, 330–31
    techniques, 266
Processing controls, 312–13, 315
Professional proficiency, 376
Programs, 7, 8, 39, 399
    evaluations, 4, 97–98, 399
    need for, 400
    results, 375–76
    similar compared, 332
Program analysis, 97
Program audit (P-audit), 4, 7–8, 39–43, 97
    GAO, selected policies for, 399–402
Program budgeting, 97–98
Program controls, 313
Program conversion costs, 327
Program effectiveness, 400
Program for the review and testing of management and internal control, 66
Program objectives, defining, 399–400
Program results audits, 4
Proof, 20
    beyond reasonable doubt, 145

Proposal letter, and engagement, 64, 377–79
    approach, 377
    basic objectives, 377
    benefits of proposed program, 377
    conclusion, 378
    example of, 379
    introduction, 377
    professional qualifications, 378
    staffing, 378
    time and fees, 378
Proposition, 20
Purchasing, 16

Quality-control review, 94
Queuing, 335, 339
Questionnaires, 281, 295–96
    value of, 295

Random numbers, 277
Random selection, 277
Recommendations, 356
Records evidence, 146
Relevancy of evidence, 75, 144, 265
Report:
    clarity and simplicity in, 434
    coherence in, 363
    constructive tone of, 435
    digest of, 357
    draft, 357
    emphasis in, 363
    and level of reader, 361–62
    logic in, 363
    organization in, 350–51
    planning of, 65
    sections in, 362
    summaries in, 173, 177
    unity in, 363
    and work done, 357
Report digest, tentative, 387
Reporting, 9, 10, 349–60, 361–66
    results of audit, 354
    standards, 373–74
Responders, selecting potential, 296
Results, 9, 21
    expected of audit, 68
Review of program results, 400
Review and testing of management control, 24, 26, 106, 121
    for M-audit, 35, 79
    for P-audit, 41
Risk, 267

Sample objectives, 266
Sample size, computation of, 270
Sampling:
    attribute, 273–74
    judgment, 264
    plan, 266
    principles of, 265
    statistical, 263–64

    stratified, 274
Scope of audit, 356
Secondary evidence, 143
Second party, 5
Significance, 21, 403, 433
Simplex method, 339
Simulation, 307, 318
Social or other management objectives, 98
Social programs, 98
Software problems, 322
Special instructions, 69
Staff and time estimates, 64
Standard deviation, 267, 270
Standard error, 269
Standards:
    for achieving valid program objective, 100
    for efficient and economical operations, 77–78
    for internal accounting control, 122
    for reporting, 349
    for work-paper preparation, 172
Stratified sampling, 274
Style of writing, 362
Subobjectives, 22
    elements of, 23
Sufficiency:
    of data, 264
    of evidence, 75, 145
Summary, 357
    levels, 176
    purpose of, 174
Supervisory review, 210
Systematic selection, 277

Tentative report digest, 387
Test decks, 316–17
Testimonial evidence, 146
Third party, 5–6
Time series, 333
Time sharing, 308
Tracing and tagging, 307, 318

Unity in report writing, 363
Universe, 266
    finite, 271
    infinite, 271
Usefulness and timeliness of report, 433

Validity of data, 400
Valid measures of policy and program consequences, 102

Weight of evidence, 145
Working papers, 161
    purpose of, 162–63
    summaries, 174
Writing style, 362

Book Order Forms

If after reading *Auditing the Performance of Management* you feel that some of your friends or colleagues should have copies, please clip out the order forms below and pass them along.

MAIL TO:

Lifetime Learning Publications
Ten Davis Drive
Belmont, California 94002

Please send me _____ copies of *Auditing the Performance of Management* at $24.95 each. I understand that if I am not satisfied, I can return the book for a complete refund within 30 days.

☐ Check enclosed   ☐ Bill my credit card account:
　　　　　　　　　　　BankAmericard or Visa # _____
　　　　　　　　　　　Master Charge # _____

_____
(signature)

Name _____

Address _____

City _____ State _____ Zip _____

MAIL TO:

Lifetime Learning Publications
Ten Davis Drive
Belmont, California 94002

Please send me _____ copies of *Auditing the Performance of Management* at $24.95 each. I understand that if I am not satisfied, I can return the book for a complete refund within 30 days.

☐ Check enclosed   ☐ Bill my credit card account:
　　　　　　　　　　　BankAmericard or Visa # _____
　　　　　　　　　　　Master Charge # _____

_____
(signature)

Name _____

Address _____

City _____ State _____ Zip _____